Principles of Operating Systems:
Design & Applications

Brian L. Stuart
FedEx Labs
University of Memphis

Australia · Canada · Mexico · Singapore · Spain · United Kingdom · United States

Principles of Operating Systems:
Design & Applications

Brian L. Stuart

Senior Product Manager:
Alyssa Pratt

Marketing Manager:
Bryant Chrzan

Cover Design:
Yvo Riezebos Designs

Acquisitions Editor:
Amy Jollymore

Editorial Assistant:
Patrick Frank

Art Director:
Beth Paquin

Development Editor:
Jim Markham

Manufacturing Coordinator:
Julio Esperas

Compositor:
Brian L. Stuart

Content Project Manager:
Matt Hutchinson

Printer:
RR Donnelley, Crawfordsville

For more information, contact Course Technology, 25 Thomson Place,
Boston, Massachusetts, 02210.

Or find us on the World Wide Web at: www.course.com

Disclaimer
Course Technology reserves the right to revise this publication and make
changes from time to time in its content without notice.

ISBN 1-4188-3769-5

for my beloved wife and daughter

Brief Contents

	Preface	xxi
1	Introduction to Operating Systems	1
2	Some Example Operating Systems	21
3	Inferno Structure and Initialization	35
4	Linux Structure and Initialization	55
5	Principles of Process Management	81
6	Some Examples of Process Management	121
7	Process Management in Inferno	141
8	Process Management in Linux	165
9	Principles of Memory Management	195
10	Some Examples of Memory Management	233
11	Memory Management in Inferno	253
12	Memory Management in Linux	281
13	Principles of I/O Device Management	307
14	Some Examples of I/O Device Management	333
15	I/O Devices in Inferno	345
16	I/O Devices in Linux	371
17	Principles of File Systems	399
18	Some Examples of File Systems	425
19	File Systems in Inferno	437

20 File Systems in Linux   **479**

21 Principles of Operating System Security   **511**

22 Principles of Distributed Systems   **537**

A Compiling Hosted Inferno   **555**

B Compiling Native Inferno   **561**

   Suggested Readings   **565**

   Index   **569**

Contents

Preface   **xxi**

1 Introduction to Operating Systems   **1**

1.1   What Is an Operating System? 1

    1.1.1   Resource Manager 2

    1.1.2   Service Provider 3

    1.1.3   Virtual Machine 3

1.2   Areas of Operating System Responsibility 3

    1.2.1   Processes 4

    1.2.2   Memory 4

    1.2.3   I/O Devices 5

    1.2.4   File Systems 6

    1.2.5   Security 6

    1.2.6   Networking 7

    1.2.7   User Interfaces 8

1.3   History of Operating Systems 8

    1.3.1   Bare Metal 9

    1.3.2   Batch Operating Systems 9

    1.3.3   Time-Sharing Operating Systems 10

    1.3.4   Distributed Operating Systems 11

1.4   Techniques of Organizing Operating Systems 12

    1.4.1   Monolithic Designs 12

    1.4.2   Layered Designs 12

    1.4.3   Microkernel Designs 12

    1.4.4   Virtual Machine Designs 14

1.5   Bootstrapping 15

1.6   System Calls 17

    1.6.1   Example System Calls 17

    1.6.2   System Call Mechanism 18

1.7   Summary 18

1.8   Exercises 19

2 Some Example Operating Systems   **21**

2.1   CTSS 21

    2.1.1   Organization 22

    2.1.2   Booting 22

2.2   Multics   22
       2.2.1   Organization   23
       2.2.2   System Calls   24
2.3   RT-11   24
       2.3.1   Organization   24
2.4   Sixth Edition UNIX   26
       2.4.1   Organization   27
       2.4.2   System Calls   27
2.5   VMS   27
       2.5.1   Organization   28
       2.5.2   Booting   28
       2.5.3   System Calls   29
2.6   4.3BSD   29
       2.6.1   Organization   30
       2.6.2   System Calls   30
2.7   Windows NT   30
       2.7.1   Organization   31
2.8   TinyOS   31
       2.8.1   Organization   32
2.9   Xen   32
       2.9.1   Organization   32
2.10   Summary   33
2.11   Exercises   33

3   **Inferno Structure and Initialization**   **35**
3.1   Origins of Inferno   35
3.2   Fundamental Concepts   36
3.3   Organization   39
       3.3.1   Basic Architecture   39
       3.3.2   Source Code Organization   40
3.4   Initialization   42
       3.4.1   Starting Inferno   43
       3.4.2   Host OS Specific Initialization   45
       3.4.3   Host OS Independent Initialization   47
       3.4.4   Starting Time-Sharing   50
3.5   System Calls   52
3.6   Summary   52
3.7   Exercises   53

4   **Linux Structure and Initialization**   **55**
4.1   The Origins of Linux   55
4.2   Organization   57
       4.2.1   Basic Architecture   57
       4.2.2   Modules   58

	4.2.3	Source Code Organization	59
4.3	Initialization	61
	4.3.1	Bootstrapping	62
	4.3.2	Processor-Specific Initialization	65
	4.3.3	Processor-Independent Initialization	68
	4.3.4	Starting Time-Sharing	73
	4.3.5	Initiating Administrative Initialization	74
4.4	System Calls	76
	4.4.1	Application-Side System Call Handling	76
	4.4.2	Kernel-Side System Call Handling	77
4.5	Summary	78
4.6	Exercises	78

5 Principles of Process Management   **81**

5.1	The Process Concept	81
5.2	Realizing Processes	82
	5.2.1	Process Operations	82
	5.2.2	Process State	84
	5.2.3	The Process Table	85
5.3	Threads	86
5.4	Scheduling	86
	5.4.1	First-Come, First-Served	87
	5.4.2	Shortest Job First	87
	5.4.3	Round-Robin	90
	5.4.4	Priority Scheduling	90
	5.4.5	Adjusting Scheduling Parameters	94
	5.4.6	Two-Level Scheduling	94
	5.4.7	Real-Time Scheduling	94
	5.4.8	Scheduling in Embedded Systems	97
5.5	Context Switching	97
5.6	Process Creation and Termination	100
5.7	Critical Sections	101
	5.7.1	Interrupt Control	102
	5.7.2	Atomic Instructions	103
	5.7.3	Peterson's Algorithm	104
	5.7.4	Semaphores	105
	5.7.5	Monitors	106
	5.7.6	Message Passing	107
	5.7.7	Examples	107
5.8	Deadlock	111
	5.8.1	Necessary and Sufficient Conditions	111
	5.8.2	Dealing with Deadlock	112
5.9	Summary	118
5.10	Exercises	118

6   Some Examples of Process Management   **121**
  6.1   CTSS 121
      6.1.1   Process State 121
      6.1.2   System Calls 122
      6.1.3   Scheduling 123
  6.2   Multics 124
      6.2.1   System Calls 124
      6.2.2   Process State 124
      6.2.3   Scheduling 125
  6.3   RT-11 126
      6.3.1   System Calls 126
      6.3.2   Process State 126
      6.3.3   Process Table 126
      6.3.4   Scheduling 127
  6.4   Sixth Edition UNIX 127
      6.4.1   System Calls 127
      6.4.2   Process State 128
      6.4.3   Process Table 128
      6.4.4   Scheduling 128
  6.5   4.3BSD 129
      6.5.1   System Calls 129
      6.5.2   Process State and Process Table 130
      6.5.3   Scheduling 130
  6.6   VMS 131
      6.6.1   System Calls 131
      6.6.2   Thread State 132
      6.6.3   Scheduling 132
  6.7   Windows NT 133
      6.7.1   System Calls 133
      6.7.2   Thread State 134
      6.7.3   Process and Thread Tables 134
      6.7.4   Scheduling 135
  6.8   TinyOS 136
  6.9   Xen 137
  6.10 Summary 138
  6.11 Exercises 138

7   Process Management in Inferno   **141**
  7.1   Processes in Inferno 141
  7.2   Process State 142
      7.2.1   Kernel Processes 142
      7.2.2   User Processes 143
  7.3   Process Data Structures 145
      7.3.1   Kernel Process Table 145

	7.3.2	Kernel Process Table Entry	147
	7.3.3	User Process Table	148
	7.3.4	User Process Table Entry	148
7.4	Process Creation		151
	7.4.1	Interpreting the Process Creation Instruction	151
	7.4.2	Implementing Process Creation	152
7.5	Process Destruction		155
7.6	Process Scheduling		157
	7.6.1	Adding to the Ready List	157
	7.6.2	Removing from the Ready List	158
	7.6.3	Time-Sharing	159
	7.6.4	Running a Time Slice	161
7.7	Summary		163
7.8	Exercises		163

8	**Process Management in Linux**		**165**
8.1	Process and Threads		165
	8.1.1	Kernel Threads in Linux	165
	8.1.2	Process Relationships	166
8.2	System Calls		166
8.3	Process State		168
8.4	Process Table		170
8.5	Process Creation		173
	8.5.1	Handling the System Call	173
	8.5.2	Creating the Process	176
	8.5.3	Architecture-Specific Steps	178
8.6	Process Scheduling		181
	8.6.1	Priorities	182
	8.6.2	Queue Structure	182
	8.6.3	Clock Ticks	184
	8.6.4	Scheduler	187
8.7	Summary		193
8.8	Exercises		193

9	**Principles of Memory Management**		**195**
9.1	The Memory Hierarchy		195
9.2	Address Translation		197
	9.2.1	Base/Limit Registers	198
	9.2.2	Segmentation	198
	9.2.3	Paging	199
9.3	Memory-Related Services		202
9.4	Memory Layouts		203
9.5	Memory Allocation Techniques		206
	9.5.1	Free Space Management	206

        9.5.2   Fragmentation   208
        9.5.3   Partitioning   208
        9.5.4   Selection Policies   209
        9.5.5   Buddy System Management   211
   9.6 Overallocation Techniques   213
        9.6.1   Swapping   214
        9.6.2   Segment Swapping   214
        9.6.3   Paging 215
        9.6.4   Paged Segments   224
        9.6.5   Memory-Mapped Files   225
        9.6.6   Copy on Write 226
        9.6.7   Performance Issues 226
   9.7 Memory Management in Embedded Systems   229
   9.8 Summary   229
   9.9 Exercises 230

10 Some Examples of Memory Management   233
   10.1 CTSS   233
   10.2 Multics 234
        10.2.1   Memory-Related System Calls   234
        10.2.2   Memory Layouts   235
        10.2.3   Segment and Page Management   235
   10.3 RT-11 235
        10.3.1   Memory-Related System Calls   236
        10.3.2   Memory Layouts   236
        10.3.3   USR and KMON Swapping   237
   10.4 Sixth Edition UNIX 238
        10.4.1   Memory-Related System Calls   238
        10.4.2   Memory Layouts   238
        10.4.3   Free Space Management   240
        10.4.4   Allocation 240
        10.4.5   Swapping   240
   10.5 4.3BSD 241
        10.5.1   Memory-Related System Calls   241
        10.5.2   Memory Layouts   241
        10.5.3   Free Space Management   243
        10.5.4   Swapping and Page Replacement   243
   10.6 VMS 245
        10.6.1   Page Tables 245
        10.6.2   Memory Layouts   245
        10.6.3   Free Space Management   245
        10.6.4   Swapping and Page Replacement   246
        10.6.5   Memory-Related System Calls   247
   10.7 Windows NT   247

	10.7.1	System Calls	248
	10.7.2	Memory Layouts	248
	10.7.3	Page Management	248
10.8	TinyOS		250
10.9	Xen		250
	10.9.1	Hypercalls	250
	10.9.2	Memory Layouts	250
	10.9.3	Page Management	251
10.10	Summary		251
10.11	Exercises		251

11 Memory Management in Inferno   **253**

11.1	Overview		253
11.2	Memory Layouts		255
11.3	Memory Management Data Structures		255
	11.3.1	Memory Pools	256
	11.3.2	Memory Blocks	258
11.4	Memory Management Implementation		261
	11.4.1	Allocating Memory	261
	11.4.2	Removing a Free Block from the Tree	267
	11.4.3	Freeing Memory	270
	11.4.4	Inserting a Free Block into the Tree	271
11.5	Garbage Collection		273
	11.5.1	Heap Structure	273
	11.5.2	Reference Counts	273
	11.5.3	Very Concurrent Garbage Collector	273
	11.5.4	Implementing VCGC	275
11.6	Summary		279
11.7	Exercises		279

12 Memory Management in Linux   **281**

12.1	Memory Layouts		281
12.2	System Calls		284
12.3	Allocation Mechanisms		285
	12.3.1	Zoned Page Allocation	285
	12.3.2	Slab Allocator	285
	12.3.3	Kernel Memory Allocation	286
12.4	Page Management		286
	12.4.1	Page Tables	286
	12.4.2	Page Replacement	287
12.5	Memory Management Data Structures		288
	12.5.1	Representing Process Allocation	288
	12.5.2	Representing Virtual Memory Areas	290
12.6	Memory Management Implementation		292

12.6.1   Handling the Allocation System Call   292
12.6.2   Adding a Region   295
12.6.3   Processing Page Faults   298
12.6.4   Resolving a Fault for a Missing Page   300
12.6.5   Handling New Page Frames   302
12.7   Summary   305
12.8   Exercises   305

13 Principles of I/O Device Management   **307**
13.1   Elements of the I/O Subsystem   307
13.2   I/O Device Hardware Characteristics   309
13.2.1   Disk Drives   309
13.2.2   Serial Communications   312
13.2.3   Controller Interface Techniques   314
13.3   Types of I/O Devices   317
13.3.1   Communication vs. Storage Devices   317
13.3.2   Stream vs. Block Devices   318
13.4   Objectives of I/O Subsystem Design   319
13.5   I/O Device Services   319
13.6   Device Driver Structure   320
13.7   Device Management Techniques   322
13.7.1   Buffering   322
13.7.2   Interleaving   323
13.7.3   Elevator Algorithm   324
13.7.4   RAID   326
13.7.5   Water Marks   328
13.7.6   Human Input Processing   330
13.7.7   Pseudo-Devices   331
13.8   Summary   331
13.9   Exercises   331

14 Some Examples of I/O Device Management   **333**
14.1   CTSS   333
14.2   Multics   334
14.3   RT-11   335
14.4   Sixth Edition UNIX   338
14.5   4.3BSD   339
14.6   VMS   340
14.7   Windows NT   341
14.8   TinyOS   342
14.9   Xen   342
14.10 Summary   343
14.11 Exercises   343

15 I/O Devices in Inferno   **345**
   15.1 Device Driver Structure 345
   15.2 Parallel Port Support 347
        15.2.1 Servicing a Write Request 347
        15.2.2 Writing a Single Byte 349
   15.3 Keyboard Support 350
        15.3.1 Initializing the Keyboard Controller 352
        15.3.2 Handling a Keyboard Interrupt 353
   15.4 IDE Disk Support 357
        15.4.1 Processing an I/O Request 359
        15.4.2 Initiating an IDE Controller Operation 362
        15.4.3 Handling an IDE Controller Interrupt 366
   15.5 Summary 369
   15.6 Exercises 369

16 I/O Devices in Linux   **371**
   16.1 Block Request Support 371
   16.2 Two-Half Interrupt Handler Structure 372
   16.3 Parallel Port Driver 374
        16.3.1 Handling the System Call 374
        16.3.2 Selecting the Proper Low-Level Write 378
        16.3.3 Writing Bytes from the Buffer 380
        16.3.4 Configuring the Controller 383
   16.4 Floppy Disk Driver 385
        16.4.1 Handling the Request 385
        16.4.2 Scheduling the Floppy Operation 386
        16.4.3 Performing a Floppy Operation 387
        16.4.4 Starting the Command 390
        16.4.5 Preparing for the Data Transfer 390
        16.4.6 Programming the Controller 392
        16.4.7 Handling a Floppy Interrupt 394
        16.4.8 Finishing the Floppy Operation 395
   16.5 Summary 397
   16.6 Exercises 397

17 Principles of File Systems   **399**
   17.1 File System Services 399
        17.1.1 Shared and Exclusive Access 400
        17.1.2 Access Patterns 401
        17.1.3 File Structure 401
        17.1.4 Metadata 403
        17.1.5 Memory-Mapped Files 403
   17.2 General File System Design 404
        17.2.1 Form of the File System 404

      17.2.2   Major Data Structures 405
  17.3 Name Spaces 406
      17.3.1   Drive Specifiers 407
      17.3.2   Account Specifiers 408
      17.3.3   Hierarchical Naming 409
      17.3.4   File Extensions 410
      17.3.5   File Versions 411
      17.3.6   Special Files and Directories 411
      17.3.7   Relative and Absolute Names 412
  17.4 Managing Storage Space 412
      17.4.1   File System Metadata 412
      17.4.2   Data Units 413
      17.4.3   Free Space Management 413
      17.4.4   Regular Files 415
      17.4.5   Sparse Files 418
      17.4.6   Forks 418
      17.4.7   Directories 419
      17.4.8   Aliases 419
  17.5 Consistency Checking 420
  17.6 Journaling and Log-Structured File Systems 421
  17.7 Block Caching 422
  17.8 Summary 423
  17.9 Exercises 424

18 Some Examples of File Systems   **425**
  18.1 CTSS 425
      18.1.1   First CTSS File System 425
      18.1.2   Second CTSS File System 426
  18.2 Multics 427
  18.3 RT-11 428
  18.4 Sixth Edition UNIX 429
  18.5 4.3BSD 431
  18.6 VMS 432
  18.7 Windows NT 434
  18.8 Summary 435
  18.9 Exercises 435

19 File Systems in Inferno   **437**
  19.1 The Role of File Servers 437
      19.1.1   The Styx Protocol 438
      19.1.2   Built-in Kernel File Servers 441
      19.1.3   User-Space File Servers 441
  19.2 The Root Device Server 442
      19.2.1   Providing the Names Served 443

19.2.2   Walking the Root Server's Tree 444
19.2.3   Reading from the Root Server 445
19.3   Generic Styx Message Handler 445
19.3.1   Creating a Directory Entry 446
19.3.2   Generating Names 446
19.3.3   Walking a Directory Tree 447
19.4   Native Inferno File System 450
19.4.1   Initialization 451
19.4.2   Main Server Process 456
19.4.3   Processing a Styx Request 456
19.4.4   Walking a Directory Tree 458
19.4.5   Searching a Directory 460
19.4.6   Reading from a File 464
19.4.7   On-Disk Data Structures 466
19.4.8   Reading a Directory Entry 471
19.4.9   Reading a File Block 471
19.4.10 Locating a File Block 472
19.4.11 Processing Indirect Blocks 474
19.4.12 Fetching from the Buffer Cache 475
19.5   Summary 477
19.6   Exercises 478

20 File Systems in Linux   479
20.1   Virtual File System 479
20.1.1   Superblocks 480
20.1.2   I-Nodes 480
20.1.3   Directory Entries 481
20.1.4   Files 481
20.2   The EXT3 File System 481
20.3   EXT3 Disk Structure 482
20.3.1   EXT3 Superblock 482
20.3.2   EXT3 I-Node 485
20.3.3   EXT3 Directory Entries 487
20.4   EXT3 Name Lookup 488
20.4.1   Walking a Path 488
20.4.2   Generic Directory Lookup (Part 1) 494
20.4.3   Generic Directory Lookup (Part 2) 495
20.4.4   EXT3 Directory Lookup 496
20.4.5   EXT3 Directory Search 498
20.4.6   EXT3 Directory Block Search 501
20.5   File Writing 502
20.5.1   Linux Write System Call 502
20.5.2   Generic File Writing 503
20.5.3   EXT3 File Writing 505

20.6   Locating File Blocks in EXT3   505
    20.6.1   Identifying the Indirect Blocks   506
    20.6.2   Reading the Indirect Blocks   508
20.7   Summary   509
20.8   Exercises   509

21 Principles of Operating System Security   **511**
21.1   User Authentication   511
    21.1.1   User Names and Passwords   512
    21.1.2   Cryptographic Hashing Functions   512
    21.1.3   Callbacks   513
    21.1.4   Challenge/Response Authentication   513
    21.1.5   One-Time Passwords   514
    21.1.6   Biometric Authentication   514
21.2   Basic Resource Protection   515
    21.2.1   Privileged Users   515
    21.2.2   Access to CPU Features   516
    21.2.3   Memory Access   517
    21.2.4   Simple Protection Codes   517
    21.2.5   Access Control Lists   519
    21.2.6   Capabilities   520
21.3   Types of Threats   520
    21.3.1   Man-in-the-Middle Attack   521
    21.3.2   Trojan Horse   521
    21.3.3   Trapdoor   521
    21.3.4   Logic/Time Bomb   522
    21.3.5   Virus   522
    21.3.6   Worm   523
    21.3.7   Covert Channel   523
    21.3.8   Denial of Service   524
21.4   Orange Book Classification   524
    21.4.1   Division D   525
    21.4.2   Division C   525
    21.4.3   Division B   526
    21.4.4   Division A   527
21.5   Encryption   527
    21.5.1   Symmetric Encryption   528
    21.5.2   Public Key Cryptography   529
21.6   Protection Rings in Multics   531
21.7   Security in Inferno   533
21.8   Security in Linux   533
21.9   Summary   535
21.10 Exercises   535

22 Principles of Distributed Systems   **537**

22.1   Basic Concepts 537

     22.1.1   Resource Sharing 538

     22.1.2   Synchronous Operation 541

     22.1.3   Consensus 541

     22.1.4   Distributed Mutual Exclusion 541

     22.1.5   Fault Tolerance 543

     22.1.6   Self-Stabilization 543

22.2   Processor Sharing 544

     22.2.1   Symmetric Multiprocessing 544

     22.2.2   Clusters 545

     22.2.3   Grids 546

22.3   Distributed Clocks 546

     22.3.1   Logical Clocks 547

     22.3.2   Physical Clocks 547

22.4   Election Algorithms 548

     22.4.1   Bully Algorithm 548

     22.4.2   Ring Algorithm 550

22.5   Summary 552

22.6   Exercises 553

A Compiling Hosted Inferno   **555**

A.1   Setting Up the Configuration 555

A.2   Compiler and Development Tools 557

A.3   The PATH Environment Variable 557

A.4   Other Environment Variables 558

A.5   Compiling the System 558

A.6   Running the New Version 559

A.7   Summary 559

B Compiling Native Inferno   **561**

B.1   Setting Up the Configuration 561

B.2   Building the Tool Chain 561

B.3   Building the Bootstrapping Code 562

B.4   Setting Up the Kernel Configuration 562

B.5   Creating the Loader Configuration 562

B.6   Building the Kernel Image 563

B.7   Making the Floppy Image 563

B.8   Running the New Kernel 563

B.9   Summary 564

Suggested Readings   **565**

Index   **569**

Preface

The seed for this book was planted over 20 years ago when I was in graduate school. During the summer of 1986, a group of students collected for an advanced operating systems seminar, under the leadership of Dr. David Cohen. We began with the intention of writing an operating system, but our focus soon shifted to writing a textbook on operating systems. As so often happens, little of our original intent was accomplished. However, along the way, we had many fruitful discussions about how to organize a book on operating systems and, by extension, how to approach teaching operating systems.

That, combined with a number of years teaching operating systems, led me to observe that there are several different approaches to teaching operating systems. It also led me to realize that no existing text really provided the instructor with the flexibility to draw on each of the different approaches as desired. The motivating objective for this book is to provide that flexibility.

Organization

Seven topics make up the body of this book. I begin with an introduction that highlights history, structure and organization, system calls, and bootstrapping. Following this introduction, I examine in some depth each of the major areas of operating system responsibility: processes, memory, I/O devices, and file systems. The final two topics are security and distributed systems.

The coverage of the first five topics is presented in sequences of four chapters each that examine each topic from a variety of perspectives. The first chapter in each sequence presents general principles associated with managing a resource. In these chapters, I introduce the relevant issues, and I present some standard techniques for addressing those issues. In some cases, the chapters devoted to general principles also include discussion of related issues. For example, the subjects of mutual exclusion and deadlock are discussed along with process management in Chapter 5 because of their relevance to interprocess communication. The second chapter in each sequence surveys a number of historic and current operating systems. The set of nine OS examples includes CTSS, Multics, RT-11, sixth edition UNIX, 4.3BSD, VMS, Windows NT, TinyOS, and Xen. My focus with these is to study in a high-level way how their developers translated available standard techniques into practice. In the third and fourth chapters of each part, I drill down further into implementational considerations. I discuss selected parts of the code for Inferno (in the third chapter) and Linux (in the fourth chapter).

However, I do not use this pattern in Chapters 21 and 22. These chapters discuss security and distributed systems, respectively. Because these topics are extensive enough for full books in their own right, I necessarily take a selective approach to them. These

chapters present only a few representative techniques. I also discuss a more restricted set
of examples in Chapter 21, illustrating applied security techniques.

I describe how you build a hosted Inferno kernel image in Appendix A. Doing this is
a part of implementing solutions to those assignments that ask for modifications to the
Inferno kernel. A kernel image built in this way can be run as an application on an existing
host OS. Appendix B shows you how to do the same for a native kernel. In particular, I
provide the steps necessary to create a bootable floppy image for an x86 PC. This image
can then be written to a floppy or used to create a bootable CD-ROM.

Intended Audience

The audience for this book consists of two groups. The first group is practitioners who
want to learn about the internals of Linux or Inferno, as well as reinforce their understanding of the basic principles. People in this group will likely come to the book with
substantial exposure and experience in their respective OS. They will also likely have
some familiarity with some of the concepts and techniques of OS operation. There is
a possibility that such readers might not have been exposed to some of the data structures discussed in this book. Any book on data structures will provide the necessary
background. Likewise, books on computer organization can provide good background in
computer hardware. For this group, the chapters on general principles will help fill in any
gaps in their knowledge, and the respective chapters on Linux and Inferno will provide
introductions to the internals of those operating systems.

The second group this book serves is instructors and students of operating systems
classes. Both introductory and advanced OS courses can make use of this book. Typical
prerequisites for OS courses include a data structures course and a computer organization
course. Some sections of this book assume that kind of background. Other sections are
connected to programming languages, their compilers, and their run-time environments.
Although courses on programming languages and compilers are helpful background, they
are not necessary to study this material.

Using the Book

A book is intended to be read straight through, from start to finish, in most cases. This
book can be used in that way. However, most instructors will not use it in that way.
Rather, the most effective way to use this book in the classroom is to take selected
material from each of the major parts. The full range of material provides each instructor
with the flexibility to select the material that best fits the style of the course and personal
preferences.

An instructor of an operating system course will choose those sections that support the
course's general pedagogical approach. For example, one approach might focus on concepts
and techniques in the abstract. Coverage of the difficulties associated with implementing
those techniques on real hardware is traded off for theoretical depth. Another approach
might trade off time used to present general principles for time used to illustrate the
application of principles through a survey of a number of real operating systems. The
final common approach to introductory classes combines a study of general principles

with an in-depth examination of the implementation of an OS. In this last type of course, students are often required to make modifications to the operating system they study. Such in-depth experience with the internals of an existing OS is also often found in advanced operating systems classes.

Now, consider a set of recommended chapters and sections for each style of course. For general principles courses, the focus should be on a thorough coverage of Chapters 1, 5, 9, 13, 17, 21, and 22. Instructors might want to supplement this material with selected examples from Chapters 2, 6, 10, 14, and 18. Similarly, these chapters can be assigned as outside readings. One particular formulation of this type of course deserves special attention. The course designated CS220 in the Computing Curriculum 2001 specifies a number of specific topics that should be covered. The following sections provide good coverage of those recommendations: 1.1–1.4, 1.6, 5.1–5.8, 9.1–9.3, 9.5–9.6, 13.1–13.4, 13.7.1, 17.1–17.4, 17.7, 21.1–21.2, 21.4–21.5, 22.1, and 22.3–22.4. Of course, instructors are not restricted to covering only these sections. Material in other sections and chapters can be included to supplement the CC2001 recommendations.

If the principles-and-survey approach is used, Chapters 2, 6, 10, 14, and 18 should be in the classroom presentation. If the additional material places too great a demand on classroom time, instructors can be selective about which topics from the principles chapters to present. For example, the proof of the optimality of shortest job first and the formalism for name spaces can be safely omitted. Other examples of existing operating systems, not included here, make for good outside reading assignments.

It is also quite common to structure operating systems courses with a "hands-on" component. In this approach, students are generally expected to familiarize themselves with and make modifications to an existing OS. Frequently, the OS that is used is a relatively small one to make the expectations more manageable. This book also provides material that supports this style of course. The instructor can choose between two existing operating systems: Inferno and Linux. Instructors using Inferno should cover Chapters 3, 7, 11, 15, and 19 in addition to the general principles. Similarly for Linux, Chapters 4, 8, 12, 16, and 20 should be included. In covering the chapters that present code, it is important not to present too much code in the classroom. Experience has shown that it doesn't take long for all code to start looking the same, and the additional benefit dwindles. It is better to present a few smaller bits that illustrate particularly important points and have the students learn the rest with outside reading and assignments. The ability to read and understand real code is a valuable benefit of this type of organization.

The last curriculum example to consider is that of an advanced operating systems course. Considering the nature of advanced courses, several parts of the book could be used well. If the students have come from an introductory course that did not cover all the principles discussed here, then classroom time could be spent presenting them and digging more deeply into any of the principles. Similarly, the survey chapters are a good launching point for a more thorough examination of any one of them or for a more encompassing survey of real operating systems. Finally, for those students whose introductory course did not include experience with operating system internals, the detailed coverage of Inferno and Linux provides a starting place for such experience. These various curriculum designs are summarized in the following table:

Chapter	Principles Only	Principles and Examples	Principles and Inferno	Principles and Linux
1	√	√	√	√
2	•	√		
3			√	
4				√
5	√	√	√	√
6	•	√		
7			√	
8				√
9	√	√	√	√
10	•	√		
11			√	
12				√
13	√	√	√	√
14	•	√		
15			√	
16				√
17	√	√	√	√
18	•	√		
19			√	
20				√
21	√	√	√	√
22	√	√	√	√

√ : The chapter is covered.
• : Selected topics from the chapter are covered.

Features of the Book

Each division of the book presents a topic from several perspectives: general principles, survey of applications, and detailed design and implementation of Inferno and Linux. The general-principles chapters include a number of key features. Several techniques are presented in the form of semiformal algorithms that are suitable for implementation. These algorithms are set apart typographically. In a number of cases, techniques are illustrated with detailed examples, also with distinct formatting. Finally, these chapters include a number of historical notes to help establish context. In those chapters that present detailed discussions of Inferno and Linux, I focus on relatively small parts of the kernel that illustrate the techniques and principles covered in the principles chapters. Each function I present is broken down in to small fragments, and I describe each of those in some detail. The result is a detailed study of some key elements of the respective kernels. These chapters also include exercises that ask the student to "get their hands dirty" making changes to Inferno and to Linux. In addition to these general features, here are some of the key topics discussed:

- *Chapter 1*: background, history, organization, bootstrapping, and system calls

- *Chapters 3, 4*: Inferno and Linux history, structure, initialization, and system calls

- *Chapter 5*: process representation, process scheduling, context switching, mutual exclusion, and deadlock

- *Chapters 7, 8*: process representation, creation, and scheduling in Inferno and Linux, including the new $O(1)$ scheduler in Linux

- *Chapter 9*: address translation techniques, variable-sized allocation techniques (including a comparative example), swapping, and paging

- *Chapter 11*: pool/block allocation and garbage collection in Inferno

- *Chapter 12*: zone/slab allocation, page tables, and page faults in Linux

- *Chapter 13*: overview of I/O hardware, techniques for controlling devices, and selected device management techniques

- *Chapter 15*: device driver structure, parallel port driver, keyboard driver, and IDE disk driver in Inferno

- *Chapter 16*: two-half interrupt handler, parallel port driver, and floppy disk driver in Linux

- *Chapter 17*: name spaces, storage management techniques, and journaled file systems

- *Chapter 19*: Inferno file server design, the Styx protocol, and the kfs file system

- *Chapter 20*: the Linux Virtual File System and the EXT3 file system

- *Chapter 21*: basic security techniques and threats, the Orange Book, encryption, and the Multics protection rings

- *Chapter 22*: resource sharing, synchronous operation, clusters, grids, distributed clocks, and election algorithms

Operating System Examples

The two operating systems discussed in detail in this book each provide their own advantages. Inferno is a relatively small operating system, making its details easier to grasp. Inferno is also somewhat unique in that it was designed to run not only as a conventional native operating system, but also as an application running on a host operating system. This hosted capability makes it significantly easier for students to install the OS on their own machines. It also simplifies the process of testing new versions as students debug their assignments. Linux, on the other hand, is a very familiar system—much more so than Inferno. Consequently, studying it provides the student with more directly applicable experience. It also provides examples of some of the more complex techniques not found in Inferno.

The version of Inferno used in this book is the release of May 10, 2007. The most recent distribution of Inferno can be found at the Vita Nuova Web site, *http://www.vitanuova.com*. Current development and recent revision history can be found on Google's code-hosting site at *http://code.google.com/p/inferno-os/*. I discuss the process of compiling and running Inferno in the appendices.

I use version 2.6.18 of the Linux kernel here. The primary site for both current and older versions of the Linux kernel is *http://www.kernel.org*. Two excellent sources of information on building a Linux kernel can be found in the "Linux Kernel HOWTO" by Brian Ward and the "Kernel Rebuild Guide" by Kwan Lowe.

Some of the source code for examples in Chapters 2, 6, 10, 14, and 18 is also available on the Web. The full source code for the CTSS operating system can be found at *http://www.piercefuller.com/library/ctss.html*. Some portions of the source code to Multics can be found at *http://www.multicians.org*. Old versions of UNIX, including the sixth edition, can be found at *http://www.tuhs.org*. The 4.3BSD version of UNIX is being maintained by the International Free Computing Task Force (IFCTF) as 4.3BSD-Quasijarus. The home for this project is *http://ifctfvax.harhan.org/Quasijarus* where these updates, as well as older versions, are all available. The primary resource for TinyOS is *http://www.tinyos.net*. Finally, the home for the Xen virtual machine monitor is *http://www.cl.cam.ac.uk/research/srg/netos/xen*.

Source Code Formatting

The source code fragments in this book are formatted using Knuth and Levy's CWEB system of structured documentation. Keywords and data types are typeset in boldface. Identifiers not in all caps are typeset in italic; identifiers in all caps are typeset in a monospace font. Several of the C language operators are multicharacter sequences that use characters from the ASCII character set. When presented here, some of these are replaced by common mathematical symbols, which in some cases express the meaning more directly. The correspondence between the C operators in ASCII and the symbols typeset in this text are summarized in the following table:

ASCII	Symbol
->	$\rightarrow$
NULL	Λ
~	$\sim$
^	$\oplus$
==	$\equiv$
!=	$\neq$
>=	$\geq$
<=	$\leq$
!	$\neg$
&&	$\wedge$
||	$\vee$
>>	$\gg$
<<	$\ll$

In addition to these conventions, `CWEB` formats octal and hexadecimal constants differently. An octal constant that would be expressed as `0123` in ASCII is typeset as °*123*, and the hexadecimal constant `0x123` is typeset as #`123`.

It might seem strange that our printed representation doesn't appear in the same form as the compiler input that is typed in a text editor. Although today we don't see this sort of difference much outside of `WEB` and `CWEB`, it has a long tradition. A number of languages allowed variation in the characters used for operators and such because not all installations used the same character sets. Some environments had very limited character sets with some not even including lowercase letters. Others had extremely rich character sets, allowing programmers to directly enter mathematical symbols, such as those we use here for "not equal to," "less than or equal to," and "greater than or equal to." C itself defines trigraphs to allow for its use in environments that do not include all needed characters. Beyond that, it has been quite common for published code to have a different look to it, much as typeset text has a different look from the output of a typewriter. In that spirit, Algol 68 formalized the difference between the published form, called the strict language, and the compiler-input form, called the reference language. It is interesting to note that Algol was one of the languages that influenced the design of C, and the typesetting practices used with Algol influenced Knuth's development of `WEB`. The two lines of influence have converged in `CWEB`, whose printed representation I use here.

Supplementary Material

Supporting material for this book can be found on the Course Technology Web site at *http://www.course.com*. This same material is included on the instructor's CD, which can be obtained from a Course Technology sales representative. Copies of the relevant versions of Inferno and Linux are included with the supplementary material. The material also includes solutions to most of the exercises. Presentation material is included as well.

Acknowledgments

No project of this magnitude can be completed without help. There are numerous people whose support, encouragement, and assistance have been invaluable. I would first like to thank my wife Mary and my daughter Rachel. They have put up with innumerable nights of my frustration and of losing me to my office. But they never stopped believing in me or in this project. They picked up the slack around the house as I wrote. The interest and support of my other family and friends have also been a much welcome source of encouragement.

Next, I would like to thank my colleagues, both at FedEx and at the University of Memphis. No matter how hard an author tries to manage time (or at least no matter how hard *I* try to manage time), writing a book like this affects other responsibilities. I would particularly like to express my appreciation to Miley Ainsworth of FedEx Labs for his support of this project. I would also like to thank my colleague at FedEx, Tim Gregory, for his assistance in understanding TinyOS and for reviewing what I wrote about it.

The next group of people I'd like to thank is all of my operating systems students over the past few years. They have been my test subjects for this book. They have made do with partial drafts, typos, and awkward grammar. Nevertheless, many of them have expressed support and encouragement for the project. I'd like to recognize a few students who provided helpful feedback. They include Bob Bradley, Jim Greer, Taliesin Penfound, and Debbie Travis.

I have also corresponded with several members of the operating systems community who provided valuable assistance and feedback. They are Charles Forsyth, of Vita Nuova Holdings Ltd.; Tom Van Vleck, former member of the Multics development team and maintainer of the multicians.org Web site; Stephen Hoffman, of the HP OpenVMS group; and Digby Tarvin, of the University of New South Wales. I would also like to thank Jim Aman at Saint Xavier University, Charles Anderson at Western Oregon University, Bob Bradley at the University of Tennessee at Martin, Thomas Liu at New Jersey City University, Chung-Horng Lung at Carleton University, Jon Weissman at the University of Minnesota, and Dongyan Xu at Purdue University. Their careful review of the early drafts led to substantial improvements in this material.

Finally, I want to express my appreciation to everyone at Course Technology. There's no way to list everyone who has contributed to this project. However, a few names must be recognized. First, I'd like to thank Mary Franz, who first saw the potential for this book and helped me through the early stages of the process. There are three people who have been there working with me all the way through the project. I am supremely grateful to Alyssa Pratt, Jim Markham, and Matt Hutchinson for everything they've done to make this book possible. Everyone's input and involvement have made this a better book. Any remaining flaws are entirely my own. I can't thank everyone enough for all the support in making this a reality.

Brian L. Stuart

Chapter 1

Introduction to Operating Systems

At some level all computer software must interface with the hardware on which it runs. It must use the central processing unit (CPU) and memory in a safe and efficient manner, and it must control input/output (I/O) devices in order to bring data in and put results out. Most applications, however, do not attempt this control directly. Instead, they are written to operate with additional underlying software that is responsible for managing the hardware. This underlying software is the **operating system**.

The study of operating systems is the study of software that directly controls hardware and provides a framework for other software. It is the study of the foundation software on which most all applications depend. It is the study of the environment in which and for which applications are written. Consequently, the study of operating systems is one of the most important foundation topics in computer science.

Because the operating system runs directly on hardware without additional supporting software, a study of operating systems also provides a good background for **embedded systems**. Embedded systems include the wide variety of applications ranging from automotive ignition control computers to electronic thermostats to medical IV pumps. Many of the same techniques that are used in embedded applications are also used in operating systems.

As we begin our study of operating systems in this chapter, we examine much of the background and questions surrounding the operating system as a whole. We first define what an operating system is and identify what it does. We also look at the development of operating systems over the history of computing. The next major topics address the question of how we organize and structure an operating system. followed by a study of how an operating system gets loaded into memory and initialized. Finally, we address the connection between applications and the operating systems on which they run.

1.1 What Is an Operating System?

In order to frame our study of the principles of operating systems (OSs), we need to ask the question, "What exactly is an operating system?" Often vendors of operating systems refer to everything included in their distribution media as their operating system. This is, however, a somewhat problematic definition for our purposes. After all, the images, sound files, and application programs are not part of the operating system per se, and are subjects of their own areas of study.

At the other end of the spectrum, the label of operating system is sometimes restricted to a program that runs on bare hardware without any supporting software. This program, often called a **kernel**, **monitor**, or **supervisor**, does provide all the functions of an operating system in many systems. However, as discussed in this book, there are a number of operating systems, where much of the traditional functionality is provided by auxiliary programs.

It seems that any attempt to define an operating system in terms of how it's packaged or how it's constructed is doomed to failure. Consequently, we define it in terms of what it does. In particular, we identify the following key functions and purposes:

- The operating system manages the sharing of resources among competing entities.

- The operating system provides a number of common services that make applications easier to write.

- The operating system serves as the interface between application programs and hardware.

With these ideas in mind, we define the operating system as follows:

> An operating system is a set of one or more programs which provides a set of services that interface applications to computer hardware and which allocates and manages resources shared among multiple processes.

The three key functions and purposes of an operating system just listed suggest three corresponding perspectives on its role. In Sections 1.1.1 through 1.1.3, we discuss these three perspectives on the concept and the role of the operating system, derived from these three functions and purposes. Think of these in the same way as we talk of a person "wearing different hats." Indeed throughout this book, we look at the functions of the operating system from each of these perspectives at various times.

1.1.1   Resource Manager

The most classic way of viewing an operating system is as a **resource manager**. From this point of view, the operating system is responsible for the system hardware. In that role, it receives requests for access to resources from applications and it either grants or denies access. When granting allocation requests, it must be careful to allocate the resources so that programs don't interfere with each other.

For example, it is a bad idea to allow programs to have unrestricted access to each other's memory. If a buggy (or malicious) program writes into the memory space of another program, the second program will crash if it's lucky, or produce incorrect results if it's not lucky. Worse yet, if the offensive program modifies the operating system's memory, it could affect the behavior of the whole system.

When we talk about an operating system as being a resource manager, we think of it as the authority figure of the system. We even refer to programs as running *under* an operating system. (This view was illustrated dramatically in the movie Tron. In that movie, the Master Control Program, MCP, operated like a despotic government impeding the freedoms of the heroic programs. The naming of this program is no accident; MCP was the name of the operating system, originally released in 1962, for some models of computers manufactured by Burroughs.)

1.1.2   Service Provider

We can imagine that the resource manager viewpoint represents that of a system owner who wants to make sure that the resources are used effectively. On the other hand, we can look at things from the viewpoint of the application (or the application's programmer). From this perspective, we want the operating system to provide a rich collection of services that make the application's job easier. In particular, we expect that much of the detail in accessing I/O devices, allocating memory, and the like will be handled by the operating system. When we think about the operating system from the service provider perspective, we often talk about programs running *on* the operating system.

1.1.3   Virtual Machine

The last perspective we examine is that of the **virtual machine**. This perspective stems from our observation of the operating system as an interface between the application and the hardware. We get the basic idea here by imagining the application software looking down toward the operating system and hardware. The application cannot tell the difference between a computer with very simple hardware with few features and a computer with very complex hardware with many features if the operating system provides the same features in both cases. In other words, as far as the application is concerned, the combination of the hardware and the operating system is the "computer" on which it runs. In Section 1.4, we see a particular way of designing an operating system we call a **virtual machine operating system** which takes this perspective to its logical conclusion. (To make matters more complicated, there's yet another common use of the term virtual machine. This other use refers to a machine that is simulated in the sense that each instruction is interpreted by the host on which it is running. Sometimes, we translate the virtual instructions into native ones on the fly. This is called just-in-time compiling. The advantage of this type of virtual machine is portability. We can compile programs to the simulated instruction set and then run those programs anywhere we have an interpreter, or virtual machine. This concept has been used in a variety of systems ranging from the P-code of UCSD Pascal in the 1970s to the more modern Java Virtual Machine (JVM) and the Dis virtual machine.)

1.2   Areas of Operating System Responsibility

Regardless of the perspective from which we're looking, the OS must deal with a variety of resources. It is along these lines of responsibility that the majority of this book is organized. Of the items described in this section, the first five (processes, memory, I/O devices, file systems, and security) are discussed in detail in subsequent chapters. As we discuss these areas of responsibility, we do so from the various perspectives discussed in the previous section.

1.2.1   Processes

The most obvious resource that needs to be managed and used effectively is the CPU. The tricky part is that the very resource we're trying to manage is the resource that's executing the code of the operating system itself. In other words, the CPU is the active entity in managing and allocating itself. Furthermore, because there's usually only one of them (or at most a few), managing the CPU is not a matter of allocating the physical resources exclusively to running programs. Rather, we manage the CPU in terms of allocating fractions of its time among competing running programs.

When managing the CPU resource, we generally work in terms of running programs. We refer to these programs in execution as **processes**. To support processes, operating systems generally provide services including:

- creating a process

- destroying a process

- changing a process's priority

- providing interprocess communication

- often providing process synchronization

In most cases, these services are used by one process to act on another. However, in some cases, a process might call a service to act on itself. For example, when a process is finished, it can call the process destruction service to remove itself. Internally, the operating system is responsible for **scheduling** and **context switching**. The scheduler is the mechanism by which the operating system chooses which process is to run next. The actual operation of transferring control of the CPU from one process to another is what we mean by context switching.

1.2.2   Memory

In many ways, one might expect that managing the memory space is one of the simplest responsibilities of the operating system. However, experience has shown that the performance of the system is probably more dependent on the behavior of the memory management subsystem than on any other. At its heart, memory management is primarily about responding to requests to allocate and to free memory. Of course, in satisfying these requests, the operating system must ensure that processes don't interfere with each other and that memory space is not wasted. These responsibilities form the basis of a typical set of memory management services, such as:

- directly requesting additional memory

- indirectly requesting memory (e.g.,when creating a new process)

- freeing (releasing) memory back to the OS

- requesting that memory areas be shared among processes

As with process management, there is a significant behind-the-scenes responsibility for the memory manager. In particular, in most environments, we wish to satisfy requests for more memory than is physically installed on the machine. Providing support for this type of overallocation (often called **virtual memory**) is typically a major part of the operating system's memory manager.

1.2.3   I/O Devices

One of the primary functions of an operating system is providing services that simplify application development. This is nowhere more evident than in the area of I/O programming. If every application program had to handle the minute details of every I/O device that it used, application programming would be far more error-prone than it is. Furthermore, I/O devices are often shared among numerous processes. For example, nearly every application running on a system has need of mass storage devices such as disk drives. This sharing complicates the interactions between a program and the devices it uses. Naturally, we assign the responsibility for preventing problems to the operating system.

In managing I/O devices, we generally provide a variety of services for processes. These services often include:

- opening a device or attaching a device to a process

- reading data from a device

- writing data to a device

- closing and releasing a device

- providing exclusive access for appropriate devices

- providing various special functions, such as rewinding tapes and setting serial line baud rates

We often also make use of I/O devices as part of other OS functions. For example, the illusion of large memory spaces is normally provided by using space on a storage device to hold less frequently used data. Likewise, if we want to start a process running a new program, we must read the binary code for that program from some device.

1.2.4   File Systems

Another area where we use I/O devices to support other functions is the area of **file systems**. Indeed, for most applications, the primary use of I/O devices is for storing and retrieving named persistent data that we usually call files. For the most part, the file system supports a set of requests similar to the I/O device subsystem:

- opening a file

- reading from a file

- writing to a file

- closing a file

- seeking to a random place within a file

- reading file metadata (e.g., file name, size, ownership, protection codes, etc.)

- modifying selected metadata

In Chapter 17, we find that in order to support these requests, the file system must also provide the service of translating names into locations of data. We also define there the idea of a **name space** as the set of names which a process can access. Indeed, as operating systems have developed, the management of name spaces has become a key element in the design and organization of operating systems.

1.2.5   Security

Virtually every other area of operating system responsibility carries with it security elements. An OS should not allow just any process to terminate another one. As we've already mentioned, we must be careful to ensure that processes cannot write indiscriminantly into each other's memory space. Likewise, requests to access I/O devices and files must be filtered through tests of ownership and permission. These measures are implemented in terms of enforcing security policies in a manner which is transparent to applications. Programs make requests of the OS, and they are determined to be either permissible or not. Some very interesting new developments in the realm of security are in networking. With the rapid proliferation of the worldwide Internet, the need for strong authentication of network requests has taken on increased importance. Finally, there are additional security responsibilities that belong to various administrative applications. These include tasks such as scanning the system for known vulnerabilities, testing the system for unauthorized access, verifying the safety of third-party software, and so on. In addition to the enforcement mechanisms operating in the background, applications can request services such as:

- setting security policies

- querying security policies

- authenticating themselves to a remote system

- listening for a remote system to authenticate itself

- encrypting and decrypting messages, especially ones carried over a network

Out of view of the applications, the OS acts as a gatekeeper. When a process requests a service of any of the subsystems, the operating system checks whether or not it has permission for the service. If it does have permission, then the request is granted, but if not, the request is denied.

1.2.6   Networking

In many ways, networking support is another application of the I/O subsystem. In addition to the details of moving bits in and out of the system, however, the operating system normally implements protocol stacks. It is quite common for networking protocols to be designed in terms of several layers, each encapsulating the other. For instance, communication using the TCP/IP suite of protocols over an Ethernet interface generally involves four protocols as illustrated in the following example.

Example 1.1: Network Protocols

In this example, consider a Web browser making a request for a file using the Hypertext Transfer Protocol (HTTP). Using this application level protocol, the client (browser) may send a message such as "`GET / HTTP/1.0\r\n\r\n`" when attempting to fetch the URL *http://www.google.com*. This application message is then encapsulated in one or more Transmission Control Protocol (TCP) segments. Each TCP segment has a header containing data used to maintain the integrity of the series of messages, followed by the data it contains. TCP segments are, in turn, encapsulated into one or more Internet Protocol (IP) datagrams. As with TCP segments, IP datagrams have a header, which ensures that the datagram gets to the right destination uncorrupted, followed by the data. Finally, the IP datagrams are further encapsulated in Ethernet frames. Each Ethernet frame has both a header and a trailer. The overall transmission looks like that shown in Figure 1-1.

Ethernet Header	IP Header	TCP Header	`GET / HTTP/1.0\r\n\r\n`	Ethernet Trailer

Figure 1-1: Example of Network Protocol Encapsulation

As with I/O programming, it makes sense to let the operating system take responsibility for these protocols. From the application perspective, networking services include:

- establishing a connection to a remote service

- listening for connections from a remote client

- sending messages to a remote system

- receiving messages from a remote system

- closing a connection to a remote system

1.2.7 User Interfaces

The last area of responsibility that we discuss is the **user interface**. While some designs have integrated the user interface into the operating system, most modern designs break the user interface out as normal application processes. This is part of the reason why we don't attempt to give user interfaces a thorough examination in this book. The other reason is that when dealing with users, things are often more complicated than when dealing with hardware and the other OS responsibilities. As a result, the area of user interfaces is a large subject unto itself.

1.3 History of Operating Systems

The history of operating systems is the story of two trends in their development. The first trend is the evolution from the operating system as a collection of disparate mechanisms to the operating system organized around unifying principles. Even though the areas of OS responsibility seem very dissimilar, operating systems research has identified a number of concepts with which they can be united.

The second major trend addresses the conceptual model of computer usage. As we see throughout this section, computer systems were originally seen as being for a single user to run a single program on a single machine. This perspective can be conceptualized with the triangle shown in Figure 1-2. While every generation of computing seems to start with this same model in mind, we always find that we need to add functionality to allow multiple users to run multiple programs and to interact with multiple computers.

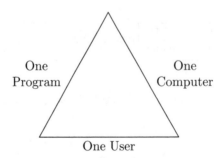

Figure 1-2: Triangle of "Ones"

1.3.1   Bare Metal

Proto-computers and the earliest computers were developed with the idea that they'd be used by one person at a time to solve one problem at a time. These one-of-a-kind machines and early, small volume production machines were built from the late 1930s to the early 1950s. It wasn't long, however, before many people had uses for these machines. So the natural thing happened. Those who administered these machines began to schedule the use of them. It was not uncommon for a sign-up sheet to be posted with a week's worth of time divided into hour-long time slots. An individual user may have been allowed to sign up for only two or three slots per week.

To our modern ears, this sounds like a painfully difficult way to work. Partly, this is because it was a painfully difficult way to work, and partly this is because the discipline of design and debugging away from the computer has largely been lost in a world of graphical debuggers and quick-and-easy compiling. Nevertheless, in a world where machines were rare and priceless, this was an effective use of the machine and programmers had little choice but to live with it.

The systems of those days had no operating system as we would think of one today. However, the seeds of the operating system were already beginning to appear. Even with the earliest machines, it was quite common for a lab to develop libraries of code fragments forming the first examples of code reuse. Using these libraries, programmers did not have to rewrite routines to compute square roots or to control a tape drive for each new application. We can see how these libraries inspired the service provision aspects of operating systems today.

1.3.2   Batch Operating Systems

There's a big problem with the scheduling described in the previous subsection. Remember that these machines were very expensive and rare. With that in mind, consider how programmers spend most of their time. For most of us, it's spent staring at the screen trying to figure out what went wrong. So the upshot was that for many of those scheduled hours, the CPU was idle and the expensive machine went to waste for most of the hour. The first real operating systems were developed in the 1950s to address this ineffective use. In order to use the machine more effectively, users had to be separated from the

---

Historical Note: ENIAC

One of the most extreme examples of a machine that could work on only one problem at a time was the Electronic Numerical Integrator and Computer (ENIAC). In fact, this machine, which went into operation in 1945, required rewiring to change the problem it solved. This was true for its initial design. In 1947, a technique, requiring a relatively minor modification to the machine, was developed that allowed a program to be entered on the switch panel originally designed to store numeric constants. This enhancement reduced the time to set up a problem from potentially several days to a matter of hours. ENIAC continued to operate this way until 1955, when it was retired.

machine so that debugging time did not prevent the machine from doing useful work for other users.

Even today, this type of noninteractive operation makes sense in some areas. Examples include periodic running of payroll, billing, group membership mailings, and so forth. The basic idea is that a user submits a job to the system and then comes back later to get the results. Groups of jobs are collected together in batches and each job is run to completion before moving on to the next. In some of the early batch systems, jobs were submitted as a deck of punched cards handed over to an operator in the computing center or perhaps fed into a card reader by the user. In more modern applications of the technique, jobs might be submitted from some form of interactive session, but still run as part of a batch. Operating systems that operate in this way are called **batch operating systems**.

In some installations, groups of jobs are collected on a small computer and put onto tape to be processed by the main computer. In these cases, it is also common for the output from the main computer to be written to a tape, which is then read by another smaller computer that prints the results. These printed outputs are then placed into output bins for users to pick up.

By developing these batch operating systems, developers began to break the one user/one program/one computer triangle. The one user leg is broken here. Even though at any point in time, the computer is working on behalf of only one user, many users can be in the process of using the overall computing facility.

1.3.3   Time-Sharing Operating Systems

As usual, we don't get something for nothing. Batch operating systems make using the computer more efficient in the sense that the CPU does useful work for a greater percentage of the time. However, this benefit comes at a cost. When people work directly with a computer, there is an interactive component that gives an immediacy making one's debugging time more effective. Even though we take this as self-evident today, the benefit of interactive use was not seen as worth the cost of less-efficient CPU usage in most early environments.

Nevertheless, there were some environments that did hold to manual scheduling of computer time. In these environments (often research), another phenomenon soon emerged. A programmer who had signed up for an hour but ran into a snag would often leave the system before the hour was up. Something of a subculture developed where other members of the computing community waited around for those times when the computer would be free for part of a scheduled hour.

As the decade of the 1960s dawned, some of the researchers in these environments noticed that the computer turned out to be more efficiently used when scheduling and turn-taking took place with more fine-grained resolution. The natural thing to do with an observation like this is to ask what happens if we take it to the limit. In effect, we ask what would happen if we moved from one user's program to another with an infinitesimal time between these switches? Two things immediately emerge from this question. First, it becomes clear that a program cannot run to completion before switching to another. Second, we see that users could not alternate the use of a single I/O device to communicate with the system. However, if we could solve these issues, we'd have a system where multiple users could run multiple programs with the illusion that all the programs would be running simultaneously.

These ideas form the basis of the next stage in operating system development. The first step is easy. We just replicate the user interface connecting numerous terminals with keyboards for input and printers or video displays for output. This easily addresses the issue of how multiple users can use the system simultaneously. In order to provide the illusion of simultaneous program execution, we approximate the theoretical model. Rather than try to switch among processes in infinitesimal time, we do the switching with a fast but finite interval. Times of one-tenth of a second between switches are not uncommon. The innovative technique of suspending a running program, saving its state, and restoring a previously saved program in order to give it the CPU is called context switching.

This new type of operating system is variously called a **time-sharing operating system**, a **multiprogramming operating system**, or a **multitasking operating system**. While we have presented these terms as being synonymous, they are often used with subtle distinctions in meaning. In particular, the term multiprogramming is often more precisely used to refer to holding multiple programs in memory at once. We generally think of this as going hand in hand with time-sharing, but it doesn't have to. Without multiprogramming, time sharing can still be implemented by writing a snapshot of the currently running program to disk on each context switch. This way, only one program is resident in memory at a time. Conversely, there have been multiprogramming batch systems that allow one program to run while another is waiting on an I/O device. In providing a mechanism for switching among a number of processes all ready to run, we break the second leg of the one user/one program/one computer triangle.

1.3.4   Distributed Operating Systems

The natural next step is to break the one-computer leg of the triangle. Allowing a user or program to use multiple CPUs or computers to cooperate on a single problem is the realm of distributed computing. The various degrees to which cooperating systems are treated as one large system form a spectrum of distributed techniques discussed in more detail in Chapter 22. At one end of the spectrum, we have **grid** computing systems, which are generally identified by their independent administrative domains. They are often more widely distributed geographically than other distributed designs. These systems cooperate by convention, but no system can assume that another is behaving according to the plan. Popular distributed projects such as SETI@home and folding@home can be classified as grids. Somewhere in the middle of the spectrum, we have **clusters**. These systems are generally administered as a single system, but each machine runs its own operating system. The individual operating systems are generally aware of each other and expect all the members of the cluster to cooperate. At the other end of the spectrum, we find environments where a single operating system treats all the CPUs and memory in multiple systems as a single resource pool. Operating systems written with the objective of coordinating multiple CPUs are generally referred to as **distributed operating systems**.

There is another type of multiple CPU support that doesn't fall into the class of distributed operating systems. Some machines have multiple CPUs sharing a single physical memory and the same set of I/O devices. We refer to these as symmetric multiprocessing

(SMP) systems. While the operating system design must account for scheduling and coordinating multiple processors, the shared memory and I/O devices separate these systems from the class of distributed system.

1.4   Techniques of Organizing Operating Systems

As with any other substantial software system, an operating system must be carefully designed. In this section, we look at a few of the general organizational techniques commonly used. Throughout this discussion, keep in mind that most often system designers use techniques in combination, even when one approach dominates their design.

1.4.1   Monolithic Designs

We begin our discussion of design techniques with **monolithic** designs. While it can be tempting to think of this as a class of designs the are characterized by a lack of any other form of organization, in reality a monolithic design is just a design organized as a single program. As with any program, such a design should be done with a well-organized structure. Most operating systems have been organized along these lines.

1.4.2   Layered Designs

We next consider a **layered** approach to OS design. The concept of layered design is not exclusive to operating systems. Many of the better software system designs are structured in a layered manner. The basic idea is that each layer increases the level of abstraction and is built on the functions provided by lower layers. For those who approach design more formally, the design can be made to follow a layering principle, which can be stated as "no function calls a function or uses a data structure defined in a higher layer." Most uses of libraries follow a layered approach.

In the context of operating system design, a layered design might place the I/O device management at the lowest layer, build memory management on top of it, put file systems as the third layer, and, finally, process management might exist at the top layer. This arrangement is illustrated in Figure 1-3. As we move from the hardware up through the layers to applications, we gain more and more functionality. In realistic designs, the layer assignment is not as simple as the example presented here. In fact, it's not uncommon for some subsystems to be split into lower and upper parts that have other functional layers between them. The XINU operating system by Comer is a good example of a system that follows a layered design.

1.4.3   Microkernel Designs

A number of designers have suggested that much of the traditional kernel functionality could be moved out of the kernel and into other processes managed by the kernel. In principle, this would make the kernel smaller and easier to write and maintain. In such a design, much of what is done through function calls in a monolithic kernel is handled by message passing with a **microkernel**. Figure 1-4 illustrates one such design. Each box

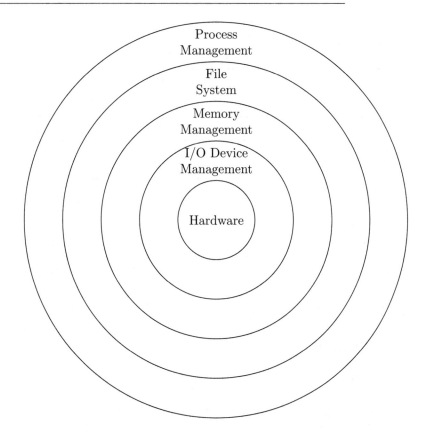

Figure 1-3: Simplified Example Layered OS Design

above the microkernel is implemented as an independent process. The primary role of the microkernel is scheduling the processes and passing messages among them.

One effect of the microkernel design is that communication between components, that might otherwise take place through parameter passing or shared variables, is carried by messages. As one might expect, this characteristic creates a greater burden on the design of the microkernel and its message passing implementation to be efficient. The risk is that the effort to create efficiencies, in a poorly designed example, can result in a microkernel that is nearly as complex as a full monolithic kernel.

Another challenge in the design of a microkernel OS lies in the issue of security. We want as much functionality as we can to operate as ordinary processes. But for much of that functionality, we don't want normal users to be able to substitute their own versions. Consider the following (admittedly contrived) example. If the memory management functions of the OS are implemented as normal processes, then we must allow (at least some) normal processes to be able to allocate memory to other processes. How then do we pre-

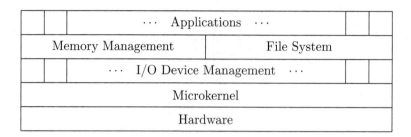

Figure 1-4: Example Microkernel OS Design

vent all normal processes from being able to do this? One of the most common answers is to give those processes that provide OS mechanisms a special status with higher privileges.

Some good examples of microkernel designs include Tanenbaum's MINIX, The Hurd (part of the GNU environment from the Free Software Foundation), and the MACH operating system, which (among other uses) serves as the foundation for Mac OS X for the Apple Macintosh. While Inferno is not built around a microkernel, we will see examples of how it also moves some traditional functions into user processes.

1.4.4   Virtual Machine Designs

Section 1.1.3 discusses the concept of a virtual machine as a way of looking at the function of an operating system. It's also possible to take that idea a step further and make it the basis of an operating system design. In particular, we can take literally the idea of providing the illusion of a machine. This approach leads us to develop an operating system which gives each process the illusion that it is running on the machine all by itself. In other words, the main function of a virtual machine operating system is to provide the illusion of many copies of the hardware. In such an environment, we can, and often do, run another operating system in each of the virtual machines. Again, as one might expect, doing this efficiently is a significant challenge. The canonical example of this approach is the VM operating system from IBM. Figure 1-5 illustrates this approach with three "guest" operating systems running on top of the virtual machine OS and a number of applications running on each of those.

	Applications		Applications		Applications	
Guest OS			Guest OS		Guest OS	
Virtual Machine OS						
Hardware						

Figure 1-5: Sample Virtual Machine OS Design

In recent years, a number of products have emerged with the purpose of allowing the user to simultaneously run more than one OS. The commercial product VMware supports several operating systems for the Intel x86 architecture. These operating systems can run unmodified. The open source project Xen provides very similar functionality. However, it requires that certain low-level operations be ported to Xen. In effect, Xen becomes the machine on which the OS is running. A number of open source operating systems have been ported to Xen. However, because only the vendor can make the necessary changes to a proprietary operating system, there is very little in the way of such OSs available for Xen. One final approach that is gaining momentum is emulating a complete computer in software and running an OS on that emulated machine. While there have been examples of this practice for several decades, it is becoming practical for more applications all the time. For example, even on a low-end commodity computer, an emulated PDP-11 is faster than any of the real ones built by Digital Equipment Corporation (DEC). (The PDP-11 is the machine on which much of the early UNIX development took place. It was manufactured from the 1970s into the 1990s.) This approach allows us to run operating systems developed for one computer architecture on another. Such an emulator can also be used to run multiple operating systems on a single machine. One of the most interesting emulators being used for running operating systems in parallel is QEMU, developed by Fabrice Bellard. When running code for the Intel x86 architecture on an x86, QEMU can run much of the code natively rather than emulating it. In doing so, it can provide much the same functionality as VMware or Xen but without requiring special hardware features or modifications to the OSs being run.

1.5   Bootstrapping

In all of our discussion up to this point, we've skipped over one challenging issue. The OS can only provide all of the services we've discussed once it's loaded in memory and running. However, allocating memory, loading code from a storage device, and starting it running are normally functions of the very operating system we need to load and start running. The net effect is we have a sort of "chicken and egg" problem. How can we get the system to a point where the operating system is running before we have the operating system available to perform the functions usually associated with loading and running a program? Getting the system from bare hardware to the point where we have a running OS is a process we often call **bootstrapping**. (The term comes from the image of the computer lifting itself up by its own bootstraps.) While the term bootstrapping is in common use today, many manufacturers have also referred to it by other terms, which are still in use with those systems. Among those are **cold start**, **dead start**, and **initial program load** (IPL).

There are three typical approaches to the bootstrapping problem.

- Up through the 1980s, many computers were manufactured with front panels. These devices provided an operator or programmer with access to the system's CPU and memory. There were usually one or more rows of lights (usually LEDs) that showed the current state of various busses and registers. For input, there were generally one or more rows of toggle switches on which the user could set an address or a data value in binary. Typically, the user could use the front panel to examine and modify memory locations and to start and stop the CPU. In some larger (especially later) designs, the front panel was replaced with another smaller computer called a console computer. This small computer gave the user a textual interface to the same functions that were provided by the front panel.

Given this type of interface, we can easily move from the computer as a lump of inactive silicon to a machine running a program. We need only enter the program on the front panel, storing it into memory, and then start the CPU running that program. Of course, entering a large program in binary, one word at a time, is rather tedious. Naturally, we don't load the whole operating system that way. Instead, the system loads a small program that knows only enough to read another small program from a storage device. This first stage program is often called the boot loader, or the bootstrap loader. The code read from the storage device is often itself another second stage loader, which knows enough to find the OS and load it.

- In a number of large-scale computer designs (especially older ones), the hardware provided the critical first step. This was especially true with devices like punched card readers. Often, the hardware was capable of loading the contents of one card into memory and causing the CPU to run that code. As with loading code from a front panel, we put a small bootstrap program on the storage medium and it knows enough to carry on with the next step of the process.

- For some installations, the system included code for a number of boot loaders in special read-only memory (ROM). This was especially common in larger installations where the incremental cost of the additional memory was relatively benign. In these systems, the front panel could be used simply to select which boot loader to use. This had the effect of selecting which storage device was used to load the second stage loader. In time, the relative costs of components changed and ROM became much less expensive than front panels. As a result, the front panel largely became extinct and nearly all machines are manufactured with code in ROM that the computer is running from the moment it is reset. This code gives the operator much the same sort of interface as a console computer provides. (In fact, most console computers start up running code in ROM.) The operator can directly interact with the machine in some cases, but the main use of this code is to load second stage loaders from storage devices.

Regardless of which method is used to get the system running, we end up running a small program that loads the operating system from disk (or some other storage device) and starts it running. In some cases, there are additional intermediate loaders. We usually refer to each of the loader programs as a stage. The most common designs use either two- or three-stage boot loaders. Typically, each loader does very little in the way of initializing the hardware. We normally leave that up to the OS itself. However, in most cases, there are a few tasks that must be performed to get the system to the state expected by the OS, and those tasks are performed by the loader code.

1.6 System Calls

The final topic covered as part of this introduction is the connection between applications and the operating system. Almost universally, this takes place through **system calls**. Conceptually, the system call is a mechanism by which a process can request one of the services mentioned in this chapter from the operating system.

1.6.1 Example System Calls

While we discuss a number of examples of system calls in later chapters, we give a few from the example of the UNIX operating system here:

- *fork( )*: creates a new process that is a copy of the existing one

- *exit( )*: terminates the requesting process

- *open( )*: opens a file for reading and/or writing

- *read( )*: retrieves data from a file or device

- *write( )*: puts data to a file or device

Note how each of these system calls corresponds to one of the system services that are described in Section 1.2. As with many systems, UNIX system calls are used in the same way as ordinary library functions. This is illustrated in Example 1.2.

Example 1.2: Using System Calls

In order to illustrate their use, consider a sample use of some system calls. Suppose we want to read the header from a file. A function to do this, coded in the C language, might look like:

```
int load_hdr(char *name, char *buf)
{
    int fd;
    fd = open(name, O_RDONLY);
    if(fd < 0)
        return(fd);
    n = read(fd, buf, HDR_SIZE);
    close(fd);
    return(n);
}
```

In this example, we start by opening the file for reading. The *open( )* system call returns an integer file descriptor which we then use for the other calls related to that file. In the *read( )* system call, we request that the OS copy data from a file into the memory space at the location pointed to by *buf*. The number of bytes requested is given by HDR_SIZE and *fd* identifies what file we want to read. Upon completion, the system call returns (and we assign to the variable n) the number of bytes actually read. If the OS detects an error and is unable to read any data, then it returns a -1 and the global variable *errno* is set to indicate which error was detected.

While every system defines its own conventions, this example illustrates the common features. First, we need a mechanism to specify which service we are requesting. Here, it is the call to a function called *read( )* that specifies the requested service. Second, most requests require that the process making the request provide some parameters. In this example, the parameters are passed (initially) through the normal function call mechanism. Finally, nearly all system calls produce some results. At the very least, they produce a status indicating whether the request was successful. In this example, the result comes back to the requesting process using the normal function return mechanism.

1.6.2   System Call Mechanism

There are a variety of ways in which the system call mechanism can be implemented, but we describe a typical one here. Notice that the examples we give in the previous subsection are all shown as function calls in a high-level language. Normally, the compiler doesn't know anything special about system calls as opposed to normal function calls. We can get away with this because the libraries we link to have small ordinary functions for each of the system calls. These small **stub** functions don't usually do much more than set up the system call parameters in a well-defined way and then switch control to the operating system.

The transfer of control is often done through some type of software interrupt (often called a trap) instruction. These special instructions cause the CPU to save the current state of the machine and transfer control to a function in the operating system. They are like a cross between an ordinary subroutine call instruction and a hardware interrupt. Upon receiving the transfer of control, the operating system will usually suspend the requesting process. At some later time when the request can be fulfilled, the requesting process is resumed with the system call results returned in a well-defined way.

1.7   Summary

Without software, a computer is just a static lump of silicon. The operating system is the base level of software on which applications run. It is responsible for managing and allocating the system hardware, including the CPU, physical memory, and I/O devices. The operating system also provides support for additional functions such as file systems and network protocols. In providing these functions, we can look at the operating system as a manager of the system's resources, as a provider of services, and as defining a virtual machine. There are several ways in which we can put the pieces together to build a complete operating system. Some systems are structured as a conventional monolithic program. Others follow a layered design. Still others are based on microkernels and some are virtual machine designs. Regardless of how the system is structured, it must be loaded into memory by some form of boot loader. After the system is loaded and running, it is ready to accept service requests from processes through the system call mechanism.

1.8   Exercises

1. List four areas for which the operating system is responsible for managing and providing services. For each, list three services that are usually requested by a system call.

2. What is the difference between a system call and a library call?

3. In what way are the resource manager viewpoint and the service provider viewpoint at odds?

4. Describe how microkernel designs are especially well suited to distributed operating systems.

5. Should an unprivileged user process be allowed to execute a system call that changes the system clock? Why or why not?

6. What are the advantages and disadvantages of integrating the user interface into the operating system?

7. What are the security aspects of memory management? Of file system management?

8. Why are special instructions used to implement system calls? Why not use normal subroutine calling instructions?

9. Virtual machine OSs and systems like Xen are often used to run multiple copies of the same guest OS. What are some advantages of this approach over running a single copy of the guest OS directly on the hardware?

10. Why do we need a special bootstrapping procedure? Why not just load the OS like we load any other program?

Chapter 2

Some Example Operating Systems

In this chapter and following in Chapters 6, 10, 14, and 18, we discuss a number of example operating systems. They represent but a small cross section of the vast variety of operating systems that have been created over the years. In general, these examples illustrate the realistic application of techniques we present in the preceding chapters. We use these specific examples in order to illustrate some particular classes of systems and to show the progression of influence over time. Some of the ones here, particularly CTSS, Multics, sixth edition UNIX, and 4.3BSD, trace the family line from one of the earliest time-sharing systems to Inferno and to Linux, which we discuss in detail starting in Chapters 3 and 4. VMS and Windows NT (and to some extent RT-11) illustrate an alternative and familiar line of influence. RT-11 provides an example of a minimal real-time operating system. TinyOS serves to illustrate the considerations in very small, embedded environments. Finally, we use Xen as an example of the growing application of virtual machine techniques. The order in which we present them is chronological. For each example system, we discuss those implementation details that are instructive in illustrating the general principles discussed in Chapter 1. In this chapter, we consider general organization, bootstrapping procedures, and system call design.

2.1 CTSS

The situation we describe in Section 1.3.3 is exactly what faced researchers at MIT when they began to use machines such as the newly introduced IBM 7094 and DEC PDP-1. Some environments used batch systems, while others used sign-up sheets. They had experience working interactively with machines they had built, such as the Whirlwind and the TX-0. By comparison, batch processing and coarse scheduling were ineffective ways to use the machines. Consequently, a number of researchers at MIT, including John McCarthy, Herb Teager, and Marvin Minsky, suggested that they develop a time-sharing OS for the IBM 7094.

The result of this effort was the Compatible Time-Sharing System (CTSS), one of the earliest time-sharing operating systems. It was developed at MIT for the IBM 7094 by

21

a team led by Fernando J. Corbató. It was first demonstrated in 1961 and continued to be used through 1973. The word "compatible" in the name comes from the fact that CTSS allowed the native batch system, FORTRAN Monitor System (FMS), to run as a background job along with time-sharing jobs.

2.1.1 Organization

CTSS is structured as a set of modules that are linked into a supervisor at load time. Each of the major OS functions is provided by one or more modules. These functions also include the command interpreter and a few programs that process system commands.

The main memory of the IBM 7094 is divided into two banks called memory A and memory B. Memory A holds the supervisor and the resident system programs. User programs run in memory B.

2.1.2 Booting

The loader for CTSS takes a punched card as input, which names a control file. This file contains a list of the file names of the modules that are to be loaded to form the supervisor. By maintaining several such control files, the system can be started with any of several configurations simply by supplying a different control card at boot time. This arrangement makes it easy to test new implementations of any module and to easily roll back to a previous version.

2.2 Multics

In the early 1960s, when the first time-sharing systems were being developed, large computer systems were still multimillion dollar investments and required highly skilled operators. One school of thought said that we should view these resources much like we do the telephone system or the power grid. Namely, for reasons of cost and efficiency, computing power should be available to customers through computing utilities.

It was into this world that Multics (**Mult**iplexed **i**nformation and **c**omputing **s**ervice) was born. Fresh from their experience with CTSS, Fernando J. Corbató and his team at MIT began the development of a new operating system that would support such a computing utility. In order to support a utility model of usage, this new operating system would need to have a number of characteristics:

- remote access

- reliable file storage

- reliable protection mechanisms

- flexible usage models for both large and small customers

While these features had largely been demonstrated in other systems, Multics would require that they be developed to a higher degree of performance and reliability. Multics was also somewhat unusual at the time in that it was implemented in a high-level language, PL/I.

In order to support this type of usage, Multics was developed on a new model of computer, the General Electric GE-645, built specially for Multics. It was based on the earlier GE-635 and included hardware features necessary to support the techniques used in Multics. Later, most Multics installations ran on the Honeywell 6180 and its follow-on machines.

Development work began on Multics in 1964 as a collaboration between MIT, GE, and Bell Labs. Bell Labs withdrew in 1969 and, in 1970, GE sold its computer division to Honeywell. Multics development was canceled in 1985. The last Multics system was shut down on October 30, 2000. Many of the major operating systems developed since have been influenced, either directly or indirectly, by Multics.

2.2.1   Organization

The Multics designers describe the organization of the system as **single-level**. This choice of terminology should not be taken to suggest that everything in the OS is thrown together into one big box wrapped around with strapping tape. On the contrary, Multics has a very well-defined structure. The term "single-level" here refers to the idea that substantial parts of the OS functionality are provided by software that is structured and behaves much like ordinary application software. Although Multics predates the term microkernel and isn't structured like a modern microkernel, it does share the objective of moving OS functionality out of a monolithic kernel.

In order to address the protection questions raised by moving OS functionality outward, Multics implements a set of **protection rings**. The closer a ring is to the hardware (lower ring number), the higher the privilege of the code in it. Only code in ring 0 can execute privileged instructions such as those necessary to modify the memory management behavior and to initiate I/O operations. Also, all interrupts invoke code in ring 0. Con-

---

Historical Note: ITS

By the late 1960s, Bell Labs was not the only group that was having second thoughts about the Multics effort. Many within the MIT Artificial Intelligence (AI) lab felt that other avenues of research were warranted. The result of their effort was the Incompatible Time-sharing System (ITS), a clear play on the name of CTSS. The ITS designers intentionally chose to make some parts of the system more primitive than Multics. Partly because of those design choices, they quickly got a system up and running that became the primary platform for other research in the AI lab. ITS itself pioneered a number of techniques including device-independent graphics and network file systems. It also served as the environment on which influential packages such as Maclisp, Macsyma, and EMACS were developed. The system and the culture around it also had a significant social influence. Much of the philosophy and ethos of the modern open source culture developed at the MIT AI lab in the ITS community, and many open source pioneers, including Richard Stallman, worked in the lab.

sequently, the Multics supervisor runs in ring 0. Other OS functions, such as higher-level I/O functions and file system functions, run in ring 1. Ring 2 is used for the main system libraries, and ring 3 is used for trusted system applications and for nonsystem libraries. Normal user applications run in ring 4 and, in some special cases, ring 5. Finally, rings 6 and 7 are special in that they are not allowed to call functions in ring 0, effectively preventing them from directly making system calls. These rings are illustrated in Figure 2-1. The primary focus of the Multics ring system is the protection it provides, but from a structural point of view, it gives the system something of a layered flavor. This viewpoint is supported by the fact that normally code requested services only from lower numbered rings. Additionally, if we look at each set of nested rings from the perspective of an outer ring, we effectively have a virtual machine. The boundary between each pair of rings defines a new virtual machine.

2.2.2 System Calls

With the virtual machine perspective in mind, we see that there is no essential distinction between the way library functions are called in upper layers and the way system calls in ring 0 are requested. In all cases, if code in one layer calls code in a lower layer, it must do so though a **call gate**, which is a special mechanism of the memory management hardware. Call gates define which entry points are valid and which rings are allowed to call them. When a function makes a call through such a gate, it is allowed to call only the valid entry points in the destination segment, and the called code runs in the new, lower ring. The effect is to transfer control to selected entry points in more privileged code, which is, after all, what system calls do.

2.3 RT-11

Throughout the over 30 years that the PDP-11 was manufactured and marketed, first by Digital Equipment Corporation (DEC) and then by Mentec, Inc., several operating systems were available for it. One of these is RT-11, a small, single-user operating system aimed at real-time applications. It developed from version 1, released in 1973, to version 5.7, released in 1999.

2.3.1 Organization

The core OS functionality in RT-11 is provided by a collection of code identified as the resident monitor (RMON), the keyboard monitor (KMON), various device handlers, and the user service routine (USR). One interesting aspect of RT-11 is its ability to run with some of these components not resident in memory. In particular, only those device handlers that are actually being used need to be loaded. Furthermore, both the USR and KMON can be swapped out when their functions are not needed. In other words, applications can run with only the subset of the OS they are actually using.

These components can be built to form three different configurations. The first is called the single job (SJ) monitor. It can run on PDP-11s without a Memory Management Unit (MMU) and, therefore, operates in 64KB of memory. It supports only a single process

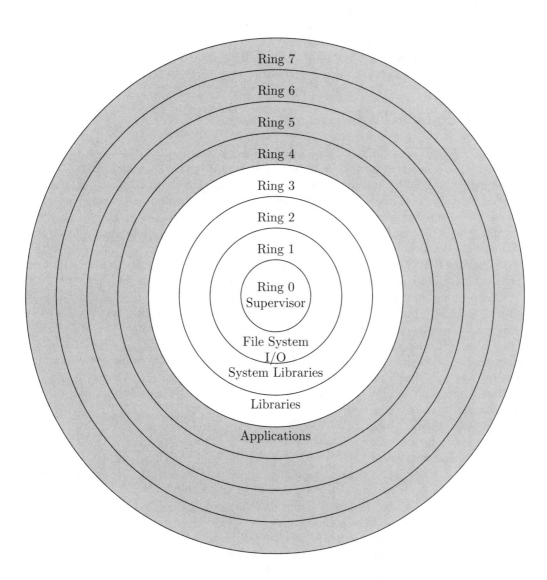

Figure 2-1: Multics Protection Rings

at a time. The foreground-background (FB) monitor also runs on systems without an MMU, but it allows a number of processes to be run in a simple time-sharing fashion. One of the processes is identified as the background process and runs as a normal user process. The other processes are called foreground processes and run in response to hardware interrupts. Finally, the foreground and background processes are also supported in the extended memory (XM) monitor. This configuration of the system makes use of a hardware MMU and, therefore, allows processes to use as much memory as available.

2.4   Sixth Edition UNIX

By the time Bell Labs pulled out of the Multics project in 1969, the Bell Labs staff involved with it included Ken Thompson and Dennis Ritchie. They and others were no longer committed to the Multics effort, but Bell Labs at that time had a very enlightened view of industrial research. The Multics refugees were not "assigned" to other projects; they were expected to generate interesting ideas and to work on them. Thompson began working with a disused PDP-7 computer developing space travel simulations. Frustrated with the development environment available to him, he decided to develop an operating system for the PDP-7 that was simpler than Multics but included some of what he thought were its better ideas. The operating system he developed there was the beginning of UNIX.

Thompson did not attempt to re-create Multics for the PDP-7. It would not have fit on that machine's limited resources even if he tried. Whereas Multics was developed to serve multiple users with a wide variety of tasks, Thompson set out to create a small, single-user OS suited primarily to his need for a software development environment. In recognition of this shift in focus, the name Unics (**Un**iplex **i**nformation and **c**omputing **s**ervice) was coined as a pun on Multics. (The origin of this pun is variously attributed to Brian Kernighan and Peter Neumann.) Very early in the system's history, the spelling was changed from Unics to UNIX.

UNIX was somewhat unusual in that it wasn't really released in versions in the usual sense. It was constantly evolving even though it was in production use within Bell Labs. As enough changes accumulated, the current manuals became less and less useful. At various points, a new edition of manuals were typeset and issued. To this day, we refer to the various versions of research UNIX by their manual editions.

By 1974, UNIX had been ported to the PDP-11, it had been rewritten in the newly developed C language, and the manuals were up to the 5th edition. At around the same time, a number of computer science faculty spent sabbaticals at Bell Labs and were exposed to UNIX. They found the system interesting and took it back with them to their respective institutions and word got around. Furthermore, that same year Thompson and Ritchie published a paper in the *Communications of the ACM* about the new system, triggering additional requests for copies. In response to the need for a system that was in a distributable form, Bell Labs produced the sixth edition of UNIX. This version of the system was distributed very widely among universities. It also became very well-known as the basis of a commentary by John Lions. Originally, Lions distributed copies to those institutions who had UNIX licenses and who requested copies. Later, Bell Labs took over the distribution of the books and sent copies along with all distributions of the sixth edition.

2.4.1   Organization

UNIX has always used a classic monolithic organization. That is not to say that it is a random collection of functions without any structure. Because most of the early development of UNIX was done on the PDP-11, and because that machine had very limited resources, the developers had to be very judicious in their choice of features to include. As a result, the system is not a very large system, and the modularity available in the C language is itself sufficient to organize the kernel. In particular, each major functional component is contained in a single source code file. Each of the device drivers are in their own source files. Process creation and scheduling are in one source file. Basic memory allocation is in one source file, and so on. The net effect is a small system with a clean and simple structure.

2.4.2   System Calls

UNIX also differs from its Multics influence in the mechanism used for system calls. In UNIX, system calls are not treated exactly the same way as ordinary function calls. In the C language, a system call such as *fork*( ) is indeed an ordinary function call, but the function called is just a small library function. This library function is the code that actually issues the system call. It does so by executing a trap instruction. The trap instruction on the PDP-11 is actually a family of instructions. The lowest eight bits of the instruction word are used to encode which system call is requested. Like other forms of interrupt, the trap instruction transfers control into the kernel, switching the processor to the privileged mode of operation necessary for the kernel to carry out its tasks.

2.5   VMS

In 1977, DEC introduced the VAX, which was designed to be its follow-on to the very successful PDP-11 line of computers. The architecture of the VAX clearly feels like a 32-bit extension of the 16-bit PDP-11 design. The biggest effect of this change is increasing the directly addressable memory space from 64KB to 4GB.

Along with the machine, they introduced a new operating system called VMS. It was developed under the leadership of Roger Gourd with Dave Cutler, Dick Hustvedt, and Peter Lipman providing additional technical leadership. VMS is meant to address the needs of all VAX applications in contrast to the many operating systems supported for the PDP-11. Consequently, it provides support for batch processing and real-time processing in addition to the usual time-sharing. In 1992, DEC introduced it's new 64-bit architecture designed to replace the VAX. This architecture is the Alpha. In anticipation of the Alpha port, VMS was given the new name of OpenVMS. Since then, development has continued on OpenVMS through the purchase of DEC by Compaq and the subsequent merger of Compaq with Hewlett-Packard. Since the Compaq/Hewlett-Packard merger, OpenVMS has also been ported to the Intel Itanium.

2.5.1 Organization

The VMS internal organization is highly modular, much like CTSS. It is written in roughly equal parts Bliss, C, and Macro-32 (which is the VAX assembly language). Contrary to what one might expect, Macro-32 continues to be used for both the Alpha and Itanium ports of OpenVMS. In those cases, the VAX assembly language is treated as if it were a high-level language and processed by a translator (a compiler, in effect) that converts the VAX assembly language into either Alpha or Itanium machine language.

One base module, contained in the file SYS.EXE, provides the foundation on which all other modules are built. It primarily consists of transfer vectors that allow code to call functions throughout the kernel without knowing the memory addresses where they actually get loaded. These vectors are mapped in each process's memory space. SYS.EXE and all other modules that make up the OS are loaded during the bootstrapping and initialization process.

The VAX supports the following four processor modes, which VMS uses to create a degree of layering and protection similar to that in Multics:

- Kernel: Most of the typical operating system functions execute in kernel mode. These functions are divided into a lower layer, a core set, and an upper layer set of system services. The system service routines are the ones that implement system calls. The core set of kernel functions are organized in three groups: the memory management subsystem, the I/O subsystem, and the process and time management subsystem.

- Executive: Executive mode is used for the record management system (RMS) and certain other high-level system calls. RMS occupies a sort of middle ground. It provides a set of functions that build record structures on top of files. However, rather than being implemented as an ordinary library, it is code contained in the system memory space and runs at a higher level of privilege than normal user code.

- Supervisor: The command-line interpreter runs in supervisor mode. In most cases, this is the interpreter for the Digital Command Language (DCL).

- User: Finally, all other user processes run in user mode. Among these are special system processes such as the swapper and some file system support.

The VMS file system design deserves special mention. File system support in VMS is mostly provided by Ancillary Control Processes (ACPs). In the case of the primary file system, Files-11, support is split into two parts. One part is provided by an ACP and the other is provided by the extended QIO processor (XQP), which runs as a thread in kernel mode.

2.5.2 Booting

VMS follows a multiple stage booting process much like that described in Section 1.5. The first stage bootstrap program is called VMB. Its primary responsibility is locating and loading the program SYSBOOT.EXE. This program loads SYS.EXE and a number of other modules that provide a basic level of kernel functionality. The system now has enough capability to run EXE$INIT, which gets the kernel running normally. It loads the remaining kernel modules and starts the memory management system. Its last step is setting itself up to return back to SCH$SCHED, which is the scheduler. This has the effect of starting time-sharing. When time-sharing begins, the only available process is the swapper. One of its jobs is starting the SYSINIT process, which carries out the remaining user-mode initializations.

2.5.3   System Calls

The system call mechanism in VMS is interesting. Normal function calls are issued into the transfer vectors in SYS.EXE, which is mapped in the process's memory space. Upon entry, the transfer vector issues a change mode instruction (chmk or chme on the VAX) to change the processor mode in the same way a software interrupt does. The kernel interrupt handler for the change mode instruction dispatches the request to the appropriate system service routine. This allows application software to be built without any special instructions being used. Any language that follows the normal VMS calling sequence can issue system calls with no special support from either the compiler or libraries. On the Alpha, the PALcode for OpenVMS provides an instruction that performs the same functions as the chmk, chme, chms, and chmu instructions.

2.6   4.3BSD

The University of California at Berkeley was one of the early licensees of UNIX. In working with the system, the faculty and students developed a number of enhancements and extensions to the system. These were released to other UNIX licensees in the form of Berkeley Software Distributions (BSD). Some of the Berkeley enhancements made their way into the Bell Labs research editions, and in return, some of the Bell Labs developments were incorporated into the BSD releases. Releases supporting the PDP-11 were identified as 1BSD and various 2BSD versions. The 3BSD and the various 4BSD versions supported the VAX architecture, and the 4.3BSD Tahoe release also included support for the Computer Consoles, Inc. (CCI) Power 6 system. The 4BSD releases ranged from 1980 to 1988.

In time, however, the two lines of development diverged, and by the time the Berkeley versions had reached 4.3BSD, there was not much Bell Labs code left in the system. In fact, subsets of 4.3BSD were released publicly. The Net 2 release, from 1991, became the foundation of the commercial BSD/386 system. BSDI (the vendor for BSD/386) was sued by UNIX Systems Laboratories (USL), who then had the rights to that previous AT&T code. In the final judgment, a small fraction of the remaining BSD code was found to be close enough to the original AT&T code that it had to be removed from the Net 2 release. The functionality of this code was quickly replaced by other developers, and the system quickly evolved. The final release from Berkeley (with the replaced code) was 4.4BSD, and this code base became the foundation of a number of freely distributed versions, including FreeBSD, NetBSD, OpenBSD, and DragonflyBSD.

2.6.1   Organization

As one would expect, the BSD UNIX organization is much like an expanded version of the original UNIX design. The biggest difference in the organization of the source code is an effect of the support for the CCI Power 6. As with most systems that support multiple architectures, 4.3BSD divides the source code into the architecture-independent parts and the architecture-dependent parts. As much as possible, code is developed in an architecture-independent manner. Any enhancements or bug fixes in the architecture-independent code then benefit all architectures. The NetBSD derivative of BSD has taken this support of multiple architectures to a very high degree. At the time of the release of NetBSD 3, the source tree included support for 56 different computer systems based on 17 different CPU architectures.

2.6.2   System Calls

The system call mechanism for VAX BSD uses the `chmk` instruction, which changes the processor mode to kernel mode. (The VAX has four processor modes: kernel, executive, supervisor, and user.) When a user process executes this instruction, it behaves much as the trap instruction in the PDP-11. It switches the CPU to kernel mode and causes a function in the kernel to execute, which looks at the instruction operand to determine which system call is being issued.

2.7   Windows NT

Microsoft's first OS for the IBM PC was based on QDOS by Tim Paterson at Seattle Computer Products. (QDOS was itself based on CP/M, marketed by Gary Kildall's company, Digital Research.) Introduced with the IBM PC in 1981, copies of the OS sold by IBM were called PC-DOS, while those sold directly by Microsoft were called MS-DOS. In 1985, Microsoft released a graphical user interface called Windows, which ran as an application on MS-DOS. This began a line of OS development resulting in distributions marketed under the name Windows, though the underlying OS was MS-DOS.

In 1988, Microsoft began development of a new operating system meant to replace both Windows 3.0 (then in development, but not released until 1990) and OS/2 in its product line. This new system was called Windows NT. Development was led by David Cutler, who had left DEC and joined Microsoft that year.

The first version was Windows NT 3.5, released in 1993. The next year, Microsoft released Windows NT 3.51, Windows NT 4.0 followed in 1996, and in 1999, Microsoft released the next version of the NT system and called it Windows 2000. Recent releases of the NT system include Windows XP, released in 2001, and Windows Server 2003, released in 2003. The most recent release of Windows is called Vista.

Over its life, the Windows NT design has run on the Intel x86 architecture, the MIPS R4000, the DEC/Compaq/HP Alpha, the IBM PowerPC, and the Intel Itanium. The most recent versions support only the two Intel architectures.

2.7.1 Organization

Like many of the example systems we discuss here, Windows NT is structured as a monolithic system with some layering. It is written predominantly in C. The core OS functionality is structured in three layers.

The bottom layer is called the Hardware Abstraction Layer (HAL). The HAL is where architecture and hardware dependencies are encapsulated. It is the principal mechanism for the portability of Windows NT. All other OS components that need to perform architecture or hardware dependent functions go through the HAL.

The second layer contains code that Microsoft calls the kernel and any loaded device drivers. This kernel code provides a base level of functionality for the OS. It provides services such as scheduling, synchronization, and interrupt handling.

The third layer is called the executive. (Together, the Windows NT HAL, kernel, and executive provide the same functionality that we call the kernel elsewhere in this text.) The executive provides the remaining usual OS functions, including memory management, file systems, and some process management. System calls are also handled by the executive.

While not a part of the OS proper, there is another interesting aspect of the environment Windows NT provides to applications. In particular, Windows NT provides three environment subsystems: Win32, POSIX, and OS/2. Applications written to any of these APIs can run on Windows NT using the appropriate subsystem to mediate between the application and the executive. The arrangement of these major components is illustrated in Figure 2-2.

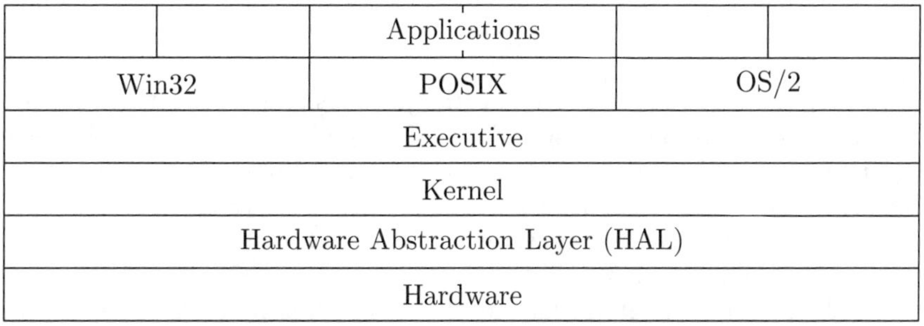

		Applications		
Win32		POSIX	OS/2	
Executive				
Kernel				
Hardware Abstraction Layer (HAL)				
Hardware				

Figure 2-2: Windows NT General Organization

2.8 TinyOS

TinyOS was created by researchers at the University of California at Berkeley. The earliest releases were made in 2002 and it continues to be developed. The focus of TinyOS is supporting applications that run on very small devices called motes. There are a couple of ways we can look at motes. First, we can think of them as very small computers whose input devices are primarily environmental sensors (for example temperature, light, shock, and so on). Alternatively, we can see them as sensors with a small amount of processing capability attached. Typically, they communicate using some form of wireless networking. These machines have very little memory and very limited computing power compared to typical desktop machines. As a result, TinyOS has to be very small compared to the other operating systems we study here.

2.8.1 Organization

TinyOS is structured in an unusual way. Application code and the core TinyOS code are all compiled together into a single image put on the mote. The main functional elements of a TinyOS system are called components. These components communicate using interfaces, and their execution is controlled by a very small scheduler. They are structured in a layered arrangement. Interfaces are defined by commands and events. Commands are requests issued by one component to a component in a lower layer, and events trigger actions in upper layers.

TinyOS and any components developed for it are written in nesC, which is based on the C language. The operating system also includes features that allow developers to define components' interfaces and to define the interconnections among components.

The TinyOS distribution comes with a number of components. Among these are a number of components that support various hardware which might be part of the mote. This hardware includes various types of radios, temperature sensors, light sensors, and I2C bus interfaces.

2.9   Xen

In 1999, the Systems Research Group at the University of Cambridge proposed the Xenoserver project. The idea behind this project is providing a collection of publicly available servers on which anyone can run their code. In some sense, it harkens back to the computing utility that originally inspired Multics. However, the Xenoserver project isn't about creating a new operating system. It is an infrastructure that supports many operating systems operating simultaneously.

As part of the project, the group has developed the Xen hypervisor. Xen is not itself an operating system, though it shares a number of characteristics with one. In fact, it is similar in some ways to VM. Xen provides a platform on which other operating systems run. It can support many different operating systems all running simultaneously on an Intel x86 processor. The earliest release of Xen was in 2003. Version 3.0 of Xen was released in 2005.

2.9.1 Organization

An operating system running on Xen is called a guest OS, and each guest OS runs in its own virtual machine, called a domain. Each domain has its own area of physical memory separate from the other domains. Not all guest OSs have direct access to I/O device hardware. That is reserved for domain 0. The OS running in domain 0 has access to all the I/O devices and manages them on behalf of the other guest OSs.

For most members of the x86 family, Xen also provides certain memory management services for the guest OSs. Consequently, operating systems must be ported to Xen much as they might be ported to other hardware. Some of the operating systems that have been ported to run on Xen are Linux, FreeBSD, NetBSD, Plan 9, and Microsoft Windows XP (however, this port is not generally available due to licensing restrictions). For members of the x86 family that support the Virtualization Technology (VT) extensions, Xen allows unmodified operating systems to run as guests. Intel's VT enhancements provide features that allow a virtual machine monitor to mediate attempts by a guest OS to access hardware features that could affect other OSs also running on the machine.

To provide this structure, Xen itself is implemented as a small kernel that provides a subset of the usual OS functions. Its main responsibilities are starting and stopping domains, allocating physical memory to domains at the time they are created, time-sharing among domains, and mediating memory management functions on processors without VT features.

2.10   Summary

The variety of operating system designs is enormous. We have selected just a few here to use as examples throughout this text. These examples serve several purposes. They illustrate the general principles discussed in this book. They provide an historical context for some of the commonly used operating systems. Finally, they show the evolution of ideas that have found their way into Inferno and Linux, the two systems we examine in detail beginning in the next two chapters.

2.11   Exercises

1. Why did the designers of CTSS design the system to allow FMS to run as a normal job?

2. What is the advantage of implementing an operating system in a high-level language (like PL/I in Multics) over implementing it in assembly language?

3. What are the advantages and disadvantages of implementing libraries using a call gate (or other system call-like mechanism) as in Multics?

4. Throughout this chapter, we have seen the trend in writing operating systems shift from assembly language to higher-level languages. We have also seen a shift from operating systems written for a single type of machine to ones that are ported to a variety of different machines. In what ways are these two trends connected?

5. In RT-11, why not just run the foreground-background (FB) monitor even if there is only one job to run instead of using a special single job (SJ) monitor?

6. On the VAX, 4.3BSD and VMS both use special instructions to change the processor mode in the system call mechanism. In 4.3BSD, these instructions are executed in

normal user code, while in VMS they are executed in the kernel. What are the considerations in choosing one scheme over the other?

7. We did not discuss system calls in TinyOS. Was this an oversight? Is it possible that TinyOS doesn't actually have system calls as we've studied them? How might the operating system work without them?

8. What services of a typical operating system are not provided by Xen?

9. UNIX was intentionally created to be more limited than Multics. Multics had a head start in development, but UNIX became more widely used than Multics. Discuss some of the possible reasons why this occurred.

10. Investigate and write a summary of the history and organization of another operating system such as MVS.

Chapter 3

Inferno Structure and Initialization

In this chapter, we begin our in-depth examination of Inferno, one of our detailed examples of operating system design. Inferno is a descendant of UNIX and is particularly interesting for a number of reasons. First, it is compact and well written, making it good for a detailed study like this. Second, it has the interesting characteristic of being available both natively on a number of platforms and hosted by a number of other operating systems. As a result, it is easier to experiment with than purely native systems, but at the same time, it provides examples of device drivers not found in purely hosted environments. The third reason Inferno is valuable to study is that it illustrates several techniques we don't often find in other systems. Among these are a file system implemented as a normal user program, the advanced use of name servers, and a virtual machine with just-in-time compiling.

Our discussion parallels that of the examples in Chapter 2 and the general design issues in Chapter 1. We begin by addressing the historical background behind Inferno. The next section presents a number of fundamental design elements in Inferno. These elements form the organizing concepts around which Inferno is built. Based on those concepts, we discuss the general structure of the system and the organization of the source code that implements it. Our first examination of code from Inferno is the system initialization. We wrap up the chapter by looking at the system call mechanism for Inferno.

3.1 Origins of Inferno

To understand the origins of Inferno, we have to look at the rest of the UNIX story. We discuss the early history of UNIX (up to about 1976) in Section 2.4. From about 1975 on, numerous universities and companies continued UNIX development beyond the work at Bell Labs. By the 1980s, UNIX existed in many different, incompatible versions. Features like networking had been added to the kernel, and multiwindowed graphical user interfaces had been added as applications. In the meantime, Bell Labs had continued developing research versions of UNIX, sometimes drawing on the work done by others. This work culminated with the publication of the manuals for the 10th edition research version of UNIX in 1990.

35

In a real sense, UNIX had run out of steam. The new computing world was no longer a central system with many users connected by peripheral terminals. Instead, it was a networked collection of many computers where users had significant computing power directly on their desks. These local workstations were interfaced into a sea of computing resources. Despite all the work that had gone into UNIX over the years, it had not adapted well to this new computing world. Furthermore, the commercial UNIX interests had ensured that even at Bell Labs, where UNIX was born, not all of the system source code was available. For those reasons, in about 1987 several of the UNIX veterans began to consider the development of a new operating system. Spearheaded by Ken Thompson and Rob Pike, the group began to take a step back and apply the lessons they had learned in almost 20 years of UNIX experience. Rather than create another UNIX, they sought to create a system where they could correct their previous mistakes and apply new ideas that had grown out of their subsequent research. The system they created is called Plan 9. (The name "Plan 9 from Bell Labs" is a play on the name *Plan 9 from Outer Space*, the name of a movie that has sometimes been called the worst film ever made.)

Like UNIX, Plan 9 is a system primarily created by and for programmers and was created as an object of research as well as a system to be used. However, in the mid-1990s, the climate at Bell Labs had changed: There was an expectation to produce results with more immediate commercial value. To that end, several of the Plan 9 researchers developed an operating system that they named Inferno, based on the ideas of Plan 9 but targeted to small computing environments, including network devices, handheld devices, robotics, and set-top boxes. After using this new operating system for several internal products, Lucent sold the rights to Inferno to Vita Nuova Holdings Limited. In 2003, Vita Nuova changed the license structure, making Inferno open source for nonprofit applications.

3.2 Fundamental Concepts

On one hand, Inferno is a fairly conventional operating system. It manages multiple processes that can be created and destroyed and that can communicate with each other. Processes can allocate memory dynamically and can request I/O services from Inferno. The system provides a conventional file system stored on disks, it supports networking, and it provides an interesting security model. Its user applications include a graphical windowing environment and a number of expected programs—even games such as Tetris. Figure 3-1 shows the graphical user interface in action.

On the other hand, Inferno is quite unusual. Because it is targeted to small environments, Inferno runs without some of the hardware usually necessary for multiuser time-sharing systems. All applications are written in the Limbo programming language, a language that is unique to Inferno. Limbo programs are compiled to the Dis virtual machine (VM). (The Dis VM is much like the P-code engine associated with UCSD Pascal or, more recently, the Java Virtual Machine, which runs bytecode compiled from Java source code.) This allows the same compiled code to run on any supported platform. Inferno not only runs natively on a number of architectures, but it also can be run as an application hosted by any of several conventional operating systems. Most of our examination of the implementation of Inferno is centered on the hosted version. The primary exception is

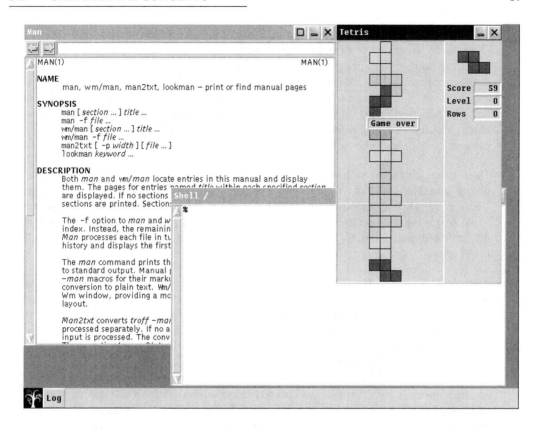

Figure 3-1: Sample Inferno Session

our study of I/O device support, which examines code that is part of the native version of Inferno.

Most of these characteristics come from a combination of several basic, but powerful, ideas. These ideas form the core of the basic design of the Inferno kernel. Some are inherited from Plan 9, and some are key to its use in small-scale environments. These key design elements include:

- *Per-process name spaces*: In most operating systems, the same set of names is available to all processes. We refer to this set of available names as the **name space**. (This concept is discussed in more detail in Chapter 17.) In Plan 9 and Inferno, however, each process may construct its own unique name space. For example, the file /foo/bar as seen by one process might not be the same file as seen by another. In fact, it might not even exist for the second process. Furthermore, these name spaces may be exported to and imported from other machines.

- *Resources as files*: Like its predecessor Plan 9, Inferno builds on the UNIX feature that the file interface can be used for more than just persistent data. In fact, most resources and services are provided in the form of names that look like files. These names are provided by file servers, some of which are built in to the kernel and some of which are normal applications. For example, instead of having special system calls for networking, in Inferno, we open special files and write control messages to them. Similarly, many normal applications, such as mail clients and text editors, present a set of files that allow other applications to communicate with them.

- *User space file servers*: Not all of the services that provide name spaces are part of the kernel in Inferno. Application programs can provide name spaces that may be used by other applications to build their name spaces. Indeed, through the use of such special file servers, almost every resource and service is provided through an interface connected to a name space and can be used through the usual file operations.

- *Portability*: Inferno runs natively on a number of hardware platforms, including the IBM-compatible PC, some models of the iPAQ, the Sun Javastation 1, and several systems built on the PowerPC CPU. The network protocol has even been ported to the Lego Mindstorms robot controller. Unlike most operating systems, however, Inferno is also implemented as an application that runs on other operating systems, including Linux, FreeBSD, Solaris, IRIX, HP-UX, Mac OS X, Plan 9, and various versions of Microsoft Windows. The version of Inferno that runs on top of another operating system is called hosted Inferno. Hosted Inferno implementations are compiled as a normal application typically called emu or emu.exe. We should note that even though there is a host OS providing the usual set of services for its processes, Inferno still provides process management, memory management, file systems, and security for its applications. Most I/O device requests are relayed by Inferno to the host OS, as are low-level networking operations.

- *Limbo and Dis*: All application programs in Inferno are written in Limbo, a modular language that compiles to a virtual machine called Dis. This characteristic contributes to several of Inferno's features. Because the Limbo language and the virtual machine interpreter are designed to limit memory accesses to only those that are safe, Inferno can run on machines with no memory management hardware. The use of a virtual machine instruction set makes compiled applications portable across hardware platforms. Finally, the compiled application code is more compact than natively compiled code. Of course, the trade-off for interpreted virtual machine instructions is performance. To offset this downside, the virtual machine interpreter provides just-in-time compilers for most platforms. This facility translates Dis instructions into native instruction on the fly, allowing applications to run at the speed of natively compiled ones.

- *Styx protocol*: Applications communicate with file servers through the Styx protocol. This is true regardless of whether the server and application reside on the same machine or on different machines. This is a bit of an oversimplification. When the server is on the local machine and provided by the kernel, the protocol stack (building the messages) is short-circuited, and Styx requests are turned into function calls. By obscuring the distinction between local and remote services, Inferno makes developing applications for distributed computing resources as straightforward and direct as developing them for single computers.

Throughout our study of the internals of Inferno, we see how these concepts work together to provide an efficient and capable platform for applications. With the exception of user space file servers, our presentation does not follow these elements, but instead follows the primary areas of OS responsibility, including processes, memory, I/O devices, and file systems. However, along the way, we see how each of these design elements comes into play forming a well-designed and powerful system.

3.3   Organization

With some of Inferno's basic design concepts in hand, we now turn our attention to the overall structure of the system. There are two aspects of this structure we highlight. First, the way in which the various subsystems fit together is a reflection of the way in which the basic design elements are realized in actual code. Second, the organization of the source code itself is important as we take our tour through the details of Inferno.

3.3.1   Basic Architecture

Because of the pervasive use of file servers and especially those that run as normal applications, we might expect to see a microkernel design. However, this is not the case. All of the servers providing services related to process management, memory management, and I/O device support are built in to the kernel. Therefore, this design is like many other systems, in essence a monolithic kernel with a conventional persistent file system implemented as an application program. Nevertheless, the use of a standard interface (Styx) for all of the built-in servers results in some of the same design advantages as microkernels enjoy.

We have already suggested the basic elements of Inferno's structure. All application programs are written in Limbo and compiled to Dis bytecode modules. Each application program is interpreted (or compiled on the fly) by the Dis virtual machine interpreter. Complete Limbo applications generally load additional support modules at run time. A number of fundamental Limbo modules are built in to the interpreter. Some of these include:

- a system module that provides an interface to the operating system services, much as system calls do in typical operating systems

- a built-in drawing module that provides the basic graphics capabilities to Limbo programs

- a keyring module for managing keys used for authenticating network connections and for data encryption

- a library of math functions that serves the same role as the standard ANSI/POSIX math library

- the Tk module, which builds on the graphics support to provide a set of user interface and window management functions based on the Tk toolkit created for the TCL scripting language

Underlying the virtual machine interpreter, we have a typical collection of facilities for managing computing resources. We have conventional process management, memory management, and I/O device management components. Somewhat unique to systems like Inferno and Plan 9 is the name space management component. Functionally, it serves much like the file system support found in other operating systems, but it only manages how the per-process directory tree is structured rather than managing normal files.

In addition to the usual resource management components, the Inferno kernel also includes a number of built-in file servers. These file servers provide services such as audio output, graphics display, access to I/O devices, and access to network facilities. An application typically incorporates the name spaces provided by each of these servers into its unique name space.

Finally, many of the components described here use the Styx protocol to interact with each other and with components on other machines. The protocol itself, which is described in more detail in Section 19.1.1, provides the infrastructure for clients to communicate with file servers. In particular, the protocol defines messages for authenticating and connecting to servers, for reading and writing data, and for creating and deleting files. In addition to these basic operations, Styx defines messages that walk a directory tree and that read and update the descriptive metadata about files. By funneling all services through a common protocol, Inferno achieves a key element of its portability objective. Applications can be written to operate equally well using local services or using remote services.

At some level, the operating system (whether hosted or native) must access physical devices and allocate physical memory. In the case of hosted Inferno, these accesses are relayed through the host operating system. In native Inferno, they are handled through conventional device drivers. The overall structure of Inferno is illustrated in Figure 3-2.

3.3.2 Source Code Organization

Almost all of the Inferno kernel code is written in the C programming language. It is divided among a number of directories, described throughout the remainder of this section. We begin with the following two:

- emu: This directory contains the core source code for the hosted kernels. The port subdirectory includes code common to all host operating systems. There are also directories named according to the various host operating systems such as Linux, Plan9, and Nt. These directories contain code unique to the corresponding host.

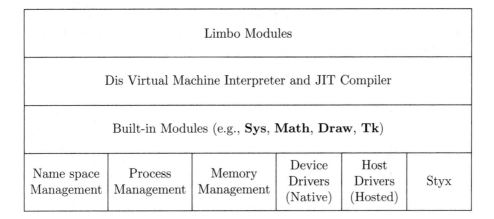

Figure 3-2: Inferno System Organization

- os: In the os directory, we find code for the native ports of Inferno. As with the hosted version, the port directory contains platform-independent code and various named directories contain code unique to the named platforms.

The following libraries contain code that is common to both the hosted and native versions of Inferno:

- lib9: This directory contains code that implements a number of functions that are part of the Plan 9 programming environment but which might not be present in other hosting environments.

- libdraw: This library provides the implementation of the built-in **Draw** module. It provides the low-level interface for drawing in Limbo.

- libfreetype: The libfreetype directory has code for rendering TrueType fonts. It was developed and is distributed by the FreeType project.

- libinterp: This library implements the Dis interpreter and just-in-time compilers.

- libkeyring: The files in this directory define several functions that are used to manage lists of keys used for authentication and encryption.

- libmath: The libmath directory contains code for the built-in math module. It provides all the floating-point support for Limbo. The library is built on a freely distributable implementation of the ANSI/POSIX math library developed by Sun Microsystems.

- libmemdraw and libmemlayer: The code contained in these two directories implements the details of the drawing device normally served in the directory tree rooted at /dev/draw.

- libtk: In this directory, we find code that implements the built-in **Tk** module. Based on the GUI toolkit developed for the TCL scripting language, this module forms the basis for GUI development in Limbo.

A selected subset of the hierarchy of source code directories is shown in Figure 3-3.

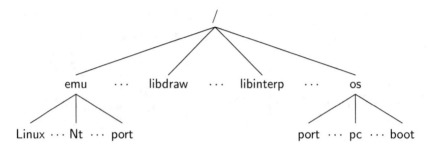

Figure 3-3: Inferno Source Code Directory Structure

3.4   Initialization

In Chapter 1, the topic of bootstrapping is discussed after that of OS structure. With Inferno, a study of system startup can take two paths. For Inferno running natively, the bootstrapping process is similar to that discussed in Section 1.5. The details, however, are very dependent on the actual system on which it's running. For a conventional computer, the Inferno kernel is loaded from disk much as with any other OS. For smaller embedded systems, the kernel is likely to be permanently stored in some form of nonvolatile memory from which it might or might not be copied into the main system memory.

Because most of our study focuses on the hosted version of Inferno, we consider here the initialization process for only that case. The native version of Inferno has a similar structure overall, but it differs substantially in details. When running natively, Inferno is responsible for initializing all of the hardware. In the hosted case, the host OS handles that for us.

Before getting into the details, however, an outline of the initialization process is in order. As the system moves from being loaded into memory to the point where it is running applications, it goes through the following steps:

1. We process the command-line arguments to set various optional parameters for the system. Some examples of these parameters are the geometry of the windowing environment, the location of Inferno's root directory, and whether to use the just-in-time compiler.

2. Identify the user who owns access to devices and other system resources, getting that information from the host operating system, if possible.

3. Initialize anything specific to the host OS environment. In the sections that follow, we use Linux as the example of a host OS. For Linux, one of our primary initializations is setting the proper behavior for any signals we might receive.

4. Create a new process that serves as the ancestor for all of the processes we may create for running Dis VMs.

5. Identify this process as being in a new process group, a new file group, and a new environment group. The effect of this step is to declare that this process does not inherit any characteristics from a parent process in Inferno.

6. Initialize any devices. Even in the case of hosted Inferno, we have components of the OS that behave like devices, and we need to initialize any that require it.

7. Build an initial name space. In doing so, we construct a root directory where everything else is attached. Then we connect several "drivers" to the directory tree. In reality, these drivers are all small file servers, and we are actually attaching each of their trees to the main one.

8. We create a new process for running a copy of the Dis VM.

9. Create an initial state for the floating-point support.

10. Initialize the Dis VM.

11. Load an initial Dis module. This module becomes the first application code to run and, in turn, becomes the ancestor for all application processes. Its main purpose is performing any application-level initialization that is necessary and starting whatever program is needed to allow users to interact with the system.

12. Set up this module to be ready to run when the VM starts and so that it can serve as a parent to any other initialization processes.

13. Start running the Dis VM, which has the effect of starting time-sharing.

Once the system has completed these steps, it no longer behaves as a single independent program. From here on out, the running Inferno system is primarily running applications and executing code providing services for those applications.

3.4.1   Starting Inferno

As described in Section 1.5, the first step in starting an OS is loading it into memory. In hosted implementations of Inferno, this is handled by the host operating system. As with usual C programs, the entry point at the source code level is *main( )*. In Inferno, this function is defined in emu/port/main.c as follows:

```
void main(int argc, char *argv[])
{
    char *opt, *p;
```

```
char *enva[20];
int envc;
```

The bulk of these first lines of *main*( ) process any environment variables that we recognize. If either INFERNO or ROOT are set, then they give the location of the Inferno root directory. However, this specification can be overridden with the EMU variable or the -r command-line option. After processing those variables, we then parse through the options given both on the command line to emu and in the environment variable EMU.

```
quotefmtinstall( );
savestartup(argc, argv);
if ((p = getenv("INFERNO")) ≠ nil ∨ (p = getenv("ROOT")) ≠ nil)
    strecpy(rootdir, rootdir + sizeof(rootdir), p);
opt = getenv("EMU");
if (opt ≠ nil ∧ *opt ≠ '\0') {
    enva[0] = "emu";
    envc = tokenize(opt, &enva[1], sizeof (enva) − 1) + 1;
    enva[envc] = 0;
    option(envc, enva, envusage);
}
option(argc, argv, usage);
```

Inferno makes use of a special user referred to as *eve*. *Eve* is also referred to as the host owner. Many security policies are based on the idea of an owner. The owner of a resource has more privileges than other users. Inferno does the same thing, and *eve* is the user that owns resources like the built-in servers, devices, and such. Until we know who we really are, we set the value of *eve* to inferno. This remains the default for native Inferno. For hosted Inferno, the user running Inferno becomes *eve*. In both cases, this can be overridden by a login process.

```
eve = strdup("inferno");
```

Now we optionally print out a startup message. This is done if the -v option is set. The message contains the Inferno version number, the host process ID, and the flag that indicates whether the virtual machine just-in-time compiler should be invoked.

```
opt = "interp";
if (cflag)
    opt = "compile";
if (vflag)
    print("Inferno %s main (pid=%d) %s\n", VERSION, getpid( ), opt);
```

Finally, we call *libinit*( ). Here is where we begin the initialization of the system. Up to this point, we have just pulled some environment and command-line parameters that will control our behavior later. Our initialization will operate in two phases, the first being that which is needed for the host OS and the second being host OS independent initialization of Inferno. This function never returns. We do not expect to fall off the end of *main*( ) to exit the program. This is somewhat typical of operating systems. We often handle system shutdown in a special way rather than returning from the entry routine. (In some cases, though, the OS does exit by returning from its entry routine. In those cases, we return back to a loader that usually halts the system when control returns.) The variable *imod* is a pointer that is initialized to point to the string `/dis/emuinit.dis`, which is the name of a file containing user-level initialization code. If `emu` is run with the `-d` option, then the parameter that follows is used as the file name of the initialization code.

>   *libinit*(*imod*);
> }

3.4.2   Host OS Specific Initialization

The *libinit*() function is defined in the per-host system code. For illustration here, we will examine the Linux version, which is defined in emu/Linux/os.c as follows:

```
void libinit(char *imod)
{
    struct termios t;
    struct sigaction act;
    sigset_t mask;
    struct passwd *pw;
    Proc *p;
    void *tos;
    char sys[64];
```

The first bit of the function establishes a new session for this process. Next we get some information from our host environment. At this point, we are interested in the host name and the user ID and group ID of the `nobody` user (if it exists).

```
    setsid();
    gethostname(sys, sizeof (sys));
    kstrdup(&ossysname, sys);
    pw = getpwnam("nobody");
    if (pw ≠ nil) {
        uidnobody = pw→pw_uid;
        gidnobody = pw→pw_gid;
    }
```

If the daemon option is not set, then we want to set the appropriate terminal modes. (For those unfamiliar with daemons, they can roughly be described as processes that are not associated with any user interface and live to provide services to other processes.) In our case, this test boils down to the question of whether we have a terminal attached. If not, then we don't want to try to set terminal parameters. Because Inferno handles most of the normal keyboard processing (echo, deleting characters, etc.), we turn most of those functions off in the host OS.

> **if** $(dflag \equiv 0)$
>   *termset*( );

The next big section of code sets up the right behavior for signals. Signals are a UNIX feature that operate like software interrupts for applications. When a signal is sent with the *kill*( ) system call, it interrupts the process and the signal is handled according to the action identified for the particular signal. Here, we set some of the signals to be ignored, but we register signal handler functions for most of them. Most of these handlers effectively throw an exception, causing the VM process that received the signal to restart.

> *memset*($\&act, 0,$ **sizeof** (act));
> *act.sa_handler* $=$ *trapUSR1*;
> *sigaction*(SIGUSR1, $\&act, nil$);
> *sigemptyset*($\&mask$);
> *sigaddset*($\&mask,$ SIGUSR2);
> *sigprocmask*(SIG_BLOCK, $\&mask, \Lambda$);
> *memset*($\&act, 0,$ **sizeof** (act));
> *act.sa_handler* $=$ *trapUSR2*;
> *sigaction*(SIGUSR2, $\&act, nil$);
> *act.sa_handler* $=$ SIG_IGN;
> *sigaction*(SIGCHLD, $\&act, nil$);
> /* For the correct functioning of devcmd in the face of exiting slaves */
> *signal*(SIGPIPE, SIG_IGN);
> **if** $(signal(\text{SIGTERM}, \text{SIG\_IGN}) \neq \text{SIG\_IGN})$
>   *signal*(SIGTERM, *cleanexit*);
> **if** $(signal(\text{SIGINT}, \text{SIG\_IGN}) \neq \text{SIG\_IGN})$
>   *signal*(SIGINT, *cleanexit*);
> **if** $(sflag \equiv 0)$ {
>   *act.sa_handler* $=$ *trapBUS*;
>   *sigaction*(SIGBUS, $\&act, nil$);
>   *act.sa_handler* $=$ *trapILL*;
>   *sigaction*(SIGILL, $\&act, nil$);
>   *act.sa_handler* $=$ *trapSEGV*;
>   *sigaction*(SIGSEGV, $\&act, nil$);
>   *act.sa_handler* $=$ *trapFPE*;
>   *sigaction*(SIGFPE, $\&act, nil$);
> }

Now we get to the Inferno-specific initialization. The upshot of the remainder of the function is that we create an initial process running the function *emuinit( )* on the initial Dis module. The function *newproc( )* creates an initial process structure and calls *addprog( )* (which we see in Chapter 7) to put the process into the ready list, meaning that it is ready to run. Next we allocate the stack space for the new process.

$$p = newproc(\,);$$
$$p{\to}kstack = stackalloc(p, \&tos);$$

At this point, we override the identity of *eve* if we are able to get the user name from the host. Similarly, we'll set the user ID and group ID if they're available.

```
pw = getpwuid(getuid());
if (pw ≠ nil)
    kstrdup(&eve, pw→pw_name);
else
    print("cannot␣getpwuid\n");
p→env→uid = getuid();
p→env→gid = getgid();
```

The final function, *executeonnewstack( )*, is a system-specific routine (in assembly language in the case of Linux). To a first approximation, this function switches to the newly allocated stack (from the earlier call to *stackalloc( )*) and calls the function *emuinit( )*.

```
    executeonnewstack(tos, emuinit, imod);
}
```

At this point, we should admit to a bit of an oversimplification. Up until now, we've presented Inferno as if every process in Inferno were the execution of a program written in Limbo and interpreted by the Dis VM interpreter. The reality is a little more complicated. There are some processes that are managed by the Inferno process management but that are actually normal host processes. The *newproc( )* function creates one of these. In Chapter 7, we discuss the distinctions and roles of these two types of processes in more detail.

3.4.3   *Host OS Independent Initialization*

Our chain of initialization now takes us back to **emu/port/main.c**, where *emuinit( )* is defined as:

```
void emuinit(void *imod)
{
  Osenv *e;
```

First we set up an environment for this initial process. The main part of this is recognizing that we aren't inheriting any process, file, or environment information from a parent process. Before going any further, this is the first time we've encountered *up*. This global variable always points to the process table entry (discussed in Chapter 5) of the currently running process.

```
e = up→env;
e→pgrp = newpgrp();
e→fgrp = newfgrp(nil);
e→egrp = newegrp();
e→errstr = e→errbuf0;
e→syserrstr = e→errbuf1;
e→user = strdup("");
```

Next we initialize the set of devices we have. The *chandevinit*() function loops through an array of devices, calling an initialization function for each one. This array is built by a script that looks at all the device source code files and extracts a structure declaration from each one, at the time the OS is compiled. We see an example of this structure definition in Chapter 19.

```
links();
chandevinit();
```

The next two lines are part of an error-handling technique that's used throughout Inferno. The way to view this is to understand that the *waserror*() "call" (it's actually a macro) tests false when we first reach this part of the code. Later, if we encounter an error in one of the functions we call, we, in turn, call the function *error*(), which transfers control back here, causing *waserror*() to evaluate as true. Those familiar with ANSI POSIX environments will recognize that this is implemented using *setjmp*() and *longjmp*() in those environments. This mechanism is somewhat like a cross between nonlocal **goto** statements and **throw/catch** mechanisms.

```
if (waserror())
    panic("setting␣root␣and␣dot");
```

Because every process may assemble its own unique name space, each process must have a place to start. For most processes, the starting point is a name space inherited from the new process's parent. Because we're setting things up for the first VM process, we don't have a parent. So here, we set up the initial root of the name space. Most of the steps here are normally done when we mount or bind. However, here there is nothing to mount or bind to, so we have to do it "by hand."

```
e→pgrp→slash = namec("#/", Atodir, 0, 0);
cnameclose(e→pgrp→slash→name);
e→pgrp→slash→name = newcname("/");
```

$e{\rightarrow}pgrp{\rightarrow}dot = cclone(e{\rightarrow}pgrp{\rightarrow}slash);$

$poperror();$

$strcpy(up{\rightarrow}text, \texttt{"main"});$

These few lines open the console for three file descriptors. As in POSIX environments, processes in Inferno generally start life with open file descriptors for the standard input, standard output, and standard error files. For our initial process, all three of these refer to the console.

```
if (kopen("#c/cons", OREAD) ≠ 0)
    fprint(2, "failed␣to␣make␣fd0␣from␣#c/cons:␣%r\n");
kopen("#c/cons", OWRITE);
kopen("#c/cons", OWRITE);
```

The next part of the code builds the name space that our initial process will need. Most of what we do here are calls to *kbind*( ). This internal kernel function serves the same role as the *bind*( ) system call available to applications. It attaches one set of names to another. In these cases, we are attaching the names provided by some of the built-in kernel file servers to the name space we are creating. This does, however, create something of a "chicken and egg" problem. How do we refer to the names we want to attach if they're not part of our name space yet? The answer is that we provide a separate, small name space that encompasses only the built-in file servers. Each built-in server has associated with it a name of the form #*x*, where *x* is a single character. Each of these servers declares the character *x* it uses. For example, the notation #c refers to the name space provided by the console device server. When we bind it to /dev, we are saying that all the names provided by that server are to be available in the directory /dev.

```
/* the setid cannot precede the bind of #U */
kbind("#U","/",MAFTER | MCREATE);
setid(eve,0);
kbind("#^","/dev",MBEFORE);       /* snarf */
kbind("#^","/chan",MBEFORE);
kbind("#m","/dev",MBEFORE);       /* pointer */
kbind("#c","/dev",MBEFORE);
kbind("#p","/prog",MREPL);
kbind("#d","/fd",MREPL);
kbind("#I","/net",MAFTER);        /* will fail on Plan 9 */
/* BUG: we actually only need to do these on Plan 9 */
kbind("#U/dev","/dev",MAFTER);
kbind("#U/net","/net",MAFTER);
kbind("#U/net.alt","/net.alt",MAFTER);
```

Now we set up some more environment data. In particular, we take the arguments for emu and set them and a couple of host details as environment values served by the environment file server.

```
if (cputype ≠ nil)
    ksetenv("cputype", cputype, 1);
putenvqv("emuargs", rebootargv, rebootargc, 1);
putenvq("emuroot", rootdir, 1);
ksetenv("emuhost", hosttype, 1);
```

This call to *kproc*( ) creates a new process to be scheduled by the host operating system. It shares memory space and files with the parent process. In many environments, this type of process is referred to as a thread. This thread runs the function *disinit*( ) on the initial Dis module. In many ways, *kproc*( ) functions much like the last lines of *libinit*( ). In fact, *kproc*( ) also calls *newproc*( ).

```
kproc("main", disinit, imod, KPDUPFDG | KPDUPPG | KPDUPENVG);
```

Here this parent process basically goes to sleep. All the *ospause*() function does is repeatedly sleep for a long time. It has its own infinite loop and is called in this infinite loop. (There's nothing wrong with wearing both a belt and suspenders.)

```
    for ( ; ; )
        ospause( );
}
```

3.4.4   Starting Time-Sharing

As the name implies, *disinit*( ) initializes the virtual machine interpreter and runs the initial module. It is defined in the file emu/port/dis.c as:

```
void disinit(void *a)
{
    Prog *p;
    Osenv *o;
    Module *root;
    char *initmod = a;
```

As in *emuinit*( ), we might generate errors in some of the functions we call, so we need a place to fall back. In this case, if we do get an error, then we call *panic*( ), which causes the OS to halt.

```
    if (waserror())
        panic("disinit error: %r");
```

Here we have another message generated if the `-v` option is given to `emu`. It reports the name of the module we're running to perform user-level initializations.

```
if (vflag)
    print("Initial␣Dis:␣\"%s\"\n", initmod);
fmtinstall('D', Dconv);
```

Here we initialize the floating-point subsystem of the Dis VM.

```
FPinit();
FPsave(&up→env→fpu);
```

These three calls finish initializing several of the internals. There's nothing particularly worthy of note in these, with one exception. The function *modinit()* isn't defined in any of the original source code files. Another source code file called `emu.c` gets created during the build process and contains the code for this function.

```
opinit();
modinit();
excinit();
```

Now, at last, we can run the code in the initial module. First, we load it into memory. Then, we call *schedmod()*, which creates an Inferno process for the module and adds it to the ready list. Finally, after a little bookkeeping, we call *vmachine()*, which is found in `emu/port/dis.c` and is the main loop of the virtual machine. We discuss *vmachine()* in Chapter 7.

```
root = load(initmod);
if (root ≡ 0) {
    kgerrstr(up→genbuf, sizeof up→genbuf);
    panic("loading␣\"%s\":␣%s", initmod, up→genbuf);
}
p = schedmod(root);
memmove(p→osenv, up→env, sizeof(Osenv));
o = p→osenv;
incref(&o→pgrp→r);
incref(&o→fgrp→r);
incref(&o→egrp→r);
if (o→sigs ≠ nil)
    incref(&o→sigs→r);
o→user = nil;
kstrdup(&o→user, up→env→user);
o→errstr = o→errbuf0;
o→syserrstr = o→errbuf1;
isched.idle = 1;
```

```
      poperror( );
      vmachine(nil);
  }
```

3.5   System Calls

With the call to *vmachine*( ) at the end of *disinit*( ), time-sharing begins. At this point, the primary role of the system is running Dis code from applications written in Limbo. As with other systems, these applications are free to make requests of Inferno for services. In Section 1.6, we call these requests system calls.

Inferno takes an unusual approach to system calls. It doesn't have them in the conventional sense. Although all applications and many other modules in Inferno are written in Limbo and compiled to Dis code, a few modules are not written in Limbo. These modules are written in C and are built in to the Dis interpreter.

One of the built-in modules is called **Sys**. The **Sys** module contains much of the functionality that we normally associate with system calls. For example, the calls to open, close, read, and write files are found in **Sys**. Some functions in **Sys** are not typical of system calls but are more typical of conventional libraries. (The *tokenize*( ) function is an example of these. It splits a string into tokens.)

Some services that normally have system calls are not found in **Sys**. Process creation and memory allocation are particularly conspicuous by their absence. The reason for this is that these operations are features of the Limbo language. The **spawn** statement in Limbo compiles to one of a pair of Dis instructions based on context. The interpretation of these instructions causes a new process to be created. Memory allocation is implicit in operations such as module loading and variable declaration.

The net effect of this structure is a system that is fully functional, but unconventional. All of the usual operating system services are available to applications, but there is no system call mechanism for transferring control to the OS. Because the Dis virtual machine interpreter is part of the OS, system calls are implemented using the Dis instructions for ordinary function calls into the **Sys** module. In turn, the file-related system calls are used to access names provided by file servers. This is the mechanism by which applications request services from the servers, whether they are built in to the kernel, implemented as local server applications, or implemented as remote server applications.

3.6   Summary

Inferno is the most recent operating system to come from the development group that created UNIX. It grew out of research that led to Plan 9, and it builds on the reemergence of virtual machine languages. It is novel in its ability to run natively on a number of platforms and to be run in its hosted form on any of a number of other operating systems. In this chapter, we have examined the details of the initialization of the Inferno system running in a hosted environment.

3.7   Exercises

1. Figure 3-2 doesn't show file system support anywhere. Why not? How are file systems handled in hosted Inferno? In native Inferno?

2. Inferno doesn't use a software interrupt instruction to initiate system calls. Would it be feasible to use such an instruction for Inferno running natively? For Inferno running hosted by another OS?

3. How many lines of code are contained in each of the directories discussed in Section 3.3.2?

4. Inferno does not have the notion of a superuser or other privileged user. Compare and contrast the role of *eve* to that of a superuser.

5. In many time-sharing operating systems (including UNIX), hardware is owned by a superuser or other administrative user. Yet the same people who developed UNIX chose to make such things owned by the logged-in user in Inferno. Why did they use a different approach with Inferno?

6. Is it possible that we could fail to open all three initial file descriptors in *emuinit*() but not print the error message? How?

7. After initializing the Dis VM interpreter floating-point support, we save its state. What reason might we have for doing so?

8. In *emuinit*(), the comments indicate that some of the binds apply only to some host OSs. Modify this code so that an initial name space is described by a file stored in the host OS and so that the file is used to control the sequence of calls to *kbind*().

9. Modify the Inferno initialization code to ask the user for an initial module to load instead of panicking if the default one cannot be loaded.

Chapter 4

Linux Structure and Initialization

We turn now to the second of our detailed case studies, the Linux operating system. Linux is a relatively modern implementation of UNIX. Like UNIX, it began as a small project of one individual. Since then, it has grown into a cornerstone of the open source movement and is one of the most widely used noncommercial operating systems in the world. The familiarity of the system makes it an interesting and worthwhile candidate for a study like this. Combining a study of the implementational details of a system with knowledge of using and programming that system builds a picture of how one affects the other.

In this chapter, we follow the outline established in Chapters 1 and 2. We begin with a look at the historical background behind Linux, followed by a study of its organizational structure. Our study of the implementational details begins with an examination of the bootstrapping and initialization mechanisms. Finally, we cover the way in which system calls are implemented in Linux.

4.1 The Origins of Linux

During the time that UNIX was in its early development, AT&T was a legal monopoly running the entire long-distance telephone system in the United States. In exchange for this status, it was highly regulated. It was also prevented from getting into other markets, such as computers. That meant that although UNIX was useful to the company internally, it had no commercial value. As a result, it did not hurt the company any for it to also be used by other organizations.

The landscape changed, however, when the U.S. Justice Department sought the breakup of the AT&T monopoly. The judgment that brought an end to the monopoly was handed down in 1982. In the meantime, significant commercial interest had developed around UNIX. With the divestiture, AT&T was allowed to get into the computer market, and it had an operating system ready to sell in UNIX.

Because UNIX was no longer just a research project, but a potential revenue stream, the inexpensive license for universities was no longer available, and the Lions' commentary was no longer distributed. This was a problem for educators. No longer did they have an accessible (both in the sense of available and in the sense of understandable) example of an operating system that they could teach in the classroom. Both in response to this situation and for other pedagogical reasons, several faculty set out to write operating systems of their own that could be used in textbooks and in the classroom. One of these was MINIX by Andrew Tanenbaum.

MINIX and its companion textbook were released in 1987. It was designed to be nearly functionally equivalent to seventh edition UNIX and to run on most IBM PC hardware available at the time. In particular, it could run on a machine as small as an 8086 with 256 KB of memory. Prentice Hall retained the distribution rights to MINIX. The general effect of this was that MINIX became quite successful as an educational system, and some people did develop extensions to it. However, because it was not freely distributable, it didn't see the widespread distributed development that some other software at the time did.

One of the students who purchased both the book and the OS was Linus Torvalds in Finland. In 1991, after having worked with MINIX, Torvalds, set out on a project of his own. His project had two objectives. First, he wanted to learn more about using some of the newer Intel 386 processor's features that MINIX (at that time) did not use. Second, he wanted to develop a terminal emulator that would allow him to use his computer to connect to and use the larger university computers.

His first step was to implement context switching on the 386 and use it to manage two processes, one to print As on the screen and one to print Bs. Once this was working, he was able to boot up his program (running without MINIX or any other OS for support), and it printed AAAAABBBBBAAAABBBBB.... As his next step, he then developed the I/O support to modify these two processes so that one copied characters from the modem to the screen and the other copied characters from the keyboard to the modem. With that step, he had his terminal emulator program.

A terminal emulator program is useful by itself, but in most cases, we also want it to be able to transfer files back and forth between the local machine and the remote one. Torvalds recognized this as well and set out to add that capability to his emulator. Because most of his work was being done on MINIX, it made sense for his terminal emulator to be able to access the MINIX file system. In addition to the file system support itself, this also meant that his code needed to support disk devices.

The astute reader no doubt sees what Torvalds saw. This terminal emulator program that ran with no underlying OS was itself beginning to take on much of the functionality of an operating system. At this point, the nature of the project changed. The objective became to develop an operating system.

In the fall of 1991, Torvalds made his nascent operating system available for free on the Internet. As the system developed, the objectives and ambitions grew as well, from a small system just for his own use, to something as functional as MINIX, to something fully POSIX-compliant. Then in the spring of 1994, version 1.0 of Linux was released. Along the way, Linux transformed from a single-person project into a large, collaborative project involving many people across the world.

Since that initial introduction, Linux has grown beyond what anyone imagined. It has been ported to over a dozen architectures. It has become the basis of a number of commercial enterprises that distribute and support it. It has grown to millions of lines of code. Numerous revisions of Linux have been released and numerous distributions have been made available.

4.2 Organization

Given the way in which Linux developed, its general structure and organization makes for an interesting study. Because Linux was in some ways inspired and modeled after MINIX, and because MINIX has a microkernel design, we might expect that Linux does too. However, this is not the case. Rather, if we look at the way in which Linux evolved from a simple terminal emulator into an operating system, it comes as no surprise that it follows a classic monolithic kernel design much like UNIX, after which both Linux and MINIX are patterned.

Through the remainder of this section, we consider how that classic UNIX design is realized in Linux. In doing so, we highlight three major aspects. First, we discuss the set of subsystems that make up the kernel and how these subsystems interact. Second, we present a design element that deviates from the classic monolithic kernel, the loadable module. Finally, we provide a high-level overview of the source code organization.

4.2.1 Basic Architecture

Overall, Linux is a conventional monolithic kernel with support for loadable modules. In 1999, Bowman, et al., reported on their attempt to extract the structure of the Linux kernel from the existing documentation and source code. Figure 4-1 shows what they describe as the Linux Conceptual Architecture. The boxes in the figure represent major subsystems of the Linux kernel. An arrow going from box x to box y indicates that subsystem x depends on subsystem y. These dependencies generally take the form of a function in subsystem x calling a function in subsystem y or using a data structure owned by subsystem y. (In our presentation, we simplify this slightly by omitting an Initialization subsystem, which depends on all the others, and a Library subsystem, on which all the others depend.)

Each of the subsystems shown in Figure 4-1 addresses a part of the general OS responsibilities discussed in Section 1.2:

- *Process Scheduler*: This subsystem provides context switching and scheduling support for process management. Although it is a relatively small subsystem in terms of the set of functions it provides, it is a very central one. As shown in Figure 4-1, all of the other subsystems depend on it.

- *Memory Manager*: The memory manager subsystem is responsible for allocating memory among the various processes on the system. It also handles those cases where the amount of memory requested is greater than that which is physically available.

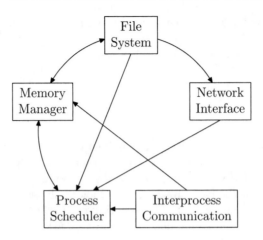

Figure 4-1: Linux Conceptual Architecture

- *File System*: Linux supports a wide variety of file system layouts. This subsystem handles the expected functions for storing and accessing files on a storage device.

- *Network Interface*: The network interface subsystem provides the various network protocols that are supported by Linux.

- *Interprocess Communication*: This subsystem allows processes to exchange data with each other. There are three mechanisms that support this exchange: direct messaging operations, shared memory areas, and primitives that support synchronization between processes.

Before we finish our look at the kernel subsystems, there's one more facet we should mention. Comparing this set of subsystems to the list of responsibilities in Chapter 1 reveals a gap. In particular, this set does not include a subsystem to handle the I/O device support discussed in Chapter 1. In Linux, I/O device support is part of the file system support. Like other implementations of the UNIX design, the file system presents I/O devices in a way that look like files. In turn, the file system depends on I/O devices for the file storage itself. As a result of this interdependence, both file systems and I/O device support are integrated in the same subsystem.

4.2.2 Modules

It is not always desirable to build an operating system with every possible feature supported. In the case of Linux, including every supported device driver, every file system, and every networking protocol would result in an unreasonably large kernel image. Even if we did that, most of that code would never get executed. However, we might like to have a particular file system available for those cases when we do need it. Similarly, there are times when we might like to add additional capabilities to the OS without rebooting the machine. To enable these types of usage, Linux supports **Loadable Kernel Modules** (LKMs).

Normally when we build an application, we compile a number of source code modules into object code modules. In doing so, when one module references another, the compiler doesn't know where the other one will be located in memory, so a placeholder is inserted into the object code. Later, a program called the **linker** resolves those references. It takes the several modules that make up the program and connects them together, replacing placeholders with the correct memory addresses. The same thing happens when we build a typical monolithic kernel.

When we build an LKM, on the other hand, we leave it in the form of an object file complete with unresolved references to other kernel code. Then, when it comes time to load the module, an application program requests that the kernel load the module. The kernel allocates memory to hold the module, loads it into memory, and resolves all the references that the linker normally would. (In kernels prior to version 2.6, symbol resolution was handled by insmod, the application that loads kernel modules.)

After being loaded and dynamically linked, a module behaves as any other part of the kernel. It can call any functions within the kernel that are not private to their own modules. It can reference any global data structures, and it can allocate kernel resources just as parts of the kernel that are statically linked. Consequently, even though LKMs are not part of a single large kernel image, they still function as part of the monolithic kernel.

4.2.3 Source Code Organization

The majority of Linux is written in C. Certain small portions of code are written in the assembly languages of the various architectures. There are a number of places where we need to use assembly language rather than C. Most of these are situations where we are using hardware features that require instructions the compiler doesn't generate or registers the compiler doesn't know.

Like most systems, the source code for Linux is organized according to functionality. In fact, we see a strong correspondence between the subsystems in Figure 4-1 and the directories containing the code. We also see a separate hierarchy of platform-dependent code similar to that found in other systems with multiple ports. Selected directories of the hierarchy are shown in Figure 4-2. The top-level source code directory of the Linux kernel contains the following directories:

- arch: This is the directory where all of the system-specific code is located. All of the other code in the system is platform-independent. Some of the architecture subdirectories are alpha, arm, i386, ia64, m68k, mips, ppc, and sparc. Most of these architecture directories contain a subdirectory called boot. This directory often contains small bits of code and scripts that are necessary to build the final kernel image as needed by the bootstrapping procedure for that particular system. Other subdirectories of the architecture directories mirror top-level source directories such as kernel or mm. These contain any architecture-specific code that supplements or overrides platform-independent code.

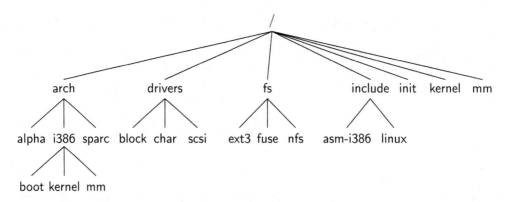

Figure 4-2: Selected Directories in the Linux Source Tree

- crypto: As its name suggests, this directory contains the source for a library of cryptographic functions. Among other applications, some of these functions are used to implement the secure internetworking protocol known as IPsec.

- drivers: This is by far the largest directory of source code. It contains the source for all the device drivers whether they can be statically linked into the kernel or compiled as loadable modules. The source files here are organized into subdirectories by the type of device. For example, the **net** directory contains the driver source code for all of the network interfaces supported by Linux. Similarly, the **scsi** directory contains the code that supports all supported SCSI devices.

- fs: As suggested by its name, this directory contains support for various file systems. This directory also contains code that handles the executable file formats.

- include: All C language header files, both platform-dependent and independent, are found in this directory.

- init: The code in this directory handles the initialization necessary to get the Linux kernel running.

- ipc: This directory contains code to support the interprocess communication mechanisms.

- kernel: Platform-independent code for core kernel functions is found in this directory. This code primarily supports process management.

- lib: The code in this directory forms a small library of utility functions used throughout the Linux kernel. Normally, we don't compile an OS kernel with the standard application libraries. Consequently, we find that most operating system source trees contain (sometimes simplified) implementations of a number of common utility functions.

- mm: The platform-independent memory management code is found in this directory. Because controlling hardware memory management units is very platform specific, the architecture directories contain subdirectories called mm, which provide necessary code.

- net: Linux supports a number of networking protocols in addition to the usual TCP/IP protocol suite. The source code for all these protocols is contained in the net directory.

- security: The code in this directory provides several optional security features. Among these is support for the NSA's security-enhanced Linux (SELinux).

- sound: This directory contains Linux kernel support for audio. Unlike other devices, the drivers for sound devices are in this directory under subdirectories such as drivers, isa, pci, pcmcia, and usb.

Not every file in these directories is compiled and linked in a build of the Linux kernel. Instead, there is a configuration process that builds a number of files that control the compilation process. These files determine which source code files are compiled for a particular configuration. In this way, the full source tree is transformed into a compiled kernel.

4.3 Initialization

We now turn from our general overview to begin an examination of portions of the Linux source code. In this chapter, we examine those code portions that parallel the topics in Chapters 1 and 2, namely the task of system bootstrapping and initialization and the task of issuing system calls.

Initialization is one of the most platform-dependent parts of an OS. As we discuss the initialization of the Linux kernel, we focus on its implementation on the IBM-compatible PC platform. Although much of the general structure of the initialization process is the same for all platforms, many of the details of this process differ on other platforms.

We follow the bootstrapping and initialization process chronologically from first loading the OS into memory to the point where user-level processes are in control of the system. In terms of the big picture, this process goes through the following steps:

1. We first load a (usually) compressed kernel image file into memory. This is generally done by a boot loader. We omit the details of boot loaders because they are not part of Linux proper.

2. As we discuss in Section 4.3.1, we begin by performing hardware initializations necessary to run the code that decompresses the kernel image.

3. The next step is decompressing the kernel.

4. Once we have an uncompressed kernel, we enter into its initialization code. The first part of this code includes initializations of the CPU itself and its associated memory management unit (MMU). These initializations are covered in Section 4.3.2.

5. After we complete the processor-dependent initializations, we move on to initialize the remainder of the hardware and various internal management structures, as discussed in Section 4.3.3.

6. After the kernel has been fully initialized, we are ready to start time-sharing with a single process. This stage is described in Section 4.3.4.

7. The last initialization code we examine is in Section 4.3.5. It is the code for the initial process, which initializes the system from the perspective of user processes. This process serves as the ultimate ancestor for all processes that are created during the lifetime of the system.

With our initialization road map in place, we now turn to the details of each step.

4.3.1 Bootstrapping

The first step in booting an IBM-compatible PC is locating and loading the boot block. The first 512-byte block of a bootable disk is the **boot block** also called the **Master Boot Record** (MBR). It contains two things: a partition table and a small boot program. The BIOS searches the list of devices identified for booting and looks at the first block of each one. If the first block contains the correct signature, then the boot program in it is loaded and executed. The most common program found in the boot block simply searches the partition table for a partition that is marked active. It then loads the first block from that partition and transfers control to it.

Although there were originally many ways to load the Linux kernel into memory, today it is nearly universally done by a boot loader such as LILO or GRUB. Most often these loaders replace the standard code in the boot block, though they may be used as the boot code in an active partition. These loaders are started by the BIOS and read the kernel image into memory from the disk. Finally, they transfer control to the loaded kernel image.

The most common type of kernel image (one with a compressed kernel) contains a number of separate parts, as illustrated in Figure 4-3. The boot sector shown here is left over from an earlier time, a time when a Linux kernel could be built to reside on a floppy disk with no file system. This 512-byte sector would be the boot block loaded by the BIOS, and it would be responsible for loading the rest of the kernel image. Today, the boot sector code simply prints out the message, "Direct booting from floppy is no longer supported." When the boot loader loads the kernel image, it transfers control to the setup code.

4.3.1.1 Setup

The setup code (represented by the second box in Figure 4-3) handles all those initializations that are necessary on an IBM-compatible PC in order to allow the kernel to run.

Boot Sector	Setup	Decompression Code	Compressed Kernel

Figure 4-3: Linux Kernel Image

There are three main parts of this initialization. First, some of the steps gather information about the system that we need later. Second, other steps initialize various features of the CPU, including the MMU and the floating point unit (FPU). Finally, the other major subset of steps initializes the other hardware that makes up an IBM-compatible PC. Rather than delve into the details of the code for setup, we summarize what it does here:

1. Check the last two words of the setup code to make sure setup was completely loaded in the right place.

2. Check to make sure that a bzImage kernel was properly loaded with a loader that would put it in the right place in memory.

3. Determine the size of extended memory. Depending on the motherboard and the amount of available memory, there are three different methods we can attempt to use. All three involve querying the BIOS through `int #15`.

4. Set the keyboard repeat rate to the maximum value.

5. Get the video configuration information.

6. Get the disk drive configuration left in memory by the BIOS.

7. Check for a PS/2 mouse.

8. Test to see if the BIOS supports advanced power management (APM). This check code is included only if the kernel has been configured to support APM.

9. If the kernel has been configured to support BIOS Enhanced Disk Drive (EDD) Services, then we request the disk configuration data through those services.

10. Turn off interrupts.

11. Move the kernel to the appropriate place in memory if necessary.

12. Enable A20. The 8086 and 8088 processors had only 20 address lines and thus could only address 1 MB of memory space. (IBM decided to divide that space into 640 KB for normal memory and 384 KB for I/O devices. This is the source of the infamous "640 KB limit.") Some early software depended on this limitation assuming that memory would wrap around at the 1 MB point. To allow such software to run on machines with processors supporting larger memory spaces, many motherboards provided a way to disable the A20 address line. However, we want to use the full memory space of the machine, and we want to enable the full address bus.

13. Set up the segment descriptor tables. All members of the x86 family start out running with the features of an 8086 for backward compatibility. Beginning with the 80286, a new memory management mode, called **protected mode**, was introduced. Linux doesn't make extensive use of the segmentation capability of the x86 family, but even so, we have to set it up. Initially, we set up the segments to describe the full 4 GB address space as both a code segment that is readable and executable and a data segment that is readable and writable.

14. Reset the math coprocessor if present.

15. Set all external interrupts to be masked in the 8259 interrupt controllers.

16. Switch the processor to protected mode. Turning this mode on enables the more complex segmented memory management.

17. Finally, jump to the entry point startup_32 in the file head.S in the decompression code.

4.3.1.2   Kernel Decompression

The last step of the setup code transfers control to the decompression code illustrated in the third box of Figure 4-3. This code, found in arch/i386/boot/compressed/head.S, performs a small amount of initialization and setup to decompress the kernel. The primary focus of these steps is setting up a call to a C language function. Most of the decompression is handled in code borrowed from the GNU application gzip. The assembly language code in head.S performs the following steps:

1. Set the segment registers for the C language decompression code.

2. Verify that the A20 gate has been enabled.

3. Clear the processor status flags.

4. Clear the data space. ANSI C requires that the global data space of a C program be clear when it starts running.

5. Set up and call *decompress_kernel( )*.

6. Finally, jump to the same startup_32 symbol in the kernel's head.S code.

The final step of the decompression code transfers control to the newly uncompressed kernel. The entry point of that code has the same name as the entry point of the decompression code. It might seem a little confusing to have two entry points, both called startup_32, but it prevents the setup code from having to know whether we're starting a compressed or an uncompressed kernel.

   In some sense, the code up to this point is support code and not the Linux kernel itself. Transferring control to the entry point of the decompressed kernel image transitions from that support code to Linux proper.

4.3.2 Processor-Specific Initialization

When control reaches here, we are ready to begin running the uncompressed Linux kernel. Our first initialization steps are concerned with properly initializing the CPU and MMU, as well as a few other initializations. These initializations for the Intel x86 processors include the following steps:

1. Set up the segment registers.

2. Clear the global data memory.

3. Make copies of the command-line parameters.

4. Initialize a kernel page table and turn paging on. (Details of page tables and paging techniques are discussed in Chapter 9.)

5. Set up the interrupt descriptor table.

6. Determine if we have a math coprocessor.

7. Initialize a global segment table.

At first glance, it appears that much of arch/i386/kernel/head.S repeats what is done in setup and in head.S for the decompression code. There are three things to keep in mind, however. First, if the kernel we're loading is not compressed, we will go directly from setup to the kernel's head code. Second, some of the code in both versions of head.S is to set up C language function calls to two different functions. Even though the code for both cases is similar, it is necessary to perform those operations for each case separately. Third, there is an apparent repetition from the setup code in the initialization of the segment tables. In the code here, we set up a more complex set of segments than we needed in the setup code for a booting environment. The first step is to set up our segment registers to refer to the segments we created in setup.

```
ENTRY(startup_32)

        cld
        lgdt boot_gdt_descr - __PAGE_OFFSET
        movl $(__BOOT_DS),%eax
        movl %eax,%ds
        movl %eax,%es
        movl %eax,%fs
        movl %eax,%gs
```

As in the previous case, we want our global data space cleared according to the ANSI C standard and in case any of the early code we run depends on it.

```
        xorl %eax,%eax
        movl $__bss_start - __PAGE_OFFSET,%edi
```

```
movl $__bss_stop - __PAGE_OFFSET,%ecx
subl %edi,%ecx
shrl $2,%ecx
rep ; stosl
```

4.3.2.1 Processing Kernel Parameters

Copy both the boot parameters and the command-line parameters into a pair of C language
arrays so we can get to them later.

```
movl $(boot_params - __PAGE_OFFSET),%edi
movl $(PARAM_SIZE/4),%ecx
cld
rep
movsl
movl boot_params - __PAGE_OFFSET + NEW_CL_POINTER,%esi
andl %esi,%esi
jnz 2f                          # New command-line protocol
cmpw $(OLD_CL_MAGIC),OLD_CL_MAGIC_ADDR
jne 1f
movzwl OLD_CL_OFFSET,%esi
addl $(OLD_CL_BASE_ADDR),%esi
2:
movl $(saved_command_line - __PAGE_OFFSET),%edi
movl $(COMMAND_LINE_SIZE/4),%ecx
rep
movsl
1:
```

4.3.2.2 Initializing Memory Management Hardware

Here, we build the first page tables. We create two for the kernel. One is the identity
mapping from virtual address 0 to physical address 0 on up through the size of the kernel.
This is used when the kernel is executing in its own right. The other table we create maps
from virtual address PAGE_OFFSET to physical address 0 through the size of the kernel. In
include/asm-i386/page.h, PAGE_OFFSET is defined to be #C0000000. This maps the kernel
to the 3 GB point in the address space.

```
page_pde_offset = (__PAGE_OFFSET >> 20);
```

```
movl $(pg0 - __PAGE_OFFSET), %edi
movl $(swapper_pg_dir - __PAGE_OFFSET), %edx
movl $0x007, %eax          /* 0x007 = PRESENT+RW+USER */
10:
leal 0x007(%edi),%ecx      /* Create PDE entry */
movl %ecx,(%edx)           /* Store identity PDE entry */
movl %ecx,page_pde_offset(%edx) /* Store kernel PDE entry */
```

```
        addl $4,%edx
        movl $1024, %ecx
11:
        stosl
        addl $0x1000,%eax
        loop 11b
        leal (INIT_MAP_BEYOND_END+0x007)(%edi),%ebp
        cmpl %ebp,%eax
        jb 10b
        movl %edi,(init_pg_tables_end - __PAGE_OFFSET)
```

Now we turn the paged memory management on. The two main steps are to set `cr3` to the address of the page directory and to set the high-order bit of `cr0`.

```
        movl $swapper_pg_dir-__PAGE_OFFSET,%eax
        movl %eax,%cr3      /* set the page table pointer.. */
        movl %cr0,%eax
        orl $0x80000000,%eax
        movl %eax,%cr0      /* ..and set paging (PG) bit */
        ljmp $__BOOT_CS,$1f /* Clear prefetch and normalize %eip */
1:
```

Next, we do a couple more little initializations, including initializing the stack pointer and clearing the processor flags.

```
        lss stack_start,%esp

        pushl $0
        popfl
```

This call to `setup_idt` initializes the interrupt descriptor table. Initially, all 256 entries point to a function called `ignore_int`, but entries that need to point to real interrupt handlers get changed as the corresponding drivers are initialized.

```
        call setup_idt
```

The next section of code determines the member of the x86 family of processors on which we're running. For later members of the family, this is a pretty easy task. There are internal registers that give that information. For older members of the family, we are forced to attempt to use features that are in one but not another. The exact set of those features that work tells us which member of the family we have. (For the sake of brevity, we omit the details of this process.)

The next call determines whether there's a math coprocessor installed. It's only a question for very early members of the x86 family. Most have it included on the same die as the CPU.

```
        call check_x87
```

4.3.2.3   Calling the C Language Initialization

Our final initialization here is setting up the new segmentation structure. In doing so, we set the global descriptor table register, the interrupt descriptor table register, and the local descriptor table register along with the segment registers. The jump to the next instruction immediately after selecting the segment descriptor tables probably looks quite strange. It's actually part of the protocol for using protected mode. If we change the segmentation, either by turning protected mode on or by changing the descriptor table we're using, we have to perform an intrasegment jump to force out any instructions in the queue from the other segment.

```
        lgdt cpu_gdt_descr
        lidt idt_descr
        ljmp $(__KERNEL_CS),$1f
1:      movl $(__KERNEL_DS),%eax # reload all the segment
        movl %eax,%ss           # registers after changing gdt.

        movl $(__USER_DS),%eax   # DS/ES contains default USER
                                 # segment
        movl %eax,%ds
        movl %eax,%es

        xorl %eax,%eax           # Clear FS/GS and LDT
        movl %eax,%fs
        movl %eax,%gs
        lldt %ax
```

Finally, we are ready to transfer control to the C language initialization code. We should never return from the *start_kernel( )* function.

```
        cld
        pushl %eax               # fake return address
        call start_kernel
```

4.3.3   Processor-Independent Initialization

The entry point for platform-independent initialization in Linux is *start_kernel( )*, which is found in init/main.c. Most of what we do here is call the initialization functions for each subsystem. The first step is to get a mutual exclusion lock on the kernel so that if we have other processors, they won't all be interfering with each other. (We discuss mutual exclusion locks in detail in Chapter 5.) At first glance, it seems like the sequence of initializations is arbitrary. However, designing code like this is like satisfying course prerequisites. Many of these initializations depend on others being done first. Getting them out of order can result in problems like dereferencing uninitialized pointers. Another way to think of the issues here is to consider a layered view. Our initialization order is from bottom up. We need to initialize the lower layers before we initialize the upper layers that depend on the lower layers. Organizing the initialization in this way results in code that doesn't seem to follow an expected order. Along the way, however, we do initialize several key parts of the system, including page table management, scheduling, and interrupt handling.

asmlinkage void __init *start_kernel*(**void**)
{
    char *command_line*;
    extern struct kernel_param *__start___param*[ ], *__stop___param*[ ];
    smp_setup_processor_id( );
    lockdep_init( );
    local_irq_disable( );
    early_boot_irqs_off( );
    early_init_irq_lock_class( );
    lock_kernel( );
    boot_cpu_init( );

The rest of this function is a series of calls to various initialization functions. Many of these are related to process management and memory management and are discussed in more detail in their respective chapters. Here, we mention them only in a very high-level way. For example, the first call initializes one of the memory management data structures.

    page_address_init( );

Next, we print out the message announcing the version of Linux we're booting.

    printk(KERN_NOTICE);
    printk(*linux_banner*);

Next, we come back to do some more platform-specific initialization. These are things that can be handled in C as opposed to the initialization in setup and in head.S that required assembly language.

    setup_arch(&*command_line*);

These next few calls initialize some of the CPU management data structures. Some of these initialize the scheduler but disable it so that no other process can run until we are finished with initialization.

    setup_per_cpu_areas( );
    smp_prepare_boot_cpu( );
    sched_init( );
    preempt_disable( );

These are more memory management initializations.

> *build_all_zonelists* ( );
> *page_alloc_init* ( );

Now we process the platform-independent, command-line options. Mostly, we just cycle through a set of "arg=value" pairs and call the function that's defined for setting the value of the arg.

> *printk* (KERN_NOTICE"Kernel␣command␣line:␣%s\n", *saved_command_line*);
> *parse_early_param* ( );
> *parse_args* ("Booting␣kernel", *command_line*, __start___param,
>   __stop___param − __start___param, &*unknown_bootoption*);

These next several calls initialize two classes of responsibilities. One of these is the interrupts, traps, and exceptions that the kernel must handle. The other is some internal data structures and management responsibilities. Among these is a hash table for quick lookup of process IDs, various timer functions, and a mechanism for assisting exclusive access to data structures.

> *sort_main_extable* ( );
> *unwind_init* ( );
> *trap_init* ( );
> *rcu_init* ( );
> *init_IRQ* ( );
> *pidhash_init* ( );
> *init_timers* ( );
> *hrtimers_init* ( );
> *softirq_init* ( );
> *timekeeping_init* ( );
> *time_init* ( );

Here are a couple more of the internal initializations. We allocate space to record the results of kernel profiling if it's enabled. At this point, we're now ready to turn on interrupts.

> *profile_init* ( );
> **if** (¬*irqs_disabled* ( ))
>   *printk* ("start_kernel():␣bug:␣interrupts␣were␣enabled␣early\n");
> *early_boot_irqs_on* ( );
> *local_irq_enable* ( );

We can now initialize the device driver for the console. Once we've done that, we can then report on any problems that might have occurred while we were going through other initializations.

       console_init ( );
     if (*panic_later*)
       panic(*panic_later*, *panic_param*);
       lockdep_info ( );
       locking_selftest ( );

Linux can be configured to run its user-level initialization in a RAM disk rather than out of a disk-based file system. If that is the case, then the kernel must be compiled with that support and the initial RAM disk image must also be specified as a kernel parameter. If those conditions are satisfied, then we initialize the RAM disk and begin using it.

     #ifdef `CONFIG_BLK_DEV_INITRD`
       if (*initrd_start* $\wedge$ ¬*initrd_below_start_ok*
           $\wedge$ *initrd_start* < *min_low_pfn* ≪ `PAGE_SHIFT`) {
       printk(`KERN_CRIT"initrd`␣`overwritten`␣`(0x%08lx`␣`<`␣`0x%08lx)`␣
         `-`␣`""disabling`␣`it.\n"`, *initrd_start*, *min_low_pfn* ≪ `PAGE_SHIFT`);
       initrd_start = 0;
     }
     #endif

Now we come back to more of the memory management initialization. Along the way, we also perform some of the initialization of the file system's caches. If we are supporting the next generation time chips found in some machines, then we can initialize their use when more of the memory management initialization is done.

       vfs_caches_init_early ( );
       cpuset_init_early ( );
       mem_init ( );
       kmem_cache_init ( );
       setup_per_cpu_pageset ( );
       numa_policy_init ( );
     if (*late_time_init*)
       late_time_init ( );

The *calibrate_delay* ( ) function is where we calculate the famous BogoMIPS value. The real purpose here is to determine the number of iterations of a simple loop that are required to achieve a specified time delay. From that value, we calculate and report a rough estimate of the processor's speed.

       calibrate_delay ( );

These calls continue the initialization of internal data structures for processes, memory management, and a priority search tree infrastructure.

```
pidmap_init( );
pgtable_cache_init( );
prio_tree_init( );
anon_vma_init( );
```

Initialize the extensible firmware interface if we've enabled it.

```
#ifdef CONFIG_X86
  if  (efi_enabled)
      efi_enter_virtual_mode( );
#endif
```

Here are yet more internal initializations. These include more process managment, memory management, file system buffering, security, and support libraries.

```
fork_init(num_physpages);
proc_caches_init( );
buffer_init( );
unnamed_dev_init( );
key_init( );
security_init( );
vfs_caches_init(num_physpages);
radix_tree_init( );
signals_init( );
page_writeback_init( );
```

If we have support for the /proc file system configured, then we initialize it.

```
#ifdef CONFIG_PROC_FS
  proc_root_init( );
#endif
```

These final calls take care of the last things we need to do before beginning time-sharing. The first initializes the way we manage groups of tasks that need to be treated together. The second looks to see if the particular version of the processor we're using has any known bugs for which we can implement work-arounds. The last begins the initialization of the Advanced Configuration and Power Interface (ACPI).

```
cpuset_init( );
taskstats_init_early( );
delayacct_init( );
check_bugs( );
acpi_early_init( );
```

The last call takes us to rest_init( ), which starts time-sharing.

> *rest_init*( );
> }

With this call, we transfer control permanently to the code that controls user processes. We never return back to *start_kernel*( ).

4.3.4   Starting Time-Sharing

The function *rest_init*( ), also in init/main.c, is where we get the time-sharing ball rolling. Our two main tasks are creating the first process (from which all others descend) and starting the scheduler.

> **static void noinline** *rest_init* (**void**) *__releases* (*kernel_lock*)
> {

Here, we create a new process running the function *init*( ). This process is the ancestor of all user processes that will ever be created during the lifetime of the system.

> *kernel_thread* (*init*, Λ, `CLONE_FS | CLONE_SIGHAND`);

Before scheduling this new thread, we have a few more steps, including setting the policy for NUMA memory management. (This applies only for multiple processor systems with a specific memory architecture.) We can now release the big kernel lock and allow other processors to execute kernel code.

> *numa_default_policy*( );
> *unlock_kernel*( );

Here, we can enable scheduling. In particular, we say that processes can be interrupted in favor of other processes. To get the whole sequence of context switching and scheduling going, we make the first call to *schedule*( ). This will have the effect of running the *init*( ) function in its newly created process.

> *preempt_enable_no_resched*( );
> *schedule*( );
> *preempt_disable*( );

As we see in more detail in Chapter 8, processes are assigned ID numbers in sequential order. The process we just created for *init*( ) is process 1. This leaves the following code to run as process 0. The *cpu_idle*( ) code runs when there are no other processes ready to run, and it just sits in an infinite loop until something needs to happen. (On processors where we can enter a power-saving mode, we do that when idle.)

> *cpu_idle*( );
> }

4.3.5   Initiating Administrative Initialization

Now that time-sharing is going, we can start the user-level initializations found on most systems. These include things like starting server processes, setting audio levels, starting login programs, and starting a windowing system. All of this typically gets handled by a program, also called init. The function *init( )*, again found in init/main.c, sets up the necessary environment and runs this program.

static int *init*(**void** *∗unused*)
{

We don't want any other processors executing kernel code while we're doing some of these initializations.

lock_kernel( );   /∗ init can run on any cpu. ∗/

There are two main things happening in this code. The bulk of the code is responsible for setting up the way we handle multiple CPUs. In the midst of it, we set the value of *child_reaper*, which identifies which process is to handle orphaned processes. When a process exits, it leaves behind an exit status that its parent picks up. If, however, the parent has already exited, we need someone who will be responsible for those children. The init process is that one.

set_cpus_allowed(*current*, CPU_MASK_ALL);
child_reaper = *current*;
smp_prepare_cpus(*max_cpus*);
do_pre_smp_initcalls( );
smp_init( );
sched_init_smp( );
cpuset_init_smp( );

The *do_basic_setup*( ) call initializes device drivers, network sockets, and other initializations that we will not cover. The rest of this code handles the case where we're running init out of a RAM disk. We uncompress the root file system image and then look to see if the specified init program is there. If it is, we keep that for later; otherwise, we set the command to Λ so we know later not to try it.

populate_rootfs( );
do_basic_setup( );
if (¬*ramdisk_execute_command*)
   ramdisk_execute_command = "/init";
if (*sys_access*((**const char** *__user∗*) *ramdisk_execute_command*, 0) ≠ 0) {
   ramdisk_execute_command = Λ;
   prepare_namespace( );
}

Now we have the system up to the point where we're ready to turn it over to the administrative initialization programs and scripts. We can now return some memory allocated just for initialization back to the free pool, we can release the big kernel lock, and we can mark the system as running.

> *free_initmem* ( );
> *unlock_kernel* ( );
> *mark_rodata_ro* ( );
> *system_state* = SYSTEM_RUNNING;
> *numa_default_policy* ( );

UNIX processes normally start with three file descriptors already open: descriptor 0 for standard input, descriptor 1 for standard output, and descriptor 2 for standard error. Unless otherwise specified, all three of these are normally attached to the terminal interface on which the process is started. For the init process, this device is the console. The call to *sys_open* ( ) gets us the standard input, and the two calls to *sys_dup* ( ) copy it as the standard output and standard error.

> **if** (*sys_open*((**const char** *__user*∗) "/dev/console", O_RDWR, 0) < 0)
>   *printk* (KERN_WARNING"Warning:␣unable␣to␣open␣an␣initial␣console.\n");
> (**void**) *sys_dup* (0);
> (**void**) *sys_dup* (0);

Now it's time to try running the init program itself. If we have one to run from the RAM disk, we try it. If no such program was specified or if we are unable to run it, then we see if a specific initialization program was specified among the command-line parameters. If so, then we attempt to run it. Failing that (the more common case), we try several possible locations for the program in turn. If we exhaust all the places where we expect to find it, we resort to just starting a shell. If that fails, there's nothing we can do but panic.

> **if** (*ramdisk_execute_command*) {
>   *run_init_process* (*ramdisk_execute_command*);
>   *printk* (KERN_WARNING"Failed␣to␣execute␣%s\n", *ramdisk_execute_command*);
> }
> **if** (*execute_command*) {
>   *run_init_process* (*execute_command*);
>   *printk* (KERN_WARNING"Failed␣to␣execute␣%s.␣␣Attempting␣"
>   "defaults...\n", *execute_command*);
> }
> *run_init_process* ("/sbin/init");
> *run_init_process* ("/etc/init");
> *run_init_process* ("/bin/init");
> *run_init_process* ("/bin/sh");

$panic(\texttt{"No\_init\_found.\_\_Try\_passing\_init=\_option\_to\_kernel."});$
}

Because the init process is the last one started by the kernel, all other processes in the system must be descendants of init. Traditionally, one of its primary responsibilities is to start another program called getty for each of the terminals (or virtual consoles) on which we want people to be able to log in. When someone enters a user name, getty then starts login, which in turn starts the shell if the user also supplies the correct password. As a result, at this point, the system has now transitioned from the boot loader to a full time-sharing environment.

4.4   System Calls

Early versions of Linux used a system call mechanism much like that described in Section 1.6. On early versions of the Intel x86 processor, the software interrupt instruction was the best way to transfer control into the kernel. Linux used the `int` #80 instruction in library stub functions for system calls. Later, Intel introduced a new instruction that makes the switch into the kernel much faster. This instruction is called `sysenter`, and during development of the version 2.5 series of kernels, Linux added support for it. (AMD introduced a similar instruction called `syscall` into its line of x86 compatible processors.)

4.4.1   Application-Side System Call Handling

To support this new mechanism in a way that can efficiently fall back on the older one when necessary, a page of kernel memory, called the vsyscall page, is mapped into each process's space. This page of memory contains the code to issue system calls. The library stub functions (sometimes compiled inline) now just issue an ordinary function call into this special page. At boot time, one of the by-products of the call to *check_bugs*( ) is to determine the model of processor on which we're running. If it's a processor that supports the `sysenter` instruction, then the kernel page defining the system call mechanism is loaded with the code to use that instruction. Otherwise, we load that page with code that uses the older `int` #80 mechanism. That way the same kernel and applications can run on both the older and newer processors with no speed penalty for each system call.

By way of example, we consider the line of code

$p=brk\,(q);$

which requests that the OS set the boundary between data and stack at the address given by q. Taking a slightly simplified view of the GNU C library, we find that this call is linked to the function $\_brk(\,)$, which contains the line:

$newbrk = \texttt{INTERNAL\_SYSCALL}(brk, err, 1, addr);$

`INTERNAL_SYSCALL` is a macro that is defined in one of several ways depending on how we want to issue the system call. One of those ways expands it to use the `int` #80 instruction. Another expands to an inline assembly language sequence that looks something like:

```
      LOADARGS_1
      movl    __NR_brk, %eax
      call    *_dl_sysinfo
      RESTOREARGS_1
```

where _dl_sysinfo points to the vsyscall page code for issuing a system call.

If we're running on a processor that supports the **sysenter** instruction, then the relevant code in the vsyscall page begins with:

```
__kernel_vsyscall:
      push    %ecx
      push    %edx
      push    %ebp
      movl    %esp,%ebp
      sysenter
```

The **sysenter** instruction operates much like a faster version of the traditional software interrupt instruction.

4.4.2   Kernel-Side System Call Handling

The interrupt handler code for the **sysenter** instruction begins with some overhead that's part of the protocol for using it.

```
ENTRY(sysenter_entry)
        movl TSS_sysenter_esp0(%esp),%esp
```

Then, we enable interrupts and save the data we need to return on the kernel stack.

```
sysenter_past_esp:
        sti
        pushl $(__USER_DS)
        pushl %ebp
        pushfl
        pushl $(__USER_CS)
        pushl $SYSENTER_RETURN
```

For simplicity, we skip over a bit of complication in supporting the very few system calls that need six arguments. We also skip over a check to see if we need to trace this system call. The next few instructions check to make sure that the process is not requesting a system call number that's greater than the largest one we support. If it's acceptable, then we call the function that is specified in the table *sys_call_table* indexed by the **eax** register. Earlier, that's the register in which we saved the value **__NR_brk**. For this value of **eax**, the function given in the table is *sys_brk( )*.

```
              cmpl $(nr_syscalls), %eax
              jae syscall_badsys
              call *sys_call_table(,%eax,4)
```

Now we are finished with servicing the request. We omit most of the detail of preparing to return to the calling process, but note that when using the **sysenter** instruction, the proper way to return is to use the instruction:

```
sysexit
```

The process for returning back to the code that originally issued the system call largely follows the reverse of the procedure described here. Along the way, we maintain the value returned from the system call in the **eax** register.

4.5   Summary

The Linux operating system grew out of the work of Linus Torvalds motivated by his desire to create a system with the capabilities of UNIX but without the licensing restrictions. The resulting system has become very widely used. It has grown into a fully functional member of the UNIX family. We have seen how the system makes the transition from a raw piece of hardware into a time-sharing system allowing user access. We have also discussed how the Linux system call mechanism has adapted to the changes made by Intel in the design of the x86 family of processors. These considerations build the foundation for the detailed examination of the Linux kernel we present in later chapters.

4.6   Exercises

1. The conceptual architecture in Figure 4-1 does not explicitly address process creation or termination. Why not? Where does it belong in Figure 4-1?

2. Are there some kernel functions that cannot be put into modules? Give some examples and explain why they cannot be put in modules.

3. What are the trade-offs in compressing the kernel image? When would we choose to use a compressed kernel and when would we choose to use an uncompressed kernel?

4. Why are the setup program and the two instances of head.S written in assembly language?

5. Describe the code that implements the int #80 system call mechanism. How does it differ from the code for the **sysenter** technique?

6. Why is the BogoMIPS a rarely useful measure of CPU performance? Under what circumstances can it be useful?

7. How many lines of code are found in each of the directories listed in Section 4.2.3?

8. In *start_kernel*( ), we disable preemption after initializing the scheduler. If there are no other processes at this time, why disable preemption?

9. Modify the Linux initialization code to print out a custom message after the standard version message.

10. Modify the Linux initialization code to ask the user for an initialization program if the standard ones are not available.

Chapter 5

Principles of Process Management

The operating system manages the resources of the computer. We begin our examination of these with the CPU. As discussed in Section 1.2, an operating system manages the CPU resource by managing the processes that use it. In Sections 5.1–5.3, we first discuss the definition and representation of processes. We then discuss how the OS creates and terminates processes in Section 5.6. However, we are most interested in the issue of time-sharing the CPU among processes. In particular, scheduling (selecting the process that gets the CPU next) is the topic we cover in the most detail in Section 5.4. In Section 5.7, we discuss mechanisms for ensuring exclusive access to data structures to prevent multiple threads of execution from interfering with each other. Finally, we consider the issue of deadlock where multiple processes are all waiting on resources locked by another process.

5.1 The Process Concept

Unlike other entities managed by the OS, a **process** is an intangible thing. Many of the more tangible things that are related to processes are very familiar. We are familiar with programs both in their source code form and in the form of compiled machine code stored on the disk. We are familiar with the idea of program instructions and data stored in memory as well as the I/O and file usage of a program. However, none of these is the process itself.

If none of these is a process, then what exactly is a process? We can describe a process as an instance of a running program. Several things about this definition are worth noting. First, as suggested previously, it's not a process when a program is just sitting on a disk or sitting in memory as data. Second, if two users are running the same program at the same time, there are two separate processes. This is true even if both processes share one copy of the program's instructions in memory.

This definition gives us a good conceptual basis for understanding a process. However, a somewhat more formal definition is sometimes useful. The formal model we usually use for describing programs is the Turing machine. In its simplest form, the Turing machine consists of a finite automaton and a tape. The automaton takes the combination of its internal state and the tape symbol under the read/write head and transforms them into a new internal state, a new tape symbol, and a direction (left or right) to move the tape head. At any point in time, the configuration of the machine consists of the contents of the tape, the automaton internal state, and the head position. As a machine progresses through a computation, it sequentially transforms one configuration into another. This sequence of transformations corresponds to the running of a program, where the changes in tape and state are like the changes in memory and registers as instructions are executed. With this formalism in mind, we can say that a process is the sequence of configurations that a machine goes through during a specific computation.

5.2   Realizing Processes

The descriptions in the previous section help us to understand what a process is. However, they are more conceptual statements than definitions suitable as a basis for design and implementation of an operating system. How do we move from the idea of an instance of a running program to the data structures and algorithms necessary to implement process management?

The first approach we take to this problem is reducing the process to a set of more concrete constituent parts. One of the earliest approaches described the process in terms of its memory space and an associated locus of control. In representing and managing processes in practice, we not only identify and describe the memory space, but also all resources, including currently used I/O devices and files. The idea of locus of control helps to bridge the gap between the nebulous notion of a progression through time (as captured in the Turing machine view) and the stacks and registers we need to manage as part of time-sharing. It captures the idea that by viewing certain registers and memory locations, we can observe the progression of a process through its sequence of configurations. By saving and restoring these values, we can temporarily stop a process and resume it later. As we see in this section, the resources used by a process and the set of values that represent and control the program's execution are major parts of our internal representation of a process.

5.2.1   Process Operations

Another perspective that helps us to develop a concrete implementation of process management is the **abstract data type**. Abstract data types are defined in terms of the operations performed on them. They are implemented as a combination of one or more data structures and a set of functions that operate on them. Although different systems define different sets of operations, we might informally define processes in terms of the following set of typical operations:

- *Create process*: In creating a new process, we have to do several things. First, we have to create the internal representation of the process. Second, we have to assign the process's initial resources. Finally, because a process is an instance of a running program, we must initialize the program that is to run in this process. We often call the process that initiates process creation the parent process. Similarly, we often call the newly created process the child process.

- *Terminate process*: Our primary task in terminating a process is releasing all of the resources it was using at the time of its termination. We often also have to handle some administrative tasks related to informing other processes of the end of this one.

- *Change program*: Typically, systems provide the ability for a process to replace the program that it is running. This would seem to violate our definition of a process. After all, if we change what program is running, would it not be a new process? However, this operation makes sense in most practical implementations, and we accept the fact that our conceptual definition only approximates real implementations.

- *Set process parameters*: There are often a number of administrative parameters we maintain for each process. For example, a process may have an associated priority. We need to provide a mechanism for setting these parameters.

- *Get process parameters*: We also need to be able to query the settable parameters. In addition to those parameters, we usually keep other information about processes. For example, often each process has a numeric identification, and we often keep a record of the amount of CPU time used by each process. We also make this information available to a process that requests it.

- *Block process*: At various points during the lifetime of a process, it might need to wait on an event before it can continue running. In addition to other events, a process will normally need to wait between the time it requests an I/O operation and the time that the operation is finished.

- *Awaken process*: After the event on which a process is waiting has occurred, we can allow the process to again run.

- *Switch process*: The next operation we define on processes is context switching. This operation takes the CPU away from one process and gives it to another.

- *Schedule process*: In most systems, the OS is responsible for selecting which process is assigned to the CPU on each context switch. This selection is called scheduling.

We should point out that we are presenting these operations from the perspective of the internals of the operating system, rather than the perspective of processes issuing system calls. Many of these operations do have corresponding system calls, such as creating and terminating processes. However, others do not. This list also does not represent all system calls an OS may support.

5.2.2 Process State

The operations to block, awaken, and switch processes all affect the **process state**. The idea of process state describes the current condition of the process in terms of how we manage it. Is this process ready to use CPU time? Is it waiting on some I/O event? Is it terminated but still being managed? We normally talk about the set of possible states of a process in terms of a state machine (finite automaton) such as the simple example shown in Figure 5-1. In this machine, we have three states:

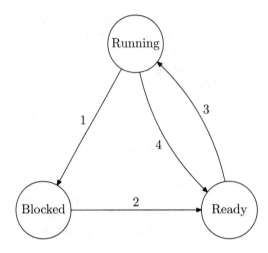

Figure 5-1: Typical Process State Machine

- *Running*: The CPU is currently executing code that is part of the process.

- *Ready*: Processes in the Ready state are not waiting for any events, but are waiting their turn on the CPU.

- *Blocked*: We identify processes that are waiting for some event (often I/O operations) as being blocked.

It also has four transitions:

1. A process makes the transition from the Running state to the Blocked state when it makes a request that cannot be immediately satisfied. While the request is being processed, the process remains in the Blocked state.

2. When a request has been satisfied and a process no longer needs to be blocked, it is transitioned to the Ready state.

3. The third transition in the diagram represents the case where a process is scheduled. In other words, a process has been selected as the next one to run on the CPU.

4. After a process is selected to be the running process, the previously running process must be returned to the Ready state. This is the case where a process is **preempted** as opposed to a case where a process is blocked.

We sometimes use the term **state** to refer to everything about a process: its memory contents, register values, internal representation, and so on. However, in this book, we use the term **configuration** to describe this information whenever there is potential for confusion.

5.2.3   The Process Table

If the process is such an intangible thing, then how does the operating system manage it? The key is much like it is for a number of application domains. We do not operate on the entities directly, but instead operate on representations. The same is true of managing processes.

The representations of all processes currently on the system are collected into a data structure we generally call a **process table**. We refer to a process's individual representation as a **process table entry**. The following are some of the items typically found in a process table entry:

- saved registers
- process state
- process ID number
- owner ID number
- group ID number
- priority
- memory usage and mapping
- status of open files
- cumulative running time

Real operating systems generally have a number of additional elements unique to their own management of processes. Rather than discuss these structure members in isolation at this point, we look at them in later sections in the context in which they are used.

Process table entries are organized into process tables using a variety of data structures. Some of the more common ones include arrays, linked lists, and hash tables. We often see these structures used in combination for efficiency. For example, a system might originally be designed with a linked list representation of the table, but later add a hash table to speed searches.

5.3   Threads

In viewing a process as a memory space and a locus of control, we identify two separate, but cooperative, components of a process. These two components are not completely independent as a locus of control is meaningful only in the context of a particular memory space. However, we can ask, "What happens if we allow more than one locus of control in a single memory space?" The answer is that we create a useful programming technique where applications can be written as multiple cooperating entities.

These separate loci of control sharing a common memory space are usually called **lightweight processes** (LWPs) or **threads**. Just as with normal processes, threads are scheduled and switched to provide time-sharing among them.

In practice, we see two methods of implementing threads. In the first form, a process manages its own threads. Here, the program is linked with a library of thread management code containing code to schedule and switch among the threads sharing the process's memory space. In this first type of implementation, the OS sees and manages a single process. The multiple threads are invisible to the kernel. The second form of implementation is often called **kernel threads**. This term is normally used to describe threads belonging to applications, but managed by the kernel. From the operating system's perspective, the unit of scheduling is the thread rather than the process. When implemented in this way, we often think of the process as a container for one or more threads.

Both approaches to implementing threads provide a set of services accessed through library and system calls. One set of calls, which is particularly worth noting, is the thread application programming interface (API) that's part of the portable operating system interface (POSIX) specification from the Institute of Electrical and Electronics Engineers (IEEE). This set of library calls can be used as the basis of portable multithreaded applications because it has been implemented on a wide variety of operating systems, including implementations of both types.

As developers have gained experience with both the use and the implementation of threads, it has become clear that both the traditional, single-threaded process and the multithreaded process are special cases of a more general notion of process. When a parent process creates a child, there are several aspects of the parent that might be relevant to the newly created child process. Some of these are the memory space, the set of open files, the name space, and the data describing the environment in which the process runs. The child either shares, inherits a copy of, or is given a replacement for each of these aspects of its parent. In the most general case, we can select at the time of process creation which are shared, which are inherited, and which are replaced. Using this approach, traditional UNIX process creation (using *fork*() as mentioned in Section 1.6) can be achieved by creating a process that inherits all aspects of its parent. Similarly, typical thread creation is equivalent to creating a process sharing all aspects of its parent.

5.4   Scheduling

One of the most studied and analyzed aspects of process management is **process scheduling**. The scheduler is the mechanism by which the operating system selects which process gets the CPU next. As we discuss the various scheduling techniques, we also consider a number of motivations and criteria for scheduling. For example, we usually say we want the scheduler to be fair, but what do we consider fair? Do we want to give preference to some processes over others? If so, how much preference should they be given? Should one process be able to run to the exclusion of others? Preventing a process from getting CPU time when it is ready is called **starvation**. The answers to these questions play a big part in establishing the details of the scheduling policy we implement.

When reduced to practice, the task of scheduling becomes one of maintaining a data structure of processes ready to run and of selecting the appropriate member of that structure. Regardless of the actual data structure used, we generally refer to this set of processes as the **ready list**. In most implementations, we keep the list arranged in such a way as to make finding the desired process fast. For example, if we use a linked list, then we usually keep it sorted in the order in which we want to run the processes in it.

5.4.1   First-Come, First-Served

The first couple of scheduling techniques we examine are suitable for batch operating systems. In batch environments, we often speak of **jobs** rather than processes. For purposes of scheduling, we consider the two terms interchangeable. When thinking about scheduling in batch systems, it is important to remember that (particularly in early systems) groups of jobs are often collected into a batch before the first of the group is executed. In keeping with this, we make a simplifying assumption in our discussion of batch scheduling. We focus on the time between starting the run of a batch of jobs and the time a job is complete.

Perhaps the most intuitive and simplest technique is to allow the first process submitted to run first. We call this approach **first-come, first-served** (FCFS) scheduling. In effect, processes are inserted into the tail of a queue when they are submitted. As each process finishes running, the next process is taken from the head of the queue. This approach is illustrated in Example 5.1. This technique applies not only to the common case of a batch being assembled prior to execution, but also to the case where we allow new jobs to be added after the batch has begun.

5.4.2   Shortest Job First

Although first-come, first-served scheduling is very straightforward, it has one rather unfortunate feature. Suppose we have one very long job and four very short jobs. If the long job happens to be submitted just before the other four, then the submitters of all five jobs will have to wait a very long time for their results. On the other hand, if the four short jobs happen to be submitted just before the long job, then the submitters of the four shorter jobs will get their results quickly. Yet, in this case, the submitter of the long job will see only a small increase in the time before receiving results. In other words, the average time to wait for results might be longer than necessary because of the order in which the jobs arrived.

We can avoid this phenomenon by executing the jobs in increasing order of their run time. In fact, this **shortest job first** (SJF) scheduling policy is optimal in the sense that the average turnaround time is minimized. To make this more precise, let the time taken to run job i be denoted by t_i, and let the processes be executed in the order $i = 1, 2, 3, \ldots, n$. For simplicity, we consider only the case where the batch is assembled prior to execution and consider time to begin when the first job begins running. This is equivalent to assuming that all the jobs arrive simultaneously. The turnaround time for job i is the total time between the time job i is submitted and the time that job i is completed. Following our assumption of simultaneous arrival, this turnaround time is given by $T_i = \sum_{j=0}^{i} t_j$. Example 5.1 illustrates the comparison between FCFS and SJF.

Example 5.1: FCFS and SJF

In this example, we compare the average turnaround time of FCFS and SJF scheduling. Suppose we receive three jobs, a, b, and c with $t_a = 20$, $t_b = 50$, and $t_c = 10$. We assume that they arrive in the order of a, b, c but that they all arrive so close together that we receive them all before we can select the first one to run. Using FCFS scheduling, we arrange them in a queue, as shown in Figure 5-2.

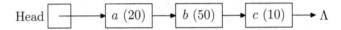

Figure 5-2: First Come, First Served Queue

The turnaround times for FCFS are

$$T_a = 20$$
$$T_b = 20 + 50 = 70$$
$$T_c = 20 + 50 + 10 = 80$$

and the average turnaround time is

$$\tau = \frac{20 + 70 + 80}{3} = 56.67$$

By comparison, if we use SJF scheduling, we run the jobs in the order c, a, b, as illustrated in Figure 5-3.

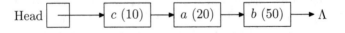

Figure 5-3: Shortest Job First Queue

The turnaround times for SJF are

$$T_c = 10$$
$$T_a = 10 + 20 = 30$$
$$T_b = 10 + 20 + 50 = 80$$

which yields an average turnaround time of

$$\tau = \frac{10 + 30 + 80}{3} = 40.00$$

In this example, we save 29% of the average turnaround time by using SJF scheduling over FCFS scheduling.

Now that we have a general understanding of SJF, we are ready to justify the claim that shortest job first is optimal. Assume to the contrary that there exists an ordering with minimum average turnaround time but which is not shortest job ordering. There must be at least one value of i where $t_i > t_{i+1}$. The average turnaround time for this sequence is given by

$$\tau = \frac{1}{n} \sum_{j=1}^{n} T_j$$

By partially expanding the summations for T_i and T_{i+1}, we obtain

$$\tau = \frac{1}{n} \left(\sum_{j=1}^{i-1} T_j + \left(\sum_{k=1}^{i-1} t_k + t_i \right) + \left(\sum_{k=1}^{i-1} t_k + t_i + t_{i+1} \right) + \sum_{j=i+2}^{n} T_j \right)$$

Now consider another order where the jobs are processed in order $1, 2, 3, \ldots, i - 1, i + 1, i, i + 2, i + 3, \ldots, n$. Here the average turnaround time is given by

$$\tau' = \frac{1}{n} \left(\sum_{j=1}^{i-1} T_j + \left(\sum_{k=1}^{i-1} t_k + t_{i+1} \right) + \left(\sum_{k=1}^{i-1} t_k + t_{i+1} + t_i \right) + \sum_{j=i+2}^{n} T_j \right)$$

By comparing the expressions for τ and τ' we see that

$$\tau' = \tau + \frac{1}{n}(-t_i + t_{i+1})$$

But because $t_i > t_{i+1}$, $\tau' < \tau$, which violates the assumption that an ordering other than the shortest job first ordering gives a minimal turnaround time.

Of course, using SJF scheduling requires that we know the time that the job will take to run. This is a little bit of an odd concept. How can the operating system know how long a program is going to take to run before it is run? The answer is that we require the user submitting the job to specify its running time. Although that sounds like a strange requirement to those coming from a time-sharing background, it was quite common in batch-processing systems. The natural question arises, why don't users just specify a very small running time so that their jobs get scheduled first? Typically, this is solved by terminating a job as soon as its specified running time is exceeded. To balance between a job being terminated prematurely and a job being scheduled later than necessary, users are motivated to provide accurate running time estimates.

5.4.3   Round-Robin

We now turn our attention to scheduling techniques applicable to time-sharing systems. In time-sharing, the approach is to run a process for a small time slice and then to select another process to get the next time slice. This cycle is repeated indefinitely. The length of a time slice is called a **quantum**. For most scheduling policies, the quantum is fixed at a value such as 0.1 or 0.01 seconds. A process's time slice can end in one of three ways. For compute-bound processes, the usual case is that the process is still running when its time slice expires and another process is scheduled. However, a process might not finish its time slice because another process becomes ready to run and is granted the CPU in favor of the current process. Another case where a process doesn't complete its time slice is the one where the process makes a request that causes it to block. We say that the process is **preempted** in the first two cases.

The time-sharing analog of first-come, first-served is a policy we call **round-robin** (RR). In round-robin scheduling, processes take turns in an equal manner. One way to define it is that the next process selected to run is the one that has been waiting the longest. The implementation is very similar to that for first-come, first-served. Processes that are preempted are added to the tail of the queue just as are new processes. (Though some systems implement a variation, where new processes are placed on the head of the queue, giving them an immediate time slice.) In other words, ready processes are kept in a circular queue, as illustrated in Figure 5-4. The net effect is that all ready processes get an equal fraction of the CPU time.

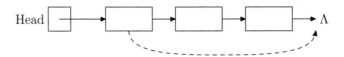

Figure 5-4: Round-Robin Circular Queue

5.4.4   Priority Scheduling

Sometimes we don't want processes to be scheduled with equal frequency of selection. Instead, we might want to set some priority on a process. For example, we might administratively define that certain users have a higher priority on all their processes than other users. Another motivation for priorities is a desire to give interactive processes preference over compute-bound processes. The rationale for this is twofold. First, it is generally assumed that interactive processes are more likely to have users waiting on the results, whereas compute-bound processes are more likely to be running without a user directly observing them. By giving preference to interactive processes, users perceive the system as more responsive. The second rationale is similar. Because interactive processes are more likely to block rather than use their entire time slice, giving them priority has somewhat the same flavor as the shortest job first policy.

Up to this point, we have intentionally left the notion of priority as an abstract concept. As a semifacetious example, suppose a process's priority is represented by a color. We might say that green processes are given preference over red processes. Despite the abstract nature of priority, systems represent priority by an integer more often than not. However, greater integer values do not universally imply higher priority. For some systems, the smaller the integer, the higher the process's priority.

To implement a priority scheduling policy, we select the ready process with the highest priority to run next. If we have more than one at the same highest priority level, we most often select among them using a round-robin policy (though other policies are also possible). This policy is shown in Example 5.2.

Example 5.2: Priority Scheduling

To illustrate priority scheduling, let us consider five processes, a, b, c, d, and e. We denote the priority of process a by $p(a)$ and likewise for the other processes. In our example, let $p(a) = 10$, $p(b) = p(c) = p(d) = 5$, and $p(e) = 1$. This set of priority assignments has the effect of giving process a the CPU whenever it's ready. When a is blocked, then processes b, c, and d are scheduled round-robin if they are ready. Process e runs only when nothing else is ready to run. Such a process is often called a background process or an idle process.

There are several approaches we can take to implementing a priority scheduling system. The simplest, though not particularly fast, method is to examine each process in the process table looking for the ready one with the highest priority. If we always begin the search at the last process that was run and search in a circular manner, then we can guarantee round-robin behavior for processes of equal priority. Slightly faster, we can keep a list of ready processes and examine each process in it. (The speed improvement comes from the fact that we don't look at those processes that are not in the Ready state.) Another common approach is to keep a structure of ready processes arranged by priority. With this representation, selecting the next process can be done in constant time, but inserting a process (each time one is preempted or a process moves from Blocked to Ready states) will typically take a longer time. For a simple linear list, insertion takes linear time. The insertion can be sped up by using a tree representation of a priority queue. Finally, we can maintain a multilevel queue, consisting of several queues each with a different priority value. Then, we just schedule among the processes in the nonempty queue with the highest priority.

Up to this point, we have not really addressed how priority values get set. Perhaps the simplest approach is to set the priorities statically according to some characteristic of the processes. For example, we might have an environment where certain users are given a higher priority than other users. As another example, consider a microkernel design. We might set the priority of processes that provide operating system functionality higher than normal user processes.

More commonly, however, priorities are set in a dynamic manner. In particular, the system adjusts the priority of a process according to rules based on the process's execution history. One common method is to raise the priority of processes that are blocked and therefore get no CPU time while lowering the priority of those that get a large amount of CPU time. This policy tends to implement the desired behavior where interactive processes get priority over compute-bound processes. In most real systems, a combination of static and dynamic priorities is used. In particular, we usually allow administrative settings to limit the minimum and maximum values that can be dynamically set. The various systems discussed in Chapter 6 exemplify a number of dynamic priority adjustment techniques.

5.4.4.1 Multilevel Feedback Queues

One particularly significant implementation of dynamic priorities is the **multilevel feedback queue**. This structure implements a priority scheduler with dynamic priority adjustments using separate queues for each priority level. One of the most common priority adjustment techniques in multilevel feedback queues schedules each priority level according to a first in, first out (FIFO) policy rather than round-robin. When a process completes a quantum, it is not placed on the tail of the queue from which it came. Rather, it is placed on the tail of the queue of next lower priority. Of course, the lowest priority queue is treated as a circular queue and scheduled round-robin. Quite commonly, individual processes are assigned a base priority below which they do not shift downward. In that case, processes that complete a quantum at their base priority are placed on the tail of the same queue. In most implementations of multilevel feedback queues, processes do not migrate toward higher priorities in the normal course of scheduling. Instead, they may be given a **priority boost** for a number of reasons. For example, a process that is added to the ready list after being blocked for some period of time may be added at a priority higher than its base priority. Similarly, a process that has been in a low priority queue for some period of time without being scheduled may be given a boost. From these boosted levels, processes then move back down to their base priorities in the normal course of scheduling.

Even though this technique dates back to some of the earliest time-sharing operating systems, it continues to be used in many priority schedulers. Figure 5-5 shows an example of this structure. The solid arrows in the figure show the linked list structure of the queue. The dashed arrows show where processes may move on completing their time slice. They show both the cases where processes stay at the same priority level and the cases where they migrate to a lower priority level.

5.4.4.2 Priority Inversion

If we're not careful, the simple policy of always selecting the highest priority process with static priorities can lead to a phenomenon called **priority inversion**. Priority inversion occurs when a high priority process is waiting on a low priority process that is starved by a medium priority process. This phenomenon is most easily understood by way of an example such as Example 5.3.

Example 5.3: Priority Inversion

Suppose we have three processes a, b, and c with priorities 3, 5, and 7, respectively. Further, let process c be waiting on process a to complete some task. The problem occurs

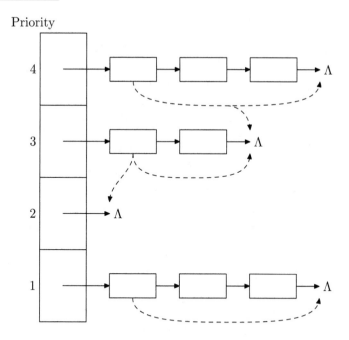

Figure 5-5: Multilevel Feedback Queue

if process b is compute-bound and never blocks. If we always select the highest priority ready process to run, then process a will never run, and consequently neither will process c. The overall behavior is as if priority 5 were higher than priority 7. In other words, their priorities are inverted.

5.4.4.3 Priority Inheritance

If we're using dynamic priority adjustments, then the priority inversion may be addressed in time as the medium and low priority processes are adjusted. However, we might want to attack the problem more directly. We can solve the priority inversion problem by applying **priority inheritance**. This technique involves temporarily elevating the priority of a process if a higher priority process blocks waiting on it, as illustrated in Example 5.4. If process x waits on process y, where the priority of x is greater than that of y, then we set the priority of y to that of x until x unblocks.

Example 5.4: Priority Inheritance

In the previous example, when process c waits on process a, we temporarily set the priority of process a to 7. In this way, process b cannot starve process a. Process a can complete the task on which process c is waiting, thus preventing the priority inversion. After a has completed the task and we unblock process c, then the priority of a returns to 3.

5.4.5   Adjusting Scheduling Parameters

Priority is not the only parameter that we can change to tune the behavior of the system. The prime example of this is the way in which the Compatible Time-Sharing System (CTSS) adjusts the process's quantum. As discussed in more detail in Section 6.1, CTSS uses a multilevel feedback queue with an exponentially increasing time slice. If the base quantum is q seconds, queue i has a time slice of length $2^i q$. In CTSS, queue 0 has the highest priority, and lower priority queues have the longer time slices.

As with other common priority adjustment techniques, CTSS gives priority to I/O-bound processes over compute-bound processes. However, the longer time slices have the effect of reducing the number of context switches for compute-bound processes.

In Section 6.7, we discuss Windows NT as another example of a system that uses different sized quanta to give preference to some processes over others. In that system, a longer quantum is used to give preference to the process that has focus in the windowing system.

5.4.6   Two-Level Scheduling

In Chapter 9, we discuss how to deal with a case where not all processes can fit into memory at once. If we need to allocate space to create a process and there is not enough memory available, it is common to write the memory of a process out to the disk. Normally, we pick the process that hasn't run in the longest time.

Now suppose that we are about to schedule a process that has been swapped out to the disk. What do we do? We respond much as we would to a request to create a process. We pick the process that hasn't run in the longest amount of time, write it out to the disk, read in the one we want to schedule, and then continue where we left off. Taking this a step further, suppose that there is not enough memory to hold all the processes in the ready list and that we are using round-robin scheduling. It should be clear that in this case, the process selected to swap out will always be the same one that we will schedule the next time around. This means that we will swap between disk and memory for each context switch! This is an example of a phenomenon called **thrashing**, and as we see in Chapter 9, this is very detrimental to system performance.

To ameliorate this problem, we can use a **two-level scheduling** technique. Using a higher-level, long-term scheduler that runs more slowly, we select which subset of processes are resident. Then, a normal, lower-level, short-term scheduler selects among only those processes that are resident in memory.

5.4.7   Real-Time Scheduling

All of the scheduling policies up to this point have been targeted to general-purpose systems. However, there are more special-purpose systems out there than there are general-purpose systems. The automotive industry is a good example. With between 10 and 40 microprocessors in each car and millions of cars produced each year, most people have many more computers in their cars than on their desks. In these special-purpose systems, we often have very strict requirements on the response time for events. For example, in an automotive ignition control computer, an error of only 3 mS in firing a spark plug represents 10% (36°) of an engine revolution at 2000 RPM In fact, errors of over 1° of a revolution can have a noticeable detrimental effect on engine performance. At 2000 RPM, 1° only takes 83 μS.

The automotive example is quite typical in that many real-time applications have a cyclic nature. Of course, if the code involved doesn't complete its work in the time allotted, then no amount of scheduling design will help.

5.4.7.1   Event-Driven Scheduling

With these concepts in mind, we can now turn our attention to the details of real-time scheduling techniques. The first case we consider is where the event to which we need to respond is signaled by a hardware interrupt. Environmental sensors are one example of the source of such interrupts. For activities that are driven by time, a clock can provide the initiating interrupt. In these cases, the process that handles the event remains blocked until the interrupt occurs. When we get the interrupt, we immediately schedule the appropriate process and let it run until it blocks again. Things get a little more complicated when we have more than one such event. Suppose we are processing one real-time event and an interrupt for another comes in. Should we preempt the running process for the one that handles the new interrupt? The answer to that question is normally given by either a priority or by specifying the timing bounds. So if the new event has a higher priority or a tighter time requirement than the currently running one, then we will preempt the current one. Otherwise, we let the current one complete before servicing the new one.

5.4.7.2   Earliest Deadline First

Our next real-time scheduling technique is **earliest deadline first** (EDF), which parallels the SJF policy for batch systems. EDF is most easily understood when we think of the work done in each time slice as being a self-contained task. For each process, we maintain a scheduling parameter that specifies the time by which the next task must be accomplished. These times are deadlines that the scheduler attempts to meet. As the policy's name suggests, the scheduler always selects the process with the earliest deadline. We can keep a simple list sorted by deadline and always take the first process from it. In effect, we have a priority scheduler where priority is the inverse of the time until a deadline.

After a process has used its time slice, we set the next deadline and add the process back to the ready list. In many cases, we set the next deadline by adding a constant period to the time at which the time slice ended. The effect of this is to cause the process to run at least as often as the period. By setting different periods for different processes, we can give each process a desired share of the CPU. We see the way this works in Example 5.5.

Example 5.5: Earliest Deadline First

To illustrate EDF scheduling, let us take a system with three processes. Each process runs for 100 mS during a time slice. Suppose that processes a, b, and c have periods of 300 mS, 500 mS, and 1000 mS, respectively. If all three are ready at time $t = 0$ and have initial deadlines equal to their periods, then the first process we select is a, and we run it for 100 mS. At time $t = 100$ mS, we set the next deadline for a to be 400 mS, which is still the earliest, so process a gets another time slice. After that time slice is finished, its deadline is set to 500 mS, and it is inserted into the queue between b and c. We place it behind b, which has the same deadline in order to treat equal deadlines in something like a round-robin fashion. Process b then runs for 100 mS, and its new deadline is set for 800 mS. The behavior of the system for the first several time slices is illustrated in Figure 5-6. Each box represents one time slice, and the letter in it identifies the process that runs during that time slice. The numbers below each step are the deadlines for processes a, b, and c, respectively at that point in time.

100	200	300	400	500	600	700	800	900	1000
a	a	b	a	a	b	a	c	a	b
300	400	500	500	700	800	800	1000	1000	1200	1200
500	500	500	800	800	800	1100	1100	1100	1100	1500
1000	1000	1000	1000	1000	1000	1000	1000	1800	1800	1800

Figure 5-6: Earliest Deadline First Scheduling Example

This example illustrates an important aspect of EDF scheduling. We generally don't attempt to hit each deadline exactly. It is acceptable for a process to finish before its deadline. This makes EDF scheduling useful for those cases where a task must be accomplished before a certain time, but where there is no problem with it being completed early.

5.4.7.3   Slotted Scheduler

When we have more stringent timing requirements and we must not run a process too early, we often turn to a scheduler with a timing loop. Each cycle through the loop is divided into a number of slots, each t_s seconds long. With n slots, the overall scheduling cycle is $T_c = nt_s$ seconds long. Processes are assigned to slots administratively. If a process does not need all of or any of one of its slots, then the CPU is idle during that time. Example 5.6 described how a slotted scheduler works.

Example 5.6: Slotted Scheduler

Let us consider a major cycle that is 100 mS long. Within the loop we identify which process gets which fraction of the loop. If in our example, each loop is divided into 10 slices, then each process can be guaranteed from 10 to 100 mS out of each 100 mS. The slices given to a particular process don't have to be contiguous. If a process needs 10 mS out of each 50, then we can give that process slots 1 and 5 out of the 10 available in our example. In Figure 5-7, we have four processes where a gets 50% of the CPU, b gets 30%, and the remaining two processes each get 10%.

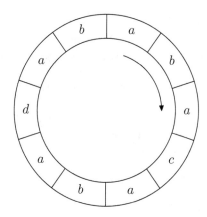

Figure 5-7: Slotted Scheduling Example

5.4.8 Scheduling in Embedded Systems

In embedded systems, we find a variety of scheduling policies dictated by the application. Some systems use typical time-sharing scheduling policies. A good example of this is the round-robin scheduling in Inferno, which we examine in detail in Chapter 7. We also find this in the cases of general-purpose operating systems configured for small, embedded environments, such as various embedded configurations of Linux and Windows.

In other embedded systems, the applications have more of a real-time character. In these applications, we often find interrupt- (or event-) driven schedulers like that in TinyOS, discussed in Section 6.8.

5.5 Context Switching

As discussed in Section 1.3, the fundamental concept behind the time-sharing operating system is the idea of reassigning the CPU among competing processes rapidly enough that

---

Historical Note: Apollo 11

The cyclic nature of real-time software was dramatically illustrated on July 20, 1969. As the Apollo 11 lunar excursion module (LEM) descended to the surface of the moon, the Apollo Guidance Computer (AGC) reported several 1201 and 1202 program alarms. These alarms indicated that the computer had run out of time in a cycle before completing the work assigned to it. Because the designers had the foresight to prioritize the work, these particular alarms indicated that only low-priority tasks had not been completed and that the landing could still take place. Why was the workload too great? It turns out that a data input device had mistakenly been left activated during the landing. This rendezvous radar was meant to be used only after leaving the moon to assist redocking with the command module.

we have the illusion that they are all running simultaneously. Of course, the fact that it is the CPU itself that must accomplish this creates the closest we get to an existential crisis. After all, how can the CPU take itself away from one process and give itself to another?

The answer turns out to be surprisingly simple based on our analogy to Turing machines in Section 5.1. If a process is a sequence of configurations over time, then taking a process from the CPU amounts to copying its configuration in such a way that we can later copy it back. Likewise, copying a process's configuration back to the CPU effectively gives the CPU to that process. **Context switching**, which is what we call the mechanism that moves the CPU from one process to another, boils down the following steps:

1. Transfer control flow from the current user process to the operating system.

2. Save the configuration of the current process.

3. Select (schedule) the next process.

4. Restore the (previously saved) configuration of the next process.

5. Return control flow to the (new) current user process.

To make this technique more concrete, we present two sample context-switching events in Example 5.7.

Example 5.7: Context Switching

In this example, we consider two processes, called A and B. In the course of our illustration, two context switches take place, as shown in Figure 5-8. Moving in a downward direction in this figure corresponds to moving forward in time. The arrows show the flow of control as we switch between the two processes.

We begin with process A running. At some point, an interrupt occurs, which transfers control to the operating system. In the course of processing the interrupt, the OS determines that a context switch is needed. This is likely because process A either used up its entire time slice or because it issued a request that caused it to block. After we have determined that we need to switch to another process, we save enough information about process A that we can later resume it. The next step is invoking the scheduler, which selects process B in our example. Before returning from the interrupt, we restore process B's previously saved context back to the registers and stack from which we saved it earlier. Upon return from the interrupt, control passes back to process B rather than to process A.

While process B is running, there might be interrupts that do not trigger a context switch. In those cases, control transfers to the kernel, which processes the interrupt. The return from interrupt instruction then transfers control back to the same code that was interrupted. We omit such interrupts from Figure 5-8 for clarity.

Eventually, an interrupt occurs that does cause us to switch from process B to another process. In this example, that other process is A. When this happens, we follow essentially the same steps we did in the previous context switch, with the roles of processes A and B reversed. After we restore process A's context and return from the interrupt, control

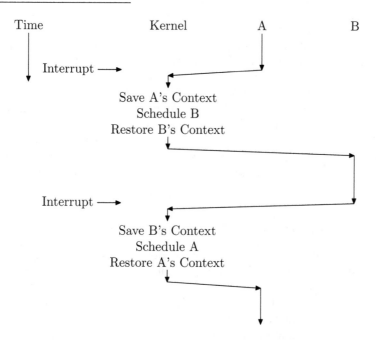

Figure 5-8: Context-Switching Example

transfers back to the same place where process A was interrupted at the beginning of our example. From process A's perspective, the only thing that has happened is a very long pause between two instructions. From the perspective of the overall system, we are time-sharing.

Although it seems straightforward enough, a number of points are worth discussing. First, it might look as if we have begged the question of how the CPU can take itself away from a process. We've already alluded to the necessary mechanism several times. When an interrupt occurs, control is transferred from a user process to the operating system. This transfer is a hardware function, the details of which vary from system to system. Typically, the interrupt causes the processor to save some registers (such as the program counter) to the stack. The processor then transfers control to an **interrupt vector**, which identifies the appropriate interrupt handler code. In the process of transferring control to the interrupt handler, the hardware also usually switches the processor to a more privileged mode necessary for the OS.

In the case where we are preempting a process that has used up its quantum, the interrupt comes from the clock, which typically interrupts 60 to 100 times per second. For most systems, interrupts also save some of the process's state onto a stack. At the very least, the hardware normally has to save at least the program counter and stack pointer so that the user process can be resumed after the interrupt. After the OS decides that a context switch is necessary, it must then save the process configuration in the process table. (There are exceptions to this. In some systems, interrupts are processed on a separate stack that can be per-process. In those cases, we often keep the process state on the interrupt stack. Sometimes we even put the interrupt stack in the process table entry!) Normally, the saved process configuration consists of all of the registers. Those which are saved on the stack by the interrupt are copied from the stack to the process table, and the rest are saved directly. As might be expected, restoring a process's configuration amounts to undoing this. We load most of the registers from their saved values in the process table and then set up the stack to look the same as it did when that process was last interrupted. Returning control to the new process is accomplished by executing the same return from interrupt instruction that is used at the end of all interrupt handlers.

5.6   Process Creation and Termination

For the most part, the task of creating a process proceeds pretty much as expected. The most obvious step is setting up the memory space with the necessary code and data as discussed in later chapters. The other step is initializing a new process table entry. Most elements of the table are either inherited from the parent process or are set to sensible initial values. Although the basic idea is straightforward, there are a number of variations on the theme of process creation. For each resource, the child may be created to share the parent's, with a copy of the parent's, or with a newly allocated resource. As an example, for the program code, we usually either allow the child to share the parent's or we start the child running a new program. We often refer to the first case as forking a process and the second as spawning a process. In most cases, we want both the parent and the child to be ready as soon as the child is created. There are, however, a few instances of systems that block the parent until the child exits or takes some other action that allows the parent to continue. As child processes create additional processes, we build a tree of processes. Although a system may impose administrative limits on the depth and breadth of the tree, many systems allow processes to be created up to the limits of resources.

There is one part of this initialization that's not quite so obvious. When the time comes to schedule this new process, the context switching works under the assumption that this process has already been interrupted. But if the process has never yet run, it can't have been interrupted. This isn't really a problem. In the case of forking a process, the child inherits a copy of the parent's saved configuration, which means that it will resume at the same place as the parent. For a spawned process, we can just set up the "saved" registers to have values that look like the process was interrupted just prior to the execution of its first instruction. Then when it gets scheduled and the registers are restored, the new process will begin executing at the beginning.

When terminating a process, our primary responsibility is releasing the resources held by the process. This includes memory, any open files, any reserved I/O devices, as well as internal data structures such as the process table entry. In some cases, the resources may be shared with other processes. When that is the case, we must be careful to free them only when all the processes using them have released them. We commonly use **reference counts** in those cases. Each time a process is created that shares the resource, we increment its reference count. Each time a process using the shared resource terminates, we decrement the resource's reference count. Only when the reference count reaches zero do we free the resource. The last factor in terminating a process is providing notification of the event. Typically, the parent (or some other process) queries for the status of the process to determine whether is has terminated and why. The OS must record that status until some process queries for it.

5.7   Critical Sections

The last major topic we cover in this chapter is not actually a management function of the operating system. Instead, it is an issue that arises frequently in operating system design and also appears in applications where more than one process (or thread) shares some resource (usually memory). The issue is that if a process is updating a data structure and another process is allowed to run before the update is completed, the results might be inconsistent.

As a simple example, consider two processes that both increment a shared variable:

$++x$;

For a number of machines, this code compiles to a sequence of instructions like:

```
ld      _x, r1
addi    #1, r1
st      r1, _x
```

As long as all three of these instructions are executed without interruption, there is no problem. On the other hand, suppose that process A executes the first instruction of the sequence and is then preempted for process B. During its time slice, process B executes all three instructions, starting with the same value of x that process A read into register r1. The effect is that process B increments x as expected. But when control returns to process A, it adds one to the old value of x and stores the result. The net effect is that process A doesn't actually change the value of x. Even though two processes incremented the variable, the net change is only one. The fundamental problem is that even though it's just a single operator in C, the operation to increment a variable is not **atomic**. Here, we use the word atomic with its meaning of indivisible. An operation that is not atomic can be interrupted, allowing another process to access the shared resource before the operation is complete.

Inserting an element into a linked list provides another common example. One typical implementation looks like:

if $(head \equiv \Lambda)$
    $head = new\_elem$;
else
    $tail\rightarrow next = new\_elem$;
$tail = new\_elem$;

There are several places in this sequence where a process can be preempted to create an inconsistent result. For example, consider a process that tests for an empty list and finds that it is empty. However, suppose that it is preempted before adding its new element. In this case, the other process will also see the list empty. Both will attempt to put their new element at the beginning of the list, resulting in one of the elements getting lost.

We call situations like this **race conditions**. The key idea with race conditions is that the correctness of the result depends on the relative timing of scheduling among two or more processes sharing some resource. Code that embodies a race condition is called a **critical section**. We identify a critical section as a sequence of code that has a race condition. Furthermore, if a critical section is executed atomically, there is no race condition. This observation identifies the means of dealing with race conditions. Namely, we need to develop techniques for making sections of code atomic.

The basic approach to adding atomicity is to use a **mutual exclusion** (mutex) lock. Before entering a critical section, we obtain a lock. If another process is already in its corresponding critical section, we are blocked until we can safely enter. As we leave the critical section, we release the lock. So our list insert code might look like:

$mutex\_lock(\&lock);$
if $(head \equiv \Lambda)$
  $head = new\_elem;$
else
   $tail\text{-}next = new\_elem;$
$tail = new\_elem;$
$mutex\_unlock(\&lock);$

5.7.1   Interrupt Control

The first approach to implementing a mutex lock is based on our understanding of context switching. We know that for a process, or any other code, to be preempted, an interrupt must occur and be serviced. From that observation, it is clear that we can lock a critical section by preventing the interrupts that could preempt us while in the critical section. For some hardware, the only control we have is the ability to disable all interrupts. For other systems, there is more fine-grained control where we can change the level of interrupts that are allowed. In cases like this, we set an interrupt priority level, and all interrupts of a higher level are allowed while all lower or equal level interrupts are blocked.

Controlling interrupts is a fundamental technique for protecting critical sections within the operating system itself, particularly when interrupt handlers share data structures with other parts of the system. However, there are several limitations and caveats in using interrupt control. First, although this approach is applicable within the operating system, we cannot allow it to be used by user processes. If a normal process were allowed to disable interrupts, then, an erroneous (or malicious) process could disable interrupts and never reenable them, preventing the first process from ever being preempted. Obviously, this would prevent the system from operating normally. Another issue with disabling interrupts is the time during which we hold the mutex lock. If the critical section is too long or has the potential to block, then we can't use the control of interrupts to directly implement the lock. One of the more obvious problems with keeping interrupts turned off too long is that we might lose clock interrupts, causing our internal measure of real time to slowly drift. Finally, the nature of interrupt control prevents multiple processes from waiting for the critical section simultaneously. This, in turn, gives us no way to prioritize among processes that might want to gain access.

5.7.2   Atomic Instructions

Manipulating interrupts works well for a single processor. However, if we have more than one processor sharing memory, stopping interrupts on one processor doesn't stop the other from accessing memory. For these cases, we need another mechanism. The next approach to implementing mutual exclusion is to build atomicity of a relatively large section of code out of a very small-scale atomic operation. In particular, we use CPU instructions that perform at least two operations atomically. Various machines have different such instructions. One typical instruction is the test-and-set instruction. This instruction tests the value of a memory location setting condition codes and then sets a value (for example, the sign bit) in the memory location. Using this type of instruction, we can implement the lock and unlock operations as follows:

```
_mutex_lock:
    tas     _lock
    blt     _mutex_lock
    ret

_mutex_unlock:
    move    #0, _lock
    ret
```

The code in this example is written assuming a system that sets the sign bit in the test-and-set (**tas**) instruction. When the sign bit is set, the lock is held by some process, and when the bit is clear, the lock is available. The key to understanding how this code works is to realize that after we execute the **tas** instruction, somebody has the lock. The only question is did we just get the lock, or did someone else already have it? We can answer this question by looking at the previous value of the lock. If it is less than zero, then somebody else had the lock before we tried to get it. The branch if less than zero (**blt**) instruction recognizes this case and loops back to try to gain the lock again. If the previous value of the lock was greater than or equal to zero, then nobody had the lock previously, so we now have it and we can return.

One important thing to notice about this example is that it still works if we are interrupted between the **tas** and **blt** instructions. We conclude this from the fact that the information about the previous value of the lock that is saved by **tas** is also saved as part of the process configuration if we are interrupted. The key to the correctness of this implementation is the atomicity of the **tas** instruction. If it were possible for another process (or processor) to access the lock variable between the time we save its value and the time we set it, then we'd be right back to where we started with a race condition.

This implementation is quite different from the case of manipulating interrupts, in that a process waiting for the lock continually executes instructions until it gains the lock. In this case, it is the tight loop of the the `tas` and `blt` instructions. This type of waiting is generally termed **busy waiting**, and this type of lock is often called a **spin lock**. Whether busy waiting is a problem depends on the situation. If the code waiting on the lock must wait for a long time, the busy waiting can consume time that could be used by other code. This is particularly an issue for normal processes on a single processor machine. When a process begins busy waiting, it is guaranteed to keep waiting (and using CPU time) until its time slice runs out. Some systems provide a special system call to yield the CPU for just such cases. This call effectively says "I know that nothing else useful can happen during this time slice, so allow another process to run."

5.7.3 Peterson's Algorithm

Both of the previous two techniques for implementing locks are based on hardware instructions that don't have a corresponding high-level language feature. The natural question arises: Are there any techniques that can be implemented on an arbitrary architecture using only normal instructions? Another way to ask this question is: Can we implement a lock in a typical systems programming language? As it turns out, the answer is yes. The most well-known such technique was discovered by Gary Peterson. His approach, presented in 1981, is based on the idea that we normally want two competing processes to take turns. However, if one process is interested in using the shared resource while the other isn't, then the first can get it even if it's not its turn. His solution can be implemented as follows:

```
int turn;
int want[2];
void mutex_lock(int who)
{
    int other;
    other = 1 - who;
    want[who] = 1;
    turn = other;
    while (want[other] ∧ turn ≠ who) ;
}
void mutex_unlock(int who)
{
    want[who] = 0;
}
```

The basic idea is pretty straightforward. We say that if we get the lock, then the next time around it will be the other process's turn. Then, we must wait as long as the other side is interested and it's not our turn. However, it is instructive to trace through the behavior when a process is preempted in the middle of *mutex_lock( )*. For example, suppose process A gets preempted between setting *want*[*who*] and setting *turn*. Then, process B goes through the full locking code and busy waits because process A wants the lock and process B had declared it to be A's turn. When process A runs again, it changes *turn*, causing it to also busy wait. But when B runs, it is able to pass the **while** statement and gets the lock. Although we cover only the two-process case here, this approach can be generalized to any number of processes.

5.7.4   Semaphores

We've already mentioned that we don't want to allow user processes to manipulate interrupts. We've also pointed out that the other two techniques employ busy waiting, which is not suitable for user processes. In general, we give user processes mutual exclusion mechanisms, which are built on top of others used by the kernel. For example, we might provide lock and unlock system calls, where the operating system uses interrupt control to protect critical sections in its implementation.

One of the most often studied and implemented models of mutual exclusion for user processes is the **semaphore**. Semaphores are best understood in terms of the operations that are performed on them. We define the semaphore by the operations *up* and *down*. Originally, these operations were called V and P, respectively. (Because they are mnemonically meaningful in Dutch, but not English, we will use *up* and *down*.) As their names imply, *up*( ) increments the semaphore and *down*( ) decrements it. We define them more formally as follows:

- *up*( ) — Increase the value of the semaphore by one.

- *down*( ) — If the semaphore is 0, block until it becomes > 0. Decrease the value of the semaphore by one.

This description does not address what happens if there are multiple threads of execution all waiting in a *down*( ) operation for the semaphore to become positive. In particular, what happens when another thread does an *up*( ) operation? We do not want all of the waiters to awaken at once. That would violate mutual exclusion. Typically, we take one of two approaches. In some implementations, we keep the waiters in a queue and wake the one that blocked first. In others, we select one to wake at random. A few implementations provide a mechanism for establishing a wake-up priority other than order of waiting.

Notice that if we initialize the semaphore to have the value of 1, then the *down*( ) becomes the same as the lock operation and the *up*( ) becomes the same as the unlock. In fact, we often define a special case called the **binary semaphore** where the value of the semaphore can take on only the values 0 and 1. If the value of a binary semaphore is already 1, then the *up*( ) operation is a no-op. Later we look at some examples of applications where the counted nature of semaphores is useful.

Before continuing, we need to point out an important caveat. Remember that critical sections arise only when we are sharing resources among two or more threads of control. Typically, there are two classes of resources that are shared among user processes. First, user processes often share files. As part of the file system support, the operating system usually provides file locking mechanisms that are separate from the techniques in this chapter. The other resource that user processes can share is memory. Normally, this type of sharing occurs only when the user processes explicitly request memory sharing, such as when they are using a multithreading mechanism like POSIX threads. Consequently, the techniques discussed throughout the rest of this chapter are somewhat specialized with respect to user processes. (However, we do see them sometimes implemented as a higher-level mutual exclusion technique within an operating system implementation.)

5.7.5 Monitors

The second mutual exclusion method suitable for user processes is the **monitor**. Even though we sometimes see the term monitor applied to implementations of locks that look much like those we discuss in previous sections, the term is more properly applied to a language feature. In particular, some languages allow us to declare a set of functions as being a monitor. When declared this way, only one process is allowed in the monitor at a time. Any other process attempting to call one of the functions in the monitor is blocked until no other processes are executing code in the monitor. Using monitors, the lock and unlock operations are implicit, relieving the programmer of the burden of using them correctly.

As an example, we show how we can implement a semaphore using a monitor. In doing so, we prove a theorem, which can be stated informally as, "Monitors are at least as powerful as semaphores in the sense that they can be used for all applications of semaphores." Thus, in any application where we use semaphores, we can use our monitor-based implementation with the same functionality.

To suggest the ideas behind a proof, we present this implementation using a C-like syntax:

```
monitor semaphore
{
    unsigned int sem;
    void up(void)
    {
        ++sem;
        signal;
    }
    void down(void)
    {
        while (sem ≡ 0)
            wait;
        --sem;
    }
}
```

Note that C itself does not provide a monitor mechanism, so this code is not valid C. It should be clear that this implementation works given that the monitor provides the necessary atomicity in the implementation of *up( )* and *down( )*.

What is not quite so clear, however, is the use of the operations **signal** and **wait**. When a process executes the **wait** statement, it blocks and gives up exclusive access to the monitor. When a process executes the **signal** statement, it immediately leaves the monitor, and one of the processes blocked in a **wait** is made ready and is again placed exclusively in the monitor. Although this type of behavior can be implemented without these special operations, it is generally more complicated and involves busy waiting. For similar reasons, the POSIX thread system provides a similar mechanism called condition variables. A process can wait on a condition much like our **wait** statement, or it can signal a condition much like our **signal** statement.

5.7.6   Message Passing

In most cases, the data that are being shared between two processes are there in order for the two processes to communicate with each other. It is natural to ask whether we can accomplish the communication more directly through some type of send and receive mechanism. The answer is yes, though it's not always the most efficient way to do it. On the last point, consider a set of processes that operate on large image data. For most implementations, passing the large images through a message passing mechanism would be much slower than sharing the memory the images occupy.

Keeping in mind that we should be careful about using message passing with large shared data, we now turn our attention to the actual mechanisms. In most implementations, sending a message is accomplished through a call like:

$$send(p, m);$$

which sends a message pointed to by m to process p. Similarly, receiving a message generally looks like:

$$sender = recv(p, m);$$

where p gives the process from which we want to receive a message and m points to the buffer where we want the message put. Normally, there is a special value we can send as the first argument to indicate that we are willing to accept a message from any sender. The return value of the call gives us which process sent the message we are receiving.

In most cases, the $recv()$ is synchronous, meaning that if there are no messages waiting to be picked up, the calling process blocks until a message comes in. The natural question then is, what happens on a $send()$ when there is no receiver waiting? If we choose to implement the operation such that a sending process blocks until a receiver comes along, then we are following the **rendezvous principle**. By following this principle, we can ensure that two processes are synchronized in the sense that they both are at known corresponding places in their code at the same time.

5.7.7   Examples

There are a myriad of standard example problems that illustrate these techniques. We consider two here: the dining philosophers problem and the producer-consumer problem.

5.7.7.1 Dining Philosophers Problem

In the classic dining philosophers problem, we have a set of n members of the philosophy department eating at a circular table in a Chinese restaurant. Between each pair of philosophers lies a chopstick; two chopsticks are required to eat. (Ignore the issues of hygiene suggested by sharing chopsticks. Further, we should note that the original formulation of this problem places the philosophers in an Italian restaurant using pairs of forks to eat spaghetti. The author prefers the Chinese restaurant formulation because, although he is not very skilled at using chopsticks, he never uses two forks to eat pasta.) Each of the philosophers operates in a simple cycle consisting of a random amount of time thinking, during which neither of the neighboring chopsticks are being used by this philosopher, alternating with a random amount of time eating, where both chopsticks are needed.

The problem seems simple enough, but there are several issues we must confront. First, we cannot have more than one philosopher holding a given chopstick at a time. This means that if a philosopher wants to get the left chopstick but it is in use, then the hungry thinker must wait for it. But what happens if all of the philosophers attempt to eat at the same time and all grab the chopstick on their left first? At this point, they must all wait for the chopstick on their right to become available, but nobody will ever finish and make it available. When this happens, we have reached **deadlock**, which we discuss in more detail in Section 5.8.

Solving the first issue is easy. Preventing both philosophers from using the shared chopstick at the same time is just a mutual exclusion issue that we can solve with our favorite locking mechanism. The second issue is more problematic. There are several solutions to it. The first is to simply limit the number of philosophers who simultaneously try to eat to $n-1$. Using this approach, we take advantage of counted semaphores and get a solution like:

```
int sticks[N];
int eat_set = N - 1;
void begin_eat(int i)
{
    down(&eat_set);
    down(&sticks[i]);
    down(&sticks[(i + 1) % N]);
}
void end_eat(int i)
{
    up(&sticks[i]);
    up(&sticks[(i + 1) % N]);
    up(&eat_set);
}
```

A second approach is to control access in terms of eaters rather than chopsticks. Here, the idea is to divide the philosophers into three sets, those thinking (represented in the following code by T), those hungry (H), and those eating (E). If a philosopher is hungry and neither neighbor is eating, then that philosopher can eat. Each time the state of a neighbor changes, we check to see if we can allow someone else to eat. We can implement this approach as follows:

```
#define T  1
#define H  2
#define E  3
int philo_lock[N], philo_state[N];
int mutex = 1;
void begin_eat(int i)
{
    down(&mutex);
    philo_state[i] = H;
    test(i);
    up(&mutex);
    down(&philo_lock[i]);
}
void end_eat(int i)
{
    down(&mutex);
    philo_state[i] = T;
    test((i + 1) % N);
    test((i - 1) % N);
    up(&mutex);
}
void test(int i)
{
    if (philo_state[i] ≡ H ∧ philo_state[(i + 1) % N] ≠ E
            ∧ philo_state[(i - 1) % N] ≠ E) {
        philo_state[i] = E;
        up(&philo_lock[i]);
    }
}
```

Notice the use of the extra mutex lock. We need this because the state changes and code within $test()$ constitute critical sections themselves.

Our last approach to the dining philosophers problem returns to the idea of controlling access to the chopsticks. Like the second solution, however, we don't artificially limit the behavior of the philosophers. Instead, we construct a rule that prevents deadlock from ever happening. In particular, notice how in the first solution every philosopher picked up the left chopstick first and the right one second. If on the other hand, we have even numbered philosophers pick them up the other way around, then the solution is quite simple and we can never get deadlock. This approach is illustrated as follows:

```
int sticks[N];
void begin_eat(int i)
{
    int first, second;
    if (i % 2) {
        first = i;
        second = (i + 1) % N;
    }
    else {
        first = (i + 1) % N;
        second = i;
    }
    down(&sticks[first]);
    down(&sticks[second]);
}
void end_eat(int i)
{
    up(&sticks[i]);
    up(&sticks[(i + 1) % N]);
}
```

Notice that we don't need to worry about order when releasing the locks. In other words, the philosopher can put the sticks down in either order and not affect the potential for deadlock.

5.7.7.2   Producer-Consumer Problem

The idea behind the producer-consumer problem is that we have one process that generates data and another that uses that data. The two processes do not operate at the same rate and, in fact, both may be somewhat erratic. Consequently, we need a buffer between them to hold those data that have been generated but not yet used. Of course, the buffer must be implemented with data structures that are shared between the two processes and, thus, are natural candidates for race conditions.

For our sample implementation, we give two functions, $put()$ and $get()$, which are called by the producer and consumer, respectively. We build these functions on top of some basic queueing code that implements an unbounded queue. Finally, we keep a counting semaphore, which keeps track of how many elements are in the queue.

```
int in_queue = 0;
int mutex = 0;
void put(int i)
{
    down(&mutex);
    enqueue(i);
    up(&in_queue);
```

```
    up(&mutex);
}
int get(void)
{
    int i;
    down(&in_queue);
    down(&mutex);
    i = dequeue();
    up(&mutex);
    return (i);
}
```

5.8   Deadlock

Any time we allow exclusive access, we run the risk of **deadlock** (also called **deadly embrace**). Regardless of whether we are locking memory, I/O devices, or files, there is the possibility that multiple entities might all be waiting on a resource held by another. It would be as if four drivers all came to a 4-way stop and each was waiting on another to go first. If no one breaks out of the waiting state, then all the drivers will be there until they run out of gas. Throughout our discussion of deadlock, we use examples of I/O devices rather than memory areas or files, because devices are easier to visualize. Also, some techniques are more useful with I/O devices than with memory or files.

Suppose we have two processes, A and B, that both need exclusive access to both the printer and the CD-ROM drive. Let's say that process A gains an exclusive lock on the printer but before it attempts to access the CD-ROM drive, process B runs and locks the CD-ROM drive. At some point B blocks waiting on access to the printer that A holds and A blocks on access to the CD-ROM drive that B holds. At that point, both processes are blocked with no hope of escape from this purgatory. This is deadlock.

5.8.1   Necessary and Sufficient Conditions

In 1971, Coffman, et al identified four necessary and sufficient conditions for deadlock:

1. Mutual Exclusion—No more than one process may hold a resource at a time.

2. Hold and Wait—A process does not voluntarily give up a resource while waiting for another.

3. No Preemption—Once we've given a process exclusive access to a resource, we do not forcibly take it away.

4. Circular Wait—The dependency graph is cyclic. The dependency graph contains a vertex for each process and a directed edge from process x to process y if y holds a resource on which x is waiting. Figure 5-9 shows such a graph where processes 1, 2, and 3 are in deadlock, and processes 4, 5, and 6 are not themselves deadlocked, even though they are waiting directly or indirectly on processes that are.

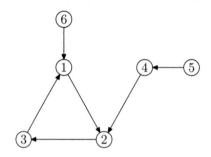

Figure 5-9: Example Dependency Graph

5.8.2   Dealing with Deadlock

While Coffman's conditions are (as a set) both necessary and sufficient, it is the necessary part that interests us. The reason is that if we can do something to make sure that one of the conditions doesn't hold, then we know we don't have deadlock. Typically, there is very little we can do about the first three conditions, however. As we've pointed out, some cases inherently require exclusive access. Similarly, we rarely know that we can safely release exclusive access or take it away once it's granted. The printer is a good example. It would be problematic for a process to be allowed to write the header of a report to the printer and then have the printer taken away and given to another process. This leaves us with handling deadlock based on handling the circular wait condition.

5.8.2.1   Ignoring Deadlock

Our first approach is simply ignoring the problem, in effect assuming that deadlock will never happen. In his classic operating systems textbook, Tanenbaum calls this the Ostrich Algorithm. Of course, leaving such a significant potential problem in a system should offend the sensibilities of any good software designer. However, there are a couple of aspects of the issue that might make just ignoring the problem the right engineering tradeoff.

The first such case is one where the only risk of deadlock is in application processes. In other words, we may know that the operating system itself is immune from deadlock. In a case like this, we may deem it more trouble than it's worth to deal with application process deadlock. After all, we can't deal with every bug that the application might exhibit. We might judge that adding code and complexity to the operating system just to deal with that one bug is not a good use of resources. We might even go so far as to object on philosophical grounds saying that it's not the operating system's responsibility to dictate that applications behave.

Even if there is a possibility that the operating system itself could deadlock, we should still decide whether to address the problem rationally. Suppose that we calculate that the expected time between occurrences of deadlock is five years, but that the expected time between reboots for other reasons is only one year. In a case like this, adding code to deal with deadlock could well be more likely to introduce bugs that would reduce the stability of the system rather than increase it. Nevertheless, most designers opt for a strategy that is far more careful about dealing with deadlock in the kernel and is more likely to let sloppy application programmers get what they deserve.

5.8.2.2   Detecting Deadlock

If we're going to handle deadlock, then how do we do so? Our first approach is to detect when it's happened and to correct it. The definition of circular wait gives us one approach to detecting deadlock. Periodically, we can build a dependency graph and test whether it is cyclic or acyclic. If it's acyclic, then there is no deadlock and we continue. If there is a cycle in the graph, then we have deadlock and we must deal with it. Since we can't do anything about the other conditions, we have no choice but to break the cycle which means we have to terminate one of the processes in it, releasing all of the resources that process has locked.

In some cases, we are not always able to determine the process on which another one is waiting. For systems like this, we can make a good guess regarding when deadlock has occurred. Periodically, we check to see how long processes have been blocked waiting for exclusive access to a resource. If we find two or more that have been blocked for longer than some threshold, then we assume that they are deadlocked. Again, we must terminate one of them, hopefully allowing the other to continue.

5.8.2.3   Preventing Deadlock

While detecting deadlock isn't particularly difficult, the action we take to "correct" it is rather Draconian. We'd be much better off if we simply never had deadlock happen in the first place. There are times when it is possible to structure the software involved so that deadlock can never occur. Because the four conditions are all necessary, this technique amounts to breaking one of them, in effect, making one of them impossible.

The first approach we sometimes take essentially says that we don't hold and wait. There are some cases where we can know all of the resources we are going to need and we can safely release one before using it. In those cases, we can attempt to lock all of our needed resources before doing anything to any of them. If we fail to gain the lock on any, we release all those we did lock and try again after some delay. In those cases where we are locking an area of memory or a file, this approach can at least be feasible if not efficient. The more resources we need to lock, the greater the probability that we will encounter at least one that is already locked by someone else. That, in turn, implies that we will need more iterations of this try and release approach before we can expect to get all the resources we need. When locking I/O devices, this approach can be even more problematic. Suppose we are locking a device with removable media, such as a CD-ROM drive or a tape drive. If the locking operation also includes placing the CD or tape in the drive, then repeatedly locking and releasing would be awkward at best. Furthermore, the locking mechanism must also provide a nonblocking lock operation. Such an operation would return whether the lock was gained or not, and it would return an indication of whether it was successful. Although these issues can sometimes be tolerated in applications, they are generally not acceptable when the OS is locking a resource for its own use.

Because of the considerations we've examined, deadlock prevention usually boils down to the idea of ensuring that we can never create a cyclic dependency graph. The simplest way to prevent dependency cycles is by imposing an ordering on the resources. Consider our original example. The deadlock only occurred because Process A attempted to lock the devices in a different order from Process B. Had they both attempted to lock the printer first, then there could not have been deadlock. This idea generalizes to many resources and many processes.

Mathematically, we say that the set of resources must be a partially ordered set where for any two resources a and b that can be exclusively held simultaneously, either $a \leq b$ or $b \leq a$. (A partially ordered set (poset), $(P, \leq)$, is defined as being reflexive ($\forall a \in P, a \leq a$), antisymmetric ($\forall a, b \in P, a \leq b \wedge b \leq a \Rightarrow a = b$) and transitive ($\forall a, b, c \in P, a \leq b \wedge b \leq c \Rightarrow a \leq c$).) The notation $a \leq b$ means that a must be locked before b if they are held simultaneously. In other words, while a lock on b is held, attempting to lock a is prohibited. (In practice, we usually assume that all pairs of resources could possibly be held simultaneously. In this case, the requirement reduces to a totally ordered set.)

Defining resource ordering is a theoretically appealing solution to deadlock, but in practice it is often unwieldy. For single application domains, such as various components of a database, defining a partial order on the resource set is not too difficult. However, asking for a partial order to be defined on the set of all possible resources at the time the operating system is written is tantamount to asking for a crystal ball. (In the realm of automata theory, we can do interesting things with oracles, but in the realm of operating systems, we eventually have to reduce our ideas to code. So far, no one has figured out how to code an oracle.)

The other major impediment we have to using resource ordering is the question of how we can be confident that the order has not been violated. In a project with a single programmer, it is an easy matter to just list the resources in order on a piece of paper that gets referenced whenever a resource lock call is coded. Even the best programmers sometimes get sloppy and in large multi-person projects, expecting that kind of discipline is hopeless. The exercises suggest a method that can be used to enforce the ordering at run time. (Any attempt to statically verify the code for compliance is doomed to run afoul of Rice's Theorem, which is a generalization of the Halting Theorem and essentially says that determining whether a program satisfies a nontrivial property is undecidable.)

5.8.2.4 Avoiding Deadlock

Our last strategy in dealing with deadlock is analyzing each lock request to determine if it would put us into a situation where deadlock is unavoidable. Those requests that would do so, are deferred until conditions change and they can be safely granted. The difference between this avoidance of deadlock and the prevention of deadlock in the previous section is whether or not it is structurally impossible for deadlock to occur. If we've designed the system so that deadlock is impossible (barring programming errors), then we have prevented deadlock. If we code the system so that it detects when deadlock is about to occur, then we can avoid it.

Consider again our first deadlock example. Once we've granted B exclusive access to the CD-ROM drive, our path to deadlock is irrevocable. This is illustrated graphically in

Figure 5-10. The shaded areas are ones that cannot be entered because they imply that mutual exclusion is violated (i.e. more than one process has access to a resource). Since the line in the graph can only extend to the right (A gets CPU time) or up (B gets CPU time), never to the left or down, entering the region marked U would be unsafe in the sense that it will eventually lead to deadlock. If we can test to see whether we are about to enter such an unsafe region, then we can avoid deadlock. Of course, in order to do so, we have to know what resources each process will be allocating in the future.

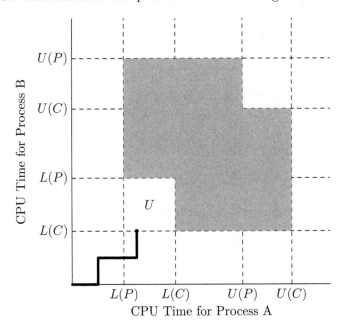

Figure 5-10: Example Trajectory Space

If we require processes to tell us ahead of time what their resource needs will be, then we can use a technique called the Banker's Algorithm to implement this test. (The algorithm is so named because it is similar to some of the considerations that bankers use to decide whether or not to grant a loan request. If a bank grants too many, then it runs the risk of becoming overextended and running out of cash.) The Banker's Algorithm can be stated quite succinctly:

Banker's Algorithm: Given matrices **N** and **A**, vector **E**, and a request from process p for a resource from class C, determine if allocating a resource from class C results in a safe configuration. **E** lists the number of each class of resource in the system. Matrices **N** and **A** each have one row per process. A row of matrix **N** lists the resources still needed by the corresponding process. Similarly, a row of **A** lists the resources currently allocated to that process. Prior to any requests we initialize **A** = **0** and set **N** to the set of requirements announced by processes as they start.

For convenience, we maintain a vector, $\mathbf{P}$, which is the column sum of $\mathbf{A}$.

1. Temporarily, decrease the value $\mathbf{N}_{(p,C)}$ by one and increase the $\mathbf{A}_{(p,C)}$ by one (implicitly increasing element $\mathbf{P}_C$ by one).

2. Select a process p' such that all elements of the row $\mathbf{N}_{p'}$ are less than or equal to $\mathbf{E} - \mathbf{P}$. If no such row exists, then the new configuration would be unsafe and the algorithm terminates with $\mathbf{N}$ and $\mathbf{A}$ restored to their values before step 1.

3. Strike rows p' of $\mathbf{A}$ and $\mathbf{N}$ from further consideration. (Here row $\mathbf{A}_{p'}$ is implicitly subtracted from $\mathbf{P}$.)

4. Repeat steps 2–3 until an unsafe configuration has been found or until all rows have been processed. In the latter case, the algorithm has verified that the request is safe and the changes of step 1 are made permanent.

Examples 5.8 and 5.9 show a simple example of the Banker's Algorithm and a more involved example, respectively.

Example 5.8: Simple Banker's Algorithm Example

Now let us apply the Banker's algorithm to our example. We let Process A be represented by row 1 and Process B by row 2. Similarly, the printer is in class 1 and the CD-ROM drive in class 2. If we have one instance in each resource class, then initially:

$$\mathbf{A} = \begin{bmatrix} 0 & 0 \\ 0 & 0 \end{bmatrix} \quad \mathbf{N} = \begin{bmatrix} 1 & 1 \\ 1 & 1 \end{bmatrix} \quad \mathbf{E} = \begin{bmatrix} 1 & 1 \end{bmatrix} \quad \mathbf{P} = \begin{bmatrix} 0 & 0 \end{bmatrix}.$$

In processing A's request for a printer, we temporarily change the configuration as follows

$$\mathbf{A} = \begin{bmatrix} 1 & 0 \\ 0 & 0 \end{bmatrix} \quad \mathbf{N} = \begin{bmatrix} 0 & 1 \\ 1 & 1 \end{bmatrix} \quad \mathbf{E} = \begin{bmatrix} 1 & 1 \end{bmatrix} \quad \mathbf{P} = \begin{bmatrix} 1 & 0 \end{bmatrix}.$$

Since $\mathbf{E} - \mathbf{P} = \begin{bmatrix} 0 & 1 \end{bmatrix}$, we can select row 1 in step 2. Then in the second iteration $\mathbf{E} - \mathbf{P} = \begin{bmatrix} 1 & 1 \end{bmatrix}$ which allows Process B to complete and we verify that the new configuration is safe. Next we evaluate B's request for a CD-ROM drive. Again we temporarily set the configuration to

$$\mathbf{A} = \begin{bmatrix} 1 & 0 \\ 0 & 1 \end{bmatrix} \quad \mathbf{N} = \begin{bmatrix} 0 & 1 \\ 1 & 0 \end{bmatrix} \quad \mathbf{E} = \begin{bmatrix} 1 & 1 \end{bmatrix} \quad \mathbf{P} = \begin{bmatrix} 1 & 1 \end{bmatrix}.$$

However, since $\mathbf{E} - \mathbf{P} = \begin{bmatrix} 0 & 0 \end{bmatrix}$, no row can be selected in step 2 meaning that the configuration is not safe. As a result, we must block Process B without giving it exclusive access to the CD-ROM drive until Process A has released the printer. Notice that we run the algorithm both for each new request that arrives and also for each suspended request when ever a process releases a resource.

Example 5.9: Another Banker's Algorithm Example

Let us now consider a slightly more complicated example with three processes and three resource classes. At some point in time, the configuration is

$$\mathbf{A} = \begin{bmatrix} 1 & 1 & 0 \\ 0 & 0 & 0 \\ 2 & 0 & 0 \end{bmatrix} \quad \mathbf{N} = \begin{bmatrix} 0 & 1 & 0 \\ 2 & 0 & 1 \\ 1 & 1 & 1 \end{bmatrix} \quad \mathbf{E} = \begin{bmatrix} 3 & 2 & 1 \end{bmatrix} \quad \mathbf{P} = \begin{bmatrix} 3 & 1 & 0 \end{bmatrix}.$$

This configuration is safe allowing processes 1, 3 and 2 to finish in that order. As we verify this, $\mathbf{E} - \mathbf{P}$ takes on the following values for each iteration of the algorithm:

Row Selected	P	E − P
	$\begin{bmatrix} 3 & 1 & 0 \end{bmatrix}$	$\begin{bmatrix} 0 & 1 & 1 \end{bmatrix}$
1	$\begin{bmatrix} 2 & 0 & 0 \end{bmatrix}$	$\begin{bmatrix} 1 & 2 & 1 \end{bmatrix}$
3	$\begin{bmatrix} 0 & 0 & 0 \end{bmatrix}$	$\begin{bmatrix} 3 & 2 & 1 \end{bmatrix}$
2	$\begin{bmatrix} 0 & 0 & 0 \end{bmatrix}$	$\begin{bmatrix} 3 & 2 & 1 \end{bmatrix}$

Notice how in each iteration, the value of $\mathbf{E} - \mathbf{P}$ is at least as large as the next row of $\mathbf{N}$ that is selected.

Now consider what would happen if process 3 attempts to allocate one of resource class 3? The new configuration would be

$$\mathbf{A} = \begin{bmatrix} 1 & 1 & 0 \\ 0 & 0 & 0 \\ 2 & 0 & 1 \end{bmatrix} \quad \mathbf{N} = \begin{bmatrix} 0 & 1 & 0 \\ 2 & 0 & 1 \\ 1 & 1 & 0 \end{bmatrix} \quad \mathbf{E} = \begin{bmatrix} 3 & 2 & 1 \end{bmatrix} \quad \mathbf{P} = \begin{bmatrix} 3 & 1 & 1 \end{bmatrix}.$$

This also turns out to be safe as verified by the algorithm:

Row Selected	P	E − P
	$\begin{bmatrix} 3 & 1 & 1 \end{bmatrix}$	$\begin{bmatrix} 0 & 1 & 0 \end{bmatrix}$
1	$\begin{bmatrix} 2 & 0 & 1 \end{bmatrix}$	$\begin{bmatrix} 1 & 2 & 0 \end{bmatrix}$
3	$\begin{bmatrix} 0 & 0 & 0 \end{bmatrix}$	$\begin{bmatrix} 3 & 2 & 1 \end{bmatrix}$
2	$\begin{bmatrix} 0 & 0 & 0 \end{bmatrix}$	$\begin{bmatrix} 3 & 2 & 1 \end{bmatrix}$

However, what if process 2 attempts to allocate one of resource class 3 instead? Then the configuration would be

$$\mathbf{A} = \begin{bmatrix} 1 & 1 & 0 \\ 0 & 0 & 1 \\ 2 & 0 & 0 \end{bmatrix} \quad \mathbf{N} = \begin{bmatrix} 0 & 1 & 0 \\ 2 & 0 & 0 \\ 1 & 1 & 1 \end{bmatrix} \quad \mathbf{E} = \begin{bmatrix} 3 & 2 & 1 \end{bmatrix} \quad \mathbf{P} = \begin{bmatrix} 3 & 1 & 1 \end{bmatrix}.$$

As before, the initial value of $\mathbf{E} - \mathbf{P} = \begin{bmatrix} 0 & 1 & 0 \end{bmatrix}$. This will allow us to pick the first rows of the matrices and to allow process 1 to complete giving us $\mathbf{E} - \mathbf{P} = \begin{bmatrix} 1 & 2 & 0 \end{bmatrix}$. In this case, however, we are unable to continue. Neither process 2, nor process 3 can complete because at least one element of their rows of $\mathbf{N}$ is greater than the corresponding element of $\mathbf{E} - \mathbf{P}$. At this point, step 2 of the algorithm declares that the new configuration would be unsafe.

5.9 Summary

One of the most critical resources the operating system must manage and allocate is the CPU. Instead of managing the resource directly, we manage the processes that use it. One of the most thoroughly studied aspects of process management is scheduling, which is the task of selecting the next process to run on the CPU. We have presented a number of scheduling techniques here along with a number of other elements of process management. In addition to the direct management of processes, we have discussed techniques for providing exclusive access to shared resources. These techniques are useful both within the operating system itself and for applications as well. When providing exclusive access, we also create the possibility of deadlock, which we have also discussed in this chapter.

5.10 Exercises

1. If a compute-bound process (it never does I/O) takes T seconds to run, will the time taken for n such processes be less than, equal to, or greater than nT on a realistic system that does round-robin scheduling? Why?

2. Extend the timeline in Example 5.5 to show which processes get scheduled for the next 10 time slices.

3. In Example 5.5, the period for process a is 300 mS with a quantum of 100 mS. This would suggest that a should get 33% of the CPU time. How much does it actually get in this example? What is the source of the discrepancy?

4. Among the mutual exclusion methods, disabling interrupts, test-and-set instructions, and semaphores, which can be used by user processes, and which should be reserved for use by the operating system? Why?

5. Describe how disabling interrupts prevents two processes from entering the critical section at the same time.

6. Suppose a batch of jobs is submitted, and they are identified as taking 100, 30, 20, 240, and 120 seconds, respectively. Assume that they have arrived in the order given but that there is no time between their arrivals. What is the average turnaround time for first-come, first-served scheduling? What is it for shortest job first?

7. What is the advantage of two-level scheduling?

8. In Example 5.6, suppose that process a only uses 75% of each of its slots, process b uses 80% of each of its slots, process c uses 20% of its slot, and process d uses 15% of its slot. What is the efficiency of the overall scheduling cycle? Ignore any scheduling and context switching overhead.

9. Suppose we have a multilevel feedback queue such as the one illustrated in Figure 5-5 with three processes, a, b, and c, where each has a base priority of 1 and where each process moves down one level on completing a time slice. Let $p(a)$ be boosted to 4,

$p(b)$ to 3, and $p(c)$ to 2. How many time slices will expire before all three processes are back to their base priority? How many will each process get in the process?

10. What is the difference between a program and a process?

11. What is the difference between a process and a thread?

12. Complete the proof of equivalence between semaphores and monitors. One approach is to show how a monitor could be automatically translated into equivalent code using only semaphores. (Ignore the use of the **wait** and **signal** statements.)

13. Show that an atomic exchange (between a register and a memory location) instruction can be used to implement a lock equivalent to the one implemented with the `tas` instruction.

14. Sketch the pseudocode for an implementation of semaphores using a test-and-set instruction.

15. Suppose we adjust a process's priority by $p' = \alpha p$ for each time slice where it is running and by $p' = 1 - \alpha(1 - p)$ when it is blocked. (There is no change for processes that are ready but not running.) If $0 < p < 1$ and $0 < \alpha < 1$, is it possible for a ready process to ever starve? Why or why not?

16. Write an implementation of the dining philosophers problem using message passing for synchronization.

17. Write an implementation of the producer-consumer problem using monitors.

18. Describe how a system that does not follow the rendezvous principle (that is, $send(\,)$ calls do not block waiting for a receiver) can be used to provide the same form of synchronization as one that does follow it.

19. When dealing with detected deadlock, we kill one of the processes in the cyclic wait. Why can we not just detect that granting a request will create deadlock and block the requesting process?

20. Draw the dependency graph for the example of Processes A and B requesting a printer and a CD-ROM after A has been granted the printer and B the CD-ROM.

21. Design the open function for a library that prevents deadlock by preventing circular dependency. Build your design around enforcing the resource ordering technique.

22. Why can the line in a trajectory such as the one exemplified in Figure 5-10 never move to the left or down?

23. Show that it doesn't matter which row we pick in the step 2 of the Banker's Algorithm when more than one is less than $\mathbf{E} - \mathbf{P}$.

24. Consider the configuration:

$$\mathbf{A} = \begin{bmatrix} 1 & 0 & 2 \\ 0 & 2 & 0 \\ 1 & 1 & 0 \\ 0 & 0 & 0 \end{bmatrix} \quad \mathbf{N} = \begin{bmatrix} 0 & 1 & 1 \\ 1 & 1 & 1 \\ 1 & 1 & 1 \\ 0 & 1 & 1 \end{bmatrix} \quad \mathbf{E} = \begin{bmatrix} 2 & 4 & 3 \end{bmatrix}$$

Is this configuration safe? Would granting a request from Process 2 for one of Resource 3 lead to a safe configuration?

25. Why do you suppose the UNIX design has a single strategy entry point for block device drivers, but separate read and write entry points for character devices?

Chapter 6

Some Examples of Process Management

In this chapter, we examine how the principles of process management are applied in our set of operating system examples. We particularly focus on the set of system calls that provide process-related services, the state machines used to manage processes, and the scheduling policies and mechanisms. In doing so, we highlight the issues found in moving principles into real systems.

6.1 CTSS

CTSS doesn't have the same concept of process that we describe in Chapter 5. In CTSS, the entity which is represented and managed is more of an instance of a logged-in user.

6.1.1 Process State

Just as the state machine in Figure 5-1 describes a process through its life, CTSS maintains a state for each user on the system. The CTSS user state machine is shown in Figure 6-1. Each of these states represents the condition of the user just as those in Figure 5-1 represent the conditions of processes:

- *Dead*: This state is the one a user enters on login. It represents a quiescent state where there is no program loaded on behalf of the user.

- *Dormant*: Users in CTSS may load programs into memory prior to issuing a command to run them. The Dormant state represents the case where the user has a program loaded but is not running it. In both the Dead and Dormant states, the command interpreter is waiting for the user to enter commands.

- *Working*: In CTSS, the Working state plays the same role as both the Ready and Running states in Figure 5-1. When the user issues the command to run the program loaded in memory, it enters the Working state.

- *Waiting Command*: Between the time a user enters a command into the command interpreter and the time the command is processed, the user is in the Waiting Command state.

- *Input Wait*: Both the Input Wait and the Output Wait states serve to identify a user as blocked in the same sense as discussed in conjunction with Figure 5-1. In CTSS, we only enter the Input Wait state for user input on a terminal. Interestingly, the speed of the CPU on early machines was relatively slow compared with the speed of disk transfers. Consequently, the designers decided that it would not be efficient to enter an Input Wait state leading to a context switch while waiting for disk data.

- *Output Wait*: This state is analogous to the Input Wait state and is entered when we are generating output on a device that cannot keep up with the speed at which the CPU can send it data. Mechanical devices, such as printers and plotters, are good examples of this type of device. However, as with the Input Wait state, transfers to disk are not significantly faster than the CPU and don't cause an Output Wait state.

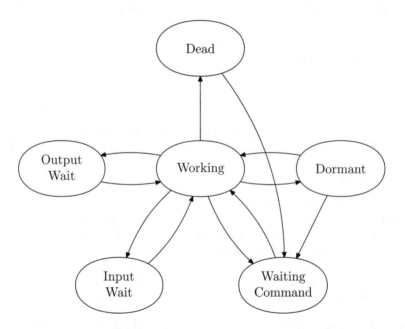

Figure 6-1: CTSS User State Machine

6.1.2 System Calls

Because processes in CTSS have a different character than those in most other systems, the set of system calls for dealing with them is also different. One effect of managing users instead of processes is the absence of a system call to create a process. However, there is the CHNCOM call (as well as other calls, such as XECOM and NEXCOM, which are built on top of CHNCOM), which starts a new sequence of commands running much as if they had been issued at the terminal. One thing that is typical, however, is the idea of a call that a program uses to terminate itself. There are two versions of this call in CTSS: EXIT and EXITM. The first one transitions the user to the Dormant state, allowing a postmortem debugger to be used. The second transitions the user to the Dead state, allowing a new program to be requested. Note that unlike most systems, these calls do not completely terminate the user (process); they terminate the program that is currently running. Finally, programs may temporarily suspend themselves using the SLEEP and WAIT calls. SLEEP places the user in the Dormant state for a specified number of seconds, whereas WAIT places the user in the specified state for up to that number of seconds. In some of the three waiting states, the program can resume due to other events before the time has elapsed.

6.1.3   Scheduling

Users in CTSS are scheduled in a multilevel feedback queue. There are nine levels, numbered 0 through 8. The scheduler always selects the process at the head of the queue in the lowest numbered nonempty level for processing. A process running in level l is given $2^l q$ time, where q is the quantum and is typically configured to be 16 mS. Upon completion of these quanta, the process is then moved to the tail of the queue at level $l+1$. Conversely, if a process goes for too long without getting selected to run, it is moved from level l to level $l-1$. This maximum waiting time is typically set to 60 S. New programs start at level

$$l_0 = \left\lfloor \log_2 \left(\left\lceil \frac{w_p}{w_q} \right\rceil + 1 \right) \right\rfloor$$

where w_p is the number of words in the new program, and w_q is the number of words that can be transferred from disk to memory in one quantum (120 words with a typical configuration). In other words, the first time the new program is scheduled, it is allowed to run for as long as it took to load it from disk. We also make the same level assignment when a program comes out of the Input Wait and Output Wait states back to the Working state. If a new program enters the queue at level $l' < l$ when a program at level l is running, the scheduler preempts the running program and selects the new (lower level) program to run.

The background job, providing batch-processing compatibility, runs at a lower priority level than all interactive processes. In effect, it is always placed at the tail of an overall queue of all processes in the Working state. With the batch process permanently placed at a lower priority than all interactive processes, there is the possibility that it could starve. There are two administrative mechanisms to prevent this. First, the operator has a console command available that forces the batch process to run and continue running until another command is entered that returns the system to normal time-sharing. The other mechanism to prevent batch job starvation is a parameter in the scheduler that guarantees it a certain percentage of the system time.

6.2   Multics

Much of our idea about what a process is was developed along with the Multics system. In early descriptions (prior to the implementation of the system), a process is described as the execution of a program. To make the idea more concrete, processes in Multics are associated with the details of memory management. In fact, Multics is the origin of our description of a process as a memory space with an associated locus of control.

In Multics, all processes are created by other processes. In principle, any process can create another. However, in practice, only an initializer process creates new processes. It and an idle process for each CPU are constructed "by hand" rather than being created by other processes. New processes are not created for each program that is run. Because process creation is time consuming, new processes are normally created only when a user logs in to the system, and all programs are run as part of that process. Users are also allowed to create a new process to replace their current one.

6.2.1   System Calls

As with CTSS, processes are created primarily as part of the mechanism for logging a user in to the system. The main call available for process management is *terminate_process_*( ), which causes the calling process to exit. An argument to this function determines whether the process should be logged out, terminated due to an error, or replaced with another process. There are additional calls, such as *get_process_id_*( ), that allow a process to request information about itself. Multics also provides a number of calls that support interprocess communication. Two key interprocess communication calls are *ipc_$block*( ), which places a process into a Blocked state, waiting on another process to wake it up, and *hcs_$wakeup*( ), which is used to wake up a blocked process.

6.2.2   Process State

Multics manages the states of processes a little differently than most systems do. The first difference we notice between the Multics state machine shown in Figure 6-2 and the generic machine shown in Figure 5-1 is the addition of the Waiting state, which parallels the Blocked state. The difference between them is one of time. The Blocked state is used when a process is waiting on a relatively long-term event such as user input. On the other hand, the Waiting state identifies a process that is waiting on an operation that is expected to occur quickly. Mutex locks and memory management operations are examples of such operations.

Another difference between the Multics state machine and the typical one is the addition of the Ineligible state. In reality, there's no Ineligible state per se. Ready processes in the queue can be either eligible or ineligible. Generally, we take the first eligible ready process from the queue when a CPU becomes available. The eligible and ineligible states and the mechanism for moving processes between them implements a two-level scheduler. The scheduler is responsible for selecting processes to make eligible.

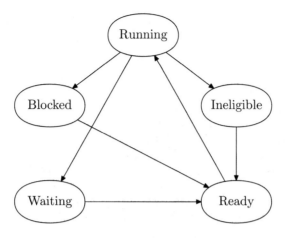

Figure 6-2: Multics Process State Machine

6.2.3   Scheduling

There are three approaches to scheduling that have been used in Multics. The first approach is a multilevel queue similar to the one used in CTSS. Each level gets twice as long a time slice as the next higher priority level. The process selected is the one at the head of the highest priority nonempty queue. Unlike CTSS, all processes enter at the highest priority queue. The lowest priority queue is called the background queue.

The second scheduler design is called a workclass scheduler. In this scheduler, a process is assigned to one of 16 groups. The group containing a process is administratively determined by the project a process is running under. Within each group, the scheduler selects processes using the original multilevel queue design. Among groups, the scheduler attempts to assign each group a percentage of the CPU time as designated administratively. If a group is assigned 20% of the CPU, then the scheduler attempts to give one out of every five quanta to processes from that group. This assumes that there are processes to run in all groups with nonzero percentages. If some groups have no ready processes, then their percentages are divided among the other groups that do have ready processes. This approach is implemented using a system of credits. When a process runs, credits that represent the time it runs are distributed among all groups according to their assigned percentage. The group with the most credits is always chosen to run. Additional details of the algorithm prevent any group from accumulating too many credits when it doesn't have any ready processes.

The final scheduling policy is a form of earliest deadline first (EDF) scheduling. The workclass groups continue to be used to give some projects preferential treatment over others. To establish deadlines, each group has a set of parameters, r_1, q_1, r_2, and q_2. For a process that becomes unblocked at time t, we set its deadline to $d = t + r_1$. When scheduled, the process is then allowed to run for a quantum of q_1. Processes that use their entire time slice ending at time t are then rescheduled according to a deadline $d = t + r_2$

and a quantum of q_2. No attempt is made to actually meet the deadlines. We use the deadlines to set process priorities. The scheduler always selects the process with the smallest value of d.

6.3   RT-11

In RT-11, processes are called jobs, but we continue to refer to them as processes in our discussion. When running the **single job** (SJ) monitor, there is only a single process, which is usually called a user job. In the **foreground-background** (FB) and **extended memory** (XM) monitors, one of the processes is identified as the background job and runs much the same as the user job in the SJ monitor. All other processes are called foreground jobs and run primarily in response to events rather than interacting with the user. This terminology may seem a little counterintuitive when approached from a perspective of an end user using a multiwindowed graphical user interface, where the window in front of others is the one interacting with the user. However, it makes sense in RT-11, where the foreground jobs are typically real-time jobs, and an interactive job is relegated to getting the CPU time that's left over.

6.3.1   System Calls

Background processes in RT-11 are created by the command interpreter in response to a user command, such as run or r. The .CHAIN system call (programmed request in RT-11 terminology) allows one background process to replace itself with another. This call reads the new program code into the same memory space used by the calling process and transfers control to it. All foreground processes are created by the frun or srun commands, with srun being used for special foreground processes called system jobs. A program terminates by issuing the .EXIT system call, which transfers control back to the command-line interpreter in the case of a background process.

6.3.2   Process State

To a first approximation, the state machine shown in Figure 5-1 describes processes in RT-11. As implemented, the Blocked state actually subsumes a number of possible blocking conditions. These possible conditions are stored in a job blocking word with one bit per condition. Among the reasons a process may be blocked are that the process is waiting on the user service routine (USR), the process is exiting and waiting on I/O to complete, or the process is waiting on normal I/O completion. We can generally interpret a zero job blocking word to mean the process is ready and a nonzero one to mean that it is blocked. There is also a job state word that records information about how this process relates to the rest of the system. It includes bits that record conditions such as the USR is running for that process or that process is being aborted.

6.3.3   Process Table

Both the job state word and the job blocking word are part of a collection of information we can think of as a process table entry. This collection also includes a substantial amount of information describing terminal input and output operations. For the XM monitor, these data include a description of the memory areas used by the process as well. Because there is only one process running on an SJ monitor, these data are kept in variables throughout the monitor. In the FB and XM monitors, each process has these data collected into a memory space called the impure area. The impure area for the background process is stored as part of the resident monitor (RMON) and the foreground process impure areas are stored adjacent to the processes' memory spaces. As a result, the process table is not collected as a single table but is distributed in memory along with the processes themselves.

6.3.4 Scheduling

RT-11 uses a simple priority scheduler, but it does not do preemptive time-sharing. The scheduler picks the highest priority process that is not blocked to run. This process continues to run until either it blocks or a higher priority process becomes unblocked. The single background process always has the lowest priority. The nonsystem foreground process always has the highest priority, and any system processes may be set to priority levels in between.

6.4 Sixth Edition UNIX

UNIX (except for the very earliest, single user version) implements processes much as we describe in Chapter 5. For each program that is run, a process is created. All processes are created by other, existing processes except for the very first process after the system is booted.

6.4.1 System Calls

All processes are created by the *fork( )* system call. It makes a copy of the calling process. The calling process is the parent, and the newly created process is the child. These two processes are identical except for the return value from *fork( )*. The return value for the child is 0, whereas the return value for the parent is the process ID of the child.

Although *fork( )* is quite capable of building an arbitrary family tree of processes, they're all running the same program. This is where the *exec( )* system call comes in. A call to *exec( )* replaces the currently running program with a new one. In fact, most calls to *fork( )* are followed closely by calls to *exec( )* because the most common reason for creating a new process is to run a new program.

Process termination is handled by two system calls. When a process is finished with its work and wants to voluntarily terminate, it calls the *exit( )* system call. Another process (with the appropriate privileges) may send a process a signal, which often results in the termination of the receiving process. Signals are sent with the *kill( )* system call.

The last process-related system call we examine is *wait( )*. When a process terminates, it produces an exit status that can be used by its parent to determine whether it was successful in its task. When a parent process is ready to pause until a child process has finished and to pick up the child's exit status, it does so with the *wait( )* system call.

6.4.2   Process State

The state machine in Figure 5-1 captures the nature of processes in UNIX fairly well. In the sixth edition implementation, there are a few additional states identified as:

- SSLEEP: This is a Blocked state where the process cannot be awakened by a signal.

- SWAIT: This Blocked state does allow the process to be awakened to handle a signal.

- SRUN: Processes in both the Ready and the Running states shown in Figure 5-1 are identified by the SRUN value. To distinguish between the running process and the other ready ones, there is a global variable, u, which contains process table information of the currently running process.

- SIDL: A process is set to this state if, during its creation, the copy of the parent's memory space cannot be made immediately and we have to resort to using the swapping mechanism to do the copy.

- SZOMB: When a child process exits, but the parent has not yet issued the *wait()* system call to pick up the exit status, the child still exists at some level. Such processes are called zombies.

- SSTOP: This state is used to identify a process that is being traced. Tracing is a facility that allows a parent process to monitor the progress of a child.

In addition to the process structure member that holds these state values, there is a member which holds a number of flags. These flags record the status of the process with respect to memory and tracing. In particular, they tell us whether the process is currently in memory, swapped out, or in the process of being swapped out.

6.4.3   Process Table

The process table data is divided into two parts. The first part is an array of structures called *proc*. These structures hold data we need, whether the process is resident in memory or swapped out. Among these data are the state information, identification information, and scheduling information.

Other process table data are not needed when the process is swapped out. These data are kept in a structure called the **user structure**. These per-process data areas are stored in each process's data segment. The user structure of the currently running process is also mapped to a fixed location in the kernel address space. User structures are swapped along with the rest of the process's memory space.

6.4.4   Scheduling

The sixth edition UNIX scheduler is a priority scheduler. The actual scheduling code is in the context switching function *swtch()*. It searches the process table for the highest priority ready process that is resident in memory. Early versions of UNIX use process swapping, as discussed in Section 9.6.1, to manage memory demands that exceed available memory. Consequently, some processes may not be resident in memory. Processes migrate between memory and disk under the control of the function *sched*( ). Together, *swtch*( ) and *sched*( ) effectively make up a two-level scheduler. Somewhat counterintuitively, the kernel uses smaller priority values to represent higher priority. In the kernel source code, the term scheduler is used to describe the code that handles swapping.

Periodically, the priority value of each process is recomputed according to the equation

$$p = \min\left(127, \frac{c}{16} + 100 + n\right)$$

where c is a cumulative CPU usage measured from the time the process was last swapped into memory. It is incremented for the currently running process on each clock interrupt up to a maximum value of 255. The value n is a parameter called **nice**. This parameter is so named because if we increase the value of nice, then the process gets a lower priority. In other words, we can be "nice" to the other processes in the system by increasing our value of nice. Normal users may set n to a positive value, but only the superuser may set it to a negative value. The effect of this algorithm is to give preference to processes with smaller amounts of cumulative CPU time. This characteristic is generally true of processes that are predominantly I/O bound.

6.5   4.3BSD

Because 4.3BSD is an evolution of sixth edition UNIX, it should come as no surprise that its general approach to process management is substantially similar. This is to be expected especially because the primary development focus in the 4BSD series is support for the larger virtual address space on VAX as compared with the PDP-11. Nevertheless, there are a few differences in process management worth pointing out.

6.5.1   System Calls

Most of the sixth edition UNIX process-related system calls are also present in 4.3BSD. However, there are some additional calls, and in a few cases, a new call replaces the older

---

Historical Note: Early UNIX Scheduling

While the UNIX scheduler as we have presented it is coded in the context switching function, *swtch*( ), there is another kernel function called *sched*( ), which is described as the scheduler. Why this seeming discrepancy? The answer goes back to the earliest versions of UNIX. In those, there was only one process in memory at a time and all other processes were stored on a mass storage medium such as a disk. So swapping and scheduling went hand in hand. In effect, the decision of which process to schedule was the decision of which process to swap in. Somewhat naturally, the function that managed swapping was called *sched*( ). As the system evolved and multiple processes could be kept in memory, the actual scheduling functionality was moved into the context switching function, but the swapping function still kept the name *sched*( ).

one. As discussed with respect to sixth edition UNIX, the *fork( )* system call makes a copy of the parent process. This requires that we copy all of the parent's writable memory space. If the *fork( )* is followed closely by a call to *exec( )*, then the work to copy the parent's memory is wasted. For that reason, the BSD developers added the *vfork( )* system call. It still creates a child process, but the child shares the parent's memory space until it issues either an *exit( )* or an *execve( )* system call. At that point, the parent resumes in the same way it would had it called *fork( )*. This variant saves the copying of the parent's memory in the common case where a *fork( )* is quickly followed by an *execve( )*.

The *exec( )* system call in sixth edition UNIX is replaced with the *execve( )* system call in 4.3BSD. The new version still replaces the calling program with a new one. However, it is more general in that it supports the use of environment variables.

4.3BSD continues to provide the older *wait( )* system call. However, there are times when a parent might want to check to see if a child has exited, but not block if it hasn't. The *wait3( )* system call allows this. It also allows the parent to ask for the child's resource usage in addition to the exit status.

6.5.2   Process State and Process Table

Little changed in the representation of process state between sixth edition UNIX and 4.3BSD. Among the actual set of possible states, the `SWAIT` state was collapsed into the `SSLEEP` state so that there is only one Blocked state. On the other hand, a number of new flags were added. Many of these are used in the implementation of new features, such as *vfork( )*. The process table structure of 4.3BSD continues the split *proc* table and user structure design.

6.5.3   Scheduling

Aside from the new system calls, the biggest changes in process management between sixth edition UNIX and 4.3BSD are the details of the scheduling algorithm. The basic concept is the same; we maintain a process priority that biases our selection of processes toward I/O bound processes. We dynamically adjust that priority based on process history and include a nice parameter that allows some user influence over scheduling.

There are a number of differences in detail, however. In 4.3BSD, we don't search the entire process list for the ready process of highest priority. Instead, we organize the ready processes into a set of queues, one for each priority level, creating a multilevel feedback queue. As a result, the search time is now proportional to the number of priority levels as opposed to proportional to the number of processes. On a PDP-11 with sixth edition UNIX, these two sizes are comparable, so the extra complexity of maintaining the queues is not justified. However, on a VAX with 4.3BSD, the number of processes on the system can be much greater, and this new organization results in a faster scheduler.

There are also differences in the details of how priorities are calculated. The update equation is similar in form, but differs in detail from that in sixth edition UNIX. In 4.3BSD, we update the priority by

$$p = \min\left(127, \frac{c}{4} + 50 + 2n\right)$$

There are also differences in the calculation of c. We continue to increment c for the currently running process on each clock tick. However, we also periodically adjust c for ready processes to bias it toward the most recent time. This update is given by

$$c' = \frac{2l}{2l+1}c + n$$

where l is the load average. This value is the average number of ready processes during the past minute. For blocked processes, we adjust c at the time the process becomes unblocked. This adjustment is given by

$$c' = \left[\frac{2l}{2l+1}\right]^{s} c$$

where s is the number of seconds the process just spent in the SSLEEP state. The net effect of this adjustment is to increase the priority of a process that's been blocked, and the longer it's been blocked, the more we increase that priority.

6.6   VMS

Like in UNIX, the command-line interpreter in VMS is written like most other applications. However, in VMS, it resides in a different part of the virtual memory space than other applications. It also differs in how it starts applications in response to user commands. Whereas in UNIX, the shell creates a new process for each command, the VMS command-line interpreter runs programs within its own process space. Most processes in VMS are created by the login program to run the command-line interpreter.

Recent versions of VMS have added threads managed by the kernel. (Threads managed by an application library were available for some time before the kernel threads were introduced.) All processes have one or more threads that are managed by the scheduler. Even a process that creates no additional threads is managed by its single kernel thread.

VMS also has the concept of jobs. A job in VMS is a set of processes including an initial process and all its descendants. Jobs allow processes to share resources other than memory. For example, processes in a job can share I/O devices.

6.6.1   System Calls

Any process can create another process by issuing the $CREPRC system call. All processes except for the initial swapper process are created by $CREPRC calls. When creating a new process, we specify the name of the file containing the code for a program to run in the new process. However, to support the POSIX *fork()* call, VMS also supports minimal process creation through the EXE$CRE_MIN_PROCESS and EXE$PSX_FORK_PROCSTRT calls.

A process can call $EXIT to voluntarily terminate. One process can force another to issue an $EXIT call by issuing a $FORCEX system call.

6.6.2 Thread State

Figure 6-3 shows the state machine for threads in VMS. Although the terminology is different, the organization of this machine is essentially the same as our generic machine shown in Figure 5-1. In VMS, the Current state corresponds to the state we call the Running state. Similarly, our Ready state is called Computable in VMS. The Waiting state shown in Figure 6-3, corresponding to our generic Blocked state, is actually not a single state in VMS. In reality, there are a number of individual states representing waits on different conditions. For clarity, we have grouped them in one Waiting state.

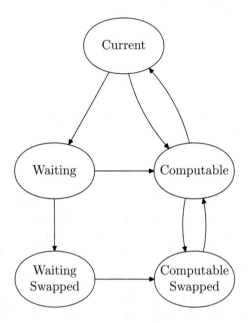

Figure 6-3: VMS Thread State Machine

The remaining two states parallel the Waiting and Computable states. They represent the situations where the thread is either waiting or is computable but is not resident in memory. As we discuss in Section 9.6, we are often forced to copy some processes to a disk to make room for other processes. When a process is swapped out, it can otherwise be ready to run, but can't be scheduled until it is read back into memory.

6.6.3 Scheduling

VMS uses a multilevel feedback queue for scheduling. In the VAX version of VMS, there are 32 levels where levels 0 through 15 are normal application priority levels and levels 16 through 31 are designated as real-time priorities. In the Alpha version of VMS, there are 64 levels, with the additional levels 32 through 63 being higher priority real-time levels. Although the higher priority levels are called real-time priorities, no attempt is made to provide guaranteed response times.

Normal processes are given a quantum that is determined by a systemwide configuration parameter. The default value of the quantum is 200 mS.

Each thread has both a base priority and a current priority. For normal processes, the default base priority, set at thread creation, is level 4. The current priority of a normal thread may be elevated above the base priority during the life of the thread. Current priorities of real-time threads are always equal to their base priorities.

As with other multilevel feedback queues, the scheduler selects the thread at the head of the highest priority nonempty queue to run next. When a thread completes a time slice, its current priority is decreased by one level if it is greater than its base priority. It is then placed on the tail of the queue corresponding to its current priority.

There are two cases where the current priority of a normal thread can be boosted above its base priority. The first case occurs when a thread becomes unblocked. The event on which the thread was waiting determines the amount of the boost, which can be either zero, two, three, four, or six priority levels above the thread's base priority. However, the priority boost is applied only if it would not boost the thread's current priority above level 15. It is also not applied if the thread's current priority is already greater than the boosted level. The second type of boost is called a PIXSCAN boost. This boosting results from a periodic scan of threads in the scheduling queues. If a thread is found that has been in a queue without getting any running time for at least two seconds, then its current priority is boosted to be equal to that of the highest priority nonempty queue.

Recent versions of VMS also provide a mechanism that allows user-provided schedulers to govern the behavior of a subset of processes. These schedulers are called class schedulers and can be used to provide special scheduling policies that are not covered by the standard multilevel feedback queue.

6.7 Windows NT

Windows NT does not have a single unit of management that corresponds to the process as we discuss in Chapter 5. Rather, it has a hierarchy of entities that collectively provide processes and threads in a number of forms. At the most coarse-grained level, we have jobs. Jobs in Windows NT are sets of processes that share certain process management parameters. Processes in Windows NT are sets of one or more threads that all share a common memory space. Threads are the units of execution that are scheduled and managed in the way we discuss process management in Chapter 5. Finally, a thread may be converted into a fiber and new fibers may be created by it. Fibers are units of execution that are managed strictly in the application and not by the kernel.

6.7.1 System Calls

The *CreateProcess( )* Win32 call creates a new process and implicitly a new thread to run in it. This call takes as an argument the name of the program to run in the newly created process. The normal call to end a process is *ExitProcess( )*. Similarly, the *CreateThread( )*

and *ExitThread()* calls start and end threads. When starting a new thread, we specify the function within the containing process that is to run rather than a new program to run.

6.7.2   Thread State

Management of threads in Windows NT follows a state machine very similar to the generic one shown in Figure 5-1. There are, however, some additional intermediary states, as shown in Figure 6-4. In this figure, the state labeled Waiting is the same as the state labeled Blocked in the typical machine discussed earlier. The state labeled Initialized identifies a thread that is in the process of being created but is not yet ready to run. Conversely, the Terminated state indicates that the thread has ended but its resources have not yet been reclaimed by the system. A thread will be in the Standby state between the time it is selected by the scheduler and the time it is given to a CPU by context switching. Finally, the Transition state identifies that the thread is no longer blocked on the condition that made it enter the Waiting state. However, it is not yet ready to run because the memory used for its kernel stack is swapped out to disk. We can also see in Figure 6-4 that the transition from Waiting to Running, which must go through the Ready state in our typical machine, can be taken directly in Windows NT.

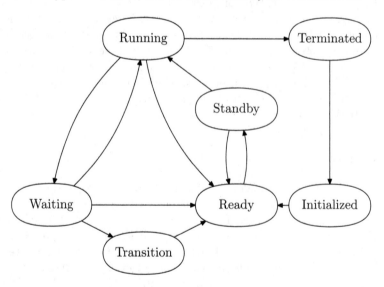

Figure 6-4: Windows NT Thread State Machine

6.7.3   Process and Thread Tables

Data used to represent and manage processes and threads are spread across a number of data structures. We start with the executive process (EPROCESS) block. There is one such block for each process, and it is maintained in the OS's memory space. Among other information, this block contains the process ID and information concerning the memory usage of the process. It also contains another structure called the kernel process (KPROCESS) block or process control block (PCB). This block points to a list of thread blocks and also contains certain default scheduling data shared by all threads in the process. One other key piece of data in the KPROCESS block is a pointer to the process's page directory, which defines the actual memory mapping for the process. The final part of the process data structure is the process environment block (PEB), which is pointed to by the EPROCESS block and is stored in the process's memory space. This block contains process management data that needs to be accessible to the application code and libraries. The primary data in this block relate to managing the heap and the thread-local storage.

For threads, there is a parallel set of data structures. The executive thread (ETHREAD) block records the address of the initial function of the thread as well as information about pending I/O requests. It also holds process ID data, including a pointer to the EPROCESS block. As with EPROCESS, the ETHREAD block is kept in the system memory space. Also in parallel to processes, the ETHREAD block includes a kernel thread (KTHREAD) block. Among the data in the KTHREAD block are the data used by the scheduler to select which thread runs next. Finally, the KTHREAD block points to the thread environment block (TEB), which lives in the process's memory space. Among other things, this block identifies the location of the thread's stack.

6.7.4   Scheduling

Scheduling in Windows NT is strictly a function of threads. Which process a thread belongs to has no effect on the scheduling of that thread, except for establishing its initial base priority. Windows NT uses a multilevel feedback queue with 32 priority levels. The lowest priority level, 0, is reserved for a special kernel thread that clears free memory pages. Levels 1–15 are designated dynamic levels. These levels are used for normal applications and are so named because the priority level of threads in these levels gets adjusted by the system to implement the desired scheduling policies. Priority levels 16–31 are called real-time levels. These are not real-time in the sense of guaranteed response time or in terms of scheduling by deadline. Rather, these levels provide a higher priority level than normal applications and a more predictable response because they are not dynamically adjusted by the system. While internally priorities are managed numerically, applications often operate in terms of a few priority classes: real-time, high, above normal, normal, below normal, and idle.

In addition to various priority levels, a thread may also have a different value of quantum. On a uniprocessor x86 system, the quantum values range from 20 mS to 120 mS. Normally, this value is set administratively for all threads in the system. However, the setting can optionally give the foreground process's threads a longer quantum. (The foreground process is identified by the windowing system as the process that owns the window currently having focus.) Regardless of how the quantum has been set, the scheduler itself doesn't change it or depend on it. It determines how long a thread is allowed to run before the scheduler is invoked to replace it.

As with all multilevel feedback queue schedulers, the actual scheduling operation is simple. We select the thread at the head of the nonempty queue of highest priority. That thread runs until one of two things happens: The thread finishes its quantum, in which case it is normally placed on the tail of the queue from which it came, or another thread of higher priority becomes ready to run, in which case the preempted thread is placed back on the head of its queue.

In addition to this, however, Windows NT also implements a number of independent mechanisms for adjusting the priority of threads with the aim of improving system performance. All of these adjustments are made only to processes in the dynamic range of priorities and in no case is the priority of such a process ever raised above 15.

- When a thread is moved to the Ready state after waiting on an I/O operation, the relevant device driver increases the thread's priority. The exact amount is up to the driver, and typical values range from 1 to 8 levels. This increase is applied to the thread's base priority but can be disabled by a Win32 call.

- Similarly, when a thread is again made ready after waiting on an executive event or semaphore, its priority is set to one level higher than its base priority. This increase can also be disabled.

- A foreground thread is one identified as belonging to the process that owns the window with current focus as determined by the windowing system. When such a thread becomes unblocked after waiting for a kernel object, it is given an increase in its current priority determined by a system parameter called *PsPrioritySeparation*. This adjustment cannot be disabled.

- Similarly, threads that own a window are given an increase of two priority levels when they move to the Ready state because of a windowing event. This increase is applied to the current priority and can be disabled.

- Threads that are being starved are given a priority increase as well. A process that has been in a ready queue for approximately 3 to 4 seconds is given a current priority of 15 and a double quantum. After the thread runs for its double quantum, its priority immediately returns to its base level.

For all priority increases except for the starvation remedy, the priority decays back to the thread's base priority in a stairstep fashion. Each time a thread completes a quantum at a current priority greater than its base priority, its current priority is decreased by one. In other words, it is placed on the tail of the next lower queue rather than back on the queue from which it was scheduled.

6.8   TinyOS

TinyOS doesn't support processes in the usual sense. In their place, components define three classes of executable code, commands, event handlers, and tasks. Commands are executed in response to requests from higher layer components. Event handlers respond to hardware events either directly or indirectly. In an abstract sense, events are messages sent from lower layers to upper ones. Unlike commands and event handlers, tasks are not run in response to external triggers. They are scheduled to be run at some later time.

Tasks and event handlers may signal events to higher layers, call commands in lower layers, and schedule tasks. To prevent cycles in event handling, commands are allowed only to call lower layer commands and to schedule tasks. They may not signal events to upper layers.

To describe how these forms of executable code are handled, we describe a scenario beginning with the system being idle. In that state, nothing can happen until a hardware interrupt is generated. This results in an event handler being called. The event handler may then generate further events handled by higher layers. It may also post a task to be executed later. The upper layer handlers may further pass on more events, post other tasks, or call commands. Unless another interrupt is generated while handling this one, the whole chain of event handlers and commands are part of a single thread of execution. All tasks that are posted are deferred until the complete chain of processing is completed.

Posting a task is something like submitting a small batch job. We schedule these "batch" jobs according to a first-come, first-served (FCFS) policy. The scheduler picks the first task from the list and runs it. When it completes, the next task on the list is selected and run. When the list becomes empty, the scheduler places the CPU into a powersave mode to wait for the next interrupt. In TinyOS 1, the scheduler is built in to the system, much as we would find it in most any OS. However, in TinyOS 2, the scheduler is actually another component. This design allows the scheduler to be easily replaced with one more suited to the problem domain.

6.9 Xen

In Xen, there are two notions of process that concern us. The first is the processes that are managed by each of the guest operating systems. Xen is unaware of the details of these processes. However, because on most versions of the x86 processor Xen does not fully virtualize the hardware, guest OSs are required to make a request of Xen to carry out the details of context switching. Most of these details are related to memory management, which we discuss in Section 10.9.

Xen's other view of a process is really a guest OS itself. Xen must switch among these OSs in the same way a conventional time-sharing OS switches among application processes. In version 3 of Xen, there are two schedulers that may be selected. They are a borrowed virtual time (BVT) scheduler and a simple earliest deadline first (SEDF) scheduler. (Version 2 of Xen provided a BVT scheduler, an atropos scheduler, which provided fixed shares of CPU time, and a simple round-robin scheduler.) Although we don't present a detailed discussion of BVT scheduling here, the basic idea is straightforward. Processes are scheduled according to their accumulated running time with a weighting factor that allows some processes to be given preference over others. When a process wakes up and needs to run quickly, time is borrowed from that process's future use by effectively subtracting a warp factor from its accumulated time. All of the BVT parameters can be set in the configuration file and by a scheduler configuration system call. In the SEDF scheduler, the deadlines are set according to a per-domain parameter called period. At the end of each time slice, the next deadline is set to the current time plus the period. In effect, the period can be used to determine the share of the CPU each domain gets. This parameter can also be set in the configuration file or by a system call.

Just as processes in most operating systems can take actions that change their process states or that affect their scheduling, domains in Xen can do the same thing. The primary interface for these changes is the *sched_op_new( )* hypercall. The first argument to this call indicates what action is to be taken. There are three actions that interest us. If the first argument is *SCHEDOP_yield*, then the domain is moved from the Running state to the Ready state, giving up the rest of its time slice but remaining available to be scheduled. If the first argument is *SCHEDOP_block*, the domain moves to the Blocked state, where it waits, ineligible for scheduling, until it receives an event. Finally, the *SCHEDOP_shutdown* operation is analogous to the guest OS shutting down or rebooting on real hardware.

6.10   Summary

Although the techniques discussed in Chapter 5 are the basis of most process management, the details typically get more involved in practice. This chapter presents a number of real systems, focusing on how processes are represented, controlled, and scheduled. These systems are a sampling of the wide variety of operating systems that have been developed and that are in use. In studying them, we see how general techniques for process management are turned into specific implementations. In the next two chapters, we dig deeper and look at the details of process management in Inferno and Linux.

6.11   Exercises

1. In CTSS, if $w_q = 120$, and the largest program is no greater than 32 K words (the size of each bank of memory), then what is the maximum queue level at which a process may enter?

2. In CTSS, the exponentially increasing time slice length has the effect of reducing the number of context switches for compute-bound processes. If t_s is the time to perform a context switch, what is the fraction of time spent in context switching overhead for a process in the level l queue?

3. Describe one way in which the workclass scheduler of Multics could be implemented. Be sure to account for the cases where one or more workclasses have no ready processes.

4. In RT-11, we have a background process that isn't guaranteed any CPU time, but which can run using any time not used by other processes. Can such a background process also be used with a slotted scheduler, as described in Section 5.4.7.3? If so, describe how.

5. Is the sixth edition UNIX scheduler susceptible to priority inversion, assuming that all three processes involved have the same value of nice? Why or why not?

6. The developers of 4.3BSD chose to implement different priority calculations from those in sixth edition UNIX. What are some undesirable behaviors that sixth edition might have exhibited that 4.3BSD corrects?

7. VMS and Windows NT both treat threads as the primary unit of management for scheduling, process table management, and state management. What role do processes play in such systems?

8. In RT-11, the background process is associated with an interactive user, whereas in Windows NT, the foreground process is the one that has focus in the user interface. Why the difference? Does one of the systems use the wrong terminology?

9. Would it be feasible to implement a shortest job first (SJF) scheduler in TinyOS instead of the FCFS one? What would be the trade-offs in such a decision?

10. TinyOS restricts some types of component interactions. In particular, commands are not allowed to generate events. What would be the problem if they were?

Chapter 7

Process Management in Inferno

Processes in Inferno are somewhat unusual owing to Inferno's use of a virtual machine. The virtual machine interpreter embedded in the OS has more control over running user programs than a typical OS has. In addition to user processes, Inferno also uses kernel processes internally. In this chapter, we discuss both user and kernel processes and some elements of managing them. For both types of processes, we discuss their representation in their respective process tables as well as the process state machines for each. Our focus, however, is primarily on how Inferno handles user processes as interpreted by the Dis virtual machine. As a result, we discuss their creation, destruction, and scheduling in more detail than kernel processes.

7.1 Processes in Inferno

Even though, as a system, Inferno has a very simple design and a straightforward implementation, there are facets that make matters a bit more involved. One of these is the variety of types of processes in Inferno. The first is the type of process we describe in Chapter 3, a user process running interpreted Dis code. For these processes, the virtual machine has complete control over the process right down to the execution of individual instructions. As we see later in this chapter, this makes operations such as context switching and determining the end of a time slice very simple.

For many platforms, Inferno includes a **just-in-time** (JIT) compiler that translates Dis code into the machine's native instruction set. This facility leads to a variation on user processes, ones that run native machine code. Because the virtual machine interpreter does not have complete control over those modules that are compiled to native code, the details of their process management are necessarily different. In the interest of space and to focus on how Inferno applies the principles of process management, we do not cover JIT code here.

Finally, we have the kernel process. Kernel processes (which we sometimes call *kprocs* after the function that is used to create them) are independent threads of control within the kernel itself. In hosted Inferno, they are threads managed by the host OS. We see one of these created in the system's initialization discussed in Chapter 3. As the system operates, others get created as needed. For example, in hosted Inferno, we create a *kproc* that listens for characters to be typed at the keyboard and puts them into the buffer that is used to serve application requests for input. We also create multiple virtual machine interpreter *kprocs* as the system runs. Processes can issue requests that cause the interpreter to block. If there are no other interpreters that can run application code, then we create a new *kproc* to continue running applications while the other interpreters are blocked. Only one interpreter at a time is actively running application code. All the others are either blocked or idle. Although we do discuss some of the elements of managing *kprocs*, the primary focus of our presentation in this chapter is on user processes interpreted by the virtual machine.

In terms of our discussion of processes and threads in Section 5.3, all of the processes in Inferno are best thought of as threads. They all run sharing a common memory space. Consequently, the set of all kernel processes make up a single multithreaded program. Normally, we wouldn't want all user processes to share a common memory space. However, the nature of the Limbo language and the Dis virtual machine design prevent applications from having unrestricted access to each other. As a result, they can safely run in a common memory space.

7.2   Process State

Because we have two general classes of processes in Inferno (kernel processes and user processes), we have two different sets of process states to manage. In keeping with our primary focus on managing user processes, we briefly discuss kernel process state and then look at the state machine for user processes in more detail.

7.2.1   Kernel Processes

For hosted Inferno, the primary issues of kernel process state are handled by the host OS because it handles much of the process creation and scheduling for us. Native Inferno maintains its own set of process states for kernel processes because it is responsible for managing these processes itself.

In both cases, however, the *kprocs* that run the virtual machine interpreter deserve special mention. In addition to the usual scheduling and process management for these *kprocs*, there is an additional level of scheduling. Each of these is capable of running user processes. To run user processes, the code in libinterp is like a CPU. There is a single set of registers, and only one *kproc* can be using it at a time. A *kproc* that doesn't need the interpreter, particularly when it's about to do something that might block, calls *release*( ) to signal that another *kproc* can use the interpreter. When a *kproc* again needs the interpreter, it calls *acquire*( ) to reclaim it. Normally, an interpreter *kproc* time-shares among all the ready user processes, as discussed in Section 7.6. If the interpreter blocks on behalf of a user process, then we need to run another interpreter. After the blocked one wakes up, then we need to be able to run it again to let it finish what it was doing

on behalf of the user process. Consequently, interpreter *kprocs* can be in the following
states, as illustrated in Figure 7-1:

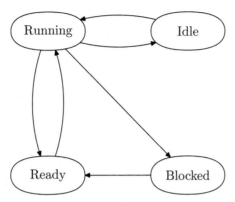

Figure 7-1: Hosted Inferno Kernel Process State Machine

- *Running*: There is only one interpreter *kproc* at a time that has control of the
  interpreter. That one is identified as being in the Running state by a global variable
  up which points to its process table entry.

- *Blocked*: As with our previous use of the term, an interpreter *kproc* that is blocked
  is one that is waiting for some event.

- *Ready*: This state represents the case where an interpreter *kproc* has been awakened
  from a Blocked state and, thus, has a user process attached to it because it is waiting
  to get the interpreter.

- *Idle*: This is the state that identifies an interpreter *kproc* that has no associated
  user process and, therefore, is available if the current one blocks.

Unlike most representations of process state, these states are not recorded in the process
table. Rather, we infer these states from the position of the *kproc's* process table entry
on various lists.

7.2.2   *User Processes*

In Inferno, the process states for user processes follow the basic model we discuss in
Section 5.2.2. The set of states for user processes is defined in include/interp.h. The main
part of the state machine for user processes is illustrated in Figure 7-2. The state names in
the figure, with the exception of Running, are those defined in the header file. No value is
defined for the Running state; it is identified as the single process on which an interpreter
is operating. In the figure, we omit two states, *Pdebug* and *Pbroken*, for clarity because
they are exceptional cases and not part of the usual process lifetime. The full set of states
is used as follows:

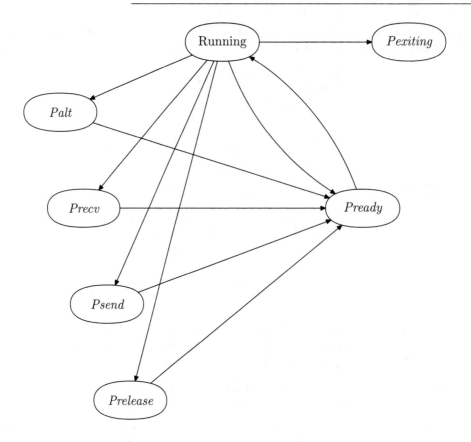

Figure 7-2: Inferno User Process State Machine

- *Palt*: This state is used when the process executes an **alt** instruction corresponding to the **alt** Limbo language construct. This is used much like *select( )*, found in most UNIX systems, which allows a process to wait on several input or output file descriptors simultaneously. In Limbo, the **alt** construct allows the process to wait on multiple communications channels.

- *Psend* and *Precv*: The *Psend* and *Precv* states are also used with communications channels. These are used for sending to or receiving from single channels. All three of these states are types of Blocked states.

- *Pdebug*: A process is placed in this state when it is under the control of a debugger.

- *Pready*: Processes that are eligible to be interpreted are in the Ready state as identified by *Pready*. If a process is in the Ready state, it will also be on a linked list of ready processes.

- *Prelease*: A process is placed in the *Prelease* state when the function *release*( ) is called. The idea here is that a process is releasing its claim on the virtual CPU, usually temporarily. Within much of the kernel we call *release*( ) immediately before making a call that may require service by the host OS and then call *acquire*( ) immediately after.

- *Pexiting*: When we are in the process of cleaning up after a process terminates, we set its state to *Pexiting* so that if anything looks at the state of this process before we're done cleaning up, there's no confusion as to the status of this process. For simplicity, we show only the transition from the Running state to the Exiting state in Figure 7-2. It is also possible for a process to be forced into the Exiting state from other states.

- *Pbroken*: We use the *Pbroken* state to mark a process that exited while under the control of a debugger. We keep the process in place so that the debugger can examine the process to determine what caused it to exit. We also use the *Pbroken* state when a process terminates as a result of most error conditions. This allows a debugger to be attached to it for postmortem analysis.

7.3   Process Data Structures

As with most other real systems, Inferno's process table is not quite as simple as the picture we painted in Chapter 5. Part of this is due to the variety of process types we manage, and part of it arises as a result of mechanisms that improve performance.

Figure 7-3 shows the complete process table and ready queue structures. In this figure, the boxes marked *a*, *b*, *c*, and *d* are kernel processes. The numerical values in boxes are process IDs of user processes. Note that both kernel processes and user processes may be on more than one linked list at a time. All instances of the same labeled box are the same data structure. For clarity, we draw them as separate boxes rather than attempt to show all list links going into and out of a single box per process.

7.3.1   Kernel Process Table

The first process data structure is the **Procs** structure. The definition for it is found in emu/port/dat.h as follows:

```
struct Procs {
    Lock l;
    Proc *head;
    Proc *tail;
};
```

It defines the doubly linked list of all kernel processes. The global variable *procs* is the only defined instance of this structure. The structure member *l* is a lock that is used to provide mutual exclusion when multiple threads attempt to access the list simultaneously.

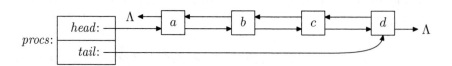

(a) Kernel Process List

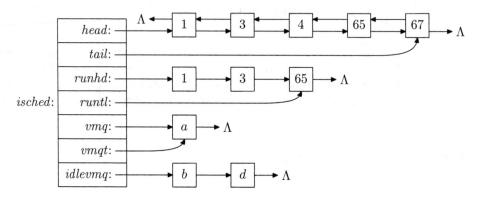

(b) User Process and Ready Queue Lists

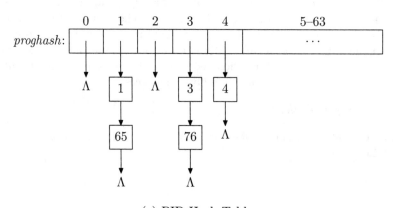

(c) PID Hash Table

Figure 7-3: Inferno Process and Ready Queue Structures

When the list is not empty, the first process and the last process in the list are pointed to by *head* and *tail* respectively. Each *kproc* is described by a **Proc** structure, described next. The list is illustrated in Figure 7-3(a).

7.3.2   Kernel Process Table Entry

The **Proc** structure, which is the process table entry for kernel processes, is declared as follows in emu/port/dat.h:

```
struct Proc {
    int type;        /* interpreter or not */
    char text[KNAMELEN];
    Proc *qnext;      /* list of processes waiting on a Qlock */
    long pid;
    Proc *next;       /* list of created processes */
    Proc *prev;
    Lock rlock;       /* sync between sleep/swiproc for r */
    Rendez *r;        /* rendezvous point slept on */
    Rendez sleep;     /* place to sleep */
    int killed;       /* by swiproc */
    int swipend;      /* software interrupt pending for Prog */
    int syscall;      /* set true under sysio for interruptable syscalls */
    int intwait;      /* spin wait for note to turn up */
    int sigid;        /* handle used for signal/note/exception */
    Lock sysio;       /* note handler lock */
    char genbuf[128];   /* buffer used e.g. for last name element from namec */
    int nerr;         /* error stack SP */
    osjmpbuf estack[NERR];     /* vector of error jump labels */
    char *kstack;
    void (*func)(void *);      /* saved trampoline pointer for kproc */
    void *arg;        /* arg for invoked kproc function */
    void *iprog;      /* work for Prog after release */
    void *prog;       /* fake prog for slaves eg. exportfs */
    Osenv *env;       /* effective operating system environment */
    Osenv defenv;     /* default env for slaves with no prog */
    osjmpbuf privstack;        /* private stack for making new kids */
    osjmpbuf sharestack;
    Proc *kid;
    void *kidsp;
    void *os;         /* host os specific data */
};
```

Because our focus is on managing user processes, we only describe a few of the members of the **Proc** structure. Whether this is an interpreter *kproc* or not is indicated by the value of the *type* member. It is equal to *Interp* for those *kprocs* that run the interpreter. The *text* field is a textual name that can be used to identify the process. The doubly linked list of all kernel processes is defined by the *next* and *prev* members of this structure. When an interpreter kernel process is blocked on behalf of a user process or when it's in a Ready state, the *iprog* member is used to point to the user process's process table entry. We use a **void**∗ type here because some code that includes the dat.h header file doesn't have access to the actual declaration of the user process table entry.

7.3.3   User Process Table

Now we turn our attention from the representation of kernel processes to the representation of user processes. Whereas kernel processes are described by a structure called **Proc**, user processes are described by a structure called **Prog**. We begin by looking at the structure that defines the lists shown in Figure 7-3(b). This *isched* structure is defined as follows in emu/port/dis.c:

```
struct {
    Lock l;
    Prog *runhd;
    Prog *runtl;
    Prog *head;
    Prog *tail;
    Rendez irend;
    int idle;
    int nyield;
    int creating;
    Proc *vmq;        /* queue of procs wanting vm */
    Proc *vmqt;
    Proc *idlevmq;    /* queue of procs wanting work */
    Atidle *idletasks;
} isched;
```

The **Lock** variable *l* is used to provide mutual exclusion for accesses to the data structure. The list of ready user processes for scheduling is identified by the *runhd* and *runtl* pointers. Because we are storing the full set of processes in a list instead of an array, we need head and tail pointers for the list. This is the function of the *head* and *tail* pointers. When the scheduler is idle (no user processes to be scheduled), we set the *idle* flag. The pointers *vmq* and *vmqt* are the head and tail of a linked list of the interpreter *kprocs* in the Ready state. These are the ones that have a user process table entry attached to the *iprog* structure member. The interpreter *kprocs* that are idle (i.e., have no associated user process) are in a linked list pointed to by *idlevmq*.

7.3.4   User Process Table Entry

Inferno represents the user process table with a combined linked list and hash table, as illustrated in Figure 7-3. The details of the Inferno user process table entry are defined in the file include/interp.h as:

```
struct Prog {
    REG R;        /* Register set */
    Prog *link;        /* Run queue */
    Channel *chan;        /* Channel pointer */
    void *ptr;        /* Channel data pointer */
    enum ProgState state;        /* Scheduler state */
    char *kill;        /* Set if prog should error */
    char *killstr;        /* kill string buffer when needed */
    int pid;        /* unique Prog id */
    int quanta;        /* time slice */
    ulong ticks;        /* time used */
    int flags;        /* error recovery flags */
    Prog *prev;
    Prog *next;
    Prog *pidlink;        /* next in pid hash chain */
    Progs *group;        /* process group */
    Prog *grpprev;        /* previous group member */
    Prog *grpnext;        /* next group member */
    void *exval;        /* current exception */
    char *exstr;        /* last exception */
    void (*addrun)(Prog *);
    void (*xec)(Prog *);
    void *osenv;
};
```

It is quite normal for a process table entry to contain a member to hold a copy of the process's registers when the process is not in the Running state. In the case of Inferno, this member is called R. This might seem a little surprising, as processes in Inferno are all run by the virtual machine interpreter. However, the virtual machine is defined with a set of registers similar to those on a typical CPU. So while the interpreter is running another process, we need to keep the registers belonging to this (noncurrent) process in the process table.

The next member of the structure, *link*, is a pointer to the next process in the ready list. Each process table entry lives on a linked list of all processes, but only those processes that are ready to run are on the linked list defined by *link*. The *link* member is ignored for processes that are blocked.

Inferno provides support for a feature of the Limbo language called **channels**. Channels are similar to the more familiar pipe and socket facilities found in most C environments except that they are typed. The *chan* member is used to record a channel on which a process is currently blocked. This allows us to clean up properly if that process gets killed while it's still blocked on the channel. Similarly, we use *ptr* to record the address of the data buffer that we are using for sending or receiving. This allows us to quickly know where to copy data when the other end performs the corresponding receive or send.

The *state* member holds the current state of the user process. It may take on the values described in Section 7.2.2.

If an application program fails due to an error detected by the OS, then we set *kill* to point to an error message describing the fault. In some cases, we allocate a buffer to hold the string and make *killstr* point to that buffer.

Inferno assigns a unique process ID number to each process when it is created. These values are assigned sequentially until the integer value rolls over to become negative. When it hits a negative number, we have run out of allowed process IDs, and the system must stop. Inferno does not reuse process IDs; however, on a 32-bit machine, there can be over two billion processes created before the system will shut down as a result of running out of process IDs. (If we create processes on average once per second, this gives us a little over 68 years of uptime.) This process ID is stored in the *pid* member of the process table entry.

User processes in Inferno can be part of a group. Normally, a process is added to the group of which its parent is a part. The list of processes in a group is described by a structure pointed to by *group*.

The *quanta* member is initialized to the value defined by **PQUANTA**, which is defined to be 2048. It is used to set the number of instructions an interpreted process is allowed to run before being preempted.

When exceptions occur in a process, sometimes we want the exception to be passed on to some of the other processes in the same group. The *flags* member of the structure allows us to control this exception handling. It is a bitmap that can have any combination of the following values: *Ppropagate*, *Pnotifyleader*, *Prestrict*, *Prestricted*, and *Pkilled*.

We have already seen that process table entries may reside on a linked list of ready processes. In addition to that data structure, there is a doubly linked list of all processes. The members *prev* and *next* are used to identify the adjacent elements of the list. Of course, searching a linked list takes $O(n)$ time (proportional to the number of items in the list), and if there are many processes, then this can become significant. To help speed things up, we also maintain a hash table of all processes in the system, as illustrated in Figure 7-3(c). Processes that hash to the same bucket are kept in another linked list, which uses the *pidlink* structure member to point to the next processes in the list. Finally, processes that are part of the same processes group are kept in another doubly linked list defined by the *prgprev* and *prgnext* members.

As with the *flags* member, the *exval* and *exstr* members are used for exception handling. They point to the strings that are used to represent the actual exception.

The next two members of the **Prog** structure are pointers to functions. The first, *addrun*, is normally *nil*, which indicates that when adding this process to the ready queue, we call the default function, which also goes by the name *addrun*( ). In a couple of cases, we set this pointer to point to another function. The other function pointer is called *xec* and is normally set to point to the function *xec*( ), which handles the interpretation of a quantum's worth of Dis instructions. As with *addrun*, there are a few special cases where we set *xec* to point to other functions.

The final part of the **Prog** structure is the member *osenv*, which points to an **Osenv** structure that contains additional information about the process. Among these data are the name space, open files, and environment variables. For hosted Inferno, we also store information about the user in the host environment.

7.4 Process Creation

New user processes in Inferno are created with the **spawn** statement in Limbo. We won't trace the complete chain of code that processes the **spawn** command. The basic idea is that the **spawn** statement is reduced to either the **spawn** or the **mspawn** Dis instruction. In the following discussion, we trace the steps of process creation from the point where the virtual machine processes the instruction to the point where the new process has been created and exists on the lists illustrated earlier in Figure 7-3. These steps can be summarized as follows:

1. Transfer control from the virtual machine code to internal kernel code.

2. Create and initialize the process table entry for the new process.

3. Add the process to the linked list and hash tables that make up the process table.

4. Make the new process ready.

The flow does not strictly follow this order, however. In particular, the initialization of the new process table entry is divided into several parts that are intermingled with some of the other steps.

7.4.1 Interpreting the Process Creation Instruction

We begin following the code with the interpretation of the **spawn** instruction in libin-terp/xec.c:

OP(*spawn*)
{
   Prog *p*;

The first step is calling *newprog( )*, described next, to create a process with the current process as the parent.

   $p = newprog(currun( ), R.M);$

Now we set the saved program counter to point to the function that was specified as part of the **spawn** statement in the application. When the new process is next scheduled, this will cause it to resume (begin) execution at the beginning of that function.

   $p\text{-}R.PC = *(\textbf{Inst} **) \ R.d;$

These last two calls create and set up the stack for the new process.

```
        newstack(p);
        unframe();
    }
```

7.4.2 Implementing Process Creation

The interpretation of both the **spawn** and the **mspawn** instructions ends up in the function *newprog*(), which is declared in **emu/port/dis.c** as follows:

```
Prog *newprog(Prog *p, Modlink *m)
{
    Heap *h;
    Prog *n, **ph;
    Osenv *on, *op;
    static int pidnum;
```

7.4.2.1 Creating the Process Table Entry

Our first step is allocating space for the process table entry (PTE) and for the structure holding environment information for the process. As usual, we are careful to check for failure before continuing.

```
    n = malloc(sizeof(Prog) + sizeof(Osenv));
    if (n ≡ 0) {
        if (p ≡ nil)
            panic("no␣memory");
        else
            error(exNomem);
    }
```

7.4.2.2 Setting the PID

Now we need to set the new process's ID number (PID). As discussed previously, the process IDs are sequentially assigned. We initially don't point to any group list. Later, we will add this process to its parent's group, if it has a parent.

```
    n→pid = ++pidnum;
    if (n→pid ≤ 0)
        panic("no␣pids");
    n→group = nil;
```

7.4.2.3   Adding to the Process Table

Next, we insert the new process at the end of the process table. As usual with insertion into a linked list, we have a special case when the list is empty. In practice, the only time the list is actually empty is when we create the first process, when we call *schedmod( )* from *disinit( )*. Otherwise, this check is defensive programming.

```
if (isched.tail ≠ nil) {
    n→prev = isched.tail;
    isched.tail→next = n;
}
else {
    isched.head = n;
    n→prev = nil;
}
isched.tail = n;
```

There are times when we want to look up a process by its PID. Searching the list linearly could get time consuming if we have a large number of processes. Instead, we keep a hash table using the PID as the key. The function *pidlook( )* returns a pointer to a pointer (double indirection) to the PTE of the process whose PID is passed as the argument. If the specified process does not exist, then *pidlook( )* returns a pointer to the last pointer it examined. This is the pointer that will be used to point to the new process. This next bit of code puts the new process into the table.

```
ph = pidlook(n→pid);
if (*ph ≠ nil)
    panic("dup␣pid");
n→pidlink = nil;
*ph = n;
```

7.4.2.4   Initializing the Process Table Entry

Here, we set the rest of the process table entry for a new process, assuming there is no parent. Later, we override some of these assignments to inherit properties from the parent process, if there is one. We make our new environment point to the space we allocated for it earlier. Also, we flag that the code for this process will be interpreted by the normal virtual machine interpreter, *xec( )*. Every process executes code that belongs to a module that we get as the parameter *m*. Because we now have a new process that uses that module code, we increment the reference count for the module.

```
n→osenv = (Osenv *) ((uchar *) n + sizeof(Prog));
n→xec = xec;
n→quanta = PQUANTA;
n→flags = 0;
n→exval = H;
```

$$h = \text{D2H}(m);$$
$$h\text{-}ref\mathbin{+\kern-0.2em+};$$
$$Setmark\,(h);$$
$$n\text{-}R.M = m;$$
$$n\text{-}R.MP = m\text{-}MP;$$
if $(m\text{-}MP \neq H)$
$\qquad Setmark\,(\text{D2H}(m\text{-}MP));$

7.4.2.5   Marking the Process Ready

Every new process starts life in the *Pready* state, and so it needs to be on the ready list. That's the purpose of *addrun( )*, which we examine later.

$$addrun\,(n);$$

7.4.2.6   Inheriting the Parent's Properties

The last part of creating a new process is inheriting from the parent process. Of course, if there's no parent, nothing is inherited. The no-parent case happens only when we create the first process in *disinit( )*, discussed in Section 3.4.4. In that case, we create a new process group and we are done. Otherwise, we need to inherit things like the flags, the environment, and the user name, and we need to add the new process to its parent's process group. As with the module data, we need to increment the reference counts for some of the data structures shared with the parent. We must also adjust the list of processes pointed to by the environment members *waitq* and *childq*. They point to queues used to communicate strings to other processes. In particular, they are used to send the exit status to a process reading the /**proc**/*n*/**wait** file, and they are used to communicate with a process in the host OS that is invoked with the command device.

if $(p \equiv nil)$ {
$\qquad newgrp\,(n);$
$\qquad$**return** $n;$
}
$addgrp\,(n, p);$
$n\text{-}flags = p\text{-}flags;$
if $(p\text{-}flags\ \&\ Prestrict)$
$\qquad n\text{-}flags\mathrel{|=} Prestricted;$
$memmove\,(n\text{-}osenv, p\text{-}osenv, \textbf{sizeof}\,(\textbf{Osenv}));$
$op = p\text{-}osenv;$
$on = n\text{-}osenv;$
$on\text{-}waitq = op\text{-}childq;$
$on\text{-}childq = nil;$
$on\text{-}debug = nil;$
$incref\,(\&on\text{-}pgrp\text{-}r);$
$incref\,(\&on\text{-}fgrp\text{-}r);$

```
    incref (&on→egrp→r);
    if (on→sigs ≠ nil)
        incref (&on→sigs→r);
    on→user = nil;
    kstrdup (&on→user, op→user);
    on→errstr = on→errbuf0;
    on→syserrstr = on→errbuf1;
    return n;
}
```

At this point, we have finished creating a new process table entry and adding the process to the ready list. Our last step is returning a pointer to the new process table entry back to the caller. In Inferno, that's about all we need to do to create the process itself. Before *newprog( )* is called, the module containing the code the new process is to run has already been loaded. Any memory allocated to the new process is handled elsewhere.

7.5 Process Destruction

A process may come to the end of its life in one of three ways. First, if the function identified in a **spawn** statement returns, then the process created by the **spawn** exits. Likewise, if a process executes the **exit** statement, then it terminates. Finally, a process can be terminated by another process that writes a `kill` or `killgrp` message to a special control file associated with the first process. In all three cases, control ends up in the *delprog( )* function, where we begin tracing the code. It is declared in emu/port/dis.c as:

```
void delprog(Prog *p, char *msg)
{
    Osenv *o;
    Prog **ph;
```

Here's where we make use of the *waitq* and the *childq* to send our exit status back to a waiting process.

```
    tellsomeone(p, msg);      /* call before being removed from prog list */
```

The main thing done in this section is letting go of the name space, open files, environment variables, and so on that are used by the process being deleted. Because these operations generally require services from the host OS, we need to bracket them with calls to *release( )* and *acquire( )*.

```
    o = p→osenv;
    release( );
    closepgrp(o→pgrp);
    closefgrp(o→fgrp);
```

$closeegrp(o{\to}egrp);$
$closesigs(o{\to}sigs);$
$acquire(\ );$

Next, we take this process out of the process groups where it may reside.

$delgrp(p);$

Now, we remove the process table entry from the linked list of all processes.

if $(p{\to}prev)$
  $p{\to}prev{\to}next = p{\to}next;$
else
  $isched.head = p{\to}next;$
if $(p{\to}next)$
  $p{\to}next{\to}prev = p{\to}prev;$
else
  $isched.tail = p{\to}prev;$

Similarly, we remove the process from the hash table w_ use to make lookups faster.

$ph = pidlook(p{\to}pid);$
if $(*ph \equiv nil)$
  $panic("lost_\sqcup pid");$
$*ph = p{\to}pidlink;$

Next, we remove the process from the ready list if it's there. It might seem strange that we don't account for the case where the process being deleted is ready but not at the head of the list. It turns out that *delprog( )* is called in only two places. One is a case where the currently running process is exiting, which is the case this code handles. The other is when a process is being killed from outside itself. In that case, ready processes are removed from the list before *delprog( )* is called.

if $(p \equiv isched.runhd)$ {
  $isched.runhd = p{\to}link;$
  if $(p{\to}link \equiv nil)$
    $isched.runtl = nil;$
}

The final stage is marking the process table entry with an invalid value for the state in case someone tries to look at this process table entry. (Note that we use the hexadecimal value spelled out by the words "dead beef" for the invalid value.) Then, we free the internal data structures allocated for this process.

```
    p⃗state = #deadbeef;
    free(o⃗user);
    if (p⃗killstr)
        free(p⃗killstr);
    if (p⃗exstr)
        free(p⃗exstr);
    free(p);
}
```

One aspect of process termination is conspicuous by its absence, namely freeing the memory used by the process. This is handled elsewhere. The code that calls *delprog( )* also calls code that goes through the memory used by the process decrementing the reference count on each block of memory. As we see in Chapter 11, these memory blocks are only become free when the reference count goes to 0.

7.6   Process Scheduling

Process scheduling in Inferno is handled in **emu/port/dis.c**. The two different types of processes are scheduled differently. Kernel processes are scheduled very differently in hosted and native Inferno. In the native case, these processes are handled much as in any other operating system. However, because there is only one interpreter *kproc* running at a time, scheduling amounts to simply selecting one of the idle *kprocs* and letting it run until it blocks or yields the CPU to another *kproc*. In a hosted environment, the kernel processes are threads in the host OS. As such, they are scheduled by the host operating system. The second type of process is the user process that is running Dis code. These processes are scheduled by the Dis interpreter. It interprets each instruction in turn. Although in most operating systems the quantum is a measure of time, for these processes, it's an instruction count. When the interpreter has executed the appropriate number of instructions, we preempt the process, schedule the next one, and switch to the new one to be interpreted.

7.6.1   Adding to the Ready List

Before looking at the scheduler itself, we look at the functions for manipulating the ready list. We've seen a few cases of adding a process to the ready list. As discussed earlier, this is handled by the *addrun( )* function. The first thing it does is call a special version of *addrun( )* if one is defined.

```
void addrun(Prog *p)
{
    if (p⃗addrun ≠ 0) {
        p⃗addrun(p);
        return;
    }
```

For the usual case, we fall through to this point. Here we set the state of the process to *Pready*.

$$p\text{-}state = Pready;$$

Finally, we insert it into the linked list of ready processes. We always add newly ready processes to the tail of the list.

```
p-link = nil;
if (isched.runhd ≡ nil)
    isched.runhd = p;
else
    isched.runtl-link = p;
isched.runtl = p;
}
```

7.6.2   Removing from the Ready List

Naturally, we also have to remove processes from the Ready state. Of course we have to specify the state to which we are transitioning.

```
Prog *delrun(int state)
{
    Prog *p;
```

Referring back to the state machine in Figure 7-2, we notice that the only transition from the Ready state is to the Running state. This implies that the current process is the only one we remove from the ready queue.

```
p = isched.runhd;
p-state = state;
```

Because we never remove any list item but the first, this list manipulation code is significantly simpler than it would be for the more general case.

```
isched.runhd = p-link;
if (p-link ≡ nil)
    isched.runtl = nil;
return p;
}
```

7.6.3   Time-Sharing

We now look at the details of the scheduler by looking at the function *vmachine*( ), which we saw called as the last initialization step from *disinit*( ). It is also the function that new interpreter kernel processes are created to run. It is defined in emu/port/dis.c.

```
void vmachine(void *a)
{
    Prog *r;
    Osenv *o;
    int cycles;
    static int gccounter;
    USED(a);
```

The function *startup*( ) gets called only here. It ensures that the current process is identified as handled by this virtual machine interpreter *kproc* and clears the *idle* flag.

```
    startup();
```

The next section is an error handler. As discussed earlier, the *waserror*( ) call uses the C *setjmp*( ) mechanism. It marks a point where control can be transferred from anywhere in the code in case of an error. The control transfer is invoked by a call to *longjmp*( ). We don't ever come back here in normal operation.

```
    while (waserror()) {
        if (up→iprog ≠ nil)
            acquire();
        if (handler(up→env→errstr) ≡ 0) {
            propex(currun(), up→env→errstr);
            progexit();
        }
        up→env = &up→defenv;
    }
```

Now we drop into the infinite loop where the operating system will sit as it does time-sharing. We schedule and give a quantum to one process each time through this loop.

```
    cycles = 0;
    for ( ; ; ) {
```

For each iteration, our first test is to see if there are any ready processes. If not, then we can fall into our idle tasks. The *execatidle*( ) function runs the garbage collector, which attempts to reclaim unused space.

```
if (tready(nil) ≡ 0) {
    execatidle();
    strcpy(up→text,"idle");
    Sleep(&isched.irend, tready, 0);
    strcpy(up→text,"dis");
}
```

If there are processes in the *vmq* list, then we want to give them a chance to run peri-odically. As described earlier, such processes are other instances of the interpreter that had been blocked but are now ready again. The *iyield()* function turns control over to another kernel process.

```
if (isched.vmq ≠ nil ∧ (isched.runhd ≡ nil ∨ ++cycles > 2)) {
    iyield();
    cycles = 0;
}
```

At last, we get to the actual scheduling of interpreted processes. We take the first pro-cess on the list and call its execution function. Normally, that is the function *xec()* in libinterp/xec.c, which is discussed in Section 7.6.4. Although *xec()* handles the saving and restoring of the Dis virtual machine registers, we take care of the floating-point reg-isters here. As a result, the context switching mechanism is split between *vmachine()* and *xec()*. Though it's a little unusual for context switching to be split in this way, the different handling of floating-point and other registers is not. For many machines, saving and restoring floating-point registers is done with different instructions than those that are used for the other registers.

```
r = isched.runhd;
if (r ≠ nil) {            .
    o = r→osenv;
    up→env = o;
    FPrestore(&o→fpu);
    r→xec(r);
    FPsave(&o→fpu);
```

Now it's time to rotate the list to make the next process on the list the one that gets run the next time through the loop. The first three lines here are guards to ensure that the list hasn't changed while we gave the current process a quantum in the sense that it's no longer the head of the list. They also ensure that there's more than one process on the list. (Reordering the list doesn't mean anything if the list is empty and is pointless if there's only one process there.) After we pass those tests, the rest is easy. We just pull the first element off the list and stick it on the end. In short, this is a simple round-robin scheduler. There is no notion of priority, and all processes are treated equally at all times.

```
    if (isched.runhd ≠ nil)
    if (r ≡ isched.runhd)
    if (isched.runhd ≠ isched.runtl) {
        isched.runhd = r→link;
        r→link = nil;
        isched.runtl→link = r;
        isched.runtl = r;
    }
    up→env = &up→defenv;
}
```

Even when we are never idle, we still need to run the garbage collector periodically. That's what the last section of this function does.

```
    if (isched.runhd ≠ nil)
    if ((++gccounter & #FF) ≡ 0 ∨ memlow()) {
        gcbusy ++;
        up→type = BusyGC;
        pushrun(up→prog);
        rungc(isched.head);
        up→type = Interp;
        delrunq(up→prog);
    }
  }
}
```

7.6.4   Running a Time Slice

The last of the Inferno process management functions we discuss is $xec()$ in libinterp/xec.c. This function is actually part of the virtual machine interpreter, but we discuss it here because it illustrates how context switching works for user processes in Inferno. Throughout, we need access to the current process's process table entry. A pointer to it is passed into the function in the parameter p.

```
void xec(Prog *p)
{
    int op;
```

The first step is copying the saved registers from the current process's process table entry to a global set of registers that is used by the virtual machine interpreter. As discussed in Section 7.3.4, the R member of the process table entry is where we save the virtual machine's registers when a process is blocked or preempted. The global variable R is a copy of the current process's registers, and it contains the ones on which all the instructions operate. This step corresponds to restoring a process's context as the last step of a context switch. At the same time, we also set the pointer to the module data. The saved register set includes the pointer M, which points to a structure describing the module of Dis code the process is currently running. That structure, in turn, contains the pointer MP, which points to the data owned by this instance of this module. We copy that pointer directly into the current register set to speed up access.

$$R = p\text{-}R;$$
$$R.MP = R.M\text{→}MP;$$

Next, we set an instruction counter to *quanta*, which was set to 2048 when the process was created. This *IC* member of the current register set is decremented for each instruction we interpret. When it reaches 0, we know the time slice is over.

$$R.IC = p\text{-}quanta;$$

If an event occurred to kill the process since it last ran, then we handle that case now.

if $(p\text{-}kill \neq nil)$ {
    char $*m$;
    $m = p\text{-}kill$;
    $p\text{-}kill = nil$;
    error (m) ;
}

Code that is just-in-time compiled is handled differently from purely interpreted code.

if $(R.M\text{→}compiled)$
    comvec( );

This loop is the core of program execution for interpreted user processes. Just like a real CPU, we repeatedly fetch an instruction and execute it. For each instruction, we increment the program counter so that it points to the next instruction each time.

    else
        do {

The next two lines get the operation code and the operands before we advance the program counter. Because there are a number of different instruction formats, the decoding for a particular instruction is handled by an array of functions called *dec*.

        $dec[R.PC\text{→}add]( )$;
        $op = R.PC\text{→}op$;

Now we can increment the program counter. Any references after this will be to the next instruction rather than the current one.

$R.PC$ ++;

The array *optab* is an array of function pointers, one for each Dis instruction. Here we call the one that corresponds to the current instruction. The value *op* we saved before incrementing the program counter is the current instruction's operation code.

$optab[op]($);

The last step of each instruction interpretation is decrementing the instruction count and asking if the time slice is finished. The *IC* member of the current register set was initialized before the loop to the value of *quanta*. When it reaches 0, we have executed that many instructions, and we preempt the process because its time slice has ended.

} **while** $(--R.IC \neq 0)$;

Before returning, we copy the registers from the virtual machine's internal set, R, back to the current process table entry's R structure.

$p\text{-}R = R$;
}

When we return from *xec*( ), we go back to *vmachine*( ), where we schedule the next process to run.

7.7   Summary

The Dis virtual machine at the heart of Inferno leads to a number of unusual process management features. We have two classes of processes in Inferno: user processes and kernel processes. Both require mechanisms for creation and scheduling. However, because the process types are fundamentally different, the mechanisms are different. In this chapter, we have given a general overview of the issues concerning and the representation of kernel processes. We have also looked in some detail at the creation, destruction, and scheduling of user processes.

7.8   Exercises

1. Why can't JIT-compiled code be handled the same way as interpreted code in terms of the quantum?

2. In the per-instruction loop of *xec*( ), why can't we call the instruction execution function with the following line?

   $optab[R.PC\text{-}op]($);

3. If *xec*( ) handles both JIT-compiled code as well as interpreted code, then what value would there be in making the *xec* member of the **Prog** structure point to a different function?

4. In the infinite scheduling loop of *vmachine*( ), we check only the *vmq* list to see if there are any processes on it. Why do we not also look at the *idlevmq* list?

5. Why do you suppose that the *isched* structure has a pointer to the tail of the *vmq* list and not to the tail of the *idlevmq* list?

6. Modify Inferno so that process ID numbers are reused when the counter rolls over. You should make sure that no two processes simultaneously have the same PID. At the same time, make sure that a process ID is not reused until all other ones have been used.

7. Extend the *isched* structure to include some statistics regarding the operation of the process management subsystem of Inferno. In particular, you should keep track of how many processes are currently in the ready queue and how many are currently in the process queue specified by the *head* and *tail* pointers. Print out both values each time one is changed. Also, whenever the scheduler becomes idle (the run queue becomes empty), check the lengths of the lists to verify the correctness of your counters. If the counts don't match, then produce a report to that effect and take any other course that is appropriate.

8. Change Inferno to use a priority scheduler. Implement the strategy discussed in Chapter 5 where interactive processes are given priority over compute-bound processes.

9. Modify Inferno to allow a limited number of interpreter kernel processes to run at once. This would allow hosted Inferno to take advantage of multiple CPUs.

10. Modify Inferno's scheduler to implement the CTSS multilevel feedback queue.

Chapter 8

Process Management in Linux

In this chapter, we examine how the process management principles discussed in Chapter 5 are applied in the Linux kernel. Our focus is on the representation, creation, and scheduling of processes. We present these techniques through selected excerpts from the Linux source code.

Over the history of Linux, there have been a number of changes in the details of its process management. Most recently, a major overhaul of the scheduler appeared in the version 2.5 series development kernels and subsequently in the version 2.6 production kernels.

We begin considering the application of process management principles to Linux with a look at some of Linux's process management system calls. The next topic we study is the representation of processes through the process table and the process state stored there. In the remainder of this chapter, we present a detailed examination of portions of the Linux version 2.6 source code that implement process creation and the Linux scheduler.

8.1 Process and Threads

Linux does not distinguish between processes and threads. Instead, it takes a unified approach like that discussed in Section 5.3. The *clone( )* system call allows us to create processes with selected parts of the parent being shared with the child. Regardless of which resources are shared, Linux treats all processes the same way and uses the same representation and scheduling for them. Internally, the Linux source code refers to these processes and threads as **tasks**. Linux does, however, provide a means of specifying that some processes (threads) are part of a group. It also supports several system calls that operate on a whole thread group. We omit coverage of these calls in keeping with our focus on individual processes and threads.

8.1.1 Kernel Threads in Linux

In Chapter 5, we use the term **kernel thread** to describe user process threads that are managed by the kernel to distinguish them from threads provided by application-level libraries. However, in Linux, the term kernel thread is used in another way. Here, it is used to describe threads of execution that operate entirely in the kernel memory space rather than having a user memory space. In effect, this version of kernel threads allows us to write the kernel itself as a multithreaded program.

8.1.2   Process Relationships

In Section 4.3.3, we discuss how the init process in Linux is created and started. In doing so, we created a kernel thread, attached it to the console for input and output, and executed the init program in it. This process is the original ancestor of all other processes and threads in the system. Every other process is created by another one. The process that initiates a new process creation is called the **parent process**, and the newly created process is called the **child process**. As a result, every process except init has a single parent and might have zero or more children resulting in a tree of processes.

8.2   System Calls

Among the nearly 300 system calls in the Intel i386 version of Linux, a substantial number of calls are related to process management. We highlight several of them that are some of the most commonly used ones and some that are relevant to later discussion in this chapter. These relevant system calls include the following:

- *fork*(): This is the original UNIX process creation system call. The newly created child process is a copy of the parent process that issued the *fork*() call. They both resume execution with the return from *fork*(), with the only difference being the return value from the call. The parent process receives the child's process ID as a return value, whereas the child receives 0 as the return value.

- *vfork*(): This variation on *fork*() was introduced in the 4BSD series of UNIX implementations. Its raison d'être is to eliminate the copy of the parent's memory space in the common case where the *fork*() is quickly followed by one of the *exec*() family of calls. The child uses the parent's memory space until it issues one of the *exec*() calls or an *exit*() call. In the meantime, the parent is suspended until the child is no longer using its memory space. In Linux, the need for this call has largely been eliminated through the use of the **copy on write** technique discussed in detail in Section 9.6.6. Using this technique, we copy only those parts of the parent's memory space that the child modifies. They share the rest of the memory space.

- *clone*(): We allude to this call in the previous section. It provides a general means of implementing process creation. It allows us to specify which of the parent's resources are to be shared with the child and which are to be copied. As such, the function underlying *clone*() is also used to implement both the *fork*() and *vfork*() calls, as well as thread creation by library calls such as the POSIX *pthread_create*() call.

- *_exit*(): Whereas *clone*() is the primary interface for creating processes in Linux, *_exit*() is the primary means for process termination. Applications that are ready to finish generally either return from the *main*( ) function or call *exit*( ). Code linked by default with applications calls *exit*( ) upon return from *main*( ). The implementation of *exit*( ) performs some application-level cleanup of open files and then issues the *_exit*( ) system call. The kernel then frees the process's resources and makes an exit status available to the terminating process's parent.

- *kill*( ): There are times when we cannot rely on a process to voluntarily terminate properly. However, Linux, like UNIX before it, does not permit one process to directly terminate another. Instead, it provides a more general mechanism called **signals** that allows one process to send another the application-level equivalent of an interrupt. The *kill*( ) system call is the means by which a process sends a signal. For some signals, the default behavior is to terminate the process. For most signals, the process may set up a signal handler that is invoked when the signal is received.

- *wait4*( ) and *waitpid*( ): These calls allow a parent process to inquire as to the state of a child. The primary purpose of these calls is to notify the parent when the child has exited and to deliver the child's exit status to the parent. These calls are also flexible enough to allow the parent to inquire about either a specific child or any children, and they allow the parent to inquire without blocking if desired.

- *execve*( ): Because all process creation takes place (directly or indirectly) through the *clone*( ) system call, which copies the parent process, we must have some mechanism for causing a process to run a program other than the one with which it started. This is the purpose of the *execve*( ) system call. It allows a process to specify a program to begin running in place of the current one. The calling process also specifies a list of strings, each of which is a parameter to the new program. This list is used by the user interface to implement command-line parameters. The *execve*( ) call also provides the interface for the calling process to pass a list of strings, each defining an environment variable for the new program. The standard C library also provides a number of variations on the *execve*( ) call. All of them are implemented using *execve*( ).

- *nice*( ): The *nice*( ) system call gives the calling process the ability to adjust its priority level. As we discuss in Section 8.6, this value biases the dynamic scheduling priority of a process. Higher values of **nice** represent lower priorities. Only the superuser may call *nice*( ) to lower the value of nice (increase the priority).

- *sched_setscheduler*( ): Linux provides three different scheduling policies, two for real-time processes and one for normal time-sharing. This call allows a process with sufficient privileges to change the policy and priority level the scheduler uses for the specified process.

- *sched_getscheduler*( ): This call allows a process to query which scheduling policy is currently in effect for the specified process.

- *sched_yield*( ): Particularly in the case of real-time scheduling, a process might want to give up the remainder of its current time slice but not enter a Blocked state. The *sched_yield*( ) system call allows a process to do just that.

8.3 Process State

The set of process states in Linux is much like that in our generic state machine illustrated in Figure 5-1. Specifically, the Linux process states can be described as follows:

- **TASK_RUNNING**: This state encompasses both the Running and Ready states in our generic state machine. As with many other OSs, the distinction between a process in the Ready state and one in the Running state is made separately from the state information kept in the process table. In particular, a macro called *current* evaluates to a pointer to the process table entry of the currently running process.

- **TASK_INTERRUPTIBLE**: This state is among the three states in Linux that represent a blocked process. The **INTERRUPTIBLE** in this state's name indicates that a process in this state can be awakened by signals sent by other processes issuing the *kill*( ) system call.

- **TASK_UNINTERRUPTIBLE**: This Blocked state differs from the interruptible one in that processes in this state do not come out of a Blocked state in response to signals.

- **TASK_STOPPED**: A process is placed in the Stopped state in response to a signal called **SIGSTOP**. The process remains in this state until it receives a **SIGCONT** signal. In effect, processes in the Stopped state are suspended until resumed by another process. These signals are used to implement **job control** in several of the user interface shells. Although there are other signals that can result in a Stopped state, these job control signals are the most common use of the Stopped state.

- **TASK_TRACED**: This state is used as part of the implementation of a tracing facility, where a process can control the execution of another process. It is used primarily in the implementation of debuggers. We largely ignore this state in our presentation here.

- **EXIT_ZOMBIE**: A process is a zombie if it has exited but its parent has not yet issued one of the *wait*( ) calls to pick up its exit status.

- **EXIT_DEAD**: This state is used very briefly in the unusual case when a process terminates and we don't need to notify its parent. Such a process can be completely removed from the system immediately.

The relationships among these states are summarized in the state machine shown in Figure 8-1. For clarity and to keep our focus on the life cycle of a typical process, we omit the ellipses that correspond to the **TASK_TRACED** and **EXIT_DEAD** states.

The file include/linux/sched.h gives a number of definitions of constants, structures, and function prototypes used in process management. Those in this file are the ones that are

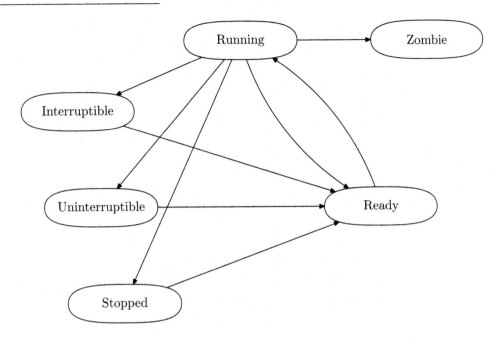

Figure 8-1: Linux Process State Machine

independent of machine architecture. Architecture-specific definitions are given in other header files. In this file, we find the Linux process states defined as:

```
#define TASK_RUNNING  0
#define TASK_INTERRUPTIBLE  1
#define TASK_UNINTERRUPTIBLE  2
#define TASK_STOPPED  4
#define TASK_TRACED  8
#define EXIT_ZOMBIE  16
#define EXIT_DEAD  32
```

(There is actually one more defined, TASK_NONINTERACTIVE, but it is used in only very rare cases.) The first thing we notice about these values is that they are all powers of 2. In other words, the binary representation of all these states are integers, each with a single bit set. From that, we might infer that a process might be in some combination of these states at some point in time. However, these values are not used that way. We do sometimes create values with more than one bit set, but these values are used to quickly test whether a process is in one of a set of states. We never set the state of a process to more than one of these at a time.

8.4   Process Table

To get a complete picture of the process table structure in Linux, we have to understand one aspect of the process's memory layout. When the kernel runs during a process's time slice, either as a result of a system call or of some other interrupt, the kernel must have a stack on which to operate. Normally, we give the kernel some stack space separate from the stack used by the process. Many architectures, including the Intel x86, provide hardware support for switching the stack on an interrupt. In Linux, we reserve a small part of each process's memory space for a stack that the kernel uses when it is executing during that process's time slice. The default size of this kernel stack is 8 KB.

Although the connection between the kernel stack and the process table might not be very clear, it turns out to be central to the implementation of the *current* macro mentioned earlier. When kernel code is executing, the current stack pointer points into the kernel stack of the current process. Because this stack is aligned on an address that is a multiple of its size, we can find the lowest address of the kernel stack by masking off the low-order bits of the stack pointer. This operation results in a pointer to the first part of the process's process table entry. At the lowest part of the kernel stack memory space, we have a structure of type **struct thread_info**. The details of the structure are defined in include/asm-i386/thread_info.h. Most of this structure does not concern our discussion here. However, the first member of the structure is declared as:

struct task_struct **task*;

This structure member points to the main part of the process table entry for this process. Now we have the last piece we need for the macro *current*. We take the current stack pointer when running kernel code, mask off the low-order bits to get a pointer to a **struct thread_info** and then dereference the *task* member of the structure to get a pointer to the main process table entry structure for the current process. This arrangement is illustrated in Figure 8-2. As mentioned earlier, the kernel stack on the left in the figure is stored in the process's memory space. The task structure on the right is kept in the kernel's memory space. We should note that this mechanism is architecture dependent. Developers for each architecture are free to implement *current* as they see fit. Our description here applies to the implementation for the Intel x86 architecture.

The *task* pointer we've just described points to a structure that's defined in the file include/linux/sched.h. This structure contains a substantial number of members that describe all of the aspects of a process we need to manage. In the interest of brevity, we focus here only on those members that are part of the process management functions we examine. The ones we discuss here represent a diverse set of process characteristics primarily related to process state, creation, termination, and scheduling.

- **volatile long** *state*; This member holds the process state discussed in the previous section. However, it holds only those that begin with **TASK_** and not those beginning with **EXIT_**. It is declared **volatile** because it can be changed in several different threads of execution. This declaration tells the compiler that it cannot do optimizations that assume its value will not change between references.

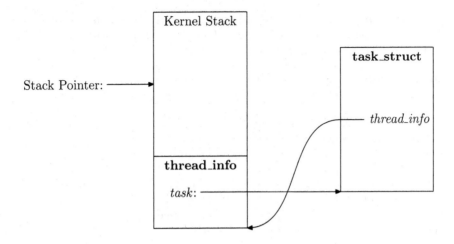

Figure 8-2: Linux Process Table Structures

- **struct thread_info** *∗thread_info*; This points back to the **thread_info** structure at the bottom of this process's kernel stack space.

- **int** *prio*, *static_prio*; These two members maintain the priorities used in the scheduler. The one called *static_prio* holds the value of the process's nice parameter, and *prio* holds the process's current dynamic priority. In reality, the situation is slightly more complicated. The value stored in *static_prio* is really $n + 120$, where n is the nice value. The reason for this is to allow a set of 100 priority values designated as real-time priorities that are all higher than the normal time-sharing priorities. Because $-20 \leq n \leq 19$, this makes all normal values of nice greater (lower priority) than all real-time priorities.

- **struct list_head** *run_list*; This structure contains the pointers (*next* and *prev*) that make up the doubly linked list of ready processes at a particular priority. The way these pointers are used is a little unusual and deserves some explanation. It might be expected that the *next* pointer in the structure would point to the **task_struct** structure for the next process on the list. However, it points instead to the *run_list* structure within that **task_struct** structure. Macros are available that allow us to access the structure that contains a **list_head** structure to which we have a pointer.

- **struct prio_array** *∗array*; As we discuss in more detail later in this chapter, processes move back and forth between two different multilevel feedback queues, one for ready processes that still have some time left to run and the other for those that have used their entire time slice. The *array* member points to the structure that describes the queue on which this process currently resides.

- **unsigned long** *sleep_avg*; The Linux scheduler gives a priority boost to processes that spend most of their time blocked. This value records a measure of how much recent time has been spent blocked.

- **unsigned long long** *timestamp*; We use *timestamp* to record the times of certain events for which we later want to know how much time has elapsed.

- **unsigned long** *policy*; This member takes on one of the three values `SCHED_FIFO`, `SCHED_RR`, and `SCHED_NORMAL` set by the *sched_setscheduler*( ) system call. We discuss these three scheduling policies in detail later in this chapter.

- **unsigned int** *time_slice*, *first_time_slice*; When a process is placed into a ready queue, its quantum (the length of its time slice) is determined and stored in *time_slice*. The *first_time_slice* flag is set prior to a process receiving its first time slice and then cleared once it has used that first time slice.

- **struct list_head** *tasks*; This structure contains the pointers that make up a doubly linked list of all processes in the system. It is used like the same-typed structure for the ready queues described earlier in this section.

- **long** *exit_state*; When a process is exiting, this is where its state (either `EXIT_ZOMBIE` or `EXIT_DEAD`) is stored.

- **int** *exit_code*, *exit_signal*; We make several references in this chapter to a process's exit status, which is retrieved by the parent process when it issues a *wait4*( ) or a *waitpid*( ) system call. This value is stored in *exit_code*, and the signal that caused the process to terminate, if any, is stored in *exit_signal*.

- **pid_t** *pid*; This is the process ID (PID) number. At any point in time, this ID is unique among all the processes that are present on the system. ID numbers do, however, get reused, so a PID is not unique over the lifetime of the system.

- **struct task_struct** *∗parent*; This member points to the process table entry of this process's parent.

- **struct list_head** *children*; The *next* part of the *children* structure serves as the head pointer to a list of the child processes.

- **struct list_head** *sibling*; The pointers in this structure define a doubly linked list of all of the children of this process's parent.

- **unsigned long** *rt_priority*; For processes that are scheduled according to either the `SCHED_FIFO` or `SCHED_RR` policies, the priority is stored in *rt_priority*.

- **struct thread_struct** *thread*; This structure holds the process's registers that are saved and restored as part of a context switch. Not all registers are stored in this structure, as some are saved on the stack as part of normal interrupt processing.

8.5   Process Creation

Processes in Linux can be created by any of the three system calls *fork( )*, *vfork( )*, or *clone( )*. For the Intel x86 version of Linux, the functions handling all three of these system calls are defined in arch/i386/kernel/process.c, and all three call the function *do_fork( )* defined in kernel/fork.c. This function has three main responsibilities, discussed here. First, *do_fork( )* calls *copy_process( )* to do the work of actually creating the child process. Even though its name contains the word copy, it uses the *clone_flags* parameter to determine which of the parent's resources are copied and which are shared. The second responsibility of *do_fork( )* is that of setting up the suspension of the parent if we get here through a *vfork( )* system call. Finally, *do_fork( )* is also responsible for setting the initial state of the child. Children can be created either in a Ready state or in a Stopped state.

8.5.1   Handling the System Call

In the following declaration for *do_fork( )*, the parameter that interests us the most is *clone_flags*. This long integer is treated as a set of one-bit flags that control the copy versus share behavior of *do_fork( )*. We don't attempt to fully describe each flag. Rather, we discuss some of them as we encounter them. In most cases, *stack_start* is the calling process's current stack pointer. The *regs* parameter points to a structure containing the machine registers saved on entry to the system call. The parameter *stack_size* ends up being unused, and the final two parameters are used only in special cases, which we do not examine here.

```
long do_fork(unsigned long clone_flags, unsigned long stack_start,
    struct pt_regs *regs, unsigned long stack_size,
    int __user *parent_tidptr, int __user *child_tidptr)
{
    struct task_struct *p;
    int trace = 0;
```

8.5.1.1   Assigning the Process ID

In this initializing declaration, we assign the PID of the new process. Rather than present the code for the implementation of *alloc_pid( )*, we describe what it basically does. It maintains a global variable called *last_pid*, which is the PID it most recently assigned. When called, it begins by setting the tentative PID to *last_pid* + 1. Because PIDs can be reused, we must ask whether this tentative PID is currently in use. Much of the complexity of *alloc_pid( )* comes from the need to make this determination quickly. It maintains a bitmap of all possible PIDs, allocating it as needed. If the tentative PID is in use, then we begin searching at that point for the next unused one. If we search all the way to the highest allowed PID (normally 32767), then we wrap around and begin searching from PID 301 up to *last_pid*. If we fail to allocate a PID, we return −EAGAIN, which indicates that the system call failed, but that the process can try again later because another process's termination will make a PID available. Assuming we find an unused one in that search, we return it and assign it to *pid*.

```
struct pid *pid = alloc_pid();
int nr;
if (¬pid)
    return −EAGAIN;
nr = pid→nr;
if (unlikely(current→ptrace)) {
    trace = fork_traceflag(clone_flags);
    if (trace)
        clone_flags |= CLONE_PTRACE;
}
```

This code fragment is also the first place we see the use of *unlikely*( ). Later, we also see its counterpart, *likely*( ). These are macros that use an extension to GCC (officially named the GNU Compiler Collection, but often called the GNU C Compiler). This extension allows us to give a hint to the compiler regarding whether we expect an **if** condition to evaluate to true or to false.

8.5.1.2 Creating the Child Process

At this point, we now call *copy_process*( ) to do most of the work in actually creating the child process. The key arguments we pass it are *clone_flags*, *stack_start*, *regs*, and the process ID (which we saved in the variable *nr* earlier). Later in this section, we discuss this copy operation in more detail. There is one detail we should note here, however. Even though the child is a copy of the parent, only the parent returns to this point in the code. As we discuss later, the child is set up to go directly to the code that returns from the process creation call that created it.

```
p = copy_process(clone_flags, stack_start, regs, stack_size, parent_tidptr,
    child_tidptr, nr);
```

8.5.1.3 Setting Up Parent Behavior

Assuming we were successful in creating the child as a copy of its parent, we can now start setting up the correct behavior of both the parent and the child. The issue we must address is the parent's behavior in the case where we got here through a *vfork*( ) system call. In that case, the parent must block until the newly created child issues an *_exit*( ) or an *execve*( ) system call. Setting the value of *p→vfork_done* sets up the mechanism we use to notify the parent that it may continue.

```
if (¬IS_ERR(p)) {
    struct completion vfork;
    if (clone_flags & CLONE_VFORK) {
        p→vfork_done = &vfork;
        init_completion(&vfork);
    }
    if ((p→ptrace & PT_PTRACED) ∨ (clone_flags & CLONE_STOPPED)) {
```

```
        sigaddset(&p→pending.signal, SIGSTOP);
        set_tsk_thread_flag(p, TIF_SIGPENDING);
}
```

8.5.1.4 Starting Child Process

Now we may start the newly created child process. Because the child is created as a copy of the parent, it inherits the parent's Ready state. However, one of the options we have available allows us to create a process that starts life in the Stopped state. If this process has been created with this flag, then we change its state to TASK_STOPPED. Otherwise, we call *wake_up_new_task( )*, which inserts the child process into the appropriate ready queue.

```
        if (¬(clone_flags & CLONE_STOPPED))
            wake_up_new_task(p, clone_flags);
        else
            p→state = TASK_STOPPED;
        if (unlikely(trace)) {
            current→ptrace_message = nr;
            ptrace_notify((trace ≪ 8) | SIGTRAP);
        }
```

8.5.1.5 Determining Parent Behavior

In the case of a *vfork( )*, we are now ready to block the parent until the child issues the necessary system call. The call to *wait_for_completion( )* sets the state of the parent to TASK_UNINTERRUPTIBLE in order to block it. We move it from the Blocked state to the Ready state when the *vfork* structure is modified, indicating that the child is finished using the parent's memory space. Notice how it is particularly critical that the child did not return back to this function upon creation.

```
        if (clone_flags & CLONE_VFORK) {
            wait_for_completion(&vfork);
            if (unlikely(current→ptrace & PT_TRACE_VFORK_DONE))
                ptrace_notify((PTRACE_EVENT_VFORK_DONE ≪ 8) | SIGTRAP);
        }
}
```

8.5.1.6 Handling the Failure Case

If the call to *copy_process( )* failed, then we must notify the would-be parent that it was unable to create a child.

```
    else {
        free_pid(pid);
        pid = PTR_ERR(p);
```

```
    }
    return nr;
}
```

8.5.2 Creating the Process

As discussed earlier, *copy_process*( ), along with the functions it calls, does the real work
of creating a new process. It is also found in kernel/fork.c. This function is quite lengthy
owing to numerous details outside the scope of our study. In the interest of keeping
our focus on presenting how Linux illustrates the principles and techniques of process
management, we discuss only selected portions of this function. Omitted code is indicated
by an ellipsis (...). As mentioned earlier, the parameters that concern us most are the
flags, the stack, the registers, and the PID. The code we omit after the local variable
declarations is largely sanity-checking to ensure we aren't given a meaningless set of flags.

```
static struct task_struct *copy_process(unsigned long clone_flags,
    unsigned long stack_start, struct pt_regs *regs,
    unsigned long stack_size, int __user *parent_tidptr,
    int __user *child_tidptr, int pid)
{
    int retval;
    struct task_struct *p = Λ;

    ...
```

8.5.2.1 Inheriting the Parent's Characteristics

This call to *dup_task_struct*( ) allocates a new task structure and copies the parent's structure into it. It also sets up the pointers between the **thread_info** structure and the new
task structure, as illustrated in Figure 8-2. At this point, we have a new process table
entry for the child process with an initial set of values. Many of the members of this
structure are changed later in this function.

```
p = dup_task_struct(current);
if (¬p)
    goto fork_out;
retval = −EAGAIN;

...
```

A newly created process has no children, so we initialize an empty list for them. We also
temporarily initialize our sibling pointers to indicate that the new process has no siblings.
Later, we insert the new process into the parent's list of children, which sets the sibling
relationships.

```
INIT_LIST_HEAD(&p→children);
INIT_LIST_HEAD(&p→sibling);
    . . .
```

After initializing numerous statistical values, locks, and timers, we reach several lines of code that call various functions which handle the actual copying or sharing of the parent's resources. Most of these handle resources such as memory and files, which are the subjects of later chapters. Others handle aspects of process management, such as signals that we do not cover in detail. The last one, *copy_thread*( ), is of interest to us, as it is where we handle the difference in the way the parent and the child return. We discuss it in more detail later in this chapter.

> **if** $((retval = copy\_semundo(clone\_flags, p)))$
>   **goto** *bad_fork_cleanup_audit*;
> **if** $((retval = copy\_files(clone\_flags, p)))$
>   **goto** *bad_fork_cleanup_semundo*;
> **if** $((retval = copy\_fs(clone\_flags, p)))$
>   **goto** *bad_fork_cleanup_files*;
> **if** $((retval = copy\_sighand(clone\_flags, p)))$
>   **goto** *bad_fork_cleanup_fs*;
> **if** $((retval = copy\_signal(clone\_flags, p)))$
>   **goto** *bad_fork_cleanup_sighand*;
> **if** $((retval = copy\_mm(clone\_flags, p)))$
>   **goto** *bad_fork_cleanup_signal*;
> **if** $((retval = copy\_keys(clone\_flags, p)))$
>   **goto** *bad_fork_cleanup_mm*;
> **if** $((retval = copy\_namespace(clone\_flags, p)))$
>   **goto** *bad_fork_cleanup_keys*;
> $retval = copy\_thread(0, clone\_flags, stack\_start, stack\_size, p, regs)$;
> **if** $(retval)$
>   **goto** *bad_fork_cleanup_namespace*;
>   . . .

8.5.2.2   Splitting the Time Slice

The primary role of *sched_fork*( ) is to split the remainder of the parent's time slice evenly between the parent and the child. We don't want other processes starved by one that continually creates children.

> $sched\_fork(p, clone\_flags)$;
>   . . .

8.5.2.3   Setting Up Family Relationships

When using the *clone*( ) system call, we have the option of specifying whether the newly
created process is a child of the calling process or of the caller's parent. Both the
CLONE_PARENT and the CLONE_THREAD flags imply that the newly created process should
be a sibling of the caller. Otherwise, the caller is the parent of the new process.

> **if** (*clone_flags* & (CLONE_PARENT | CLONE_THREAD))
>   *p→real_parent* = *current→real_parent*;
> **else**
>   *p→real_parent* = *current*;
> *p→parent* = *p→real_parent*;
>   . . .

8.5.2.4   Wrapping Up

Now we are ready to return back to *do_fork*( ). If we encountered any errors along the
way, we end up jumping to the label *fork_out* and we return that error. Otherwise, we
return the pointer to the process table entry for the newly created process.

> **return** *p*;
>   . . .
> *fork_out*:
>   **return** ERR_PTR(*retval*);
> }

8.5.3   Architecture-Specific Steps

The last function we examine as part of the creation of processes in Linux is *copy_thread*( ).
This function is responsible for three major parts of creating a process. First, it handles
copying some of the parent's registers to the child. Second, it is responsible for copying
the hardware segment descriptor tables if necessary. (These descriptor tables are part of
the memory management responsibilities of the OS.) Finally, it sets up the child's return
so that the child receives a 0 return value and so that the child process skips the processing
described previously in the parent's thread of execution. The first two parts are clearly
architecture dependent. Although it might not appear so at first glance, so is the third
part. In particular, setting the child's return value requires knowledge of the architecture-
specific return mechanism. Furthermore, setting the child to skip directly to the system
call return requires modifying its stored program counter. As a result, this code is found
in the architecture-dependent part of the source tree in the file arch/i386/kernel/process.c.

> **int** *copy_thread*(**int** *nr*, **unsigned long** *clone_flags*, **unsigned long** *esp*,
>   **unsigned long** *unused*, **struct task_struct** *∗p*, **struct pt_regs** *∗regs*)
> {
>   **struct pt_regs** *∗childregs*;

struct task_struct **tsk*;
int *err*;

8.5.3.1   Setting Up Child's Registers

The next two lines of code make a copy of the parent's saved registers just above the **thread_info** structure at the bottom of the kernel stack space.

childregs = task_pt_regs(p);
*childregs = *regs;

The following assignments seem simple enough. At one level, they are fairly straightforward. The first assignment sets the value of what will ultimately be returned to the child process as the return value from the system call. The assignment of the value *ret_from_fork* sets a stored program counter value to the address of code labeled *ret_from_fork*. This will at some point in the future cause the child process to resume execution at that point, which then immediately returns from the system call. The subtlety lies in the fact that we're dealing with two different sets of saved registers. The first set, which we just copied, are those register values that were saved on entry to the system call handler. The other set are those stored in the *p→thread* structure. These are the registers that were last saved on a context switch. In particular, they are the ones that were saved the last time the parent was preempted. (The child process got a copy of them when it was given a copy of the parent's task structure.) The net effect of these assignments is to set up the following steps for the completion of the system call in the newly created child process:

1. When the child is next scheduled, it will begin running the code at label *ret_from_fork* because that's what we've set in the saved program counter.

2. When the child begins running that code, it will use the block of saved registers pointed to by *childregs* as its stack.

3. The code at *ret_from_fork* assumes that the stack contains the registers that were saved on entry to the system call handler and thus that will need to be restored as part of the return from the system call.

4. In returning from the system call, the **eax** register will hold the value 0. This register value is interpreted as the system call's return value by the library code that issued the system call.

5. On return from the system call, the child process will use the specified stack. Usually, this is the same stack that the parent used when it issued the process creation system call.

childregs→eax = 0;
childregs→esp = esp;
p→thread.esp = (**unsigned long**) *childregs;*

$$p\text{-}thread.esp0 = (\textbf{unsigned long})(childregs + 1);$$
$$p\text{-}thread.eip = (\textbf{unsigned long})\ ret\_from\_fork;$$

8.5.3.2   Setting Up Child's Memory

The remainder of this function handles copying the segment descriptors if necessary.

```
savesegment(fs, p-thread.fs);
savesegment(gs, p-thread.gs);
tsk = current;
if (unlikely(test_tsk_thread_flag(tsk, TIF_IO_BITMAP))) {
    p-thread.io_bitmap_ptr = kmalloc(IO_BITMAP_BYTES, GFP_KERNEL);
    if (¬p-thread.io_bitmap_ptr) {
        p-thread.io_bitmap_max = 0;
        return −ENOMEM;
    }
    memcpy(p-thread.io_bitmap_ptr, tsk→thread.io_bitmap_ptr,
        IO_BITMAP_BYTES);
        set_tsk_thread_flag(p, TIF_IO_BITMAP);
}
if (clone_flags & CLONE_SETTLS) {
    struct desc_struct *desc;
    struct user_desc info;
    int idx;

    err = −EFAULT;
    if (copy_from_user(&info, (void __user *) childregs→esi, sizeof (info)))
        goto out;
    err = −EINVAL;
    if (LDT_empty(&info))
        goto out;
    idx = info.entry_number;
    if (idx < GDT_ENTRY_TLS_MIN ∨ idx > GDT_ENTRY_TLS_MAX)
        goto out;
    desc = p-thread.tls_array + idx − GDT_ENTRY_TLS_MIN;
    desc→a = LDT_entry_a(&info);
    desc→b = LDT_entry_b(&info);
}
    err = 0;
out:
    if (err ∧ p-thread.io_bitmap_ptr) {
        kfree(p-thread.io_bitmap_ptr);
        p-thread.io_bitmap_max = 0;
    }
```

```
        return err;
}
```

8.6   Process Scheduling

Beginning with work introduced in the version 2.5 series of development kernels, Linux uses a multilevel feedback queue in its scheduling. (As we see later in this section, it is more precise to say that it uses a pair of multilevel feedback queues per CPU.) This version of the Linux scheduler is often referred to as the $O(1)$ scheduler in recognition of the fact that it operates in time bounded by a constant, independent of the number of processes either in the system or in the ready list.

Although it is organized and operates a little differently than other schedulers in UNIX-like systems, the current Linux scheduler still gives preference to interactive processes and to processes with lower nice values. The key elements of the Linux scheduler include the following:

- There are two multilevel feedback queues: one for processes that are designated as active and one for processes that are designated as expired.

- As with other multilevel feedback queue implementations, the Linux scheduler picks the process at the head of the queue for the highest nonempty priority. It uses a bitmap to quickly determine which queue is the highest priority nonempty one.

- Interactive processes that use their complete time slice are placed back into the active queue and are scheduled round-robin with other processes at the same priority. (These are processes that have recently spent a significant amount of time blocked.)

- Compute-bound processes that use their complete time slice are moved to the expired queue.

- When the active queue becomes empty, it is swapped with the expired queue.

- Priority and time slice length are computed each time a process is placed into a queue.

- Processes scheduled according to the SCHED_FIFO policy are real-time processes with a higher priority than any time-sharing processes. These processes are scheduled in a first in, first out (FIFO) manner, with each process running until it yields the CPU.

- Processes scheduled according to the SCHED_RR policy are also real-time processes with a higher priority than any time-sharing processes. However, these processes are scheduled in a round-robin fashion with finite time slices.

In the following subsections, we discuss the details of the implementation of the Linux scheduler.

8.6.1   Priorities

From a priority perspective, Linux has two classes of processes: real-time processes and time-sharing processes. Real-time processes are those that are scheduled according to the `SCHED_FIFO` or `SCHED_RR` policies. They each have a static priority value in the range 0–99. Time-sharing processes are scheduled according to the `SCHED_NORMAL` policy. They have priorities in the range −20 to 19. Internally, the priorities of time-sharing processes are scaled to the range 100–139. Smaller priority values represent higher actual priority.

As discussed in connection with system calls, each time-sharing process has a parameter called nice. In addition to that, we maintain a value in the process table called *sleep_avg*, which is the amount of recent time spent blocked. Specifically, on a transition to the Ready state, we increment *sleep_avg* by the amount of time spent blocked up to a maximum of `MAX_SLEEP_AVG` (which defaults to one second in this version of the kernel). For each clock tick the process spends running, the value of *sleep_avg* is decremented by some period of time down to zero. From this measure, we calculate an effective priority as

$$p = n + \frac{s}{M_s} M_b - \frac{M_b}{2}$$

where n is the value of nice using the internal representation in the range 100–139, s is the average sleep time, M_s is the maximum average sleep time, and M_b is the maximum bonus, which is 10. The effect of this calculation is to linearly map the range of average sleep times, 0–`MAX_SLEEP_AVG` onto the range −5 to 5, and add that to the value of nice. If the computed value of p would fall outside the range of 100–139, it is set to the corresponding end of the range. As a result, processes that have spent more recent time blocked are deemed to be interactive and are given a priority boost.

In addition to priority adjustments, Linux also makes adjustments to the length of a time slice based on nice. The length of the time slice is computed as

$$t = \begin{cases} 5(140 - n), & n \geq 120 \\ 20(140 - n), & \text{otherwise} \end{cases}$$

in milliseconds. This has the effect of giving processes with nonnegative nice (0–19 as specified by the user, 120–139 when represented internally) time slices ranging from 5 mS to 100 mS. Processes with negative values of nice (−20 to −1 as specified by the user, 100–119 represented internally) are given time slices ranging from 420 mS to 800 mS.

8.6.2   Queue Structure

The primary data structure for the scheduler is the **rq** (standing for runqueue) structure. Several of the members of this structure are particularly interesting to us. First, there is a member called *lock*, which we use for mutual exclusion. The other members we highlight are *active*, *expired*, and *arrays*. Both elements of *arrays* are multilevel feedback queues. At any point in time, *active* points to one element, and *expired* points to the other. So for some of the time, *active* ≡ &*arrays*[0] and *expired* ≡ &*arrays*[1]. Then when it comes time to swap, we reset the pointers such that *active* ≡ &*arrays*[1] and

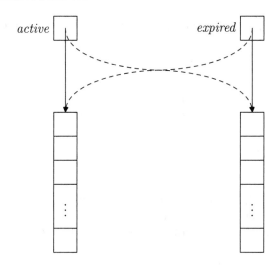

Figure 8-3: Linux Multilevel Feedback Queue Structure

$expired \equiv \& arrays[0]$. Figure 8-3 shows these two scenarios. The **rq** structure is defined in kernel/sched.c as follows:

```
struct rq {
    spinlock_t lock;
    unsigned long nr_running;
    unsigned long raw_weighted_load;
    unsigned long long nr_switches;
    unsigned long nr_uninterruptible;
    unsigned long expired_timestamp;
    unsigned long long timestamp_last_tick;
    struct task_struct *curr, *idle;
    struct mm_struct *prev_mm;
    struct prio_array *active, *expired, arrays[2];
    int best_expired_prio;
    atomic_t nr_iowait;
    struct lock_class_key rq_lock_key;
};
```

The multilevel feedback queue structure itself is also declared in kernel/sched.c. The first of the three members of this structure simply records the number of processes in all priority levels of the queue. The *bitmap* contains one bit for each priority level. On a 32-bit machine, each word can accommodate 32 priority levels. With 140 total priority levels, *bitmap* contains five words on a 32-bit machine. If the queue for a particular priority level is empty, then the corresponding bit is 0. This allows us to determine which is the highest priority nonempty queue very quickly. Finally, the actual queue structures are in the array *queue*.

```
struct prio_array {
    unsigned int nr_active;
    DECLARE_BITMAP(bitmap, MAX_PRIO + 1);
    struct list_head queue[MAX_PRIO];
};
```

8.6.3 Clock Ticks

Now that we have examined the scheduler data structures, we turn our attention to the code that implements the Linux scheduler. We start with the code that is called for each clock tick. This code is found in *scheduler_tick( )* in kernel/sched.c.

```
void scheduler_tick(void)
{
    unsigned long long now = sched_clock( );
    task_t *p = current;
    int cpu = smp_processor_id( );
    struct rq *rq = cpu_rq(cpu);
```

We start out with some bookkeeping. If the current process is the idle process, we handle that as a special case. As discussed in Section 4.3.4, at the end of *rest_init( )*, we call *cpu_idle( )*, which is the idle process and runs when no other process is ready. We never adjust the priorities or move that process around in the queues. It's possible that even though this processor is idle, other processors may have some ready processes. The *rebalance_tick( )* function does nothing on a single processor machine. On a system with more than one CPU, this function moves processes among CPUs to balance the load among them.

```
    update_cpu_clock(p, rq, now);
    rq→timestamp_last_tick = now;
    if (p ≡ rq→idle) {
        if (wake_priority_sleeper(rq))
            goto out;
        rebalance_tick(cpu, rq, SCHED_IDLE);
        return;
    }
```

8.6.3.1 Special Error Condition

If we find that the current process is in the expired queue rather than the active one, then the metaphorical rug has been pulled out from under us. We need to preempt this process and reschedule.

```
    if (p→array ≠ rq→active) {
        set_tsk_need_resched(p);
        goto out;
    }
```

8.6.3.2 Handling Real-Time Processes

After gaining a mutual exclusion lock on the **rq** data structure, we handle the case of a real-time process. The priorities of these processes are never adjusted, and they never move to the expired queue. Processes scheduled according to the SCHED_FIFO policy are especially easy to handle. They are allowed to run until they yield the CPU. For them, we don't need to do anything. For a round-robin, real-time process, we count off another tick. If that means that its time slice is finished, we set the reschedule-needed flag and put it at the back of its queue.

```
    spin_lock(&rq→lock);
    if (rt_task(p)) {
        if ((p→policy ≡ SCHED_RR) ∧ ¬--p→time_slice) {
            p→time_slice = task_timeslice(p);
            p→first_time_slice = 0;
            set_tsk_need_resched(p);
            requeue_task(p, rq→active);
        }
        goto out_unlock;
    }
```

8.6.3.3 Time-Sharing Processes

The major portion of this function concerns time-sharing processes. As with the round-robin, real-time case, we count off a tick and ask whether the time slice is finished. If it is, then we pull the current process out of its queue and recompute its priority and time slice. The reference to *jiffies* deserves note. This variable is global to the kernel and is incremented once for each clock tick. Consequently, it is a measure of how long the system has been up, measured in clock ticks.

```
    if (¬--p→time_slice) {
        dequeue_task(p, rq→active);
        set_tsk_need_resched(p);
        p→prio = effective_prio(p);
        p→time_slice = task_timeslice(p);
        p→first_time_slice = 0;
        if (¬rq→expired_timestamp)
            rq→expired_timestamp = jiffies;
```

At this point, we have preempted the currently running process because its time slice
expired and we have removed it from the active queue. However, because it is still in the
Ready state, we need to put it back into a queue. Our next step is to determine whether
to put it back into the active queue or move it to the expired queue. This decision can be
described in simple terms by saying that if the process is compute-bound or if processes in
the expired queue are starving, then we move this process to the expired queue. The first
condition is based on the current priority boost and on the current process's nice value.
The higher the value of nice, the more the priority boost must be for the process to be
considered interactive. For the starvation condition, we ask if enough time has passed that
all of the ready processes have had a chance to get as much time as the maximum sleep
average. If that amount of time has passed since we last swapped the active and expired
queues, then we stop putting processes back into the active queue and begin putting them
into the expired queue, irrespective of their degree of interactivity.

$$
\begin{aligned}
&\textbf{if } (\neg\texttt{TASK\_INTERACTIVE}(p) \lor \textit{expired\_starving}(rq)) \ \{ \\
&\quad \textit{enqueue\_task}(p, rq\text{-}expired); \\
&\quad \textbf{if } (p\text{-}static\_prio < rq\text{-}best\_expired\_prio) \\
&\quad\quad rq\text{-}best\_expired\_prio = p\text{-}static\_prio; \\
&\ \} \\
&\textbf{else} \\
&\quad \textit{enqueue\_task}(p, rq\text{-}active); \\
&\} \\
&\textbf{else } \{
\end{aligned}
$$

If we have a process with a very long time slice and there are other processes at the same
priority, we can split the time slice and let the other processes get some time. In this case,
we always put the preempted process back into the active queue.

$$
\begin{aligned}
&\textbf{if } (\texttt{TASK\_INTERACTIVE}(p) \\
&\qquad \land \neg((\textit{task\_timeslice}(p) - p\text{-}time\_slice)\ \%\ \texttt{TIMESLICE\_GRANULARITY}(p)) \\
&\qquad \land (p\text{-}time\_slice \geq \texttt{TIMESLICE\_GRANULARITY}(p)) \\
&\qquad \land (p\text{-}array \equiv rq\text{-}active)) \ \{ \\
&\quad \textit{requeue\_task}(p, rq\text{-}active); \\
&\quad \textit{set\_tsk\_need\_resched}(p); \\
&\ \} \\
&\}
\end{aligned}
$$

At this point, we're ready to unlock the **rq** data structure and return from the clock
interrupt.

$$
\begin{aligned}
&\textit{out\_unlock}: \\
&\quad \textit{spin\_unlock}(\&rq\text{-}lock); \\
&\textit{out}: \\
&\quad \textit{rebalance\_tick}(cpu, rq, \texttt{NOT\_IDLE}); \\
&\}
\end{aligned}
$$

If *scheduler_tick()* determines that a new process needs to be scheduled, it sets a flag in the current process that says a reschedule is needed. Before returning from the clock interrupt, the kernel checks to see if that flag is set. If the flag is clear, then the kernel proceeds to complete the return from interrupt. If the flag is set, then the kernel calls *schedule()*, discussed in the next section, prior to returning from the interrupt.

8.6.4   Scheduler

The function *schedule()* in kernel/sched.c contains the code triggered by setting the reschedule-needed flag. There is one feature of this code that we should highlight here. There are no loops in this function. This is one of the key elements to our earlier observation that the running time of the Linux scheduler is bounded by a constant. (The other part of justifying that claim is showing that all the functions called by *schedule()* are also constant time.) An $O(1)$ scheduler can be a significant benefit in large-scale deployments where there may be thousands of ready processes. A scheduler whose running time is proportional to the number of ready processes would be significantly slower in such cases.

The kernel follows the general strategy of identifying when a scheduling operation should take place and then recording that fact. When it comes time to return from the interrupt that transferred control to the kernel back to the process that was interrupted, the scheduler is then invoked to select the process to which we should return. The first thing to notice in the declaration of *schedule()* is the **asmlinkage** keyword. This reflects the fact that *schedule()* is called from the interrupt return code, which is written in assembly language. Function calls in languages like C often involve some setup on the part of the caller. Using **asmlinkage** allows us to call the function using a simple subroutine jump instruction without the setup.

```
asmlinkage void __sched schedule(void)
{
    struct task_struct *prev, *next;
    struct prio_array *array;
    struct list_head *queue;
    unsigned long long now;
    unsigned long run_time;
    int cpu, idx, new_prio;
    long *switch_count;
    struct rq *rq;
```

The first thing we do on entry to the scheduler is to check for an error condition. If the current process is flagged as nonpreemptible at the present time, then we should not run the scheduler. Normally, we should never get here in that case, but just in case we do, we want to check for that case and report the error.

```
    if (unlikely (in_atomic() ∧ ¬current→exit_state)) {
        printk(KERN_ERR"BUG:_scheduling_while_atomic:_%s/0x%08x/%d\n",
```

```
        current→comm, preempt_count( ), current→pid);
    dump_stack( );
}
```

To observe the performance of software, we often profile it. If we have profiling for the kernel turned on, then *profile_hit*( ) increments a counter. The first argument specifies what operation we're profiling and, consequently, which counter is incremented.

```
    profile_hit(SCHED_PROFILING, __builtin_return_address(0));
```

8.6.4.1 Preempting the Current Process

Because we're about to select a new process to run, the current one becomes the previous process. We set *prev* to point to its process table entry. The remaining lines in this fragment all support symmetric multiprocessing (SMP) on multiple processors. One of these is relevant to our presentation. In particular, each processor has its own **rq** structure. We set *rq* to point to the one that contains the current process we're about to replace.

```
    need_resched:
    preempt_disable( );
    prev = current;
    release_kernel_lock(prev);
    need_resched_nonpreemptible:
    rq = this_rq( );
```

Here we have another error case. Just as we should never be called if the current process is nonpreemptible, we should never be called if the current process is the idle process and it's not running.

```
    if (unlikely(prev ≡ rq→idle) ∧ prev→state ≠ TASK_RUNNING) {
        printk(KERN_ERR"bad:␣scheduling␣from␣the␣idle␣thread!\n");
        dump_stack( );
    }
```

There are several places in kernel/sched.c that support gathering and reporting scheduling statistics. This line is a part of that functionality. It records the number of scheduling operations that take place in each runqueue.

```
    schedstat_inc(rq, sched_cnt);
```

8.6.4.2 Updating Run Time

We want to know how long the current process has been running since we scheduled it to adjust the measure of recent sleep time. This time is given by the current time minus the time we recorded in the *timestamp* field when we scheduled this process. However, we want to bound this value by 0 and by NS_MAX_SLEEP_AVG, which is one second (10 mS in earlier versions of the kernel).

$now = sched\_clock();$
if $(likely((\textbf{long long})(now - prev\text{-}timestamp) < \texttt{NS\_MAX\_SLEEP\_AVG}))$ {
  $run\_time = now - prev\text{-}timestamp;$
  if $(unlikely((\textbf{long long})(now - prev\text{-}timestamp) < 0))$
    $run\_time = 0;$
}
else
  $run\_time = \texttt{NS\_MAX\_SLEEP\_AVG};$

The more interactive a process is, the less we let the running time affect the measure of recent sleep time. The result is that the measure of recent sleep time decays very slowly at first and then reaches the point where we reduce the sleep average at the full rate of the running time as we approach zero. The `CURRENT_BONUS` macro evaluates the expression $\frac{s}{M_s}M_b$ in the effective priority calculation discussed earlier. This line of code might seem strange because there is no expression between the question mark and the colon of the conditional expression. The GCC compiler supports this as an extension. In this case, the result of the expression is the same as the condition if it is nonzero. As usual, if the condition evaluates to zero, then the third expression is the value of the conditional expression. The effect of this particular usage is to divide *run_time* by the current bonus, but if the bonus is zero, we obviously cannot divide by zero, so we divide by one.

$run\_time \mathrel{/{=}} (\texttt{CURRENT\_BONUS}(prev)\ ?\!: 1);$

8.6.4.3 Adjusting the Queues

Here we lock the **rq** data structure in case another processor attempts to access it. This might seem an unexpected thing to do if there is one runqueue per processor. However, any processor may move processes from one runqueue to another to balance the load. When that happens, another processor may access our runqueue.

$spin\_lock\_irq(\&rq\text{-}lock);$
if $(unlikely(prev\text{-}flags\ \&\ \texttt{PF\_DEAD}))$
  $prev\text{-}state = \texttt{EXIT\_DEAD};$

If the previous process has just blocked, then we need to handle that case. In most cases, we want to take this process out of the runqueue, which is handled by the *deactivate_task()* call. The one exception is the case where we have an interruptible Blocked state but where a signal for this process has arrived before we get here. In that case, we go ahead and make the transition back to the Ready state and leave the process in the queue.

$switch\_count = \&prev\text{-}nivcsw;$
if $(prev\text{-}state \land \neg(preempt\_count()\ \&\ \texttt{PREEMPT\_ACTIVE}))$ {
  $switch\_count = \&prev\text{-}nvcsw;$
  if $(unlikely((prev\text{-}state\ \&\ \texttt{TASK\_INTERRUPTIBLE})$
      $\land\ unlikely(signal\_pending(prev))))$

```
    prev→state = TASK_RUNNING;
  else {
    if (prev→state ≡ TASK_UNINTERRUPTIBLE)
      rq→nr_uninterruptible ++;
    deactivate_task(prev, rq);
  }
}
```

If there are no processes in the Ready state on this CPU, then we attempt to rebalance the load. If afterwards, there still aren't any ready processes, then we switch to the idle process. The call to *wake_sleeping_dependent*( ) has an effect only if we are running the special scheduling support for the hyperthreading feature of later models of the Intel x86 processor. Hyperthreaded CPUs duplicate a number of elements including the register set. When one thread of execution is stalled waiting on a memory access, the other register set is used to execute instructions from another thread. We treat such a CPU as two processors, but we also recognize that two complete CPUs still give better performance. The details of its use are beyond the scope of our discussion here.

```
  cpu = smp_processor_id( );
  if (unlikely(¬rq→nr_running)) {
    idle_balance(cpu, rq);
    if (¬rq→nr_running) {
      next = rq→idle;
      rq→expired_timestamp = 0;
      wake_sleeping_dependent(cpu);
      goto switch_tasks;
    }
  }
```

Now it is time to determine whether to swap the queues pointed to by *active* and *expired*. If there are no more processes in the active array, then we know it's time to swap.

```
  array = rq→active;
  if (unlikely(¬array→nr_active)) {
    schedstat_inc(rq, sched_switch);
    rq→active = rq→expired;
    rq→expired = array;
    array = rq→active;
    rq→expired_timestamp = 0;
    rq→best_expired_prio = MAX_PRIO;
  }
```

8.6.4.4   Selecting the Next Process

Whether we swapped or not, at this point, *array* should point to a multilevel feedback queue that has some ready processes. We can now pick the process at the head of the highest priority nonempty queue. The first step is to find that queue. The function *sched_find_first_bit*( ) is architecture-dependent to take advantage of any special features found in the processor's instruction set. Many processors have an instruction that will tell us which bit in a word is the first one that is set to 1. Such an instruction makes it very easy to find the first bit in the *bitmap* array that is 1. After we know the highest nonempty priority level, we set *next* to point to the first process table entry in the list. This is the core of the actual scheduling implementation.

$$idx = sched\_find\_first\_bit(array{\rightarrow}bitmap);$$
$$queue = array{\rightarrow}queue + idx;$$
$$next = list\_entry(queue{\rightarrow}next, \mathbf{struct\,task\_struct}, run\_list);$$

The next section of code handles a rather special case. When a process is made ready after being blocked for some time, we recompute its priority, taking into account the time it was asleep. However, depending on the new priority we calculate for it, there may be considerable time that it sits in the queue still not being scheduled. If the process we just selected to run is such a process, then we adjust its priority to take into account the additional time it was sitting in the queue.

$$\mathbf{if}\ (\neg rt\_task(next) \wedge interactive\_sleep(next{\rightarrow}sleep\_type)\ \{$$
$$\quad \mathbf{unsigned\ long\ long}\ delta = now - next{\rightarrow}timestamp;$$
$$\quad \mathbf{if}\ (unlikely((\mathbf{long\ long})(now - next{\rightarrow}timestamp) < 0))$$
$$\quad\quad delta = 0;$$
$$\quad \mathbf{if}\ (next{\rightarrow}sleep\_type \equiv \mathtt{SLEEP\_INACTIVE})$$
$$\quad\quad delta = delta * (\mathtt{ON\_RUNQUEUE\_WEIGHT} * 128/100)/128;$$
$$\quad array = next{\rightarrow}array;$$
$$\quad new\_prio = recalc\_task\_prio(next, next{\rightarrow}timestamp + delta);$$
$$\quad \mathbf{if}\ (unlikely(next{\rightarrow}prio \neq new\_prio))\ \{$$
$$\quad\quad dequeue\_task(next, array);$$
$$\quad\quad next{\rightarrow}prio = new\_prio;$$
$$\quad\quad enqueue\_task(next, array);$$
$$\quad \}$$
$$\}$$
$$next{\rightarrow}sleep\_type = \mathtt{SLEEP\_NORMAL};$$
$$\mathbf{if}(dependent\_sleeper(cpu, rq, next))$$
$$\quad next = rq{\rightarrow}idle;$$

8.6.4.5   Preparing to Context Switch

Now that we have the next process we want to run, it's time to do the context switch. There is a fair amount of bookkeeping we need to do in preparation for the actual switch.

```
switch_tasks:
    if (next ≡ rq→idle)
        schedstat_inc(rq, sched_goidle);
```

These two calls issue instructions that improve the performance of the cache on the context switch. Not all processors have such prefetching instructions, but if we have them, we use them.

```
prefetch(next);
prefetch_stack(next);
```

We always get to the scheduler when a flag is set that indicates a rescheduling operation is needed before returning from an interrupt. Now that we are ready to switch, we can clear that flag.

```
clear_tsk_need_resched(prev);
rcu_qsctr_inc(task_cpu(prev));
update_cpu_clock(prev, rq, now);
```

At this point, we now use the value of *run_time* we computed previously to adjust the recent average sleep time for the process we're preempting.

```
prev→sleep_avg −= run_time;
if ((long) prev→sleep_avg ≤ 0)
    prev→sleep_avg = 0;
```

Now we record the current time so that later we'll be able to know how long the previous process went between schedulings. If the process has just blocked, then we'll use this time to determine how long it was asleep when it is awakened.

```
prev→timestamp = prev→last_ran = now;
```

If it turns out that we selected the same process to continue running, then we don't actually need to perform the switch. The primary work of the switch is done in the function *context_switch()*. Its work is divided into two parts. The first step is to switch all the memory management details to the new process. The second step is switching the registers and stack so that the return from interrupt goes back to the new process. This is handled by an architecture-specific function called *switch_to()*. (The call to *barrier()* enforces execution order, preventing the optimizer from reordering memory accesses. All memory accesses in code before the call are made before any specified after the call.)

```
sched_info_switch(prev, next);
if (likely(prev ≠ next)) {
    next→timestamp = now;
    rq→nr_switches ++;
    rq→curr = next;
```

```
            ++*switch_count;
            prepare_task_switch(rq, next);
            prev = context_switch(rq, prev, next);
            barrier();
            finish_task_switch(this_rq(), prev);
        }
        else
            spin_unlock_irq(&rq⁻lock);
        prev = current;
        if (unlikely(reacquire_kernel_lock(prev) < 0))
            goto need_resched_nonpreemptible;
        preempt_enable_no_resched();
        if (unlikely(test_thread_flag(TIF_NEED_RESCHED)))
            goto need_resched;
    }
```

As we mention in Section 8.6.3, *schedule*() is called immediately before returning from the clock interrupt. This means that at the end of this function, control transfers to code that ends in a return from interrupt instruction. When that instruction is executed, control is transferred to the newly scheduled process at the point where it was last interrupted.

8.7   Summary

Linux provides a good example of a modern implementation of a mainstream approach to processes. It takes advantage of the underlying commonality between processes and threads and consequently doesn't make a distinction between them. The set of system calls and process states is typical of other UNIX-like systems. The process table follows a two-part structure in a linked list organization. In this chapter, we have examined some of the details of the process states and of the process table. We have also discussed the way in which the general principles of process creation have been implemented in Linux. The details of the new Linux scheduler design have also been covered. We have seen how Linux implements a pair of multilevel feedback queues that alternate between storing active and expired processes and how priority adjustments are used to give preference to interactive processes.

8.8   Exercises

1. In Section 8.5, we point out that the code assumes that the newly created child process does not return to *do_fork*() as the parent does. What would happen if it did?

2. In Section 8.6, we examine the computation of time slice length. The code contains a check to set the value to 5 mS if the computation resulted in a smaller value. Is that possible with the equation we have given? Why or why not?

3. We did not show the **EXIT_DEAD** state in Figure 8-1. Where should it be added?

4. From an examination of the code discussed in Section 8.5, at what state in Figure 8-1 do new processes enter?

5. Consider two compute-bound processes, one with nice 0 and one with nice 10. If each process is moved from the active queue to the expired queue at the end of each time slice, then how does the process with nice 0 get preference over the one with nice 10?

6. What purpose does using the expired multilevel feedback queue serve? In particular, what undesirable behavior does it avoid?

7. In *schedule( )*, the value of *run_time* is scaled by **CURRENT_BONUS**. What is the maximum amount by which we divide *run_time*? What effect does this have on the scheduling of the process?

8. Modify the Linux scheduler to eliminate *bitmap* from the **prio_array** structure. How will you determine the highest priority nonempty queue? How much of a performance penalty do you incur?

9. Modify *schedule( )* so that *sleep_avg* is not decreased based on *run_time* and the **CURRENT_BONUS**. Instead, decrease *sleep_avg* based on the fraction of CPU time that the current process has gotten. In particular, use *last_run* and *timestamp* to determine a percentage of CPU time used in the last scheduling cycle and decrease *sleep_avg* in proportion to that percentage. What effect, if any, does that have on the scheduling behavior?

10. Add an earliest deadline first real-time scheduler to Linux. Define a new value **SCHED_EDF** to use in *sched_setscheduler( )* for it.

Chapter 9

Principles of Memory Management

At first thought, we might expect that memory management is the simplest area of responsibility. After all, memory is usually just a regular array of bytes, each with a unique address. As we see in this chapter, the task of managing memory can be fairly straightforward when we have memory to spare. However, if we try to operate in a memory-starved environment, then our task becomes much more difficult. This is particularly true when we must resort to using the disk to provide the illusion that there's more memory than we really have. Because disk accesses can be up to a million times slower than memory accesses, making the right decisions about what to copy from memory to disk and back again is critical.

We begin this study with an overview of the concept of the memory hierarchy. Following that, we discuss the various approaches to memory management hardware. Our look at memory management support in the operating system, then, begins with a look at typical memory management services, and then we look at the way the memory space is divided into various regions. The largest part of this chapter is devoted to a study of various memory allocation techniques, with particular attention given to page replacement policies.

9.1   The Memory Hierarchy

Over the years, various forms of data storage have evolved to meet a variety of design demands. We often call this set of storage technologies the **memory hierarchy** and view it as shown in Figure 9-1. Each level of the hierarchy has its own characteristics:

- *Registers*: These storage locations are part of the CPU itself. They are designed to be accessed in less time than it takes to execute an instruction. Typically, there are between a very few and a very few hundred of them. In most CPU designs, they are implemented on the same chip as the other parts of the CPU.

- *Cache*: The reality of hardware design dictates that the CPU is generally able to request and to process data from memory faster than the memory can supply it. For

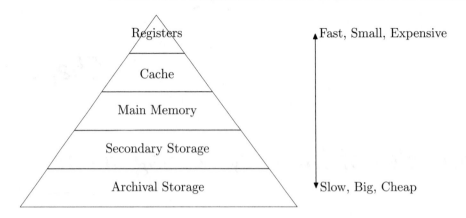

Figure 9-1: The Memory Hierarchy

that reason, we generally include one or more levels of a buffer called **cache** memory. In terms of speed, cache is slower than the registers but is faster than main memory. Typical cache sizes range from a few kilobytes to a few megabytes with cache sizes getting larger with each new design. This increase in size is driven by two factors. As time progresses, application designs tend to consume more memory, which requires larger caches to get the same hit rates (the fraction of the time that the desired data is found in the cache). In addition, the disparity between the speed at which the CPU can process data and the speed at which the memory can supply it is increasing. As a result, the hit rates must increase for the expected access time to stay low.

- *Main memory*: This level of the hierarchy is also sometimes called **primary storage**. It is the central focus of the memory management component of the operating system and occupies something of a middle ground with respect to size and speed. For some embedded applications, the main memory might be only a few kilobytes, whereas for large-scale systems there might be many gigabytes of memory.

- *Secondary storage*: **Secondary storage** is also often called **backing store**. This storage is usually realized with mechanical magnetic devices such as disk drives. Although it is much slower than main memory, even small systems often have tens of gigabytes of secondary storage. In the context of memory management, we often use a small fraction of the secondary storage for swapping data between memory and disk when the demands of applications exceed the available physical memory. As address spaces continue to get larger, the idea of considering all of a system's secondary storage space as part of its addressable memory space becomes quite appealing. Consequently, even though we usually treat the file system management as a separate part of the operating system, future designs could consider it to be part of the secondary storage that is our swapping space.

- *Archival storage*: We often treat our backup data storage as a separate issue. It is usually assumed to be a system administration problem and not an inherent function of the operating system. It is certainly rarely considered as part of an operating system's memory management responsibilities. However, there have been some recent research projects where the structure of the overall secondary storage management has been designed around the idea of long-term permanent storage. In effect, all data is stored in a way that it is automatically preserved for archival purposes. Data is never deleted in this type of storage subsystem. It has even been observed that for many application domains, the manufacturers are producing storage capacity faster than the users can create data to fill it.

Notice that as we move up and down the hierarchy we trade speed for size and economy. The realities of physical systems dictate that the faster we make data storage, the more resources it consumes. This is true both in terms of the number of cubic inches per bit and in terms of the power consumed while the memory is in operation. The net effect is that we find that faster memory is larger and more expensive per bit. Consequently, we build systems with small capacities of fast memory to save cost and physical space. Otherwise, we'd just build the entire memory hierarchy out of the same stuff we build the registers.

There is one additional reason why we have different technologies for different levels of the hierarchy. The fastest memory technologies are **volatile**. This means that when the power is removed, the data is lost. Obviously, we must have some other technologies that allow data to be **persistent**. Along similar lines, we want at least a part of our archival storage to be removable. If we can't separate copies of the data from the physical computer, then disasters such as fire and storms would destroy the value of the archival storage. Most computing centers keep copies of important data in separate locations to reduce the possibility of completely losing it. However, the design requirements for building devices where the media are removable tend to be at odds with speed of data retrieval.

9.2   Address Translation

Later in this chapter, we discuss typical memory layouts both in terms of the overall system and in terms of individual processes. We illustrate both types of layouts starting at address 0 and going up from there. In doing so, however, we fail to highlight the distinction between the address spaces of the overall layout and the process layout. They obviously cannot be the same space because the low memory space can't be both interrupt vectors and program code. In the case of the overall layout, we talk in terms of **physical addresses** or **real addresses**. These are the addresses that directly determine which memory locations are addressed. On the other hand, the process layout is specified in terms of **virtual addresses**. These are the addresses that are generated by the running program. We call the set of possible physical addresses the **physical address space** (or **real address space**) and the set of possible virtual addresses the **virtual address space**.

As discussed in the following subsections, the discrepancy between these two address spaces is reconciled through various forms of **address translation** (sometimes also called **relocation**). In addition to address translation, the **memory management unit** (MMU) is also responsible for protection. We usually require that processes be prevented from accessing the memory belonging to other processes or to the operating system.

9.2.1   Base/Limit Registers

The first, and simplest, method of providing address translation is by the use of base registers. The simplest realization of this technique is a single base register, the contents of which is added to each virtual address, giving the physical address. This is illustrated in Figure 9-2.

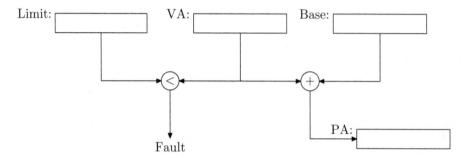

Figure 9-2: Base Register Address Translation

As described, the base register technique of address translation has a significant problem: It doesn't do a very good job of providing protection. If a process is using less physical memory than the size of the virtual space, then it could access memory beyond the end of its allocated space. This is where the limit register comes in. Limit registers come in two forms. In the first case, they specify the last accessible address. For this type of limit register, we compare the computed physical address to the limit register, and if it is greater, we disallow the access and generate a memory fault interrupt. The other type of limit register specifies the size of the allocated memory space. For this type, we compare the virtual address to the limit register and, if it is greater, we disallow the access and generate a memory fault interrupt. Figure 9-2 illustrates this second use of the limit register. The second form is the more common because the comparison and the addition can be performed in hardware in parallel, making the implementation faster than an addition followed by a comparison.

9.2.2   Segmentation

Quite often, we want to manage the various parts of a process separately. For example, consider the case where we have more than one process that uses the same program code. If we do address translation for the code segment separately from the data and stack segments, then we can save memory by having the two processes share the code space. This motivation leads us to a segmented memory management system. One of the simplest ways of implementing such a system is to use separate base and limit registers for each segment. This type of memory management is called **segmentation**. As we see later in this chapter, this term is also used to describe techniques for dividing data into a number of distinct functional regions. When there is potential for confusion, we refer to the address translation technique as **hardware segmentation**.

There are two common ways of selecting which base/limit pair to use for a given address. In the first case, we use the registers appropriate to the particular type of access. If we are fetching an instruction, we use the base and limit registers for the code segment. On the other hand, if we are pushing a return address onto the stack, we use the register pair for the stack segment. The second common approach is to organize the base/limit registers in a table indexed by high-order bits of the virtual address. This second approach is illustrated in Figure 9-3.

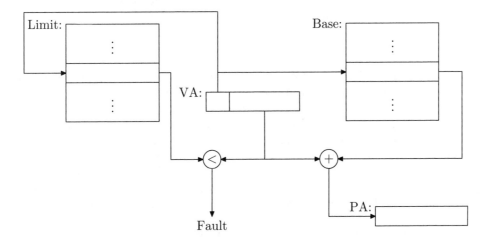

Figure 9-3: Segmentation Address Translation

9.2.3 Paging

Segmentation schemes usually have a relatively small number of relatively large variable-sized segments. However, if we reverse all these attributes, we get another, even more commonly used, memory management scheme. We call schemes that manage memory in a large number of relatively small fixed-sized units **paging** schemes.

In a system that uses a paged memory management unit, the virtual address space is divided into **pages** each of 2^k bytes. If the virtual address is n bits, then the virtual memory space consists of 2^{n-k} pages. The upper $n - k$ bits form a **page number**, and the lower k bits are an offset into the page. In the physical memory space, a 2^k byte space where a page may be mapped is called a **page frame**.

9.2.3.1   Page Tables

Just as the registers that define the segment address translation can be collected in a table, so too can the data that defines the address translation in a paging system. We call these tables **page tables**. A page table is indexed by the page number in a virtual address, and the **page table entry** (PTE) in the table defines the translation. A complete set of PTE fields typically includes:

- *Page frame number (PFN)*: This field determines the page frame to which the page in question is mapped. This field is concatenated with the offset to give the physical address.

- *Protection bits*: We generally want to be able to restrict the use of some pages. Just as we talked about sharing portions of memory in a segmented scheme, we also want to be able to do so in a paged system. Usually, we want to mark the pages that are shared as read-only. Similarly, we often want to be able to prevent data pages from being executed like instructions.

- *Present bit (P)*: This bit is sometimes called the **valid bit**. It is set when there is a translation of this page number into a page frame number. If an attempt is made to access a memory location in a page for which there is no valid translation, an interrupt is generated. This interrupt is called a **page fault**. Page faults indicate one of two conditions. The first interpretation of a page fault is that the requested memory is not allocated to the process. In this case, it must either be automatically allocated, or, more often, we say that the process has performed an illegal operation and must be terminated. The other interpretation is that the page is not present in memory, but is stored on the disk and should be read into memory in response to the fault. This latter case is discussed in more detail in Section 9.6.3.

- *Dirty bit (D)*: This bit is often called the **modified bit**. When set (by the hardware), it means that a write access has been made to that page since the last time the bit was cleared. We often use that information to tell us whether we need to save the page back to disk before reallocating its frame.

- *Accessed Bit (A)*: Not all systems include this bit. When it is implemented, it gets set by the hardware to indicate that the page has been accessed (for read or write) since the last time the bit was cleared.

Putting these pieces together, we get the address translation scheme illustrated in Figure 9-4.

Suppose we have a machine with 32-bit virtual addresses and $2^{12} = 4096$ byte pages. This implies that there are $2^{20} = 1,048,576$ pages and, thus, page table entries. If each PTE is 4 bytes, then the page table is 4 MB. Even with modern, large physical memory spaces, it is still wasteful to allocate a full page table for each process if we are using only a small fraction of the pages. There are a couple of ways in which we reduce the need for page table space. First, we often use a base and limit register approach to define the page

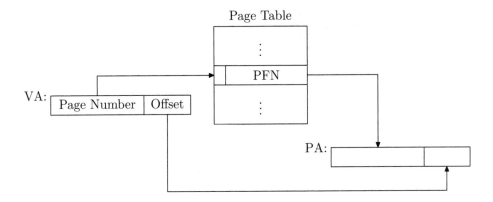

Figure 9-4: Single-Level Page Table Translation

table. This works best if we have allocated the bottom part of the virtual address space to the process.

Dividing the virtual memory space into a hierarchy is another method for dealing with the large page tables. This hierarchy leads us to a two-level page table. Using our example, we divide the 20 bits of the page number into two sets of 10. The most significant 10 bits index a page table, often called a **page directory**. The page frame number stored in the selected PTE identifies the page holding the page table, which is then indexed by the other 10 bits of the page number. Figure 9-5 shows this two-level paging scheme.

9.2.3.2   Translation Lookaside Buffers

Because page tables are stored in memory, a significant performance issue arises. To complete a memory access, we must first look up the PTE for that memory location, which involves a memory access itself (two in the case of a two-level page table). The result is that every memory access takes two or three times as long as it would if there were no page table address translation.

Needless to say, this exacerbates the mismatch between the rate at which the processor can request and process data and the rate at which the memory subsystem can supply it. Just as we use a cache to bridge that performance gap, we use a special cache to improve the speed of the paging system. This cache is called the **translation lookaside buffer** (TLB). It is addressed by a lookup on the page number, and if the PTE is contained in the TLB, then it saves us a memory access. Otherwise, the page table in memory is indexed to locate the PTE.

9.2.3.3   Inverted Page Tables

The basic idea of a paged memory management unit makes sense for systems with 32-bit addresses. However, if the system uses 64-bit addresses, the size of the table can get prohibitively large. Consider the case where our pages are 65,536 bytes each. This means that the offset part of the virtual address is 16 bits. If we use a two-level page table, each level is addressed by a 24-bit number meaning that each table has about 16 million

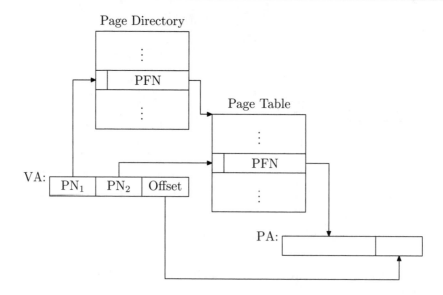

Figure 9-5: Two-Level Page Table Translation

entries. Each PTE would likely be 8 bytes, making these tables 128 MB each! Even if we went to a three-level page table, each table would still take half a megabyte, and we'd have to deal with the fact that page references could take up to four memory accesses.

To deal with this issue, we can employ **inverted page tables**, sometimes called **frame tables**. Where a normal page table maps page numbers to page frame numbers, an inverted page table maps page frame numbers to page numbers. Using these tables, the operation of the TLB remains the same. Of course, this does not permit the hardware technique of using the page number as an index into the table. Instead, when we have a TLB miss, the operating system is responsible for locating the appropriate PTE and loading it into the TLB.

9.3 Memory-Related Services

Earlier in this chapter, we discuss the concept of the memory hierarchy. In a broad sense, the operating system is responsible for managing this hierarchy. Ultimately, we must decide what data is to reside in each level. For some levels, this is determined by hardware, but in most cases, it is the operating system that must make those decisions. Every memory-related service that the OS provides to applications ultimately boils down to determining both in which level of the hierarchy and where within that level data is to reside.

At its heart, the operating system provides two primary memory services for processes: allocation and deallocation. Memory allocation follows two general approaches. In the first, which can be called **explicit allocation**, the requesting process specifies exactly which memory addresses are required. For example, the system call might specify the highest address that is to be used for the memory space. The presumption is that all lower addresses will also be used. As we might expect, the other approach can be termed **implicit allocation**. With this approach, the requesting process asks for a particular sized block of memory, but it does not specify where that memory should be. The system call returns the address of the newly allocated block. Either way, applications often further subdivide the allocated space with their own memory management. However, from the operating system's perspective, these spaces are just allocated blocks. We don't care how the application uses them.

Similarly, we can identify deallocation strategies that are explicit and those that are implicit. In some cases, the application issues a system call specifying which memory is to be freed. This specification is typically made either by passing the address of the block or by reducing the size of the memory space. On the other hand, we sometimes design systems in such a way that deallocation is implicit. The idea here is that we can determine which memory is still in use by analyzing all memory references in the system. We start with known blocks of memory and follow any references contained in them. This process is carried out recursively, looking at all the references contained in each block we've identified. At the end of this process, any blocks of memory that we didn't visit must no longer be used and, thus, can be freed. This type of **mark and sweep** algorithm is a form of **garbage collection**.

Some operating systems additionally provide services that control memory sharing. We sometimes want to allow a process to declare that some part of its memory space coincides with some part of another process's. Although we might consider this to be a special case of an allocation request, the typical set of services provides distinct system calls for controlling sharing. For example, we might provide a system call where the application passes the address and size of already allocated memory and declares it to be available for sharing. The result of this call is that the OS allocates a systemwide unique identifier and returns it to the calling process. Then, another process can issue another system call where it states that it would like to incorporate the shared memory block with a certain ID number into its address space. After this mapping has been established, anything that one process writes to the shared memory space, the other process can read. Naturally, the processes involved use mutual exclusion techniques, such as those discussed in Section 5.7, to coordinate access to the shared resource.

One last service provided by some operating systems is the **memory-mapped file**. Suppose that we have a file stored on the disk in a file system, as discussed in Chapter 17, and that we request that it be mapped into memory. If we are programming in C and the mapping request returns a pointer p that points to the mapped file, then an expression like $p[10]$ refers to byte 10 of the file. The effect is that we can read and write the file using normal memory access operations, rather than file system–specific system calls.

9.4   Memory Layouts

Before delving into the details of how the operating system provides memory services, it is helpful to establish the context for them. First, we examine the overall memory layout of the system. In what follows, it is important to remember that for most of what we say about the general principles of memory layouts, there are systems that provide exceptions. Nevertheless, certain features are common enough for us to build a picture of a typical layout.

We start with the memory space defined by the hardware. If the architecture defines addresses to be n bits wide, then the possible memory addresses are 0 through $2^n - 1$. Other aspects of the system design might limit the amount of that address space which we can access. For example, although the architecture might define n bits, the actual implementation might bring out only m bits to access real memory, leaving the other $n - m$ bits to be ignored. In addition to these restrictions, other parts of the memory space are often reserved for specific purposes. Space for interrupt vectors is a common example of such reservations. Usually, these are placed either at the bottom or at the top of the memory space. Similarly, many system designs define a part of the upper memory space for I/O devices. Putting these pieces together, we get a layout like that shown in Figure 9-6. Keep in mind that this layout is specified in terms of physical memory addresses.

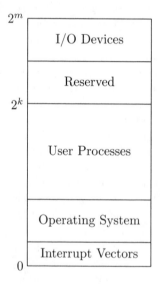

Figure 9-6: Typical System Memory Layout

Just as we can make some general statements about the overall system layout, we can say some things about the way in which processes are laid out in memory. For most environments, the memory space of a process is divided into a number of **segments**. One typical segment contains the process's code. Bytes in the **code segment** are those that make up the executable instructions of the program. Another segment is the **data segment**, which contains some of the process's data. In particular, the data segment typically contains those data that are global data or those that are dynamically allocated by allocation system calls. Finally, there is usually a **stack segment**, which is used to store activation records. These records (also called stack frames) hold arguments, local variables, return addresses, and other administrative overhead related to function calls and interrupts. Some systems subdivide one or more of these segments, and some have additional segments.

There are two main approaches to positioning segments in the memory space. In discussing these techniques, we focus on the three primary segments described earlier. First, in systems with large virtual memory spaces, the segments are sometimes positioned at fixed virtual address boundaries. For example, in a system with a 32-bit address space, we might position the code segment at virtual address 0 and allow up to 1 GB for it. Similarly, the next gigabyte might be reserved for the data segment and the third for the stack segment, with the final gigabyte prohibited. The second main layout is created by allocating the code segment only as needed. Then, the data segment starts at the end of the code segment and can grow upward, whereas the stack starts at the top of the address space and can grow downward. This second approach is illustrated in Figure 9-7. In both of these cases, the layout is described in terms of virtual address spaces. Even though we've illustrated these per-process layouts as contiguous, remember that address translation might well break them up and spread them out across the physical memory space. As discussed in Section 9.2, hardware segmentation or paging or both can be used to effect the address translation.

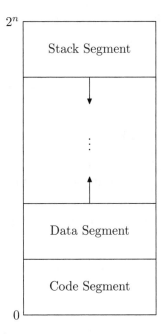

Figure 9-7: Typical Process Memory Layout

9.5   Memory Allocation Techniques

The primary role of the memory management system is to satisfy requests for memory allocation. Sometimes this is implicit, as when a new process is created. At other times, processes explicitly request memory. Either way, the system must locate enough unallocated memory and assign it to the process.

9.5.1   Free Space Management

Before we can allocate memory, we must locate the free memory. Naturally, we want to represent the free memory blocks in a way that makes the search efficient.

Before getting into the details, however, we should ask whether we are talking about locating free memory in the physical memory space or the virtual memory space. Throughout this chapter, we look at memory management techniques primarily from the perspective of the operating system managing the physical memory resource. Consequently, these techniques can all be viewed as operating in the physical memory space. However, many of these techniques can also be used to manage virtual memory space. Application-level dynamic memory allocation, using familiar operations such as the *malloc*( ) call in C or the **new** operator in C++, often allocate large blocks from the OS and then subdivide them into smaller allocations. They may well use some of these same techniques to manage their own usage of memory. The operating system, however, does not concern itself with that use of these techniques.

9.5.1.1   Free Bitmaps

If we are operating in an environment with fixed-sized pages, then the search becomes easy. We don't care which page, because they're all the same size. It's quite common in this case to simply store one bit per page frame, which is set to one if the page frame is free, and zero if it is allocated. With this representation, we can mark a page as either free or allocated in constant time by just indexing into this **free bitmap**. Finding a free page is simply a matter of locating the first nonzero bit in the map. To make this search easier, we often keep track of the first available page. When we allocate it, we search from that point on to find the next available one.

The memory overhead for a free bitmap representation is quite small. For example, if we have pages that are 4096 bytes each, the bitmap uses 1 bit for each 32,768 bits of memory, a 0.003% overhead.

Generally, when we allocate in an environment that uses paging address translation, we don't care which page frame we give a process, and the process never needs to have control over the physical relationship among pages. However, there are exceptions. One exception is a case where we do allocate memory in fixed sized units, but where there is no address translation. Another is where not all page frames are created equally. In both cases, we might need to request a number of physically contiguous page frames. When we allocate multiple contiguous page frames, we look not for the first available page, but for a run of available pages at least as large as the allocation request.

9.5.1.2   Free Lists

We can also represent the set of free memory blocks by keeping them in a linked list. When dealing with fixed-sized pages, allocation is again quite easy. We just grab the first page off the list. When pages are returned to the free set, we simply add them to the list. Both of these are constant time operations.

If we are allocating memory in variable-sized units, then we need to search the list to find a suitable block. In general, this process can take an amount of time proportional to the number of free memory blocks. Depending on whether we choose to keep the list sorted, adding a new memory block to the free list can also take $O(n)$ time (proportional to the number of free blocks). To speed the search for particular sized blocks, we often use more complex data structures. Standard data structures such as binary search trees and hash tables are among the more commonly used ones.

Using the usual linked list representation, we have a structure that contains the starting address, the size, and a pointer to the next element in the list. In a typical 32-bit system, this structure takes 12 bytes. So if the average size of a block is 4096 bytes, the free list would take about 0.3% of the available free space. However, there's a classic trick we can play to reduce this overhead to nothing except for a pointer to the head of the list. This trick is based on finding some other way to keep track of the starting address, the size, and the pointers that define the list structure. Because each element of the list represents free space, we can store the size and pointer to the next one in the free block itself. (The starting address is implicit.) This technique is illustrated in Example 9.1.

Example 9.1: Free List Structure

Consider a free list with three free blocks, of sizes 3, 8, and 16. If the block of size 16 is first in memory, followed by the blocks of sizes 3 and 8, then the list structure shown in Figure 9-8 stores the list in ascending order of size.

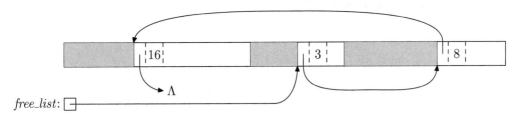

Figure 9-8: Free List Example

There are several things in this example we should note. First, except for the global pointer *free_list*, we store everything in the free blocks themselves. The only overhead is this pointer. Second, if a block is of size 16 KB and the pointers and sizes are stored in 4-byte integers, then the unused space while the block is in the free list is $16384 - 8 = 16376$. However, the full 16,384 bytes are available to be allocated to a requesting process. Third, we do not store the starting address of a block in its descriptive information. When we follow a pointer to a block, that pointer gives us the starting address.

9.5.2 Fragmentation

When allocating memory, we can end up with some wasted space. This happens in two ways. First, if we allocate memory in such a way that we actually allocate more than is requested, some of the allocated block will go unused. This type of waste is called **internal fragmentation**. The other type of waste is unused memory outside of any allocated unit. This can happen if there are available free blocks that are too small to satisfy any request. Wasted memory that lies outside allocation units is called **external fragmentation**.

9.5.3 Partitioning

The simplest methods of allocating memory are based on dividing memory into areas with fixed **partitions**. Typically, we administratively define fixed partitions between blocks of varying size. These partitions are in effect from the time the system starts to the time it is shut down. Memory requests are all satisfied from the fixed set of defined partitions. This approach is illustrated in Example 9.2.

Example 9.2: Fixed Partitioning

Although fixed partitioning is not commonly found in modern, general-purpose systems, it is seeing a sort of revival. Some of the virtualization systems use simple, fixed partitions between the various virtual systems. One good example of this is Xen. In Xen, the memory used by the OS identified as the Domain 0 OS is specified with the option dom0_mem in whatever boot loader is used to load the Xen hypervisor into memory. For example, when using grub, the line

```
kernel=/xen.gz dom0_mem=262144 console=vga
```

declares that the Domain 0 OS has 256 MB reserved for it. For OSs run in other domains, the line

```
memory = 128
```

in a configuration file reserves 128 MB for the corresponding domain.

More commonly, however, we want the flexibility of allocating memory in either large or small units as needed. When we allocate memory in these systems, we pick a free block and split it into two parts. The first part is the memory we allocate to the requesting process, and the second part is returned to the set of free memory blocks. When allocating in such a variable partition scheme, we allocate in multiples of some minimum allocation unit. This unit is a design parameter of the OS and is not a function of the hardware MMU design. This helps to reduce external fragmentation. In most cases, these allocation units are relatively small—usually smaller than the page frame sizes we typically see in systems that use paging. Furthermore, if we are using a free list data structure stored in the free blocks, then we must ensure that each free block is large enough to hold the structure.

9.5.4   Selection Policies

If more than one free block can satisfy a request, then which one should we pick? There are several schemes that are frequently studied and are commonly used.

9.5.4.1   First Fit

The first of these is called **first fit**. The basic idea with first fit allocation is that we begin searching the list and take the first block whose size is greater than or equal to the request size, as illustrated in Example 9.3. If we reach the end of the list without finding a suitable block, then the request fails. Because the list is often kept sorted in order of address, a first fit policy tends to cause allocations to be clustered toward the low memory addresses. The net effect is that the low memory area tends to get fragmented, while the upper memory area tends to have larger free blocks.

Example 9.3: First Fit Allocation

To illustrate the behavior of first fit allocation, as well as the other allocation policies later, we trace their behavior on a set of allocation and deallocation requests. We denote this sequence as A20, A15, A10, A25, D20, D10, A8, A30, D15, A15, where An denotes an allocation request for n KB and Dn denotes a deallocation request for the allocated block of size n KB. (For simplicity of notation, we have only one block of a given size allocated at a time. None of the policies depend on this property; it is used here merely for clarity.) In these examples, the memory space from which we serve requests is 128 KB. Each row of Figure 9-9 shows the state of memory after the operation labeling it on the left. Shaded blocks are allocated and unshaded blocks are free. The size of each block is shown in the corresponding box in the figure. In this, and other allocation figures in this chapter, time moves downward in the figure. In other words, each operation happens prior to the one below it.

A20	20			108		
A15	20	15		93		
A10	20	15	10	83		
A25	20	15	10	25	58	
D20	20	15	10	25	58	
D10	20	15	10	25	58	
A8	8 · 12	15	10	25	58	
A30	8 · 12	15	10	25	30	28
D15	8	37		25	30	28
A15	8 · 15	22		25	30	28

Figure 9-9: First Fit Allocation

9.5.4.2   Next Fit

If we want to spread the allocations out more evenly across the memory space, we often use a policy called **next fit**. This scheme is very similar to the first fit approach, except for the place where the search starts. In next fit, we begin the search with the free block that was next on the list after the last allocation. During the search, we treat the list as a circular one. If we come back to the place where we started without finding a suitable block, then the search fails. Example 9.4 illustrates this technique.

Example 9.4: Next Fit Allocation

For the next three allocation policies in this section, the results after the first six requests (up through the D10 request) are the same. In Figure 9-10, we show the the results after each of the other requests when following the next fit policy.

A8	20	15	10	25	8	50		
A30	20	15	10	25	8	30	20	
D15	45			25	8	30	20	
A15	45			25	8	30	15	5

Figure 9-10: Next Fit Allocation

9.5.4.3   Best Fit

In many ways, the most natural approach is to allocate the free block that is closest in size to the request. This technique is called **best fit**. In best fit, we search the list for the block that is smallest but greater than or equal to the request size. This is illustrated in Example 9.5. Like first fit, best fit tends to create significant external fragmentation, but keeps large blocks available for potential large allocation requests.

Example 9.5: Best Fit Allocation

As with the next fit example, we show only the final four steps of best fit allocation for our example. The memory layouts for these requests is shown in Figure 9-11.

A8	20	15	8	2	25	58		
A30	20	15	8	2	25	30	28	
D15	35		8	2	25	30	28	
A15	35		8	2	25	30	15	13

Figure 9-11: Best Fit Allocation

9.5.4.4   Worst Fit

If best fit allocates the smallest block that satisfies the request, then **worst fit** allocates the largest block for every request. Although the name would suggest that we would never use the worst fit policy, it does have one advantage: If most of the requests are of similar size, a worst fit policy tends to minimize external fragmentation. We illustrate this technique in Example 9.6.

Example 9.6: Worst Fit Allocation

Finally, Figure 9-12 shows the memory layout after each of the last four requests in our example for worst fit allocation.

A8	20	15	10	25	8	50		
A30	20	15	10	25	8	30	20	
D15	45			25	8	30	20	
A15	15	30		25	8	30	20	

Figure 9-12: Worst Fit Allocation

9.5.5   Buddy System Management

There is another memory allocation system, which is very elegant and which tends to have very little external fragmentation. This approach is called the **buddy system** and is based on the idea that all allocated blocks are a power of 2 in size. The buddy system allocation algorithm can be described as follows:

Buddy System Allocation: Let n be the size of the request. Locate a block of at least n bytes and return it to the requesting process.

1. If n is less than the smallest allocation unit, set n to be that smallest size.

2. Round n up to the nearest power of 2. In particular, select the smallest k such that $2^k \geq n$.

3. If there is no free block of size 2^k, then recursively allocate a block of size 2^{k+1} and split it into two free blocks of size 2^k.

4. Return the first free block of size 2^k in response to the request.

We call this technique the buddy system because each time we split a block, we create a pair of buddies that will always either be split or paired together. Neither will ever be paired with another block. From the offset of a block, we know whether it is the left buddy or the right buddy in a pair. In particular, if we have a block of size 2^k, then bit k of the offset (numbered from the least significant bit starting at 0) is 0 if the block is a left buddy and 1 if it is a right buddy. For instance, a block of 32 bytes will start at an offset whose last six bits are either 000000 or 100000. In the first case, it is the left buddy and in the second, it is the right. To find a block's buddy, we only need to complement bit k of the offset. So when freeing a block, we can easily find which block can be combined to make a larger block. If we do find that the block's buddy is also free and combine the two, then we will recursively attempt to combine the new block with its buddy. This method is illustrated in Example 9.7.

Buddy system allocation is very straightforward and tends to have very low external fragmentation. However, the price we pay for that is increased internal fragmentation. In the worst case, each allocation request is 1 byte greater than a power of 2. In this case, every allocation is nearly twice as large as the size requested. Of course, in practice, the actual internal fragmentation is substantially smaller, but still tends to be larger than what we find with the other variable-sized block techniques.

Example 9.7: Buddy System Allocation

We return again to the allocation requests in the previous examples to see how the buddy system would handle them. Figure 9-13 shows the memory allocations under the buddy system. Within each allocated block, both the size of the allocated block and the size of the request are given to illustrate the internal fragmentation.

	128					
A20	32:20	32			64	
A15	32:20	16:15	16		64	
A10	32:20	16:15	16:10		64	
A25	32:20	16:15	16:10		32:25	32
D20	32	16:15	16:10		32:25	32
D10	32	16:15	16		32:25	32
A8	32	16:15	8:8	8	32:25	32
A30	32:30	16:15	8:8	8	32:25	32
D15	32:30	16	8:8	8	32:25	32
A15	32:30	16:15	8:8	8	32:25	32
D8	32:30	16:15	16		32:25	32
D30	32	16:15	16		32:25	32
D15	64				32:25	32

Figure 9-13: Buddy System Allocation

The set of allocations and deallocations in this example illustrate a number of aspects of this technique. In the first request, we want to allocate a block of size 20, that we round up to the nearest power of 2, which is 32. There are no free blocks of that size, so we take the only free block there is (size 128) and split it into two free blocks of size 64. We still don't have a block of size 32, so we take the recursion one more step and split one of the blocks of size 64 into two of size 32. Now we have a block we can use to satisfy the request. The other allocation requests are comparatively straightforward in that they can all be satisfied either with an available free block or with one split. The last three deallocations (beyond those in the earlier examples) also deserve note. In each of these three cases, the block that is deallocated is a buddy to free block. In these cases, we combine them into a bigger free block. The last deallocation is especially interesting. We deallocate the block of size 16 (of which the application used 15). Because its buddy (also of size 16) is free, we combine them into a free block of size 32. The buddy of this new free block is also free, so we recursively combine the two blocks of size 32 into one of size 64.

9.6 Overallocation Techniques

Up to this point, we have assumed that we can just deny an allocation request if there is no suitable free block available. In some environments (for example, supercomputers) this is a reasonable policy. However, in most general-purpose systems, we want to be able to overextend ourselves a bit. Our justification is that it is very rare that every block of allocated memory is currently in use, in that it is frequently accessed. If we can identify blocks that are not in current use and temporarily store them to disk, then, in most cases, we'll have enough memory to hold everything that is currently active.

In dealing with overallocation, we often encounter the term **virtual memory**. From our previous discussion, it would be quite reasonable for the term virtual memory to refer to the memory addressable with a virtual address. However, we have been careful to use the term virtual memory space to describe this, because in common usage, the

---

Historical Note: Overlays

In addition to the swapping and paging techniques discussed here, there is another overallocation technique that has been largely lost to history. There was a time when programmers provided their own overallocation management as part of the applications themselves. The most common mechanism was the **overlay**. Suppose the program's structure can be broken up into a number of distinct phases. A compiler is a good example of this. One design calls for the parsing phase to produce an intermediate representation that is then operated on by the code generation phase, and the output of the code generator is operated on by the optimizer. Upon completion of the parser, we no longer need that code to be resident in memory. If we're short of either virtual memory space or physical memory, we can start the program with just the parser code resident, then overlay that code with code for the code generator after the parser is finished. Similarly, when the code generator completes its task, we read the code for the optimizer into memory on top of the code generator. The application itself will read the new code into memory and transfer control to it. The operating system isn't responsible for managing memory except for allocating space for the process as a whole. Like many techniques, overlays were used for several generations of computers, including mainframes, minicomputers, and microcomputers, where the technique was used with operating systems such as CP/M and MS-DOS. Between large virtual address spaces on modern systems and demand paging, programmers are very rarely burdened with implementing overlays today.

term virtual memory has a related, but subtly different, meaning. When we use the term virtual memory, we are usually referring to that part of the virtual memory space that is being used by a process, whether any or all of that memory is currently stored in physical memory. This usage is particularly common when discussing the paging techniques we cover later. In some cases, the term is used primarily to refer to that part of the virtual memory space which is not currently stored in physical memory. When it's used this way, it's often seen as synonymous with the storage (such as disks) used to hold that data, a concept we also call the **backing store**. Because this term can be a little ambiguous, we try to be more specific here, using terms such as virtual memory space, resident memory, and nonresident memory.

9.6.1   Swapping

Suppose we have a process that has been waiting for user input for quite some time because the user has minimized the process's window while doing other things. If we need to free up some memory to satisfy an allocation request, then we can simply copy this idle process's memory contents to disk and put its memory back into the free set. When this process is scheduled at some later point, we read it back from disk into memory and continue as if nothing happened. Of course, when we read it back into memory, we might have to pick some other process to evict in order to make room for the one we're reloading. This type of copying between main memory (primary storage) and disk (secondary or backing storage) is called **swapping**.

There are a couple of issues that make swapping a little more involved than we've described. First, we often set our address translation to map the same physical memory holding a code segment into all processes that are running the same program, implicitly sharing that memory among them. If the process we're swapping out shares its code segment with another process, we probably want to swap out only the data and stack segments and leave the code segment where it is. The second issue is a more interesting subject of study. How do we pick the process we're going to swap out? Ideally, we want one that we're not going to be using for a while. However, unless we make substantial advances in crystal ball technology, we're stuck basing our decision on information about the past rather than the future. When dealing with variable-sized blocks, one of the big issues we must keep in mind is the size of the request. It does us no good to swap out a process that doesn't free up enough memory to satisfy the request. Aside from the size issue, the matter of using usage patterns to determine the process to swap out is very similar to the matter of choosing a page to swap out, as discussed in Section 9.6.3.

9.6.2   Segment Swapping

The idea that we might leave the code segment in memory when swapping out the rest of a process suggests that we might also be more selective about the rest of a process's memory space. How selective we can be is primarily a function of the memory management hardware. If the hardware provides for only a few functional segments like code, data, and stack, then the type of swapping described earlier is about the best we can do. On the other hand, if we have an MMU that translates addresses in a moderate to large number of segments (as illustrated in Figure 9-3), then we have more flexibility. By swapping out only parts of a process, we save disk read and write time, and we open up the possibility that the process might be able to continue without the parts that are swapped out. As in the case of swapping whole processes, the size of a segment is one of the factors in deciding which segments are good candidates to swap out. Otherwise, the considerations for selecting which segments to swap out are much like those for pages, as discussed in the next section.

9.6.3   Paging

As discussed in Section 9.2, paged MMUs manage memory in terms of relatively small fixed-sized pages. These characteristics allow us to carry the flexibility of swapping segments (either in the sense of functionally related subsets of the address space, or in the sense of hardware segments) even further. In particular, because page frames are all the same size, they are interchangeable. The question of size doesn't enter the picture, because any page will serve equally well in terms of what it contributes to satisfying the request. (This is mostly a correct statement. To be precise, accesses to different page frames will have different effects on the cache. However, this also depends on past accesses. Few systems attempt to factor this into the choice of page to swap out.) Therefore, it is very natural to copy individual pages between memory and disk. In effect, we can swap pages in much the same way as we can swap entire processes or segments. Pages are the natural unit to swap in systems with paged MMUs, making this technique the dominant approach for overallocation in current, general-purpose systems. This form of page swapping is most often called **paging**, despite the potential confusion coming from our use of that same term in reference to the address translation technique used by paged MMUs. To avoid that confusion and to highlight its similarity to other forms of swapping, we sometimes use the phrases **swapping pages** and **page swapping** to refer to copying pages between memory and disk.

There are a couple of big advantages to swapping pages over swapping entire processes or even segments. First, by making decisions at a finer-grained level, we can limit our swapping to only enough pages as are needed to satisfy the request. In other words, if the request is for 10 pages, then why spend the time swapping out the 100 pages that make up a whole process? Similarly, if we are looking at individual pages of a process, we can choose to swap out the parts of a process not currently in use. It's entirely possible that the process might be able to use its next time slice without having to swap those pages back in.

When operating this way, we use the present (P) bit (as discussed in Section 9.2) to indicate whether the page is currently resident in memory or the page is currently in the backing store. If the page has been swapped out to disk, we clear the P bit, causing a page fault if it is accessed. When a page fault occurs, the operating system must decide whether the process was trying to access a page not allocated to it or whether it was trying to access a page currently swapped out. In the latter case, the operating system must swap the page back in, possibly picking another page to be swapped out to make room for it. This loading of pages when they are needed is called **demand paging**.

In the extreme case, suppose we start executing a process by jumping to the starting memory location without loading any code into memory. Then, the first instruction fetch causes a page fault, so we load the page and begin executing code. In principle, responding to page faults, including one generated on the first instruction fetch, is all we have to do to run a program. However, this would seem to cause more page faults than we would desire. After all, we would expect that very quickly we'd incur additional page faults as we reach a "critical mass" of pages loaded into memory. For that reason, we often employ some form of **prepaging** (also called **prefetching** or **preloading**). For example, we might predict that the first n pages of the code segment will be needed soon and load them all at once. Similarly, when loading a page of the data segment, we might guess that the following pages will also be needed soon and load them at the same time.

Choosing which page to swap out is the main focus of study in paging. Most of the following subsections catalog some of the more commonly studied and implemented page replacement policies.

Historical Note: Ferranti Atlas

Although we often think of paged virtual memory as a feature of large computers starting in the '70s and of small computers starting in the '80s and '90s, the world was originally introduced to the concept in 1961 when Kilburn published a description of the Ferranti Atlas. This computer used 512-byte pages, which were swapped to drum storage, providing a larger virtual memory space than the 16 KWord to 48 KWord configurations that were shipped. The Atlas collection of page address registers (P.A.R.s) resembles the inverted page tables in modern systems. However, the comparison between the requested page number and all 32 to 96 P.A.R.s was done in hardware.

The page replacement algorithm (called the drum transfer learning program) sweeps the set of page frames once every 1024 instructions executed saving the values of the A bits (called the "use" digits) and clearing them. These samples are used to calculate two parameters for each page frame, the time since last access, t, and the length of the last inactive time, T. Pages are selected for swapping according to the following:

1. If a page has been idle longer than its previous period of inactivity, indicated by $t > T + 1$, then it has probably fallen out of use and is selected.

2. If no page satisfies criteria 1, then select the page with maximum $T - t$ among those with $t \neq 0$.

3. If all pages have $t = 0$, then select the page with maximum T.

Although this algorithm doesn't exactly match any of the policies discussed here, it seems to have some similarity to the Not Frequently Used (NFU) policy, which is discussed in Section 9.6.3.9.

Only three full scale Atlases and two scaled-down machines were delivered by Ferranti (and later ICT). However, this early foray into paged memory management influenced nearly every later paging design either directly or indirectly.

9.6.3.1 Page Reference Strings

When studying page replacement policies, we often want to examine what happens when the policy is applied to particular examples or test cases. We specify these cases by an ordered sequence of page accesses. These lists of page numbers are called **page reference strings**. In some cases, we distinguish the references that are reads from those that are writes. In other cases, we treat the string as a sequence of accesses without regard to whether we are reading or writing.

9.6.3.2 Local vs. Global Policies

In designing or selecting a page replacement policy, there is a major question we face. That is, do we select a page for replacement from all processes on the system or only from the process that is needing a page? The first case, called a **global replacement** policy, allows processes to grow the number of pages they have in memory. In effect, as one process needs a new page, it can "steal" a page frame from another process. On the other hand, we might want to keep processes from affecting each other in this way and use a **local replacement** policy, choosing among only those pages the process already has. Many of the techniques we discuss in the remainder of this section can be applied either locally or globally.

9.6.3.3 Belady's Min

We have already suggested that a good strategy is to pick the page that will be used least soon. In other words, if t_i is the time at which page i will next be accessed, we pick the page p defined by $p = \text{argmax}_i t_i$ to be swapped out. In fact, this policy is not only a good strategy, it is an optimal strategy. It ensures that the number of page faults is minimized. We call this policy **Belady's min**, named after Laszlo Belady, who carried out seminal research in paging while at IBM. While not a proof, there is some intuition behind why we might think that this policy is a good candidate for being optimal. We consider the extreme cases. If a page is never used (its next use is infinitely far away), then it is an ideal choice to swap out. On the other hand, if a page is going to be referenced next, then it is the worst choice of page to swap out.

Of course, Belady's min is not a realizable policy. We cannot look into the future to determine the values of t_i. However, because we know that it is optimal and because we can implement it in simulations, it serves as a reference against which we can measure other, realizable policies. By comparing them to Belady's min, we can say by what percentage they differ from optimal. We show this "policy" as well as the following ones in Example 9.8.

9.6.3.4 First In, First Out

Most realizable policies are based on the idea that pages are used for a finite amount of time, and that if a page is in some sense "old," it has a good chance of not being used again soon. The first policy we consider is the **first in, first out** (FIFO) policy, which is one of the simplest policies we can imagine. As the name implies, we take "old" to be defined in terms of the amount of time since the page was loaded into memory. So we pick the page that has been in memory the longest to be swapped out.

Implementing the FIFO policy is very simple. We keep a queue of all pages in memory. Pages are added to the tail of the queue when they are read into memory, and the page to be swapped out is always taken from the head of the queue.

9.6.3.5   Second Chance

The obvious weakness in the FIFO policy is that we don't make any allowance for the fact that a page might be loaded and then used continually for a very long time. One way to address this is the **second chance** policy. The idea is that we look at a page in the queue, and if it's been accessed since the last time we checked, it is spared being swapped out.

Implementation of the second chance policy is a pretty simple extension of the FIFO implementation. When we pull a page off the head of the queue, we examine the accessed (A) bit of the PTE. If the bit is 0, then we swap the page out as with the FIFO policy. If it is 1, then we clear the bit and reinsert the page at the tail of the queue. Notice that we are guaranteed to find a page to swap out. Even if we start with all pages having been accessed, after a complete pass over the queue, we will reexamine the first page a second time and will swap it out. In this extreme case, the second chance policy is equivalent to the FIFO policy.

9.6.3.6   The Clock Algorithm

In its simplest form, the **clock algorithm** is just another way to look at the second chance policy. Imagine the set of pages arranged in a circle. We have a "hand" that rotates around the circle of pages. When we need to pick a page to swap out, we look at the page under the hand and look at its A bit acting on it as with the second chance policy. This scenario is illustrated in Figure 9-14.

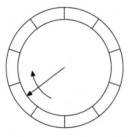

Figure 9-14: Single Hand Clock Algorithm

We've already mentioned that the second chance algorithm (and by extension the clock algorithm) performs correctly if all pages have been accessed. However, this is not the best situation in which to be. After all, if we've gone so long since clearing the A bits that they're all set, we can't really tell which ones have been accessed recently. This can easily happen if we have a large number of page frames. Even if most of the A bits are set, there is still a good chance the clock hand will encounter some page with A = 0. As a result, it will take the hand quite a long time to make a complete revolution. To get a good sense of what has and has not been recently accessed, we want to shorten the amount of time between clearing the A bit and checking it. We can do this by implementing a two-handed clock. The two hands move in lock-step, and the distance between them determines how long the page is given to be accessed. If it has not been accessed within that time, we can pick it to be swapped out. Figure 9-15 shows the relationship between the hands in a two-handed clock.

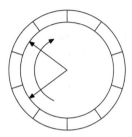

Figure 9-15: Two Hand Clock Algorithm

In many implementations of the two-handed clock, we don't move the hands just when a page fault occurs. Instead, we periodically advance the pair of hands some number of pages (up to the size of the gap) and keep a record of those we found where $A = 0$. When a page fault does occur and we need to pick one to evict, we do so from the set we've recorded.

9.6.3.7 Not Recently Used

Suppose we have several pages in a clock algorithm which have $A = 0$. Which one is best to swap out? Up to this point, we've assumed that a FIFO policy is best to fall back on. However, there is another factor to consider. If the page we are swapping out has not been modified since the last time it was written to disk, then there's no need for us to write it again when we swap it out. In other words, if we have two pages with $A = 0$, but one has $M = 1$ and the other has $M = 0$, we can swap the page with $M = 0$ twice as fast as the other. (This factor of two comes from the fact that we need to write a page and read a page if the page being swapped out has been modified. If it hasn't, then we can just read the new page on top of it.)

This observation is the basis of the **not recently used** (NRU) policy. If we treat the bits AM as a two-bit number labeling the pages, then we want to pick a page with the smallest label. So we'll pick pages with the label 00 over those with the label 01, over 10, over 11. This policy works well in conjunction with the two-handed clock. The second hand records both the A and M bits during its pass and keeps the list sorted by AM. Then we just pick one off of the end of the list with the lowest value of AM.

9.6.3.8 Least Recently Used

In a sense, these techniques are based on approximating how long it's been since a page has been accessed. Thinking about the problem this way, we really want to ask what page has been idle the longest. In other words, we want to pick the **least recently used** (LRU) page to swap out.

LRU is good as a concept, but it is rarely used in practice for page swapping. The reason is that we must answer the question, how long has it been since a page was last accessed? However, we can't timestamp each access in software because the accesses are happening at the rate of one or more per instruction. This would mean that the hardware would have to record a timestamp for each access of a page. Although this is possible in principle, it's not generally a feature we find in real hardware.

As a result, we find that we often approximate LRU in software using more coarse measurement. One of the more direct approximations to LRU is based on inducing additional page faults. The idea is that we periodically mark pages as not present (set P to 0). When a page is accessed, it causes a page fault. The operating system then checks to see if the page is actually present, and if it is, then the access time is recorded. At the same time, we set P to 1 to avoid page faults on future accesses. Using this approach, we get actual access times, though not necessarily the most recent ones. However, we would expect that on each sweep setting the P bits to 0, we would find several pages that still had P = 0, that is, pages that had not been accessed since the last time we marked them. If that is the case, then the access times of all the others are not particularly relevant. All of these untouched pages have been used less recently than all those we have access times for. In other words, we really just want to know when was the most recent pass where we found it was accessed. If we have an A bit, we can do this without inducing additional page faults. We can periodically sweep setting A to 0, and as we do, we check to see if it has been accessed since the last sweep. Then, the pages that were last accessed the furthest in the past are the ones we select to replace.

9.6.3.9   Not Frequently Used

Another approximation to LRU is based on counting references. In implementing the **not frequently used** (NFU) policy, we periodically sweep all of the pages in memory, and for each one where A = 1, we clear A and increment the page's counter. When it comes time to pick a page to swap out, we pick the page with the smallest value of the counter.

Unfortunately, this policy tends to unduly penalize newly loaded pages and to keep heavily used pages around longer than we want. We can improve on NFU by weighing recent references more heavily than older references. We call the technique **aging**. The usual approach is to compute a new value of the reference count according to the equation:

$$c' = \alpha c + (1 - \alpha)A$$

where $0 < \alpha < 1$. Frequently, we set $\alpha = 0.5$ and we represent c as a fixed point fraction with the binary point to the left of the most significant bit. Using this representation, we can implement the aging technique by shifting the value of c one bit to the right and shifting the value of A into the most significant bit. There are several subtleties that need to be addressed when implementing aging. First, the actual aging process (updating the value of c) should be applied to all pages, not just those resident in memory. Second, when looking for the page to evict, we should be careful about those pages that have been loaded and accessed since the last update pass. The page to swap out should be chosen from among those for which $A = 0$ (unless all pages have $A = 1$). Since $0 \leq c < 1$, we can search all pages for the one with minimum value of $c + A$ and swap it out.

Example 9.8: Paging Policies

As a way of illustrating these paging policies, we compare how they behave when processing an example of a set of page references. For this example, we have a system with only four page frames, all initially empty, and seven pages currently in use. The pages are referenced in the following order: 1, 2, 3, 4, 1, **2**, 5, 6, 2, 7, **3**, **4**, **2**, 6, **7**, 2, 7. In this page reference string, the pages listed in a normal Roman font are read accesses and those in bold are write accesses. In Figures 9-16 and 9-17, the page reference string is given vertically in the first column. In each row, the four blocks represent the four page frames, and the number in each frame is the page number in that frame after the reference labeling that line. Page numbers in italic are those for which the A bit is set, and those in a Roman font have the A bit cleared. Dirty pages are represented by a shaded box. Finally, those references that result in a page fault are labeled with the letter F to the right of the page frames.

For simplicity of presentation, this example uses NRU with a single-handed clock algorithm. Furthermore, Figure 9-17, illustrating the NFU policy, deserves special attention. The binary strings to the right of and between each pair of rows in the figure are the fixed point representations of the value c given earlier. Also, we follow the common case where $\alpha = 0.5$. Each page frame's value of c is given as a four-bit fraction, with an implied binary point to the left of the most significant bit. We sweep the set of pages and updating c after every other page reference (an update frequency that is much more frequent than we would use in practice). The values that are omitted (and replaced by a horizontal rule) are for pages that have not yet been loaded. Finally, when more than one page has the same minimum value of $c + A$, we select the page with the smallest page number.

Because this is only an example, it does not prove any general properties. Nevertheless, we can make some observations that do turn out to be frequently true:

- Because Belady's min is known to be optimal, we should certainly see that it has the fewest page faults, and this is indeed the case in this example.

- Because Belady's min, FIFO, and LRU don't use the A bit in any way, we don't see the bit ever being cleared.

- Because the FIFO policy doesn't take into account how much or when pages get used, we would expect that it would perform poorly. In this example, we see that it is the worst performing of the six policies.

- Because the NRU policy avoids swapping out pages that are dirty, it should be no surprise that it has more dirty pages after the last reference than the other policies.

- Remember that NFU is an approximation to LRU. Because of this, and because we are updating the measure of usage frequently, we find that the results of NFU and LRU are the same in this example.

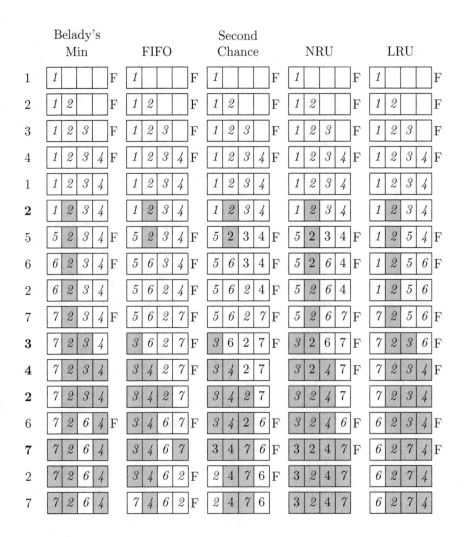

Figure 9-16: Paging Policy Comparison (Part 1)

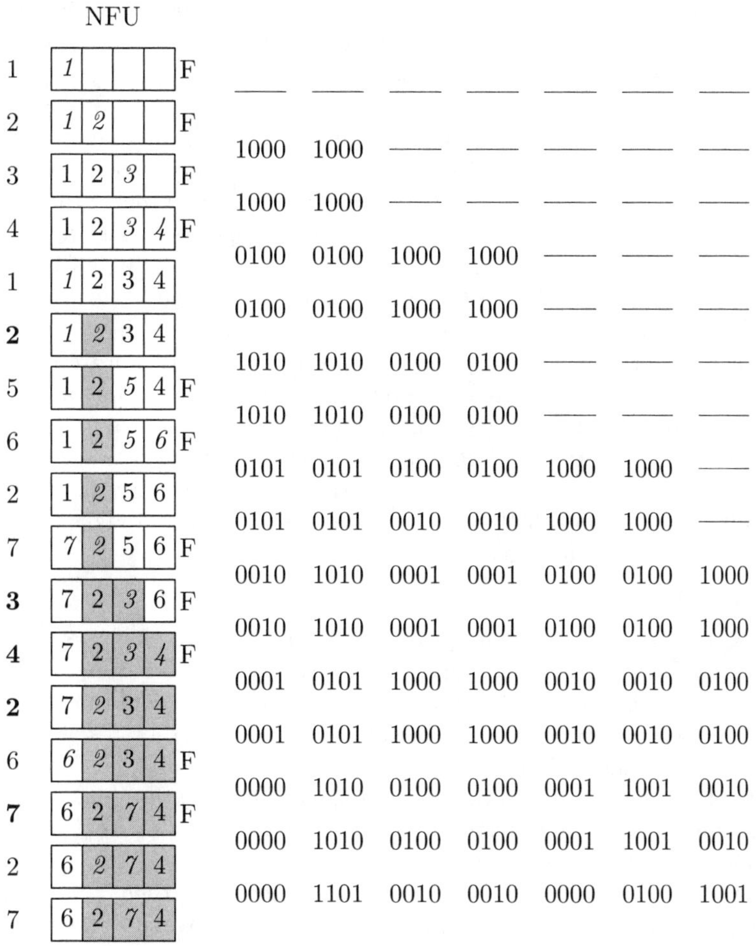

NFU

1	[1 _ _ _] F	
2	[1 2 _ _] F	
3	[1 2 3 _] F	1000 1000 — — — — —
4	[1 2 3 4] F	1000 1000 — — — — —
1	[1 2 3 4]	0100 0100 1000 1000 — — —
2	[1 2 3 4]	0100 0100 1000 1000 — — —
5	[1 2 5 4] F	1010 1010 0100 0100 — — —
6	[1 2 5 6] F	1010 1010 0100 0100 — — —
2	[1 2 5 6]	0101 0101 0100 0100 1000 1000 —
7	[7 2 5 6] F	0101 0101 0010 0010 1000 1000 —
3	[7 2 3 6] F	0010 1010 0001 0001 0100 0100 1000
4	[7 2 3 4] F	0010 1010 0001 0001 0100 0100 1000
2	[7 2 3 4]	0001 0101 1000 1000 0010 0010 0100
6	[6 2 3 4] F	0001 0101 1000 1000 0010 0010 0100
7	[6 2 7 4] F	0000 1010 0100 0100 0001 1001 0010
2	[6 2 7 4]	0000 1010 0100 0100 0001 1001 0010
7	[6 2 7 4]	0000 1101 0010 0010 0000 0100 1001

Figure 9-17: Paging Policy Comparison (Part 2)

9.6.3.10 The Working Set

In discussing the concept of prepaging, we suggest that there is some "critical mass" of pages that would be necessary to keep us from generating page faults too frequently. This intuitive observation leads us to the concept of the **working set**. We generally define the working set as those pages that a process is using at a particular point in time. However, if we take the idea of a point in time too literally, then during any infinitesimal time interval, we are using only one page. At the other extreme, if we consider the time in question to be the entire lifetime of a process, then all the pages it ever uses are in the working set. Clearly, we need to find a happy medium.

Fortunately, the value of the working set concept is not in precisely enumerating the working set at any particular time. Rather, we are primarily interested in what constitutes a reasonable range of working set sizes. Suppose we have one process that is blocked for a long time. As we use the page replacement policies discussed here to make room for new allocations and for swapping pages in, we find ourselves picking off the pages of this blocked process one by one. When the hapless process does get scheduled again, it will generate page faults at a high rate until its working set is once again loaded into memory.

The working set concept can help us deal with such situations. For example, we can set a pair of thresholds (often called **watermarks**), which establish upper and lower bounds on the allowed working set size. If we allocate and load pages for a process such that it exceeds its maximum working set size, then the next time we need to find a page to swap out, we select it from that process. On the other hand, if we are taking pages from a process and its working set falls below the lower bound, then we might as well swap the rest of it out and free up all its pages.

9.6.3.11 Page Fault Frequency

In discussing the working set concept, there is one aspect which we've conveniently skipped, namely how we establish the working set limits. For some systems, we set those limits administratively. However, it would be nice if we could in some way adjust the working set size of a process automatically. That is the objective of the **page fault frequency** policy. The basic idea is that if a process generates page faults too often, then it probably needs to have more pages allocated. On the other hand, if a process has generated no page faults, then it may well have stopped using some pages it has loaded and can stand to have them swapped out.

To be more precise, if t_i is the time of the ith page fault, then $f_i = 1/(t_{i+1} - t_i)$ is an estimate of the frequency of page faults. We normally average these estimates over several consecutive page faults and compare that average, f, to a pair of thresholds, F_l and F_u where $F_l < F_u$. If $f > F_u$, then we add a page to the process's working set size. If $f < F_l$, then we subtract a page from the process's working set size. Otherwise, we leave the size alone. Those processes for which the number of resident pages is greater than their working set size are examined first for pages to swap out.

9.6.4 Paged Segments

Some hardware includes support for both hardware segmentation and paging. In most cases, the virtual address space is carved up relatively coarsely into segments and then each segment is divided into relatively fine-grained pages. In terms of managing overallocation in such a system, one option is to ignore the segmentation and to just swap pages using the techniques of the previous section. However, from a working set perspective, the segmentation can potentially give us additional information about what pages should be swapped together. Suppose that the compiler places each major data structure in its own segment. Similarly, we can collect all the interdependent functions of a library into a segment. If the virtual memory space is organized in this way, it becomes fairly clear that entire segments are either part of the working set or not. In other words, we should make our swapping decisions on whole segments rather than individual pages.

In some sense, this scheme gives us the best of both worlds. By basing our swapping decisions on coarser units, we are more likely to have the complete working set resident. We are less likely to have one page from each major data structure swapped out, thus practically forcing the process to incur a page fault on the next time slice. However, by using fine-grained units of allocation, we gain flexibility in satisfying requests. The pages belonging to two swapped-out segments can be mixed and matched among one or more allocation requests. Similarly, when it comes time to swap a segment back in, we don't need a contiguous free block; we need only an appropriate number of free page frames, wherever they might be.

If paged segments have such nice advantages, then why do most systems use straight paging? The answer lies in the reality that mechanisms don't come for free. Adding segmentation hardware requires additional transistors, which takes additional real estate on the CPU chip. However, that same real estate could be used for other things like additional cache. Furthermore, adding a stage to the address translation process increases the average memory access time. On the software side, handling segments, as well as pages, adds complexity to the operating system. Additional complexity opens additional chances for flaws, both in software and in hardware. Finally, optimizing swapping performance is simply not as critical as it once was. Physical memory capacities have grown dramatically, while the number of users per machine has dropped. (We would, however, be remiss if we failed to notice that application sizes have also grown dramatically. Software, we might call "bloatware," accounts for a large part of the typical computing environment. The exact set of applications one uses determines whether it appears that the hardware designers or the application developers are winning the memory size war.) When the working set of all active processes is significantly less than the physical memory, the choices of pages to swap out can be less than optimal without being too detrimental to system performance.

9.6.5   Memory-Mapped Files

Demand loading of pages (or segments) provides a natural mechanism for implementing memory-mapped files. When a request to map a file arrives, the operating system allocates the necessary number of pages in the process's virtual memory space and marks them all as being swapped out. The key is that instead of identifying them as being swapped out to the normal paging area on the disk, we mark them as being swapped out to the areas of the file system where the file being mapped is stored.

When the process accesses one of the pages, a page fault occurs and the appropriate block of the file is read into memory. When pages are selected to be swapped out, the dirty ones are written back to the file. Similarly, when the file is closed by unmapping the memory area or by terminating the process, all the dirty pages are written back to the file.

9.6.6 Copy on Write

There are a number of cases where we find ourselves copying large amounts of memory. The UNIX *fork( )* system call is a good example of this as it creates a child process that is a copy of the parent. Most current systems implement this copy using a technique called **copy on write** (COW). Rather than literally make a second copy of the parent's memory space, we set up the memory management unit to map the child's virtual memory space to the same physical memory as the parent's. However, we mark all of the memory as read-only for both the parent and the child. As a result, any attempt to write by either the parent or the child will cause a protection fault from the MMU. When we get such an interrupt for a page or segment that would normally be read/write, we then make a new copy mapping the new copy into the child's memory space. Both copies are marked read/write and the instruction that caused the interrupt continues. The net effect is that we make copies of only those pages that end up being written.

9.6.7 Performance Issues

The illusion of a memory space larger than our physical memory doesn't come for free. If we're not careful in choosing allocation and replacement policies, system performance can suffer. In addition, many overallocation techniques have potential pitfalls that can also affect performance. This section discusses some of the more fundamental issues we face in implementing the techniques described here.

9.6.7.1 Access Times

Whereas access time to memory is measured in nanoseconds (billionths of a second), access time for disks is measured in milliseconds (thousandths of a second). We let the memory access time be given by t_m. The term t_d includes the disk access time and the time to process the page fault. Finally, f is the fraction of memory accesses that result in page faults. Then

$$t = t_m + f t_d$$

gives the average access time if none of the pages being replaced are dirty. (For that fraction of pages which are dirty, we add an additional t_d term.) Because of the vast discrepancy between t_d and t_m, f must be extremely small for t to be close to t_m. In other words, if the overall system is to have reasonable performance, then very few memory accesses can induce page faults. We see this in Example 9.9.

Example 9.9: Average Access Time

To put this into perspective, consider straight-line executable code, ignoring any data accesses. If each page is 4096 bytes and each instruction is 4 bytes, then we cross a page boundary every 1024 instructions. This implies that $f = 0.000976$ if no pages are already loaded. If $t_m = 50$ nS and $t_d = 10$ mS, then $t = 9760$ nS. The net effect is that instruction execution is 200 times slower than it would be if all of the instructions were resident in memory.

We should point out that if the paging system is working well and the code has a typical looping structure, then f, and hence the speed penalty, will generally be smaller. Another factor to consider is that on a busy time-sharing system, the situation is not as bleak as it seems. While the disk hardware is writing the old page and reading the new one, the CPU can be executing code that belongs to another process.

9.6.7.2   Thrashing

Another issue we consider is a phenomenon known as **thrashing**. This behavior occurs when there is not enough physical memory to support the set of ready processes. Rather than attempt to formulate a precise definition for thrashing, we discuss it in broad terms. Generally, we say that a system or a process is thrashing if it is getting little or no productive work done as a result of excessive paging. A couple of examples can help to make this clear. Suppose that we have a degenerate situation where every (otherwise) ready process is waiting on a page to be loaded from disk. Suppose that the first process to get its page loaded generates another page fault before the next process gets its page loaded. If this situation continues, then the system will not get much accomplished. Much of the time, the ready list will be empty and the CPU will be idle while the disk subsystem will be in heavy use, as illustrated in Example 9.10.

Example 9.10: Thrashing

As another example, consider a process that operates on a 4096×4096 image array, where each element of the array is a single byte grayscale value. The rows of the array are laid out so that adjacent elements in the same row are at consecutive memory addresses. Further, suppose that the process is limited to use no more than 4096 pages of 4096 bytes each and that the code to process the array resides in a single page. Thus, we have each row contained in a single page. If we go through the array a row at a time with none of the array already loaded into memory, then we incur one page fault per row. On the other hand, if we go through the array one column at a time, then by the time we get to the end of the first column, we will have to swap a page out. Because the least recently used page was the one for the first row, that is the one that gets swapped out. However, that's the very page we attempt to access next. The net effect is that every reference to the array generates a page fault. In this case, the process spends far more time waiting for pages to be loaded than it does executing instructions.

9.6.7.3   Belady's Anomaly

The final performance issue we discuss is a strange phenomenon called **Belady's anomaly**. It is quite reasonable to expect that if we increase the number of available page frames, we should have no more page faults. After all, we could just ignore the additional page frames and operate with exactly the same number of page faults as before. As it turns out, however, for some page replacement policies, this expectation can be violated. Belady's anomaly describes the case where even though $m > n$, the same page replacement policy can lead to more page faults with m pages than with n. Example 9.11 presents an example of this unexpected behavior.

Example 9.11: Belady's Anomaly

Belady's anomaly is most often illustrated with the reference string 1 2 3 4 1 2 5 1 2 3 4 5. (The reason this string is so commonly used is that it is the same string presented in both Belady's original paper on the anomaly and a later paper, where the idea of stack algorithms is presented.) Figure 9-18 illustrates this phenomenon using the FIFO page replacement policy. If we have only three page frames, we end up with nine page faults, but if we have four frames, there are 10 faults. For the first seven page references, we see

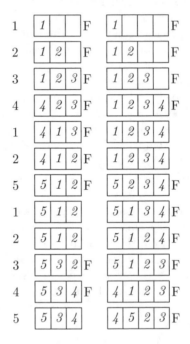

Figure 9-18: Belady's Anomaly

the behavior we would expect, namely that the larger number of page frames yields fewer page faults. However, for the final five references, we never have the right pages in place in the case of four frames and every reference induces a fault. On the other hand, in the case of three frames, only two of the last five references result in page faults.

It has been shown that it is both necessary and sufficient that a page replacement policy be implemented by a **stack algorithm** in order that it be immune to Belady's anomaly. Stack algorithms are those for which the **inclusion property** holds. The inclusion property basically holds for algorithms where all the pages that are resident would also be resident if there were more page frames. More formally, if $B_t(C)$ is the set of pages resident in C page frames at time t, then an algorithm for which $B_t(C) \subseteq B_t(C+1), \forall t, C$ is one which satisfies the inclusion property. Without proof, we observe that LRU does satisfy this property and is, thus, immune to the anomaly. Similarly, the NFU approximation to LRU is also a stack algorithm. However, because the second chance policy reduces to FIFO when all pages are used, it is not hard to show that for any page reference string that exhibits the anomaly in FIFO, there is at least one that exhibits the anomaly in second chance. Similarly, if all references are reads (or writes), then NRU is equivalent to second chance and, thus, can exhibit Belady's anomaly.

9.7   Memory Management in Embedded Systems

Most of the discussion in this chapter looks at memory management from the perspective of general-purpose systems. The memory management tasks in an embedded system are usually simpler than those in general-purpose systems. There are several reasons for this. First, in many embedded systems, the set of processes is determined at the time the system is compiled and linked. Going hand-in-hand with this, we generally provide enough physical memory to meet the needs of all the processes that are on the system. Furthermore, many embedded systems don't have any mass storage devices that could be used as secondary storage. All of these factors lead us to develop embedded systems without any form of overallocation of memory. We generally don't do swapping of either processes or pages on such systems.

In addition to these factors, embedded systems rarely have the memory management hardware we find in larger systems. Often there is no address translation at all. In these cases, we usually take one of two approaches. The first approach allocates all memory statically at compile and link time. In those cases, we don't need any run-time memory allocation policy. In the second approach, we generally use one of the simple variable-sized allocation policies like first fit. In Chapter 11, we look at the details of a system that shares much with embedded systems (though the set of processes isn't fixed when we build the system).

9.8   Summary

Every process needs a portion of the memory resources provided by the hardware. At the same time, processes accessing each other's memory represent one of the biggest security risks in a system. Thus, an operating system bears the responsibility for working with the hardware in allocating memory to processes according to their needs, while preventing processes from accessing memory indiscriminately.

The nature of the OS's allocation strategy generally depends on the nature of the memory management hardware. For systems that translate addresses for variable-sized segments, we often use one of the first fit, next fit, best fit, and worst fit strategies. For those systems where address translation operates in units of fixed-sized pages, the choice of which free page to allocate is usually arbitrary.

Things get more complicated when we want to support processes that, in total, require more memory than is physically present in the hardware. The two main approaches to supporting this are swapping and paging, both of which use secondary storage (such as disk space) to substitute for main memory. In swapping, we copy the entire memory space of a process to secondary storage when there is not enough physical memory to satisfy requests. When we swap individual pages, we operate on only parts of the memory space of a process. That way we can have parts of more (or even all) processes resident in memory.

For page swapping, the primary issue is which pages to choose to page out when we need to make room to satisfy requests. All practical policies are attempts to approximate the optimal Belady's min policy. The ones surveyed in this chapter include first in, first out, second chance, the clock algorithm (in one and two-handed variations), not recently used, least recently used, not frequently used, and page fault frequency. The last of these aims to balance the memory allocated to processes so that all processes have their working sets in memory at the same time.

The secondary storage devices can be slower than main memory by factors as high as one hundred thousand or even one million. Because of this vast discrepancy in access time, it is critical that our choices of pages to swap out don't result in thrashing, where the system spends most of its time swapping pages back and forth between main memory and secondary storage. When this happens, the system as a whole operates very slowly. Consequently, how well the OS handles its memory management task is one of the most important factors in overall system performance.

9.9　Exercises

1. Suppose we have a hardware segmentation system like that shown in Figure 9-3 where the base and limit tables have eight entries. Base register i (numbered from 0) contains the value $i \times 2^{10} + \text{0x100}$ and each limit register contains the hexadecimal value 0x200. If the 16-bit virtual address is 0x605f, then what physical address is computed? Does this address generate a fault?

2. Is it good design to make the minimum memory allocation size be a single byte? Why or why not?

3. The process memory layout shown in Figure 9-7 is based on hardware that decrements the stack pointer when pushing onto the stack. How would the design change if the hardware incremented the stack pointer instead?

4. Assuming a uniform distribution of request sizes, what percentage of internal fragmentation would we see on average if the minimum allocation unit is 32 bytes and the average request size is 1 KB?

5. In a buddy system design, how could we structure the representation of our free space to ensure that we can locate a free block of a given size (or determine that no such free block exists) in constant time? How much memory is used in overhead with this approach?

6. Consider a system with 64-bit addressing. If the page size is 64 KB, how many levels must the paging system have so that each table fits within one page? (Take the PTE size to be 8 bytes.)

7. If we have a machine with a 32-bit virtual address and a 1-KB page size, then how many pages are in the virtual address space? If each PTE takes 4 bytes, then how many pages are required to hold a complete page table? If the physical address space is 256 MB, then how many bits are needed for the page frame number (PFN) in the PTE?

8. Suppose that you have a system with 128 MB of memory with no memory initially allocated. Given the sequence of allocations (A) and deallocations (D): A 10 MB, A 20 MB, A 15 MB, D 20 MB, A 12 MB, A 30 MB, D 15 MB, and A 17 MB, show the free list at each stage for each of first fit, next fit, best fit, and worst fit.

9. Assume that you have 128 KB of memory. Give a sequence of allocations and deallocations that will succeed with first fit, but will fail with worst fit. Give a sequence that will succeed with worst fit, but fail with first fit.

10. An early version of UNIX was developed for small PDP-11 computers without memory management hardware. It held only one process in memory at a time; a swap was needed on each context switch. An early disk drive for such systems was the RL01. This drive took 55 mS to seek to access the data, and that data could be transferred at a rate of 512 KB/S. If each process was 32 KB in size and the quantum was 0.3 S, what fraction of the time was the system doing useful work?

11. Most of the examples we have studied use the paging system to map a large virtual address space onto a smaller physical space. Could it be useful to map a small virtual space onto a larger physical space? Why or why not?

12. Does using paged memory management hardware have any value even if we never swap pages to disk and back?

13. Write the pseudocode to implement an allocate and a deallocate operation using the buddy system.

14. If memory access time is 70 nS and disk access time is 12 mS, then what is the maximum fraction of memory accesses that can generate page faults and maintain an expected memory access time of no more than 100 nS?

15. A system with four page frames has six currently active pages where no pages are currently loaded. Using the second chance page replacement policy, which pages are resident at each step for the sequence of page accesses 1, 2, 3, 4, 1, 2, 5, 6, 3, 2, 6, 1? What about LRU?

16. Suppose that for a given job, Belady's min would result in a 99.99% hit rate, that memory access time is 70 nS, and that disk access time is 12 mS. If NFU results

in 20% more page faults than Belady's min, and second chance results in 30% more page faults than Belady's min, how much is the average access time degraded for each of these page replacement policies?

17. If a system has a 4-MB address space, where each page is 4 KB, and page table accesses take 100 nS, how long does it take to load a complete page table? What fraction of a 100 mS time slice does this take?

18. Show that the page reference string used in Figure 9-18 also exhibits Belady's anomaly under the second chance replacement policy.

19. Most systems don't swap out pages that are part of a read-only text segment because they can be reread from the original executable file. Would there be any advantage to doing so?

Chapter 10

Some Examples of Memory Management

In moving from basic principles and simple examples to real implementations, things are rarely as straightforward as they would seem. This is just as true in memory management as in other parts of the OS. In this chapter, we use our set of nine operating systems examples to illustrate variations in implementation of memory management techniques. Some examples apply the techniques discussed in the previous chapter directly, while others use combinations or modifications of the basic techniques.

10.1 CTSS

The machine on which CTSS runs has two 32 KWord banks of memory called **memory A** and **memory B** (sometimes called A-core and B-core). The system also includes memory relocation and protection registers, used to limit the memory accessed by a process. The supervisor is kept in memory A along with certain system commands. Memory B is used for all other programs run by user processes.

The approach CTSS takes to managing its memory space is very straightforward. After the system is loaded, the contents of memory A are fixed, and no swapping takes place for that bank of memory. Memory B is also managed with a rather simple policy. At any time, only one program can be fully resident in memory B. This means that on any scheduling that switches to a program running in memory B, we must read that program in from the swap space, unless it happens to already be the one in memory. (Swapped processes are stored on a drum device. Drums are similar to disks, but the recording medium is on a cylinder rather than a platter. Generally, drums have one read/write head per track, rather than moving the head as in typical disk drives. This makes access to data on drums faster than on disks.)

To improve efficiency, CTSS uses an interesting optimization called the "onion-skin" algorithm. When swapping a process out to drum, we don't necessarily swap all of it out. Suppose that we are swapping out a process that occupies n words, but the process we are about to swap in from the drum has $m < n$ words. In this case, we swap out only the

233

first m words of the first process, and then we load the second process into memory. The memory protection register is set to limit the second process's memory accesses to prevent it from accessing the first process's data still in memory. Although the basic idea of the onion skin algorithm is simple, things can get a little more complicated as the system runs. If we schedule a series of processes, each smaller than the one before, we end up with fragments of several processes in memory all at once. Then, if we swap the first large process back in, we have to swap out all the fragments, keeping track of which process each belongs to.

10.2   Multics

If there is any single feature of Multics which distinguishes it from other operating systems and makes it a worthy subject of study, that would be its memory management design. We should remember, however, that Multics is a little bit of an unusual case. The developers of Multics are the ones who added segmentation and paging hardware to the GE-635 resulting in the GE-645. In other words, the memory management unit (MMU) of the GE 645 was designed specifically for Multics rather than Multics being developed for existing hardware. Similarly, the Honeywell 6180, on which most installations of Multics ran, was designed with the same memory management organization.

To understand memory management in Multics, we need to put ourselves into the mindset of its creators. They wanted the system as a whole as well as individual processes in the system to see an unlimited number of segments, each with its own name and each unlimited in size. Of course, there must be limits in any practical system. However, in the mid-1960s, using 18 bits to specify the segment's name and 18 bits to specify the word within it was as close to unlimited as the designers could reasonably hope for. This arrangement means that our segment "names" are, in fact, the segment numbers. As we discuss later, however, from the application perspective, segments actually do have textual names. Furthermore, segments are divided into pages, so the 18-bit segment offset is itself divided into a page number and page offset, as illustrated in Figure 10-1.

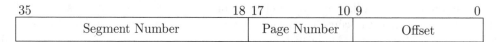

35	18	17	10	9	0
Segment Number		Page Number		Offset	

Figure 10-1: Multics Virtual Address Format

10.2.1   Memory-Related System Calls

Because all memory in Multics is divided into segments, we don't talk in terms of allocating or freeing memory. Rather, Multics provides system calls to create and delete segments. Processes also have the ability to modify the access rights of a segment. The size of a segment is determined by how much data we write to it. Multics dynamically allocates new pages to segments as they are accessed, up to a limit that is set per segment. Because segment offsets are specified with 18 bits, the maximum limit for a segment is 2^{18} words. Notice that from the application perspective, segmentation is very visible, but paging is hidden.

Multics doesn't need system calls for mapping a file into memory in the usual sense. This is because there is a one-to-one correspondence between segments and files. Creating a segment also creates a file. Similarly, files are accessed by accessing their segments. This also means that every segment has a name in a hierarchical name space, like those described in Chapter 17. Because the number of possible files in the system is larger than the number of available segment numbers, each process assigns a segment number to a file as it is needed.

10.2.2   Memory Layouts

Because segment numbers are assigned as segments are referenced, there is no fixed layout in the virtual address space. The primary exception is that the kernel is mapped into the first few hundred segments of all processes. This arrangement makes all the system call entry points of the kernel available in the process's memory space. Protection, preventing improper access to kernel internals, is provided by the ring access controls and call gates, as discussed in Section 21.6.

10.2.3   Segment and Page Management

With both segmentation and paging, processes in Multics can incur both segment faults and page faults. A segment fault normally indicates that a segment is being accessed for the first time. In other words, there is no mapping from path name to segment number. Establishing this mapping is the responsibility of the segment fault handler. Because segment path names are also file path names, we defer the details of the lookup process to Chapter 17. After the mapping from path name to segment number has been established, it is stored in the Known Segment Table to speed future references to the same segment. At the same time, the corresponding Segment Descriptor Word is loaded with the address of the segment's Page Table.

As with most paging systems, page faults are normally caused by accesses to pages that are not resident in main memory but are in secondary storage. The set of all page frames is kept in two lists, one of used frames and one of free frames. Pages that need to be swapped in are read into free frames. When the number of available free frames drops too low, more frames are identified as free using the clock algorithm.

10.3   RT-11

The primary distinction among the three RT-11 monitors is their memory usage. The SJ (single job) monitor reserves space for only one process. In the FB (foreground-background) monitor, there is room for multiple processes, one large background process and one or more smaller foreground processes. Both the SJ and FB monitors can run on PDP-11s without memory management hardware and are limited to 64 KB of memory. The XM (extended memory) monitor operates much like the FB monitor but also includes support for the MMU, allowing the system to access up to 4 MB of memory.

10.3.1   Memory-Related System Calls

Because part of the objective of RT-11 is giving applications nearly complete control over the hardware, there is very little in the way of system calls that allocate and free memory. However, there are a few system calls that allow applications to have some control over the system's memory layout. The primary one of these is .SETTOP. This call allows an application (the background application in the case of an FB or XM monitor) to declare, or change, the highest memory address that it will use. In effect, it tells the OS that any addresses above that point are available for the OS to use.

The XM monitor also provides additional calls that allow a process to directly control the mapping between virtual memory windows and physical memory regions. A process can allocate (or create) a region with the .CRRG call and can free (or eliminate) that region with the .ELRG call. Similarly, the .CRAW and .ELAW calls allocate and free virtual windows. The .MAP call requests that the OS set up the MMU to map between a given window and a given region. Mappings can be removed with the .UNMAP call.

There are also some system calls that deal more with process management but which have memory implications. Among these are the .CHAIN call for replacing one process with another and the .EXIT system call for terminating a process.

Finally, the .LOCK call can be used to force the User Service Routine (USR) to be resident in memory. To allow the USR to be swapped out, the application issues the .UNLOCK system call. (Swapping and the role of the USR are described in more detail in the following sections.)

10.3.2   Memory Layouts

Figure 10-2 shows the most general memory layout in an RT-11 system, as used in the XM monitor. Both the SJ and FB monitors use a subset of the components shown here. Because RT-11 can run on hardware without an MMU, the figure shows the memory layout in terms of physical addresses only and is given in units of words. The lowest 32 bytes are trap vectors as defined by the hardware. Just above the trap vectors, we find 16 bytes that are used to describe the current background job. Interrupt vectors for various I/O devices occupy the next 272 bytes. Most of the space below the 28 KW point is occupied by the current background job. In this area, a fixed-sized stack space is at the bottom of the address space. The rest of the job's address space is laid out in a fairly typical manner with code just above the stack. Data space, the top of which is set by the .SETTOP system call, occupies the memory directly above the code. The Keyboard Monitor (KMON) is located just above the background job. This code provides the command-line interpreter and a number of built-in commands. It is typically a little less than 4 KW in size. The USR occupies the next 2 KW of memory. It contains the code that supports a subset of the system calls. In particular, the USR contains code that implements file system operations such as creating, opening, reading, writing, and closing files. It also handles dynamically loading and retrieving the status of device handlers. In FB and XM monitors, the next memory area holds any foreground jobs. The SJ monitor doesn't support foreground jobs. Any additional device handlers reside above the foreground processes. The Resident Monitor (RMON) occupies the next area of memory. This monitor, which occupies about 2 KW in an SJ monitor and about 4 KW in a FB monitor, provides the remaining system calls, I/O buffering, timer handling, and scheduling in FB monitors. The final bit of software in the lower 28 KW of memory is the system device handler. This is the device driver for the device where all other device handlers are stored and where we find the swap area for the USR and KMON. In the SJ and FB monitors, the memory management hardware is not used, and the I/O devices are mapped to the region between 28 KW and 32 KW. In the XM monitor, any physical memory between 28 KW and 124 KW is available for applications to map and use.

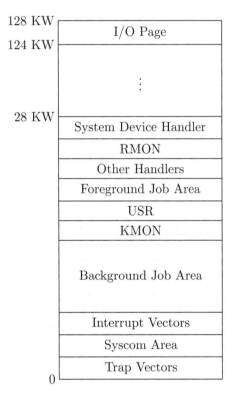

Figure 10-2: RT-11 XM Monitor Memory Layout

10.3.3   *USR and KMON Swapping*

Much like the shell in UNIX systems, the RT-11 KMON is written to operate like a normal background job. Because there can be only one background job in RT-11 at a time, a newly started background job can use the memory previously occupied by KMON for its own purposes. When a background job exits, the system reloads KMON and transfers control to it. In this way, KMON is effectively swapped on each background job load and exit.

As another provision to allow a background job to use as much memory as possible in SJ and FB monitors, RT-11 allows a background job to swap out the USR. (In XM systems, the ability to use virtual memory eliminates the need to swap the USR.) It is swapped out automatically whenever a job is loaded that is large enough to require it or when a .SETTOP call is issued that would use that space. A job can prevent the USR from being swapped by issuing a .LOCK call, and the user can do so by issuing the SET USR NOSWAP command. Jobs must be careful not to allow the USR to be swapped during times that they need to execute file system–related system calls or to load drivers as the code to support those functions resides in the USR.

10.4   Sixth Edition UNIX

By the time that UNIX had matured to the sixth edition, it had already been ported to several hardware platforms. However, the predominant platform for running UNIX was, by far, the PDP-11 from Digital Equipment Corporation (DEC). Although there were versions that could run without any memory management hardware, we concentrate here on the system running on a PDP-11 with memory management hardware.

10.4.1   Memory-Related System Calls

In the basic UNIX design, only four system calls allow processes to affect the allocation of memory. Three of these, *fork*( ), *exec*( ), and *exit*( ), are primarily process management system calls. When creating a new process with *fork*( ), we allocate space for and copy the parent's data and stack segments. Because the child is a copy of the parent, it is configured to share the memory allocated to the parent's text segment. When replacing a process's program with *exec*( ), memory is allocated for the text, data, and stack segments and is appropriately initialized. If there is already a process running the same program, then we configure the caller to share the other process's text segment. If the program is identified as not having a sharable text segment, then we pretend that there is no text segment and set up the data segment so that it includes both the code and the data. Finally, the *exit*( ) system call frees the data and stack segments that belong to the process making the call. If it is the last process using its text segment (there are no other existing processes sharing it), then we free the text segment as well.

The *brk*( ) system call is the only call by which a process may change the size of its memory allocation. The argument to this call establishes the boundary that separates data from stack in the virtual address space. All virtual addresses from the top of the text segment to the break are allocated to data. From the top virtual address (177777_8) down to the break is a memory area into which the stack can grow. The familiar *malloc*( ) and *free*( ) family of calls (and the **new** and **delete** operators in C++ in later implementations) are built on the *brk*( ) system call.

10.4.2   Memory Layouts

The PDP-11's MMU translates virtual addresses to physical ones using a scheme like that illustrated in Figure 9-3. Although we've labeled this approach segmentation, DEC referred to their memory regions as pages. In their later designs (the VAX and the Alpha), they used the term page in the same way that we have. A table of eight segments is indexed by the upper three bits of the 16-bit virtual address. Segment sizes can range from 64 to 8192 bytes. For most PDP-11 models, the physical address is either 18 bits or 22 bits. Two such tables exist, one used when the processor is running in user mode and one when it is running in kernel mode. (On some models, a third supervisor mode is also available.) Furthermore, some models provide for separate virtual address spaces for instructions and data. In these cases, there are two address translation tables in each mode.

In the PDP-11 design, the first 512 bytes of physical memory is reserved for interrupt vectors, and the top 8 KB of the physical space is reserved for I/O devices. Any available memory in between is fair game for the operating system to use as it sees fit. The sixth edition UNIX kernel resides in the low part of physical memory, just above the interrupt vectors. It initializes the kernel mode memory mapping to that shown in Figure 10-3 (using C-style octal notation and assuming 18-bit addressing). The effect of these settings is to create an identity mapping on the first 48 KB of memory. Because the kernel is smaller than this, it can function regardless of whether address translation is enabled. The last segment maps the I/O controller registers into the kernel's highest 8 KB of virtual address space (160000_8–177777_8). Segment 6 is used as a small window into the rest of the system's memory. We use it to access data that needs to be shared between user processes and the operating system. This windowing is necessary only because the physical address space is larger than the virtual one.

Segment	Base	Size	Access
0	0000000	8 KB	R/W
1	0020000	8 KB	R/W
2	0040000	8 KB	R/W
3	0060000	8 KB	R/W
4	0100000	8 KB	R/W
5	0120000	8 KB	R/W
6	User Process Dependent	1 KB	R/W
7	0730000	8 KB	R/W

Figure 10-3: Sixth Edition UNIX Kernel Memory Mapping

Per-process memory is allocated in two contiguous areas. The first, which is located at the bottom of the virtual space, is the text segment. This area is mapped as read-only and uses enough of the segment descriptors to fully define it. For example, if the process uses 20 KB of code space, then the first three hardware segments are set up for the text segment. The first two hardware segments are both 8 KB in size and the third is 4 KB. All three are specified as read-only. Because we've identified the text segment as read-only, it is safe to share this space among all processes that are running the same code. Therefore, all processes running this program have the same values in the first three pairs of segment registers.

The other contiguous memory area is for the data and stack segments. The data area occupies the lower hardware segments, and the stack occupies the upper segments. Continuing in this example, suppose that we have 15 KB of data space and 6 KB of stack space currently in use. To accommodate this need, we allocate a 21-KB area in memory and set up the fourth and fifth hardware segments to map to the lower 15 KB of the area. The stack in the upper 6 KB is mapped by the eighth hardware segment, leaving the sixth and seventh hardware segments unused. Because the data and stack segments are adjacent, changing their sizes adds complication. If a process issues a $brk(\ )$ system call to change the size of the data segment, then we must enlarge the combined data and stack segment area and copy the stack up to the new top of the enlarged area. Furthermore, if the memory immediately above this combined area is not free, then we must find a new free area large enough to accommodate the new area and then copy both data and stack to that newly allocated area. It turns out that the easiest way for us to handle this expansion is to take advantage of the swapping infrastructure discussed in Section 10.4.5.

10.4.3   Free Space Management

Free space in sixth edition UNIX is represented by an array of structures, each of which identifies the size and address of a free block. The array has room for 50 such structures, but the last one in the list is a sentinel with the size set to 0. Therefore, there can be only 49 distinct free areas in the system. Structures in the array are kept sorted by address. When a block is freed, if it is adjacent to one or two other free blocks, then the contiguous free blocks are coalesced into one larger free block. If the newly freed block is distinct from all others, then structures representing blocks at higher addresses are shifted in the array to make room for the new one.

10.4.4   Allocation

Allocation requests are handled with a first-fit policy. The array of free blocks is searched sequentially until a block is found whose size is greater than or equal to the size of the request. If the free block is larger than the request size, then it is split into two parts, the first of which is returned to satisfy the request. The remaining part of the block remains in the free list. Allocation and free space is managed in units of 64 bytes, so no fragments smaller than 64 bytes are ever created.

If an attempt is made to push data onto the stack, but doing so would use memory not allocated to the process, an addressing fault interrupts the system. In this case (assuming that there is available virtual space between the current top of the stack and the break), we implicitly allocate memory for the stack and resume the instruction that was interrupted.

10.4.5   Swapping

When the total memory allocated to processes in the system exceeds available physical memory, sixth edition UNIX swaps processes between memory and disk. In many cases, only the data and stack segments are written to disk. However, if all of the processes sharing a particular text segment are swapped out, then the memory occupied by that segment is freed. To simplify the swapping of text spaces, program code is copied to the swap space for each program run with the *exec()* system call. When a text segment is "swapped out," it is not actually written because all such segments are configured as read-only, which implies that the copy on the disk always matches the one in memory. Finally, to keep common programs from being copied to swap space frequently, UNIX implements a "sticky" bit that can be set for executable programs. If a process using the text segment of a program with the sticky bit set is the last such process to exit, then the copy in swap space is not removed in anticipation of another process running this program in the near future.

10.5   4.3BSD

We turn now from early UNIX to 4.3BSD, one of the nine examples we are studying. In terms of memory management, the biggest difference between earlier versions of UNIX and the 4BSD distributions is the use of paging. The 4BSD UNIX distribution from Berkeley was originally targeted to the DEC VAX hardware, which introduced paging hardware to the DEC computer products. Later, these distributions were ported to other hardware and formed the foundation of both commercial and open source distributions, such as SunOS, NetBSD, FreeBSD, OpenBSD, and DragonflyBSD.

10.5.1   Memory-Related System Calls

For the most part, the BSD distributions retained the same system calls for memory allocation. One of the biggest differences is the introduction of the *vfork()* system call. As discussed in Section 10.4.1, the traditional *fork()* system call makes a complete copy of the parent process's memory space (except for the text segment if it is shared and read-only). However, a *fork()* is very often followed quickly by an *exec()* call. The effect of this pairing is that the OS makes a copy of the parent's data and stack spaces just before freeing them and allocating new memory for the program being loaded. Eliminating the copy in this common case is the purpose of *vfork()*. When a process issues this system call, the process is suspended, and the newly created child process runs using the parent's memory space until it exits or issues an *exec()*. Of course, this places some restrictions on what the child process can do between returning from *vfork()* and calling *exec()*. Anything it does to change the global data space is seen by the parent process. More seriously, if the child returns from the function that called *vfork()*, then the stack the parent expects to see on return is destroyed.

10.5.2   Memory Layouts

The original 4BSD releases targeted the DEC VAX computer. In terms of physical memory, BSD UNIX on a VAX uses much the same layout as illustrated in Figure 9-6. The interrupt vectors occupy the first page (512 bytes) of physical memory space. When the system is loaded, the BSD kernel then occupies the low memory area. The top of this kernel memory is identified by the variable *firstfree*. During system initialization, the kernel determines how much physical memory is installed on the system and sets the variable *maxfree* to the top of physical memory, leaving a little bit of room for storing console messages that can be used to debug after a system crash.

The VAX 32-bit virtual address consists of three fields, as illustrated in Figure 10-4. The low-order 9 bits specify a byte offset within a page. As a result, each page is $2^9 = 512$ bytes. Bits 9–29 form a 21-bit page number. The final two bits (30 and 31) specify a region number. Each region can have up to $2^{21} = 2,097,152$ pages for a total of 1 GB. The four possible values for the region field are interpreted as follows:

- 00: This is defined as the per-process program region. It is often called the P0 region.

- 01: Region 01 is the per-process control region, also called the P1 region.

- 10: The system region is identified by the value 10. All processes share the same address mapping for the system region.

- 11: This region is reserved and not used.

Addresses within each region are translated by a single-level page table. All processes share the same page table for the system region. Each process has its own tables for the P0 and P1 regions. The location and extent of the page tables are specified by a form of base and limit register pair. Because each PTE is 4 bytes, a fully populated page table for each region would occupy 8 MB. All page tables are stored in the system region.

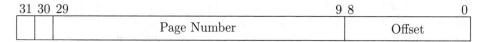

Figure 10-4: VAX Virtual Address Format

The virtual memory space seen by processes is something of a cross between the two techniques described in Section 9.4. The memory management hardware divides the virtual space into four regions. In the P0 region, covering addresses 00000000_{16}–$3FFFFFFF_{16}$, the text and data segments are laid out as in Figure 9-7. Process code occupies the low-order virtual addresses starting at address 0. Starting on the next page boundary, static data is allocated to the next addresses in the P0 region. Finally, the heap area (dynamically allocated memory) is allocated from the remainder of the P0 region, growing toward higher memory addresses. The stack segment is located in the P1 region (addresses 40000000_{16}–$7FFFFFFF_{16}$), starting at the top of the region and growing downward toward the P0 region. There are actually three structures in this region. At the top of the region, there is a fixed space reserved for the kernel stack, which is used when handling system calls. A per-process data structure is stored just below the kernel stack. The user mode stack grows downward from there. Finally, the kernel is also mapped into each process's virtual space in the system region, which spans addresses 80000000_{16}–$BFFFFFFF_{16}$. This layout is illustrated in Figure 10-5.

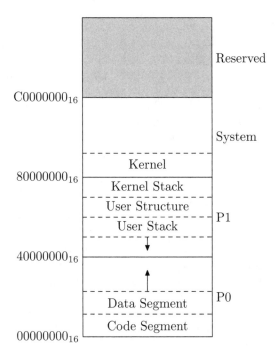

Figure 10-5: Virtual Memory Layout in 4BSD

10.5.3   Free Space Management

The earlier 3BSD version of UNIX managed memory in terms of 512-byte pages as defined by the memory management hardware. However, with a large physical memory space, the number of pages to manage is also large. Consequently, in 4BSD, memory management was changed to operate in units of clusters, each of which is an integral number of hardware pages. (For the VAX running 4.3BSD, the cluster size is two pages or 1 KB.) This clustering effectively creates a larger page size, which is used for all page management.

The set of clusters that span physical memory are represented by an array called the core map. Each element of the array is a *cmap* structure representing a single cluster. Free clusters in the array are kept in a doubly linked list, which is sorted in least recently used (LRU) order. Allocations are taken from the least recently used clusters. This allocation policy allows us to reuse a cluster without rereading it from disk if we find that a cluster was freed prematurely.

10.5.4   Swapping and Page Replacement

The 4BSD distributions use a combination of page (cluster) swapping and whole-process swapping. Normally, the system operates with page swapping as long as it can keep free memory available to satisfy requests. However, if memory becomes especially scarce, then the system will resort to swapping whole processes to make room. To simplify swap space management, we allocate swap space to hold the complete memory space of all processes, regardless of whether that space gets used.

Memory in 4BSD is normally demand paged. That is, when a page fault occurs, the OS reads the desired page from the disk. In the case of a process's code segment, we can read the desired page directly from the executable file rather than from swap space. Furthermore, we also do some prefetching. We load up to 16 adjacent clusters along with the desired one. Only those clusters that are adjacent both on the disk and in virtual memory are loaded as part of the page read. The preloaded pages are placed on the free list but at the tail (implying that they have been recently accessed, but are still free). If they do get referenced before the free list gets used up, then we can mark them as in use without incurring disk read overhead.

The page replacement policy in 4.3BSD is implemented by a two-handed clock as described in Section 9.6.3. Two MB separate the hands in most systems. (On very small systems with less than 2 MB of physical memory, the distance is set equal to the physical memory size, and the algorithm reduces to the one-handed clock.) The frequency and speed of sweeping is determined by comparing the current size of the free list to a threshold called *lotsfree* (normally set to 512 KB). This comparison takes place four times a second. If there is more than *lotsfree* memory in the free list, then nothing is done with the clock, and the hands stay where they were last left. If the amount of free space is less than *lotsfree*, then the scanning rate is set to

$$r = f - \frac{(f - s)}{l}m$$

where f is the maximum scanning rate (normally 200 pages per second), s is the minimum scanning rate (normally 100 pages per second), l is *lotsfree*, and m is the amount of free memory.

None of this is surprising, given our discussion in the previous chapter. However, there's a facet of the VAX hardware that keeps things from being simple. The VAX MMU doesn't have an accessed (A) bit. However, in Section 9.6.3, the clock algorithm is described using the A bit to determine if a page has been used since the hand last passed it. So, how did the BSD developers deal with this dilemma? The answer is that they simulated the A bit. When the front hand of the clock would normally clear the A bit, they cleared the P bit. If the page was then accessed, a page fault would occur, and this case would be recognized, recording the access and setting the P bit back to 1. Further accesses would not incur additional page faults, and the P bit could be examined by the back hand as if it were the A bit.

There are certain circumstances when a 4.3BSD system resorts to swapping entire processes. The first case is when the amount of free memory drops below the value of the *minfree* parameter (normally 64 KB), despite the clock sweeping at essentially the maximum rate. A process that is idle for over 20 seconds is the second case where we will swap. The final case is an artifact of the way in which 4.3BSD manages page tables. If they become fragmented, the only way to reorganize them is to swap processes out and back in.

10.6   VMS

When DEC introduced the VAX and the VAX/VMS operating system, it did so with an interesting approach to memory management. In comparing it to the approach taken by the BSD developers, we get a glimpse into how the hardware design determines some choices for the OS developer. At the same time, we get to see room for creativity and originality. Furthermore, in VMS, we see how a system can evolve to accommodate major changes in its hardware platform. In moving from a 32-bit VAX to a 64-bit Alpha, the VMS designers had to balance the need for change in the memory management design with the need to retain as much commonality as possible.

10.6.1   Page Tables

Where the VAX uses a 512-byte page size, the Alpha design allows for pages ranging from 8 KB to 64 KB. However, all implementations of the architecture use 8-KB pages. The page table design is also different. The VAX uses one single-level page table per region of virtual memory space. On the Alpha, the page table is organized as a three-level table, where each table is exactly one page in size. For an 8-KB page size and an 8-byte PTE, each table holds 1024 entries, taking 10 bits of the address to index. With three levels of such tables, there are a total of 30 bits specifying the page number. The lowest 13 bits of the address are the page offset, meaning that 43 bits of the address are used. The upper 21 bits are a sign extension of the 43rd bit. That is, the 43rd bit is copied into bits 43–63.

10.6.2   Memory Layouts

Because they both run on the same hardware, it is not surprising that 4.3BSD and VAX/VMS use similar virtual memory layouts. Both place a process's code and data in the P0, or program, region, as shown in Figure 10-5. Similarly, both place the operating system code and data in the system region and the process's stack in the P1, or control, region. Unlike BSD, VMS uses all four processor modes (user, supervisor, executive, and kernel). Stacks for all four modes are also include in the P1 space. Whereas BSD places the user structure in the control region just above the process stack, VMS includes process structures among the OS data structures in the system region. VMS doesn't actually have a user structure exactly like BSD UNIX; however, the Process Control Block (PCB) and the Process Header (PHD) serve much the same function in VMS.

VMS on Alpha uses a similar layout, but with a much larger virtual address space. The P0, P1, and system (S0) regions from the VAX map directly to regions on the Alpha. The system region is placed at the top of the virtual memory space as a result of the sign extension in the virtual address. The area between the P1 region and the S0 region is filled with two new regions, the P2 region and the S2 region. This design allows as much code as possible written for the VAX to run unchanged on the Alpha.

10.6.3   Free Space Management

Free space management is another area where BSD and VMS are similar. Both use a queue to maintain the list of free pages. (VMS keeps individual pages in the queue, as opposed to the BSD clusters.) As pages are marked free, they are added to the tail of the queue, and pages are allocated from the head of the list. If a page is referenced again while it is moving from the tail to the head, it can be removed from the list and marked active again without incurring the penalty of a disk access. Maintaining the list in this way results in a free list that is sorted in LRU order. Freed pages that are modified are first placed on a modified list, from which they can also be reclaimed. One function of the swapper process is to take pages from the modified list, write them to disk, and move them to the free list. In addition to this, VMS also implements a mechanism whereby it maintains a number of zero pages available to satisfy requests for new empty pages. Another low priority process takes pages from the free list, zeros them, and places them on the zero page list.

10.6.4   Swapping and Page Replacement

VMS and BSD also both provide a combination of whole-process swapping and individual page swapping. One of the biggest differences, however, is the page replacement policy. Section 10.5.4 describes how the BSD designers went to some effort to simulate the A bit on the VAX so that they could implement a two-handed clock policy. Assuming the hardware and software development groups in DEC were on good terms, we would expect that VMS uses a page replacement policy that doesn't need the A bit. In fact, it uses an interesting combination of FIFO and LRU, which DEC calls Segmented FIFO.

To understand VMS paging, it is important that we understand how memory is partitioned. The set of physical page frames is partitioned into a number of subsets, one for the global free list and one for each resident process. The free list is kept around 20% to 30% of physical memory. (Simulation studies done at DEC indicate that the performance of the policy is not particularly sensitive to the exact balance between active pages and those in the LRU free list.) VMS uses the working set model, so individual processes are limited to a maximum working set size.

If a process needs a new page and its current working set size is less than its upper limit, then one is taken from the head of the free list and added to the process. On the other hand, if a process is already at its maximum working set size when it needs a new page, then it must give one up before one is added. The page taken from the process is the oldest one in the working set. As with the free list, maintaining this FIFO behavior is a simple queue application. Newly allocated pages are added to the tail of the process's working set list. When we must take a page away from a process, we take the page at the head of the list and add it to the tail of the global free list (after writing it to disk if it's dirty). The net effect of this policy is that we get performance close to that of LRU with an implementation similar to the simplicity of FIFO.

In all versions of VMS except for the first, there is an additional optimization to the FIFO policy. When looking at the working set, if we find that the page we would otherwise choose to swap out is in the translation lookaside buffer (TLB), as discussed in Section 9.2.3.2, we skip it and move on to the next. This is somewhat similar to a second chance policy. Because the nature of a TLB is to store recent page translations, any page whose PTE is in the TLB must have been recently accessed. Consequently, we consider it a poor candidate to swap out.

In the earliest versions of VMS, the working set size limits were established administratively. The maximum working set size was a per-user parameter, which was stored in the user authorization file (UAF). Later versions of VMS added a working set size adjustment policy based on the ideas of the page fault frequency technique, discussed in Section 9.6.3.

If the free list becomes too small (drops below an administrative threshold), then VMS resorts to swapping out the entire working set of one or more processes to restore the free list. Processes that are blocked waiting on I/O are swapped before those that are blocked waiting on paging before those that are ready. The last two groups are swapped out only if a higher-priority process needs to be swapped back in. Processes that are swapped out and transition to the Ready state are swapped in if there is enough free memory to hold their working set. If not, then they wait until enough memory can be freed by swapping out blocked processes and lower priority processes. In addition to whole-process swapping, VMS also implements a working set trimming mechanism. If there are processes that have grown their working sets when there was low demand on memory, we can take pages away from their working sets to increase the free list without swapping them out altogether. However, if all processes are at their working set minimum already, then we must select one to swap out.

10.6.5   Memory-Related System Calls

The first two memory-related VMS system calls we consider are SYS$EXPREG and SYS$CNTREG. The first of these is used to expand either the program or control region, and the second is used to contract it. As with the layout illustrated in Figure 10-5, the program region grows upward when SYS$EXPREG is called, and the control region grows from the top of the region downward. A process that wants to use an arbitrary area of the virtual address space calls SYS$CRETVA to allocate such a space and SYS$DELTVA to free it. VMS also supports memory-mapped files. It provides a number of system calls that manage these sections, as the mapped memory areas are called. There are also a number of system calls that control the behavior of the working set management. Some of these include SYS$LKWSET to lock pages in the working set, SYS$ADJWSL to change the working set limit, and SYS$LCKPAG to lock pages in memory. Of course, the working set size cannot be set outside the limits administratively established for that process. The protection codes for a page can be changed with the SYS$SETPRT system call. To control swapping, the SYS$SETSWM call allows a process to declare that it should not be swapped out. Finally, the SYS$SETSTK call gives a process control over the size of its stacks. However, processes are not allowed to change the stacks belonging to processor modes that are more privileged than the mode in which the process is running.

10.7   Windows NT

One of the additions to the Windows NT series over previous Windows products is the thorough use of paged memory management. In Windows products prior to the NT series of kernels, the physical memory space accessible by applications was not limited to memory allocated to that process. As a result, these applications often had dangerous access to other processes and to the operating system.

10.7.1 System Calls

At the lowest level, Win32 memory calls operate on pages. Allocation is handled through the *VirtualAlloc* and *VirtualAllocEx* calls. The *VirtualFree* and *VirtualFreeEx* calls release memory. The application can also mark pages as immune from swapping with the *VirtualLock* call. Although each allocation request results in the assignment of some number of pages to the process, all such allocations begin on a 64-KB boundary. Finally, the *CreateFileMapping* call is used both to map files to memory and to establish memory areas shared by multiple processes.

10.7.2 Memory Layouts

There are several variations on the layout of a process's virtual memory space in Windows NT. The most common one occurs when we are running the default configuration on an Intel x86 processor. (We consider only the details of systems with 32-bit addressing. Those with 64-bit addresses have a different memory layout.) In this case, the first 2 GB (addresses 00000000_{16} through $7FFFFFFF_{16}$) are allocated to the user process. All code, per-process data, per-thread data, and dynamically allocated pages reside in this area. The next 1 GB (addresses 8000000_{16} through $BFFFFFFF_{16}$) hold the OS, including the Hardware Abstraction Layer (HAL), the kernel, and the executive. The 8-MB region, ranging from address $C0000000_{16}$ through $C07FFFFF_{16}$, is primarily used for process page tables. Finally, the remainder of the virtual address space is used for various buffers, free space management structures, and the system page tables. Although the upper 2 GB of the virtual address space for all processes contains the OS code and data structures, this part of the memory space is not accessible by processes running in user mode.

10.7.3 Page Management

Windows NT uses a working set page management technique. Each process has an administratively determined minimum and maximum working set size. The default values are based on the amount of physical memory in the system. When a process needs to read a page and is using its maximum working set size, then the choice of page to replace comes from its working set. Normally, a process that is below its maximum working set size and needs to read a page in gets that new page added to its working set. To keep enough free pages available for this, the system periodically checks the number of free pages, and if there are too few, it runs the working set manager. This code trims the working sets of processes that are above their minimum size and frees the trimmed pages.

The page replacement policies in Windows NT apply both to the case where a process must lose one from its working set so that a new page may be read in and to the case where a page is selected for trimming by the working set manager. These policies have evolved through the various versions of Windows NT. The policy found in the earliest versions is a modified FIFO policy like that in VMS. The page selected for removal is the one that has been in the working set the longest. However, removed pages are first placed on a list from which they can be re-added to the working set if they are referenced before their frames are reallocated. Over time, beginning with uniprocessor server versions, then to all uniprocessor versions, and finally to all versions of the system, the FIFO policy has been replaced with an NFU policy. Pages are periodically scanned, and if they have been accessed since the last scan, a usage count is incremented. The count is also aged so as to weigh recent accesses more heavily than older accesses. Pages selected according to this policy are still added to a list from which they can be reallocated if needed.

The management of pages in Windows NT can best be described with the state machine illustrated in Figure 10-6. These states function as follows:

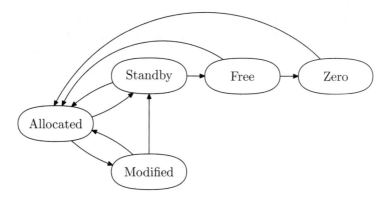

Figure 10-6: Windows NT Page Frame State Machine

- *Allocated*: Page frames in this state hold pages that are part of a process's working set.

- *Modified*: When a page is selected to be removed from a working set, its frame is moved to the Modified list if the page's modified bit is set

- *Standby*: Similarly, when a page with the modified bit cleared is taken out of a working set, it is moved to the Standby list. Furthermore, there is a thread that takes pages from the Modified list and writes them to the paging space. As they are written to disk, pages are moved from the Modified list to the Standby list.

- *Free*: Page frames on this list are available for allocation. For page frames that satisfy kernel requests and for those that will be loaded with pages read from the disk, we can allocate directly from this list, as the previous contents are not important.

- *Zero*: The page zero thread moves pages from the Free list to the Zero list by clearing them. Those frames on this list are available for allocation for user processes that request frames through the *VirtualAlloc* call. The previous data on these pages must not be available to the process that allocates the frame.

Page frames can move from the Modified and Standby lists back to working sets if the pages are referenced before they are added to the Free list. The page faults that trigger this move are called soft page faults. Frames moving from the Free or Zero lists to working sets are those that are being allocated.

10.8   TinyOS

In terms of memory management, TinyOS represents an extreme, but common, case in the embedded world. The systems on which TinyOS runs have exceptionally small amounts of memory and no memory management hardware. In environments like that, there is generally little or no value in supporting dynamic memory allocation. In fact, the NesC language, in which TinyOS components are written, does not support dynamic memory allocation. Furthermore, because TinyOS applications are composed of a number of components compiled together, processes are not created or destroyed. Consequently, there are no memory allocation features in the code that makes up the operating system. The layout of components in memory is determined at build-time by the linker.

10.9   Xen

Memory management is one of the key areas where Xen provides support for the operating systems running in its domains. In effect, Xen owns the page tables and hardware segment tables of the x86 hardware, and operating systems that run on top of it make requests of Xen to change those tables.

10.9.1   Hypercalls

Accordingly, Xen provides a number of hypercalls that allow guest OSs to request changes to the page tables. The primary calls are *mmu_update*( ) and *update_va_mapping*( ). Similarly, Xen allows changes to the segment tables with the *set_gdt*( ) call and the *update_descriptor*( ) call. Domains may use the *memory_op*( ) call to change the amount of memory they have allocated to them. There is one additional address translation hypercall. The *vm_assist*( ) call can be used to turn on a mode where the guest OS can make page table changes "directly" without using the *mm_update*( ) or *update_va_mapping*( ) calls. When this mode is enabled and the guest OS attempts to write to the page table, Xen traps the operation and takes the page table out of use long enough for the guest OS to make its changes. Then, Xen later verifies that the change is permissible and places the page table back into use.

Finally, Xen provides one additional memory management call that is central to the context switching mechanism. The *stack_switch*( ) call requests that the hypervisor change the kernel stack. Normally, this is done in the OS kernel, but guest OSs run in a privilege mode where direct access to the kernel stack pointer is prohibited.

10.9.2   Memory Layouts

On system startup, Xen is loaded into memory, and it reserves a small area for itself. Normally, as domains are created, their size is specified and used to allocate an area of physical memory to them. The effect is a simple memory partitioning. In Example 9.2, we suggested that these partitions are fixed. Although domains often treat these partitions as fixed, it is possible for a domain to request a change in its size. If a domain issues a hypercall to change its size, things get more complicated. In general, satisfying a domain's request for more memory might create a situation where its physical memory is not contiguous. Allocation is done in units of pages, and Xen implements the allocation of pages using a buddy system allocator.

10.9.3   Page Management

Many OSs that can run as guests in Xen are written with the assumption that their physical memory is contiguous. To assist in porting these OSs, Xen maintains a set of tables that provide something like virtual-to-physical and physical-to-virtual address mappings. However, the concept of virtual-to-physical translation already exists in the guest OSs. In Xen, we refer to machine memory as the actual physical memory on the machine. The memory assigned to a domain, which it uses as if it were the physical memory of the system, is called pseudo-physical memory in Xen. Xen maintains a global machine-to-physical table for the whole system and a physical-to-machine table for each domain. The code in a domain's memory manager can then continue to work with the assumption of contiguous physical memory and then use the tables to translate from pseudo-physical to machine page frame numbers just before issuing the call to modify the page table. This reduces the amount of code that has to change in the guest OS when ported to Xen.

10.10   Summary

Although the principles of memory management are generally straightforward, in real systems, there are often factors that complicate implementation. The systems discussed in this chapter illustrate this. For example, the absence of the reference bit on the VAX made implementing a clock algorithm more difficult for the BSD developers. We also see in these examples how developers of different systems choose different policies and techniques even on the same hardware. Despite our tendency to view memory as a relatively simple resource, the systems discussed here represent only a sampling of the variety of techniques of memory management.

10.11   Exercises

1. Would the CTSS "onion-skin" algorithm have benefit on other systems that do full process swapping? What about those that swap only pages?

2. From time to time, it has been suggested that Multics be reimplemented for commodity microprocessors, such as the Intel x86. What effect would a 32-bit virtual address have on the design of Multics? How many segments would there be, and how big would they be?

3. Normally, the segment table entry contains a field that specifies the physical base address of the segment. However, the combined segmentation/paging approach used in Multics does not. What does the segment table entry store instead of the segment's base address? How many bits are required for this field? With the bits

required for segment protection, size, and so on, what is the natural size of a segment table entry? How many are stored in a page?

4. The RT-11 memory management design is optimized both for machines with small amounts of memory and for fast, real-time processing. Discuss how its design trade-offs would be different on a more modern machine with 32-bit addressing and a paged MMU.

5. Consider the example in Section 10.4.2 with 20 KB of read-only code, 15 KB of data, and 6 KB of stack. If the disk uses 512-byte blocks, how many disk blocks must be written to swap the process out if there is another process sharing the code space? An early, experimental, version of UNIX on the PDP-11 implemented demand paging with all pages being 8 KB. What is the minimum number of blocks that must be written to swap out a part of this process? How many bytes of internal fragmentation are created for this process as a result of the fixed page size?

6. On 4.3BSD, what is the scanning rate if we have 2 MB of free memory, when using the default value of *lostfree*? What if we have 1 MB free, 512 KB free, and 4 MB free?

7. Systems that use the working set model generally combine both swapping of individual pages and swapping of whole processes. 4.3BSD also implements both of these mechanisms, but it doesn't use the working set model. Discuss the similarities and differences between the 4.3BSD approach and the working set model.

8. Like VMS, successors to 4BSD have been ported to the Alpha. If the general virtual memory space layout is divided up the same way as on the VAX, then how big are the equivalent of the P0, P1, and System spaces when using the 43 bits of virtual address on the Alpha?

9. Both VMS and Windows NT have low-priority threads that zero free pages. What advantage does this give over zeroing them at the time they're allocated? How about zeroing them at the time they're reclaimed from the working set?

10. In Windows NT, pages can move to the Allocated state both from the Standby state and from the Free state. But no change is made to the page's contents when moving from Standby to Free. What, then, is the difference between these states?

Chapter 11

Memory Management in Inferno

The predominant characteristic of memory management in Inferno is simplicity, which arises from the nature of Inferno's target platforms. For example, neither PDAs nor embedded platforms usually use the paged memory management hardware that is so often found in general-purpose computers. Systems like these often lack any form of address translation at all. It is also quite common for them to have no mass storage devices that can be used for a backing store. Similarly, when Inferno is hosted by another operating system, it is running in the address space of a process or several processes sharing a single memory space. The upshot of all this is that Inferno has been designed to operate with a minimal memory model. There is a single address space managed by the Inferno kernel and allocated as needed to various processes. No use is made of address translation hardware or memory protection hardware, and no attempt is made to swap processes either in whole or in part.

If Inferno does not use any form of address translation or hardware protection, then how do we keep processes from stepping on each other's toes? The answer lies in the use of the Limbo programming language. All application processes in Inferno are written in Limbo and execute on a virtual machine managed by the Inferno kernel. The design of the language, the compiler, and the virtual machine all prohibit processes from attempting to access memory outside that which is allocated to them.

We begin our examination of Inferno memory management with a high-level look at the way in which memory is allocated in Inferno, focusing on three different units of memory management. We follow this with a brief discussion of memory layouts. The next topic we cover is a detailed examination of the data structures Inferno uses in managing memory. Finally, we trace through a number of functions that perform the actual memory allocation and deallocation, finishing with Inferno's garbage collector.

11.1 Overview

In Inferno, memory is managed in three different levels of granularity. The three units of allocation and management are called **pools**, **arenas**, and **blocks**. Figure 11-1 illustrates the relationship among them. Pools are made up of arenas, which, in turn, are divided into blocks. In this figure, the solid boxes are arenas, and the boxes identified by dashed lines are blocks. The shaded blocks are free, and the unshaded blocks are allocated. As we describe these three memory structures in more detail, we highlight further features of Inferno memory management illustrated in this figure.

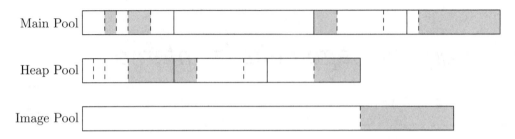

Figure 11-1: Relationship Among Pools, Arenas, and Blocks

At the highest level, there are three pools: the main pool, the image pool, and the heap pool. Most allocation requests are satisfied from the main pool. The image pool is used by the drawing library, and the heap pool is used for some allocations by the Dis virtual machine.

Each pool consists of one or more arenas. An arena is a relatively large area of memory allocated from a level underlying the rest of the kernel. In the case of a hosted implementation, arenas are allocated from the host OS. In native Inferno, arenas are similar to partitions. In a simplified view, we can imagine that all memory starts as free. When a new arena is needed, it is taken from the beginning of the remaining free memory. After an arena is allocated to a pool, it remains a part of that pool until the system is shut down. Consequently, the memory not yet allocated to any pool is always a contiguous region. As illustrated in Figure 11-1, arenas for a given pool are generally the same size, with two exceptions. If an arena is allocated to satisfy a request larger than that pool's arena size, a larger arena is allocated. The other exception arises when a newly allocated arena is adjacent to one already belonging to the same pool. In that case, they are combined into one large pool. This last case implies one additional feature. Contrary to the appearance in the figure, two arenas belonging to the same pool are never adjacent in physical memory.

Arenas are further subdivided dynamically into blocks. Blocks are allocated to satisfy requests for memory. Requests can come from the kernel itself or from applications, and are satisfied with single appropriately sized blocks, as illustrated in Figure 11-1. They are allocated according to a best-fit policy, with consideration given to avoiding external fragmentation. The free blocks are stored in a binary search tree to speed the best-fit search. If no free block is available to satisfy a request, then a request is made to allocate a new arena to the pool. As also illustrated in the figure, free blocks are never subdivided into smaller blocks; they are always single, contiguous blocks.

Internally, the kernel uses this block allocation mechanism through calls that operate like the familiar *malloc( )* and *free( )* routines. User programs written in Limbo don't directly allocate memory like UNIX processes do using the *brk( )* system call or the *malloc( )* library call. Consequently, Inferno does not provide any form of memory allocation system call for user processes. There are, however, a number of Limbo constructs that do implicitly allocate memory. The **spawn** statement implicitly allocates memory when creating a new process. Similarly, the **load** statement must allocate space to load a new module into memory. As with most systems, stack space grows automatically with usage. Finally, there are two Dis instructions, `new` and `newa`, which are used when a program dynamically creates a new data structure or a new array. Limbo programs do not directly free any memory they allocate. Instead, Inferno uses a combination of reference counts and mark-and-sweep garbage collection to identify and free memory no longer used by user processes.

11.2   Memory Layouts

Most of our discussions of memory layouts make a distinction between virtual memory space and physical memory space. Because Inferno doesn't use any address translation, these two spaces are the same, and we refer to it simply as the memory space.

The pool/arena allocation strategy has significant implications for the overall memory layout. Aside from the kernel image itself, memory is simply sliced up into arenas according to the sizes of the requests as they are issued. There are no fixed assignments of components in the memory space.

As in most systems, processes in Inferno have separate areas of memory for code and for data. However, unlike most systems, Inferno does not place these areas in particular locations in the address space. Each of the modules used by a process has its own code that occupies the memory block where it was loaded. Similarly, each module has a global data block. All dynamic data items and stack also occupy the blocks that are allocated for them. Because no address translation is done, a process cannot depend on these various memory areas being at known locations. Furthermore, because Limbo does not provide the capability of manipulating arbitrary pointers, a user process doesn't have any way to use that information anyway.

The remainder of this chapter presents a detailed examination of the implementation of Inferno memory management. We begin with the data structures used to represent memory and move on to the functions that handle block allocation and deallocation.

11.3   Memory Management Data Structures

We turn now to the details of how the general memory management techniques in Inferno are implemented. There are two main data structures representing memory in Inferno. The first of these represents pools. There is an array of these, one for each pool. The second is used to represent both arenas and blocks. Blocks are represented by a pair of structures that form a header and a tail. Arenas don't have their own data structure to describe them. Instead, they are treated much like large blocks that are then subdivided into smaller blocks.

11.3.1 Memory Pools

As explained earlier, blocks of memory are allocated from the **main pool**, the **heap pool**, and the **image pool**. For allocations made within the kernel, as well as allocations in some of the built-in modules, the main pool is used. The image pool is used by the code in libdraw for storing image data. The heap pool is used by the code in libinterp for some allocations needed in interpreting Dis bytecode.

Each pool is represented by the following data structure defined in emu/port/alloc.c for hosted builds and os/port/alloc.c for native builds:

```
struct Pool {
    char *name;
    int pnum;
    ulong maxsize;
    int quanta;
    int chunk;
    int monitor;
    ulong ressize;      /* restricted size */
    ulong cursize;
    ulong arenasize;
    ulong hw;
    Lock l;
    Bhdr *root;
    Bhdr *chain;
    ulong nalloc;
    ulong nfree;
    int nbrk;
    int lastfree;
    void (*move)(void *, void *);
};
```

Before looking at each structure member, we examine how the instances of this structure are initialized:

```
struct {
    int n;
    Pool pool[MAXPOOL];
        /* Lock l; */
} table = {
    3,
    {
        {"main", 0, 32 * 1024 * 1024, 31, 512 * 1024, 0, 31 * 1024 * 1024},
        {"heap", 1, 32 * 1024 * 1024, 31, 512 * 1024, 0, 31 * 1024 * 1024},
        {"image", 2, 32 * 1024 * 1024 + 256, 31, 4 * 1024 * 1024, 1,
            31 * 1024 * 1024},
```

```
    }
};
Pool *mainmem = &table.pool[0];
Pool *heapmem = &table.pool[1];
Pool *imagmem = &table.pool[2];
```

In this structure named *table*, the member n is the number of pools. As indicated previously, there are three pools. The remainder of *table* is an array of three pool structures that are partially initialized.

In the **Pool** structure, the *name* member holds a descriptive string for that pool. Here, we have the pools named `main`, `heap`, and `image`. The *pnum* member is a numeric identifier and is equal to the index into the array of pool structures. When allocating new arenas for the pool, we are careful never to exceed *maxsize* bytes for the pool. In the declarations given earlier, each of the pools is limited to 32 MB. For a hosted implementation, these maximum sizes can be overridden by command-line arguments. Generally, any memory allocation system will allocate only in multiples of some minimum allocation size. We specify that minimum size with the *quanta* member. However, this value does not give the allocation unit directly. Instead, the value stored here is actually $2^q - 1$, where 2^q is the minimum allocation size. Another way to think about this is that *quanta* is a mask with 1s in the bits that must all be 0 for any valid allocation size. We see exactly how this gets used later. Similarly, when allocating a new arena for the pool, we allocate with a minimum size specified by the *chunk* structure member. The *monitor* flag is used as a switch to enable or disable calling a monitoring function when memory is allocated or freed from that pool. This is enabled only for the image pool. The last structure member initialized at declaration time is *ressize*. As the comment indicates, this is a restricted size for the pool. The effect of these values of restricted size is that only certain processes may allocate the last megabyte of the pool's allowable space.

As we might guess, *cursize* is used to record the amount of memory currently allocated from the pool. On the other hand, *arenasize* gives the total amount of memory allocated to the pool. For bookkeeping purposes, we use *hw* to record the peak amount of memory allocated out of the pool over the history of the system (a high water mark). Because updating a data structure like this is a complex operation, there are inevitably race conditions with allocation and freeing. We use the lock variable l to provide exclusive access. In the next subsection, we discuss how free blocks are stored in a binary tree. A pool's *root* structure member points to the root of the free block tree. The *chain* member points to a linked list of **Bhdr** structures (discussed next) that describe the arenas allocated to the pool. Figure 11-2 shows the relationship between the **Pool** structure and the various **Bhdr** structures. In this figure, the *clink* pointer is part of the **Bhdr** structure. The next three structure members are used for mostly statistical purposes, where *nalloc* records the number of times a block is allocated from the pool, *nfree* does the same for calls to free blocks, and *nbrk* records the number of times a new arena is added to the pool. The *lastfree* member records the number of frees that had occurred as of the last time the pool was compacted. It is used so that we don't go to the trouble of compacting again if there have been no freeing operations in the meantime. The last member of the structure is a function pointer called *move*. This function is used as part of the pool compacting operation.

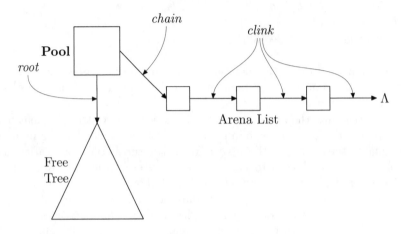

Figure 11-2: Pool Data Structure, Arena List, and Free Tree

11.3.2 *Memory Blocks*

We now move to the structure of the header at the beginning of each block. This block header is declared in include/pool.h as follows:

```
struct Bhdr {
    ulong magic;
    ulong size;
    union {
        uchar data[1];
        struct {
            Bhdr *bhl;
            Bhdr *bhr;
            Bhdr *bhp;
            Bhdr *bhv;
            Bhdr *bhf;
        } s;
#define clink  u.l.link
#define csize  u.l.size
        struct {
            Bhdr *link;
            int size;
        } l;
```

```
        } u;
};
```

The *size* member of the **Bhdr** structure gives the size of the block in bytes. The *magic* member of the structure is used to record the current status of this block. It may take on one of the following values:

```
enum {
    MAGIC_A = #a110c,      /* Allocated block */
    MAGIC_F = #badc0c0a,     /* Free block */
    MAGIC_E = #deadbabe,     /* End of arena */
    MAGIC_I = #abba      /* Block is immutable (hidden from gc) */
};
```

As the comments imply, `MAGIC_A` is used to mark a block that is assigned to a particular use, whether it be internal to the kernel or as part of a user process. Blocks that are available to be assigned are marked with `MAGIC_F`. The `MAGIC_E` value is used as a marker to identify the end of an arena we subdivide for allocation. Finally, blocks marked with the value `MAGIC_I` are allocated only within the system rather than in response to process requests for memory. The difference between an immutable block and a regular allocated one is that we skip the immutable ones when scanning for garbage collection. In other words, we don't need to have any explicit references to such a block to keep it allocated.

These values are similar to the hexadecimal "dead beef" used in Chapter 7 to mark terminated processes. Here, we see that allocated blocks are identified with the word *alloc* if we accept the abuse of a 1 (one) for the letter "l" and a 0 (zero) for the letter "o". Similarly, the free blocks are identified as *bad cocoa,* the end of the arena is identified as a *dead babe,* and a block that we do not allow to be garbage collected is an homage to the 1970s musical group AꓭBA.

The rest of the data structure deserves a little more explanation. The basic idea is pretty straightforward. When a block is allocated, we have a minimal header (the size and magic number) followed by the data itself. However, when a block is unallocated, we are free to use the data space of the block for our free list bookkeeping. So at times, the bytes that follow the size are used for data whose type is determined by the process to which the block is allocated, and at other times, we use those same bytes as administrative values. This type of multiplicity of purposes is exactly the role for which the **union** type in C was created. Here, we have a union called *u* with three elements. The first element, *data*, is used when the block is allocated. This array of one element serves to provide us with a pointer to the data area of an allocated block. For example, we use it in the macro:

```
#define B2D(bp)   ((void *) bp⁓u.data)
```

to provide a mapping from a pointer to a block to a pointer to its data area.

The structure, *s*, is used for those blocks marked with the `MAGIC_F` magic number—namely those that are normal free blocks. The pointers that make up this structure are used to maintain a tree of free blocks, where each node in the tree is a doubly linked list of blocks of equal size. If the blocks attached to a given node have *size* $\equiv n$, then the blocks in the left subtree have *size* $< n$, and the blocks in the right subtree have *size* $> n$. With the following definitions found in emu/port/alloc.c:

#**define** *left   u.s.bhl*
#**define** *right   u.s.bhr*
#**define** *fwd   u.s.bhf*
#**define** *prev   u.s.bhv*
#**define** *parent   u.s.bhp*

we can use *left* and *right* for a node's children in the tree. The *parent* macro identifies a pointer to the node's parent in the tree. Similarly, the *fwd* and *prev* macros are pointers that make up the doubly linked list of equal-sized blocks. The net effect of this arrangement is a binary search tree, where each node represents a given size of free block. Multiple free blocks of the same size are kept in a doubly linked list where only the head of the list is part of the tree structure. Figure 11-3 illustrates this design with a small example of a free tree (or a portion of a larger tree). In this figure, the number in a box is the size of free block represented by that box. We label all the pointers to show the mapping from the figure to the structure definition, but the linked list structure is shown only for the central node. Notice that all free blocks in the right subtree below the block of 128 are larger. Also notice that all the blocks in the linked list in the middle of the figure are the same size.

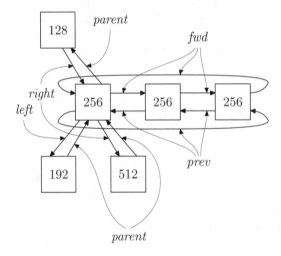

Figure 11-3: Free Blocks

The last structure in the union, called *l*, is used in those block headers marked with the MAGIC_E magic number. These block headers are used as part of the bookkeeping when a new arena is added to the pool. In particular, the number of bytes in the arena is kept in *size*, and *link* points to the block header structure of the next arena in the list.

Each block also contains a **Btail** structure at the end. The only member of this structure is a pointer, *hdr*, which points back to the **Bhdr** structure at the beginning of the block. This block trailer allows us to quickly find the header that belongs to the block immediately preceding the one we are using.

11.4   Memory Management Implementation

With the data structures representing memory defined, we now turn our attention to the code that manipulates those structures to allocate and free memory. In a very real sense, all memory management operations boil down to adding and removing free blocks from a tree.

11.4.1   Allocating Memory

Most allocations of memory inside the Inferno kernel are made through variations on the familiar *malloc()* call, but all allocations are ultimately handled by the function *dopoolalloc()*, defined in emu/port/alloc.c. It is in this function where we concentrate our study. The basic strategy in *dopoolalloc()* can be summarized in the following steps:

1. Traverse the tree to find the best-fit block.

2. If the size of the block we found is close enough to the requested size, we return the block.

3. If we found a block that is much larger, then we split it into an allocated block to return and a free block to put back in the tree.

4. If we didn't find any block at least as large as the request, then we try to allocate a new arena for this pool and repeat the allocation attempt.

The function is declared as follows:

static void *∗dopoolalloc(***Pool** *∗p,* **ulong** *asize,* **ulong** *pc)*
{

where *p* points to the **Pool** structure describing the pool from which we are allocating, and *asize* gives the size of the allocation request in bytes. The third argument, *pc*, is the program counter of the caller. It is used only when tracing the behavior of the memory manager. Upon successful allocation, *dopoolalloc()* returns a pointer to the newly allocated block. On failure, it returns *nil*. Next, we have some typical local variables that we use as we manage the free space.

Bhdr *∗q, ∗t;*
int *alloc, ldr, ns, frag;*
int *osize, size;*

Good programming practice always requires that we be careful to keep from acting on unreasonable parameters. In this case, we check to make sure that *asize* is not outside the realm of reason.

> **if** ($asize \geq 1024 * 1024 * 1024$)   /* for sanity and to avoid overflow */
>   **return** nil;

11.4.1.1   Adjusting Request Size

Now comes the time to adjust the size of the request. We need to round the request up to the nearest greater quantum, being careful not to forget to make room for the block header structure.

> $size = asize$;
> $osize = size$;
> $size = (size + \textbf{BHDRSIZE} + p\text{-}quanta)\ \&\ \sim(p\text{-}quanta)$;

The next two lines represent some administrative overhead. First, we have to gain the mutual exclusion lock to prevent any other thread of control from interfering with us as we work on the data structure. Then, we record the fact that our allocation count has now gone up by one.

> $lock(\&p\text{-}l)$;
> $p\text{-}nalloc$++;

11.4.1.2   Searching for the Best Fit

The basic allocation technique in Inferno follows a best-fit strategy. This first loop searches for the case where we have a block in our pool that is an exact fit. If we ignore the large **if**( ) statement inside the loop for now, then the loop is a pretty typical search through a tree that is kept in sorted order. Along the way, we keep the variable q pointing to the smallest block that is larger than the one we're seeking.

> $t = p\text{-}root$;
> $q = nil$;
> **while** (t) {
>   **if** ($t\text{-}size \equiv size$) {
> $t = t\text{-}fwd$;
> $pooldel(p, t)$;
> $t\text{-}magic = \textbf{MAGIC\_A}$;
> $p\text{-}cursize\ += t\text{-}size$;
>   **if** ($p\text{-}cursize > p\text{-}hw$)
> $p\text{-}hw = p\text{-}cursize$;
> $unlock(\&p\text{-}l)$;
>   **if** ($p\text{-}monitor$)
> $\text{MM}(p\text{-}pnum, pc, (\textbf{ulong})\ \text{B2D}(t), size)$;

```
        return B2D(t);
    }
    if (size < t→size) {
        q = t;
        t = t→left;
    }
    else
        t = t→right;
}
```

Now we turn our attention to the **if**( ) statement that we skipped previously. This is the case where we actually find an exact match. In this case, we only need to remove the block from the pool and update *cursize*. It is worth noting here that we advance *t* to the second element in the list if there is one. (If there's only one element, *t→fwd* leaves *t* unchanged.) This reduces the amount of work we have to do in taking the block out of the data structure, because only the head of the list is part of the tree structure. Finally, before we return we must release the mutual exclusion lock.

11.4.1.3   Splitting a Large Free Block

However, what happens if we don't find an exact match but have at least one block larger than the one we're seeking? In that case, we may return the block as it is, or we may split the block into two pieces, one of which is the size of the request, and one of which is the remaining free space. First, we remove the block from the pool and calculate how much would be left if we split.

```
if (q ≠ nil) {
    pooldel(p, q);
    q→magic = MAGIC_A;
    frag = q→size − size;
```

There's no need to bother splitting the block if the remaining free space would be too small to be useful. We define this condition by saying that if the fragment would be less than 32 KB and also less than one-quarter the size of the allocation, it's too small to be useful. The hexadecimal value 8000 is 2^{15}, which is 32 K. In this case, we just return the whole thing.

```
    if (frag < (size ≫ 2) ∧ frag < #8000) {
        p→cursize += q→size;
        if (p→cursize > p→hw)
            p→hw = p→cursize;
        unlock(&p→l);
        if (p→monitor)
            MM(p→pnum, pc, (ulong) B2D(q), size);
        return B2D(q);
    }
```

If the fragment would be useful, then we split the block into two parts. We do this by constructing new tail and header structures in the middle of the block so that we now have two adjacent blocks. The allocated one is returned, and the remainder is placed back in the pool's free block structure.

$$ns = q\text{-}size - size;$$
$$q\text{-}size = size;$$
$$\text{B2T}(q)\text{-}hdr = q;$$
$$t = \text{B2NB}(q);$$
$$t\text{-}size = ns;$$
$$\text{B2T}(t)\text{-}hdr = t;$$
$$pooladd(p, t);$$
$$p\text{-}cursize \mathrel{+}= q\text{-}size;$$
$$\textbf{if } (p\text{-}cursize > p\text{-}hw)$$
$$\quad p\text{-}hw = p\text{-}cursize;$$
$$unlock(\&p\text{-}l);$$
$$\textbf{if } (p\text{-}monitor)$$
$$\quad \text{MM}(p\text{-}pnum, pc, (\textbf{ulong}) \text{ B2D}(q), size);$$
$$\quad \textbf{return } \text{B2D}(q);$$
$$\}$$

11.4.1.4 Allocating a New Arena

Now comes the most complex of the scenarios we could encounter. Namely, we didn't find any block as large as the one requested. This means we need to get more memory allocated to the pool. We begin by calculating how big the arena needs to be. We want the larger of *chunk* (from the **Pool** structure) and *size* (the adjusted request size).

$$ns = p\text{-}chunk;$$
$$\textbf{if } (size > ns)$$
$$\quad ns = size;$$
$$ldr = p\text{-}quanta + 1;$$
$$alloc = ns + ldr + ldr;$$
$$p\text{-}arenasize \mathrel{+}= alloc;$$

It's possible that adding enough to this pool will cause us to exceed the *maxsize* limit on the pool size. In that case, we try compacting the pool with the function *poolcompact( )*. If we made some progress compacting, then we recursively attempt to allocate again. If not, then there's nothing we can do except deny the allocation request.

$$\textbf{if } (p\text{-}arenasize > p\text{-}maxsize) \text{ } \{$$
$$\quad p\text{-}arenasize \mathrel{-}= alloc;$$
$$\quad ns = p\text{-}maxsize - p\text{-}arenasize - ldr - ldr;$$
$$\quad ns \mathrel{\&}= \sim p\text{-}quanta;$$

```
    if (ns < size) {
        if (poolcompact(p)) {
            unlock(&p⊣l);
            return poolalloc(p, osize);
        }
        unlock(&p⊣l);
        print("arena␣%s␣too␣large:␣size␣%d␣cursize␣%lud
            ␣arenasize␣%lud␣maxsize␣%lud\n", p⊣name, size,
            p⊣cursize, p⊣arenasize, p⊣maxsize);
        return nil;
    }
    alloc = ns + ldr + ldr;
    p⊣arenasize += alloc;
}
```

Finally, we come to the point where we attempt to add more memory to the pool. In native Inferno, we call a function, *xalloc*( ), which is specific to the hardware platform and knows how to permanently allocate large memory blocks to pools. In hosted Inferno, we request that the hosting OS give us more memory. We do this through the traditional UNIX call *sbrk*( ), which incrementally moves the border between the data and stack spaces. For host operating systems that do not directly support *sbrk*( ), a function is provided to emulate it.

```
p⊣nbrk++;
t = (Bhdr *) sbrk(alloc);
if (t ≡ (void *) −1) {
    p⊣nbrk−−;
    unlock(&p⊣l);
    return nil;
}
t = (Bhdr *) (((ulong) t + 7) & ~7);
```

With the new arena added to the pool, it's time to add it to the linked list of these arenas. However, if it turns out that this one abuts the last one we added to this pool, we can just combine them. With the original *sbrk*( ), this will happen exactly when there are no intervening allocations for other pools. The actual mechanism of combination is pretty simple. We pretend that the new block was previously allocated, we mark the older block as being bigger by *alloc* bytes, and, finally, we request that the newly allocated block be freed. As with the compaction case, after we've finished the work, we recursively attempt to satisfy the allocation request.

```
if (p⊣chain ≠ nil ∧ (char *) t − (char *) B2LIMIT(p⊣chain) − ldr ≡ 0) {
    if (0)
        print("merging␣chains␣%p␣and␣%p␣in␣%s\n", p⊣chain, t,
            p⊣name);
```

```
    q = B2LIMIT(p↝chain);
    q↝magic = MAGIC_A;
    q↝size = alloc;
    B2T(q)↝hdr = q;
    t = B2NB(q);
    t↝magic = MAGIC_E;
    p↝chain↝csize += alloc;
    p↝cursize += alloc;
    unlock(&p↝l);
    poolfree(p, B2D(q));      /* for backward merge */
    return poolalloc(p, osize);
}
```

If, on the other hand, the newly added arena is not adjacent to an old one, we add it as a separate arena to the pool. We do this by building the block header structure for this arena and inserting it at the beginning of the pool's list. At the end, we reset t to point to the data area following the newly created header.

```
    t↝magic = MAGIC_E;      /* Make a leader */
    t↝size = ldr;
    t↝csize = ns + ldr;
    t↝clink = p↝chain;
    p↝chain = t;
    B2T(t)↝hdr = t;
    t = B2NB(t);
```

Now that the arena management is done, we can carve out of the data area the space we need to satisfy the allocation request.

```
    t↝magic = MAGIC_A;      /* Make the block we are going to return */
    t↝size = size;
    B2T(t)↝hdr = t;
    q = t;
```

In the case that the request doesn't use the entire new arena, we'll add the remainder to the free tree. Finally, we clean everything up and return.

```
    ns -= size;      /* Free the rest */
    if (ns > 0) {
        q = B2NB(t);
        q↝size = ns;
        B2T(q)↝hdr = q;
        pooladd(p, q);
    }
    B2NB(q)↝magic = MAGIC_E;      /* Mark the end of the chunk */
```

```
    p⁻cursize += t⁻size;
    if (p⁻cursize > p⁻hw)
        p⁻hw = p⁻cursize;
    unlock(&p⁻l);
    if (p⁻monitor)
        MM(p⁻pnum, pc, (ulong) B2D(t), size);
    return B2D(t);
}
```

The result of all the slicing and dicing of the newly allocated arena is shown in Figure 11-4. In the figure, the boxes marked E are the **Bhdr** structures with *magic* ≡ MAGIC_E. In other words, these are the markers at the beginning and the end of the arena, with the first one being placed in the linked list of arenas attached to the **Pool** structure. The box marked A is the **Bhdr** structure for the allocated block, and the one marked F is for the free block. The arrows show the pointers from the block trailers back to the headers.

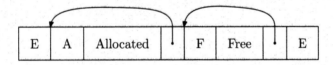

Figure 11-4: A New Arena Divided into Allocated (A) and Free (F) Blocks with Arena Markers (E)

11.4.2 Removing a Free Block from the Tree

In *dopoolalloc()*, we make use of two functions that update the free block tree. These are *pooldel()* and *pooladd()*. Because satisfying an allocation request implies that we must remove a free block from the tree, we examine *pooldel()* here and save *pooladd()* for the next section.

The easiest case is the one where the block we want to remove is part of a linked list but is not the head of that list. In determining that this is the case, we have to be careful to treat the root list differently. All other list heads point to their parent. For this case, we just remove it from the linked list and we're done.

```
    void pooldel(Pool *p, Bhdr *t)
    {
        Bhdr *s, *f, *rp, *q;
        if (t⁻parent ≡ nil ∧ p⁻root ≠ t) {
            t⁻prev⁻fwd = t⁻fwd;
            t⁻fwd⁻prev = t⁻prev;
```

```
        return;
   }
```

11.4.2.1   Removing a List Head

We divide what's left into two cases. The first case occurs when the block we're removing is the list head but is not the only block in a list. (The list is kept as a circular one, so if the next item in the list isn't the same as the one we're removing, we know it isn't the only item.) This means we don't need to move a child up to take its place. On the other hand, we do need to establish the next item on the list as the parent's new child and the children's new parent.

```
if (t→fwd ≠ t) {
    f = t→fwd;
    s = t→parent;
    f→parent = s;
    if (s ≡ nil)
        p→root = f;
    else {
        if (s→left ≡ t)
            s→left = f;
        else
            s→right = f;
    }
    rp = t→left;
    f→left = rp;
    if (rp ≠ nil)
        rp→parent = f;
    rp = t→right;
    f→right = rp;
    if (rp ≠ nil)
        rp→parent = f;
    t→prev→fwd = t→fwd;
    t→fwd→prev = t→prev;
    return;
}
```

11.4.2.2   Removing a Single Free Block

This is the final case. Here we have a block that is in a list by itself. Because we don't represent empty lists, we need to move one of this block's descendants up in its place. If either subtree is empty, then the other one can move up.

```
if (t→left ≡ nil)
    rp = t→right;
```

```
else {
    if (t→right ≡ nil)
        rp = t→left;
    else {
```

If both subtrees are present, we run down the left edge of the right subtree to find the smallest node larger than the one we're removing.

```
        f = t;
        rp = t→right;
        s = rp→left;
        while (s ≠ nil) {
            f = rp;
            rp = s;
            s = rp→left;
        }
```

If there was a left branch in the right subtree, then we remove the leftmost descendant in the right subtree and use it to replace the block we're deleting.

```
        if (f ≠ t) {
            s = rp→right;
            f→left = s;
            if (s ≠ nil)
                s→parent = f;
            s = t→right;
            rp→right = s;
            if (s ≠ nil)
                s→parent = rp;
        }
        s = t→left;
        rp→left = s;
        s→parent = rp;
    }
}
q = t→parent;
if (q ≡ nil)
    p→root = rp;
else {
    if (t ≡ q→left)
        q→left = rp;
    else
        q→right = rp;
}
```

```
    if (rp ≠ nil)
        rp⁻parent = q;
}
```

11.4.3 Freeing Memory

By comparison, the main function for freeing memory is quite straightforward. The entry point, *poolfree*( ), is declared in **emu/port/alloc.c**. Most of the code in this function is concerned with combining adjacent free blocks into larger free blocks. It is declared as:

```
    void poolfree(Pool *p, void *v)
    {
        Bhdr *b, *c;
        extern Bhdr *ptr;
```

As with *dopoolalloc*(), we have some administrative tasks, including locking the pool data structure.

```
    D2B(b, v);
    if (p⁻monitor)
        MM(p⁻pnum | (1 ≪ 8), getcallerpc(&p), (ulong) v, b⁻size);
    lock(&p⁻l);
    p⁻nfree ++;
    p⁻cursize -= b⁻size;
```

11.4.3.1 Coalescing Adjacent Free Blocks

Now, if the block immediately before this one is free or the one after it is free, then we combine this block with them. For the time being, those free blocks are taken out of the free data structure so that we add back exactly the right block.

```
    c = B2NB(b);
    if (c⁻magic ≡ MAGIC_F) {      /* Join forward */
        if (c ≡ ptr)
            ptr = b;
        pooldel(p, c);
        c⁻magic = 0;
        b⁻size += c⁻size;
        B2T(b)⁻hdr = b;
    }
    c = B2PT(b)⁻hdr;
    if (c⁻magic ≡ MAGIC_F) {      /* Join backward */
        if (b ≡ ptr)
            ptr = c;
```

```
        pooldel(p, c);
        b⟶magic = 0;
        c⟶size += b⟶size;
        b = c;
        B2T(b)⟶hdr = b;
    }
```

Finally, we return our (possibly enlarged) newly freed block to the free tree, and then unlock the data structure.

```
    pooladd(p, b);
    unlock(&p⟶l);
}
```

Because *poolfree()* handles the combination of adjacent free blocks, it is the primary interface for returning memory back to the free list.

11.4.4   Inserting a Free Block into the Tree

As mentioned earlier, both *dopoolalloc()* and *poolfree()* make use of *pooladd()* to place free blocks into the free block tree.

```
    void pooladd(Pool *p, Bhdr *q)
    {
        int size;
        Bhdr *tp, *t;
```

The first step is setting the block up as the sole free block of its size. (We change that later if necessary.)

```
        q⟶magic = MAGIC_F;
        q⟶left = nil;
        q⟶right = nil;
        q⟶parent = nil;
        q⟶fwd = q;
        q⟶prev = q;
```

11.4.4.1   Locating the Insertion Point

Now, we search through the binary search tree for the place in the tree where this block should go. If it turns out that the tree is empty, then life is easy; our new free block is the root of the tree.

```
        t = p⟶root;
        if (t ≡ nil) {
            p⟶root = q;
```

```
        return;
   }
```

11.4.4.2 Adding to an Existing List

There are two other cases. In the first, we find an existing node of the tree where there are already free blocks of the same size. If we find this case, we insert this block at the end of the list.

$$size = q\text{-}size;$$
$$tp = nil;$$
while $(t \neq nil)$ {
   if $(size \equiv t\text{-}size)$ {
      $q\text{-}prev = t\text{-}prev;$
      $q\text{-}prev\text{-}fwd = q;$
      $q\text{-}fwd = t;$
      $t\text{-}prev = q;$
      return;
   }
   $tp = t;$
   if $(size < t\text{-}size)$
      $t = t\text{-}left;$
   else
      $t = t\text{-}right;$
}

11.4.4.3 Creating a New List

In the last case, we don't have any other blocks of the same size, and we need to add a new leaf node to the tree. This new node will contain a linked list containing only the new block.

$$q\text{-}parent = tp;$$
if $(size < tp\text{-}size)$
   $tp\text{-}left = q;$
else
   $tp\text{-}right = q;$
}

When we return from *pooladd*( ), the block we got as a parameter has been added to the tree. This operation is needed when we release a block back to the free list, when we add new free space as a result of an arena allocation, and when we move blocks of memory around to reduce fragmentation. Most instances of returning a block to the free list, such as that in the next section, go through *poolfree*( ) so that the newly freed block can be combined with any adjacent free blocks.

11.5   Garbage Collection

For the main and image pools, all the memory allocation and freeing is done through calls that directly invoke the code we just covered. In other words, all allocation and freeing is explicitly controlled by the kernel and the built-in Limbo modules. However, the heap pool is handled differently. Whenever a process dynamically creates an array or list or other data structure, the memory for this data structure is allocated from the heap. There are Limbo language features that result in these allocations. However, there are no Limbo language features that destroy or free these structures. So how, then, is the memory for these data structures recovered when they are no longer used? That is the focus of this section.

11.5.1   Heap Structure

Each block allocated for the heap has a descriptive structure of type **Heap** at the beginning. There are three members of this structure that interest us here. First, there is a member called *color*. This integer is used to label each heap block during garbage collection. We discuss its use in detail later. The second item of interest is a reference count, *ref*, which we also discuss later. Finally, there is a pointer to a type descriptor, *t*. From our perspective, the most important part of a type descriptor is a map of all pointers within the data structure. Because the Limbo language does not allow a programmer to take the address of an arbitrary object nor directly manipulate pointers, we can know with certainty every pointer in the heap.

11.5.2   Reference Counts

The primary mechanism for managing heap allocation is the reference count in the **Heap** structure. Each time a new heap block is allocated through *dopoolalloc( )*, the reference count is set to 1, representing the variable to which the address of the structure is assigned. Whenever that address is copied, such as when an allocated structure is passed as a reference parameter, we increment the reference count. Each time a reference goes away, as in the case of local variables and parameters at the end of a function, the reference count is decremented. When the count reaches 0, we can free that block using the *poolfree( )* call covered earlier.

This reference count approach to managing heap blocks works well and covers about 98% of the cases. There is one scenario where it doesn't work. If there is a cyclic set of references, then the reference count will never reach 0. For example, if we have a circular linked list, each element has at least one reference to it. To access the list, though, there must also be one more reference from outside the list referring to one of the elements. If that reference goes away, then we cannot access the list, but all the elements still have a reference count greater than 0.

11.5.3   Very Concurrent Garbage Collector

We deal with the cases that reference counts can't by using garbage collection. Most garbage collection techniques are variations on the mark-and-sweep approach. The basic idea is that we go through all the blocks of memory, clearing the flags that indicate they are reachable. Next, we go through all the references to data structures, marking as reachable all of the data structures that have references. Finally, we then sweep through memory looking for all those that still have the reachable flag cleared, and we free them. The Inferno garbage collection technique is built on this basic mark-and-sweep approach. It is a variation on an algorithm called Very Concurrent Garbage Collection (VCGC).

VCGC is one of those algorithms where it is imperative that we understand it at a high level before delving into the code. As suggested earlier, the algorithm operates on heap blocks by coloring them. There are four colors we use in the Inferno implementation: **mutator**, **marker**, **sweeper**, and **propagator**. (The original VCGC formulation did not include the **propagator** color found in the Inferno implementation.) The colors, in effect, represent what type of thread of control "owns" a block, and in doing so, tells us something about the reachability of the block.

Each pass through the heap is called an **epoch**. As we examine each block during an epoch, we identify which are known to be reachable, which are known not to be reachable and can be freed, and which appear to be unreachable and can be freed in the next epoch. These identifications are associated with the colors as follows:

- *mutator*: A mutator can change the allocation of a block. Mutators are the user processes that allocate data structures. Blocks marked with the mutator color are known to be reachable. Newly allocated blocks are colored with the mutator color.

- *marker*: The marker color controls the marking of reachable blocks. The best way to think about it is that at the beginning of each epoch, all the mutator blocks are changed to marker blocks. Each reachable marker block is recolored as a mutator. When we reach the end of an epoch, all those blocks that are still marker blocks are unreachable.

- *sweeper*: The sweeper is then a conceptual thread that goes through all the marker blocks at the end of an epoch and frees them. The actual implementation is a little more clever. At the beginning of an epoch, all the marker blocks are recolored as sweeper blocks. Then as we go through all the heap blocks, any we encounter that are colored as sweeper blocks can be freed as we go. We know we are safe in freeing them because we determined that they were unreachable in the last epoch.

- *propagator*: We can think of the propagator as a flag on the marker color. When we first follow a pointer to a marker block, we change it to a propagator block. This marks the fact that we know it is reachable, but we haven't yet recursively marked any blocks it points to. When we do that recursive marking, then we change the propagator to mutator. This allows us to set a limit on how many blocks we visit in one pass, to unroll the recursion, but not lose track of which ones still need to be processed. It does mean, however, that we may have to make more than one pass over all the blocks to clear up any propagators. On the first pass where we don't mark any new propagators, we know we have finished, and we can move on to the next epoch.

In addition to the roles of the colors, there are four observations that tie it all together for us.

1. The way in which pools are composed of arenas and arenas are broken into blocks makes it possible for us to easily look at every heap block. We simply start at the beginning of an arena, look at the first block, then move on to the next by using the B2NB macro that gives us a pointer to the next block.

2. The type descriptors identify for us every pointer to a data structure. By following these recursively, we can locate every reachable block.

3. We do not have to process an entire epoch at one time. We can do part of an epoch and then come back later and do more of it. Only two changes could take place along the way. If a new block is allocated, it's marked as a mutator block, and, as such, it is correctly identified as reachable during the epoch. If a structure loses its last outside reference but we've already passed it marking it as reachable, we'll simply identify it as unreachable in the next epoch.

4. We don't need to explicitly sweep through all the blocks changing their colors. We can represent colors with integers and change the association between integers and colors each time. For example, suppose the mutator color is identifed as 0, the sweeper as 1, and the marker as 2. By renumbering the colors so that the mutator is 1, the sweeper 2, and the marker 0, we have made all the changes in color that are required at the beginning of an epoch.

11.5.4   Implementing VCGC

In *vmachine( )*, described in Chapter 7, we find two ways *rungc( )* is called. First, we force garbage collection once every 256 time slices or when memory is getting low. Second, there is also a call to *rungc( )* in *execatidle( )*, which is run when there are neither any *kprocs* nor user processes ready to run.

The function *rungc( )* is the main entry point for the garbage collector. It runs the VCGC algorithm on some number of blocks before returning. If it succeeds in completing a pass over the heap pool (regardless of whether it is the end of the epoch), it also returns. This function is found in libinterp/gc.c.

```
void rungc(Prog *p)
{
  Type *t;
  Heap *h;
  Bhdr *b;
  gcnruns ++;
  if (gchalt) {
    gchalted ++;
    return;
  }
```

11.5.4.1   Initializing a Pass

We keep the global variable *base* pointing to the next block to process at all times. If we have no next block, it must be because this is the first time we've run, or because the last time we were called, we finished a complete pass over the pool. So here, we initialize *base* to point to the beginning of the first arena and set *limit* to the end of the arena.

```
if (base ≡ nil) {
    gcsweeps ++;
    b = poolchain(heapmem);
    base = b;
    ptr = b;
    limit = B2LIMIT(b);
}
```

Just in case we've had some kind of corruption of the pool, we'll check to make sure that the block header we see is valid. In particular, it must have one of the defined magic values.

```
if (¬okbhdr(ptr)) {
    base = nil;
    gcbroken ++;
    return;
}
```

11.5.4.2   Processing the Heap Blocks

The bulk of this function is contained in this **for** loop. We look at *quanta* blocks before giving control back to *vmachine*( ). However, we skip free blocks altogether; we don't process them, and we don't count them against *quanta*.

```
for (visit = quanta; visit > 0; ) {
    if (ptr→magic ≡ MAGIC_A) {
        visit --;
        gct ++;
        gcinspects ++;
```

If we find a block that is marked as a propagator, then we know that in a previous pass, we found it to be reachable, but we haven't yet processed any of the blocks it points to. The call to *t→mark*( ) calls a marking function appropriate to the type of data in this heap block. These marker functions take the blocks marked with the marker color, mark them as propagators, and recursively process any blocks they point to. At the point where we descend into the recursion, we change the color from propagator to mutator.

```
h = B2D(ptr);
t = h→t;
```

```
    if (h⟶color ≡ propagator) {
      gce --;
      h⟶color = mutator;
      if (t ≠ nil)
        t⟶mark(t, H2D(void *, h));
    }
```

We know that any block marked with the sweeper color is unreachable and can, therefore, be freed. We use the *poolfree()* function discussed earlier. Also, if this block points to a type descriptor, we need to free that as well.

```
    else if (h⟶color ≡ sweeper) {
      gce ++;
      if (0 ∧ mflag)
        domflag(h);
      if (heapmonitor ≠ nil)
        heapmonitor(2, h, 0);
      if (t ≠ nil) {
        gclock();
        t⟶free(h, 1);
        gcunlock();
        freetype(t);
      }
      gcdestroys ++;
      poolfree(heapmem, h);
    }
  }
```

11.5.4.3 Processing the Next Arena

Here, we check the *limit* we set earlier. If we have hit it, then that means we've also hit the end of this arena. Because there may be multiple arenas in this pool, we now move on to the next one and continue.

```
  ptr = B2NB(ptr);
  if (ptr ≥ limit) {
    base = base⟶clink;
    if (base ≡ nil)
      break;
    ptr = base;
    limit = B2LIMIT(base);
  }
}
```

11.5.4.4   Finishing Off the Pass

At this point, we have fallen out of the **for** loop, indicating that we have processed as many blocks as we're allowed on this call. The first step in cleaning up is setting the number of blocks we'll process next time. The ratio of *gce* to *gct* measures the fraction of the blocks we processed that were freed versus the fraction that were found to be propagators. The idea is that if we're getting a lot of memory recovered, then we are willing to spend more of the system's time on garbage collection. If we're getting very little, then we want to get in and out of the garbage collector as fast as we can.

$$quanta = (MaxQuanta + Quanta)/2$$
$$\quad + ((MaxQuanta - Quanta)/20) * ((100 * gce)/gct);$$
if $(quanta < Quanta)$
$\quad quanta = Quanta;$
if $(quanta > MaxQuanta)$
$\quad quanta = MaxQuanta;$

Because we made sure that we moved on to the next arena at the end of the loop, the only way *base* will be *nil* at this point is if we've reached the end of the last arena. That means that most of the time we return at this point, because we still have more to do in this pass.

if $(base \neq nil)$ /* Completed this iteration ? */
$\quad$ **return**;

However, if we have reached the end of the last arena, then we know we've finished a complete pass through all the blocks of the heap pool. If in this last pass we did not mark any new propagators, then we also know we're at the end of this epoch. We know this because *nprop* is cleared. It is a flag that is set anytime we mark a block as a propagator. If we are at the end of the epoch, we increment *gccolor* and call *rootset*( ). Together, these first have the effect of reassigning the colors, making all markers sweepers and all mutators markers. After that, *rootset*( ) goes through the whole process table and looks at each module of each process, marking the module data spaces as propagator blocks. Likewise, it does the same with the process's stack frames. These blocks will then be the starting points for recursively marking blocks in the next epoch.

if $(nprop \equiv 0)$ {   /* Completed the epoch ? */
$\quad gcepochs ++;$
$\quad gccolor ++;$
$\quad rootset(p);$
$\quad gce = 0;$
$\quad gct = 1;$
$\quad$ **return**;
}
$nprop = 0;$
}

At this point, we return back to *vmachine*( ) to resume time-sharing. At some later time, *rungc*( ) will be called again to continue this epoch or to start a new one. When it is called from *execatidle*( ), it is called multiple times to ensure that all the unreachable blocks are freed.

11.6   Summary

Inferno is targeted toward two run-time environments that do not require extensive memory management. In hosted Inferno, we rely on the host OS to do much of the memory management task for us by providing memory allocated to emu. Native Inferno runs on a variety of hardware platforms, some of which have no hardware support for address translation or memory protection. As a result, Inferno itself is responsible for dividing the physical memory into the three pools. However, in doing so, Inferno doesn't need to implement paging or swapping. The net effect is that we have a relatively simple memory management system in Inferno.

Our look at memory management in Inferno illustrates a particular implementation of best-fit memory allocation. We use a binary search tree to speed the search for the best fit. The space in each tree comes from one or more arenas, which are allocated from the run-time environment. There is one such tree for each of three memory pools. Overall, Inferno uses an efficient implementation of one of the simple variable-sized allocation strategies described in Chapter 9. Finally, it incorporates a combination of reference counts and garbage collection to manage blocks allocated as part of Limbo operations.

11.7   Exercises

1. Given our discussion of memory usage in Inferno, can Inferno support shared code between processes? Can multiple processes share the global data of a module?

2. What constrains the value of the *quanta* member of the **Pool** structure? Could we make it smaller than 31? If so, how small? If not, why not?

3. Could 31 be too small to be useful as a value for *quanta*? Devise a way to determine if it is.

4. When adding a block back to the free tree for a pool, we check to see if adjacent blocks are also free and coalesce them if they are. Is it possible that we might accidentally coalesce free blocks belonging to different pools in this way? Why or why not?

5. Add debugging output to the *dopoolalloc*( ) function. In particular, print out the pool and the size of the request on entry. On both entry and exit, you should print out a list of sizes and counts for the specified pool. One possible form of output would look like:

```
Requesting 1024 bytes from main pool
Free blocks before allocation:
1x256, 3x394, 2x512, 1x16384
Free blocks after allocation:
1x256, 3x394, 2x512, 1x15360
```

where the $n \times m$ terms refer to n blocks of m bytes each. (Note that these exact numbers are not what you will see when you run your revised hosted kernel.) You can get the value of n by counting the length of the linked list and the value of m from the block header.

6. Gather statistics to determine the average allocation request and the average free block size. Print these values each time a block is allocated.

7. Modify Inferno to do worst-fit memory allocation instead of best-fit allocation.

8. Write a function that produces a list of all memory blocks used by a particular process.

9. Replace the binary search tree of linked lists with a single linked list of free blocks. How much performance do you lose with this new design?

10. Replace the binary search tree of linked lists with a hash table of free blocks. Does this new design improve the performance of the system?

Chapter 12

Memory Management in Linux

The Linux memory management subsystem is quite involved. Processes may allocate memory implicitly as part of process creation and as a result of stack growth. They may also request memory explicitly through two different system calls. Furthermore, the kernel itself does a substantial amount of dynamic memory allocation. To support all these forms of allocation, Linux implements a number of mechanisms that operate both on fixed-sized pages and on variable-sized blocks. Variable allocation can be in the form of multiple contiguous pages or in the form of smaller allocations within pages.

Like most modern systems, Linux uses demand paging and page swapping to support a greater demand for memory than is physically available. It also implements the copy-on-write mechanism, discussed in Section 9.6.6, to reduce unnecessary page allocation and copying.

We begin our examination of memory management in Linux with the way in which it assigns both physical and virtual address spaces. A discussion of memory-related system calls follows. We then present general overviews of the internal allocation mechanisms and of the page management infrastructure. Finally, the majority of this chapter is devoted to a small sampling of the code that implements Linux memory management. Our look at the implementation focuses on the data structures that represent memory allocations, on the allocation of memory in response to process requests, and on page fault handling.

12.1 Memory Layouts

The physical memory layout for any system is highly dependent on the design of the hardware as well as the design of the operating system. Both the design of the CPU and the design of the overall system influence the use of physical memory. For our examination of memory management in Linux, we focus on the implementation on the IBM-compatible systems using the Intel x86 architecture. The physical memory usage of Linux on this platform is shown in Figure 12-1. Because of various limitations on the overall system design, different areas of memory have different capabilities. In Linux, we use the term **zones** to identify these areas.

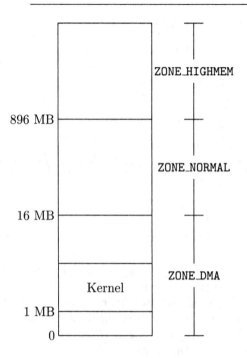

Figure 12-1: Linux Physical Memory Layout

The first megabyte of memory is largely unused except during booting and except for the 360 KB of the physical memory space used for accessing memory-mapped I/O controllers. The next several megabytes hold the uncompressed kernel image. On an IBM PC, the direct memory access (DMA) controller is capable of addressing only the first 16 MB of memory. Thus, the area between the top of the kernel and the end of the first 16 MB area is used primarily for I/O buffers. The full first 16 MB is identified as ZONE_DMA. On machines with relatively small memory spaces, the remainder of the memory is identified as ZONE_NORMAL. However, the kernel maps only 1 GB of virtual space. Therefore, on systems with a large amount of memory (more than 1 GB), we divide the remainder of the memory space into a ZONE_NORMAL, which ends at the 896 MB point, and a ZONE_HIGHMEM, which occupies the remainder of the memory space. The kernel maps the ZONE_HIGHMEM memory into the upper 128 MB of its virtual memory space as needed.

A Linux process's virtual memory layout looks like that illustrated in Figure 12-2. Overall, it is quite similar to the generic layout we see in Figure 9-7. In this case, however, the lowest memory addresses are not used. The first 128 MB of virtual space is not mapped by the MMU except in some less common applications. Normally, we leave this area unmapped so that a common class of programming bug can be found quickly. Frequently, pointers that are not set to useful values are set to relatively small addresses. A particularly common case is the null pointer, which points to address 0. If we leave the low part of the memory space unmapped, then any attempt to dereference such a pointer

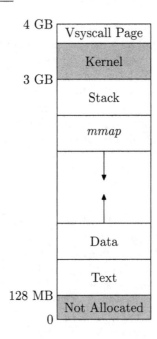

Figure 12-2: Linux Process Virtual Address Space Layout

results in a page fault. Consequently, the OS can detect the problem and terminate the program. The text and data segments follow the general approach we outlined in Section 9.4, with the data space growing toward higher memory addresses as needed. (In Linux, these segments are called **sections** to distinguish them from the hardware defined segmentation of the x86 processor. However, we continue to refer to them as segments in keeping with the terminology established in Chapter 9.) Because Linux has two mechanisms for processes to allocate memory dynamically, we need two regions that can grow. The higher of these two regions is used to support the *mmap( )* system call that allows a file to be mapped into memory, as described in the next section. In older versions of the system, we started the section that *mmap( )* uses at a fixed address, allowing normal heap allocation up to that point and allowing *mmap( )* allocation up to the stack. However, the limitations that created were more inconvenient than those imposed by a limit on the size of the stack. In fact, there was always a limit on the size of the stack. We have described stack growth as taking place automatically whenever an attempt is made to push onto the stack beyond the available space. Real systems, however, limit this. If a program has a bug that causes it to use up stack space in an uncontrolled manner, then we want to stop it. Therefore, most systems check the stack allocation against some limit before allocating a new page to it. In Linux, we simply reserve the maximum amount of space we would allow for the stack, and then let the *mmap( )* section grow downward toward the traditional data segment. The area above the 3 GB point in the address space is the kernel memory space. This region between 3 GB and 4 GB gives room for the kernel's 1 GB virtual address space, as described earlier. Despite the kernel being mapped this way in the process's page tables, it is not readable when the processor is running in user mode. When the processor switches into kernel mode on a system call, though, the kernel memory space is already mapped and available. The last page in the virtual memory space is accessible to the process and contains the vsyscall page described in Section 4.4. This page contains the code that uses the appropriate system call mechanism for the version of the processor on which we are running.

12.2   System Calls

As with other implementations of the UNIX design, Linux provides a number of system calls that affect the memory usage of a process. Some of these, such as *fork*() and *execve*(), are primarily process management system calls but have major implications for memory management. In processing the *fork*() system call, we must, in some way, make a copy of the parent's memory space. In Linux, this is done using the copy on write (COW) technique discussed in Section 9.6.6. Not only does this reduce the amount of copying to only the necessary pages, it also permits sharing of text (code) segments as a by-product. The *execve*() system call requires that we release all of the memory previously used by the process and then allocate memory to hold the new program and the new data space. Because a process often shares much of its memory space with its parent, releasing memory is a matter of reducing a count of the number of processes sharing each page. In contrast to earlier descriptions of starting a new program, Linux does not directly load the executable code into memory in response to the *execve*() call. Rather, it treats the executable essentially as a memory-mapped file, and it then relies on the demand paging mechanism to load executable pages as needed. As described in Section 9.6.5 and as created by the *mmap*() call described shortly, memory-mapped files are files that are assigned to a region of the virtual memory space. Accesses to memory in that region become accesses to the mapped file.

There are two more system calls that more directly affect a process's memory usage. The first of these is the traditional UNIX *brk*() system call. Its sole parameter specifies the first address that is not part of the data segment. In its traditional usage, everything else in the combined data and stack part of the virtual address space is available for the stack. In Linux, however, the break point defines the separation between data and the area used by the *mmap*() call. The kernel still grows the stack when an attempt is made to push data into a page not allocated to the stack. However, the maximum size of the stack is not dependent on the size of the data segment, as in the traditional UNIX process memory model. The other main system call for directly organizing a process's memory space is *mmap*(). Its primary raison d'être is mapping a file into the process's memory space. If, however, no file is specified, then the system creates a mapping to an anonymous area, which is composed of anonymous pages not associated with any file. These pages are allocated by the function *do_anonymous_page*(), covered later in this chapter. The effect of this mapping is a normal memory allocation, which may be shared with other processes. Internally, the $brk()$ system call is implemented very much like an anonymous mapping.

12.3 Allocation Mechanisms

Even though Linux provides only two primary mechanisms for processes to request memory, a number of mechanisms are defined for internal allocation. In fact, we see in later sections that the allocation mechanisms for user processes are some of the simplest ones.

12.3.1 Zoned Page Allocation

The heart of all memory allocation in Linux is page allocation. Although user processes need only pages that are mapped to certain ranges of virtual addresses, there are memory needs within the kernel that require pages that are contiguous in physical memory. Consequently, the page allocation mechanism must behave much like a variable-sized memory allocator. In Linux, this is implemented with a buddy system allocator.

In Section 12.1, we note that on many systems, including the IBM PC, there are restrictions on how we use some parts of memory. The buddy system page allocator supports this by allowing the requesting code to specify which zone should be used to satisfy the request. If the caller requests pages from ZONE_DMA by using the __GFP_DMA flag, then the request must be satisfied from that zone or it fails. If the caller requests pages from ZONE_HIGHMEM by using the __GFP_HIGHMEM flag, then the allocator attempts to satisfy the request from that zone. If there is no free block of pages large enough in that zone, then we attempt to satisfy the request out of ZONE_NORMAL; we attempt to allocate from ZONE_DMA if that fails. Finally, we request pages from ZONE_NORMAL if we set neither flag. If no appropriately sized block of pages is available in that zone, then we fall back to ZONE_DMA to satisfy the request. If no appropriate zone has the necessary free pages, then we attempt to swap pages out to disk to create enough free pages to satisfy the request.

12.3.2 Slab Allocator

Of course, not all allocation needs are multiple pages, or even a full page, in size. We often need to allocate space for an instance of a data structure that might be only a few tens of bytes. To accommodate these requests, Linux implements a mechanism called the **slab** allocator. The motivation behind the slab allocator is the observation that not all sizes are equally likely in kernel allocation. In fact, we generally have a relatively small number of possible sizes that are the sizes of the structures defined when the kernel is written. Take process table entries, for example. When we create a new process, we allocate space for such an entry. When the process terminates and the exit status is reaped, we free that memory. If we then reuse that memory for the process table entry of the next process we create, we save ourselves the work of locating and constructing a block of the appropriate size.

Slabs are collections of free memory blocks of a particular size. When a request is made for that size, we satisfy it from the slab. If the slab is empty, we allocate one or more pages dividing them into blocks of the required size and add them to the slab. When a block is freed, it is added back to the slab for its size. The full set of slabs can be examined by reading the file /proc/slabinfo.

12.3.3   Kernel Memory Allocation

Most requests for memory in the kernel are not made directly of the page allocator or the slab allocator. There is a function called *kmalloc( )*, which is similar to the *malloc( )* call in the standard C library. In addition to specifying the size of the request, this call allows the caller to pass a number of flags, which control the details of the allocation. For instance, if the set of flags defined as GFP_KERNEL is specified, the memory is allocated for the kernel. The zone from which we are requesting memory can also be specified in the flags. As one might expect, there is a *kfree( )* function, which releases the memory allocated with *kmalloc( )*.

12.4   Page Management

The implementation of page table management and page swapping in Linux is quite complex. As a result, we present only an overview of these parts of Linux memory management. In particular, we look first at the structure of page tables in Linux and at how they are generalized across a wide variety of architectures. We follow this with a discussion of the page replacement policy and implementation in Linux. Because of the size and complexity of the code, we settle for only a descriptive overview here.

12.4.1   Page Tables

For portability, Linux abstracts its paging management away from any particular page table representation. It uses a four-level page table design. (Versions prior to 2.6.11 used a three-level design.) In this abstraction, the uppermost bits of the virtual address (VA) index a **page global directory** (pgd). The entry selected points to a **page upper directory** (pud), which is indexed by the next most significant bits of the virtual address. This pud entry, in turn, points to a **page mid-level directory** (pmd), indexed by the third group of bits. Finally, the pmd entry points to a **page table** (pt), indexed by the fourth group of bits. The least significant bits of the virtual address give the offset into the page frame pointed to by the selected page table entry, which includes the page frame number part of the physical address (PA). Figure 12-3 illustrates this address translation design.

The basic design does not specify the number of bits used for each of the fields in either the virtual address or the physical address. For hardware such as the Intel x86, which has fewer levels of page tables, Linux merges levels together. On the Intel x86, the pud and pmd tables are merged into the pgd, resulting in a two-level table that matches the hardware. Both the pgd and the pt are indexed by 10 bits of the 32-bit virtual address. This leaves 12 bits to specify the page offset, giving a page size of 4096 bytes.

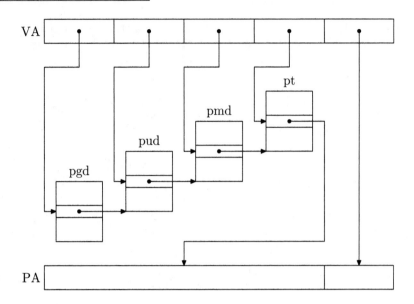

Figure 12-3: Linux Four-Level Page Table Design

12.4.2   Page Replacement

The page replacement policy in Linux is something of a combination of techniques discussed in Chapter 9. Internally, the data structures and function names refer to an LRU policy. However, the actual policy is a combination of second chance (or clock algorithm) with multiple lists vaguely similar to those in VMS and Windows NT. The lists of pages are also similar to a technique called LRU 2Q. In addition, there is consideration given to clean versus dirty pages much as NRU gives.

Linux maintains two per-zone lists of pages, an **active** list and an **inactive** list. As the names imply, we expect the active list to contain the working sets of all processes and the inactive list to contain pages available for allocation. The system attempts to maintain a balance between the sizes of these two lists. When the number of pages in the inactive list drops, the function *refill_inactive_zone( )* transfers pages from the active list to the inactive list. This transfer uses a second chance policy. Pages are taken from the end of the active list. If they have been marked referenced since being put on the list, they are marked unreferenced and placed back on the beginning of the list. Pages that are removed from the active list unreferenced are moved to the inactive list. Pages are added to the beginning of the inactive list, and pages are freed from the end of it.

When a page is to be marked as accessed, the function *mark_page_accessed( )* is often called. This function steps a page through a series of states. A page on the inactive list that is unreferenced is left on the list but marked referenced. A page on the inactive list marked referenced is moved to the active list but marked unreferenced. A page on the active list but unreferenced is marked referenced. The consequence is that a page must be marked accessed three times before it can be kept in the second chance policy if it starts out as unreferenced on the inactive list. This behavior of *mark_page_accessed*( ) is

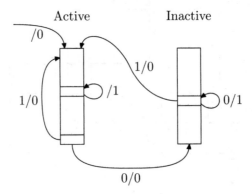

Figure 12-4: Linux Page Lists

illustrated in Figure 12-4. Each arrow represents a transition carried out by the function. The numbers adjacent to each arrow show the behavior of the accessed (A) bit. The number before the slash (/) shows the value of A prior to the transition and the number after the slash show the value of A after the transition.

The kswapd kernel thread scans memory looking for pages that can be made available when free memory gets low. Most of the time kswapd is sleeping. It is awakened by an attempt to allocate pages when there are not enough free pages to satisfy the request. It attempts to shrink each zone to make pages available. Two of its main sources of pages are process pages on the inactive list and unallocated pages in slabs. After being awakened, kswapd processes the memory allocations until each zone has enough free pages.

12.5   Memory Management Data Structures

We turn now from the overall design of Linux memory management to the specifics of implementation. We start with the data structures that represent the memory we manage. The structures that we examine are those that are used most in the code we discuss later in this chapter. One represents all of the areas of memory that are allocated to a process, and one represents one of these memory areas.

12.5.1   Representing Process Allocation

The first data structure we examine is **mm_struct**, which defines a process's memory usage and is declared in include/linux/sched.h. Each process table entry contains a pointer to one of these structures. In particular, this pointer is a member of the **task_struct** part of the process table entry. For each new process that is created, this structure is copied as part of the work done by *copy_process*( ). During the creation of a new thread which

shares its parent's memory space, the child's process table entry points to the parent's
mm_struct, causing both threads to share the structure.

```
struct mm_struct {
    struct vm_area_struct *mmap;        /* list of VMAs */
    struct rb_root mm_rb;
    struct vm_area_struct *mmap_cache;     /* last find_vma result */
    unsigned long (*get_unmapped_area)(struct file *filp,
        unsigned long addr, unsigned long len, unsigned long pgoff,
        unsigned long flags);
    void (*unmap_area)(struct mm_struct *mm, unsigned long addr);
    unsigned long mmap_base;        /* base of mmap area */
    unsigned long task_size;
    unsigned long cached_hole_size;
    unsigned long free_area_cache;
    pgd_t *pgd;
    atomic_t mm_users;
    atomic_t mm_count;
    int map_count;        /* number of VMAs */
    struct rw_semaphore mmap_sem;
    spinlock_t page_table_lock;
    struct list_head mmlist;
    mm_counter_t _file_rss;
    mm_counter_t _anon_rss;
    unsigned long hiwater_rss;        /* High-watermark of RSS usage */
    unsigned long hiwater_vm;        /* High-water virtual memory usage */
    unsigned long total_vm, locked_vm, shared_vm, exec_vm;
    unsigned long stack_vm, reserved_vm, def_flags, nr_ptes;
    unsigned long start_code, end_code, start_data, end_data;
    unsigned long start_brk, brk, start_stack;
    unsigned long arg_start, arg_end, env_start, env_end;
    unsigned long saved_auxv[AT_VECTOR_SIZE];
    unsigned dumpable:2;
    cpumask_t cpu_vm_mask;        /* Architecture-specific MM context */
    mm_context_t context;        /* Token based thrashing protection. */
    unsigned long swap_token_time;
    char recent_pagein;        /* coredumping support */
    int core_waiters;
    struct completion *core_startup_done, *core_done;        /* aio bits */
    rwlock_t ioctx_list_lock;
    struct kioctx *ioctx_list;
};
```

Some members of the structure that illustrate the application of memory management principles in Linux include:

- *mmap* and *mm_rb*: These two structure members are pointers to data structures that represent the set of all memory **areas**. For each process, a range of contiguous virtual memory addresses is called an area. The *mmap* structure points to a linked list of structures describing the areas belonging to this process. The *mm_rb* member points to a red-black tree of the same structures. (A red-black tree is a binary tree representation of a 2-3-4 tree, which is a variation on the balanced 2-3 tree found in most textbooks on data structures.) Because the red-black tree is balanced, we can use it to do operations on areas in $O(\log n)$ time rather than $O(n)$ time, where n is the number of areas for this process.

- *mmap_cache*: We find that about 30% of the requests for looking up a memory area locate the same area as the previous request. This member keeps the results of the last lookup to gain a performance advantage when we do repeat a request.

- *mmap_base*: This value identifies the boundary between the area used by the *mmap* system call and the area used for the process's stack. New allocations to this area grow downward from that point, as illustrated in Figure 12-2.

- *pgd*: A pointer to the page global directory definition is stored in this member. On the Intel x86, this definition is a structure that holds just the virtual address of the pgd itself. Because it is a data structure in the kernel, its virtual address is above 3 GB.

- *mm_users* and *mm_count*: Because these structures can be shared when we create threads, we maintain a count of the number of processes using this memory management structure so that we know when the last process has finished, indicating that we can free the structure.

- *map_count*: This member holds the number of virtual memory areas used in this structure.

- *mmap_sem* and *page_table_lock*: These provide mutual exclusion locking for the memory management data structures.

- *start_code*, *end_code*, *start_data*, *end_data*, *start_brk*, *brk*, and *start_stack*: The code, data, and stack segments shown earlier in Figure 12-2 are defined by these members.

12.5.2   Representing Virtual Memory Areas

The next memory management structure we examine is **vm_area_struct** mentioned earlier. This structure defines a contiguous memory area in the virtual address space. Its declaration is given in include/linux/mm.h. As we see in our following discussion of the structure members, while all areas are contiguous, a contiguous range of virtual addresses may be represented by more than one area structure.

```
struct vm_area_struct {
  struct mm_struct *vm_mm;
  unsigned long vm_start;
  unsigned long vm_end;
  struct vm_area_struct *vm_next;
  pgprot_t vm_page_prot;
  unsigned long vm_flags;
  struct rb_node vm_rb;
  union {
    struct {
      struct list_head list;
      void *parent;
      struct vm_area_struct *head;
    } vm_set;
    struct raw_prio_tree_node prio_tree_node;
  } shared;
  struct list_head anon_vma_node;
  struct anon_vma *anon_vma;
  struct vm_operations_struct *vm_ops;
  unsigned long vm_pgoff;
  struct file *vm_file;
  void *vm_private_data;
  unsigned long vm_truncate_count;
  atomic_t vm_usage;
};
```

Some of the relevant structure members include:

- *vm_mm*: This pointer is a link back to the **mm_struct** of which this area is a part.

- *vm_start* and *vm_end*: These two members give the starting and ending virtual addresses of this area. Because each area is a contiguous region of virtual memory, these are sufficient to describe the whole area.

- *vm_next* and *vm_rb*: As discussed in the context of the **mm_struct** structure, each memory area structure is kept on both a linked list and a red-black tree. These two members implement those data structures.

- *vm_page_prot*: Each virtual memory area has its own set of access permissions. These are stored in *vm_page_prot*. All pages belonging to this area share these permissions. Adjacent areas with different permissions are not combined even though they are contiguous in virtual addresses.

- *shared*: This union is used in maintaining another data structure containing areas. The structure is a radix priority search tree, which is used to quickly look up an area structure by the area's virtual address.

- *vm_pgoff* and *vm_file*: If this area is mapped to a file, it is specified by *vm_file*, and the offset within the file is given by *vm_pgoff*.

12.6   Memory Management Implementation

To illustrate the implementation of memory management in Linux, we follow the sequence of events that takes place when a process allocates additional data space and then accesses that new memory. At a high level, this sequence of events includes the following steps:

1. Adjust the virtual memory areas to account for this new memory allocation. Normally, we increase the size of the existing memory area for the data segment.

2. Return to the requesting process. At this point, we do not allocate physical memory to correspond to the newly allocated virtual memory.

3. The process accesses the new memory, which then causes a page fault.

4. In the page fault handler, we determine that this fault was caused by an access to a page allocated in virtual space, but not yet in physical space.

5. If a free page is available to give to this process, we do so.

6. If no free page is available, we trigger the page swapper to get a free page.

To make our discussion more concrete, we consider a specific example as we examine the code. In our example, we have a process that has 254 KB of code and 510 KB of data. The code segment, then, occupies virtual addresses #00000000 through #0007f7ff, and the data segment occupies addresses #00080000 through #000bf7ff, with the current break set at #000bf800. (All addresses are given for the 32-bit addresses on the x86 architecture and in hexadecimal notation.) The process needs to increase its data space by 256 KB. Adding 256 KB (#00040000) to the current break gives a new break of #000ff800. So the process makes a system call to set the new break with a statement such as:

$p = brk(\#000\mathtt{ff}800);$

The discussion that follows traces the kernel's response to this system call.

12.6.1   Handling the Allocation System Call

The starting point in this process is the function *sys_brk( )*, which is defined in mm/mmap.c. This is the function called on the *brk( )* system call. The argument is the new break point separating data space from the space allocated by *mmap( )*.

asmlinkage unsigned long *sys_brk*(**unsigned long** *brk*)
{
    unsigned long *rlim*, *retval*;
    unsigned long *newbrk*, *oldbrk*;

We are operating on the memory space of the process that just issued the system call. This means that we are operating on the kernel stack that is part of that process's memory space, which, in turn, means that the *current* macro described in Chapter 8 points to the relevant process's process table entry. For convenience and efficiency, we set the variable *mm* to point to the current process's **mm_struct** structure.

struct mm_struct *∗mm = current→mm*;

As we might expect, we need to lock this data structure so that no other threads can touch it while we're working.

down_write(&*mm→mmap_sem*);

12.6.1.1   Checking the Call

This error check ensures that we are not attempting to push the break down into the code segment. Doing so would cause us to release memory containing code, which would cause major problems if we tried to execute instructions from those addresses. If we had not allocated new data memory in the meantime, we would simply generate a page fault that would result in the process's termination. If we had allocated new data space where the code space used to be, then we would attempt to execute that data as if they were instructions with almost certainly undesired consequences. In our example, *mm→end_code* is #0007f800, so the test fails and we proceed with the rest of the function.

if (*brk* < *mm→end_code*)
    goto *out*;

At this point, we want to make sure that the process is not exceeding any administrative limits placed on it. If it is, then we fail. So that our example will be interesting, let us assume that the limit is not being violated.

rlim = current→signal→rlim[RLIMIT_DATA].*rlim_cur*;
if (*rlim* < RLIM_INFINITY ∧ *brk − mm→start_data* > *rlim*)
    goto *out*;

Even though the break point parameter is specified in terms of bytes, internally, all allocation is done in terms of pages. So we need to round up to the nearest page boundary. Because the x86 uses 4096-byte pages, these steps round the two values up to the nearest multiple of 4096. This makes *newbrk* #00100000 and *oldbrk* #000c0000.

newbrk = PAGE_ALIGN(*brk*);
oldbrk = PAGE_ALIGN(*mm→brk*);

After rounding up both the old and new break points, if we find that they are, in fact, the same, then we don't actually need to adjust any of our memory allocations. Because our new break is greater than our old one, we pass over the next two tests and proceed to the case of expanding the data segment.

if $(oldbrk \equiv newbrk)$
    goto set_brk;

12.6.1.2 Shrinking the Data Segment

On the other hand, if it turns out that the new break point is at a lower address than the old one, we know we are releasing memory. In that case, we call $do\_munmap(\ )$ to do the dirty work of adjusting the relevant area structure, freeing pages and adjusting page tables.

if $(brk \leq mm{\rightarrow}brk)$ {
    if $(\neg do\_munmap(mm, newbrk, oldbrk - newbrk))$
        goto set_brk;
    goto out;
}

12.6.1.3 Expanding the Data Segment

The next test checks to see whether the new data space we are requesting is already part of an existing virtual memory area. If it is, then we don't need to do anything and can return.

if $(find\_vma\_intersection(mm, oldbrk, newbrk + \texttt{PAGE\_SIZE}))$
    goto out;

Most of the actual work in increasing the size of our data area is done in $do\_brk(\ )$. Perhaps unexpectedly, it returns the old break point on success. If we don't get the old break point back, then it's a failure, and the break point is unchanged. Because of the assumptions we just made, we reach this point in the code. In the call to $do\_brk(\ )$, the second argument is calculated to be $^{\#}00040000$.

if $(do\_brk(oldbrk, newbrk - oldbrk) \neq oldbrk)$
    goto out;

At this point, we know we have successfully changed the break point, and we can update our **mm_struct** accordingly. In particular, we set $mm{\rightarrow}brk$ to $^{\#}000\texttt{ff}800$ and return that value back to the calling process.

set_brk:
    $mm{\rightarrow}brk = brk$;
out:
    $retval = mm{\rightarrow}brk$;
    $up\_write(\&mm{\rightarrow}mmap\_sem)$;
    return $retval$;
}

12.6.2   Adding a Region

The primary purpose of *do_brk*( ) is determining exactly how to go about adding a new region of virtual address space. If there is an existing area that partially covers it, we need to remove it before adding this one. If there is an existing area either immediately before or immediately after this one, we can merge them together. Finally, if there is no existing one to merge with, we create a new area for this region. The new area is identified by its *addr* and its *len*. In our example, *addr* is the old break, which is #000c0000, and *len* is #00040000.

> **unsigned long** *do_brk*(**unsigned long** *addr*, **unsigned long** *len*)
> {

As with *sys_brk*( ), we set *mm* to point to the requesting process's **mm_struct**.

> **struct mm_struct** **mm* = *current→mm*;
> **struct vm_area_struct** **vma*, **prev*;
> **unsigned long** *flags*;
> **struct rb_node** ***rb_link*, **rb_parent*;

The best way to think about *pgoff* is as the page number of the first page of the new area. This is #000002fe in our example.

> **pgoff_t** *pgoff* = *addr* ≫ PAGE_SHIFT;
> **int** *error*;

We want the size to be an integer number of pages, so we round up. If it turns out that there are no pages to add, then our job has been easy and we are done.

> *len* = PAGE_ALIGN(*len*);
> **if** (¬*len*)
>   **return** *addr*;

This test determines if we're asking for unreasonable amounts of memory. If it would put us over the limit, or if *len* is so large that it rolls over to a negative number, then we must deny the request. Neither of these conditions apply in our example.

> **if** ((*addr* + *len*) > TASK_SIZE ∨ (*addr* + *len*) < *addr*)
>   **return** −EINVAL;

Because we are expanding the data segment, we set the flags for this new area accordingly. On most architectures, including the x86, *arch_mmap_check*( ) is a null operation.

> *flags* = VM_DATA_DEFAULT_FLAGS | VM_ACCOUNT | *mm→def_flags*;
> *error* = *arch_mmap_check*(*addr*, *len*, *flags*);
> **if**(*error*)
>   **return** *error*;

12.6.2.1 Handling Physically Locked Regions

This next section of code handles special limit checks and bookkeeping in the case where the request is for a virtual memory area that is to be locked into physical memory (meaning that the system is not allowed to swap those pages out).

> **if** (mm→def_flags & VM_LOCKED) {
>   **unsigned long** $locked$, $lock\_limit$;
>
> $locked = len \gg$ PAGE_SHIFT;
> $locked\ += mm$→$locked\_vm$;
> $lock\_limit = current$→$signal$→$rlim$[RLIMIT_MEMLOCK]$.rlim\_cur$;
> $lock\_limit \gg=$ PAGE_SHIFT;
>   **if** ($locked > lock\_limit \wedge \neg capable$(CAP_IPC_LOCK))
>   **return** $-$EAGAIN;
> }

We should not be here unless we have the **mm_struct** structure mutex locked. This call checks to ensure that it is, and it warns us if not. However, the actual function $verify\_mm\_writelocked$( ) is empty unless we've compiled the kernel with an appropriate debugging flag.

> $verify\_mm\_writelocked$(mm);

12.6.2.2 Removing Overlapping Areas

This section of code is really a loop that tests to see if there is an existing area that includes the beginning address of the area we want to add. If there is, we delete its mapping and check again. After we've removed all areas that include the starting point of the new area, we may proceed to add it.

> $munmap\_back$:
> $vma = find\_vma\_prepare$(mm, $addr$, &$prev$, &rb_link, &rb_parent);
>   **if** ($vma \wedge vma$→$vm\_start < addr + len$) {
>   **if** (do_munmap(mm, $addr$, len))
>   **return** $-$ENOMEM;
>   **goto** $munmap\_back$;
>   }

12.6.2.3 Checking the Validity of the Call

If this request would put this process above a per-process administrative limit for the number of pages in the data segment, then we deny the request. Likewise, we must deny the request if the number of virtual memory areas is already at the maximum. Finally, we check the request against another limit that is part of the system security policy. Only when we pass all these tests can we move on to the next stage.

> **if** ($\neg may\_expand\_vm(mm, len \gg$ PAGE_SHIFT))
>   **return** $-$ENOMEM;
> **if** ($mm\rightarrow map\_count > sysctl\_max\_map\_count$)
>   **return** $-$ENOMEM;
> **if** ($security\_vm\_enough\_memory(len \gg$ PAGE_SHIFT))
>   **return** $-$ENOMEM;

12.6.2.4   Combining with Adjacent Areas

The function *vma_merge*( ) handles the case where there is an existing area that is adjacent (either before or after) to the new one. This function checks to see if there is an area immediately before the new one that can be expanded to include the new one. Similarly, it checks for an existing one immediately after the new one. If either free adjacent area exists, then *vma_merge*( ) expands the adjacent one to include the new area. If both adjacent areas are free, the function combines all three areas into one. If neither free adjacent area exists, then the function returns Λ. When expanding an existing data segment, the existing virtual memory area, including the existing data segment, is indeed adjacent to the new area being allocated. In our case, the existing area ends and the new area begins at address #000c0000, and *vma_merge*( ) handles the expansion.

> **if** ($vma\_merge(mm, prev, addr, addr + len, flags, \Lambda, \Lambda, pgoff, \Lambda)$)
>   **goto** *out*;

12.6.2.5   Creating a New Area

If we get here, it is because there is not an existing area to which we could add the new address range. Although this is not the case in our example, it means we must create a new area. The first step is allocating space for the new structure using the slab allocator.

> $vma = kmem\_cache\_zalloc(vm\_area\_cachep,$ GFP_KERNEL$)$;
> **if** ($\neg vma$) {
> $vm\_unacct\_memory(len \gg$ PAGE_SHIFT$)$;
>   **return** $-$ENOMEM;
> }

Now that we have a valid structure, we initialize it to describe this new area.

> $vma\rightarrow vm\_mm = mm$;
> $vma\rightarrow vm\_start = addr$;
> $vma\rightarrow vm\_end = addr + len$;
> $vma\rightarrow vm\_pgoff = pgoff$;
> $vma\rightarrow vm\_flags = flags$;
> $vma\rightarrow vm\_page\_prot = protection\_map[flags$ &
>   (VM_READ | VM_WRITE | VM_EXEC | VM_SHARED)$)]$;

Now we add the new structure into the linked list and the red-black tree for the current process's memory mapping structure.

$vma\_link(mm, vma, prev, rb\_link, rb\_parent);$

The processing of our example call picks up again here. When we get here, it's time to wrap up the allocation process. First, we need to account for the new space in the total memory used by this process.

$out:$
$\quad mm{\rightarrow}total\_vm\ +=\ len \gg$ `PAGE_SHIFT`;

Finally, if this area is to be locked in memory (not swapped), then we make sure all the virtual pages are mapped to physical page frames. After we've taken care of that, we can return successfully.

```
if (flags & VM_LOCKED) {
    mm→locked_vm += len ≫ PAGE_SHIFT;
    make_pages_present(addr, addr + len);
}
return addr;
}
```

12.6.3   Processing Page Faults

Normally, when a process allocates new data space, it soon attempts to access that memory space. Unless the area we just allocated is flagged as `VM_LOCKED`, however, we have not yet associated any physical page frames with the new virtual pages. This means that when the process attempts to access this memory, it will cause a page fault. On the Intel x86, the primary interface for handling page faults is the function *do_page_fault*( ), defined in arch/i386/mm/fault.c. This function is somewhat complex, as it is responsible for determining which of several possible causes led to this page fault. It triages the fault and calls a function appropriate to the particular action the system needs to take. For some faults, the proper action is to send the process a signal with the default action of terminating the process. These faults include those that result from an attempt to write to a read-only area of memory or from an attempt to dereference a pointer into the bottom 128 MB of the virtual address space. If the fault is caused by an attempt to push onto the stack, and doing so crosses from an allocated page into an unallocated one, then the system automatically allocates a new page to the process's stack.

12.6.3.1   Handling Nonresident Pages

The case that primarily interests us is the case where an attempt is made to access virtual memory which has been allocated, but for which there is no mapping to physical memory. Two common reasons for this case are when the page is swapped out and when the page has not yet been allocated. Continuing with our example of allocating additional data space, let us suppose that immediately after allocating the space, the process writes into the first page of the newly allocated space, say at address #000c0020. This is an example of the second reason. Both reasons are handled by *__handle_mm_fault()* in mm/memory.c. The primary role of this function is ensuring that the page tables include the mappings necessary for the memory we attempted to reference.

> **int** *__handle_mm_fault*(**struct mm_struct** **mm*,
> **struct vm_area_struct** **vma*, **unsigned long** *address*,
> **int** *write_access*)
> {
>   **pgd_t** **pgd*;
>   **pud_t** **pud*;
>   **pmd_t** **pmd*;
>   **pte_t** **pte*;

We start by ensuring that the process is in the Ready state. When we return from handling the fault, we will resume the instruction that caused the fault.

> *__set_current_state*(**TASK_RUNNING**);

This line records the page fault for record keeping purposes.

> *count_vm_event*(**PGFAULT**);

Linux can support very large pages in certain contexts. These are handled by the various *hugetlb* calls. Because these large pages are not normally used in the data area, we continue to focus on the more common case of normal pages.

> **if** (*unlikely*(*is_vm_hugetlb_page*(*vma*)))
>   **return** *hugetlb_fault*(*mm*, *vma*, *address*, *write_access*);

12.6.3.2   Setting Up the Page Tables

Here, we set *pgd* to point to the page global directory entry for the address that caused the fault. Note that this is the address the process attempted to access, not the address of the instruction that was executing at the time. On 32-bit x86 systems, the top-level page table is indexed by the uppermost 10 bits of the virtual address. For our example, this index is 0, so *pgd* points to the 0th entry of the top-level page table.

> *pgd* = *pgd_offset*(*mm*, *address*);

On processors that have three- or four-level page tables, these next several lines of code ensure that we have the pud and pmd tables corresponding to the faulting address. Because the x86 uses a two-level page table, these are effectively null operations.

$pud = pud\_alloc(mm, pgd, address);$
if $(\neg pud)$
    return VM_FAULT_OOM;
$pmd = pmd\_alloc(mm, pud, address);$
if $(\neg pmd)$
    return VM_FAULT_OOM;

The call to *pte_alloc_map*( ) first allocates a page table if necessary. It then sets the pmd entry to point to the newly allocated page table. The second role of *pte_alloc_map*( ) is similar to that of *pgd_offset*( ). It returns a pointer to the bottom-level page table entry for the faulting address. In our case, the index into that table is the second 10 bits of the address, which is #000000c0.

$pte = pte\_alloc\_map(mm, pmd, address);$
if $(\neg pte)$
    return VM_FAULT_OOM;

The last step of this function is calling *handle_pte_fault*( ), which is responsible either for swapping the needed page back into memory or for allocating a page.

    return *handle_pte_fault*(*mm, vma, address, pte, pmd, write_access*);
}

12.6.4   Resolving a Fault for a Missing Page

This function, found in mm/memory.c, determines the correct way to satisfy the need for access to a page that is not currently in physical memory. The primary two cases are pages that are currently swapped out and new pages that have been allocated in virtual space, but not physical space. In addition to these cases, this function also catches the copy-on-write (COW) case.

static inline int *handle_pte_fault*(**struct mm_struct** **mm,*
    struct vm_area_struct **vma,* **unsigned long** *address,* **pte_t** **pte,*
    pmd_t **pmd,* **int** *write_access*)
{
    pte_t *entry;*
    pte_t *old_entry;*
    spinlock_t **ptl;*
    old_entry = entry = *pte;

We first determine whether this is a case where we need to COW or a case where we need to address a page not physically present. If the PTE present bit is set, then it's a COW case. Otherwise, we need to deal with a page that's not in memory. This latter case applies to newly allocated memory as a result of a *brk*( ) system call.

      if (¬*pte_present*(*entry*)) {

12.6.4.1   Allocating a Page Frame

If there is no page present in memory, the first case we consider is the one where we've never allocated a page frame to the page. In following our example of a process moving its break point up, this is the case we hit. We know that there is no PTE yet mapping this page to a page frame. Consequently, we need to allocate a physical page frame for it. For some memory areas, we define special functions for such operations. The call to *do_no_page*() takes care of invoking such a special function. However, in the case of allocating regular data memory, we don't use such a special function, but instead call *do_anonymous_page*().

        if (*pte_none*(*entry*)) {
          if (¬*vma*→*vm_ops* ∨ ¬*vma*→*vm_ops*→*nopage*)
            return *do_anonymous_page*(*mm*, *vma*, *address*, *pte*, *pmd*,
              write_access);
          return *do_no_page*(*mm*, *vma*, *address*, *pte*, *pmd*, *write_access*);
        }

12.6.4.2   Bringing a Page into Memory

If the page has been mapped but is not currently resident, then it can either be mapped to a file, or it can be swapped out to normal swap space. These next few lines identify which of these cases we have and call the appropriate function.

        if (*pte_file*(*entry*))
          return *do_file_page*(*mm*, *vma*, *address*, *pte*, *pmd*, *write_access*, *entry*);
        return *do_swap_page*(*mm*, *vma*, *address*, *pte*, *pmd*, *write_access*, *entry*);
      }

12.6.4.3   Handling Copy-on-Write

At this point, we are about to directly manipulate the memory management data structures. As usual, we need to gain a mutual exclusion lock on them.

      ptl = *pte_lockptr*(*mm*, *pmd*);
      spin_lock(*ptl*);

This might seem an odd condition to check. After all, *entry* was set to *pte at the beginning of the function and has not been changed. However, during this time, the data structures have not been locked. As a result, the page table entry to which *pte* points could well have changed out from under us. If it has, then we don't want to do anything that could be potentially harmful.

```
    if (unlikely(¬pte_same(*pte, entry)))
        goto unlock;
```

Here we take care of the COW case. The actual copying is handled by the function *do_wp_page( )*. If it turns out that we have a fault writing to a page that is actually writable, then we're implementing the dirty bit ourselves.

```
    if (write_access) {
        if (¬pte_write(entry))
            return do_wp_page(mm, vma, address, pte, pmd, ptl, entry);
        entry = pte_mkdirty(entry);
    }
```

12.6.4.4 Faking Missing MMU Features

The remainder of this function supports those cases where we use page faults to implement dirty bits and accessed bits on machines that don't do so in hardware.

```
    entry = pte_mkyoung(entry);
    if (¬pte_same(old_entry, entry)) {
        ptep_set_access_flags(vma, address, pte, entry, write_access);
        update_mmu_cache(vma, address, entry);
        lazy_mmu_prot_update(entry);
    }
    else {
        if (write_access)
            flush_tlb_page(vma, address);
    }
unlock:
    pte_unmap_unlock(pte, ptl);
    return VM_FAULT_MINOR;
}
```

12.6.5 Handling New Page Frames

Before tracing the details of *do_anonymous_page( )*, we summarize its behavior. It operates differently depending on whether the faulting operation is a read or a write. In the case where the process is attempting to write to the unallocated page, we allocate a zeroed page frame and set up the page table entry for it. This is the case for our example of writing to virtual address #000c0020. On the other hand, if the process is reading from the page, we map a fixed page of zeros into the process's memory space. This page is marked read-only, but copy-on-write. As long as the process continues to only read from the page, everything continues without page faults. When the process then attempts to write to the page, another page fault is triggered, and the COW mechanism is invoked.

```
static int do_anonymous_page(struct mm_struct *mm,
    struct vm_area_struct *vma, unsigned long address,
    pte_t *page_table, pmd_t *pmd, int write_access)
{
  struct page *page;
  spinlock_t *ptl;
  pte_t entry;
```

12.6.5.1   Allocating for a Write Access

As described previously, the case where we fault on a write is different than the one where we fault on a read. We would normally expect that the fault would be a write fault because we don't normally expect processes to read uninitialized data. The first few lines of this case are ones we can safely ignore. The call to *pte_unmap( )* applies only for certain configurations, and *anon_vma_prepare( )* is a macro defined to be 0.

```
if (write_access) {
  pte_unmap(page_table);
  if (unlikely(anon_vma_prepare(vma)))
    goto oom;
```

Here, we allocate a page for the process, making sure that it's zeroed. For security reasons, it's standard practice to make sure all new allocations are zeroed so that a process can't look at old data that another process has freed. At this point, we also create a page table entry for the new page, marking it as writable and dirty.

```
page = alloc_zeroed_user_highpage(vma, address);
if (¬page)
  goto oom;
entry = mk_pte(page, vma→vm_page_prot);
entry = maybe_mkwrite(pte_mkdirty(entry), vma);
```

Now we look to see if there is already a page mapped here. Normally there shouldn't be. At the same time, we gain a lock on the PTE so that no other thread can touch it while we're working.

```
page_table = pte_offset_map_lock(mm, pmd, address, &ptl);
if (¬pte_none(*page_table))
  goto release;
```

Because we're accessing this page, we mark it as referenced and put it on the active list. We also also create a reverse mapping for it so that we can easily find the virtual addresses that map to it.

```
    inc_mm_counter(mm, anon_rss);
    lru_cache_add_active(page);
    page_add_anon_rmap(page, vma, address);
}
```

12.6.5.2 Mapping a Zero Page for a Read Access

Now we turn to the case of a fault on a read. It is similar to the write in that we create
a PTE to point to an appropriate page. In this case, however, the page we use is a fixed
page of all zeros, which is marked COW. As before, we lock the PTE and check to see if
there was already a mapping in place.

```
else {
    page = ZERO_PAGE(address);
    page_cache_get(page);
    entry = mk_pte(page, vma→vm_page_prot);
    ptl = pte_lockptr(mm, pmd);
    spin_lock(ptl);
    if (¬pte_none(*page_table))
        goto release;
    inc_mm_counter(mm, file_rss);
    page_add_file_rmap(page);
}
```

At this point, we can write the new PTE into the page table, release the lock, and return.

```
    set_pte_at(mm, address, page_table, entry);
    update_mmu_cache(vma, address, entry);
    lazy_mmu_prot_update(entry);
unlock:
    pte_unmap_unlock(page_table, ptl);
    return VM_FAULT_MINOR;
release:
    page_cache_release(page);
    goto unlock;
oom:
    return VM_FAULT_OOM;
}
```

After we return from *do_anonymous_page( )*, we are ready to return all the way back
through *handle_pte_fault( )* and *__handle_mm_fault( )*, and ultimately to return from the
interrupt back to the faulting process. At that point, the CPU continues the instruction
the process executed that caused the page fault. This time, the necessary page is mapped
into the process's memory space, and the instruction can complete successfully.

12.7   Summary

Memory management can be conceptually straightforward, but the practicalities of creating a high-performance memory management system can be quite complex. Linux certainly is an example of this. It provides multiple mechanisms for processes to allocate memory and even more for allocation internal to the kernel. To support a variety of processors and large memory spaces, Linux uses a four-level page table as an abstraction. On most hardware, however, one or more levels must be folded into another to match page tables with fewer levels. The Linux page swapping design is another example of how basic techniques become more complex and are combined with other techniques when implemented in practice. Even the code to implement these features is quite involved, as evidenced by the small sample we detail here.

12.8   Exercises

1. If in addition to the 128 MB not mapped at the bottom of the virtual address space, Linux reserves a 128 MB buffer between the stack and the area for the *mmap( )* call, then what percentage of a process's usable memory space is not available in this way?

2. In Figure 12-1, the ZONE_HIGHMEM is shown as starting at 896 MB. If a machine has exactly 1 GB of memory, does it still need a ZONE_HIGHMEM? Why or why not?

3. The *pgd* member of the **mm_struct** structure points to a structure that has a pointer to the process's pgd. This pointer points into the kernel memory space above 3 GB. Can a process have access to its own pgd? Is this a desirable arrangement? Why or why not?

4. In *sys_brk( )*, if the values of *oldbrk* and *newbrk* are equal, we still update *mm→brk* rather than just return. Why do we need to do this? Why do we jump to *set_brk* instead of *out*?

5. When we create a new area in *do_brk( )*, we initialize only some parts of the newly allocated **vm_area_struct**. Why do we not need to set values for the other structure members?

6. In *do_anonymous_page( )*, Linux directly allocates a new page if the process faulted on a write access, but it maps a COW zero page if it faulted on a read access. Another alternative is allocating a new page in both cases. What are the trade-offs between these options? Does it matter whether the process later writes to the page? How likely is it that the process will not write to the page?

7. What changes would be necessary in the active and inactive list structure to support the working set model? How do pages allocated to the kernel fit into this?

8. Add some record keeping to **mm_struct** to track the number of *brk*( ) calls that increased the data segment and the number that decreased it. On each *brk*( ) system call, print out the process's PID and these two statistics.

9. Modify *do_anonymous_page*( ) so that it directly allocates a new page for both read and write faults.

10. Modify *do_brk*( ) so that page allocations are made immediately rather than waiting for a page fault.

Chapter 13

Principles of I/O Device Management

As we discussed in Chapter 1, providing a clean interface between the CPU and input/output (I/O) devices is one of the most central elements of an operating system. The first operating systems evolved out of libraries of I/O routines designed to make the programmer's job easier. Even if there is only one program that owns all the memory in the system, we still want the operating system to help us by making the interface to I/O devices cleaner.

However, this central role of I/O device management doesn't come for free. The reason we want to make the I/O interface cleaner is that every device is different. Code that handles the nuances of one disk drive often doesn't help us in accessing another. The same can be said of network interfaces, video interfaces, and so on. Consequently, the operating system must have code for all the different types of devices we might want to attach. This makes the collection of device drivers the biggest and most complex part of most operating systems.

The diversity of I/O devices affects our approach to design in another way as well. Because there are so few mechanisms in common, there are fewer general principles and techniques that apply to I/O devices than apply to other parts of systems. Nevertheless, in this chapter, we attempt to summarize the more common techniques and designs. We begin this examination with a very high-level overview of I/O device hardware, including techniques for programming I/O controllers. We follow this with a look at the classification of devices, a look at the desirable characteristics of an I/O subsystem, and some discussion of I/O-related system calls. The largest part of the chapter is a discussion of device drivers and a sampling of techniques used in them.

13.1 Elements of the I/O Subsystem

To prevent confusion, we need to be specific about some of the terms we use when dealing with I/O systems. When we speak of a **device**, we are talking about the thing that actually stores the data or the thing with which we are communicating. For example, a disk drive or a printer is a device. The device, however, is not the hardware that we actually control with the operating system. Instead, there is an interface between the CPU and the device called the **device controller**. Figure 13-1 shows a typical configuration of a CPU and several devices with their controllers. The controller is the part of the system that software speaks to. Some controllers provide only simple control over basic operations, while others allow the software to program complex sequences of operations that are carried out by the controller itself, independent of the CPU. In some systems, especially mainframe systems from IBM, controllers are called channels and are typically very flexible computers in their own right. In other systems, independent computers that control I/O devices are called I/O Processors (IOPs). Finally, we note that there is a trend in controller design to develop controller-device interfaces that are generalized and not specific to particular devices. The Small Computer System Interface (SCSI), Universal Serial Bus (USB), and IEEE 1394 (also known as FireWire) are all examples of this trend. Devices ranging from disk drives to cameras can be connected to these interfaces.

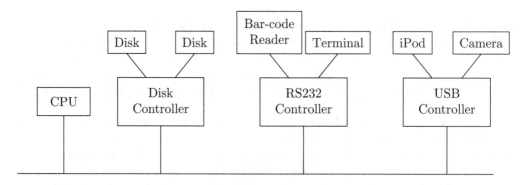

Figure 13-1: Typical I/O Device Configuration

The software that speaks to the controller is called the **device driver**. It is in the device driver that we encapsulate specific knowledge of the I/O hardware we are managing. The last piece of the puzzle is the **interrupt handler**. This is actually a part of the device driver that responds to signals that the device controller generates to request service.

Having given these definitions, we must, however, acknowledge that the terminology is not always used as precisely as we've implied. For example, when talking about network interfaces, we often think of the network interface as the device itself. According to the terminology we've defined, we should call the interface the controller and the network the device. Similarly, when we have a very generic interface, such as an RS-232 serial interface, we often ignore what actual device is attached to the other end of the cable. As far as we're concerned, we're programming to the controller alone. This perspective arises as a consequence of the set of possibly connected devices not being established before we write the operating system. Instead, the operating system must provide a general facility for communicating with serial devices, leaving applications responsible for knowing about the details of the device. In other generalized cases, such as USB, the OS does provide support for a number of specific devices as well as the controller itself. Another example that blurs the lines is the **integrated drive electronics** (IDE) (also known as **integrated device electronics**) disk drive. Most of the functionality normally associated with the controller is present on the drive. The device called an IDE controller is actually little more than buffer circuitry. From the driver's perspective, there is still a controller with a drive attached, but opening the box, we don't find the electronics that implement the controller where they're expected.

13.2   I/O Device Hardware Characteristics

In the following subsections, we highlight some of the key characteristics of I/O devices that affect the way we write I/O support in an operating system. The first two discuss representative storage and communications devices. In the third, we examine the interface between the software of the device driver and the hardware of the device controller.

13.2.1   Disk Drives

Disk drives are used to support both memory management and file systems. They provide the secondary storage where the memory manager can swap either pages or whole processes. The file system, of course, implements the most familiar use of disk drives, storing persistent data in files. In some less common cases, applications such as databases use disk drives for storage, independent of a file system. All of these users of disks issue their requests to the disk driver.

13.2.1.1   Physical Characteristics

A disk drive consists of some number of **platters**, typically made from aluminum or glass and coated with a substance that can be magnetized in small regions. In early disk

---

Historical Note: CDC-6000 Series IOPs

The Control Data Corporation 6000 series machines had a very interesting I/O Processor design. The IOP design had one instance of most of the CPU elements, such as the arithmetic logic unit (ALU) and instruction decode and control. There were, however, 10 copies of the registers and 10 independent interfaces to memory. The ALU could carry out an operation in 100 nS, while access to memory took 1 μS. When a memory operation was started on one memory interface with one set of registers, the CPU hardware would then go and execute operations on the other nine and come back around to the starting point just in time for the memory operation to be completed and to execute an operation on that data. In this way, the CPU was shared in a way that looked like there were 10 I/O Processors; they were called Peripheral Processors (PPs). This arrangement was called a barrel processor. One of the more interesting aspects of this design was that the operating system didn't run on the main CPUs. Instead, it ran on one of the PPs which had a special instruction that could carry out the context switch on the main processors.

drives, this coating was similar to that used on audio and video tapes. The platters are all mounted to a **spindle** and turn together. Early drives rotated at 3600 RPM (as a result of the 60 Hz line voltage in the United States). More modern drives rotate at higher speeds, such as 7200 RPM and 10,000 RPM. There are a number of **heads** that fly above the surface of a platter and that read and write the data. Typically, there is one head per surface of each platter. The heads are connected to an **arm** that moves the heads from close to the outer edge of the platter to close to the center of the platter. At each position of the arm, a head covers a circle on a surface of a platter. This circle where data can be stored is called a **track**. The set of tracks that are inscribed by all the heads at a given arm position is called a **cylinder**. These elements of a disk drive are illustrated in Figure 13-2. For clarity, we show only the heads on the top surfaces of the platters; normally there are also heads on the bottom surfaces.

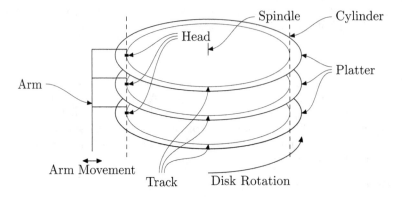

Figure 13-2: Disk Drive Structure

13.2.1.2   Programming Considerations

The first predominant characteristic of disk drives that affects our approach is the block nature of data transfers. Because of the nature of magnetic recording and the way in which data are laid out on a track, reading and writing always takes place in units of blocks, which we generally call **sectors**. For the type of disk drives commonly called "hard drives" (that is, those with rigid platters), sectors are typically 512 bytes. Although floppy disks can be formatted in a number of different ways, 256-byte sectors are quite common.

The block structured read and write operations of disk drives imply certain constraints on the behavior of the driver. Typically, drivers take one of two approaches to interfacing between the rest of the system and the disk controller. Most driver designs define disk I/O requests to be specified in multiples of sectors rather than bytes. It is then up to the code that issues the request to identify the appropriate block. That code must also deal with excess data delivered on a read and preparing the full block for a write. Some driver designs, however, take care of those issues for the requesting code. In those designs, if a read request is received that is not one or more whole blocks, then the driver must read all the blocks that contain the request but return only the data actually requested. Writes of incomplete blocks are more complicated. In these cases, we must read the containing blocks, change the specified data, and then write the blocks back out to the disk.

The second characteristic of disks that significantly affects driver design is latency in accessing data. Disk drives are mechanical devices, and as a result, they are much slower than electronics. To access a particular block, the drive must position the arm to the proper cylinder, select the appropriate surface, and then wait for the platter to rotate around to the correct sector. The total access time is then $t_a = t_h + t_s + t_r$, where t_h is the time to select the correct head, t_s is the seek time to move the arm, and t_r is the rotational latency. Selecting the correct head is an electronic operation, and as such is not a significant fraction of the overall access time. Furthermore, even that small amount of time can be overlapped with the other times. As a result, we normally omit t_h in our calculations. Seek time (the time to move the arm) is complex, involving the time to accelerate the arm, the time for the arm to travel to the desired cylinder, the time to decelerate the arm, and the time for its position to be fine-tuned. However, the seek time is usually quoted as a single average time. The rotational latency is simple to understand. After the arm has been positioned on the correct cylinder, the disk must rotate 180° on average to get to the correct sector. Thus, the average rotational latency is one-half of the time for a full rotation. All of these factors are illustrated in Example 13.1.

Example 13.1: Disk Access Time

Suppose we have a disk drive that rotates at 10,000 RPM with an average seek time of 10 mS. At 10,000 RPM, one full rotation of the disk takes 6 mS, so the average rotational latency is 3 mS. That makes the average access time $t_a = 10$ mS $+ 3$ mS $= 13$ mS. By comparison, consider access to memory. If the system's memory can be accessed in 50 nS, then the disk is 260,000 times slower than memory for accessing a single data item. Of course, the disk gets us a full sector for each such access. If the sector is 512 bytes, and we compare to reading each byte in a separate memory access, the disk is still slower by a factor of 508.

The final area we consider where disk characteristics affect the design of a driver is error handling. Generally, we assume that a CPU operates flawlessly or that any internal errors are corrected by the hardware. The same is true of the main system memory. However, disk drives are less reliable. By the nature of magnetic recording, we sometimes see errors in reading a block from the disk. Most drives or controllers have some built-in error correction, but there are also times when the drive detects an uncorrectable error. In these cases, the controller signals the uncorrectable error and the driver is responsible for handling it. Usually drivers are written to retry the operation until either the controller shows a successful transfer or some maximum number of retries is reached. In this way, the driver provides as much reliability as possible to the rest of the system.

13.2.1.3   Disk Interfaces

On first thought, we would expect that the operating system need not be concerned with the interface between the controller and the disk drive. What we find in practice, however, is that controllers for a given type of interface tend to have similar programming characteristics. For example, SCSI controllers specify the desired block with just a block number, without regard to the cylinder, head, and sector where that block resides. On the other hand, an IDE controller often allows us to specify a block either with the cylinder, head, and sector numbers or with a block number. For IDE interfaces, specifying a single block number is known as **large block addressing** (LBA). As a result of these differences, it behooves us to know something about the variety of disk interfaces.

At the large-system end of the scale, we often see manufacturer-specific interface designs on mainframes and older minicomputers. Because of this, and because most people don't encounter those systems, we won't say any more about them. In today's data centers, we often find machines designated as servers. These machines are not substantially different from those we call workstations or personal computers, except that they typically can physically accommodate more disk drives and sometimes more memory as well. In these environments, we most often see SCSI in its various implementations. Increasingly, we see the disk storage in data centers being provided by **storage area networks** (SANs). In these networks, storage subsystems, often with many disk drives, are connected to client systems over conventional networks, such as Ethernet. Messages across these networks talk about blocks rather than files, as are found in network file systems. One of the most common protocols used in SANs is iSCSI, which transports SCSI control messages using the TCP/IP network protocols.

On smaller systems, ranging from laptops to workstations, we find a mix of technologies. Some, such as the **enhanced small disk interface** (ESDI), have largely disappeared from the landscape. Particularly in workstations, we do find SCSI disk drives being used. However, the most prevalent interfaces we see in smaller computers is the IDE interface. This interface evolved from the original disk controller on the IBM PC/AT. Later, the controller was incorporated on the drive itself, creating the IDE drive. The IDE interface is also called the **advanced technology attachment** (ATA) interface. IDE drives are connected to the rest of the system by a set of signals very much like those on the **industry standard architecture** (ISA) bus. Over time, the details of the controller evolved through several iterations to accommodate larger and larger drives. The most recent incarnation of the IDE approach is called **serial ATA** (SATA) and uses a very high-speed serial interface in contrast to the parallel communication of the original ATA interface.

13.2.2   Serial Communications

We now turn from the issues often encountered with storage devices to those often encountered with communication devices. Unlike disk drives, there is no communication device that is so ubiquitous that it is representative of most others. There is, however, one communications interface that has been used to connect nearly every type of communications device, whether terminals, printers, networks, bar-code readers, and so on. This is the RS-232 serial interface. The USB interface was created to serve much the same function with much higher data transfer rates. Many new device designs use a USB interface rather than an RS-232 interface. However, we use the RS-232 interface for our example because it is easier to understand and because there are still a large (albeit decreasing) number of devices that use it.

One relevant issue is communication speed. By its nature, serial communication takes place one bit at a time. In the RS-232 standard, each byte is started by a **start bit** and followed by one or more **stop bits**. We find that serial ports can be configured to operate on a variety of numbers of data bits, most often seven or eight. We can also select whether the transmission includes a parity bit. If we take the case where we transmit eight bits, no parity, and one stop bit, then there are 10 bit times for each byte we send, as illustrated in Figure 13-3. Although there are some serial interface standards that operate at very high speeds, RS-232 usually operates in the thousands of bits per second. In the example of 10 bit times per byte, if the interface operates at 19,200 bits per second (bps), then a maximum of 1920 bytes/sec can be transferred. (Sometimes the units of bits per second is referred to as **baud**. Technically, a baud is a symbol per second. When communicating directly over an RS-232 interface, each bit is a single symbol. However, with modems, several bits are generally combined into a single symbol. So, a modem operating at 19,200 bps may well actually communicate with the other modem at a baud rate of 4800 if each symbol encodes four bits.)

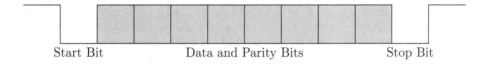

Start Bit   Data and Parity Bits   Stop Bit

Figure 13-3: RS-232 Serial Data Transmission

The next interesting issue is buffering. With disk drives, we get only what we have requested and prepared to receive. On the other hand, with communication devices, we receive a stream of data at the rate that the sender chooses to send. This observation leads to several aspects of driver design. First, the driver must be capable of processing the data at the rate at which it arrives. Most RS-232 interfaces generate interrupts for each byte (or in some cases every few bytes) received. This means that the interrupt handler must handle an incoming byte in no more time than it takes to transmit the next one. Buffer size is another issue that arises from the streaming nature of communications. If we don't know what data to expect, we don't know how much space to reserve for it. Rarely, however, is it practical to dynamically increase the buffer as more data arrives.

Several of these issues lead to a technique called **flow control**. In general, flow control provides the receiver with a mechanism to tell the transmitter to pause until the receiver is able to take more data. In some cases, this signal is made through electrical connections other than the ones used for data transmission. In these cases, we say we are using **hardware flow control** or **out-of-band flow control**. Sometimes, we transmit a special byte from the receiver to the transmitter to say stop. When using the ASCII character set, we generally use the Ctrl-S character (13_{16}) for this. The Ctrl-Q character (11_{16}) signals that the transmitter should resume transmission. Using special characters to control flow goes by a number of different names, including **XON/XOFF flow control**, **software flow control**, and **in-band flow control**.

As with storage devices, data transfer over communication devices is not perfect. A number of errors can arise in the process. For example, if the driver does not respond to an interrupt for an incoming byte fast enough, then the next byte can arrive before the previous one has been read from the controller. This generally signals a **receiver overrun error**. In cases where the transmission rate must be maintained, a **transmitter underrun error** can also occur. If the rate at which the transmitter generates bits is not the same as the rate at which the receiver is expecting bits, then the stop bit may not appear when expected, leading to a **framing error**. This error can also occur if there is a failure in the electrical connection between the transmitter and receiver during a transmission. If the two ends are using parity to check the integrity of transmission, then a **parity error** signifies that the received bits did not have the expected parity. The device driver is responsible for properly handling all these types of errors. In most cases, they are reported to the software that is requesting service from the driver.

13.2.3   Controller Interface Techniques

The software view of a controller is typically a collection of registers. These registers are used to define what operation we want the controller to perform. Take, for example, a disk controller. There may be a register, often called the **control status register** (CSR), that gives us information about the status of the controller when we read from it. When we write to the CSR, we tell the controller to perform a particular operation. To identify where on the disk we want to read or write data, some controllers have one or more registers where we specify a cylinder, head, and sector on the disk. Other controllers have a register where we specify a block number. Similarly, we need to specify a memory location that identifies where we get data to write to the disk and where we put data read from the disk. This address will also occupy one of the registers. In addition to these, it is quite common for there to be other registers for things like sector count, error handling, and additional status information.

Programming a controller tends to follow a general pattern. When initializing the device driver and when opening new access to the device, the driver writes any initialization commands that are necessary to the controller. For each request, we write any necessary parameters for the operation into the appropriate registers and then initiate the operation by writing the command to the control register (or sometimes by setting a particular bit in the control register). In some cases, the operation (command) is implicit, and we initiate the operation by writing a piece of data to be transmitted.

To alert the system to the fact that an operation has been completed, nearly all controllers generate an interrupt that the operating system must handle. For those cases where the controller doesn't generate an interrupt, the system must **poll** the controller periodically to determine when the operation is complete.

Another common element of the controller function is **direct memory access** (DMA). Controllers that support DMA write the results of read operations to the specified memory area without intervention of the CPU. Similarly, they take the data needed for write operations directly from a specified memory area. This feature is particularly common for block devices like disks and for network interfaces that operate a packet at a time. There are a couple of alternatives to DMA. The simplest alternative is interrupting the CPU for each byte (or word) transferred. Needless to say, this approach takes a substantial fraction of the CPU's time for devices that transfer data at a high rate. Another approach occupies a middle ground. The controller may maintain its own buffer that the CPU uses for a full block. When writing a block, the CPU copies the block into the controller's buffer and then initiates the write operation. Similarly, on a read, the CPU initiates the read, and then copies the data from the buffer in response to the completion interrupt. In all cases, the details of the transfer are programmed through the controller registers.

There are a variety of mechanisms by which we access the controller registers. On some machines, the registers are mapped into the normal memory space. In our disk controller example, the CSR might be mapped to memory location $FF000100_{16}$, the disk addressing register at location $FF000104_{16}$, and the memory address register at location $FF000108_{16}$. Normal load and store instructions that access these memory locations provide the means to tell the controller what we want to do. On other machines, the instruction set includes special I/O instructions. The operands for these instructions are typically a port number and a register. An out instruction will write the value of the register to the port. If the registers of our example of a disk controller are mapped to ports 100_{16}, 101_{16}, and 102_{16}, then an instruction like out r1, 101 performs the same operation as the instruction st r1, ff000104 in the memory-mapped case. In particular, both instructions write the value of register r1 to the disk addressing register of the controller.

For both memory-mapped I/O and special I/O instructions, we sometimes find that the controller is designed to not present all of the registers in the normal access scheme. In other words, we don't have distinct addresses (ports) for each of the registers. In these cases, it is typical to provide two registers: one that specifies which internal register we are accessing and one to provide data for that register. So instead of reading the controller status directly from port 100_{16}, we first write 0 into port 100_{16} and then read the status from port 101_{16}. (In this case, port 101_{16} is no longer the disk addressing register; it is the data port that is used for accessing all registers.) Both styles of I/O controller programming are illustrated in Example 13.2.

Example 13.2: Device Controller Programming

To illustrate the various techniques for programming a device controller, suppose we have three variables that describe the operation we want to perform. The variable *addr* gives the memory address where the first byte of the data is to be found on a write or to be placed on a read. The number of bytes to transfer is given by *count*. Finally, we have the operation we want to perform in the variable *cmd*. We assume that all of these variables hold the values in the same form as expected by the controller. Further, we assume that the command must be written last.

The first case we consider is the one where the controller registers are memory-mapped in the order of the command register, the address register, and the count register. If all the registers are an integer in size, we can define the following C structure that maps to the controller registers.

```
struct ctlr {
    int csr;
```

```
    int address;
    int count;
};
```

With this definition, we can create a pointer initialized to point to the controller registers in memory. In this example, the controller is positioned in the high part of a 64-bit address space.

struct ctlr *∗ctl*=#ffff800100000000;

Using this pointer, we can then write our request to the controller as follows:

ctl→address = *addr*;
ctl→count = *count*;
ctl→csr = *cmd*;

The second case is the one where each register has its own port that we access with a special output instruction. We assume that we have defined macros for CTL_CSR, CTL_ADDRESS, and CTL_COUNT, which give the respective port numbers. We also assume a small function callable from C called *out*( ) that puts the value of the second argument to the port given in the first. Systems taking this approach generally also include a function called *in*( ) that returns a value read from the specified port on the controller. With these in place, we can then program the controller with a sequence like:

out(CTL_ADDRESS, *addr*);
out(CTL_COUNT, *count*);
out(CTL_CSR, *cmd*);

The last case we consider is the one where we use special output instructions to write to a controller where we must identify the appropriate register on one port and the value on another. For this case, we need two more defined values, which we call CTL_PORT and CTL_DATA, and which give the two ports where we actually write. A typical code sequence for programming such a controller would look like:

out(CTL_PORT, CTL_ADDRESS);
out(CTL_DATA, *addr*);
out(CTL_PORT, CTL_COUNT);
out(CTL_DATA, *count*);
out(CTL_PORT, CTL_CSR);
out(CTL_DATA, *cmd*);

In all three cases, the code examples just initiate the operation. There must also be code that queries the state of the controller and handles any interrupts that the controller generates.

13.3   Types of I/O Devices

There are a couple of different classifications we can apply to I/O devices. The first is based on the role the device plays in the overall system. In particular, is it used for data storage or data communication? The second is based on how we interact with the device, whether one byte at a time or in blocks of bytes. These differences affect the way we design the device drivers and interact with the controllers. Consequently, many of the techniques we cover later in this chapter apply to one class of devices or another, but are not really applicable to all devices.

13.3.1   Communication vs. Storage Devices

Remember that an algorithm is defined as having at least one output; computers would be useless if there were no mechanism by which data could be transmitted to the outside world. This observation points us to our first class of devices, namely **communication devices**. Communication devices such as keyboards, video displays, printers, and network interfaces are familiar. Some of the simplest devices, though, are those used in embedded systems to control the physical world. The computerized thermostat moves air dampers and turns compressors on and off. The ignition control computer in a car controls the firing of spark plugs. All of these devices pass information between the CPU and the outside world, which consists of users and other devices.

The other type of device is the **storage device**. Rarely do we develop a system that does not produce data that needs to persist. Without storage devices, everything would have to live in memory. There would be no data kept from one run of a word processor to the next. Programs would have to be written anew each time we started the system up. (We're ignoring the fact that certain memory technologies can indeed keep data without

---

Historical Note: Hybrid Computers

Perhaps one of the most interesting devices to be attached to a digital computer is an **analog computer**. Analog computers, also known as differential analyzers, were machines designed to solve systems of differential equations. In contrast to stored-program digital computers, analog computers generally required rewiring to change the problem being solved. Despite the difficulty in programming, they were very good for generating curves that displayed the behavior of a system over time. For a given level of accuracy, they could do so faster than the digital computers of the day. In recognizing that each type of computer had its own strengths, it was natural to put them together to create **hybrid computers**. To the software running on the digital computer, the analog computer looked like an I/O device. The digital computer was typically capable of starting and stopping the analog computer and of setting parameters on the analog computer. In addition, the digital computer could generally use analog-to-digital (A/D) and digital-to-analog (D/A) converters to read signals from and feed signals into the analog computer. These hybrid computers were in common use through the 1960s and 1970s and special-purpose hybrid systems have been used in everything from music synthesis to automotive ignition control well into the 1990s.

power. Although we can use these types of memory to store code and data, they have
their own limitations that keep us from using them universally for all long-term storage.)
Disk drives, tape drives, CD-ROMs, and some types of memory devices are all examples of
the storage devices the operating system manages. Although our look at storage devices
here focuses on the programming details of the devices themselves, keep in mind that in
Chapter 17, we look at the file systems that organize data we store there.

We should note that these definitions are not hard and fast. Indeed, we are quite willing
to accept the fact that some devices might well be ambiguous in their role. For example,
if we record data onto a punched card, have we used a storage device or a communications
device? If we later read that card on a different computer, it seems to have followed the
idea of a communications device. On the other hand, if we later read the card on the
same computer, it seems more like a storage device. To make the waters even muddier,
the methods we use to control card punches are more similar to those used to control
most communications devices. The bottom line is that while we often find convenience
in distinguishing between storage and communications devices, don't let the distinction
become a point of confusion or conflict.

There is one particularly important class of devices that doesn't fall neatly into either
the communication or the storage classification. That type of device is the **clock** or **timer**.
A clock generates interrupts at a regular interval. For many systems, this clock is driven
by the line voltage that powers the system. In the United States, such clocks generate
an interrupt 60 times per second. Timers are devices that can be set to generate an
interrupt after some programmed interval. Most timer hardware can operate in either a
mode of generating a single interrupt or in a clock mode where they generate interrupts at
a regular rate. Clocks are particularly important because clock interrupts are the events
that trigger preemptive scheduling.

13.3.2   Stream vs. Block Devices

Although the role of the I/O device determines how the user sees it, it is the way we
interact with the device that determines how we program it. Some types of devices allow
us to randomly position ourselves anywhere on the device to read or write data. These
devices usually require that we communicate with them in terms of data units called
blocks. Most often, these **block devices** are also storage devices.

On the other hand, communications devices most often fall into the classification of
stream or **character devices**. The way to think about stream devices is to imagine
that data always passes through them one byte at a time. After a piece data has passed
through, we have no way to back up and look at it again. Neither do we have a way to
look ahead at data that has not yet arrived. There's an inherent temporal component to
data we pass over a stream device.

As with the distinction between storage devices and communications devices, we don't
want to get dogmatic about the distinction between block devices and stream devices. For
example, data are read and written to various forms of data tapes in blocks, but tapes are
very rarely randomly accessible. However, because we can rewind them and read the data
again, they don't fit the idea of a stream device. In fact, even though the code we write
to control a particular device might have the character of one type, we may present an

interface to the rest of the system that looks like the other. One notable example is the network interface. By their very nature, network interfaces are primarily communication devices. However, most networking is defined around groups of bytes variously called **frames**, **packets**, and **datagrams**. In terms of OS support, these frames can be treated much like the blocks on a disk. However, the data blocks cannot be accessed randomly but must be processed as a stream.

13.4   Objectives of I/O Subsystem Design

Even more than other subsystems, I/O device support embodies the nature of an OS as a collection of services. After all, we wouldn't want to have to include code for every device into every application. In providing I/O services, our design objectives capture a number of desirable characteristics of those services.

One of the first, and most important, objectives is **reliability**. Most I/O devices are inherently less reliable than other system components, like the CPU and memory. To deal with device unreliability, the OS's device support generally handles detecting errors, retrying operations, and reporting errors to the code making the request.

Providing **device independence** is another important objective. Programming for different types of devices involves different sets of details. However, we don't want applications to be responsible for implementing the details of all the various devices they might use. Instead, the OS I/O subsystem presents a consistent interface, allowing applications to use similar, and often the same, code to access all devices. In many cases, the design goes so far as to allow devices to be accessed in the same way as files.

Like the other subsystems of an operating system, the I/O subsystem should be efficient and fair. Again, the details of what makes for efficient use of a device varies depending on the type of device. By implementing those details in the OS, all applications can take advantage of them. Furthermore, the OS can optimize the use of devices across processes in ways the processes themselves cannot.

13.5   I/O Device Services

To a large extent, the services that we need for I/O devices are much the same as those we need for files. Applications need to gain and release access much as when opening and closing files. They also need to be able to transfer data to the device in a write operation and retrieve data from the device by reading it. Applications and other parts of the OS need to gain exclusive access to devices even more often than they do with files. After all, if several processes write to a printer simultaneously, the results would be gibberish. It's tempting to imagine users with razor blades and paste reassembling their output.

When designing read and write operations, there is a basic question we must answer. If the device is not ready for the read or write operation, do we block the requesting process or do we return control to the requesting process? The first case is referred to as **blocking** reads and writes. Most application code is written assuming that a read request does not return until the requested data are available. On the other hand, we can implement a

nonblocking policy and allow processes to continue doing other work while the data are being read. Most systems implement blocking reads and a sort of compromise on writes. The system usually puts the write data into a buffer and then returns immediately to the process. However, if there is not room in the buffer (because previous writes have not yet been transmitted to the device), then the process is blocked until buffer space is available. We sometimes refer to blocking operations as **synchronous** and nonblocking as **asynchronous**. (Because those terms are also sometimes used with slightly different meanings, we use the terms blocking and nonblocking here.)

In contrast to the similarities with files, however, devices often require additional control operations. Two examples of this are rewinding a tape and ejecting a CD-ROM. Devices also often have operational parameters that need to be set, such as the baud rate of a serial port or the volume of an audio output device. Systems vary considerably on how these functions are supported. For some, special system calls are implemented for each special function. For others, a general "catchall" system call is used. In one of the more interesting approaches, ordinary read and write operations are used. Special operations are initiated by opening a special control interface and writing control messages there.

13.6   Device Driver Structure

The key purpose of a device driver is providing an interface between a device controller and the rest of the software on the system. It must accept requests from multiple processes and other parts of the OS, and it must translate them into the parameters and commands that drive the controller. For motivation for the structure of this software, let us consider a scenario where several requests arrive faster than a device can accommodate them. We begin with Process A requesting a disk read. The device driver translates the generic read parameters into parameters that are appropriate to the disk controller and writes them into the controller's registers. Then, the driver initiates the read by writing the read command into the controller's control register. Of course, one of the main benefits of a time-sharing operating system is that while an I/O device is off doing its thing, the CPU can be working on other processes. So while the disk drive is seeking and transferring data, we schedule Process B and allow it to run. During its time slice, it issues a request to write to the same disk that is currently busy with Process A's read request. So the device driver queues up the request so that it can be processed later.

After the disk controller has finished with Process A's read request, it alerts the device driver by issuing an interrupt. The interrupt handler's first task is to arrange for Process A to be unblocked and to have its data delivered to the memory location it specified in the original request. After that's done, the interrupt handler next looks at the queue of outstanding requests. If the queue is not empty, the interrupt handler takes a request off of the queue and programs the controller to service that request. After starting the controller, the interrupt handler returns from the interrupt, and the system continues where it left off.

With this motivation in mind, how do we organize the code that makes up the device driver? The first thing to keep in mind as we design our driver structure is that we have two cooperating entities that share a data structure. We have one thread of control that is executed on behalf of a user process requesting I/O service, and we have a thread of control that is executed in response to interrupts. Because the thread on behalf of user processes can be interrupted in most cases, these two threads must coordinate their access to the request queue that they share. Similarly, they must be careful not to attempt to command the controller at the same time.

The first technique for organizing a device driver is also the most common. We conceptually divide the driver into two halves, an upper half and a lower half, as illustrated in Figure 13-4. The upper half is the part that understands the user request side of things, and the lower half is the part that understands the controller. When the upper half receives a request, it places the request into the queue, and if the queue had been empty (indicating that the controller is idle), it also calls code in the lower half to initiate the operation. When an interrupt is generated, the lower half code calls on the upper half code to unblock the process and deliver the results. Then, it removes the just-completed request from the queue, picks another one (if there are any), and initiates it. The two threads of control use mutual exclusion techniques, such as those discussed in Section 5.7, to prevent corruption of the shared queue.

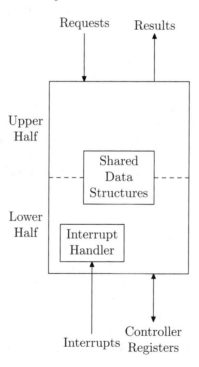

Figure 13-4: General Device Driver Structure

For those controllers that can connect to a wide variety of devices, such as SCSI and USB, the device driver's design is a little more complicated. In these cases, we add more layers of driver code, creating a stack of driver elements. The two-half design illustrated in Figure 13-4 is still commonly used. This driver provides a raw, low-level interface to the controller, independent of the type of device connected to it. However, when other software reads or writes a device, it needs to do so in the manner appropriate to the actual device. Therefore, we add another layer of driver functionality on top of the low-level driver. We might have one such driver element that knows about disk drives, another that knows about printers, and another that knows about cameras. The request is routed to the component that is appropriate for the device connected to the controller. This component, then, creates the appropriate device control message and uses the low-level driver to send the message to the device.

Some systems use another organization based on the message-passing techniques discussed in Section 5.7. In these systems, device drivers are organized as message processors. User requests come to the driver as messages, which are then processed in much the same way as in a traditional two-half driver. Interrupts in such a message-passing system are handled by a small piece of code that turns the interrupt into another type of message for the device driver. The steps for handling these interrupt messages are the same as for handling interrupts in a traditional device driver. By designing the system so that the message handler processes only one message at a time, we ensure that there is never more than one thread of control that has access to the request queue.

13.7   Device Management Techniques

Every type of device has its own set of standard techniques and even tricks. We have nowhere near enough space to provide an exhaustive survey of these techniques. However, we do present a few representative ones, including techniques for managing buffers, techniques for organizing and seeking data on disk drives, special considerations when receiving data entered by human operators, and finally pseudo-devices.

13.7.1   Buffering

We have already mentioned the idea of buffering. Anytime there is a discrepancy between the rate at which a producer generates data and the rate at which a consumer is processing that data, we use a buffer as an interface between the generator and the consumer. In the case of a device driver, these buffers often play two roles. First, as the upper half receives requests, we store them in a buffer from which the lower half takes them as it is able. Second, when reading data from a device, we often need to store it until an application is ready to take it. In these roles, the buffers are part of the data structures shared between the upper half and the lower half of the device driver. As such, access to them is normally controlled through some form of mutual exclusion locking, most often through disabling interrupts.

In both cases, we usually treat the buffers as queues. The data taken from the buffer are the oldest data in it. This results in requests being handled in a first-come, first-served (FCFS) order. It also preserves the order in which data arrives on a stream device. In a later subsection, we examine a technique where we reorder requests as a means of improving performance.

Because we usually prefer static data structures within the kernel, these buffers are most often implemented with arrays. More often than not, these buffers are treated as circular arrays. In circular arrays, both the head and tail pointers (or indices) move in the same direction as we add or remove data. When a pointer gets to the end of the array, it wraps back to the beginning.

13.7.2   Interleaving

Suppose we are reading consecutive sectors from a track of a disk drive, one at a time. After we read sector 0, we get the interrupt telling us that the operation is complete, and the driver sets up the next request. However, during interrupt processing, the platters have continued to rotate. Because of this, at least part of sector 1 very likely will already have passed under the head before the request to read it is carried out by the controller. As a result, the disk will have to make nearly a full rotation before sector 1 can be read. Reading eight sectors this way takes eight rotations of the disk where we might expect to be able to read those eight sectors in one rotation or less (depending on how many sectors there are per track).

We often address this issue by **interleaving** the sectors on a track. Instead of laying the sectors out consecutively, we skip sectors in the numbering and wrap back around to fill in the ones we skipped. By doing so, we give the interrupt handler time to process the next request before the data for the next request is under the head. Using 1:1 interleaving (one sector skipped for one sector assigned), the sector ordering would be 0, 4, 1, 5, 2, 6, 3, 7, where with no interleaving it would be 0, 1, 2, 3, 4, 5, 6, 7. Using this arrangement, it takes two rotations to read eight sectors, rather than eight rotations. Similarly, with 2:1 interleaving, the order would be 0, 3, 6, 1, 4, 7, 2, 5, and it would take three rotations to read the whole track. Figure 13-5 illustrates this for the case of eight sectors per track.

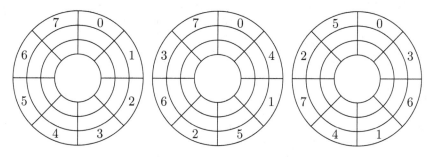

Figure 13-5: No Interleaving, 1:1 Interleaving, and 2:1 Interleaving

This figure illustrates a couple of general properties we can observe here. First, if we have $x : 1$ interleaving, then it takes $x + 1$ rotations to read the full track if we read the sectors consecutively. The second observation is that if the number of sectors per track is evenly divisible by $x + 1$, then we won't be able to maintain an even spacing of the sectors on the track. Whether this is an issue depends on whether we would try to read consecutively two sectors that are closer than normal.

Interleaving can be implemented in a couple of ways that affect the design of a device driver. If the interleaving is implemented in the controller, then the device driver's primary responsibility is configuring the controller to specify what the interleaving factor is. On the other hand, we may choose to implement interleaving completely within the driver. One simple approach is to compute the desired sector number as usual and then translate it to a physical sector number. We can do this by creating an array, indexed by the logical sector number, where each element contains the physical sector number. Such an array for 1:1 interleaving of eight sectors per track would contain the elements 0, 2, 4, 6, 1, 3, 5, 7.

Interleaving is unnecessary on most modern disk drives. The first reason is that many modern drives implement interleaving themselves in a way that is completely transparent to the driver software. The second reason is that we rarely specify the cylinder, head, and sector numbers directly with modern drives. Instead, we normally specify simply a block number treating the whole disk as a linear array of blocks. The drive determines the corresponding cylinder, head, and sector internally. The final reason that interleaving is not a typical concern of modern drivers is that many modern drives implement track caching. When we access a sector on these drives, they read the whole track into an internal buffer and satisfy future requests from that buffer until another track's data are placed there. With the data in such a buffer, the order in which we read sectors does not affect the access time.

13.7.3   Elevator Algorithm

In our discussion up to this point, we've been somewhat ambiguous about the behavior of the interrupt handler. Specifically, we keep saying that it picks a request from the request queue, but we don't really say which one. Because we've called it a queue, the implication is that we process requests in a first-come, first-served manner. For many types of devices,

---

Historical Note: Walking Disk Drives

Although it is natural to think of the elevator algorithm in terms of improving access times, there was another consideration for reducing arm travel in older disk drives. The arm had much farther to move in older drives, owing to the much larger platter sizes. The technology used in those drives also meant that the arms were much larger than those in modern drives. Because these arms had a substantial amount of mass, a substantial amount of force was required to start and stop them quickly. According to Newton's third law of motion, the rest of the disk drive assembly experiences the opposite force when starting and stopping the arm. Even though these drives were often the size of small washing machines, if this force was repeated at the right rate, the drive could begin to vibrate in much the same way as an off-balance washing machine does. This was especially true when the arm was moved back and forth across the whole disk surface. In the most extreme cases, the vibration would become so great that the drive would begin to "walk" across the floor.

this is exactly what we do. However, for disk drives, we might ask if we can reduce the amount of time spent seeking by servicing the requests in some other order.

The answer turns out to be yes, and the strategy we use to pick the next one to process follows a very familiar policy. When we walk up to an elevator, we must announce whether we want to go up or down. When we get into the elevator, we must then announce the floor to which we want to go. One might think that the first statement of direction is needlessly redundant, but it's not. The elevator uses the direction information to decide whether to stop at a given floor. Suppose that we are wanting to go up, but the elevator is currently moving downward. As it passes our floor, it skips over us. It stops only to pick up passengers who are going in the same direction it is. When there's no more to do in that direction, then it reverses and begins to follow the same policy in the opposite direction.

At first glance, it wouldn't appear that the habits of elevators would have anything to do with disk drives. After all, disk access requests don't arrive at the device driver with directions attached. If we look at the rest of the policy, however, we do see a parallel. Let the disk arm play the role of the elevator car, and let the cylinders play the roles of floors in the building. Now, we can imagine that the arm moves in a given direction, and as it passes each cylinder, it services any outstanding requests for that cylinder. If there are no more requests in that direction, then we reverse the arm and begin to follow the same policy in the other direction. In following this policy, we don't pay attention to the order in which the requests arrived. Note that this policy affects only the behavior of the interrupt handler. If a request comes into the upper half and there are no other requests being processed, the controller is commanded to move the arm to the appropriate cylinder, regardless of which direction it's in. To make our selection algorithm a little more precise, we run the following **elevator algorithm** after removing a just-completed request from the queue.

Elevator Algorithm: The interrupt handler follows the following algorithm. Requests are placed into the queue by the upper half of the driver, which also sets the initial direction when adding a request to an empty queue.

1. If the queue is empty, then exit the interrupt handler.

2. Let the current cylinder be c.

3. If current direction is UP, then select a request with minimum requested cylinder, $n \geq c$.

4. If the current direction is DOWN, then select a request with maximum requested cylinder $n \leq c$.

5. If no cylinder n satisfied the criteria, then switch the direction and repeat Steps 3 and 4.

This technique is not unlike the shortest job first (SJF) scheduling policy discussed in Section 5.4. Indeed, there is a direct parallel called **shortest seek time first** (SSTF), where we always select the request with the cylinder closest to the current one. There are a couple of problems with the SSTF approach, however. First, if we keep the disk busy, then outliers (very high cylinder numbers and very low cylinder numbers) might never get serviced. Second, each time a request is processed, the arm moves, changing the distance to other requested cylinders. In effect, the act of selecting a request changes the order in which they should be satisfied. The elevator algorithm provides a sort of compromise between serving the nearest cylinder next and serving requests in the order they are received, as illustrated in Example 13.3.

Example 13.3: Elevator Algorithm

Suppose that the driver has just completed one request, and the list of outstanding requests contains requests for cylinders 10, 30, 22, 100, 15, 6, 42, 90, and 74, listed in the order received. Also suppose the arm last moved from a lower cylinder to cylinder 40. If the requests are processed in first-come, first-served (FCFS) order, then the number of cylinders the arm must move is

$$30 + 20 + 8 + 78 + 85 + 9 + 36 + 48 + 16 = 330$$

On the other hand, if we apply the elevator algorithm, we process the requests in the order 42, 74, 90, 100, 30, 22, 16, 10, and 6. In this case, the number of cylinders the arm moves is

$$2 + 32 + 16 + 10 + 70 + 8 + 6 + 6 + 4 = 154$$

Both of these cases are illustrated in Figure 13-6, where the x-axis represents time measured in the number of cylinders the arm crosses, and the y-axis represents the arm position.

Modern disk drives throw a monkey wrench into our good intentions here. We assume several things when using the elevator algorithm. First, we assume that we know the cylinder where we are going for a given request. That's not always entirely true. Not all drives are designed so that we know in which cylinder a given block resides. To make matters more complicated, drives often do bad block, or bad track, relocation. So even if we did have a good idea where a certain block should be, we might have no idea where it really is. The other big complicating factor is the fact that drives often provide their own cache to enhance performance. As a result, we might defer satisfying a request for a block because of its distance from the current cylinder, when all the time it is really in the cache just waiting to be read out. The exercises ask for some thoughts on whether these features completely invalidate the elevator algorithm or whether we can still expect some performance improvement from it.

13.7.4 RAID

In 1988, Patterson, Gibson, and Katz presented a paper that described a technique for using multiple disks as if they were a single disk. The term they coined is **redundant array of inexpensive disks** (RAID). (More recently, the concept is often described as a redundant array of independent disks.) There are several advantages to using multiple disks in this way. The most obvious is increased capacity. Increased performance is

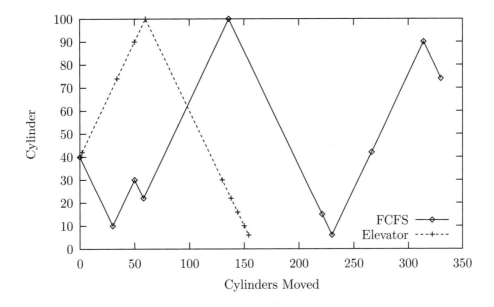

Figure 13-6: Elevator Versus FCFS Disk Scheduling

another benefit. Finally, if we record redundant data across the disks, then we can make the array more fault tolerant than a single disk.

The highest performance implementations of RAID are done in the controller. To the OS, the whole RAID array looks like a single disk. For the most part with a hardware implementation of RAID, the device driver need not be concerned with the RAID nature of the "disk." However, some operating systems provide support for software implementations of RAID. The idea is that the device driver presents an interface that looks like it is driving a single disk, but internally it operates on numerous drives through one or more controllers.

Historical Note: Connection Machine-2 DataVault

One of the most interesting, even extreme, examples of disk arrays was found on the Connection Machine-2 (CM-2) supercomputer from Thinking Machines Inc. The DataVault, introduced in 1985, used an organization, which is essentially what was later identified as RAID-2, with a total of 42 drives. Each 64-bit word was divided into two 32-bit parts, and each bit was written to one of 32 drives. Seven drives held error-correcting codes (ECC) for the 32-bit half word. The remaining three drives were spares that could be used to replace any of the other 39 drives that failed. To further enhance the system's performance, the design allowed up to eight DataVaults to be used in a striped configuration. For its time, the DataVault provided a very high-capacity and high-performance storage system for supercomputers.

Although RAID Levels 0, 1, 2, 3, 4, and 5 have been formally specified, the most commonly used levels are 0, 1, and 5.

- *RAID Level 0*: In RAID Level 0, the data is **striped** across multiple disks. This means that consecutive blocks of data are written to different drives. If we have three disks in the array, then blocks 0, 3, 6, 9,... are written to the first drive, blocks 1, 4, 7, 10,... to the second, and blocks 2, 5, 8, 11,... to the third. Because there is no redundant data, this level does not provide any increased fault tolerance. However, because seeks and transfers can happen in parallel on multiple drives, this level provides increased performance.

- *RAID Level 1*: **Mirrored** data is the primary characteristic of RAID Level 1. With mirroring, the data are replicated on multiple drives. A two-disk RAID Level 1 implementation takes twice the amount of space to store the data, but it provides the ability to access the data even if one of the drives malfunctions. Also, because the same data can be read from either drive, reads can be performed in parallel, increasing performance.

- *RAID Level 5*: RAID Level 5 provides fault tolerance without so drastic an increase in required space. It does this by storing parity information along with the data. The data itself is striped as with RAID Level 0. For each stripe, a parity block is calculated and stored on one of the drives. The parity blocks are rotated among the drives so that no one drive holds all parity blocks. Suppose we have four drives. Blocks 0, 1, and 2 form the first stripe and are stored on the first three drives. A parity block for these three data blocks is placed on the fourth drive. For the next stripe (blocks 3, 4, and 5), the parity block is placed on the third drive, and the data blocks are spread across the other three drives. Reading any data within a stripe requires that we read the whole stripe so that we may check the parity. As a result, RAID 5 implementations do not have performance advantages over single drives. This level is used primarily for its fault tolerance.

Several informal extensions and combinations of these techniques also exist. For example, by striping multiple RAID 5 arrays, we can have both the fault tolerance of RAID 5 and the performance benefit of RAID 0.

13.7.5   Water Marks

The next technique applies to many cases where we have a producer and a consumer of information and where they might operate at different speeds. Our natural approach for handling the speed mismatch is providing a buffer that allows the producer to temporarily move ahead of the consumer. It's easy enough to imagine that we can stop the producer when the buffer is full and restart it when the buffer is empty, as in the flow control used with serial communications devices. However, if it's the receiver's buffer that's getting full, and if there's significant communications latency, then the producer might send more before it gets the stop message.

We deal with this by setting two marks on the buffer. The mark closer to the full end of the buffer is called the **high water mark**, and the other one is called the **low water**

mark. If we add an item to the buffer and it results in the buffer being as full as the high water mark, then the stop message is sent to the transmitter. Similarly, if we remove an item from the buffer and it results in the buffer having no more items than the low water mark, we send the start message.

The exact values of the high and low water marks are not critical. However, if the high water mark is too high, the sender might send enough items before processing the stop that the buffer overflows. Likewise, if the low water mark is too low, then the buffer might become empty before the sender can respond to the start message. This case would result in an idle receiver wasting time that could be used to process input. On the other hand, if we have the two marks too close together, then we will send too many start and stop messages. Not only will that use more of the communications channel than necessary, but it will cause unnecessary processing in both the sender and the receiver. We show how water marks work in Example 13.4.

Example 13.4: Water Marks

To illustrate the use of water marks, consider an application where the transmitter sends 1 Byte/mS when transmitting. As those bytes arrive at the receiver, the receiver places them into a buffer. An application on the receiving system takes data from the buffer 100 bytes at a time and does so every 150 mS. Also, suppose that the receiver takes 0.25 mS to process an incoming byte to determine if it needs to send a stop signal to the transmitter, and suppose that the stop signal takes 1 mS to transmit. Similarly, when the receiver satisfies an application request and signals the transmitter to resume transmitting, it takes 1 mS to transmit the start signal. Finally, assume that the transmitter takes 1 mS to process a start or stop signal and to start or stop transmitting accordingly.

Because we know that the transmitter sends data faster than the application takes it, and because we know how much data the application reads each time, we can set the buffer size to a convenient value greater than the application request size. One such value is 128 bytes.

For setting the high water mark, observe that we expect it to take 2.25 mS to handle the full buffer condition. This means that by the time we can expect transmission to stop, the third byte past the high water mark is already being sent. As a result, we need to allow at least 3 bytes between the high water mark and the top of the buffer. Systems frequently don't respond in the expected time, however. If the transmitting system is busier than usual, it might take longer to process the stop signal than expected. Another potential source of delay comes when we use in-band flow control. The byte that signals a stop might not be received by the transmitter correctly. Consequently, it might not react until another stop signal is sent. To account for these potential problems, we usually build in a margin for error. For example, we might set the high water mark 6 or even 8 bytes below the top of the buffer rather than the minimum three. In our case, it is quite reasonable to set the high water mark at 120.

In setting the low water mark, there is one case we want to avoid. We do not want to get into a situation where there is not enough data in the buffer to satisfy an application request and at the same time not have the buffer empty enough to restart the transmitter. One way to look at the problem is to say that we want the low water mark at the request size. That way any time there are not enough bytes in the buffer, we tell the transmitter to restart. This sets our low water mark at 99. (The exercises ask what happens if we have other application request sizes.)

13.7.6   Human Input Processing

One more communication issue we consider deals with receiving input from users. When receiving input from a device such as a bar-code reader or from another computer through a communications device, we can reasonably assume that the input we receive is "meant" for us. In those cases, we can safely pass the received data on to an application without concern that the sender will "change its mind." However, when receiving input from users, we can't make those kinds of assumptions. Humans do have a tendency to make mistakes and change their minds. Consequently, a device driver for user input must make provision for these behaviors.

There are several features we generally see in such drivers. The first is **echo**. When a user types characters on a keyboard, the driver should usually send those same characters back out so that the user can see what is actually received. This feature is generally not needed (and is often troublesome) when dealing with other machines generating input. Even when dealing with users, we sometimes want to disable echo, such as when reading a password. Thus, a typical device driver for an input device that can be used by a human user provides the ability to selectively enable echo.

In addition to seeing what they type, users also like the ability to delete what they typed, either for correcting mistakes or because they change their minds about what to type. This behavior is typically supported through the use of a buffer. As characters are received, they are accumulated into the buffer. Even if an application is waiting on them, no characters are delivered by the driver until an end-of-line character (typically a carriage return or a linefeed) is received. In the meantime, certain characters are interpreted as erasing characters or the whole line. Typically, if a character such as backspace or delete is received, then the previous character is removed from the buffer. For purposes of echo, we generally output a backspace character followed by a space and another backspace. This three-character sequence has the effect of erasing the character on the screen. Of course, it doesn't work on a hard copy terminal where we use other techniques to display the changes. We must also be careful to make sure that we don't blindly back up in our buffer if the user attempts to back up beyond the beginning. If the driver receives a character such as a Ctrl-U, then it interprets the character as meaning that the whole line should be discarded.

Even though this type of input processing is normally what we want when applications deal with users, there are times when we don't want it. For example, there are applications that operate a character at a time rather than a line at a time. We might also want to use the same hardware interface for a device that is not a human input device. For example, we might connect a bar-code reader to the same RS-232 port to which we might connect a terminal. For those cases where we don't want this type of processing, the device driver needs to support what is often called a **raw mode**. In raw mode, input characters are placed into a buffer without being interpreted. Application requests for input are satisfied

Chapter 14

Some Examples of I/O Device Management

We now turn our attention to our set of examples to see how I/O device support is implemented in them. Our focus is on the structure and design of the overall I/O subsystem rather than on individual device details. It is instructive in this chapter to note both the variations in I/O subsystem design as well as the similarities in family lines.

14.1 CTSS

Though not extensive by modern standards, the final version of CTSS supports a good variety of I/O devices. Among these devices are the following:

- a clock generating regular interrupts to drive the scheduler

- numerous typewriter terminals of several types

- a graphical display system with light pens connected through a PDP-7 computer

- magnetic tape drives

- two magnetic disk drives

- magnetic drums

- printers

- punched card readers and punches

CTSS makes a distinction in design between character devices and block devices. It provides some degree of device independence, particularly when dealing with disks and drums.

CTSS provides a variety of system calls for various devices, including calls to set various device parameters. The call for writing a line of output to a terminal is different from the call to write a block to a tape. In some cases, the system provides both buffered and unbuffered versions of read and write operations. In this case, the buffering is a block-level buffering similar to the file system buffering we discuss in Chapter 17.

There are several interesting aspects of the design of CTSS device drivers. The first of these is the division of labor among various components of the I/O system. Particularly when dealing with files, I/O calls first go through the File Coordinator. This module verifies the validity of the request and passes it on to the appropriate I/O module. In the cases of block-structured devices, the next step is the Buffer Control Module, which implements the buffering described previously. Part of that responsibility is determining whether a read or write operation should be handled directly out of the user process's memory space or out of the kernel's buffer space. The Buffer Control Module uses this information to construct a request that is issued to the appropriate device's Strategy Module. The CTSS Strategy Modules are essentially the upper halves of device drivers. They take requests and place them into queues to be processed by the I/O Adapters, which serve the roles of the device driver lower halves. Strategy Modules are also where any request scheduling, such as the elevator algorithm, is implemented. The I/O Adapters provide the interface between the rest of the system and the device hardware. They also include the interrupt handlers. When an operation completes, the I/O Adapter signals the Strategy Module to relay the results back to the Buffer Control Module.

Another interesting element of the CTSS I/O design is the way in which it handles character-oriented input. All terminals are connected to a separate IBM 7750 computer, which communicates with the 7094 via a data channel. For each character that is received, the data channel writes into an adapter input buffer the character and an indication of the terminal line over which the character was received. As is typical for most character device controllers, the channel generates an interrupt after the character has been placed in the buffer. However, most of the normal character processing is not done in the interrupt handler. Instead, this interrupt handler only transfers the characters from the adapter input buffer to a character pool buffer and translates from the physical terminal line number to the user who is logged in on that line. One of the duties of the clock interrupt handler is calling a function that performs the rest of the usual interrupt handling. This function reads characters from the character pool buffer and puts them into the input buffers for their respective users. After this transfer is completed, the input buffers are checked to see if they contain any special characters. Among these special characters are line break characters, such as carriage returns, and input line editing characters, such as erase and kill. If there is a line break character, then a line of characters is moved to another buffer from which user program input requests are satisfied.

14.2   Multics

Like its predecessor, CTSS, Multics supports a variety of I/O devices, including terminals, disks, drums, tapes, printers, and punched card devices. The design of the Multics I/O subsystem also bears some similarity to that of its predecessor. However, the Multics I/O design also represents a significant advance, particularly in terms of device independence. User programs are written in terms of **streams** with no predefined correspondence between a stream and an I/O device. In this way, a program's output can go to the terminal on which the program is run, to a file, or to the printer, without the program having been written to account for all these cases. Multics also provides similar flexibility for input.

All I/O requests from user processes go to the I/O Switch. One of the primary responsibilities of the I/O Switch is managing the correspondence between streams and devices or files. These correspondences, which can be established at the time the program is run, are held in the Attach Table. By default, a standard input stream and a standard output stream are associated with the terminal on which the program is run. The I/O Switch uses the information in the Attach Table to dispatch the request to an appropriate Device Interface Module (DIM). DIMs provide much the same functionality as the CTSS Strategy Modules. For file operations, the I/O Switch forwards the request to the File System Interface Module (FSIM), which operates like a special DIM without an associated physical device. The FISM does not, however, go back through this same I/O infrastructure to access the disk. Instead, it uses the same infrastructure that supports paging. The paging system is implemented separate from the rest of the I/O infrastructure for reasons of performance. Figure 14-1 illustrates this organization for a simple set of devices, including only terminal, tape, and printer.

The figure shows the DIMs all feeding into the GIOC Interface Module (GIM). The GIM is a driver for the General I/O Controller (GIOC). This controller is found only on the GE-645 and provides a uniform programming interface for a wide variety of devices. On the Honeywell 6180 the GIOC was replaced by the I/O Multiplexer (IOM), which served much the same purpose. Interrupts are handled in the reverse of the flow for requests. For devices attached to the GIOC, the GIM initially handles any interrupts coming from the GIOC. If an interrupt requires attention from a higher level of the I/O subsystem, it is passed upward through the DIM until all necessary modules are informed of the event.

There is one more feature of the Multics I/O subsystem that we need to discuss. That is the I/O Interfacer. This facility allows code running in user rings (outside the kernel) to be interfaced into the rest of the I/O infrastructure. The effect of this design is that device drivers can be implemented in application code in the same way as in the kernel. Although this ability to control devices directly from applications is common among embedded and real-time operating systems, it is very rare among general-purpose operating systems, despite being implemented in Multics over 30 years ago. Nevertheless, much of the Multics design has influenced many OS designs since.

14.3   RT-11

Because RT-11 is designed for environments where direct control of I/O devices can be important, it has a number of characteristics that are not typical of most time-sharing operating systems. One of these unusual characteristics is the fact that it provides both blocking and nonblocking read and write system calls. Another unusual feature is the ability for a program to directly access a device controller. In effect, such a program

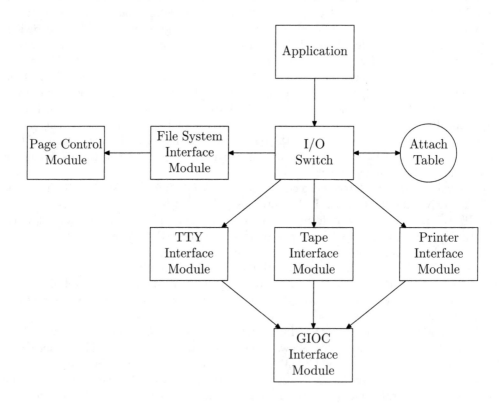

Figure 14-1: Multics I/O Subsystem Organization

includes its own device driver, possibly including the interrupt handler. Such direct access allows a program to use a device in time-critical situations where a normal device driver might be too slow. This direct access arises from a combination of the fact that all device controllers are memory mapped in the PDP-11 and of the lack of address translation when using the single job (SJ) and foreground-background (FB) monitors. Even in the extended memory (XM) monitor, some processes can have direct access to the device controller registers.

Most device access, however, takes place through device drivers, or **handlers** in RT-11 terminology. Through these drivers, most I/O in RT-11 is device-independent, using the same .READ and .WRITE system calls that are used for files. This device independence is implemented through a table that translates from device names to pointers to the entry points of the associated device drivers. This table is built at system initialization time by looking at all the drivers that were configured when the system was generated and testing to see which ones have the necessary hardware installed.

The overall structure of the RT-11 I/O subsystem is a little unusual. Device support is a combination of the resident monitor (RMON) and the dynamically loaded device handlers. RMON contains two major elements of the I/O subsystem. The first of these is the support for terminal I/O. This code is focused on supporting human users on terminals connected to RS-232 ports. It is the one major exception to the device independence, as it provides a separate set of system calls for terminal I/O. (A separate device handler, the TT device handler, is provided to support normal read and write operations. It is used when interfacing to a device attached to an RS-232 port that does not need to use human input processing.)

The other major element of I/O support in RMON is a queuing facility for I/O requests. In effect, RMON serves the role of the upper half of all device drivers. As requests come into RMON, it places them in queues, one for each device. It then turns control over to the appropriate handler whenever a new request reaches the head of the respective queue. It orders requests by process number, with the higher process numbers getting priority over lower ones. Requests from the same process are taken in FCFS order.

The device handlers, then, provide the functionality of the lower halves of device drivers. They contain the code that programs the controller registers and the code that makes up the interrupt handlers. These handlers are assembled into the files that are loaded dynamically as needed. One special handler is always loaded: the system device handler, which is the handler for the device containing the file system from which the system was booted. These system device handlers have an interesting special feature. They contain the code necessary for the bootstrapping process. When a disk (or other block device) is initialized for booting, the bootstrap code from the associated device handler is copied to a fixed place on the disk. This bootstrap code is not loaded into memory when a device handler is loaded.

There is one final interesting aspect of device handlers we examine here. Many device handlers have parameters that can be set by the user. These parameters are stored in the first two blocks of the file containing the handler's executable code. A standard command called SET allows the user to change these parameters by modifying the relevant data in the handler files. Each parameter has a routine in the handler code that checks the validity of the requested value and sets the proper value in the parameter tables. After the parameter is set, the two blocks are then written back to the file. As a result, these parameters are set for all processes in the system and remain in force until they are changed, even across reboots.

Although the overall design of the RT-11 I/O subsystem is not typical, it is well suited to its intended purpose. It makes it very easy for developers to add support for new devices. It also allows programs to be written that bypass the standard means of accessing a device and to use special techniques uniquely suited to the application.

14.4   Sixth Edition UNIX

UNIX continues the evolution of device independence begun by its CTSS and Multics ancestors. All input and output operations are carried out through the same *read*( ) and *write*( ) system calls that are used for file operations. Devices are also opened in the same way as files, using names that are managed by the file system (even to the point of being represented by data structures on the disk). Querying and setting serial port parameters is handled through the *gtty*( ) and *stty*( ) system calls, respectively. Device drivers in UNIX are generally structured as we have described drivers in Chapter 13. Unlike some of the other systems we discuss here, however, device drivers in UNIX are not loaded dynamically while the system is running. They are included as part of the kernel image loaded at boot time.

Devices in UNIX are grouped into block devices and character devices. Normally, applications directly open, close, read, and write only character devices. Access to block devices is normally handled through the file system, which, in turn, is processed through a block I/O buffer layer. Sometimes, however, we need to access a block device without going through the file system interface, such as when building a new file system on a device. To support this, most block device drivers also support a raw interface that provides the same interface as for character devices.

The representation of devices in the file system is at the heart of UNIX device independence. When a device's name, such as /dev/tty, is referenced, the file system translates it to three data items: a major device number, a minor device number, and a flag indicating whether the device is a character device or a block device. In handling a system call issued by a process, the block/character flag is used to select one of two tables, *bdevsw* and *cdevsw*, that determine how the call is processed. The major device number is used to index the selected table. Each entry in the table is a structure containing pointers to functions for handling specific operations. (Readers more familiar with object-oriented terminology than with function pointers can think of these tables much like arrays of objects, each with a method for each operation.) The minor device number is passed to the driver, which may use it as it sees fit. In most cases, at least one use of the minor device number is determining which among several devices connected to a controller is being accessed. In some other cases, the minor device number can determine other things, like whether a tape is rewound when closed.

Block device drivers have three entry points through the device switch structure: an open routine, a close routine, and a strategy routine. The open routine is most often called to prepare the device when the file system it contains is mounted (attached to the overall file system directory tree). Similarly, the close routine's primary function is handling any cleanup needed when a file system is unmounted. The strategy routine is the main entry point for all reads and writes. If the driver does any scheduling optimizations, they are done in the strategy routine. The strategy routine also starts the controller if it is idle when a request arrives. Otherwise, incoming requests are queued up to be handled by the interrupt handler.

Character device drivers have five entry points called through the device switch table. Four of the five routines correspond directly to the *open*( ), *close*( ), *read*( ), and *write*( ) system calls. The fifth routine is called for both the *gtty*( ) and *stty*( ) system calls.

UNIX uses an interesting approach to managing buffer space for character devices. Rather than attempt to manage variable-sized allocations or set a priori limits on arrays, it uses a variable number of fixed-sized blocks called **cblocks**. In sixth edition UNIX, the **cblock** contains a 2-byte pointer to the next **cblock** in the buffer and six characters. The full buffer is represented by a **clist**, which contains a character count, a pointer to the first character, and a pointer to the last character in the buffer. By ensuring that each **cblock** is stored on an 8-byte boundary, the system can easily determine if the last character is being removed from a **cblock** or if a character is to be added to a full **cblock**. This alignment also makes it easy to map from a pointer to a character in a **cblock** to the pointer to the next **cblock**.

The last element of early UNIX I/O design we consider is the handling of input character processing. Clearly, we don't want to implement the same user input processing in the drivers for every controller to which we can connect a terminal. Such repetition would be error-prone and wasteful. In UNIX, there is a separate module that handles input processing. The functions of this module are called from all device drivers that handle user input.

14.5   4.3BSD

The design of the UNIX I/O subsystem didn't change much between sixth edition and 4.3BSD. Consequently, we focus here on the changes to those features we've discussed. One of the most visible changes is the addition of the *ioctl*( ) system call. This call was actually introduced in the seventh edition system. It provides a more general interface for device control than the *gtty*( ) and *stty*( ) calls in sixth edition. The *ioctl*( ) call is rarely described as elegant. However, it has provided a mechanism for supporting numerous special functions like rewinding tapes and ejecting CDs without adding new system calls.

4.3BSD continues to use the **clist** mechanism for managing character buffers. As system memory capacities have increased, it has become appropriate to increase the size of the **cblock**. In 4.3BSD, **cblock**s have 60 characters of buffer and a 4-byte pointer to the next **cblock**.

There is also enhanced character handling in 4.3BSD. Serial interfaces are not always used for human interfaces. Sometimes they are used for computer-to-computer communication over modems. Sometimes they are used for attaching devices like printers or bar-code readers. Consequently, character device processing may have different requirements, depending on the use of the interface. In 4.3BSD, the different types of processing are handled through a generalization of the same character processing design in earlier UNIX systems. Several such processing modules provide a variety of **line disciplines**. A line discipline can be selected on a per-interface basis. The implementation of the line discipline uses a line switch table much like the device switch tables that select entry points in device drivers.

14.6   VMS

VMS provides a device-independent interface for applications to access them. Devices are identified by name. However, the system calls for accessing devices are, in part, distinct from those for accessing files. The primary system calls for devices include:

- $ALLOC requests exclusive access to a device.

- $DALLOC releases exclusive control of a device.

- $ASSIGN creates a correspondence between a device and an I/O channel. This call effectively opens a device.

- $DASSGN is much like a close operation that removes the link between device and channel.

- $QIO is a general queued read-and-write interface. The $QIO version of a call is nonblocking. Calls to $QIOW perform blocking reads and writes.

I/O devices, controllers, drivers, and requests are all managed through a collection of internal data structures known as the I/O database. Of particular interest to us are the tables that support device drivers. The first of these is the driver prolog table (DPT), which provides the information necessary to load drivers dynamically. The second is the driver dispatch table (DDT). There is one of these tables for each driver, and it gives the entry points for certain routines that are necessary for all drivers. Finally, the function decision table (FDT) for a driver provides a mapping from most I/O operations to the functions that implement them. It also includes a bit mask that specifies which I/O operations are supported by the given driver.

Drivers in VMS are structured in one of two ways. The first structure follows the upper/lower half structure we discuss in Chapter 13. Requests enter the driver through the $QIO system call, and the driver does any necessary processing prior to servicing the request. It then passes the request back to support $QIO code for placing the request into a queue. If the device is idle, then the queuing code calls the driver's routine for starting I/O. At that point, the driver waits for an interrupt to occur, indicating the completion of the operation. After completing its response to the interrupt, the interrupt handler passes control back to the $QIO support code to return the results back to the requesting process.

The other driver organization divides drivers into two parts—a class driver and a port driver. Terminal support provides an instructive example of this. Because so much of the support necessary for terminals is independent of the details of the hardware interface, we wouldn't want to repeat the line editing code for each driver. The higher-level class driver includes the implementation of policies related to a particular class of devices, such as terminals. When a lower-level operation is required, such as transmitting a string of bytes out the port, the class driver calls on the port driver for the specific hardware involved. One particularly interesting result of this organization is that by using a suitable port driver that relays requests across a network, the same class driver can use both local devices and remote devices.

VMS supports a number of pseudo-devices, such as the null device. Mailboxes are a particularly noteworthy example of pseudo-devices in VMS. These "devices" allow processes to communicate with each other using the same system calls as they use to exchange data with other devices. Special system calls allow processes to create mailboxes and give them names, which can be referenced by other processes. Any process that wants to use the mailbox can then open it with the usual $ASSIGN call and use $QIO calls to read and write to it.

14.7 Windows NT

I/O operations in Windows NT involve several layers of processing. When an application issues an I/O request, the subsystem layer is responsible for the first stage of processing. If the application is reading from a device or file, it might issue the *read*( ) call if running on the POSIX subsystem, or the *ReadFile*( ) call if running on the Win32 subsystem. The environment subsystem then issues a call into the OS. In this case, the call is *NtReadFile*( ). It is handled by the I/O manager, which handles queuing and dispatching of requests to drivers. Both blocking and nonblocking I/O calls are supported. The I/O manager may pass control to a single device driver or to a set of several layered drivers. In fact, the file system is treated as a top-level driver. Drivers are written independently of most processor and interrupt controller details. They call routines in the Hardware Abstraction Layer (HAL) to deal with those details.

Individual device drivers are themselves often implemented in layers. At the top layer, we find class drivers that handle a type of device, such as a CD or a disk. These drivers then request service from a port driver that handles the details of a particular type of interface. The disk class driver may call on different port drivers for IDE disks as opposed to SCSI disks. The particular make and model of controller is handled by the miniport driver, which receives requests from the port driver. In terms of implementation, the miniport driver is the code we usually think of as a device driver, and it calls the library of functions that make up the port driver code.

Beginning with the Windows 2000 version of the Windows NT design, another division of driver responsibility has been added with the Windows Driver Model (WDM). This model defines three types of drivers. Bus drivers handle the details of a particular type of interconnection bus. This includes traditional internal busses, such as PCI or ISA, as well as external interfaces like USB or IEEE 1394 (also known as FireWire). Any Plug and Play (PnP) or power management features of these busses are handled by the bus drivers. The usual device driver responsibilities are found in the drivers called function drivers in the WDM. Finally, other drivers can be added to provide additional features and functions. These additional drivers are called filter drivers. For example, we could include a filter driver that provides encryption of data sent over a USB port.

Another element of Windows NT device handling that deserves mention is its interrupt handling mechanism. The actual interrupt handlers don't do all the processing necessary to deal with the completion of an I/O operation. Instead, they do a minimum of work to minimize the amount of time that interrupts are blocked. After the interrupt handler has recorded the details of the interrupt and has performed any necessary acknowledgment of the controller, it then issues a deferred procedure call (DPC). This call references another routine in the driver that finishes processing the interrupt. The general DPC infrastructure issues the actual call a short time later. The routine called by the DPC handles awakening the thread blocked on that operation and delivering any results to the thread. After this, it takes the next operation from the queue and issues it to the controller, just as a normal interrupt routine would.

14.8   TinyOS

Even more than with other operating systems, the whole point of TinyOS is handling I/O devices. The devices handled by TinyOS are generally of three types. The first type, sensory devices, include hardware to measure temperature, light, motion, and so on. Often the primary role of the motes, on which TinyOS runs, is gathering environmental information in this way. This is much of the reason that they are often called sensors. The second type of device is the simple indicator output. Most often, these are one or a few light emitting diodes (LEDs), though other output devices are possible. The final group of devices are communications devices, most often RF network devices, such as Bluetooth, 802.11b, or 802.15.

Just like other parts of the system, device drivers are written as components. They take requests from higher-level components in the form of commands. These commands can result in the driver component returning data collected from a device, or they can result in the component taking some action in the hardware. Interrupts come into driver components as events. Depending on the driver design, the events can be handled completely within the component, or more often, they can result in other events being passed on to higher-level components.

14.9   Xen

Xen does not manage I/O devices itself. That responsibility belongs to one of the guest operating systems running on it. In particular, the OS running in a domain called the driver domain (usually Domain 0) has a special status. It has access to the system's I/O devices in the same way as any other OS running directly on the hardware.

OSs running in other domains use a two-part device driver to access the devices owned by the OS in the driver domain. The two parts of these drivers are called the frontend and the backend. The frontend runs on the OSs without direct device access. It presents the same interface to the OS as do other drivers for the same type of device. However, its only real function is to relay the requests to the backend driver through a block of shared memory. This memory serves as the interface between the frontend on a nonprivileged OS and the backend running on the OS in the driver domain. The backend driver takes the requests from the shared memory block, and after verifying their validity, serves them through the normal device drivers in that OS.

Networking is usually handled a little differently. The networking backend implements an interface that allows each of the guest OSs to communicate with each other through their network interfaces. In practice, some of the I/O that would normally be handled through device drivers is handled through network protocols in Xen. For example, even though each guest OS might normally want to directly control a frame buffer to provide a windowing system, only one can in Xen. Through the single guest that provides a windowing system, the user may then access virtual windowing environments on the other systems using an application such as VNC.

14.10   Summary

As we have seen with processes and memory, real implementations of I/O device support build on, but vary from, the widely studied general principles. In this chapter, we have looked at our nine-system cross-section of OS designs and how I/O devices are supported in each. We have seen how the target application domain dictates part of the design. We have also seen how various techniques and principles of I/O support have evolved over time as each generation of OS has influenced successive ones. Overall, we have seen the trend toward generic interfaces and techniques that hide device details. This trend even includes designs where I/O devices and files are unified to some degree.

14.11   Exercises

1. In moving from CTSS to Multics, the developers moved from unique system calls for different devices to a more generic approach where the same calls are used regardless of device. What are the advantages and disadvantages of this move?

2. The first stop for I/O requests in CTSS is the File Coordinator. In Multics, it is the UIM. Do these two elements do the same thing? What are the differences between them?

3. When implementing generic device interfaces, we don't want to lose the opportunity to include device-specific techniques, such as the elevator algorithm. How can we get the best of both worlds, where applications see the same interface for all devices, but internally each device can be supported with the appropriate optimizations?

4. The sixth edition UNIX buffer implementation seems a bit complicated. In most applications, either we dynamically allocate buffers as needed, or we use fixed buffers

with limits set at implementation time. Why did the designers include the **cblock** approach to buffering rather than a more typical application approach? What advantages do **cblock**s have over those approaches?

5. The systems that run 4.3BSD have much larger physical memory spaces than those that run sixth edition UNIX. One effect of this difference is larger **cblock**s. Are there other ways in which additional physical memory affects buffer design? Does "cheap" memory obviate the need for **cblock**s altogether? Why or why not?

6. Some of the systems we discuss implement only blocking I/O operations, and some implement both blocking and nonblocking operations. Is there a substantial difference in driver complexity between these two design choices? How can blocking operations be implemented on top of nonblocking operations?

7. Both VMS and Windows NT exhibit a trend to separate device-type and bus support from device-specific support. How do these designs affect the basic driver design, illustrated in Figure 13-4?

8. In VMS, we see a lot of interaction between the device driver and the $QIO code. Do all of these back-and-forth calls violate good layered design? Is there a way to look at the $QIO code and the device driver as a well-layered design?

9. We point out that TinyOS doesn't include any I/O support in the OS itself. Yet, nearly all other systems provide substantial infrastructures in addition to specific device drivers. Why did the TinyOS developers not include such infrastructure? Would there be some advantage in including such? How could generic techniques be supported with the current design?

10. Traditionally, particularly in the world of IBM PCs, each operating system has to include code to support a very wide variety of devices. This means that OS developers implement much the same code over and over again, and it adds substantial demand on the development teams. Does the increasing use of Xen affect this? How can smaller development groups use Xen to utilize all the devices out there without having to implement drivers for all of them?

Chapter 15

I/O Devices in Inferno

Unlike the rest of our examination of Inferno, in this chapter we examine primarily native code. The reason for this is simple. In hosted Inferno, most of the work in controlling devices is done by the host operating system. So to study the details of programming devices, we need to focus on native Inferno implementations, where Inferno itself is responsible for managing them.

15.1   Device Driver Structure

Nearly all device support in Inferno is handled through special file servers that present devices as resources in the name space. We examine the file server aspect of these device drivers in more detail in Chapter 19. Here, we focus primarily on the device control aspects of our drivers. However, some elements of the general structure of Inferno device drivers will help establish some context.

Device drivers in Inferno have a somewhat unusual structure as a result of their server functionality. This alternative structure results in drivers that are quite straightforward when compared to many other systems. When viewed from the rest of the kernel, device drivers are a collection of functions that provide a standard set of entry points. One function is called to initialize the device, and another is called to shut it down. There are functions that are called to read data, write data, and perform a number of other operations. To a large extent, these functions correspond to messages in the Styx protocol, detailed in Section 19.1.1. Each driver defines a structure that contains pointers to these functions. These structures form a consistent interface between all drivers and the rest of the system.

In the case of storage devices, we take this abstraction one step further. A substantial amount of processing for storage devices is independent of the physical device. Rather than implement this common functionality in each storage device driver, we create a driver that handles it, and this driver implements the functions that respond to Styx messages. Then, in response to the Styx messages, this driver calls on code specific to the physical

345

device. The interface between the device-independent code and the device-dependent code
is similar to the interface between Styx and the device drivers. In particular, each device-
dependent module defines a structure containing a set of function pointers providing a
standard set of calls into each device-dependent driver.

In comparison to the upper/lower half driver structure in Figure 13-4, most of the
upper half functionality is provided by the general Styx handling infrastructure. The code
identified as the device driver itself provides mostly lower half functionality. This code also
contains the interrupt handler if one is needed for this device. The device's initialization
function is responsible for connecting the function that implements the interrupt handler
with the hardware interrupt.

To illustrate the operation of an Inferno driver, we consider an example of a request
issued to the driver, which is illustrated in Figure 15-1. The arrows show the flow of
control, and the numbers beside the arrows indicate the order of events. All of the code
from the dashed line down is part of the device driver. Again, for storage devices, the row
of functions that process Styx operations is divided into a device-independent row and a
device-dependent row.

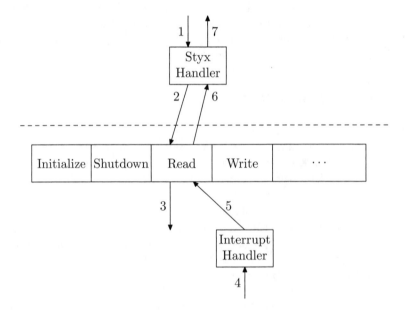

Figure 15-1: Inferno Device Driver Operation

We begin with a Styx message, say to read from the device, indicated by arrow 1 in
the figure. This message could be generated locally through a system call, or it could
arrive over a network connection. To make it more specific, let us consider the case of a
system call. Either way, the Styx handling code recognizes this as a read request and calls
the function for reading from among those function pointers mentioned earlier (arrow 2).

Before accessing an internal data structure associated with the specific device, the read function obtains a mutual exclusion lock on it. This code is running as part of a *kproc*. In particular, for a system call, it is the *kproc* that was interpreting the application that issued the system call. Further, suppose that this is a driver for a device that might take some time to fulfill the request. In this case, the *kproc* which called the read function will block in the read function after setting up the controller to read the requested data (arrow 3).

While our original *kproc* is blocked, other processes might make requests of the same device. Because they will not be able to get the mutex lock, they will be blocked. When the data are available, the controller generates an interrupt. During initialization, this driver associated one of its functions with the relevant interrupt, so that function gets called now, corresponding to arrow 4. It is, of course, not running as part of the *kproc* that issued the original request. The interrupt handler code wakes the original *kproc* thread up to complete the operation. We denote the wakeup operation by arrow 5 in the figure, but note that this is not a typical transfer of control resulting from a call or a return.

Before returning control back to the application that issued the system call (arrows 6 and 7), the driver code unlocks the data structure for that device. If there are any other *kproc*s waiting for the lock, the next one is unblocked and given the lock. We use a locking operation that preserves the order of the lock requests. As a result, the lock code implements the queue of outstanding operations for us. Individual drivers don't have to include queueing code.

15.2 Parallel Port Support

We begin our examination of specific device driver examples with one of the simplest devices in the system. It is the hardware that interfaces to printers and other parallel devices. The code for this device driver is found in the file os/pc/devlpt.c.

The first part of the code we consider is the declaration of an array listing the addresses of the controller registers for each interface. We list the register sets for up to three interfaces. If we have fewer than three devices actually installed on the system, we'll just ignore the extras.

```
/* base addresses */
static int lptbase[] = {
    #378,     /* lpt1 */
    #3bc,     /* lpt2 */
    #278      /* lpt3 (sic) */
};
```

15.2.1 Servicing a Write Request

Even though modern parallel ports can be used for bidirectional communication (both input and output), the traditional use of parallel ports is for output. Consequently, we

restrict our attention to the case of writing to the port. We get to this point as a result
of a Styx write message, as described earlier.

The function for writing to the parallel port is declared as follows, where a is a pointer
to the data that need to be written to the port, and n gives the number of bytes to
be written. The channel parameter c points to a structure that identifies, among other
things, which port we're accessing.

```
static long lptwrite(Chan *c, void *a, long n, vlong)
{
    char str[16], *p;
    long base, k;
    if (n ≤ 0)
        return 0;
```

15.2.1.1   Handling Control Operations

It turns out that some writes are not data to be sent out over the port. Instead, these
writes are intended to directly modify the control registers of the device controller. In
these cases, we write the requested data to the register corresponding to the open file.
We can tell whether it's a data or control access by which file is opened. The *qid* part of
the c structure is a unique identification of an open file. When the data file is opened, its
path member is set to *Qdata*. There are other defined values for the control files.

```
    if (c→qid.path ≠ Qdata) {
        if (n > sizeof str − 1)
            n = sizeof str − 1;
        memmove(str, a, n);
        str[n] = 0;
        outb(c→qid.path, strtoul(str, 0, 0));
        return n;
    }
```

15.2.1.2   Writing the Output Buffer

If the write request is on a channel attached to the actual port, then we get to this point
in the code. The first three lines just set up some variables that make our life easier when
writing the data.

```
    p = a;
    k = n;
    base = lptbase[c→dev];
```

As described in earlier chapters, we set this as a point where we can catch error conditions.
If we do detect an error condition, we want to reset the port output signals to a normal
idle state. *Qpcr* is defined to be the offset from the base I/O port to the one for the

control register. Similarly, *Qpsr*, which we see later, refers to the status register. In this and the next function, we also see a number of constants with names that begin with "F," such as *Finitbar*. These all correspond to specific control and status bits in the control and status registers.

```
if (waserror()) {
    outb(base + Qpcr, Finitbar);
    nexterror();
}
```

In the normal flow of control, we reach this point where we have n bytes to write out to the port. Most of the work doing the actual writing is handled in the function *outch*().

```
    while (--k ≥ 0)
        outch(base, *p++);
    poperror();
    return n;
}
```

15.2.2   Writing a Single Byte

Here, then, is the function that transfers a byte to the parallel port. It's at this point where we talk directly to the hardware using the calls *inb*() and *outb*(). These fetch a byte from an I/O port address and write a byte to an I/O port address, respectively.

```
static void outch(int base, int c)
{
    int status, tries;
```

15.2.2.1   Waiting for an Idle Controller

We can't write a byte to the port if the busy signal on the interface is active. So, we poll that signal until it is deasserted. Along the way, we look for out-of-paper and error signals.

```
    for (tries = 0; ; tries++) {
        status = inb(base + Qpsr);
        if (status & Fnotbusy)
            break;
        if ((status & Fpe) ≡ 0 ∧ (status & (Fselect | Fnoerror)) ≠ (Fselect | Fnoerror))
            error(Eio);
```

So that we don't hog the CPU while polling the busy signals, we delay 1 mS each of the first 10 times. After the first 10 mS of polling, we sleep for 100 mS each time. We also enable the interrupt from the controller so that we can be woken out of our sleep when the interface is available.

```
      if (tries < 10)
          tsleep(&lptrendez, return0, nil, 1);
      else {
          outb(base + Qpcr, Finitbar | Fie);
          tsleep(&lptrendez, lptready, (void *) base, 100);
      }
  }
```

15.2.2.2 Sending the Byte

Now that we know we can safely write to the port, we send the byte out to the port and momentarily activate the strobe signal. The strobe signals the connected device that a new data byte is available on the data lines.

```
      outb(base + Qdlr, c);
      outb(base + Qpcr, Finitbar | Fstrobe);
      outb(base + Qpcr, Finitbar);
  }
```

At this point, we return back to the tight, per-character loop in *lptwrite( )*. Notice that we don't use the interrupt generated when a character is sent to trigger sending another byte. Instead, we poll the controller to determine when it's safe to send another character. However, because we yield the CPU by sleeping and poll only periodically, we don't incur the usual negative effects of polling. However, we do use the interrupt to wake us from the sleep so that we don't wait any longer than necessary. The effect of this design is simpler code than the traditional use of interrupts but still greatly reduces the inefficiency of traditional polling.

15.3   Keyboard Support

We next examine the driver for the built-in keyboard for IBM-compatible PCs, as defined in os/pc/kbd.c. The keyboard on these machines is actually connected to a separate Intel 8042 microprocessor. In newer implementations of the IBM-compatible design, this microprocessor is but one of many functions incorporated into one or a few chips that contain most of the original interface functions. For our purposes, the main function of this keyboard processor is interrupting the main CPU and delivering keycodes for each keyboard event. These events include each depression and each release of any key on the keyboard. The same keycode is produced for each event regardless of whether any modifier is active. For example, the keycode we get when the "A" key is pressed doesn't tell us whether it's to be a lowercase "a," an uppercase "A," or a Ctrl-A. The keycode also does not match the American Standard Code for Information Interchange (ASCII) value of the corresponding character. To deal with these vagaries, we define the following three arrays that map keycodes to characters and modifier functions. In these arrays, the notation [#00] is an extension of C supported by the compiler used to build native Inferno.

It allows the programmer to specify which element of the array gets the next initializer. In these particular cases, we aren't skipping any values, so they serve mostly as an aid to the reader.

Rune *kbtab*[] =
{
[#00]*No*, #1b, '1', '2', '3', '4', '5', '6',
[#08]'7', '8', '9', '0', '-', '=', '\b', '\t',
[#10]'q', 'w', 'e', 'r', 't', 'y', 'u', 'i',
[#18]'o', 'p', '[', ']', '\n', *Ctrl*, 'a', 's',
[#20]'d', 'f', 'g', 'h', 'j', 'k', 'l', ';',
[#28]'\'', '`', *Shift*, '\\', 'z', 'x', 'c', 'v',
[#30]'b', 'n', 'm', ',', '.', '/', *Shift*, '*',
[#38]*Latin*, '␣', *Ctrl*, KF | 1, KF | 2, KF | 3, KF | 4, KF | 5,
[#40]KF | 6, KF | 7, KF | 8, KF | 9, KF | 10, *Num*, *Scroll*, '7',
[#48]'8', '9', '-', '4', '5', '6', '+', '1',
[#50]'2', '3', '0', '.', *No*, *No*, *No*, KF | 11,
[#58]KF | 12, *No*, *No*, *No*, *No*, *No*, *No*, *No*,
[#60]*No*, *No*, *No*, *No*, *No*, *No*, *No*, *No*,
[#68]*No*, *No*, *No*, *No*, *No*, *No*, *No*, *No*,
[#70]*No*, *No*, *No*, *No*, *No*, *No*, *No*, *No*,
[#78]*No*, *View*, *No*, *Up*, *No*, *No*, *No*, *No*,
};

Rune *kbtabshift*[] =
{
[#00]*No*, #1b, '!', '@', '#', '$', '%', '^',
[#08]'&', '*', '(', ')', '_', '+', '\b', '\t',
[#10]'Q', 'W', 'E', 'R', 'T', 'Y', 'U', 'I',
[#18]'O', 'P', '{', '}', '\n', *Ctrl*, 'A', 'S',
[#20]'D', 'F', 'G', 'H', 'J', 'K', 'L', ':',
[#28]'"', '~', *Shift*, '|', 'Z', 'X', 'C', 'V',
[#30]'B', 'N', 'M', '<', '>', '?', *Shift*, '*',
[#38]*Latin*, '␣', *Ctrl*, KF | 1, KF | 2, KF | 3, KF | 4, KF | 5,
[#40]KF | 6, KF | 7, KF | 8, KF | 9, KF | 10, *Num*, *Scroll*, '7',
[#48]'8', '9', '-', '4', '5', '6', '+', '1',
[#50]'2', '3', '0', '.', *No*, *No*, *No*, KF | 11,
[#58]KF | 12, *No*, *No*, *No*, *No*, *No*, *No*, *No*,
[#60]*No*, *No*, *No*, *No*, *No*, *No*, *No*, *No*,
[#68]*No*, *No*, *No*, *No*, *No*, *No*, *No*, *No*,
[#70]*No*, *No*, *No*, *No*, *No*, *No*, *No*, *No*,
[#78]*No*, *Up*, *No*, *Up*, *No*, *No*, *No*, *No*,
};

Rune *kbtabesc1*[] =
{

[#00] *No, No, No, No, No, No, No, No,*
[#08] *No, No, No, No, No, No, No, No,*
[#10] *No, No, No, No, No, No, No, No,*
[#18] *No, No, No, No,* '\n', *Ctrl, No, No,*
[#20] *No, No, No, No, No, No, No, No,*
[#28] *No, No, Shift, No, No, No, No, No,*
[#30] *No, No, No, No, No,* '/', *No, Print,*
[#38] *Latin, No, No, No, No, No, No, No,*
[#40] *No, No, No, No, No, No, Break, Home,*
[#48] *Up, Pgup, No, Left, No, Right, No, End,*
[#50] *Down, Pgdown, Ins, Del, No, No, No, No,*
[#58] *No, No, No, No, No, No, No, No,*
[#60] *No, No, No, No, No, No, No, No,*
[#68] *No, No, No, No, No, No, No, No,*
[#70] *No, No, No, No, No, No, No, No,*
[#78] *No, Up, No, No, No, No, No, No,*
};

15.3.1   Initializing the Keyboard Controller

The first function we examine is the one that initializes the keyboard controller. The first little bit of code is pretty common in device drivers, especially when initializing or initiating operations. Often, device controllers are unable to take new commands while they are busy handling another operation. Here, we poll the status of the controller until we find that it is not busy. Each time around, if the status indicates that the controller has a new input event, we need to take, but ignore, it. The values of *Status* and *Data* are the corresponding port numbers.

```
void kbdinit(void)
{
    int c;
    /* wait for a quiescent controller */
    while ((c = inb(Status)) & (Outbusy | Inready))
        if (c & Inready)
            inb(Data);
```

The remainder of this function configures the keyboard controller, enabling the keyboard functionality, enabling an interrupt on output buffer full, and setting the keyboard to an IBM-compatibility mode. Notice that we first have to write 20_{16} to the command port before we read the current configuration value, and we have to write 60_{16} to write a new configuration value. This is an example of one of the common techniques discussed in Chapter 13. To reduce the number of ports we use, or to simplify the hardware design, the controller will often have a two-step process for reading and writing its internal registers.

```
/* get current controller command byte */
outb(Cmd, #20);
if (inready() < 0) {
    print("kbdinit:␣can't␣read␣ccc\n");
    ccc = 0;
}
else
    ccc = inb(Data);
/* enable kbd xfers and interrupts */
/* disable mouse */
ccc &= ~Ckbddis;
ccc |= Csf | Ckbdint | Cscs1;
if (outready() < 0)
    print("kbd␣init␣failed\n");
outb(Cmd, #60);
if (outready() < 0)
    print("kbd␣init␣failed\n");
outb(Data, ccc);
outready();
}
```

15.3.2   Handling a Keyboard Interrupt

Now we turn to the meat of the keyboard driver: the interrupt handler. In the previous function, we enable interrupts to be generated for each keyboard event (press or release), and elsewhere we arrange for those interrupts to call this function. This function, as most interrupt handlers do, ignores its arguments. The first argument is a pointer to a structure containing the interrupted process's registers in case the handler needs access to them. The second argument is a data value defined when the handler is registered. This allows the same handler function to be associated with more than one interrupt and for it to be able to tell which interrupt caused it to be called.

```
/* keyboard interrupt */
static void i8042intr(Ureg *, void *)
{
    int s, c, i;
    static int esc1, esc2;
    static int alt, caps, ctl, num, shift;
    static int collecting, nk;
    static Rune kc[5];
    int keyup;
```

It's possible to get interrupts for things other than keyboard events. So if we don't actually have input waiting on us, we ignore the interrupt. The lock variable, *i8042lock*, is global and is, therefore, shared by all threads that could execute this code.

```
/* get status */
lock(&i8042lock);
s = inb(Status);
if (¬(s & Inready)) {
    unlock(&i8042lock);
    return;
}
```

15.3.2.1   Fetching the Keycode

Now we retrieve the input from the controller. After we've done so, we can release the locks we have.

```
/* get the character */
c = inb(Data);
unlock(&i8042lock);
```

If this input comes from the mouse, then we put the byte into the input queue for the mouse driver; otherwise, we continue on to handle it as a real keyboard event.

```
/* if it's the aux port... */
if (s & Minready) {
    if (auxputc ≠ nil)
        auxputc(c, shift);
    return;
}
```

15.3.2.2   Handling Composite Character Escapes

The values $E0_{16}$ and $E1_{16}$ are used as prefixes for multibyte character values. These values are used for keys like Page Up and not for ASCII characters.

```
/* e0's is the first of a 2 character sequence */
if (c ≡ #e0) {
    esc1 = 1;
    return;
}
else if (c ≡ #e1) {
    esc2 = 2;
    return;
}
```

15.3.2.3   Differentiating Key Press and Release

If the most significant bit of the input byte is set, then the event is a key release. The lower seven bits indicate the scan code for either the press or the release. (The scan code essentially indicates which physical key is being pressed or released.)

```
keyup = c & #80;
c &= #7f;
if (c > sizeof kbtab) {
    c |= keyup;
    if (c ≠ #FF)        /* these come fairly often: CAPSLOCK U Y */
        print("unknown key %ux\n", c);
    return;
}
```

15.3.2.4   Translating Keycode to Character

Now we use the tables defined earlier to convert the keycode to the ASCII character that we want for that key. Notice that we use the *shift* state variable to determine which array we look into.

```
if (esc1) {
    c = kbtabesc1[c];
    esc1 = 0;
}
else if (esc2) {
    esc2 --;
    return;
}
else if (shift)
    c = kbtabshift[c];
else
    c = kbtab[c];
if (caps ∧ c ≤ 'z' ∧ c ≥ 'a')
    c += 'A' − 'a';
```

15.3.2.5   Handling Modifiers

For normal characters, we care only about the press of a key. For the modifier keys like Shift and Control, however, we need to know whether the key is currently pressed. So for these, we care about releases as well as presses.

```
/* keyup only important for shifts */
if (keyup) {
    switch (c) {
    case Latin:
```

```
        alt = 0;
        break;
    case Shift:
        shift = 0;
        mouseshifted = 0;
        break;
    case Ctrl:
        ctl = 0;
        break;
    }
    return;
}
```

15.3.2.6   Sending the Character Back

For the most part, for regular keys, we just put them into the queue to be picked up by
the function that handles read requests. This function is part of the machine-independent
console device driver. There are a few special cases we need to handle. If the Control key
is pressed, then we keep only the bottom five bits of the character. Of course, we follow
convention and treat the Ctrl-Alt-Delete combination specially. Just as the standard
library function *exit*( ) transfers control back to the code that started running the program,
the call to *exit*( ) here transfers control back to the bootstrapping code that started the
kernel. Such bootstrapping code normally restarts or halts the computer in such a case.
Finally, if the press is of a modifier, then we flip the appropriate state variable.

```
if (¬(c & (Spec | KF))) {
    if (ctl) {
        if (alt ∧ c ≡ Del)
            exit(0);
        c &= #1f;
    }
    if (¬collecting) {
        kbdputc(kbdq, c);
        return;
    }
    kc[nk++] = c;
    c = latin1(kc, nk);
    if (c < -1)      /* need more keystrokes */
        return;
    if (c ≠ -1)      /* valid sequence */
        kbdputc(kbdq, c);
    else      /* dump characters */
        for (i = 0; i < nk; i++)
            kbdputc(kbdq, kc[i]);
```

```
        nk = 0;
        collecting = 0;
        return;
    }
    else {
      switch (c) {
      case Caps:
        caps ⊕= 1;
        return;
      case Num:
        num ⊕= 1;
        return;
      case Shift:
        shift = 1;
        mouseshifted = 1;
        return;
      case Latin:
        alt = 1;
        if (¬ctl) {
          collecting = 1;
          nk = 0;
        }
        return;
      case Ctrl:
        collecting = 0;
        nk = 0;
        ctl = 1;
        return;
      }
    }
    kbdputc(kbdq, c);
  }
```

At this point, we have passed the character just typed to *kbdputc( )*. This function handles echoing the character to the screen and adds the character to a queue. Input editing is done by the console driver's read function when an application reads from the keyboard device.

15.4   IDE Disk Support

Our final device driver in this chapter is the Integrated Device Electronics (IDE) disk driver. Although the code we show in this section is more extensive than the other two drivers in this chapter, don't let this be misleading. The details of programming the

device are indeed more complex than those for the keyboard. However, the code we
haven't shown for the rest of the console device is nearly as complex as the overall disk
driver. This is typical. The components of a system that interact with human users
are often more complex than those that interact strictly with mechanical and electronic
devices.

We find the code for this driver in **os/pc/sdata.c**. The first thing we examine here is
the method we use to manage multiple controllers. The IDE controller design supports
up to two drives per controller, so to support more than two drives, we need to support
multiple controllers. These structures are initialized by a probing process that attempts to
write to standard controller addresses and see whether the presumed controller responds
as expected. If so, then we believe that there is a controller there, and we initialize one
of these structures for it.

```
typedef struct Ctlr {
    int cmdport;
    int ctlport;
    int irq;
    int tbdf;
    int bmiba;        /* bus master interface base address */
    Pcidev *pcidev;
    void (*ienable)(Ctlr *);
    void (*idisable)(Ctlr *);
    SDev *sdev;
    Drive *drive[2];
    Prd *prdt;        /* physical region descriptor table */
    void *prdtbase;
    QLock;        /* current command */
    Drive *curdrive;
    int command;        /* last command issued (debugging) */
    Rendez;
    int done;
    Lock;        /* register access */
} Ctlr;
```

Several members of this structure are of particular interest in the following code. First,
the two members *cmdport* and *ctlport* are used to hold the I/O port numbers we use to
communicate with the controller. The array *drive* holds pointers to up to two structures,
each of which describes an attached drive. The reason we have an array of two elements
for the drives is that the IDE controller specification allows only up to two drives per
controller. It also specifies that only one drive can be active at once, so we use the
member *curdrive* to keep track of which drive is currently active.

15.4.1   *Processing an I/O Request*

The IDE driver is part of the more general storage device support in Inferno. Requests get passed through most of the levels of abstraction for storage devices in terms of SCSI commands. We pick up with the function *atagenio*( ), which gets called after we know the drive for which the request has been issued and that it is an IDE drive. Here, we translate a SCSI command structure to the command parameters we need to talk directly to an IDE controller.

```
static int atagenio(Drive *drive, uchar *cmd, int)
{
    uchar *p;
    Ctlr *ctlr;
    int count, max;
    vlong lba, len;
    if ((cmd[1] ≫ 5) ∧ cmd[0] ≠ #12)
        return atasetsense(drive, SDcheck, #05, #25, 0);
```

15.4.1.1   *Interpreting a SCSI Command Message*

We are focusing on the read and write operations that make up most of our use of these devices. Therefore, we will skip over this **switch** statement, which handles most of the rest of the SCSI commands.

```
    switch (cmd[0]) {
    default:
        return atasetsense(drive, SDcheck, #05, #20, 0);
    case #00:      /* test unit ready */
        return SDok;
    case #03:      /* request sense */
        ...
        return SDok;
    case #12:      /* inquiry */
        ...
        return SDok;
    case #1B:      /* start/stop unit */
        /* NOP for now, can use the power management feature set later. */
        return SDok;
    case #25:      /* read capacity */
        ...
        return SDok;
    case #9E:      /* long read capacity */
        ...
        return SDok;
    case #28:      /* read */
```

```
case #2A:      /* write */
  break;
case #5A:
  return atamodesense(drive, cmd);
}
```

15.4.1.2 Extracting Request Parameters

We get here for read and for write requests. Our first task is extracting out of the SCSI command string the actual parameters. This extraction mostly takes the form of pasting individual bytes together into integers of various sizes.

```
ctlr = drive→ctlr;
lba = (cmd[2] ≪ 24) | (cmd[3] ≪ 16) | (cmd[4] ≪ 8) | cmd[5];
count = (cmd[7] ≪ 8) | cmd[8];
if (drive→data ≡ nil)
  return SDok;
if (drive→dlen < count * drive→secsize)
  count = drive→dlen/drive→secsize;
```

We don't want anyone else touching our control structures while we're working. As mentioned earlier, this lock also provides for queueing of any outstanding requests.

```
qlock(ctlr);
```

15.4.1.3 Processing the Request in Parts

Although the upper levels of abstraction can request that a very large number of sectors be transferred, the controller has a more strict limit on the number of sectors that can be transferred in one request. The exact limit depends on which version of the IDE specification this controller uses.

```
while (count) {
  max = (drive→flags & Lba48) ? 65536 : 256;
  if (count > max)
    drive→count = max;
  else
    drive→count = count;
```

This call to *atageniostart( )* is where we actually write to the controller registers to make things happen. If something goes wrong, we clean up and retry.

```
if (atageniostart(drive, lba)) {
  ilock(ctlr);
  atanop(drive, 0);
  iunlock(ctlr);
```

```
        qunlock(ctlr);
        return atagenioretry(drive);
    }
```

Next, we set the point that we come back to if an error occurs along the way, using the *waserror*( ) operation we first encountered in Section 3.4.3.

```
    while (waserror())
        ;
```

15.4.1.4 Processing the Next Part

Now we wait for the request to complete. If it hasn't done so in 30 seconds, then the controller won't show that we're done, and we'll attempt resetting the controller and retrying the operation.

```
        tsleep(ctlr, atadone, ctlr, 30 * 1000);
        poperror();
        if (¬ctlr→done) {
            atadumpstate(drive, cmd, lba, count);
            ataabort(drive, 1);
            qunlock(ctlr);
            return atagenioretry(drive);
        }
```

If the controller did not detect an error, then we can move ahead to the next set of sectors.

```
        if (drive→status & Err) {
            qunlock(ctlr);
            return atasetsense(drive, SDcheck, 4, 8, drive→error);
        }
        count -= drive→count;
        lba += drive→count;
    }
```

Now we're done with the loop, which means that we're finished with all sectors of the transfer. Consequently, we can unlock the data structures and return with an indication of success.

```
        qunlock(ctlr);
        return SDok;
    }
```

15.4.2   Initiating an IDE Controller Operation

The *atageniostart*( ) function is responsible for communicating with the controller and
setting up the actual transfer.

> **static int** *atageniostart*(**Drive** *∗drive*, **vlong** *lba*)
> {
>   **Ctlr** *∗ctlr*;
>   **uchar** *cmd*;
>   **int** *as*, *c*, *cmdport*, *ctlport*, *h*, *len*, *s*, *use48*;

15.4.2.1   Setting Transfer Parameters

The original IBM PC/AT disk interface (on which the IDE design is based) was designed
at a time when a typical small computer disk drive held about 20 MB of data. Today,
one can purchase drives off the shelf at a local discount store with capacities in excess
of 100 GB. With a 5000-to-1 ratio like that, it should be no surprise that the details of the
interface specification have changed over the years. There are currently three ways we can
specify which disk block we're accessing, and because most of the controller electronics
are contained on the drive itself, each drive may use a different method. The original
method for specifying a block involved identifying which cylinder, which head, and which
sector within the track is required. In total, there are 28 bits used to specify the cylinder,
head, and sector. Because the number of bits allocated to each of the three geometric
parameters didn't match the way drive capacities grew, a new form of addressing called
large block addressing (LBA) was specified, wherein all 28 bits are used to specify an
absolute block number. With LBA, it is up to the drive to determine where a particular
block is located. Even with 28 bits, however, a drive can only access $2^{28} \times 512$ bytes,
or about 128 GB. (Each disk block typically contains 512 bytes.) The newest standard
specifies a 48-bit number for the block address, allowing disks beyond this limit. With
this number of bits, we can now address 128 PB of data. (A PB is approximately 10^{15}
bytes.) The first of these cases we handle is the last one, where we have a 48-bit block
address. We just flag this case and work from the *lba* variable when it comes time to
program the controller.

> *use48* = 0;
> **if** ((*drive–flags* & *Lba48always*) ∨ (*lba* ≫ 28) ∨ *drive–count* > 256) {
>   **if** (¬(*drive–flags* & *Lba48*))
>   **return** −1;
>   *use48* = 1;
>   *c* = *h* = *s* = 0;
> }

The second case is 28-bit LBA addressing. Here, we split the bits of the block address into
the values we program into the registers used for the cylinder number, the head number,
and the sector number in the old-style addressing scheme. The high-order four bits go

into the head number, the low-order eight bits are programmed into the sector register, and the middle 16 bits are stored where the cylinder would be.

> **else if** (*drive⁻dev* & *Lba*) {
>   *c* = (*lba* ≫ 8) & #FFFF;
>   *h* = (*lba* ≫ 24) & #0F;
>   *s* = *lba* & #FF;
> }

In the last case, we determine the proper cylinder, head, and sector that correspond to the requested block number. We lay consecutive sectors along a single track. When we run out of a track, we move to the next head in the same cylinder and fill that track. Upon hitting the end of the last track of a cylinder, we move to the next cylinder. Thus, the cylinder number is the block number divided by the number of blocks per cylinder. The head number is the block number divided by the number of sectors per track modulo the number of heads. Finally, the sector number is the block number modulo the number of sectors per track.

> **else** {
>   *c* = *lba*/(*drive⁻s* * *drive⁻h*);
>   *h* = ((*lba*/*drive⁻s*) % *drive⁻h*);
>   *s* = (*lba* % *drive⁻s*) + 1;
> }

15.4.2.2   Waiting for a Quiescent Controller

Now that we have the variations in specifying the block number sorted out, we need to make sure that the controller is ready for us to give it a command.

> *ctlr* = *drive⁻ctlr*;
> *cmdport* = *ctlr⁻cmdport*;
> *ctlport* = *ctlr⁻ctlport*;
> **if** (*ataready*(*cmdport*, *ctlport*, *drive⁻dev*, *Bsy* | *Drq*, 0, 101 * 1000) < 0)
>   **return** −1;

15.4.2.3   Setting Up Controller Command

The next step is determining which command we're going to send the controller. This command not only depends on whether we're reading or writing, but also on some of the capabilities of the controller. We want to take advantage of those controllers that can do direct memory access (DMA) as well as those that can work with multiple sectors.

> *ilock*(*ctlr*);
> **if** (*drive⁻dmactl* ∧ ¬*atadmasetup*(*drive*, *drive⁻count* * *drive⁻secsize*)) {
>   **if** (*drive⁻write*)
>   *drive⁻command* = *Cwd*;

```
        else
            drive→command = Crd;
    }
    else if (drive→rwmctl) {
        drive→block = drive→rwm * drive→secsize;
        if (drive→write)
            drive→command = Cwsm;
        else
            drive→command = Crsm;
    }
    else {
        drive→block = drive→secsize;
        if (drive→write)
            drive→command = Cws;
        else
            drive→command = Crs;
    }
    drive→limit = drive→data + drive→count * drive→secsize;
    cmd = drive→command;
```

15.4.2.4 Programming the Controller

We have now arrived at the heart of the driver, the controller programming. The drives
that use LBA48 use a little different programming scheme than those using the earlier
methods. When using LBA48, we write two bytes in a row to each of the geometry
registers, whereas in the other cases, we write one byte to each register. Also notice
that the last thing we write is the command. The act of writing the command register
triggers the controller to execute the command using the parameters that have already
been written into the other registers.

```
    if (use48) {
        outb(cmdport + Count, (drive→count >> 8) & #FF);
        outb(cmdport + Count, drive→count & #FF);
        outb(cmdport + Lbalo, (lba >> 24) & #FF);
        outb(cmdport + Lbalo, lba & #FF);
        outb(cmdport + Lbamid, (lba >> 32) & #FF);
        outb(cmdport + Lbamid, (lba >> 8) & #FF);
        outb(cmdport + Lbahi, (lba >> 40) & #FF);
        outb(cmdport + Lbahi, (lba >> 16) & #FF);
        outb(cmdport + Dh, drive→dev | Lba);
        cmd = cmd48[cmd];
        if (DEBUG & Dbg48BIT)
            print("using␣48-bit␣commands\n");
    }
```

```
    else {
        outb(cmdport + Count, drive→count);
        outb(cmdport + Sector, s);
        outb(cmdport + Cyllo, c);
        outb(cmdport + Cylhi, c ≫ 8);
        outb(cmdport + Dh, drive→dev | h);
    }
    ctlr→done = 0;
    ctlr→curdrive = drive;
    ctlr→command = drive→command;        /* debugging */
    outb(cmdport + Command, cmd);
```

If we are reading without DMA, then we've done everything we need to initiate the transfer. However, if we are doing DMA, then we need to start the DMA controller. Similarly, if we are writing to the drive without DMA, then we need to start the ball rolling by copying the first block of data to the controller.

```
    switch (drive→command) {
    case Cws:
    case Cwsm:
        microdelay(1);
        as = ataready(cmdport, ctlport, 0, Bsy, Drq | Err, 1000);
        if (as < 0 ∨ (as & Err)) {
            iunlock(ctlr);
            return −1;
        }
        len = drive→block;
        if (drive→data + len > drive→limit)
            len = drive→limit − drive→data;
        outss(cmdport + Data, drive→data, len/2);
        break;
    case Crd:
    case Cwd:
        atadmastart(ctlr, drive→write);
        break;
    }
```

We are now done programming the controller to carry out the read or write. It's time to unlock the data structures and return. We have only initiated the read or write operation; no data have actually been transferred to or from the disk. This, of course, is the function of the controller.

```
    iunlock(ctlr);
    return 0;
}
```

15.4.3   Handling an IDE Controller Interrupt

Finally, we get to the ATA driver interrupt handler. In the context of the code we've been studying, we get here after a read or write request has been carried out. It's now time for us to handle the completion of that request. We could either be completely done with the overall transfer, or we have some more to transfer and need to set up another block.

```
static void atainterrupt ( Ureg *, void *arg )
{
    Ctlr *ctlr;
    Drive *drive;
    int cmdport, len, status;

    ctlr = arg;
    ilock(ctlr);
```

15.4.3.1   Checking for Error Conditions

Because we normally expect that we'll get an interrupt only when the controller has completed an operation, we'll just return if the controller is still busy. Although such spurious interrupts may be unexpected, good software design requires that we account for such cases.

```
    if (inb(ctlr→ctlport + As) & Bsy) {
        iunlock(ctlr);
        if (DEBUG & DbgBsy)
            print("IBsy+");
        return;
    }
```

Similarly, if we get here but we don't have a current drive, then something is definitely not right. We need to return immediately.

```
    cmdport = ctlr→cmdport;
    status = inb(cmdport + Status);
    if ((drive = ctlr→curdrive) ≡ nil) {
        iunlock(ctlr);
        if ((DEBUG & DbgINL) ∧ ctlr→command ≠ Cedd)
            print("Inil%2.2uX+", ctlr→command);
        return;
    }
```

If we get the interrupt because the controller detects an error rather than finishes a complete transfer, we want to retrieve the exact error from the controller and move on.

```
if (status & Err)
   drive→error = inb(cmdport + Error);
else
   switch (drive→command) {
   default:
      drive→error = Abrt;
      break;
```

15.4.3.2   Transferring the Data

If the current operation is a read without using DMA, then the controller has read the requested sector(s) into an internal buffer, and the next step is to copy that data from the controller's buffer into the requester's memory space.

```
case Crs:
case Crsm:
   if (¬(status & Drq)) {
      drive→error = Abrt;
      break;
   }
   len = drive→block;
   if (drive→data + len > drive→limit)
      len = drive→limit − drive→data;
   inss(cmdport + Data, drive→data, len/2);
   drive→data += len;
   if (drive→data ≥ drive→limit)
      ctlr→done = 1;
   break;
```

On the other hand, if we're doing a write, then the interrupt means that the controller has finished writing the sector(s) in its buffer to the disk. If we still have any sectors left to write, then we can load up another buffer's worth.

```
case Cws:
case Cwsm:
   len = drive→block;
   if (drive→data + len > drive→limit)
      len = drive→limit − drive→data;
   drive→data += len;
   if (drive→data ≥ drive→limit) {
      ctlr→done = 1;
      break;
   }
   if (¬(status & Drq)) {
      drive→error = Abrt;
```

```
        break;
    }
    len = drive→block;
    if (drive→data + len > drive→limit)
        len = drive→limit − drive→data;
    outss(cmdport + Data, drive→data, len/2);
    break;
case Cpkt:
    atapktinterrupt(drive);
    break;
```

These two cases represent the cases where the current operation is a read or write using DMA. In those cases, we don't have to programmatically transfer the data, so our interrupt handling is primarily a matter of programming the DMA controller for the next transfer.

```
    case Crd:
    case Cwd:
        atadmainterrupt(drive, drive→count * drive→secsize);
        break;
    case Cstandby:
        ctlr→done = 1;
        break;
    }
    iunlock(ctlr);
    if (drive→error) {
        status |= Err;
        ctlr→done = 1;
    }
```

15.4.3.3 Waking Up the Driver

If the controller is successful with the requested transfer, then we can wake the driver up from the *tsleep*( ) where it waits for the operation to complete.

```
    if (ctlr→done) {
        ctlr→curdrive = nil;
        drive→status = status;
        wakeup(ctlr);
    }
}
```

At this point, the handling of the interrupt is complete. If another transfer has been started, then the system returns to running user processes until the controller generates another interrupt for the new transfer. Otherwise, the thread of control that initiated the original transfer is awakened to get the results.

15.5   Summary

The general structure of device drivers in native implementations of Inferno is a little unconventional. These drivers accept requests, program controllers, and handle interrupts, but they do not maintain their own request queues. Unlike drivers in most systems, drivers in Inferno are implemented as servers, accepting Styx requests. In this chapter, we consider elements of three driver examples, including support for the parallel port, for the keyboard, and for IDE disk drives.

15.6   Exercises

1. What is the maximum number of keys (not counting function keys) that can be supported on a keyboard on an IBM-compatible machine?

2. In the extended binary coded decimal interchange code (EBCDIC), the letters are not contiguous (for example, there are character values between the letters "i" and "j"). However, the difference between an uppercase letter and the corresponding lowercase one is still a constant. Would the technique for handling the Caps Lock, used in *i8042intr*( ), still work for EBCDIC? Why or why not?

3. How many bits are used to specify the sector count for transfers when using LBA48? How many are used in the cases of LBA or cylinder-head-sector addressing?

4. Using old-style cylinder-head-sector addressing, consider a disk with 1024 cylinders, 4 two-sided platters, and 34 sectors per track. What is the total number of sectors on this disk? What are the cylinder, head, and sector number corresponding to block number 100,000?

5. In the calls to *outss*( ) and *inss*( ), the final argument is $len/2$. If there are *len* bytes that need to be transferred, is it a mistake to divide it by two? Why or why not? (This question is best answered by locating the definition of *inss*( ) in the Inferno source code.)

6. In *outch*( ), while waiting for the port to become ready, we don't enable interrupts for the first 10 tries at 1 mS each. Why not just start directly sleeping 100 mS at a time and let an interrupt wake us up?

7. At the beginning of *kbdinit*( ), we wait for the controller to be ready to receive commands. There is no fail-safe condition. In particular, if the controller never becomes ready, we are stuck in an infinite loop. Is this a problem? Why or why not?

8. How would you add disk arm scheduling, such as with the Elevator Algorithm, to Inferno? Think about how the queueing of requests is handled, and design a mechanism that would allow for an ordering other than FIFO.

9. Extend the functionality of the console device file server to include a zero device. The code for this server is in **emu/port/devcons.c**. The zero device should be served on the file /dev/zero. Its function is similar to both the null and the random devices. When writing to it, it should accept any data successfully, but should discard that data. When reading from it, it should return a buffer full of bytes with the integer value 0.

10. As in Exercise 9, extend the functionality of the console device file server to include a procq device. When a process reads from this new device file, it should get back two numbers separated by a space. The first number should be the count of the number of processes in the full process list, and the second should be the number in the ready queue.

11. For native Inferno only: Modify the keyboard driver to allow the user to select between two different keyboard mappings. Use the Ctrl-Alt-Insert sequence to switch between them. Use the Dvorak keyboard layout as the alternative mapping.

Chapter 16

I/O Devices in Linux

In this chapter, we take a look at the way Linux handles device management responsibilities. Because even simple device drivers in Linux involve a substantial amount of code, we cover only the highlights in this chapter. In keeping with the focus we present in Chapter 13, we primarily discuss the general organization and structure of Linux device drivers, and we explore some details of device interaction. We begin with a look at a portion of the I/O subsystem that supports many of the block devices, and then we examine the two-part design of interrupt handlers. The remainder of this chapter is devoted to an examination of portions of an example of a character device and an example of a block device. Although nearly all Linux device drivers can be compiled as dynamically loadable modules, we do not discuss the details of module design and implementation here.

16.1 Block Request Support

Because most of the details of managing I/O requests for block devices are independent of the device, Linux abstracts those details out of the block device drivers into a **block I/O layer**. This layer provides two primary areas of support. First, it provides functions that manage request queues. Requests of type **struct request** are added to a queue by the file system. They are then broken down into one or more structures of type **struct bio**. Each of these structures represents one I/O operation. Block device drivers specify a function to be called each time there is a block I/O operation that becomes available for processing. This happens when a new request is added to an empty queue and when a request has been completed and is removed from the queue. As we see in Section 16.4, this callback function is the starting point for the driver's work in processing requests.

The second major area of block request support is a set of **I/O schedulers**. Linux supports several variations on the elevator algorithm, as discussed in Section 13.7.3:

- *Noop scheduler*: As its name implies, this scheduler does not really do any meaningful seek optimization. It does, however, merge adjacent requests. When a request is added to the queue and that request accesses sectors adjacent to those accessed by a request already in the queue, the two requests are combined into a single request.

- *Deadline scheduler*: This scheduler is a variation on the Linus elevator scheduler found in the older 2.4 versions of Linux. It merges requests as in the noop scheduler and maintains three queues: one that contains all read requests in first-in, first-out (FIFO) order, one that contains all write requests in FIFO order, and one that contains all requests sorted according to the criteria of the Linus elevator. In the sorted queue (and in the Linus elevator), new requests are inserted into the queue, sorted by sector number. However, if the queue contains any request that is old enough, then all new requests are inserted at the tail of the queue until the old requests have been serviced. This last condition prevents requests from starving.

  When being inserted, each request has an expiration time attached. For read requests, this expiration time is 500 mS from the time of insertion, and for write requests, it is five seconds from the time of insertion. Unless the requests at the heads of the read or write queues have expired, the scheduler takes requests from the sorted queue as the driver becomes available to handle them. However, if there are expired requests on either of the other queues, they are processed until there are no more expired requests in the queues. The expiration times are selected to give preference to reads over writes. The reason for this is that processes must block until reads are completed. However, writes are buffered so that processes may continue while the write request is handled at a later time.

- *Anticipatory scheduler*: The anticipatory scheduler is a variation of the deadline scheduler. It recognizes that when we service a request from an application and then return to that application, there is a good chance it will issue another request for nearby sectors very soon. This scheduler then introduces a delay of a few milliseconds (by default, six) at the end of each request service. If another request arrives for the same area of the disk in that time, it is handled immediately. Otherwise, the delay expires and the scheduler goes back to processing the queues normally.

- *Complete fair queuing scheduler*: This scheduler maintains a separate queue per process. Requests are merged and inserted in order of sector number. It schedules among the queues in round-robin order, taking a configurable number of requests from each queue. By default, it processes up to four requests from a process's queue before moving on to the next. In this way, no single process can starve other processes of disk access.

At the time the system is initialized, one of these I/O schedulers is selected for use for all block I/O layer activities. This selection is not changed while the system is running.

16.2   Two-Half Interrupt Handler Structure

Particularly in block device drivers in Linux, the functionality we describe as the upper half in Section 13.6, and illustrated in Figure 13-4, is largely handled by the block I/O layer.

Most of the functionality in the device driver itself is lower half functionality. However, in Linux, interrupt handlers are themselves designed in two halves, referred to as the top half and the bottom half. The top half is the part invoked directly by the interrupt. It does a minimum of work to acknowledge the interrupt in the hardware and to retrieve the controller status. The top half then schedules the bottom half to run at some later time. This deferred bottom half code handles the rest of the work of the interrupt handler. This choice of terminology might seem odd in view of our placing the interrupt handler in the lower half of our generic overall driver design. However, it does make sense from a layered design point of view. In particular, the top half depends on the bottom half in the sense that it causes the lower half code to run, much as if it had been run by a function call. Figure 16-1 illustrates the complete device driver structure for block devices.

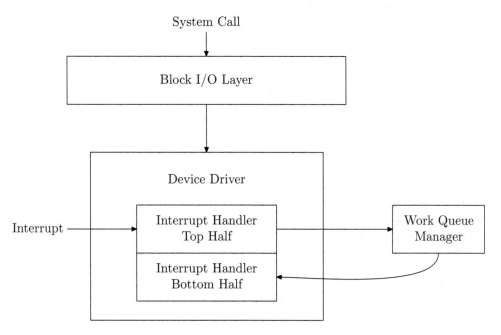

Figure 16-1: Linux Device Driver Structure

There are three mechanisms in the version 2.6 kernel design for running these bottom halves. The first are soft interrupt requests, often called **softirqs**. At various points in time, the kernel checks to see if any softirqs need to be handled, and it calls the appropriate handler. The set of available softirqs is limited and established at compile time. One of the softirqs is itself the manager for the second type of deferred function, the **tasklet**. The third mechanism is the **work queue**. For both tasklets and work queues, any driver can declare, either at compile time or at run time, the appropriate function to be executed later. The floppy disk driver (discussed in Section 16.4) illustrates the use of work queues in driver design.

16.3   Parallel Port Driver

We begin by looking at a relatively simple character driver, namely the parallel port driver. Printer ports on PCs have evolved from simple devices that pass data in only one direction with relatively simple control signals to more complex devices that can transfer data both into and out of the system. These various behaviors have been standardized in the IEEE 1284 standard, which specifies a number of different operating modes. The behavior of this driver can get quite complex when supporting various bidirectional modes. To keep the discussion manageable, we restrict ourselves to the case where the hardware operates as that on the original IBM-compatible machines. This, in part, means that we examine only output, as the original hardware could not directly be used for input. This behavior is called the **compatibility mode** in the IEEE 1284 standard.

16.3.1   Handling the System Call

When an application issues a *write*( ) system call on a file descriptor attached to a parallel port, the *lp_write*( ) function of the driver gets called. It takes as arguments a pointer to a structure that describes the open file, a pointer to the data in the user process's memory space, and a count giving the number of bytes to write. The source code for this function is found in drivers/char/lp.c.

```
static ssize_t lp_write(struct file *file, const char __user *buf, size_t count,
    loff_t *ppos)
{
    unsigned int minor = iminor(file→f_dentry→d_inode);
    struct parport *port = lp_table[minor].dev→port;
    char *kbuf = lp_table[minor].lp_buffer;
    ssize_t retv = 0;
    ssize_t written;
    size_t copy_size = count;
    int nonblock = ((file→f_flags & O_NONBLOCK) ∨ (LP_F(minor) & LP_ABORT));
```

16.3.1.1   Preparing to Service the Request

The first step is limiting the size of the operation to that of the available buffer. This size is set to the same as the size of a page. We break the request into a series of write operations, each one page in size.

```
    if (copy_size > LP_BUFFER_SIZE)
        copy_size = LP_BUFFER_SIZE;
```

Because we're about to manipulate the data structures for this port, we want to gain exclusive access to them. The mutual exclusion lock used for this is a binary semaphore. After we successfully gain the lock, any exit from this function goes through the unlock code at the end.

```
if (down_interruptible(&lp_table[minor].port_mutex))
    return −EINTR;
```

16.3.1.2   Fetching the Data for the Write

Now we copy the data from the user process's memory space into our own buffer. There are a couple of reasons for this. First, it makes us immune to whether this process's memory space is mapped into the kernel's memory space. After copying the data to the kernel's own memory space, we can then access it without needing to manipulate the memory management hardware. Second, after we've made a copy of the data, the page that contains the original data can be safely swapped out without affecting our ability to carry out the request.

```
if (copy_from_user(kbuf, buf, copy_size)) {
    retv = −EFAULT;
    goto out_unlock;
}
```

16.3.1.3   Setting Up the Hardware

At this point, we want to gain exclusive access to the hardware port. If multiple threads of control attempt to access the port simultaneously, they can interfere with each other and cause the port to function improperly.

```
lp_claim_parport_or_block(&lp_table[minor]);
```

This next call attempts to determine which of several modes is the proper one to use. To keep our discussion focused on general driver techniques, we assume that the port operates in compatibility mode, where it behaves like the original parallel port hardware.

```
lp_table[minor].current_mode = lp_negotiate(port, lp_table[minor].best_mode);
```

The last step in preparing to transfer data is setting a time out. If we attempt to write a byte to the port, but the hardware doesn't respond to that byte, we don't want to end up waiting forever.

```
parport_set_timeout(lp_table[minor].dev,
    (nonblock ? PARPORT_INACTIVITY_O_NONBLOCK : lp_table[minor].timeout));
```

When operating in compatibility mode, we need to check the port to determine if the controller is ready to receive output bytes. The call *lp_wait_ready*( ) loops checking the controller status until it indicates that the controller is ready to take output data.

```
if ((retv = lp_wait_ready(minor, nonblock)) ≡ 0)
```

16.3.1.4   Writing Pages of Data

This is where we call *parport_write( )* once for each page of output data. The underlying function is responsible for copying the bytes in the manner needed by the specific hardware on this port.

```
do {
    written = parport_write(port, kbuf, copy_size);
```

If anything was written, then we made some progress and we adjust the necessary counters and pointers by the number of bytes written.

```
if (written > 0) {
    copy_size −= written;
    count −= written;
    buf += written;
    retv += written;
}
```

If the requesting process received a signal while we were writing bytes to the port, then we stop and set our return value to indicate we were interrupted.

```
if (signal_pending(current)) {
    if (retv ≡ 0)
        retv = −EINTR;
    break;
}
```

16.3.1.5   Sharing Resources

If we wrote less than the full buffer, then we take that as an indication that we need to allow someone else to have access to the port if needed. We reset the port to compatibility mode first, and then give anyone else who's waiting on the port a chance to use it. After regaining control, we set the port back to the mode we were using.

```
if (copy_size > 0) {
    int error;

    parport_negotiate(lp_table[minor].dev→port, IEEE1284_MODE_COMPAT);
    lp_table[minor].current_mode = IEEE1284_MODE_COMPAT;
    error = lp_wait_ready(minor, nonblock);
    if (error) {
        if (retv ≡ 0)
            retv = error;
        break;
    }
    else if (nonblock) {
```

```
            if (retv ≡ 0)
                retv = −EAGAIN;
            break;
        }
        parport_yield_blocking(lp_table[minor].dev);
        lp_table[minor].current_mode = lp_negotiate(port,
            lp_table[minor].best_mode);
    }
```

We let the scheduler run if needed.

```
        else if (need_resched())
            schedule();
```

16.3.1.6   Fetching the Next Page

If that was not the last of the data we needed to write, we prepare to repeat the process by fetching up to another page from the process's memory space. We continue this as long as there's still data left to write.

```
    if (count) {
        copy_size = count;
        if (copy_size > LP_BUFFER_SIZE)
            copy_size = LP_BUFFER_SIZE;
        if (copy_from_user(kbuf, buf, copy_size)) {
            if (retv ≡ 0)
                retv = −EFAULT;
            break;
        }
    }
} while (count > 0);
```

16.3.1.7   Cleaning Up

If there's anyone waiting on the port, we release it because we're done.

```
    if (test_and_clear_bit(LP_PREEMPT_REQUEST, &lp_table[minor].bits)) {
        printk(KERN_INFO"lp%d␣releasing␣parport\n", minor);
        parport_negotiate(lp_table[minor].dev→port, IEEE1284_MODE_COMPAT);
        lp_table[minor].current_mode = IEEE1284_MODE_COMPAT;
        lp_release_parport(&lp_table[minor]);
    }
```

Before returning, we release the mutex lock on this port's data structure. Along the way, *retv* accumulated the total number of bytes written, unless we set it to an error value. This is the value we return back to the requesting process.

```
out_unlock:
  up(&lp_table[minor].port_mutex);
  return retv;
}
```

16.3.2   Selecting the Proper Low-Level Write

The next function we examine is *parport_write*( ), which is called from *lp_write*( ) to transfer data from our internal buffer to the controller. Its primary purpose is identifying and calling the function appropriate to the specific hardware and operating mode. It is found in drivers/parport/ieee1284.c.

```
ssize_t parport_write(struct parport *port, const void *buffer, size_t len)
{
```

The kernel can be built with or without support for the advanced modes. If it is built without such support, then we always call the function for compatibility mode.

```
#ifndef CONFIG_PARPORT_1284
  return port→ops→compat_write_data(port, buffer, len, 0);
#else
```

The general approach for the rest of the function is to set the function pointer *fn* to point to the appropriate function based on the mode. For each port, the *port→ops* structure contains pointers to the functions appropriate to that hardware.

```
ssize_t retval;
int mode = port→ieee1284.mode;
int addr = mode & IEEE1284_ADDR;
size_t (*fn)(struct parport *, const void *, size_t, int);
mode &= ~(IEEE1284_DEVICEID | IEEE1284_ADDR);
switch (mode) {
```

For two of the more basic modes, we always fall back on the compatibilty mode.

```
case IEEE1284_MODE_NIBBLE:
case IEEE1284_MODE_BYTE:
  parport_negotiate(port, IEEE1284_MODE_COMPAT);
```

Here, we have either fallen through to compatibility mode from the nibble or byte modes, or the port is directly set to compatibility mode. In either case, we set *fn* to point to the same compatibility function that we call if the kernel is compiled without the advance mode support.

```
case IEEE1284_MODE_COMPAT:
    DPRINTK(KERN_DEBUG"%s:␣Using␣compatibility␣mode\n", port→name);
    fn = port→ops→compat_write_data;
    break;
```

Each of the other modes is handled similarly. Because our focus is on the compatibility case, we don't examine them in detail.

```
case IEEE1284_MODE_EPP:
    DPRINTK(KERN_DEBUG"%s:␣Using␣EPP␣mode\n", port→name);
    if (addr) {
        fn = port→ops→epp_write_addr;
    }
    else {
        fn = port→ops→epp_write_data;
    }
    break;
case IEEE1284_MODE_EPPSWE:
    DPRINTK(KERN_DEBUG"%s:␣Using␣software-emulated␣EPP␣mode\n",
        port→name);
    if (addr) {
        fn = parport_ieee1284_epp_write_addr;
    }
    else {
        fn = parport_ieee1284_epp_write_data;
    }
    break;
case IEEE1284_MODE_ECP:
case IEEE1284_MODE_ECPRLE:
    DPRINTK(KERN_DEBUG"%s:␣Using␣ECP␣mode\n", port→name);
    if (addr) {
        fn = port→ops→ecp_write_addr;
    }
    else {
        fn = port→ops→ecp_write_data;
    }
    break;
case IEEE1284_MODE_ECPSWE:
    DPRINTK(KERN_DEBUG"%s:␣Using␣software-emulated␣ECP␣mode\n",
        port→name);
    if (addr) {
        fn = parport_ieee1284_ecp_write_addr;
    }
    else {
```

```
        fn = parport_ieee1284_ecp_write_data;
      }
      break;
    default:
      DPRINTK(KERN_DEBUG"%s:␣Unknown␣mode␣0x%02x\n", port→name,
        port→ieee1284.mode);
      return −ENOSYS;
    }
```

Finally, we call the function to which *fn* now points. Its return value gives us the number of bytes sucessfully written.

```
    retval = (*fn)(port, buffer, len, 0);
    DPRINTK(KERN_DEBUG"%s:␣wrote␣%d/%d␣bytes\n", port→name, retval, len);
    return retval;
  #endif
  }
```

16.3.3   Writing Bytes from the Buffer

In drivers/parport/parport_pc.c, the *compat_write_data* structure member is set to the function *parport_ieee1284_write_compat*( ). This function handles the details of writing to a parallel port in compatibility mode and is defined in drivers/parport/ieee1284_ops.c.

```
  size_t parport_ieee1284_write_compat(struct parport *port, const void *buffer,
    size_t len, int flags)
  {
    int no_irq = 1;
    ssize_t count = 0;
    const unsigned char *addr = buffer;
    unsigned char byte;
    struct pardevice *dev = port→physport→cad;
    unsigned char ctl = (PARPORT_CONTROL_SELECT | PARPORT_CONTROL_INIT);
```

16.3.3.1   Setting Up the Hardware

If we have an interrupt vector for this controller, then we turn interrupts on in the controller.

```
    if (port→irq ≠ PARPORT_IRQ_NONE) {
      parport_enable_irq(port);
      no_irq = 0;
    }
```

The next few lines make sure the port is set for output. In the case of hardware that can do only output, this is unnecessary but harmless.

> *port→physport→ieee1284 .phase* = `IEEE1284_PH_FWD_DATA`;
> *parport_write_control* (*port, ctl*);
> *parport_data_forward* (*port*);

16.3.3.2   *Processing the Buffer*

At this point, we are ready to start sending bytes out the port. This loop continues until we have written them all or until we encounter a reason to quit early.

> **while** (*count < len*) {
>   **unsigned long** *expire* = *jiffies* + *dev→timeout*;
>   **long** *wait* = *msecs_to_jiffies* (10);
>   **unsigned char** *mask* = (`PARPORT_STATUS_ERROR` | `PARPORT_STATUS_BUSY`);
>   **unsigned char** *val* = (`PARPORT_STATUS_ERROR` | `PARPORT_STATUS_BUSY`);

This inner loop waits until the device connected to the port is ready. If the device is a printer, then we might not be able to send it data because it's out of paper or because there's some error condition. When *parport_wait_peripheral*( ) returns 0, then we know that the device is neither busy nor showing an error condition. At that point, we can proceed to send a byte. Otherwise, we wait until the timeout value has expired.

>   **do** {
>   **if** (¬*parport_wait_peripheral* (*port, mask, val*))
>   **goto** *ready*;
>   **if** ((*parport_read_status* (*port*)
>   & (`PARPORT_STATUS_PAPEROUT` | `PARPORT_STATUS_SELECT`
> | `PARPORT_STATUS_ERROR`)) ≠ (`PARPORT_STATUS_SELECT`
> | `PARPORT_STATUS_ERROR`))
>   **goto** *stop*;
>   **if** (¬*time_before* (*jiffies, expire*))
>   **break**;
>   **if** (*count* ∧ *no_irq*) {
>   *parport_release* (*dev*);
>   *schedule_timeout_interruptible* (*wait*);
>   *parport_claim_or_block* (*dev*);
>   }
>   **else**
>   *parport_wait_event* (*port, wait*);
>   **if** (*signal_pending* (*current*))
>   **break**;
>   *wait* ∗= 2;
>   } **while** (*time_before* (*jiffies, expire*));

If we get to this point, it's because we waited until the time-out period expired without the device becoming ready. We have no choice but to give up. The following code is a little strange, however. We break out of the loop to exit unconditionally. Nevertheless, we still check to see if there is a signal pending. The only difference between a signal and no signal is whether we print a debugging message. If we broke out of the loop because of a signal rather than a time out, it is not an error condition.

```
if (signal_pending(current))
    break;
DPRINTK(KERN_DEBUG "%s:␣Timed␣out\n", port→name);
break;
```

16.3.3.3   Transmitting a Byte

The following short section of code is the heart of the parallel port driver. It is the code that actually transmits the byte out the port. The basic steps are:

1. Write the byte to the port.

2. Burn 1 μS in a tight loop.

3. Turn on the strobe signal.

4. Wait another μS.

5. Turn off the strobe signal.

6. Wait another μS.

```
ready:
    byte = *addr ++;
    parport_write_data(port, byte);
    udelay(1);
    parport_write_control(port, ctl | PARPORT_CONTROL_STROBE);
    udelay(1);
    parport_write_control(port, ctl);
    udelay(1);
    count ++;
```

16.3.3.4   Cleaning Up

Check to see if we need to give the CPU to another process.

```
    if (time_before(jiffies, expire))
        if (¬parport_yield_blocking(dev) ∧ need_resched())
            schedule();
}
```

We get here under several conditions. First, we can get here if we have successfully written all the bytes we are supposed to. Second, we can get here if we time out waiting on the device to become ready. Third, we can get here if the device showed some type of error that we know will not clear while we wait. In all cases, we mark the port as idle and return the number of bytes we successfully wrote.

> *stop*:
>   *port→physport→ieee1284*.*phase* = IEEE1284_PH_FWD_IDLE;
>   **return** *count*;
> }

16.3.3.5   *Writing Data to the Controller*

The symbol *parport_write_data* is defined to be *parport_pc_write_data* for IBM-compatible machines. In include/linux/parport_pc.h, this function is defined as follows. The one functional line of code just calls a function that executes the **out** instruction to write the data byte to the data port of the controller.

> **static __inline__ void** *parport_pc_write_data*(**struct parport** *∗p*,
>   **unsigned char** *d*)
> {
> #**ifdef** DEBUG_PARPORT
>   *printk*(KERN_DEBUG "parport_pc_write_data(%p,0x%02x)\n", *p*, *d*);
> #**endif**
>   *outb*(*d*, DATA(*p*));
> }

16.3.4   *Configuring the Controller*

There are a couple more functions we have used that illustrate typical control techniques.

16.3.4.1   *Enabling Interrupts*

The first of these enables interrupt generation in the controller. This is done by setting bit 4 (numbered from 0, the least significant bit) of the control register.

> **static __inline__ void** *parport_pc_enable_irq*(**struct parport** *∗p*)
> {
>   *__parport_pc_frob_control*(*p*, #10, #10);
> }

16.3.4.2 Setting the Port Direction

This one sets the parallel signals to be outputs. We set this mode by clearing bit 5 of the control register. For older controllers that don't support bidirectional modes, this bit is ignored.

```
static __inline__ void parport_pc_data_forward(struct parport *p)
{
    __parport_pc_frob_control(p, #20, #00);
}
```

16.3.4.3 Manipulating the Control Register

Both of these functions call *__parport_pc_frob_control*( ), which modifies the control register of the port described by the first argument. Bits of the second argument that are set are cleared in the new control register. Bits of the third argument that are set are complemented in the new control register. Adjustments are made to the value of the control register stored in the port structure. Although it's common to read the current value and adjust it, the parallel port controller does not support reading back the control register.

```
static __inline__ unsigned char __parport_pc_frob_control(struct parport *p,
    unsigned char mask, unsigned char val)
{
    struct parport_pc_private *priv = p→physport→private_data;
    unsigned char ctr = priv→ctr;
```

The next line does the actual updating. Anding the control register value with the one's complement of the mask clears the bits we want to turn off. Then, we take the exclusive or of the result with the third argument.

$$ctr = (ctr \mathbin{\&} \sim mask) \oplus val;$$

Some bits of the control register can't be written. We clear these bits before going further.

$$ctr \mathbin{\&}= priv\text{→}ctr\_writable;$$

Finally, we write the newly computed value to the controller's control register. We also save this value for future use and return the newly computed value.

```
    outb(ctr, CONTROL(p));
    priv→ctr = ctr;
    return ctr;
}
```

16.4   Floppy Disk Driver

The driver for the floppy disk is a good example of a driver that uses work queues to manage its activity. In this section, we examine parts of the driver that illustrate a number of details of managing such a device. We omit a number of details in the interest of focusing on organizational techniques in Linux device drivers and on techniques of controlling I/O devices. All of the code we discuss here is found in drivers/block/floppy.c.

Because the floppy driver makes use of the block I/O layer, it does not need to handle most upper half driver tasks and does not have entry points for all the system calls. However, it must inform the block I/O layer of the entry points it does have in some way. There are basically three mechanisms for doing this that interest us here. The first identifies the entry point for the driver's initialization function. This entry point is established by a definition in the driver source code. This definition depends heavily on features of the compiler and linker. Its result is placing a pointer to the initialization function into an array that is used during system initialization to initialize all built-in drivers. The second mechanism is setting up a structure with the entry points to a few functions handling operations like *open*( ), *close*( ), and *ioctl*( ). During initialization, drivers for disk drives identify these structures with the relevant major device number through calls to the block I/O layer. These structures give the block I/O layer the ability to call the right driver functions in response to those system calls. The final mechanism for connecting the driver and the block I/O layer addresses read and write operations. This is also handled during initialization. The driver creates a queue for managing outstanding requests. As part of the creation call, the driver passes the pointer to a function that is called whenever the block I/O layer adds a request to an empty queue. With this pointer, the block I/O layer is able to transfer control to the driver's read and write entry point.

16.4.1   Handling the Request

For the floppy driver, the initialization function associates the function *do_fd_request*( ) with the request queue. As mentioned earlier, it is called any time a request is added to an empty queue and any time a request is removed from a queue.

> **static void** *do_fd_request*(**request_queue_t** *∗q*)
> {

16.4.1.1   Checking for Errors

As usual, the first thing we do is check for errors. If the device hasn't been opened, the global variable *max_buffer_sectors* will not have been set. That makes a convenient test to determine whether we can allow any requests at all. Similarly, when the floppy driver opens a device and when it does certain initializations, it allocates the interrupt request (IRQ) and direct memory access (DMA) channel. At that time, it increments *usage_count*. If it is zero, then we don't have any currently active floppy devices.

> **if** (*max_buffer_sectors* ≡ 0) {
>   *printk*("VFS:␣do_fd_request␣called␣on␣non-open␣device\n");

```
        return;
    }
    if (usage_count ≡ 0) {
        printk("warning:␣usage␣count=0,␣current_req=%p␣exiting\n",
            current_req);
        printk("sect=%ld␣flags=%lx\n", (long) current_req→sector,
            current_req→flags);
        return;
    }
```

16.4.1.2 Passing On the Request

On the other hand, the controller might actually be currently busy handling another request. If we get called in that unexpected case, then we cannot handle the request either.

```
    if (test_bit(0, &fdc_busy)) {
        is_alive("do␣fd␣request,␣old␣request␣running");
        return;
    }
```

At this point, we know we can handle the request. To do so, we request a lock and call *process_fd_request*( ) to schedule the real processing.

```
        lock_fdc(MAXTIMEOUT, 0);
        process_fd_request();
        is_alive("do␣fd␣request");
    }
```

16.4.2 Scheduling the Floppy Operation

The main purpose of this function is setting up work to be run at some later time for processing the request. The function *schedule_bh*( ) is mostly a call to *schedule_work*( ), which queues the function *redo_fd_request*( ) to be run as soon as it is reasonable. The structure *rw_cont* contains a set of pointers to functions that are called for handling interrupts and errors that might occur during the handling of this request. It also contains a pointer to the function we will call when the request is completed.

```
    static void process_fd_request(void)
    {
        cont = &rw_cont;
        schedule_bh(redo_fd_request);
    }
```

16.4.3   Performing a Floppy Operation

Given our description of how control reaches this function, it might seem strange that it is named *redo_fd_request*( ). The reason for the name is that this is also the entry point, where control transfers if we need to retry a request. However, the name notwithstanding we run this code the first time we attempt to process the request.

```
static void redo_fd_request(void)
{
#define REPEAT { request_done(0); continue; }
    int drive;
    int tmp;
```

We'll record the current time so that we'll be able to tell later how long it's been since we started trying to process this request.

```
    lastredo = jiffies;
```

16.4.3.1   Scheduling the Floppy Motor Off

Contrary to what we might expect from the name, *floppy_off*( ) doesn't actually turn anything off directly. Instead, if the motor for the current drive is running, it sets an inactivity timer. If we don't cancel the timer due to activity on the drive, the callback function will turn the motor off when the timer expires. Of course, if *current_drive* doesn't identify a valid drive, we don't want to attempt to turn its motor off.

```
    if (current_drive < N_DRIVE)
        floppy_off(current_drive);
```

16.4.3.2   Cycling Through Outstanding Requests

Now we enter a loop that continually attempts to get a request and set it up for processing. If we are successful, we return directly from the body of the loop.

```
    for ( ; ; ) {
```

16.4.3.3   Getting a Request to Process

Here we check to see if the driver has a request it's currently processing. If not, then we lock the queue and get the next request. Notice that we're calling a function called *elv_next_request*( ) to retrieve the request. Although the name implies that the function uses an elevator algorithm, it is a little more involved than that. It calls on functions defined as part of the I/O scheduler that was invoked when the system was booted. With the exception of the noop scheduler, they do, in fact, use some variation on the elevator algorithm.

```
if (¬current_req) {
    struct request *req;

    spin_lock_irq(floppy_queue→queue_lock);
    req = elv_next_request(floppy_queue);
    spin_unlock_irq(floppy_queue→queue_lock);
```

If we didn't get a request back, the queue must be empty, and we can return the driver to an idle state. Otherwise, we'll set *current_req* to point to the new request.

```
    if (¬req) {
        do_floppy = Λ;
        unlock_fdc();
        return;
    }
    current_req = req;
}
```

16.4.3.4 Selecting the Drive

The call to *set_fdc()* identifies the controller we need to use for this request and sets the global variable *fdc* to point to its descriptive structure. Similarly, the call to *set_floppy()* sets the global variable *_floppy* to point to a structure describing the format of the floppy in the drive. This floppy type information identifies the disk's geometry as well as some other information necessary to properly program the controller.

```
    drive = (long) current_req→rq_disk→private_data;
    set_fdc(drive);
    reschedule_timeout(current_reqD, "redo␣fd␣request", 0);
    set_floppy(drive);
```

We'll set up the real command sequence for this operation later, but some intermediate calls require a valid command structure.

```
    raw_cmd = &default_raw_cmd;
    raw_cmd→flags = 0;
```

16.4.3.5 Starting the Motor

For simplicity, let us consider the case where the drive motor is already running. Then, *start_motor()* returns 0, and we fall through to the rest of the code. In the case where the motor is not already running, *start_motor()* starts a timer and returns 1. We return from the function at that time. However, when the timer expires, the function called is this one. We go back through the same code to get to this point, but of course, we already have a request to process. Then we call *start_motor()* again, and this time it returns 0, indicating that the motor is running.

> **if** (*start_motor* (*redo_fd_request*))
>   **return**;

16.4.3.6 Verifying the Correct Disk

The call to *disk_change*( ) queries the controller to determine if the floppy disk that was last in the drive has been removed. If it has, or if we have set a flag to act as though it has, then we repeat the loop. The main purpose of repeating the loop is resetting _floppy now that the old format information might not be valid.

> *disk_change* (*current_drive*);
> **if** (*test_bit* (*current_drive*, &*fake_change*) ∨ TESTF(FD_DISK_CHANGED)) {
>   DPRINT("disk␣absent␣or␣changed␣during␣operation\n");
>   REPEAT;
> }

If we don't have format information on the floppy currently in the drive, then we begin attempting to access the disk using different formats until we find one that works. We refer to this process as **probing** the disk.

> **if** (¬_floppy) {
>   **if** (¬probing) {
>   DRS→probed_format = 0;
>   **if** (next_valid_format( )) {
>   DPRINT("no␣autodetectable␣formats\n");
>   _floppy = Λ;
>   REPEAT;
>   }
>   }
>   probing = 1;
>   _floppy = floppy_type + DP→autodetect[DRS→probed_format];
> }
> **else**
>   probing = 0;

16.4.3.7 Preparing the Commands

Now we are ready to format the actual command bytes that need to be written to the controller. The call to *make_raw_rw_request*( ) determines the proper cylinder, head, and sector, and it puts those into the correct format for the controller registers.

> errors = &(current_req→errors);
> tmp = make_raw_rw_request( );
> **if** (tmp < 2) {
>   request_done (tmp);

```
        continue;
    }
```

Here we test to see if we need to shut the motor off and then immediately reset it to the value we have stored in our internal copy of the control register. This process is referred to as "twaddling" in the Linux source code. It is done here only in the case where we receive an interrupt and the status registers indicate that there is no data read at all.

```
    if (TESTF(FD_NEED_TWADDLE))
        twaddle( );
```

16.4.3.8   Scheduling the Command

Finally, we schedule the actual execution of the command using the normal work queues. The function we will momentarily run to carry out the request is *floppy_start*( ).

```
        schedule_bh(floppy_start);
        debugt("queue fd request");
        return;
    }
#undef REPEAT
}
```

16.4.4   Starting the Command

The function *floppy_start*( ) does not do very much itself. For our purposes, it simply calls *floppy_ready*( ). It is not called directly, but is placed on a work queue by *redo_fd_request*( ) just before returning back to its caller.

```
    static void floppy_start(void)
    {
        reschedule_timeout(current_reqD, "floppy start", 0);
        scandrives( );
        SETF(FD_DISK_NEWCHANGE);
        floppy_ready( );
    }
```

16.4.5   Preparing for the Data Transfer

This function checks to make sure that everything is ready for the request to be carried out and then calls the appropriate function to do so.

```
    static void floppy_ready(void)
    {
        CHECK_RESET;
```

16.4.5.1   Readying the Drive

Here we make sure that the motor is running. Notice that we use the same trick we did in *redo_fd_request( )*, where we let this function be called again after the motor has had time to spin up.

> **if** (*start_motor*(*floppy_ready*))
> > **return**;

Next, we set the data transfer rate. If it's not already set to the right value, then *fdc_dtr( )* starts a timer, which calls *floppy_read( )* when it expires.

> **if** (*fdc_dtr*( ))
> > **return**;

At this point, we should have taken care of any real disk changes that have taken place. However, sometimes we see the disk change line still showing a change. Twaddling the drive clears that line for some hardware.

> **if** ($\neg$(*raw_cmd*$\rightarrow$*flags* & FD_RAW_NO_MOTOR) $\wedge$ *disk_change*(*current_drive*)
> > $\wedge$ $\neg$DP$\rightarrow$*select_delay*)
> > *twaddle*( );

16.4.5.2   Handling Fake DMA

On architectures such as the Intel x86, DMA is restricted to certain areas of memory. Furthermore, the DMA controller used on IBM-compatible machines has additional limitations. If we are running on such a machine, then we check to see if we can do real DMA or if we need to fake it by doing DMA into an internal buffer and then copying the sector to the ultimate destination.

```
#ifdef fd_chose_dma_mode
    if ((raw_cmd→flags & FD_RAW_READ) ∨ (raw_cmd→flags & FD_RAW_WRITE)) {
        unsigned long flags = claim_dma_lock( );
        fd_chose_dma_mode(raw_cmd→kernel_data, raw_cmd→length);
        release_dma_lock(flags);
    }
#endif
```

16.4.5.3   Seeking to the Correct Cylinder

At this point, we are either on the right cylinder and can do the read or write operation, or we need to seek to the right cylinder. In the latter case, we call *seek_floppy( )*, which commands the controller to seek to the correct cylinder. When we get an interrupt indicating that the seek is completed, the interrupt handler then schedules *floppy_ready( )* again. When we get to this point in the code again, we are back to the former case and we call *setup_rw_floppy( )* to initiate the read or write operation.

```
if (raw_cmd→flags & (FD_RAW_NEED_SEEK | FD_RAW_NEED_DISK)) {
    perpendicular_mode( );
    fdc_specify( );
    seek_floppy( );
}
else {
    if ((raw_cmd→flags & FD_RAW_READ) ∨ (raw_cmd→flags & FD_RAW_WRITE))
        fdc_specify( );
    setup_rw_floppy( );
}
}
```

16.4.6 Programming the Controller

This function finally initiates the request. Before actually commanding the controller to start the operation, we set up the DMA transfer and the interrupt handler that will be called when the operation finishes.

```
static void setup_rw_floppy(void)
{
    int i, r, flags, dflags;
    unsigned long ready_date;
    timeout_fn function;

    flags = raw_cmd→flags;
```

Reads and writes are operations that result in interrupts. We distinguish between interrupting and noninterrupting operations later in the function.

```
if (flags & (FD_RAW_READ | FD_RAW_WRITE))
    flags |= FD_RAW_INTR;
```

16.4.6.1 Checking the Motor

Make sure we've given the motor long enough to spin up since we last turned it on. If we haven't yet, we set a timer that brings us back here either directly or indirectly through *floppy_start( )*.

```
if ((flags & FD_RAW_SPIN) ∧ ¬(flags & FD_RAW_NO_MOTOR)) {
    ready_date = DRS→spinup_date + DP→spinup;
    if (time_after(ready_date, jiffies + DP→select_delay)) {
        ready_date -= DP→select_delay;
        function = (timeout_fn) floppy_start;
    }
    else
        function = (timeout_fn) setup_rw_floppy;
```

```
      if (fd_wait_for_completion(ready_date, function))
         return;
}
```

16.4.6.2 Configuring for the Operation

Configure the DMA controller for this operation.

```
      dflags = DRS→flags;
      if ((flags & FD_RAW_READ) ∨ (flags & FD_RAW_WRITE))
         setup_DMA();
```

For reads and writes, we want our interrupts handled by *main_command_interrupt()*. (For some other operations, such as seeks, we have other handlers that are scheduled from the top half interrupt handler.)

```
      if (flags & FD_RAW_INTR)
         do_floppy = main_command_interrupt;
```

16.4.6.3 Programming the Controller

These next few lines are the ones that actually program the controller and initiate the operation. We merely cycle through the bytes of the command and write them to the appropriate controller registers one at a time. If we encounter an error trying to talk to the controller, there's not much we can do other than reset the controller and try again. Of course, if we have had too many errors, we have no choice but to give up.

```
      r = 0;
      for (i = 0; i < raw_cmd→cmd_count; i++)
         r |= output_byte(raw_cmd→cmd[i]);
      debugt("rw_command:␣");
      if (r) {
         cont→error();
         reset_fdc();
         return;
      }
```

We're done for now. If this is a noninterrupting operation, then we call the bottom half interrupt work function as if we had been interrupted. If it's an interrupting one (in particular, a read or write), then we start a timer to make sure we do get interrupted in the expected time frame.

```
      if (¬(flags & FD_RAW_INTR)) {
         inr = result();
         cont→interrupt();
      }
```

```
    else if (flags & FD_RAW_NEED_DISK)
        fd_watchdog();
}
```

16.4.7 Handling a Floppy Interrupt

Just before programming the controller in *setup_rw_floppy*( ), we set *do_floppy* to point
to *main_command_interrupt*( ). When the floppy controller issues an interrupt, the function *floppy_interrupt*( ) is executed. It shuts down the DMA operation, checks to make
sure that we got a meaningful interrupt, retrieves the results from the controller, and
schedules the function pointed to by *do_floppy* to be run later. In our case, that function
is *main_command_interrupt*( ), which deletes the watchdog timer and calls the interrupt
function for this operation. For reads and writes, that is *rw_interrupt*( ). After a significant amount of error checking, *rw_interrupt*( ) then calls the function identified as the
one to be run when the request is done. For read and write requests, that function is
request_done( ).

```
    static void request_done(int uptodate)
    {
        struct request_queue *q = floppy_queue;
        struct request *req = current_req;
        unsigned long flags;
        int block;
```

In case we were attempting to determine the floppy format, we turn off the probing flag.

```
        probing = 0;
        reschedule_timeout(MAXTIMEOUT, "request␣done␣%d", uptodate);
```

16.4.7.1 Checking for Spurious Interrupts

Just in case we get called with no current request active, we don't want to mess things
up by dereferencing null pointers and the like.

```
        if (¬req) {
            printk("floppy.c:␣no␣request␣in␣request_done\n");
            return;
        }
```

16.4.7.2 Checking Operation Success

We take *uptodate* ≡ 1 to mean that the transfer completed successfully and we can
wrap up this request. Otherwise, we have an error and we need to let the request queue
management code try again. (The code technically treats any nonzero value for *uptodate*
as indicating a successful transfer. However, this function is called only with the argument

being 0 or 1. This is why we talk in terms of whether it is 1.) In either case, we call *floppy_end_request*( ). Calling it with an argument of 1 indicates a successful transfer and with an argument of 0 indicates an error.

```
if (uptodate) {
    block = current_count_sectors + req→sector;
    INFBOUND(DRS→maxblock, block);
    if (block > _floppy→sect)
        DRS→maxtrack = 1;
    spin_lock_irqsave(q→queue_lock, flags);
    floppy_end_request(req, 1);
    spin_unlock_irqrestore(q→queue_lock, flags);
}
else {
    if (rq_data_dir(req) ≡ WRITE) {
        DRWE→write_errors ++;
        if (DRWE→write_errors ≡ 1) {
            DRWE→first_error_sector = req→sector;
            DRWE→first_error_generation = DRS→generation;
        }
        DRWE→last_error_sector = req→sector;
        DRWE→last_error_generation = DRS→generation;
    }
    spin_lock_irqsave(q→queue_lock, flags);
    floppy_end_request(req, 0);
    spin_unlock_irqrestore(q→queue_lock, flags);
}
}
```

16.4.8   Finishing the Floppy Operation

This is the final function in the floppy driver for handling a request. It turns control for the request back over to the block request management code.

```
static void floppy_end_request(struct request *req, int uptodate)
{
    unsigned int nr_sectors = current_count_sectors;
    if (¬uptodate)
        nr_sectors = req→current_nr_sectors;
```

16.4.8.1   Checking for Complete Operations

The function *end_that_request_first*( ), which is found in block/ll_rw_blk.c, looks at the request and the number of bytes that are transferred, and it determines whether the request has been completed. If the request has not been completed, then it returns 1, and we return. It is then up to the request scheduler to issue a new call to *do_fd_request*( ) to finish the request. If the request has been completed, then *end_that_request_first*( ) returns 0, and we continue.

> **if** (*end_that_request_first* (*req*, *uptodate*, *nr_sectors*))
>   **return**;

Various device drivers in the kernel contribute to an internal random number generator through the unpredictability of their events. Here is where the floppy driver contributes to the generator's entropy.

> *add_disk_randomness* (*req*→*rq_disk*);

16.4.8.2   Scheduling the Motor Off

Now that the request is completed, we can schedule the disk motor to be turned off if no more requests are processed in the next few seconds.

> *floppy_off* ((**long**) *req*→*rq_disk*→*private_data*);

16.4.8.3   Updating the Request Queue

Completed requests can be removed from the queue.

> *blkdev_dequeue_request* (*req*);

This next call tells the request scheduler that we're done with the request we just removed from the queue.

> *end_that_request_last* (*req*, *uptodate*);

The last step of the process is to clear the pointer to the current request. This indicates that the driver is idle and ready to receive another request.

> *current_req* = Λ;
> }

16.5   Summary

Linux includes support for a wide variety of I/O devices. It provides substantial infrastructure to aid in device driver development. Block device drivers can rely on the queue management and request scheduling in the block I/O layer. All drivers can minimize the time spent with interrupts disabled and can simplify their design through the use of deferred work in the bottom halves of their interrupt handlers. We have examined selected details of the parallel port driver as an example of a character device driver and the floppy disk driver as an example of a block device driver. Although both of these drivers are some of the simpler examples of their class, they both illustrate a number of significant and common techniques found in all device drivers.

16.6   Exercises

1. Why do we want to minimize the amount of work done in the top half of the interrupt handler?

2. In the anticipatory scheduler, would it make sense to distinguish between reads and writes when deciding whether to delay before resuming queue processing? Why or why not?

3. Suppose it was suggested that the write FIFO queue in the deadline scheduler is eliminated. Is there any danger in this? Could this cause any problems?

4. Would there be any value in modifying the complete fair queuing scheduler to use three queues as the deadline scheduler does? Why or why not?

5. In *__parport_pc_frob_control*( ), we use the exclusive or on the parameter *val* rather than an inclusive or. Speculate on why we do that. What advantage does it give us? How can we force a bit to be turned on as we would with an inclusive or?

6. At several points, the floppy device driver makes timer calls that result in the same function being called again at the end of the timer period. Would it be better to split the function into two, where one does the work before the timer is started, and the other does the work after it expires? Why or why not?

7. Study the code for the functions *end_that_request_first*( ), *blkdev_dequeue_request*( ), and *end_that_request_last*( ) and describe how the next request is taken from the queue and passed to *do_fd_request*( ).

8. In addition to probing the disk to automatically determine its format, the user process can also specify a specific format using the minor device number. Study the other code in the floppy driver and describe how this is handled. What prevents us from probing in that case?

9. Research the Linux design and implementation and write a description of how an interface like USB is supported. In particular, how does the system support the variety of devices that can be attached while at the same time implementing a single driver for the controller?

Chapter 17

Principles of File Systems

Aside from a user interface, the most recognizable aspect of an operating system is its file system. This is to be expected. After all, every program we run, every image that is displayed, and all of our own data are managed by the file system. It is the file system that determines how these files are stored and how they can be identified.

Notice that we've been careful to describe the function of the file system in two parts: providing storage services and providing a naming system. Classically, when we talk about file systems, we focus on the storage management and think of names simply as attributes of files. However, more modern designs take advantage of the opportunities afforded by providing these two services independently. Although it's hard to imagine the utility of stored files without names, we see in this chapter that names can exist without traditional files.

This chapter examines various aspects of file system design. First, we examine the set of services typically provided by a file system and then look at the general structure of a file system implementation. With that perspective established, we look at managing storage space and name space. Throughout this discussion, we must be careful about potentially ambiguous terminology. At times, we use the term file system to refer to the code and data structures within the operating system that implements these naming and storage services. At other times, we use the term to describe the set of data structures on a storage device. In most cases, it is clear from context which we mean; however, in those cases where it is not, we attempt to make it clear with other descriptive terms.

17.1 File System Services

In one form or another, all file systems provide applications with the ability to:

- create a file

- remove a file

- open an existing file

- read from an open file

- write to an open file

- close an open file

- fetch metadata of a file

- modify metadata of a file

Aside from those dealing with metadata, these operations are familiar and don't really need much elaboration. However, there are several variations worth mentioning. First, notice that we have listed the create and the open operations separately. Some systems do provide these as separate services. On the other hand, some also, or only, provide file creation as a special case of the open service. Typically, in the latter case, if we are opening a file for writing and it doesn't exist, then it is created for us as part of the opening process.

17.1.1 Shared and Exclusive Access

If we already have a file open and another process wants to open the file too, then we have a decision to make. Do we allow both processes to share the open file, or do we enforce exclusive access to the file? In practice, we find cases where each approach is desirable. Certainly, if both processes are only reading from the file, then there is no danger in allowing both of them access. However, as with shared data in memory, allowing one or more of the processes to write to the file can result in inconsistent data being read by others. If more than one writes to the file, then we can have a conflict where the file does not match the results we would get if the two processes accessed the file sequentially.

Consequently, most file system designs support both shared and exclusive access to files. Often, the implementation defaults to shared access. Two methods of requesting exclusive access are common. In the first, the system call to open the file is passed a flag indicating that the file is to be opened exclusively. In other words, if the file is already opened by another process, then this open request waits until it is available. Similarly, if another process tries to open the file while we have it open, it too must wait until we are finished. The second common method for requesting exclusive access is provided by an additional system call. This call provides a process with the ability to lock a file or parts of a file. This locking is similar to the mutual exclusion locking discussed in Section 5.7. Processes request exclusive access to a file and block if another process already has exclusive access.

We do see one difference in the approach to locking a file as compared with locking an area of memory. Because processes often declare whether they intend to write to the file, we have the information necessary to allow multiple readers to have access simultaneously. So, if a process requests exclusive access for the purpose of reading only, it can be given access, even if there are other readers currently with access. However, if a writer has access, then the reader must wait until the writer is finished. Any request for exclusive write access must wait until all other processes with access have finished using the file. This policy can be summarized in the following algorithm:

Exclusive File Access: When a process, P, requests exclusive access to a file, we determine whether to grant the access or to block the process. We maintain a queue, Q, of processes awaiting access.

1. If Q is nonempty, then add P to the tail of Q and return.

2. If no process currently has exclusive access to the file, give P access to the file and return.

3. If P requests read-only access and Q is empty and the processes with current access are readers, then give P access to the file and return.

4. Add P to the tail of Q and return.

This algorithm preserves the order of requests. Specifically, no process is granted exclusive access ahead of one that issued a request earlier. However, within this constraint, the algorithm permits as many simultaneous readers as possible, keeping the number of blocked processes to a minimum.

17.1.2   Access Patterns

It might seem that we've omitted from the list any means of positioning ourselves in the file. More often than not, a process expects to open a file and begin reading or writing at the beginning. Each subsequent read or write takes place where the last one left off. This type of **sequential access** implies that the operating system keeps a **current position**, which is used to determine the location of the next access. There are, however, times when we want to use a **random access** pattern with files. We can design the read and write operations so that the file position is specified explicitly each time. As we have seen in previous chapters, the lower-level device handling for storage devices works in terms of explicit positions. In many systems, however, we attempt to provide the best of both worlds. Reads and writes default to sequential access and don't require the application programmer to keep track of the current position. In these systems, file position can be changed by one or more additional system calls. Sometimes a form of a **rewind** operation is provided. Rewinding a file is much like rewinding a tape; it makes the current position the beginning of the file. This is sufficient in general, because to get to any random position, we can rewind and then read up to the desired position. However, getting to a random position is quite inefficient this way. For this reason, most systems give applications a way to **seek** to a random file position by means of another system call. Commonly, the application might seek either to an absolute location within the file or to a position specified relative to the current position.

17.1.3   File Structure

There are a number of approaches an operating system designer can take to the question of how data within a file are structured. The decision made on this issue tends to reflect the designer's general philosophical approach to the relationship between the OS and applications.

At one extreme, we treat the contents of each file as an unstructured collection of bytes. The operating system itself does not need to know and does not care how the application that wrote those bytes intended for them to be used. It is left completely up to each application how data within a file are to be organized. This minimalistic approach has the advantage that the file system design and implementation is simpler. It does not require that the file system designer identify a comprehensive set of structures and organizations at the time the file system is created. Indeed, even when file systems provide more complex data structures, they often also provide an unstructured byte stream as a fallback. The disadvantage of the unstructured byte stream is in moving complexity to applications. Instead of implementing the details of data structures once, they are implemented for each application. Even when those details are encapsulated in libraries that many applications can use, there is no guarantee that all applications will treat the same type of data with the same structures.

One way to add structure to file contents is based on the evolution of early data processing systems. In early systems where most input was presented on punched cards, it was natural to store and process data in terms of **records** of 80 (or some other fixed number of) characters. Just as was done then, we often subdivide records into fixed-sized fields. For example, the first nine characters might be a Social Security number (SSN), the next 15 might be a first name, and so on. When dealing with such fixed-sized records, the record size is usually either stored in the file's metadata or specified when the file is opened. After it is opened, reads from and writes to the file are specified in units of records rather than bytes. In some cases, the system supports a mix of variable-sized records in a single file. In these cases, the size of a given record is often stored in the file as a prefix to the record itself.

We can take this a step further and design a file system around indexed access. If the file is a linear array of n records, we can index the file with the integers 0 to $n - 1$. However, we might be more interested in indexing the file by the SSN. In other words, instead of issuing a system call to read record number i, we can issue a call to read the record with SSN s, and the file system itself locates the correct record. As in databases, the index is typically implemented using data structures such as hash tables and B-trees. Naturally, these more complex file structures have the opposite set of trade-offs when compared to the unstructured byte stream designs. They result in a more complex file system design and implementation, and they do not always meet the needs of every application. However, for those applications that do fit a record-oriented model, these file system designs considerably simplify the development of applications and supporting libraries.

One particularly interesting special case of these issues is the normal text file. Storing the text itself is not a particularly big issue; it's representing the line-oriented nature of text files that raises issues. Almost every approach imaginable has been used. In a record-oriented approach, we can set an upper limit on line size and used fixed-length records, with shorter lines padded with trailing spaces. Alternatively, we can use a variable-length record approach and prefix the line data with the line's length. Some systems use a byte stream and mark the end of each line with one or more special characters. Among the options for terminating a line are the null byte, the line feed, the carriage return, or both the line feed and the carriage return. Of course, this variety of approaches to representing lines makes writing applications that are portable to a variety of systems something of a challenge.

17.1.4   Metadata

Another item worth discussing is the subject of **metadata**. Metadata are the data about a file. For example, most systems maintain a list of file attributes, such as name, size, last modification date, owner, and protection codes. In addition, the file system might include data such as an append-only flag, a file lock flag, the record length, the creation time, the last access time, or various size or access limits. Although these data are maintained primarily for use by the operating system itself, there are also services allowing applications to query and to modify these data.

In many systems, the set of metadata is defined by the file system design as part of a fixed structure describing a file. Other systems allow for more flexibility. Some file system designs allow for any metadata an application wants to assign to a file.

We highlight now one particular piece of metadata—the file type. Before considering the file type, we should note that not all systems support any notion of file type. These systems leave the interpretation of a file up to whatever application opens that file. For those systems that do support the concept of a file type, the type identifies for us whether the file is a text file, a graphical image, an executable program, a word-processing document, a PDF file, or any of a number of other types of files. File types are used in a number of ways. For example, they can be used to control certain aspects of reading and writing, such as end-of-line conventions for text files. Similarly, files that are identified as being compressed might be automatically decompressed when read. One other major use of file types is assigning an application to the file. Particularly when using a graphical user interface, we often want to select a file and have it opened in an application that is in some sense a natural one for the file. In the case of a graphical image, for example, the default application could be an image viewer. There are two common ways this association is realized. The application can be given as an additional piece of metadata, which is often set by the program that creates the file. Alternatively, we might define a separate application, possibly part of the user interface, that is aware of the associations between files and applications. This application is responsible for turning a file selection by the user into the act of running a program with that file as input.

17.1.5   Memory-Mapped Files

Reads and writes are not the only mechanisms we can use to access the data in a file. Many systems provide applications with the ability to map a file into the process's memory space. In effect, the contents of the file become process data just as any other data the process accesses. The file contents are accessed using normal memory load and store instructions.

This technique can easily be implemented in a system with paging. We just allocate the virtual pages for the file and mark them as nonresident but record that they are "paged out" to the file we are mapping. Then when the process attempts to access the memory space for the mapped file, we get a page fault and swap the needed page into memory from the file.

It is interesting to consider using this elegant technique in place of reads and writes altogether. As we see in Section 18.2, Multics did exactly that. There are, however, a couple of issues, both related to virtual memory space, that must be addressed if we are to do that. First, if all file accesses are mapped, we restrict file sizes to be no larger than the size of our virtual memory space (or the size of a segment in Multics). For machines with 32 and fewer address bits, this can be a significant limitation. With 32-bit addresses, only 4 GB of virtual space can be addressed. All code, data, and all memory-mapped files can total no more than 4 GB. However, with 64-bit and larger memory spaces, this technique can be quite practical. With a 64-bit address, the total virtual usage can be up to approximately 16×10^{18}, or 16 exabytes. The second issue we face is that of extending the size of a file. In a segmented system, we can simply say that writes beyond the size of a file, but within the same segment, extend the size of the file. However, if we don't have a segmentation structure, there are a few things we can do. First, we can simulate the segments by defining a maximum file size that is smaller than our virtual memory space. If we have a 64-bit machine, we can use 48 bits to address the contents of a file. This allows up to 65,536 files up to 2^{48} bytes (256 TB) each. If we map all files on boundaries that are a multiple of 2^{48}, each file can grow to its maximum size without colliding with another file. Alternatively, we can place a number of unmapped pages beyond the maximum size of a file. If the process attempts to write into these guard pages, the page fault indicates that the file has gotten too large.

17.2   General File System Design

From an examination of the services provided by a file system, we now turn to the question of how a file system fits into the overall operating system structure. The first aspect that deserves notice is that the file system does not stand on its own. File system support is the primary client of device drivers for storage devices. The file system component of the OS does not generally attempt to control storage devices directly. It is written to be independent of the actual device details and uses the storage device drivers as do applications that need access to those devices.

17.2.1   Form of the File System

From even early designs, the question of whether the file system should be part of the kernel has been a thorny question. On the one hand, it seems natural to implement the file system in the kernel. It provides some of the primary file system services in response to system calls. It reads data from and writes data to the memory space of processes—and except when explicitly sharing memory, we want only the kernel to have access to a process's memory. Finally, the file system needs access to some of the information about a process that we normally keep in the kernel's process table.

On the other hand, it seems natural to move the file system out of the kernel and let it operate as a normal application. If the file system accesses storage devices only through device drivers in the kernel, then it does not need any special access to hardware. It can run as a normal process, making requests of the I/O subsystem for access to the raw storage devices. Although we would expect that separating the file system from the kernel would be most common with microkernel designs, as discussed in Section 1.4, we find that file systems are also implemented outside of a number of monolithic kernels. However, there are a few issues that have to be addressed to make this possible. If it is a normal process rather than part of the kernel, then how does it handle system calls? Second, what do we do about the issue of access to the requesting process's memory space? Third, what do we do about process information the file system needs from the process table? Finally, for those designs where devices are identified as part of the normal file name space, we end up with a sort of dilemma. If the file system is an application and has no special connection to device drivers, and if applications all go through the file system to access device drivers, then how does the file system access the device drivers that support it?

For those systems that do move the file system outside the kernel, these issues have to be addressed. In reality, they are not as problematic as we have suggested. A number of systems address several issues all at once by defining a message passing protocol between processes. In particular, that protocol can be used to make requests of the file system and to get results. Naturally, the message passing services are provided by the kernel, so it becomes easy for system calls to be turned into messages and for the message data to be copied to and from a process's memory space. Furthermore, if we define the messages in such a way that they operate over a network as well as locally, then processes can access file systems on remote machines just as easily as they do on the local machine.

17.2.2   Major Data Structures

Regardless of whether the file system is in the kernel, there are several key things the file system must manage. Typically, there are two data structures around which these management functions are organized. The first is the **open file table**. For each file that any process has open, the file system maintains a number of attributes. Some of these are in-memory copies of the file's metadata. For example, it is very convenient to have the current file size available when handling read and write requests. We also keep track of the location of the file's metadata so that any updates can be written out to the

---

Historical Note: Mars Rover: Spirit

On January 21, 2004, file system problems struck the highly successful Spirit rover on Mars. When it should have acknowledged a retransmission of a partially successful software update, it didn't respond at all. It turns out that the total number of files on the system included not only the partial update, but all data collected up to that point and numerous files from updates sent while in flight. Earlier in the day, the rover had attempted to allocate more files for data, but the number of files had exceeded the capacity of in-memory data structures. This caused the system to reset. When it rebooted, it attempted to mount the file system, which now had too many files. The allocation for the in-memory data structures again failed, leading to repeated resets. NASA was able to finally gain control of the rover and correct the problem by commanding it to boot without mounting the file system and working from there.

storage device. The file system also needs to keep track of the device on which each file is stored. The file system support code in the OS often manages multiple file systems as stored on disk. Knowing which device holds a file tells us which device driver to use and what parameters to give it when accessing the file. In the case of open files shared among multiple processes, we generally need to keep track of which processes have the file open and which have parts of the file locked. Only when all processes that share a file have closed it can we release our internal data structures related to that file. Although the items we discuss here are typical and representative, most real implementations store additional information in the open file table.

The other major data structure is the **mount table**. Because there might be multiple storage devices (or partitions on one or more devices), there can be multiple file systems available. At any point in time, the files on some or all of these file systems can be accessed by processes. In most cases, the set of accessible file systems can change while the system is running. Making a file system accessible is called **mounting**. We use the term **unmounting** to refer to removing a file system from the accessible set. We can think of mounting a file system as attaching it to the rest of the system. The details of mounting a file system vary considerably from one system to another. For some systems, there is not much to be done in mounting a file system. In these systems, a device (or partition) is referenced explicitly, and the file system metadata are read at that time. For other systems, we need to add the new file system into an overall uniform naming scheme. In these systems, the names that identify files in the newly mounted file system are determined by the mount operation rather than by the physical device.

The mount table then contains data structures that describe the set of currently mounted file systems. These data structures include information such as where in the name space the file system is mounted, the total capacity of the file system, the amount of free space in the file system, and so on. One key piece of information in the mount table is the device on which the file system is stored. When we access data on a file system, the associated device determines which device driver we call to handle the details of the request.

17.3   Name Spaces

As suggested in the introduction, one of the key responsibilities of a file system is providing names that are associated with persistent data or other resources. Each file system design defines the set of all possible names and the rules by which names can be constructed. This set of possible names is what we call the **name space**. In the common case of persistent data files, the file system must translate from elements of the name space to locations on storage devices. In other cases, the names can translate to device drivers, to communication channels, or to interfaces that control other processes. Even though we can identify a number of common uses of names, it is best not to try to define the idea of a name by the things names can reference. Names might refer to tangible data, to data generated on the fly, or to no data at all. As we see later, we can even have aliases, where multiple names can refer to the same thing. Like variables in algebra, names in a name space should be thought of as abstract entities with any number of possible meanings.

The term name space comes from the mathematical idea of a space. In mathematics, we usually think of a space as a set of possible values subject to some constraint. For example, the Cartesian coordinate system, $\mathbf{R}^2 = \{(x,y)|x,y \in \mathbf{R}\}$ is a space. Alternatively, we often define a space in terms of the set of results of some operation. For example, we might define a space that is the set of all linear combinations of two basis vectors $\mathbf{e}_1$ and $\mathbf{e}_2$, $S = \{\alpha\mathbf{e}_1 + \beta\mathbf{e}_2|\alpha,\beta \in \mathbf{R}\}$. Similarly, we define a name space using operations on alphabets of symbols.

Before discussing name spaces more deeply, we begin with some notation that is similar to that used in automata theory and programming language design. We use uppercase, italic letters (A, B, C, ..., Z) to denote sets of symbols or sets of strings, and the usual set theoretic operations are used to operate on these sets. Likewise, we use parentheses in their usual role of grouping expressions. Furthermore, we define concatenation between two sets, A and B as $AB = \{ab|a \in A, b \in B\}$. We use exponentiation as a shorthand for concatenation between a set and itself. Specifically, $A^1 = A$, $A^2 = AA$, $A^3 = AAA$, and so on. A^0 is the empty string we denote as ϵ. Other shorthand notation includes A^* to denote a string of zero or more elements from A ($A^* = \bigcup_{i=0}^{\infty} A^i$), A^+ to denote a string with one or more elements from A ($A^+ = AA^*$), and $A^{[j,k]}$ to refer to a string of between j and k elements, inclusive, from A ($A^{[j,k]} = \bigcup_{i=j}^{k} A^i$). Finally, we use the subscript opt to denote an optional element.

With this notation in hand, we can now give some examples of typical name spaces. It was quite common in early systems to define the alphabet as consisting of letters and digits, with no distinction between upper- and lowercase letters, specifically $A = \{A, B, C, \ldots Z, 0, 1, 2, \ldots, 9\}$. It was frequently the case that the names were also restricted in the number of characters in a name. For example, a name might be specified by six characters, a dot, and three more characters, as in $N = A^{[1,6]}.A^3$. In some cases, the first part might allow for eight characters, as in $N = A^{[1,8]}.A^3$.

Naturally, it is not the syntactical construction of file names that interests us the most. It is the meaning we ascribe to a name that we want to study. The remainder of this section looks at a subset of the variety of ways in which file system designers have used the name of a file to specify something about the file.

17.3.1   Drive Specifiers

On the earliest systems, file storage was predominantly in the form of tapes. Files were simply organized by the tape on which they resided. There was little motivation to develop a formal naming scheme that identified how the files were organized. Instead, the files on a tape were just strung out one after another, identified only by name. The one time when we did have to specify more than just a file name was when we had more than one tape drive and when we had more than one tape mounted simultaneously. Even though tapes often had a logical volume name associated with them, references to files were normally by a combination of the physical drive and the file name.

When disks became common, it was natural to continue this same naming scheme. Often, the only organization of files in these early systems was the physical organization on different disk drives. Of course, there had to be a way to specify which drive contained the desired file. Here it was fairly common to use a name space like $N = (A :)_{\text{opt}} A^{[1,6]}.A^3$ or $N = (A^3 :)_{\text{opt}} A^{[1,6]}.A^3$. In a case like this, a file name such as DX0:FOO.TXT refers to a file called FOO.TXT on a drive referred to as DX0. In terms of design, the choice of a colon (or other character not otherwise found in a file name) makes parsing the name easier. If no colon is present, then neither is the optional drive specifier. Otherwise, we split the string at the colon. The part before the colon is the drive, and the part after the colon is the file.

As disk drives became larger, designers began to partition them so that one physical drive would be divided into several logical drives. Although somewhat crude, it was an effective means of imposing some organization onto a set of files. In a partitioned system, drive specifiers no longer identify a physical drive, but identify a drive partition instead.

17.3.2   Account Specifiers

As time-sharing systems evolved, designers needed a way to distinguish the files owned by one user from those owned by another. Some designers looked at the idea of a drive specifier referring to a partition and extended the idea to allow drive specifiers to refer to more fine-grained subsets of the disk. In effect, they created a logical drive for each user.

Other designers approached the identification of users as a separate problem. It was common for users to be identified as accounts and given either an account number or a pair of numbers that identified the account. When using a pair of numbers, often one number identified a project and the other an individual working on that project. The project numbers in early systems evolved into the more general idea of groups we find in many systems today. If we define the set of digits, $D = \{0, 1, 2, \ldots, 9\}$, then the name space for files with an account pair might look like, $N = ([D^+, D^+])_{\text{opt}} A^{[1,6]}.A^3$. One example of such a name is [130,14]FORTH.ASM. Although our specification of N allows for arbitrarily large numbers in the account, most systems limited the numbers to a smaller range such as three or four digits each.

We should be careful here not to confuse account specifiers in names with the ownership information found in a file's metadata. In the first case, we use information about a user in organizing the name space and in preventing collisions between names used by different users. In the second case, we use the file ownership in determining access rights. This type of resource protection is discussed in more detail in Chapter 21.

It's not a far stretch to implement named accounts rather than numbered accounts. So if we allow for account names up to eight characters of both letters and digits, then our name space is defined by $N = ([A^{[1,8]}])_{\text{opt}} A^{[1,6]}.A^3$, and our earlier file name example might instead be [STUART]FORTH.ASM.

It's also easy to see how we might use both drive specifiers and account specifiers in the same system. If our name space is defined by

$$N = (A^3 :)_{\text{opt}} ([D^+, D^+])_{\text{opt}} A^{[1,6]}.A^3$$

then we could have a name such as DX0:[130,14]FORTH.ASM. This construction allows us to have separate user areas on each physical drive. Again notice how the use of characters not normally allowed in file names makes the parsing easy. We can quickly determine

which optional components are present and can easily break the whole string down into
its component parts.

17.3.3   Hierarchical Naming

In using account specifiers, we effectively give each user a name space distinct from that
of all the other users. A file called TEST.C belonging to one user is different from one of
the same name belonging to another. This is good as far as it goes. However, we might
want to take it further and allow users to organize their files in separate name spaces.
For example, a user might want to group some files under the heading of DOCUMENTS
and some under the heading of PROJECTS. In fact, under the heading of PROJECTS,
the user might want to divide the name space further yet into names of projects, such as
CALVIN, HOBBS, and LUTHER.

In this description, notice how we've naturally gravitated to a hierarchical view of the
name spaces. This leads us to a tree structure for them, as illustrated in Figure 17-1. Over
the years, a number of file system designers have flirted with the idea of using the more
general directed graph as the basis for name space organization. From an implementational point of view, there is no problem with this. However, most designers return to the
tree structured name space organization because the administrative difficulties inherent
with possibly cyclic graphs outweigh the benefits of the more general structure.

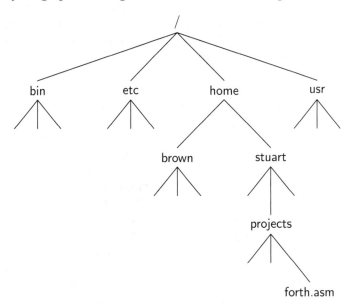

Figure 17-1: Hierarchical Name Space

By way of example, suppose we define a hierarchical name space by

$$N = /_{\text{opt}}(A^{[1,14]}/)^* A^{[1,14]}/_{\text{opt}}$$

where our alphabet is given by $A = \{A, B, C, \ldots, Z, a, b, c \ldots, z, 0, 1, 2, \ldots, 9, .\}$. In this case, the name space consists of an optional leading slash, followed by one or more names separated by slashes, followed by an optional trailing slash. Each of the names can be no more than 14 characters long. A name such as /home/stuart/forth.asm is a valid name in this name space.

Notice how this type of organization subsumes the special case of an account specifier. Although some systems use a combination of drive specifiers and hierarchical directories, this hierarchical name space can also subsume the drive notation. At an administrative level, we might establish that the tree rooted at /home is stored on a drive distinct from the drive that stores files in the /usr tree. This association is made at the time we mount the file systems contained on the various drives.

17.3.4   File Extensions

Up to this point, many of the examples of file names have been based on two-part names where the second part consists of three characters. In this common technique, the second part of the name is called the **extension**, and the extension often identifies the type of file. This approach is usually an alternative to file type metadata, as discussed in Section 17.1.4. For example, many of the files that make up this book have the extension .tex, which identifies them as being source files for the TEX typesetting package. For example, the file containing the text of this chapter is called fs_princ.tex. Similarly, C language source code is contained in files ending in .c in most environments. We have seen examples of this convention in chapters describing the details of Inferno and Linux. A number of systems also have extensions, such as .exe, which indicates that a file is an executable binary.

The critical design issue of the file name extensions is, "At what level is the identification made?" In some designs, these identifications are purely a matter of convention, and the association between extension and type is solely in the mind of the user.

The next step along the range of possible designs gives applications the power to use extensions as they see fit. Turning again to the example of .tex files, the tex and latex commands assume an extension of .tex if no extension is given. Similarly, the default behavior of a C compiler given the −c option is to create an output file whose name is the same as the source code file name where the .c is replaced with .o. For example, compiling a file called dis.c will create an object file called dis.o.

It is also possible to design applications that know about extensions that don't "belong" to them. One common realization of this technique is a file browser that allows a file to be acted on in some appropriate way when it is selected. Suppose we have such an application that allows us to select a file by clicking on it with a mouse. If we click on a file with extension .tex, it might cause an editor to be opened for modifying that file, whereas if we click on a file ending in .jpg, such as friend.jpg, an image viewer might be started to display the image contained in the file. Another example is the frequently used .doc extension, used for files generated by word processors. Clicking on the file outline.doc would start the word processor running with that file loaded. Applications of this form typically give the user a mechanism to define the mapping between extension and action.

The extreme end of the the extension interpretation scale is the case where the operating system itself knows about the extensions. One example of this type of design is an operating system where a file cannot be executed unless its name ends in .exe. Similarly, directories in some systems have the extension of .dir. Systems where the kernel does not use the extension usually use either other metadata or a magic number in the file contents.

17.3.5   File Versions

What programmer hasn't encountered a case where some change just didn't work out as expected? In these cases, we often want to revert back to the previous (or some earlier) version of the file. In most operating systems, it is the responsibility of the user to save a backup copy in case such a fallback is needed. Some applications, such as text editors, will do this for us. However, some operating systems provide this mechanism automatically. When a file is written, the previous version is kept along with the new one. One technique for identifying a particular version of a file is by using a version number separated from the file name by a semicolon. Here the space of names might look something like $N = A^{[1,6]}.A^3(; D^{[1,3]})_{\text{opt}}$. Although we've identified the version number as optional here, every file does have a version number. If we specify a file without a version number, it is taken to refer to the most recent (highest version number).

17.3.6   Special Files and Directories

As suggested earlier, the idea of the name space can be extended beyond the persistent data we usually think about when discussing files. Giving names of interior tree nodes in a hierarchical name space is the first step outside the box. These interior nodes are called **directories**. The next step is to define the means of referring to devices through names in the name space. We've already seen examples of identifying disk drives such as DY0: as part of a file name. If we allow DY0: to exist by itself and to be used in the same calls for opening files, then we have a way of addressing the whole disk drive. Likewise, we might specify the third indexterminalterminal line as TT3:. In systems that provide a uniform name space, we might have names like /dev/hda and /dev/tty02.

So far, all of our examples of names have referred to relatively concrete things such as data stored on a disk, directories of file names, and physical devices. The next step in the development of the name space is to envision ways of identifying ephemeral aspects of the system through the name space. One of the first ways we can do this is to provide a directory hierarchy that represents processes. In such a system, the directory /proc/35 represents the process whose PID is 35. Depending on the design, that directory might contain files such as mem, from which one process can ready a snapshot of another process's memory space, or it might contain a directory called fd, which contains information about all the open file descriptors. It's not uncommon to also put a number of names into /proc that refer to the system as a whole.

Now that we've made the leap of thinking of names as referring to resources other than persistent data and devices, we can begin to envision all services, such as networking and windowing systems, as candidates for names. The last big conceptual jump is a new perspective on who serves the names. Up to this point, it's been the kernel that was responsible for providing the names and their interpretation. However, by providing the right mechanisms, we make it possible for applications to provide much of that functionality. We've already seen examples of the kernel providing this type of service in Chapter 15, and we see applications doing the same in Chapter 19.

17.3.7   Relative and Absolute Names

There is one more aspect of interpreting names that is nearly universal among operating systems that have hierarchical directory structures. Imagine how painful it would be to give the full path name for every file reference. Instead of simply referring to the file fs_princ.tex, we would have to refer to:

/usr/stuart/inferno/book/fs_princ.tex

Of course, we expect the context to differentiate between this instance of the name fs_princ.tex and any other one. The idea of a **current directory** handles that. Each process is effectively running "in" a current directory, and all path names that don't start at the root are evaluated relative to that current directory. Processes often inherit their current directory from their parent but might change it later.

In the example here, names that begin with the slash character (/) are **absolute path names**. They describe the path from the root of the name space all the way down to the file being referenced. On the other hand, if the current directory is /usr/stuart, then the name inferno/fs_princ.tex refers to the same file. Such names are called **relative path names**. As we've described things, we have a way to absolutely refer to any name in the name space and a relative way to refer to anything in the tree rooted at our current directory. The only thing missing is a relative way to break out of that tree. All we need for this is a way to identify the parent directory. If we use the .. name to identify the parent, then we can use the name ../inferno/fs_princ.tex to refer to our file if our current directory is /usr/stuart/etc.

17.4   Managing Storage Space

The previous section provides a pretty thorough look at names and how they can describe resources. However, we haven't yet addressed the question of how we actually store persistent data on a disk and later retrieve that data by name. That's the focus of this section. In discussing names, we've already identified the major task of storage management. In particular, the file system must provide a means to translate from the name of a file to the locations on the disk where that file's data are stored. Beyond that, the majority of the file system's responsibility is managing the allocation of disk space.

17.4.1   File System Metadata

Just as some files, network packets, and other data often have headers, most file systems also have a header. This collection of data describes the file system as a whole and gives us a starting point for locating files in the file system. In other words, these are metadata for the file system, and it is these data that we use when mounting a file system to build the internal data structures necessary for using the file system. Typically, these metadata includes such items as the total size of the file system, the amount of free space in the file system, the date of the last mount, the location of the free space data structures, and the location of the starting point for any name lookups.

Of course, the OS must know where to find a file system's metadata. Most systems take one of two approaches. The first approach places the metadata at a fixed location, such as the first block of the disk or partition containing the file system. Alternatively, some systems put a pointer in a fixed location, such as the first block. It points to an ordinary file containing the metadata. The key to both approaches is that the OS is able to gather the necessary information before it knows the details of the file system's layout. It is also not uncommon for there to be duplicate copies of the metadata scattered across the file system. That way, if the main one gets corrupted, one of the backup copies can be used in its place.

17.4.2 Data Units

In dealing with file systems as stored on storage devices, data are allocated and transferred in units much larger than a byte. As discussed in Chapter 13, most magnetic disks store and transfer data in units of sectors. For most disk drives with rigid disks, sectors are 512 bytes in size, whereas many floppy disk drives operate on 256-byte sectors.

Most file systems operate in units of one or more sectors. We usually call these units **blocks**. (Unfortunately, the terminology is sometimes less than precise. We also sometimes speak of disk blocks when we are talking about data the same size as sectors.) It is common to see file system designs with block sizes ranging from 512 bytes to 8192 bytes. Most early designs defined a fixed block size, used by all instances of that file system. For some newer file systems designs, the block size is a parameter that is set when the file system is first initialized on the storage device. In these cases, the administrator who creates the file system has a choice of several allowed block sizes.

17.4.3 Free Space Management

Because the allocation of space in a file system is done in fixed-sized blocks, managing the free space is similar in some ways to managing pages in memory, as discussed in Chapter 9. There are, however, some significant differences. First, we do not need a replacement policy for disk blocks. If we do not have a free block to allocate, then the file system is full, and it's an error. As a result, we can simply pick an arbitrary free block— usually the first one on the list. However, as with the elevator algorithm, we often select free blocks to reduce seeks. Frequently, files are read sequentially from the beginning to the end. If we can keep all the blocks of a file close together, then we will incur shorter total seek time in the case when no other process requests disk service while we are reading the file. To help keep the blocks of a file close, if we are extending an existing file, we can pick the free block that is closest to the last existing block of the file. Similarly, when creating a new file, we can pick a free block at the beginning of several free blocks in a row, on the assumption that the new file is likely to use several blocks.

The actual representation of the set of free blocks generally takes one of several forms. First, we have the **free bitmap**. In this representation, each block is represented by a single bit, which is 1 if the block is free and 0 if it is allocated. Here, the free bitmap is often a fixed area on the disk. As such, it is overhead and occupies space that cannot be used for data. In some designs, the free bitmap is stored in an ordinary file.

The second representation is a **free list**, normally implemented as a linked list. As with free memory blocks, we can embed the links in the free blocks themselves. If we represent our free space in this way, we need only have a single pointer to the head of the list as overhead.

The third basic representation for free blocks is a simple list of free blocks. We could reserve space to hold the list just as we do for a bitmap. However, this is not necessary. Notice that unless the list is empty, we have at least one free block on the disk. Consequently, we can store the list in the free blocks themselves. Of course, we need a way to identify other blocks if the entire free list doesn't fit into one block. One simple approach is to create a linked list of these list blocks using the last pointer in the block to point to the next block in the list. Notice that it is also correct to interpret this block as a free one because we use only free blocks to store the free list. As with the linked list, this approach has only a single pointer to the first such block in overhead. These three methods of representing the free list are illustrated in Example 17.1.

Example 17.1: File System Free Lists

For the purposes of illustrating the various methods of representing the free list, we consider a very small file system. We have only eight blocks in our file system, and each block can hold only four block numbers. In this example, blocks 0, 1, 4, 5, and 7 are free. Figure 17-2 shows a bitmap representation of the free list, where free blocks are identified with a 1. In this representation, the actual block numbers don't appear anywhere.

$$\boxed{1\,|\,1\,|\,0\,|\,0\,|\,1\,|\,1\,|\,0\,|\,1}$$

Figure 17-2: Block Free Bitmap

Making a linked list from the blocks gives us the arrangement shown in Figure 17-3.

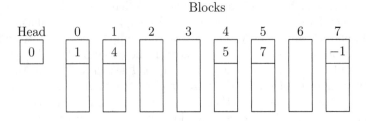

Figure 17-3: Free Block Linked List

Finally, if we store the list of free blocks as a simple list, the set of free blocks looks like that illustrated in Figure 17-4. There are several approaches to the details of such a

list. In this example, we use the list as follows. The *head* holds the block number of the
first block containing a list of free blocks. Because this block is itself implicitly free, we
do not list it. So, in this example, that block is block 5, and it lists blocks 0, 1, and 4
as free blocks. The last entry gives us the block number of the next block containing a
list of free blocks. When we need a free block, we look at the list in the block identified
by *head*. If the only entry in that list is the last one, which is the block number of the
next list, then we allocate the block identified by *head* and set *head* to the next list block.
If we encounter a −1, we know we are at the end of the list and there are no more free
blocks available.

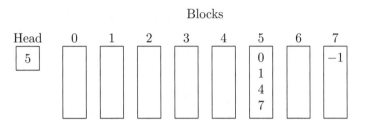

Figure 17-4: Free Block List

17.4.4   Regular Files

Given that free disk blocks have been allocated to a file, we need a way to locate those
blocks. In other words, how do we store the list of blocks that belong to a file? In the
simplest file system designs, we require that the blocks of a file be contiguous. Thus if
a file starts at block x and it takes n blocks to hold the file, then all of the blocks in
the interval $[x, x + n - 1]$ belong to that file. Knowing the starting block and the size is
enough for us to find the complete contents of the file. The two advantages of contiguous
allocation are simplicity and performance. It is trivial to locate a random byte within
a contiguous file. When reading an entire file (with no other intervening disk accesses),
contiguous storage ensures that we will move the head the smallest possible distance.

The primary disadvantage of contiguous allocation becomes evident when we want to
grow an existing file. One of two things must happen. Either we have enough free disk
space immediately after the last existing block of the file, or we copy the entire file to a
new disk location where there is enough contiguous space. It is difficult at best to ensure
that the first alternative is true for every file we might want to extend, and the second is
not a very pleasant alternative. Consequently, we generally design file systems that allow
a file to be spread out among arbitrary blocks on the disk, but we attempt to keep file
blocks as close to contiguous as we can.

A linked list is a natural means of representing the blocks of a file while allowing them
to be spread out across the disk. As with representing a free list, we can either embed the
links into the data blocks themselves, or we can maintain a separate data structure. As

an example of the first case, suppose each disk block is 512 bytes and blocks are identified with a 4-byte index. In each of these blocks, 508 bytes can be used for data and the first four bytes give the location of the next block in the file. Figure 17-5 shows this approach.

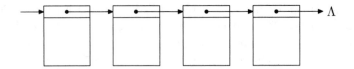

Figure 17-5: File Allocation With Embedded List

If we opt to maintain a separate data structure, we naturally think in terms of a data structure containing a block number and a pointer to the next such structure. However, because all data on a disk are allocated in units of blocks, we want to pack as many such structures into one block as possible. If we keep the structures sorted, then the pointer to the next structure is redundant, and our representation reduces to a list of block numbers. If there are more file blocks than can be listed in such a disk block, then we can chain the index blocks by using the last block index to identify the next index block. This arrangement is illustrated in Figure 17-6. Notice the similarity to the single-level page table design discussed in Chapter 9.

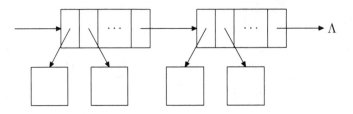

Figure 17-6: List-Structured File Allocation

A variation on this second approach uses a single array of pointers, one for each data block in the file system. The array is indexed by the same block numbers as the set of data blocks. Each entry in the array gives the next block in the file. The last block in a file is identified with a special value. Some systems refer to this as a **file allocation table** (FAT). Suppose we have two files in a very small file system. The first file uses blocks 5, 3, 2, and 6, in that order. Blocks 4, 1, and 8 comprise the second file. The only free block in this small file system is 7. The table for this case looks like Figure 17-7.

Continuing to use the example of a 512-byte block, we find that the first form of the list structure allows us to organize files up to 63.5 KB with a single index block. For files larger than this, we must linearly access each index block to read the block that indexes a randomly selected block in the file. As usual, we can use a tree structure to make our access time logarithmic instead of linear. Suppose we have a tree with two levels of

1:	8
2:	6
3:	2
4:	1
5:	3
6:	0
7:	−1
8:	0

Figure 17-7: Alternative List-Structured File Allocation

index blocks. With our 512-byte block size, the root index block contains 128 indirect pointers addressing 128 index blocks, each of which indexes 128 data blocks of 512 bytes each. This arrangement allows for files up to 8 MB in size. If we design our tree to have three levels of index blocks, we can have files as large as 1 GB. In this case, the root block contains double-indirect pointers to blocks of single-indirect pointers to data blocks. Figure 17-8 shows this structure. Although this structure allows us to manage fairly large files, randomly addressing any block in the file requires four disk reads regardless of how large or how small the file is. In Chapters 18, 19 and 20, we see examples of hybrid designs that provide random access of smaller files with fewer disk accesses while still allowing large files to be represented.

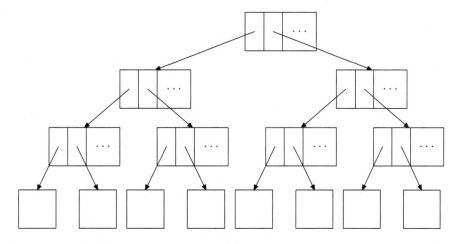

Figure 17-8: Tree-Structured File Allocation

17.4.5 Sparse Files

When a process writes past the end of a file, we naturally allocate a new block for the file and attach it to whichever of the data structures we use to represent the file. An interesting question arises, however. What if the process seeks well beyond the end of the file and then writes? What should we do about all the data between the old end of file and the newly written data? If we use the list representation as illustrated in Figure 17-6 or the tree as illustrated in Figure 17-8, we can actually avoid allocating blocks for that area. We can put null pointers for the blocks that have never been written. On a read, we return zeros for any bytes that would be found in such blocks. Such **sparse files** allow an application to use a large range of indices for records in a file but not use any more disk blocks than are actually needed.

17.4.6 Forks

Frequently, the set of metadata stored in a file system is determined when the file system is designed. This means that if an application could use additional descriptive information, it must either find a way to store it in the file itself or in some auxiliary file. One approach to providing more general metadata storage is called **forks**. The idea is that each file is effectively split into multiple parts, or forks. One holds the usual file data, and others hold the file's metadata. In addition to usual information such as ownership, the metadata fork can include things such as the icon to display for the file in a windowing system, the user who last modified the file, and any other auxiliary data an application might want to use. Mac OS for the Apple Macintosh is a primary early example of a system that uses forks. Early designs of the file system supported only two forks, where the metadata fork was called the resource fork.

If we accept the idea that a file can be more than just data and predefined metadata, we can start to see it as an arbitrary collection of labeled data, regardless of the role of the data. Some data could be the persistent data we normally associate with a file. Some data could be metadata, such as the file's name, the file's owner, or the application that created the file. Some of the data we described earlier as being metadata in a fork, such as an icon image, isn't really metadata in the usual sense. Such an image would be better described as auxiliary data.

In fact, if we consider the file as a collection of labeled data, there's no reason why we need to think in terms of only one area of persistent data. Consider, for example, a file containing an executable program. One of the data forks could contain the bytecode compiled from a language like Limbo or Java. Then, additional data forks could contain the results of just-in-time compiling, with each fork containing the results on a different architecture. At run time, the system loads the code from only the appropriate fork. In such a scenario, one approach is to continue the distinction between each of several data forks and one special fork containing everything else, including the metadata. Alternatively, we could take the abstraction one step further and consider each labeled data item as its own fork. Recent versions of HFS+ (the Mac OS file system) support additional forks. Also, Section 18.7 discusses the NTFS file system for the Windows NT design and how it also supports an arbitrary collection of labeled data.

17.4.7   Directories

For translating names to file locations, the central data structure is the **directory**. In a general sense, a directory maps a subset of names from the name space to additional file metadata. In particular, the directory gives us what we need to find the size of the file, file ownership, security characteristics, and where the blocks of the file are located. The directory might make that information available directly in a directory entry, or it might make the information available indirectly by pointing to some external data structure. In practice, a directory is usually implemented as any other file, but one with a particular structure. Figure 17-9 shows a very simple case without any concept of file ownership or protection. We also assume here that the disk blocks that make up a file are all stored contiguously on the disk. In this and the following example, we show the metadata found by way of a directory lookup, regardless of whether the metadata are stored in the directory entry or in a separate data structure.

Name	Starting Block	Size
FOO.TXT	1024	8043
REPORT.RNO	306	14365
FORTH.ASM	2964	18292

Figure 17-9: Simple Directory Structure

More complicated examples are like that shown in Figure 17-10. In this example, each file or directory has an owner and a group to which the file belongs. The column we label Alloc. gives the block number of the first block of the data structure that lists the blocks allocated to the file. We also specify a set of allowed accesses. (For space, we show only the privileges for the owner. Usually, there are privileges specified for other classes of users as well.) The last column of the figure shows a file type. In this example, we have two types of files: regular files and directories.

Name	Alloc.	Size	Owner	Group	Protection	Type
mybook.cls	1025	3224	stuart	faculty	R/W	reg.
os_inferno.ps	2958	1454722	stuart	faculty	R	reg.
backup	3333	1024	stuart	faculty	R/W/S	dir.

Figure 17-10: Complex Directory Structure

17.4.8   Aliases

Notice in our description of directories, we allow for a separation between the name and the allocation data structure. With this arrangement, there is no reason why we cannot have more than one name (possibly in different directories) identify the same allocated blocks. In other words, we have multiple names that refer to the same file data. These multiple names are called **aliases** or **links**. (We sometimes refer to these as hard links to distinguish them from the symbolic links we discuss next.) Some systems use these links to easily identify a directory's parent in the tree. Each directory then (except for the root) has one link from its parent and one from each of its children.

Some systems define a different type of link called a **symbolic link**. Whereas regular links (or hard links) are like aliased pointers, the symbolic link is more like a macro. When we use a symbolic link, we do a name substitution. For example, if we want the name /usr/stuart/foo to be an alias for the name /etc/bar, then we associate the string /etc/bar with the name /usr/stuart/foo, in such a way that given the name /usr/stuart/foo, we can easily find the string /etc/bar. With this mapping in place, a reference to the file name /usr/stuart/foo/baz is translated into a reference to the name /etc/bar/baz, and the requested operation is carried out on that name. If /etc/bar does not exist when we attempt to access foo, then the access fails. Notice that in this example, we are linking to a directory rather than a regular file.

Aliases move the idea of a hierarchical name space from being a tree to being a more general directed graph. If we allow links to point to directories (as in our symbolic link example), the graph can have cycles. In discussing hierarchical name spaces, we pointed out that cycles in the name space can cause administrative difficulties. For example, if we are traversing the whole name space for the purpose of running a backup, keeping from getting into an infinite loop due to the cycle adds an extra complication. To avoid the problems associated with cycles, we normally disallow hard links that point to directories (except for the special one for the parent directory). Symbolic links, on the other hand, are different from regular directory entries, allowing us to skip them in name space traversals.

17.5   Consistency Checking

When everything is working properly, all of the file system's data structures tell the same story. No blocks listed in the free block structure are also listed as blocks belonging to a file. Every free block is listed in the free block data structure. No blocks are listed as belonging to more than one file. Every file allocation structure is connected with a directory entry.

Often, however, reality is not perfect. A number of things can happen to lead to inconsistent file system data structures. Certainly, bugs in the file system implementation can cause problems. More commonly, the operating system crashes or the hardware loses power at a point in time when one set of data structures has been modified and another hasn't. For this reason, we sometimes run programs that scan the file system looking for and fixing any problems. On earlier systems, these file system checks were often run every time the system was booted. However, as disks, and, hence, file systems, became larger, these file system checks began to take long enough that they became an inconvenience. Today, most file systems contain a flag in the metadata that indicates whether the file system was unmounted cleanly. In particular, we want to know whether the file system was explicitly unmounted or the system went down with the file system still mounted. In the latter case, there might have been buffers of data that were never written to the file system, leaving it in an inconsistent state. When the file system is mounted, we look at that flag, and if it is set, we mount the file system without checking it. If the flag is not set, then we run consistency checks on it. Either way, we clear the flag until the file system is unmounted when we set the flag again. In addition to checking the file system when we suspect a problem, many systems also check periodically based on the number of times the file system has been mounted. Such a system might run the check every 20 times the file system is mounted, for example.

17.6   Journaling and Log-Structured File Systems

Although not completely eliminating the need for any form of checking, there is a file system design technique that does reduce the need for checking and that speeds up the process of checking and recovering. These **journaling file systems** are inspired by techniques used in database design that preserve database consistency. In a journaling file system, we treat the storage device as an unbounded linear array of blocks. In this array of blocks, we keep a journal that records information about every update to the file system. This update information is sufficient to replay each update, ensuring that the update is complete and results in a consistent file system. Consider the case of removing a file in a file system where directory entries point to separate metadata structures. To complete the removal, we must remove the directory entry, free the data blocks, and free the metadata structure. If the system crashes during any of those operations, the file system is left in an inconsistent state. By recording enough information to ensure that the operation is either fully carried out or not carried out at all, we can keep the file system consistent.

There are two basic approaches to implementing a journal. In the first approach, we record to the journal a description of our intentions. This is done before making any changes to the file system itself. If the system crashes while we're writing the journal, we don't carry out the operation at all, and it is the same as if the system had crashed before requesting the operation. If the system crashes after writing the journal but while updating

---

Historical Note: Sources of Inconsistency

The PDP-11, on which much of the early UNIX development took place, had an interesting characteristic that could lead to inconsistencies in the file system. When writing to a disk using DMA, some of the control of the DMA memory accesses went through the CPU. However, if the machine was halted, then the CPU did not perform the operations necessary to support DMA. If the processor was halted while a block was being written, then the remainder of the data for the block would not be fetched from memory, and zeros would be written to the block instead. Of course, if this took place while the system was updating file system metadata, then the file system would end up in an inconsistent state. Worse yet, if it was updating the overall file system metadata, the entire file system might be unusable. Many veterans of early UNIX systems can vividly remember going back to the distribution tapes to reinstall the operating system when this happened.

the file system, the journal contains enough information to complete the operation when the system comes back up. In the second approach, we journal the blocks themselves. Instead of writing a description of the update, we write a copy of the data that will be updated after the journal entry is complete. In both approaches, whenever we need to write a block, we always append it to the end of the device. After a set of blocks that represents a consistent set of changes is written, we then mark those blocks as being valid, and future writes are appended to these. If the system crashes before we have marked these blocks as valid, then it is as if they were never written, and the system operates with the state that was last consistent before it crashed.

Looking at the second approach to journaling, it appears to be redundant and inefficient to write the same data block twice. Alternatively, we could use the disk blocks in the journal itself for the file system. A file system journaled in this way is known as a **log-structured file system**. Notice that in a purely journaled file system, changes are made in place just as with a nonjournaled file system. As a result, both data and metadata remain in the same place all the time. In the case of a log-structured file system, however, as blocks are written, they migrate to other locations on the disk.

There are a couple of issues that make things more complicated, particularly in log-structured file systems. First, real disks aren't unbounded. As we keep appending to them, we eventually run out of disk space. When that happens, we treat them much like a circular buffer; we start over again at the beginning of the disk. Along the way, we made numerous blocks unnecessary when updates were completed. These blocks are now free, and we can use them as if they were at the end of the disk. The only time we have no free blocks is when the disk is truly full, just as with any other file system design.

The second issue that we face is updating every data structure that depends on a block's location. When we write a modified data block, we have to modify the data structure that points to it. The block containing that structure, then, is also modified and must be written to the disk. This means that the block containing a pointer to the structure must also be modified and written, and so on. As a result, whenever we modify any data, we have a cascade of updates that must be made, and all of them must be completed before we can mark the structures consistent.

Because of these issues, many implementations do not attempt to do full journaling. Instead, only the metadata and file allocation structures are treated as a journal. Data blocks are modified in place just as in a nonjournaled file system. This arrangement gives us most of the benefits of a journaled file system with fewer negative side effects.

17.7   Block Caching

File systems and device drivers for storage devices naturally work in units of blocks. However, most applications are not written to operate in units of blocks. They read and write data in sizes natural to the application. Some even read and write one byte at a time. As we've described things up to this point, each access requires that we access the on-disk data structures to locate the appropriate block, read that block into memory, and then write it back out on a write operation. This sequence of events occurs regardless of the size of the read or write operation. Needless to say, if we really did this for every byte read, it would take a very long time to read an entire file.

Virtually every operating system design includes some form of **block caching**. By keeping copies of some number of the most recently accessed blocks in memory, most requests can be satisfied from this cache rather than requiring disk accesses. Typically, a system will reserve some amount of the physical memory space at boot time for the file system to use as a cache. For systems that are configured to primarily serve files over a network, most of the physical memory might be allocated to this purpose. In some designs, the OS attempts to dynamically use whatever memory is not being used by processes for the cache, keeping some minimum number of blocks in the cache at all times.

As usual, we don't get something for nothing. There are a couple of issues we need to address in designing a block cache. The first is primarily an issue for write requests. If we store the write data in the cache, then as far as the application is concerned, the write has happened. However, if that's where the data stays, the storage device will quickly grow out of date with respect to the data. If the system stayed up forever, this wouldn't be a problem, but if the system ever crashes, then all of those changes get lost. For this reason, we generally have a process, kernel thread, or some other control structure that periodically triggers some synchronization operation. Each of the blocks in the cache that are marked modified are queued to be written to the storage device, and after they are, they are marked as clean. We also force a synchronization when a file system is unmounted, including being unmounted when the system is shut down.

The second issue we face is a result of the finite amount of cache space we have. Needless to say, as the system operates, this cache fills up. When it does, we have to pick a block to remove from the cache to make room for any new ones. This problem is very much the same as the one faced by the paging system. In fact, many of the page replacement policies are suitable for this task as well. However, there is one difference here. Because the access frequency for blocks is much lower than that for pages, we can directly use a least recently used (LRU) policy rather than approximating it. One simple implementation keeps all the blocks in a linked list. Whenever a block is referenced, we remove it from the list and reinsert it at the tail of the list. When a block must be selected for replacement, we just select the block at the head of the list. This ensures that the cache contains the most recently accessed blocks. When freeing a block in the cache, if it contains the result of a write operation, then it must be written to the disk before the block can be resued.

17.8   Summary

File systems have evolved from primitive means of storing persistent data on storage devices to flexible and sophisticated tools for accessing other operating system services. The issue of representing file data on a storage device is still a significant one. In this chapter, we saw a number of different approaches to this problem. We also saw a number of approaches to representing each file's metadata. Beyond that, we saw the development of naming systems and techniques for mapping names to both files and services. This generalization of the function of a file system provides the basis of a continuing evolution in uniformly referencing and using system services.

17.9   Exercises

1. Define the concept of a name space.

2. What are the advantages of a uniform name space design?

3. The name space example described in Section 17.3.3 is similar to that used in UNIX. Give a description of the name space for MS-DOS.

4. Is it necessary to provide both absolute and relative position seeking service? Why or why not?

5. Suppose we use a list of free blocks where each block is identified by a 32-bit number and each block contains 512 bytes. How many blocks are required to store the free list on a 20-GB disk if the disk is empty?

6. If disk blocks are 1024 bytes in size, what percentage of the disk is overhead imposed by a free bitmap?

7. What are the advantages and disadvantages of using a double-indirect pointer over multiple single-indirect pointers?

8. What percentage of the storage space is overhead in a list-structured allocation structure, as illustrated in Figure 17-6?

9. If we have a three-level tree-structured allocation structure as in Figure 17-8, where each block is 1024 bytes and each block pointer is 4 bytes, how large is the largest file that can be represented?

10. Depending on the design of the directory, aliases might have their own metadata, or they might share one set of metadata for the file. What are the advantages and disadvantages of each approach?

11. Describe how symbolic links could be implemented.

12. We suggested that in doing backups, we need not follow symbolic links in traversing the name space. Why not? How do we ensure we do not miss any files?

13. Describe some of the security risks associated with defining the executability of a file in terms of its file name.

14. Why would it be a problem to remove a USB storage device without unmounting it first?

15. Can a file allocation table scheme represent sparse files? Why or why not?

16. There was a period of time when very high-capacity storage systems were made from Write Once, Read Many (WORM) optical discs. Given that any single block on a WORM disc can be written only once, discuss how journaled and log-structured file systems are suited to WORM discs.

Chapter 18

Some Examples of File Systems

In this chapter, we return to our set of operating systems examples and examine the file system designs of each. However, we omit Xen and TinyOS because neither incorporates any file system support. In the remaining set, we see a variety of approaches, and at the same time we see some family resemblances. Within those families, we trace a number of evolutionary trends in file system design.

18.1 CTSS

Over the course of its life, CTSS had two different, but related, file system designs. The second was developed as a result of the lessons learned with the first. It served as a prototype and development environment for work on Multics. We discuss both versions of the file system to illustrate the evolution of file system ideas from early direct device accesses to the more modern file abstractions and uniform access mechanisms.

18.1.1 First CTSS File System

The first CTSS file system supported a rich set of system calls. However, many calls could be implemented in terms of others. For example, an entire file could be read or written using the .LOAD and the .DUMP calls, respectively. Unlike most later systems, the first CTSS file system used different calls for opening and closing a file depending on whether the intended use was reading, writing, or both. For creating a file to write, .ASIGN was the call to open the file; but for appending to an existing file, .APEND was used. In both cases, .FILE closed the file. For reading an existing file, .SEEK performed the open, and .ENDRD performed the close. If a process wanted to open the file for both reading and writing, it used the .RELRW call, and either .FILE or .ENDRD could be used to close it. In all cases, the .READK and .WRITE calls were used to carry out the actual reads and writes.

   File names in CTSS were composed of two parts, each with up to six characters. When written out, the two parts were normally separated by a space. Thus, the name space for

425

CTSS was given by $N = A^{[1,6]} {\scriptstyle\sqcup} A^{[1,6]}$. Although the system didn't enforce any meaning or interpretation of the two parts, by convention the first part of the name was a descriptive name, and the second indicated the file's type.

Each user had a private directory of files. These directories were single level. In other words, subdirectories were not supported. No user had access to another user's private files. To facilitate sharing, there were limited mechanisms providing common directories for programmers sharing the same problem number and for globally common directories. For one user to share a file with another, the first user would copy the file from the private area to a common area. Then, the second user would copy the file from the common area to the private area. Even in common directories, only one user at a time could be using a directory as its current directory.

Unlike many of the other systems we study, CTSS allocated disk space in units of tracks rather than blocks. This matched a record-per-track mode provided by the early disk hardware used on the system. Tracks were managed by several data structures. There was a track usage table that identified which tracks were used and which were free. The Master File Directory (MFD) was another key data structure. It mapped from programmer/problem ID numbers to the locations of the corresponding User File Directories (UFDs). The MFD also included the number of tracks allocated to each user. A UFD entry contained a file's metadata, which included the name, last access date, document number, and file mode, which indicated whether a file is read/write, read-only, append-only, and so on. The UFD entry also pointed to the first track in a file. Tracks in a file formed a linked list with the first word of each track pointing to the next track in the file. For the last track of a file, the next track pointer pointed to the end of the track itself.

18.1.2 Second CTSS File System

One of the enhancements in the second CTSS file system was a redesigned set of system calls. The newer calls represented a step in the evolution toward a simpler and more uniform interface for files. It included the now familiar OPEN. and CLOSE. calls. Both blocking and nonblocking reads and writes were provided through the RDFILE., RDWAIT., WRFILE., and WRWAIT. calls.

The two-part file naming was unchanged between the first and second file system designs. However, the details of access, particularly with respect to sharing files, did change significantly. One such change was the addition of more flexibility when dealing with common directories. In particular, more than one user could use a common directory at a time in the second version system. More significantly, the second file system design supported aliases. An entry in one UFD could be identified as a link to another entry, typically in another UFD.

The internal implementation of the second CTSS file system also represented a step forward. It was made more modular than its predecessor and followed a structure incorporating elements we discussed in Chapter 17. Overall, the second CTSS file system represented a link between the earlier experimental file system and the production file system of Multics.

18.2   Multics

In many ways, the Multics file system is one of the most interesting ones we consider. To really understand it, we need to recall the segmented memory system described in Section 10.2. From the application point of view, and largely from an internal implementation perspective, segments and files are the same thing. When we are being careful, referring to a segment refers to data stored in memory in one or more pages that share a segment number. A file is the data as stored on a storage device. However, there is always a one-to-one correspondence between them. Every segment in memory corresponds to a file, even if it's a temporary file that is removed when a process terminates. Every file can be accessed when mapped to a segment. One result of this structure is that all segments are represented by names in the name space as well as by segment numbers. Another is that the action of allocating and loading a segment and the action of opening and reading a file are really the same operation in Multics.

We highlight this last point because it means that all file references can be made through normal segment accesses. When a function in another segment is called, its segment is mapped by a segment table (described in more detail later) and is given a segment number. From that point, normal demand paging loads the needed segment pages into memory. This results in a very general and elegant scheme for dynamic loading and sharing of libraries. The same can be done with data files. Referencing a file as a data structure causes its segment to be made known to the process and the relevant pages to be swapped in. The original design for Multics recognized that this was sufficient for all file accesses. In later versions, there also exist more conventional character-, line-, and record-oriented read and write operations.

Names in Multics can contain any ASCII characters except >. However, in normal usage, only the upper- and lowercase letters, the digits, the underscore (_), and the period (.) are used. Other ASCII characters are interpreted specially in some contexts, and others are troublesome in regular usage. File names can be up to 32 characters long. Multics supports a hierarchical directory structure with up to 16 levels of directories. The > character is used to delimit directories in a path name. Thus, the name space for Multics is roughly $N = >_{\text{opt}}(A^{[1,32]}>)^{[0,15]}A^{[1,32]}$. If the leading character is >, then the path name is absolute and specifies all directories from the root down to the final name. Otherwise, it is relative to the process's current working directory. The < character can be used in relative path names to indicate the parent or other ancestor directory. For example, the path name <a refers to the file called a, which is a sibling of the current working directory. Similarly, <<a refers to a file called a, which is contained in the current working directory's grandparent directory. Names given without any path characters (> or <) are located by searching a set of directories defined by a set of systemwide search rules.

Multics supports two different types of aliases as we have described them. In the first case, each file can have several names in its directory entry. This type of alias makes it easy to load segment on demand when one of its functions is called. The other type of alias is the more familiar link. Entries in one directory can point to entries in another, much like we've described as symbolic links. All metadata for the file are maintained with the original copy. Although not exactly an alias, there is one more way in which a file (segment) can be given an alternative name. It can be assigned a **reference name**, which can then be used in both commands and in programs run after the assignment.

Multics directory entries contain a rich set of metadata for each file. Much of it exists to support security and is discussed in more detail in Chapter 21. Other metadata include a list of names by which the file is known, an indication of the file's type (directory, regular file, or link), the author of the file, the current and maximum sizes of the file, various timestamps, the type of device that stores the file, and a unique ID number for the entry.

One other directory-related matter is that of multisegment files. Because a segment can be no larger than $2^{18} = 256$ K words, any files larger than this must be spread across multiple segments. However, because there is a one-to-one correspondence between files and segments, a multisegment file must be spread across multiple regular files. Multics handles this by representing a multisegment file by a directory that contains the various regular files that comprise it. Directory entries have a flag to indicate whether the entry refers to a multisegment file, and most code that deals with files is aware of this convention and does the right thing.

The last aspect of the Multics file system we consider here is the set of data structures used to manage the relationship between files and segments. We focus our attention on two key tables. The first is called the Known Segment Table (KST) and lists all segments that have been assigned segment numbers in the process. The second is called the Descriptor Segment (DS) and is a table of segment descriptors. These tables run in parallel and are both indexed by the segment number. A KST entry contains the path name for that segment and a pointer to its directory entry. DS entries contain those elements needed for the memory management aspects of segments. In particular, they contain the pointers to the page tables for segments.

When a segment is first referenced, there is no segment number yet assigned to it, and a fault is generated, causing the dynamic linker to run. The linker uses the symbolic name (either the path name or the reference name) for the needed segment and makes calls to make the segment known. This procedure searches the KST for the desired segment. If it is found, then the linker can resolve the references to that segment with the appropriate segment number. If the segment is not found, then the search rules are applied to find the correct file for this reference, and a free segment number is allocated for this new segment. The KST and DS entries are then initialized to indicate that we have a known but invalid segment. With the allocated segment number, the linker can then resolve references to the segment. When the process attempts to reference the newly allocated segment number, a segment fault occurs, and the segment is made valid by assigning a page table to it. After the initial segment resolution is accomplished in this way, future references to that segment are handled through the normal memory management techniques discussed in Section 10.2.

18.3   RT-11

As with other subsystems, the file system of RT-11 is designed primarily for simplicity and efficiency. The set of system calls is pretty conventional. Files are created by the .ENTER call, and existing files can be opened with .LOOKUP. I/O operations can then be carried out using the .READ and .WRITE calls. Finally, programs call .CLOSE when they are finished with a file. The name space is similarly straightforward. RT-11 uses a device specifier, and directories are nonhierarchical. File names are up to six characters, followed by an extension of up to three characters. Thus, $N = (LLD :)_{\text{opt}} A^{[1,6]}.A^{[0,3]}$, where L is the set of letters and D is the set of digits.

The overall layout of the file system is also similar to other designs, but simpler. Blocks 0–5 of the disk are reserved, with block 0 normally containing bootstrap code, and block 1 being designated as the **home block** containing file system metadata. The home block contains a bad block replacement table, the location of the first directory block, three identification strings, and a checksum. Beginning with block 6, there are n directory segments, each two blocks in size. All remaining blocks on the disk are available for data.

Each directory segment contains up to 72 entries and describes the files in a particular range of disk blocks. At the beginning of each segment, there is a header that describes the list of segments and includes the total number of segments, the number of the next segment in the list, and the number of the last segment currently in use. The header also includes the number of optional extra bytes used in each of its directory entries. In most cases, this is zero. Finally, the header gives the starting data block number of the region described by that segment. Each directory entry contains seven 16-bit words, which include a file status word, the file name, the file size, the creation date, and a word with information used only for files designated as tentative.

Files in RT-11 are stored in contiguous blocks. This means that the maximum size of the file must be specified and the space reserved at the time the file is created. However, it also means that there is no overhead either in terms of space or processing time to locate the blocks that belong to a file. Because we know where a file starts and how large it is, we know all the blocks that belong to it. It might seem strange that the directory entry does not tell us the starting block for a file. However, we can calculate it relatively easily by taking the starting block number for the segment and adding the file sizes of all the files that precede the desired one in the directory. From this, it is correct to infer that the files are stored on the disk in the same order as their directory entries appear in the segment. Although this arrangement can be inconvenient (because the maximum file size has to be specified ahead of time) and can lead to significant fragmentation, the simplicity of it is ideal for the intended real-time applications of RT-11.

18.4   Sixth Edition UNIX

The early UNIX file system is one of the more clear examples of the influence Multics had on its designers. It is certainly different from its predecessor, reflecting the very different hardware environment of the two systems. However, features such as the hierarchical directory structure, the similar name spaces, and links show their similarities, particularly in contrast to most other file systems of the time.

One of the places where UNIX differs most from Multics is the area of file system services. The PDP-11, on which much of early UNIX development was done, has a much smaller virtual address space and limited hardware support for segmentation when compared with machines that supported Multics. Consequently, the segment-file correspondence we see in Multics is not a good fit for UNIX. (Later versions of UNIX do provide a mechanism for memory-mapped files, however.) Instead, UNIX uses a pretty conventional set of file-related system calls. A new file can be created with the *creat*( ) system call, and an existing file can be opened with *open*( ). After being opened by either call, a file can be read with *read*( ) and written with *write*( ). The current file position can be set with *seek*( ). When a process is finished with a file, it can close the file with the *close*( ) system call. The kernel implicitly closes any files remaining open when a process exits.

There is another way a process can get a file descriptor used by *read*( ) and *write*( ). The *pipe*( ) system call creates a communications channel that can be used to communicate between a pair of processes. A pipe, like other open files, is inherited by any child processes that are created. Thus, a parent can use a pipe to communicate with a descendant, or can create a pipe to be used between two descendants. After the pipe is created, *read*( ), *write*( ), and *close*( ) can be used just as with a file. Although pipes are not files in the traditional sense, the UNIX implementation uses the same system calls for them and uses most of the file system infrastructure to implement them.

As we've already suggested, the name space for UNIX is similar to that of Multics. Names can be composed of any ASCII characters except slash (/), but normally letters, digits, underscores, and periods are used. In sixth edition UNIX, file names are restricted to 14 characters. The slash (/) character is used to delimit directory names. Unlike Multics, UNIX doesn't set an upper bound on the depth of a directory. Consequently, the name space for sixth edition UNIX looks something like $N = /_{\text{opt}}(A^{[1,14]}/)^* A[1,14]/_{\text{opt}}$.

Unlike many systems, the correspondence in UNIX isn't between directory entries and files. There is a one-to-one correspondence between i-nodes and files, and many directory entries can refer to the same i-node. Each i-node in sixth edition UNIX includes expected metadata such as protection and ownership information, the file size, the last access time, and the last modification time. It also includes a count of the number of directory entries (links) that refer to it. Finally, the i-node includes the pointers necessary to locate the disk blocks that make up the file. UNIX uses a hybrid scheme based on the tree-structured allocation illustrated in Figure 17-8. There are eight block pointers in the i-node. Files in sixth edition UNIX can be designated as either small or large (and promoted from small to large automatically if needed). For small files, all eight pointers point directly to data blocks of 512 bytes each. For large files, the first seven pointers identify seven indirect blocks. Each indirect block holds 256 pointers to data blocks. The eighth pointer in a large file points to a double-indirect block. Each of the 256 pointers in it points to an indirect block of 256 pointers, each of which points to a data block.

In UNIX, directories are managed on the disk just as are ordinary files; however, care is taken to prevent them from being arbitrarily manipulated by processes. They can be modified only by way of the various system calls that create, remove, and rename files. Directories themselves are simply linear arrays of structures, each with 16 bytes. Fourteen bytes are used for the file name, with shorter names being null-terminated. The remaining two bytes form a 16-bit i-number, which points to the rest of the file's metadata. The i-number stored in a directory entry is used as an index into the table of i-nodes. Each directory has two special entries, dot (.) and dot-dot(..), placed there when the directory is created. The dot(.) entry always refers to the directory itself, and the dot-dot(..) entry always refers to the parent directory. In this way, references to files other than descendants of the current directory can be made without resorting to special characters or special parsing rules. A path name such as ../../foo can be resolved using the same path resolution as any other name.

For the most part, every file system in sixth edition UNIX is stored on one disk drive and occupies the whole disk, or it occupies a portion of the disk, with the remainder reserved for swap space. (Although some people did write device drivers that partitioned disks, this was not common.) Typically, the first block of each disk contains bootstrapping code that loads the kernel into memory. Beginning with the second block, the file system starts with a special block called the superblock, which contains certain metadata for the file system as a whole. Among these data are the number of blocks reserved for i-nodes, the number of data blocks, a partial list of free i-nodes, a partial list of free data blocks (for quick look up), a read-only flag, and a timestamp indicating the time of the last update. Immediately following the superblock are one or more blocks giving a free bitmap for the i-nodes. The next several blocks are those for the i-nodes. The remaining blocks in the file system are data blocks. A free block list is stored within the free blocks themselves.

In addition to regular data files, i-nodes can also identify devices. Two of the bits in the protection word are used to identify such a file as a character special file or a block special file. If a file is a special file, then the first two block pointers of its i-node are used to store the major and minor device numbers. When a system call is issued on such a file, the request is passed on to the device driver identified by the major device number. The minor device number is passed to the driver as an argument it can use any way it sees fit. Typically, the minor device number identifies at least which physical device of those supported by the driver is being used.

18.5   4.3BSD

To a large extent, the changes that appear in the development between sixth edition UNIX and the BSD series represent the sort of evolution one would expect as efforts are made to accommodate larger capacity systems and to increase performance. Some of these changes are reflected in updated system calls. One change allows the *open*( ) system call to also create files. Although *creat*( ) is still supported in 4.3BSD, its use has largely fallen by the wayside. The *seek*( ) call has been replaced by *lseek*( ), which supports larger files.

The only real difference in the name space of 4.3BSD compared wth sixth edition UNIX is longer file names. The maximum file name is 255 characters in 4.3BSD. Consequently, the name space can be defined by $N = /_{\text{opt}}(A^{[1,255]}/_{\text{opt}})^* A^{[1,255]}/_{\text{opt}}$. This change necessitates a change in the design of directories. A directory entry begins with a 4-byte i-number followed by the size of the entry (to locate the next entry), the number of characters in the name, and, finally, the name itself. The space reserved for the name is rounded up to the nearest larger multiple of four. Thus, directory entries in 4.3BSD are variable sized to allow for large names without wasting space for short names.

The BSD series of UNIX versions has also added a new type of link. Although the traditional hard links are still supported, symbolic links are also supported. Hard links have the restriction that they must refer to a file on the same file system. Symbolic links get around that restriction by simply mapping a directory entry to a path name rather than mapping it to an i-node. When resolving a path name that contains a symbolic link, the name of the link is replaced with the path to which it maps, and the name resolution continues.

This Fast File System (FFS) was introduced in 4.2BSD and continues to use the same basic i-node structure as in earlier versions, but with a few enhancements. First, a new timestamp has been added, recording the time of the last update of the i-node. Another change is a simplification of the block pointer design. The FFS no longer identifies files as large or small. Instead, there are a total of 15 block pointers in the i-node. The first 12 are direct pointers to data blocks, usually of 4096 bytes each. The exact size is selected at the time the file system is initialized. The 13th pointer points to an indirect block. If the data blocks are 4096 bytes each, then the indirect block points to 1024 data blocks. The 14th pointer in the i-node points to a double-indirect block, which, in turn, points to a number of indirect blocks, which, in turn, point to a number of data blocks. The 15th pointer is reserved for use in pointing to a triple-indirect block. However, this feature is not implemented in 4.3BSD.

As disk sizes have grown larger, and in particular as the number of cylinders has grown, the distance between the i-nodes and the data blocks they reference has grown as well. This leads to longer seek times. To combat this, the BSD FFS has introduced the idea of **cylinder groups**, which involves dividing the disk into concentric groups of contiguous cylinders much like partitioning does. The difference is that the whole space is one file system, rather than each cylinder group being its own file system. Nevertheless, each cylinder group contains most of what constitutes a file system, including a copy of the superblock, some number of i-node blocks, a free data block bitmap, and some number of data blocks. Because all the groups together make up a single file system, a file can be placed in any cylinder group. However, an attempt is made to keep data blocks close to the metadata describing them. By spreading the metadata out across the disk, the blocks can be closer to their metadata, reducing the average distance we need to seek.

18.6   VMS

The VMS file system is one of a family of file systems from Digital Equipment Corporation (DEC) that goes under the name Files-11. It originated with DEC's RSX-11 operating system in a form known as on-disk structure-1 (ODS-1). For VMS, the design was extended, producing a version called ODS-2. Although an extension called ODS-5 has been developed, ODS-2 is the most commonly used version of the file system. Therefore, that is the version we examine here.

Direct access to file system services in VMS follows much of the same structure as for I/O devices, as was described in Section 14.6. In particular, the $ASSIGN, $DASSIGN, and $QIO interfaces can be used with files as well. Most applications, however, use the services of the Record Management Services (RMS) subsystem. Although not part of the operating system proper, RMS does have a more privileged status than normal libraries.

Names in VMS can have a device specifier, a directory path, a file name and extension, and a version number. The name space can roughly be described by

$$N = (A^+ :)_{\text{opt}}([A^{[1,39]}(.A^{[1,39]})^{[0,7]}])_{\text{opt}}A^{[0,39]}(.A^{[0,39]})_{\text{opt}}(; D^{[1,5]})_{\text{opt}}$$

For example, [a.b]foo.txt;1 is a valid name. The optional device specifier (not found in this example) is the first part of the name, ending in a colon. Although the syntax for actual devices is fairly rigid, a user can also define a logical name and use that in place of the actual device name. As a result, we have allowed that specifier to be freely formatted in our specification. The dot-separated list of up to eight names in square brackets specifies the file's location in the hierarchical directory tree. (ODS-5 removes the limitation of eight levels.) The root of the tree is specified by [00000]. Following the semicolon is a version number. The VMS file system allows users to keep several versions of the same file at a time.

As with the RT-11 file system, block 0 of the disk normally contains the bootstrap loader, and block 1 (unless it is a bad block) contains the home block. The home block contains a variety of file system metadata, including several identification strings and the locations of other metadata. From these metadata, we can locate the file header for a special file called the **index file**, which has the file name INDEXF.SYS;1 and contains nearly all the metadata for the entire file system. Its first two blocks are mapped to the boot block and the home block. It also contains at least one (and usually several) additional copies of the home block. The next item it contains is a backup copy of its own file header, followed by a bitmap for other file headers. At least 16 such headers follow the bitmap. All of these data are contiguous in the index file. All other file headers for the whole file system are part of the index file but can be allocated anywhere on the disk.

Each file in Files-11 ODS-2 is assigned a unique file identifier (FID), which is a 48-bit number with a particular structure. Twenty-four bits of the FID are used as an index into the list of file headers to locate the file's metadata. To a first approximation, directories are lists of name-FID pairs. More precisely, a directory is a set of directory records sorted in alphabetical order by the file name. Each record contains the file name and one or more entries. Each entry lists a version number and an FID for that version of the file. Because multiple directory entries can use the same FID, the VMS file system supports aliases similar to the hard links in UNIX. The root of the file system is described by the Master File Directory (MFD), which is named 00000.DIR;1. The MFD lists, among others, itself, INDEXF.SYS;1, BITMAP.SYS;1 (the free bitmap for data blocks in the file system), and BADBLK.SYS;1 (the list of bad blocks on the disk). Any User File Directories (UFDs) are also listed in the MFD.

File headers are fairly complex data structures containing several areas. The first area is itself a header. The header area contains several items, including the FID of the file, the FID of an extension header if necessary, the FID of the parent directory, the file owner, the file characteristics, the protection information, and the locations of the other areas. One optional area is the access control list (ACL) area, which is used only for security. The Ident area lists the file name, the revision number, and several timestamps. Note that the revision number is not the same as the version number. The revision number is the number of times the file has been accessed for writing. The other area of interest to us is the Map area, which lists the data blocks that make up the file. It consists of a number of items called retrieval pointers. These pointers give the starting block number and length of each extent in the file. **Extents** are contiguous groups of blocks that make up the file. This representation is not unlike the list representation shown in Figure 17-6, except that each pointer in the list points not to a single block but to a contiguous region of blocks. Thus, a contiguous file contains only one extent, regardless of its size.

18.7   Windows NT

The NT File System (NTFS) is a replacement for the various FAT file systems used in other Microsoft offerings. It is much better suited to larger computing environments than FAT. Furthermore, it provides better failure recovery as a result of its use of journaling of metadata.

The system calls for files in Windows NT are the same as those discussed for I/O devices in Section 14.7. At the kernel level, there are calls such as *NtOpenFile( )*, *NtCreateFile( )*, *NtReadFile( )*, *NtWriteFile( )*, and *NtCloseFile( )*. These are made available to applications through the various environment subsystems. For the Win32 subsystem, the *WriteFile( )* call causes the *NtWriteFile( )* call to be issued, as does *write( )* in the POSIX subsystem.

The subsystem design also affects the details of the name space. Because the most general name space of the subsystems belongs to POSIX, internally Windows NT supports the same set of file names as does POSIX. In general, any file name can be up to 255 Unicode characters. A path name can be prefixed by a single letter drive specifier, and directories within a path are delimited by the backslash (\). This results in a name space that can be defined as $N = (L :)_{opt} \backslash_{opt} (A^{[1,255]} \backslash)^* A^{[1,255]}$. Interestingly, internally, the sequence \??\ is prepended to full path names before they are resolved. For instance, the path C:\Temp\foo.txt becomes \??\C:\Temp\foo.txt internally. If we recognize that the colon can be just another character in a file name, then this modification results in a more uniform name space, where disks are mounted to directories in \??\ that happen to have the same names as the drive specifiers.

NTFS forces little in the way of an overall file system layout. The first several (often 16) blocks are used for bootstrapping code. One of the items in the first block of boot code is a pointer to the Master File Table (MFT). The MFT file contains much of the metadata for the whole file system and identifies files containing the rest. This file is organized as a set of 1 KB **file records**. There is one file record for each file in the file system, including the MFT, plus several records that hold additional metadata. Some of the other records identify general descriptive information for the file system as a whole, such as the file containing the root directory and the file containing the bitmap of free blocks.

Each file is identified by a 64-bit reference number. The low-order 48 bits of the reference number are the file number that is used to index the MFT for the file record for that file. Directories in NTFS are primarily mappings from names to reference numbers. The directories are organized as B+ trees to reduce the number of blocks that must be read to search for a file.

Each file record is a set of attribute-value pairs. For most entries, one of the attributes is the file name. For regular file entries and directories, another attribute is called Standard Information. This contains the usual file metadata such as owner, size, and protection information. The Data attribute holds the contents of a regular file. The file system design allows multiple Data attributes, where each attribute (aside from a default Data attribute) is given a name. These additional Data attributes are also known as Alternate Data Streams. For directories, there are attributes that are used to describe the B+ tree. In principle, any of the attributes can be resident in the record or nonresident, and thus stored in data blocks on the disk. If the value for the attribute (including the Data attribute or the attributes that make up a directory) will fit within the 1 KB record along with other attributes, then it is stored there. Otherwise, the value is stored in other data blocks. For the attributes like the file name and the Standard Information, the value is generally stored in the record. For all but the smallest regular files, the data are, however, stored in other disk blocks. In the case of a nonresident value (such as most file data), the value stored in the file record is a list of **runs** or **extents**, which are sets of starting block numbers and block counts.

18.8 Summary

As with the other areas of OS responsibility we've studied, we find a significant number of variations on the basic techniques of file system design. In this chapter, we have considered those variations in seven of the operating system examples we have used throughout this book. Within those variations, we also see certain techniques continuing through family lines, including the CTSS/Multics/UNIX line and the VMS/Windows NT line. These file systems provide a significant contribution to the distinctive character of each of these operating systems.

18.9 Exercises

1. Why would accessing a random byte of a file be faster with RT-11 than with UNIX?

2. What limits the maximum size of a file in CTSS? What limits the maximum size in Multics? What about RT-11?

3. With 512-byte blocks, how large can a file be in sixth edition UNIX and still be identified as a small file? How large can a large file be using only the set of single-indirect blocks? How large can a large file be using both the single- and double-indirect blocks?

4. How large can a file be in 4.3BSD using only the direct block pointers, assuming a 4096-byte block? How large can it be using the direct block pointers and the indirect block? How large can it be using the direct block pointers, the indirect block, and the double-indirect block? How large could it be if the triple-indirect block were implemented?

5. The designers of the UNIX file system had experience with the CTSS file system. Why might they have chosen to implement the block pointers in i-nodes rather than the linked list approach found in CTSS? Is the same benefit found in using extents such as those in VMS and Windows NT?

6. Suppose we have a system that allows the semicolon as a character in file names, but does not support file versions. Outline a library function called *vcreate( )* that implements a form of versioning. If, for example, it is called to create a file called foo.txt, then it adds a new version of foo.txt to the current directory.

7. Describe a method for using the drive specifiers in RT-11 to provide separate user areas, similar to those in CTSS.

8. How could you support file forks in a UNIX file system design? In particular, design an approach where a file could have up to seven forks. A regular *open( )* call would read from fork 0. An additional system call, *forkopen( )* works like *open( )*, but provides one more argument that specifies the fork to be opened.

9. Normally, the directory separator character is not stored in the on-disk data structures. In principle, therefore, any character could be used. In fact, Windows NT internally allows both the forward slash (/) and the backslash (\) as separators. Outline a path name parsing algorithm that uses a per-process separator character.

Chapter 19

File Systems in Inferno

In a number of places, we have suggested that Inferno is somewhat unusual with respect to its file system design. Indeed, device drivers in Inferno are forms of file systems in their own right. We have also alluded to the fact that much of the file system support is provided by normal applications. In this chapter, we look at several aspects of file systems in Inferno. We begin by looking at the general design and role of file systems in the OS. Inferno adopts a unified interface to file systems, in which all file system requests are conveyed by means of a protocol called **Styx**. After looking at the overall structure, we next look at one of the file servers which is built in to the kernel. Finally, we consider a conventional disk-based file system implemented as a normal application program.

19.1 The Role of File Servers

All file system–related services in Inferno are provided by **file servers**, which take two forms. The first type of server is one that is built in to the kernel. The other type is implemented as a normal application program. Whether they run as part of the kernel or as stand-alone applications, all file servers accept requests from and deliver results to client processes in the same way. This common interface is provided by the Styx protocol we examine in detail in Section 19.1.1. Furthermore, this is true whether the process that originates the request is running on the local machine or on another machine connected by a network.

File servers provide their own name space in the form of a small directory tree. Using the *bind*( ) and *mount*( ) system calls, processes can assemble the various name spaces provided by a variety of servers into a complete name space. Although most processes work within the name space they inherit from their parents, each process is free to construct its own name space independently of any other. Of course, in building a name space, we must have a place to start. This is the role of the root file server discussed in this chapter.

Ultimately, the Inferno kernel is responsible for four services: process management, memory management, Styx message handling, and the Dis virtual machine. I/O device handling and file system services are provided through file servers.

437

19.1.1   The Styx Protocol

Although our focus in this book is not on operating system support of networking, we need to take a look at the Styx protocol to understand Inferno file servers. Styx is a protocol that is used between file servers and clients. It is used universally regardless of whether the client and server reside on the same machine or on different machines. The complete set of messages in Styx is:

- *Tversion/Rversion*: Establish which protocol version to use.

- *Tauth/Rauth*: Authenticate the client.

- *Rerror*: Return an error to the client.

- *Tflush/Rflush*: Abort a request.

- *Tattach/Rattach*: Establish a connection to the server.

- *Twalk/Rwalk*: Move to another node of the name space.

- *Topen/Ropen*: Open an existing file for reading or writing.

- *Tcreate/Rcreate*: Create a new file.

- *Tread/Rread*: Read from a file.

- *Twrite/Rwrite*: Write to a file.

- *Tclunk/Rclunk*: Drop a connection.

- *Tremove/Rremove*: Remove a file.

- *Tstat/Rstat*: Get a file's metadata.

- *Twstat/Rwstat*: Modify a file's metadata.

In each of these pairs, the T message is a request sent from the client to the server, and the R message is the server's response after completing the request. The use of these messages and how Styx fits into the overall design of the set of file servers is illustrated in Examples 19.1 and 19.2.

Example 19.1: Styx Messages

To illustrate the application of these messages, we examine a typical operation. In particular, we consider what happens when acme opens the file /emu/port/dis.c for editing.

1. The first step of the protocol is the client contacting the root file server and sending the Tversion message to indicate which version of the protocol it wants to use. When it receives the Rversion message in response, then it is ready to continue. At the present time, there is only one version defined. This part of the protocol exists to support compatibility as new versions are defined.

2. For those file servers that require it, the client then sends the Tauth message and waits for the Rauth response.

3. The initial protocol exchange is completed with the Tattach and Rattach messages. As a result of these messages, the client now has an fid (file identifier) that refers to the root of the server—in this case, the root of the whole name space.

4. To get to the file we want to open, the client divides /emu/port/dis.c into the three strings that represent the elements of the path and passes those file names to the server through the Twalk message. The server then traverses its tree one element at a time until it reaches the final element of the path name. It then returns the Rwalk message to the client, and the client now has an fid that refers to the file /emu/port/dis.c.

5. Next, the client sends a Topen message indicating that the file is being opened for reading and writing. As usual, on success the server returns the Ropen message to indicate that the file is available for reading and writing.

6. Finally, the client issues a series of Tread calls requesting data to be read from the file and returned. In response, the server returns the data in Rread messages. These read requests are continued until the count returned by the server is 0, which indicates that we've reached the end of the file. (The client can also use the Tstat message to determine the size of the file from the server and use that value to control the read requests.)

At this point, the file has been read and acme displays it for the user to edit. When the user selects the Put operation, acme writes the file resulting in a series of Twrite and Rwrite messages analogous to the read operation. Similarly, when the user selects Del, acme closes the file. This is performed by sending the Tclunk message, indicating that we won't be doing any other operations to this file. Note that future file operations to the same server do not need to repeat Steps 1–3, because we still have a valid fid for the server's root. Having this fid effectively means that we have an established connection to the server.

Example 19.2: Inferno File Server Interaction

To establish the big picture of Inferno file servers and Styx, consider what happens when an application attempts to open a file in the context of the small set of servers shown in Figure 19-1. In this figure, the disk device driver is the sdata (IDE) driver we examined in Section 15.4, the root file server is covered in Section 19.2, and the kfs server is discussed in Section 19.4. We consider the case where the root file server provides a small name space, which forms the root of the application process's whole name space. In particular, it includes the directory usr at the top level of the hierarchy. On the usr directory, we have mounted the name space provided by the kfs file server, which includes all the files under the /usr/stuart node in the name space tree.

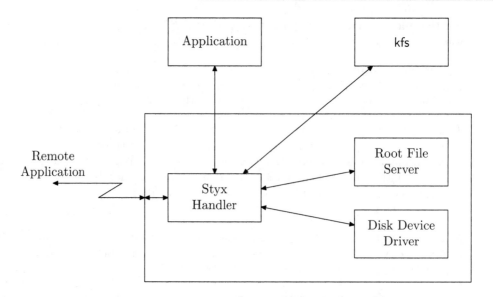

Figure 19-1: Inferno File Server Communication

To consider a specific example, suppose we are opening the file /usr/stuart/game.b. The file-opening system call first issues a Styx request to walk the path from the root to the requested file. This walking process involves a number of interactions among the various components in Figure 19-1:

1. The application (by means of the system call it issues) sends the request to walk to the root server.

2. The root server walks only the /usr part of the path, because that's the only part of the path in its name space. Consequently, it returns to the kernel's Styx handler code the results of that walk, indicating that it had to stop at /usr.

3. The Styx handler code recognizes that the file system served by another file server (kfs in this case) is mounted on /usr. It then continues the walk by sending a walk request for the path /stuart/game.b to the kfs server.

4. As part of the walk, kfs issues requests to the disk device driver, which is itself a file server.

5. The disk device driver returns the results of reading specific data from the disk back to kfs.

6. After reading enough data to complete the walk, kfs returns the remainder of the walk result back to the main Styx code.

7. This kfs walk result is then returned as the result of the walk request issued by the file-opening system call, which continues with additional requests to complete the open.

As indicated in the figure, the application issuing the original request could be on the same machine as the servers or on a remote machine connected over a network. All of the communication requests described here take the form of Styx messages carried over the arrows in the figure.

19.1.2   Built-in Kernel File Servers

The kernel provides a number of built-in file servers. Among them are the device drivers discussed in Chapter 15. However, a number of other services are also provided by file servers. For example, the server defined in the file /emu/port/devprog.c provides access to mechanisms for monitoring and controlling processes. In the /prog directory, it provides a subdirectory, named by the process's PID, for each process. In each of those subdirectories, the server provides a number of files such as, ctl, status, and fd. The ctl file provides a mechanism for controlling the state of a process, whereas status allows a process to query the state of another process. Information about a process's open file descriptors is available through the fd directory. Similar servers provide access to networking services, graphical drawing services, environment variables, and so on.

Built-in file servers do not run as separate processes, but instead receive their Styx requests through function calls. Each such server defines a structure of type **Dev**, which includes a single character name, a string name, and a set of function pointers. Most of these function pointers correspond to the Styx messages discussed in the previous subsection. When a server receives a request, the corresponding function is called and is passed arguments that come from the data in the message.

19.1.3   User-Space File Servers

Given that we have established a design where name space services are provided through a protocol, it is a small step to make that protocol available to application processes. Because all applications in Inferno are written in Limbo, we need only a Limbo module to provide that interface. The **Styx** module does exactly that. Processes using the **Styx** module listen for messages on a Limbo channel. The type of the message corresponds to the type of Styx protocol message and dictates how the message is to be handled. Responses are sent back to the client over the channel as well.

Pretty much any functionality that does not require direct access to the hardware or to operating system internals can be implemented as a user-space file server. The user-space server in this chapter, for example, implements a conventional persistent storage file system. It needs only a name in its name space that provides access to a random access "device" large enough to store the file system. Normally, this is provided by the server for the hard disk, as discussed in Chapter 15. However, in a hosted Inferno implementation, it could just as easily be provided in the form of an ordinary file in the host OS, access to which is provided by another built-in server.

There are also a number of less conventional file servers in Inferno. For example, the primary means of using the File Transfer Protocol (FTP) is through a file server called ftpfs. Access to tar format archive files can be had through the tarfs file server. Even the primary text editor, called acme, provides names by which it can be controlled. Because all these servers use the Styx protocol, client processes can reside on remote machines just as easily as on the local machine.

19.2   The Root Device Server

The first file server we examine is the server for the root "device." The files served by this server form the directory tree upon which all other name spaces are mounted and bound. It is the only part of a process's name space that is not attached via the *mount*( ) or *bind*( ) calls, either by the process itself or by one of its ancestors.

Each file server built in to the kernel has an entry in a "device" table. (This table is so named because the majority of built-in servers provide support for device access and control.) These entries contain a number of function pointers that define how the various Styx messages are handled. The first two entries, however, are descriptive. The first is a character that is used to identify this file server. The root of a built-in file server can be referred to by the string #*c*, where *c* is one of the identifying characters. (In the case of the root file server, we never actually make use of the name #/ that is defined for it.) The second element of the structure is an identifying string for the server.

```
Dev rootdevtab = {
    '/',
    "root",
    devinit,
    rootattach,
    rootwalk,
    rootstat,
    rootopen,
    devcreate,
    rootclose,
    rootread,
    devbread,
    rootwrite,
    devbwrite,
    devremove,
    devwstat,
};
```

Most of the function pointers here clearly mirror messages in Styx. However, *devbread*( ) and *devbwrite*( ) do not have any direct parallels. These are variations on the normal read and write routines. Normally, the memory containing the data for a write and where the data are put on a read is already allocated, and a pointer to it is given to the function implementing the read or write. The *devbread*( ) function first allocates space where the data can be put and then calls the normal read function. Conversely, *devbwrite*( ) calls the normal write function and then frees the buffer from which the data were written.

19.2.1   Providing the Names Served

Because the files and directories named by these file servers do not exist in the typical persistent storage (like on a disk drive), we need to be able to generate the contents of a directory on the fly. For the case of the root file server, defined in /emu/port/devroot.c, we need to make available a list of directories that normally serve as mount points for other file servers that will be attached during system initialization. These directories include chan, dev, env, net, net.alt, nvfs, and prog. In addition to those directories, native Inferno builds will include a file called osinit.dis (and often others as well). The code in this file is run to carry out the system initialization.

Basically, *rootgen*( ) first handles the special cases of dot (.) and dot-dot(..), which are not kept in the list of names served. If the request is not for one of these special cases, then we locate the name requested (or, alternatively, the position in the list) and create a directory entry for it on the fly. It takes the channel on which this request is being served as an argument. The channel also identifies which directory we're generating files for. Either the *name* or the *s* parameter will be set to identify which file in the directory we want. If *name* is set, then we search for that name in the list of files served. Otherwise, *s* gives the index into the list for the file we want. The list itself is given by the *tab* parameter and contains *nd* elements. Finally, *dp* points to a directory entry structure where we'll put the directory entry we synthesize.

```
static int rootgen(Chan *c, char *name, Dirtab *tab, int nd, int s, Dir *dp)
{
    int p, i;
    Rootdata *r;
```

19.2.1.1   Handling the Parent Directory

If we're in one of the served directories, and we're looking up one level in the tree, then we need to generate the appropriate directory. In most cases, this means we generate the root directory itself. The call to *devdir*( ) loads the structure pointed to by *dp* with a description of the directory that we are building.

```
if (s ≡ DEVDOTDOT) {
    p = rootdata[c⤳qid.path].dotdot;
    c⤳qid.path = p;
    c⤳qid.type = QTDIR;
    name = "#/";
    if (p ≠ 0) {
        for (i = 0; i < rootmaxq; i++)
            if (roottab[i].qid.path ≡ c⤳qid.path) {
                name = roottab[i].name;
```

```
        break;
      }
    }
  devdir(c, c⁓qid, name, 0, eve, °555, dp);
  return 1;
}
```

19.2.1.2 Searching for a Name

In this case (*name* being non*nil*), we need to look to see if that name is in the list of names that we are serving. If so, then we can generate that directory entry. Otherwise, it's an error.

```
if (name ≠ nil) {
  isdir(c);
  r = &rootdata[(int) c⁓qid.path];
  tab = r⁓ptr;
  for (i = 0; i < r⁓size; i++, tab++)
    if (strcmp(tab⁓name, name) ≡ 0) {
      devdir(c, tab⁓qid, tab⁓name, tab⁓length, eve, tab⁓perm, dp);
      return 1;
    }
  return -1;
}
```

The final case is used where we want to examine a file name served by the server but not walk into a subdirectory. For example, if we are doing an open or a stat, then we need to search for the file name and get the appropriate status. In these cases, we get here because *rootgen*( ) is called repeatedly with increasing values of an index into the array of names. If the caller finds that the result matches the search criteria, then the search is terminated.

```
if (s ≥ nd)
  return -1;
tab += s;
devdir(c, tab⁓qid, tab⁓name, tab⁓length, eve, tab⁓perm, dp);
return 1;
}
```

19.2.2 Walking the Root Server's Tree

The implementation of the handler for the walk message is typical of several in that nearly all the work is handed off to a generic handler. We look at the implementation of some of these generic handlers in Section 19.3.

```
static Walkqid *rootwalk(Chan *c, Chan *nc, char **name, int nname)
{
    ulong p;

    p = c⁓qid.path;
    if (nname ≡ 0)
        p = rootdata[p].dotdot;
    return devwalk(c, nc, name, nname, rootdata[p].ptr, rootdata[p].size, rootgen);
}
```

19.2.3   Reading from the Root Server

The case of handling the **Tread** message is a little more interesting. It is, however, not
very complex. In the case of reading from a directory, we pass the call off to the generic
directory read handler. Otherwise, we're reading a regular file. Because we're serving a
file that's not stored on a persistent storage device, it must be in memory. Because it is
in memory, we can just copy the requested data to the specified buffer, after first limiting
the request to data actually present in the file.

```
static long rootread(Chan *c, void *buf, long n, vlong offset)
{
    ulong p, len;
    uchar *data;

    p = c⁓qid.path;
    if (c⁓qid.type & QTDIR)
        return devdirread(c, buf, n, rootdata[p].ptr, rootdata[p].size, rootgen);
    len = rootdata[p].size;
    if (offset < 0 ∨ offset ≥ len)
        return 0;
    if (offset + n > len)
        n = len − offset;
    data = rootdata[p].ptr;
    memmove(buf, data + offset, n);
    return n;
}
```

19.3   Generic Styx Message Handler

In this section, we examine the code in /emu/port/dev.c that implements a number of Styx
message handlers. Think of these functions as an example of code factoring. We have
a significant amount of code that would otherwise be repeated in numerous file servers.
By collecting those common cases here, servers can point to these functions in their **Dev**
structures, simplifying the code for them.

19.3.1   Creating a Directory Entry

We are looking at only a few functions in this file. The first one we examine is *devdir*( ), which is used extensively in the previous section. It effectively builds a directory entry for a file named in the third argument. Directory entries in Inferno contain all the metadata describing the file. This function simply sets all the members of a directory entry structure. For the most part, the metadata we need are passed in the arguments.

```
void devdir(Chan *c, Qid qid, char *n, long length, char *user, long perm,
    Dir *db)
{
    db→name = n;
    if (c→flag & CMSG)
        qid.type |= QTMOUNT;
    db→qid = qid;
    db→type = devtab[c→type]→dc;
    db→dev = c→dev;
    db→mode = perm | (qid.type ≪ 24);
    db→atime = time(0);
    db→mtime = kerndate;
    db→length = length;
    db→uid = user;
    db→gid = eve;
    db→muid = user;
}
```

19.3.2   Generating Names

In Section 19.2, we saw that the root file server has its own implementation of a directory generator. Part of the reason is that some things (like the .. entry) are handled differently for the root file server than for other servers. For some other servers, however, the following generic generator is sufficient. Notice that it is mostly the same as the last case of the generator we saw for the root file server. In particular, it generates a directory entry for the table entry with index i. The comment about the zeroth element explains why if i is DOTDOT we don't adjust the value of *tab*. Calling *devdir*( ) in this case, we end up generating a directory entry for the zeroth element.

```
/* the zeroth element of the table MUST be the directory itself for .. */
int devgen(Chan *c, char *name, Dirtab *tab, int ntab, int i, Dir *dp)
{
    USED(name);
    if (tab ≡ 0)
        return −1;
    if (i ≠ DEVDOTDOT) {
        /* skip over the first element, that for . itself */
```

```
      i++;
      if (i ≥ ntab)
         return −1;
      tab += i;
   }
   devdir(c, tab→qid, tab→name, tab→length, eve, tab→perm, dp);
   return 1;
}
```

19.3.3   Walking a Directory Tree

Now we come to a significantly more involved case—handling the walk message. The
sender of the message has to have already parsed the path name into components, which
we receive in *name*. If successful, we want to return an array of IDs, one for each of
the directories along the way and one for the file or directory at the end of the search.
Although this function is quite complex, the basic algorithm is straightforward. After
setting up the result array, we loop through each of the names in *name*. For each of them,
we search the relevant directory for that name (assuming it's not either of the special
cases . or ..). If the name does exist, then we move to it, and if it is a directory, we can
continue searching with the next name in the path.

```
Walkqid *devwalk(Chan *c, Chan *nc, char **name, int nname, Dirtab *tab,
      int ntab, Devgen *gen)
{
   int i, j, alloc;
   Walkqid *wq;
   char *n;
   Dir dir;
   if (nname > 0)
      isdir(c);
```

19.3.3.1   Preparing the Result Buffer

First, we make space for the results assuming we'll be successful in doing the complete
walk. If we end up being only partially successful, some of this space will go wasted,
but being a little wasteful in the error case is better than additional special case code for
handling that case.

```
   alloc = 0;
   wq = smalloc(sizeof(Walkqid) + (nname − 1) * sizeof (Qid));
   if (waserror()) {
      if (alloc ∧ wq→clone ≠ nil)
         cclose(wq→clone);
      free(wq);
```

```
    return nil;
}
```

As described in the man page for walk, the client can send a proposed fid for the results of this walk. If we don't get one, we just clone the one that represents the client's connection to the root of this server.

```
if (nc ≡ nil) {
    nc = devclone(c);
    nc→type = 0;      /* device doesn't know about this channel yet */
    alloc = 1;
}
wq→clone = nc;
```

19.3.3.2   Parsing the Path Name

Now we fall into the main part of the function, which is a loop that is iterated once for each name in the path. Because the role of walk is similar to changing the working directory, we need the names along the way to be directory names. We can't expect to be successful in changing into a subdirectory of a regular file.

```
for (j = 0; j < nname; j++) {
    if (¬(nc→qid.type & QTDIR)) {
        if (j ≡ 0)
            error(Enotdir);
        goto Done;
    }
    n = name[j];
```

Those who are familiar with UNIX will likely expect that the directories have entries for . (the directory itself) and .. (the parent directory). Even though the original designers of the UNIX file system designed the Plan 9 file system (after which Inferno is modeled), they chose not to repeat that design feature. Consequently, we need to handle those two names as special cases. The case of . is easy; we just repeat the current ID in the sequence. The case of .. is more interesting, though nearly as easy. Notice that the last argument to *devwalk*( ) is a pointer to a function. In particular, each server must provide a function that generates the contents of the directory tree it serves (even if it uses the function *devgen*( ) described earlier). When processing .., we call that function to generate ..'s directory entry. It is up to the generator to handle the parent directory case properly as we saw in *rootgen*( ).

```
    if (strcmp(n, ".") ≡ 0) {
Accept:
        wq→qid[wq→nqid++] = nc→qid;
        continue;
```

```
    }
    if (strcmp(n, "..") ≡ 0) {
        (*gen)(nc, nil, tab, ntab, DEVDOTDOT, &dir);
        nc→qid = dir.qid;
        goto Accept;
    }
```

For the most part, we'll let the comments to this bit of code speak for themselves. Keep in mind that *devgen()* is the generic directory generator we saw earlier.

```
    /*
     * Ugly problem: If we're using devgen, make sure we're walking the
     * directory itself, represented by the first entry in the table, and not trying
     * to step into a sub-directory of the table, e.g. /net/net. Devgen itself
     * should take care of the problem, but it doesn't have the necessary
     * information (that we're doing a walk).
     */
    if (gen ≡ devgen ∧ nc→qid.path ≠ tab[0].qid.path)
        goto Notfound;
```

19.3.3.3   Searching a Directory

Now that we've made it through all the filters, we know we have a good name along the path we want to look up. This loop goes through the list of names in the directory that we've reached, calling the generator function on each. If we get a −1 back, it means that we weren't able to find the name in the directory. On the other hand, if we get a 1 back, we check to make sure that the name has indeed been found correctly, at which point we add the ID for this name to the list.

```
    for (i = 0; ; i++) {
        switch ((*gen)(nc, n, tab, ntab, i, &dir)) {
        case −1 :
        Notfound:
            if (j ≡ 0)
                error(Enonexist);
            kstrcpy(up→env→errstr, Enonexist, ERRMAX);
            goto Done;
        case 0:
            continue;
        case 1:
            if (strcmp(n, dir.name) ≡ 0) {
                nc→qid = dir.qid;
                goto Accept;
            }
            continue;
```

```
            }
          }
        }
```

After processing the whole name list, we are ready to return the ID list we generated along the way.

```
      /*
       * We processed at least one name, so will return some data. If we didn't
       * process all nname entries successfully, we drop the cloned channel and
       * return just the Qids of the walks.
       */
    Done: poperror();
      if (wq→nqid < nname) {
        if (alloc)
          cclose(wq→clone);
        wq→clone = nil;
      }
      else if (wq→clone) {
        /* attach cloned channel to same device */
        wq→clone→type = c→type;
      }
      return wq;
    }
```

19.4   Native Inferno File System

In this section, we examine the Inferno file system as stored on disk (or other nonvolatile media). The file system is known as kfs, which stands for "Ken's file system," because it is based on the original Plan 9 file system design developed by Ken Thompson. The revisions in the fourth edition of Inferno include moving the native file system from kernel code to user space code. As such, this version of the file system is written in Limbo. As we go through the discussion of kfs, we describe those features of Limbo that differ from C. However, these remarks are neither a tutorial nor a reference for Limbo. Papers on the Vita Nuova Web site and included in the Inferno distribution provide much more detail on Limbo. The code for this program is found in /appl/cmd/disk/kfs.b.

Overall, kfs is structured as two (three if we enable disk block buffering) cooperating processes. One of these processes is a single thread that takes Styx messages and processes them using data from the disk. This main process serves the role shown in Figure 19-1. The other process is a control and management interface, which provides files where we can initiate file system checks, shut the server down, and perform other similar operations. A new file system is created by running kfs with a command-line option that initializes the on-disk data structures prior to beginning its normal file server activity. Creating a new file system is referred to as **reaming** in Inferno.

On disk, the first block, called the superblock, contains metadata describing the file system as a whole. Free space is represented by free block lists similar to that illustrated in Figure 17-4. Blocks in files are managed using a hybrid list-structured allocation and tree-structured allocation in a way that is very similar to UNIX file systems. Unlike UNIX, however, Inferno expects all of a file's metadata to be in its directory entry, as we saw in *devdir*( ) in Section 19.3. This leads to the kfs directory structure where all of a file's metadata is kept in its on-disk directory entry. Therefore, there are no i-nodes as found in UNIX file systems. Rather than cover the details of these on-disk data structures here, we cover them later in this section as we use them.

19.4.1   Initialization

As with all Limbo programs, control in kfs begins with a function called *init*( ) (note the difference from the function *main*( ) in C), where we initialize the Styx support module. There are several features of Limbo that need explanation. First, the use of the symbol *nil* in the parameter list indicates that this function ignores that argument. Also, note that declarations in Limbo are similar to those in Pascal, where the identifier is followed by a colon and the type. Limbo programs are composed of a number of modules that are loaded at run time. The **load** keyword is used to do that loading, and the PATH member of each ADT gives the location of the module binary file.

> *init*(*nil* : **ref Draw**$\rightarrow$*Context*, *args* : **list of string**)
> {
>   *sys* = **load Sys Sys**$\rightarrow$PATH;
>   *styx* = **load Styx Styx**$\rightarrow$PATH;
>   *daytime* = **load Daytime Daytime**$\rightarrow$PATH;
>   *styx*$\rightarrow$*init*( );

In this next section of code, we use the argument processing module called **Arg** to process the command-line argument list. For the most part, we just set flags to indicate that an option has been selected. We discuss those options that are important to us as we use them. This code fragment also illustrates a few additional Limbo features. First, the symbol *nil* used in an expression is like the NULL defined constant in C. The second interesting feature is the colon-equal (:=) form of assignment. This operator both declares a variable and assigns it at the same time. The type of the new variable is the same as the type of the expression on the right-hand side. The last new feature here is the **case** statement, which functions much like the **switch** statement in C, but is syntactically more similar to the **case** statement in Pascal. There is no keyword before values, and no **break** statement is needed. The double arrow (an equal character followed by a greater than character, =>) operator separates a list of values from the code to execute for those values. Finally, the asterisk (∗) is used like the **default** keyword in C.

> *arg* := **load Arg Arg**$\rightarrow$PATH;
> **if** (*arq* ≡ *nil*)

$$error\,(sys{\rightarrow}sprint\,(\texttt{"can't load \%s: \%r"}, \mathbf{Arg}{\rightarrow}\texttt{PATH}));$$

$$arg{\rightarrow}init\,(args\,);$$

$$arg{\rightarrow}setusage\,(\texttt{"disk/kfs [-r [-b bufsize]] [-cADPRW]"} +$$
$$\texttt{" [-n name] kfsfile"});$$

$$bufsize := 1024;$$

$$nocheck := 0;$$

while $((o := arg{\rightarrow}opt\,()) \neq 0)$

  case o {

   $\texttt{'c'} \;\Rightarrow\; nocheck = 1;$

   $\texttt{'r'} \;\Rightarrow\; ream = 1;$

   $\texttt{'b'} \;\Rightarrow\; bufsize = \mathbf{int}\; arg{\rightarrow}earg\,();$

   $\texttt{'D'} \;\Rightarrow\; debug = \neg debug;$

   $\texttt{'P'} \;\Rightarrow\; writeallow = 1;$

   $\texttt{'W'} \;\Rightarrow\; wstatallow = 1;$

   $\texttt{'R'} \;\Rightarrow\; readonly = 1;$

   $\texttt{'A'} \;\Rightarrow\; noatime = 1; \quad \texttt{\# mainly useful for flash}$

   $\texttt{'n'} \;\Rightarrow\; kfsname = arg{\rightarrow}earg\,();$

   $* \;\Rightarrow\; arg{\rightarrow}usage\,();$

  }

$$args = arg{\rightarrow}argv\,();$$

if $(args \equiv nil)$

  $arg{\rightarrow}usage\,();$

$$arg = nil;$$

19.4.1.1 Initializing the File Server

The next several lines create the main data structures we'll be using. The major one is the **Device** ADT that we call *thedevice* and that represents the disk partition containing the file system. (Technically, kfs can serve a file system on a form of block storage other than a disk partition. In fact, code like this is often tested serving a file system within a file of another file system. Of course, the primary raison d'être for kfs is serving a file system on a disk.) There are two new Limbo features here. The **ref** keyword creates a reference, which is much like a pointer in C. However, Limbo does not allow the sort of manipulations to references that C allows for pointers. The other new feature is the **hd** operator. Limbo supports lists as a native data type, and **hd** gives the first element on the list.

$$devnone = \mathbf{ref}\; \mathbf{Device}(nil, 1);$$

$$mainlock = \mathbf{Lock}.new\,();$$

$$conschan = \mathbf{Chan}.new\,(nil);$$

$$conschan.msize = \mathbf{Styx}{\rightarrow}\texttt{MAXRPC};$$

$$mode := \mathbf{Sys}{\rightarrow}\texttt{ORDWR};$$

if $(readonly)$

  $mode = \mathbf{Sys}{\rightarrow}\texttt{OREAD};$

$wrenfd = sys\text{-}open(\mathbf{hd}\ args, mode);$
$\mathbf{if}\ (wrenfd \equiv nil)$
    $error(sys\text{-}sprint(\texttt{"can't open \%s: \%r"}, \mathbf{hd}\ args));$
$thedevice = \mathbf{ref}\ \mathbf{Device}(wrenfd, readonly);$

19.4.1.2   Fetching the Superblock

At this point, it's time to get the first block of the file system. Depending on the options, we either read that block from the disk, or we write a new initial block. If the server is started with the **-r** option, we are to **ream** (initialize) the file system. In that case, we write an initial block to the disk. In reality, at this point, we only make sure that the superblock has the correct magic string and that we know the block size of the file system. Later, we will finish setting up the initial file system if necessary.

$\mathbf{if}\ (ream)\ \{$
    $\mathbf{if}\ (bufsize \leq 0 \vee bufsize \mathbin{\%} 512 \vee bufsize > \texttt{MAXBUFSIZE})$
        $error(sys\text{-}sprint(\texttt{"invalid block size \%d"}, bufsize));$
    $RBUFSIZE = bufsize;$
    $wrenream(thedevice);$
$\}$
$\mathbf{else}\{$
    $\mathbf{if}\ (\neg wreninit(thedevice))$
        $error(\texttt{"kfs magic in trouble"});$
$\}$

Next, we initialize a number of globals that define all of the important block sizes and numbers of pointers per buffer. Then, we initialize the internal buffer system. The **array** operator in Limbo creates an array dynamically at run time, and the **of** gives the type of data in the array. The code $\{* => \mathbf{byte}\ 0\}$ in this case says that the array should be an array of bytes, and all elements of the array are initialized to 0.

$BUFSIZE = RBUFSIZE - \texttt{Tagsize};$
$DIRPERBUF = BUFSIZE/\texttt{Dentrysize};$
$INDPERBUF = BUFSIZE/4;$
$NDPERBUF2 = INDPERBUF * INDPERBUF;$
$FEPERBUF = (BUFSIZE - \texttt{Super1size} - 4)/4;$
$emptyblock = \mathbf{array}[RBUFSIZE]\ \mathbf{of}\ \{* => \mathbf{byte}\ 0\};$
$iobufinit(30);$

19.4.1.3   Building a New File System

Now that the buffer system has been set up, we can finish the initialization of the file system if we're reaming it. In doing this, we finish setting up the superblock, and we create an initial root directory.

if (*ream*) {
   superream(*thedevice*, SUPERADDR);
   rootream(*thedevice*, ROOTADDR);
   wstatallow = *writeallow* = 1;
}

At this point, we are in the same position whether we are reaming the file system or not. So we read the superblock and root directory and make sure that they have the correct tags. We also look at the *fsok* flag in the superblock to see if the file system was shut down in an orderly fashion the last time.

if (*wrencheck*(*wrenfd*))
   error("kfs super/root in trouble");
if ($\neg$*ream* $\wedge$ $\neg$*superok*(0)) {
   sys→print("kfs needs check\n");
   if ($\neg$*nocheck*)
     check(*thedevice*, *Cquiet* | *Cfree*);
}

19.4.1.4   Loading the Root Directory

Now that we know that the file system integrity is good, we can load the root directory in the normal way. The *geta*( ) call of the **Dentry** ADT loads a directory entry into a buffer. If there is already a buffer that contains the entry, then we don't bother reading it from the disk. As usual, we also do some error checking to make sure that we got a valid directory entry. The final call in this sequence is to *put*( ) the directory entry we just read. This function is generally used to apply any updates to the directory structure and to update the copy on the disk if there is a reason to do so immediately. The current version of the code considers any change to be reason to immediately write to the disk, but after support for write buffering is implemented, then this will be changed. Normally, we don't want to access the disk for every change to a buffer; instead, we want to let the buffers accumulate changes and write them out occasionally. Here, we see the first instance of tuples in Limbo. An ordered set of data items can be treated as a single value in many contexts. In this case, **Dentry**.*geta* returns a pair, where the first element of the pair, *d*, gives the directory entry, and the second element, *e*, gives an error string if the call was not successful.

(d, e) := **Dentry**.*geta*(*thedevice*, ROOTADDR, 0, QPROOT, Bread);
if ($d \neq nil \wedge \neg$(d.*mode* $\wedge$ DDIR))
   e = "not a directory";
if($e \neq nil$)
   error("bad root: " + e);
if (*debug*)
   d.*print*( );
d.*put*( );

19.4.1.5   *Creating the Child Processes*

The final part of the initialization starts child processes that continue the work of the file server. We begin with a couple of calls to the process control system call (*pctl*()). In the first one, we create a new process group for the file system server, and we declare that processes in that group do not share their open file descriptors. (We still share the environment, name space, and most data structures.) In the second call, we close all open file descriptors except the standard input, output, and error files and the disk containing the file system. The upshot of all this is that when we create the child processes, they will start out with just the file descriptors they need opened, but any changes they make to those open files will not be seen by the other processes. The double colon (::) operator in the second line is a list constructor operator.

```
sys→pctl(Sys→FORKFD | Sys→NEWPGRP, nil);
sys→pctl(Sys→NEWFD, wrenfd.fd :: 0 :: 1 :: 2 :: nil);
wrenfd = sys→fildes(wrenfd.fd);
thedevice.fd = wrenfd;
```

We create up to three children. The first is created only if we are doing the usual buffering of writes. Its purpose is to periodically flush the changes in the buffers to the disk. We refer to this as synchronizing (or syncing) the disk. The second child process listens for administrative commands. We use this process to force syncs, to force file system integrity checks, and to shut the file system down. The final child process we create is the file system server proper. This code fragment illustrates a couple of new Limbo features. The first line is an example of the channel data type. A channel in Limbo is a communications path that carries typed data. This is also the first time we've seen the **spawn** statement. It is used to create child processes, and is used much like thread creation operations in other languages.

```
c := chan of int;
if (Buffering) {
    spawn syncproc(c);
    pid :=<- c;
    if (pid)
        pids = pid :: pids;
}
spawn consinit(c);
pid :=<- c;
if (pid)
    pids = pid :: pids;
spawn kfs(sys→fildes(0));
}
```

19.4.2   Main Server Process

We now turn our attention to the last child process: the file system server itself. For the most part, it's pretty straightforward. As with all servers, the main function is to read a request, execute the request, and write a reply. Most of the code here is actually error handling. The request is received though the call to **Tmsg**.*read*( ). It is executed in the call to *apply*( ), and the response is formatted and sent in the calls to *pack*( ) and *write*( ).

```
kfs(rfd : ref Sys→FD)
{
    cp := Chan.new(rfd);
    while ((t := Tmsg.read(rfd, cp.msize)) ≠ nil) {
        if (debug)
            sys→print("<- %s\n", t.text());
        r := apply(cp, t);
        pick m := r {
        Error =>
            r.tag = t.tag;
        }
        if (debug)
            sys→print("-> %s\n", r.text());
        rbuf := r.pack();
        if (rbuf ≡ nil)
            panic("Rmsg.pack");
        if (sys→write(rfd, rbuf, len rbuf) ≤ len rbuf)
            panic("mount write");
    }
    shutdown();
}
```

19.4.3   Processing a Styx Request

It should come as no surprise that the implementation of the *apply*( ) call is just a big **pick** statement with calls to a function for each type of message. The only other bit of code is the locking and unlocking around the whole thing. We don't want more than one process active in these functions at a time. Although the previous code fragment was the first use of **pick**, we discuss it here, because this use is more typical. To understand **pick**, we need to know that ATDs in Limbo can contain varying types of data. More specifically, we can have an ADT that at any point in time contains one of a set of possible ADTs. This feature is much like a **union** in C or a variant record in Pascal. The type **Tmsg** is one such ADT. The **pick** statement operates much like the **case** statement, where we are selecting an action based on which type of ADT is contained in the other. Thus, if t is a reference to a **Tmsg** ADT that is currently holding an ADT that in turn describes an **Open** message in Styx, then we call the *ropen*( ) function.

```
apply(cp : ref Chan, t : ref Tmsg) : ref Rmsg
{
    mainlock.lock( );  # TO DO: this is just to keep console and kfs from colliding
    r : ref Rmsg;
    pick m := t {
    Readerror =>
        error(sys→sprint("mount read error: %s", m.error));
    Version =>
        r = rversion(cp, m);
    Auth =>
        r = rauth(cp, m);
    Flush =>
        r = rflush(cp, m);
    Attach =>
        r = rattach(cp, m);
    Walk =>
        r = rwalk(cp, m);
    Open =>
        r = ropen(cp, m);
    Create =>
        r = rcreate(cp, m);
    Read =>
        r = rread(cp, m);
    Write =>
        r = rwrite(cp, m);
    Clunk =>
        r = rclunk(cp, m);
    Remove =>
        r = rremove(cp, m);
    Stat =>
        r = rstat(cp, m);
    Wstat =>
        r = rwstat(cp, m);
    * =>
        panic("Styx mtype");
        return nil;
    }
    mainlock.unlock( );
    return r;
}
```

19.4.4   Walking a Directory Tree

As a point of focus, we will restrict our detailed examination to the code that implements the **Twalk** and **Tread** Styx messages. We start with the walk handler.

```
rwalk(cp : ref Chan, t : ref Tmsg.Walk) : ref Rmsg
{
    nfile, tfile : ref File;
    q : Qid;
```

The comment for this next piece of code refers to the fact that when we read a Styx message using **Tmsg**.*read*( ), we get back a file descriptor as part of the message that's passed in to this function as *t*. We should only be called with a file descriptor obtained in this way. It is an error to call this function with a file descriptor obtained by a normal open or create operation. This fragment turns out to be the first one we examine with comments. Comments in Limbo are started by the # character and continue to the end of the line.

```
    # The file identified by t.fid must be valid in the
    # current session and must not have been opened for I/O
    # by an open or create message.
    if ((file := cp.getfid(t.fid, 0)) ≡ nil)
        return err(t, Efid);
    if (file.open ≠ 0)
        return ferr(t, Emode, file, nil);
```

For the most part, the comment for this piece of code is self-explanatory. The Styx walk message allows the sender to specify a proposed fid to use for the result of the walk. If the sender doesn't propose one, then it's up to the server to assign one. The **len** operator we see here gives the number of elements in a list.

```
    # If newfid is not the same as fid, allocate a new file;
    # a side effect is checking newfid is not already in use (error);
    # if there are no names to walk this will be equivalent to a
    # simple 'clone' operation.
    # Otherwise, fid and newfid are the same and if there are names
    # to walk make a copy of 'file' to be used during the walk
    # as 'file' must only be updated on success.
    # Finally, it's a no-op if newfid is the same as fid and t.nwname
    # is 0.
    nwqid := 0;
    if (t.newfid ≠ t.fid) {
        if ((nfile = cp.getfid(t.newfid, 1)) ≡ nil)
            return ferr(t, Efidinuse, file, nil);
    }
```

> **else if** (**len** *t.names* $\neq$ 0)
>   *nfile* = *tfile* = **File**.*new* (NOFID);
> **else** {
>   *file.unlock* ( );
>   **return ref Rmsg.Walk** (*t.tag*, *nil*);
> }
> *clone* (*nfile*, *file*);

19.4.4.1   Walking Each Name in the Path

Next, we create an empty response message. The second line of this fragment is an example of Limbo's built-in **string** data type.

> *r* := **ref Rmsg.Walk** (*t.tag*, **array** [**len** *t.names*] **of Qid**);
> *error* : **string**;

For each name in the list, we call *walkname* ( ) to do the actual directory walking. If we have any failures along the line, then we're done.

> **for** (*nwname* := 0; *nwname* < **len** *t.names*; *nwname* ++) {
>   (*error*, *q*) = *walkname* (*nfilet.names* [*nwname*]);
>   **if** (*error* $\neq$ *nil*)
>   **break**;
>   *r.qids* [*nwqid* ++] = *q*;
> }

19.4.4.2   Preparing the Response

At this point, we need to set up an appropriate return message based on which of the terminal conditions we have. If there are no names to walk, then we have a simple clone operation. If we have an error and don't complete the walk, then we need to return an error message. Otherwise, we need to send a message that identifies the successful result of the walk. This fragment contains our first example of a Limbo feature called **slices**. The array indexing expression [0 : *nwqid*] indicates that we are to take elements 0 to (but not including) *nwqid* as a new array. This particular usage effectively drops from the array all elements from *nwqid* to the end.

> **if** (**len** *t.names* $\equiv$ 0) {
>   # Newfid must be different to fid (see above)
>   # so this is a simple 'clone' operation - there's
>   # nothing to do except unlock unless there's
>   # an error.
>   *nfile.unlock* ( );
>   **if** (*error* $\neq$ *nil*)
>   *cp.putfid* (*nfile*);
> }

```
    else if (nwqid < len t.names) {
        #
        # Didn't walk all elements, 'clunk' nfile
        # and leave 'file' alone.
        # Clear error if some of the elements were
        # walked OK.
        #
        if (nfile != tfile)
            cp.putfid(nfile);
        if (nwqid != 0)
            error = nil;
        r.qids = r.qids[0 : nwqid];
    }
    else {
        #
        # Walked all elements. If newfid is the same
        # as fid must update 'file' from the temporary
        # copy used during the walk.
        # Otherwise just unlock (when using tfile there's
        # no need to unlock as it's a local).
        #
        if (nfile ≡ tfile) {
            file.qid = nfile.qid;
            file.wpath = nfile.wpath;
            file.addr = nfile.addr;
            file.slot = nfile.slot;
        }
        else
            nfile.unlock();
    }
    file.unlock();
    if (error != nil)
        return err(t, error);
    return r;
}
```

19.4.5 Searching a Directory

As mentioned in the previous subsection, the main work of the walk is done by *walkname()*.
We start with the same sort of error check as we did in *rwalk()*.

```
walkname(file : ref File, wname : string) : (string, Qid)
{
    #
```

```
# File must not have been opened for I/O by an open
# or create message and must represent a directory.
#
if (file.open ≠ 0)
    return (Emode, noqid);
```

19.4.5.1 Checking the Validity of the Call

The first thing we do is retrieve the directory entry for the fid we get as input. It's an error if the entry isn't valid or if the entry doesn't describe a directory. After all, we can't walk down into a regular file.

```
(d, e) := Dentry.getd(file, Bread);
if (d ≡ nil)
    return (e, noqid);
if (¬(d.mode & DDIR)) {
    d.put();
    return (Edir1, noqid);
}
```

Now we make sure that we have permission to go into the requested directory.

```
#
# For walked elements the implied user must
# have permission to search the directory.
#
if (file.access(d, DEXEC)) {
    d.put();
    return (Eaccess, noqid);
}
d.access(FREAD, file.uid);
```

19.4.5.2 Handling Special Names

Because Inferno doesn't explicitly store the . and .. entries, we have to handle them as special cases. Handling . is pretty easy, but handling .. is more complex. Because we don't have a directory entry that we can follow, we have to look at the path that represents where we are. We have that information because we've kept track as walk messages were processed.

```
if (wname ≡ "." ∨ wname ≡ ".." ∧ file.wpath ≡ nil) {
    d.put();
    return (nil, file.qid);
}
```

Here, we get the directory entry for the parent node and adjust the record of our current location in the file system.

```
d1 : ref Dentry;    # entry for wname, if found
slot : int;
if (wname ≡ "..") {
    d.put();
    addr := file.wpath.addr;
    slot = file.wpath.slot;
    (d1, e) = Dentry.geta(file.fs, addr, slot, QPNONE, Bread);
    if (d1 ≡ nil)
        return (e, noqid);
    file.wpath = file.wpath.up;
}
```

19.4.5.3 Cycling Through the Directory Blocks

Now we fall into the normal case. In particular, we are searching a directory for the name that we were called to search. The outer loop is executed once for each block that makes up the current directory. The label *Search* on the **for** statement allows us to specify which enclosing loop a **break** statement takes us out of.

```
else {
Search :
    for (addr := 0; ; addr ++) {
```

This little bit of code should end up being executed only in the unusual case that we don't already have the directory entry for the current directory in memory.

```
if (d.iob ≡ nil) {
    (d, e) = Dentry.getd(file, Bread);
    if (d ≡ nil)
        return (e, noqid);
}
```

Here, we read the next block of the current directory and check for any error conditions. It's at this point where we handle the case of not finding the name that we were to search. In this case, the *d.getblk1*() call will fail, returning *nil*.

```
p1 := d.getblk1(addr, 0);
if (p1 ≡ nil ∨ p1.checktag(Tdir, int d.qid.path)) {
    if (p1 ≠ nil)
        p1.put();
    return (Eentry, noqid);
}
```

19.4.5.4   Searching in a Directory Block

This looks at each directory entry that is contained in the block we just read. If an entry isn't being used or if it doesn't match the name we're looking for, then we just keep looking. If we run out of entries, then we fall out of the loop and go to the next iteration of the outer loop.

```
for (slot = 0; slot < DIRPERBUF; slot++) {
    d1 = Dentry.get(p1, slot);
    if (¬(d1.mode & DALLOC))
        continue;
    if (wname ≠ d1.name)
        continue;
```

We get here only if we find a matching directory entry. In that case, we create a record of this step of the walk and break out of not just this loop, but the outer loop as well. In C, the **break** statement always breaks out of the innermost enclosing loop (except when used in a **switch** statement). Limbo allows us to break out of multiple levels of nesting by allowing **break** to take a label specifying which loop we're leaving.

```
        #
        # update walk path
        #
        file.wpath = ref Wpath(file.wpath, file.addr, file.slot);
        slot += DIRPERBUF * addr;
        break Search;
    }
    p1.put();
  }
  d.put();
}
```

At this point, we have completed our search by finding the name for which we were called to search. So we set up the proper information to return.

```
file.addr = d1.iob.addr;
file.slot = slot;
file.qid = d1.qid;
d1.put();
return (nil, file.qid);
}
```

19.4.6   Reading from a File

The next function we examine is the one that handles the **Tread** Styx message sent by a client requesting data from a file.

$rread(cp : \textbf{ref Chan}, f : \textbf{ref Tmsg.Read}) : \textbf{ref Rmsg}$
{

19.4.6.1   Checking the Validity of the Call

As usual, we need to check to make sure we're not being asked to carry out an illegal operation. In particular, here we check to make sure that the file is actually open and that we're not being asked to read a negative amount or from a negative starting point.

> **if** $((\textit{file} := cp.getfid(f.fid, 0)) \equiv \textit{nil})$
>   **return** $err(f, \texttt{Efid})$;
> **if** $(\neg(\textit{file.open} \, \& \, \texttt{FREAD}))$
>   **return** $ferr(f, \texttt{Eopen}, \textit{file}, \textit{nil})$;
> $count := f.count$;
> $iounit := cp.msize - \texttt{IOHDRSZ}$;
> **if** $(count < 0 \vee count > iounit)$
>   **return** $ferr(f, \texttt{Ecount}, \textit{file}, \textit{nil})$;
> $offset := f.offset$;
> **if** $(offset < \textbf{big} \; 0)$
>   **return** $ferr(f, \texttt{Eoffset}, \textit{file}, \textit{nil})$;

Next, we get the directory entry for this file and make sure that it's valid.

> $(d, e) := \textbf{Dentry}.getd(\textit{file}, \texttt{Bread})$;
> **if** $(d \equiv \textit{nil})$
>   **return** $ferr(f, e, \textit{file}, \textit{nil})$;

The lock we have here is used in implementing an exclusive-use flag when opening the file. It's easy enough to prevent one client from opening the file when another has it open. However, there's one scenario we must be careful about. If one client opens the file and then goes away (crashes) without closing it, we don't want to keep it locked forever. This bit of code takes care of that case. If the file is locked, we update a timer each time we read or write it. The timer is set for five minutes, as defined by the value of TLOCK (300) in units of seconds. If it expires, then we consider the lock expired, and the file can be accessed by other clients.

> **if** $((t := \textit{file.tlock}) \neq \textit{nil})$ {
> $tim := now()$;
>   **if** $(t.time < tim \vee t.file \neq \textit{file})$ {
> $d.put()$;
>   **return** $ferr(f, \texttt{Ebroken}, \textit{file}, \textit{nil})$;

```
        }
        # renew the lock
        t.time = tim + TLOCK;
}
```

Make sure we have read access to the file.

$$d.access(\textbf{FREAD}, file.uid);$$

We don't do reads the same way for directories as we do for regular files. So if it is a directory, we jump to the code that handles that case.

```
if (d.mode & DDIR)
    return dirread(cp, f, file, d);
```

The last check we need to make before carrying out the actual read is making sure that we read only up to the end of the file.

```
if (offset + big count > d.size)
    count = int (d.size − offset);
if (count < 0)
    count = 0;
```

19.4.6.2   Reading Data from the File

The details of the read are handled in this loop. It is executed once for each block that contains data for the read. The basic idea is that we compute where in the block the needed data reside. Then, we fetch the block in question and copy the data from the block to a buffer that we'll send back. Finally, we release the buffer and update our counts and position for the next block. The slice notation [*nread* :] we see in this fragment indicates that we are referring to the elements from *nread* to the end of the array.

```
data := array[count] of byte;
nread := 0;
while (count > 0) {
    if (d.iob ≡ nil) {
        # must check and reacquire entry
        (d, e) = Dentry.getd(file, Bread);
        if (d ≡ nil)
            return ferr(f, e, file, nil);
    }
    addr := int (offset/big BUFSIZE);
    if (addr ≡ file.lastra + 1)
        ; # dbufread(p, d, addr + 1);
    file.lastra = addr;
    o := int (offset%big BUFSIZE);
```

$$n := BUFSIZE - o;$$
if $(n > count)$
    $n = count;$
$p1 := d.getblk1 (addr, 0);$
if $(p1 \neq nil)$ {
    if $(p1.checktag(\textbf{Tfile}, \texttt{QPNONE}))$ {
        $p1.put();$
        return $ferr(f, \texttt{Ephase}, file, nil);$
    }
    $data[nread :] = p1.iobuf[o : o + n];$
    $p1.put();$
}
else
    $data[nread :] = emptyblock[0 : n];$
$count -= n;$
$nread += n;$
$offset += \textbf{big } n;$
}
$d.put();$
$file.unlock();$
return ref Rmsg.Read$(f.tag, data[0 : nread]);$
}

19.4.7   On-Disk Data Structures

All blocks in the Inferno file system are prefixed by a tag that indicates the role of the block in the system. We store two integers in the tag: one that tells what type of block it is and one that stores a path ID like that used in a QID. The tag takes 8 bytes on the disk: 2 bytes of padding, 2 bytes for the block type tag, and 4 for the path ID. In memory, the tag is stored in an ADT (similar to a structure or a class) defined as follows, where the **con** keyword is used to define a constant:

```
#
# disc structure:
# Tag: pad[2] tag[2] path[4]
Tagsize : con 2 + 2 + 4;
Tag : adt
{
    tag : int;
    path : int;

    unpack : fn(a : array of byte) : Tag;
    pack : fn(t : self Tag, a : array of byte);
};
```

The construction **con iota** assigns successive values to each of the symbolic constants in that declaration. The allowable values for *tag* are:

```
#
# tags on block
#
Tnone,
Tsuper,   # the super block
Tdir,  # directory contents
Tind1,  # points to blocks
Tind2,  # points to Tind1
Tfile,  # file contents
Tfree,  # in free list
Tbuck,  # cache fs bucket
Tvirgo,  # fake worm virgin bits
Tcache,  # cw cache things
MAXTAG: con iota;
```

The *pack* ( ) and *unpack* ( ) functions are defined in most of the ADTs that represent data on the disk. They are used to translate between the on-disk representation and the in-memory representation of the same data. So when reading a block from the disk, we call the *unpack* ( ) function to take the bytes we read from the disk and to return a **Tag** ADT. When writing to the disk, we do the converse, calling *pack* ( ) to build the array of bytes that we write to the disk.

19.4.7.1   The Superblock

Like its ancestor UNIX, Inferno stores a superblock in the first block of a file system. The primary things that we maintain in the superblock are the range of blocks that make up this file system and the list of free blocks. In memory, we represent the superblock with the following ADT.

```
Superb: adt
{
  iob : ref Iobuf;
  fstart : int;
  fsize : int;
  tfree : int;
  qidgen : int;   # generator for unique ids
  fsok : int;
  fbuf : array of byte;   #nfree[4]free[FEPERBLK * 4]; aliased into containing block
  get : fn(dev : ref Device, flags : int) : ref Superb;
  touched : fn(s : self ref Superb);
  put : fn(s : self ref Superb);
  print : fn(s : self ref Superb);
  pack : fn(s : self ref Superb, a : array of byte);
```

```
    unpack : fn(a : array of byte) : ref Superb;
};
```

The superblock as stored on the disk is described by the following set of offsets. In this and later definitions of on-disk structures, we define each of the data items only in terms of offsets, where in C we might use a structure definition. That works in C because that language has a defined relationship between the structure declaration and the corresponding memory layout. No parallel construct exists in Limbo. Notice that each offset is defined in terms of the previous one by adding the size of the previous data item.

```
Ofstart : con 0;
Ofsize : con Ofstart + 4;
Otfree : con Ofsize + 4;
Oqidgen : con Otfree + 4;
Ofsok : con Oqidgen + 4;
Ororaddr : con Ofsok + 4;
Olast : con Ororaddr + 4;
Onext : con Olast + 4;
Super1size : con Onext + 4;
```

As an abstract data type, the superblock is defined by the functions *get*( ), *touched*( ), *put*( ), *print*( ), *pack*( ), and *unpack*( ). The function *get*( ) gets the buffer containing the superblock (reading it from the disk if necessary), checks the tag, calls *unpack*( ) to extract the data, and then returns a reference to a **Superb** ADT. A call to *touched*( ) simply marks the buffer containing the superblock as dirty, indicating that it should be written back to disk at the next appropriate time. The *put*( ) function is used to flush any changes made to the superblock. It uses *pack*( ) to transfer the ADT data into the buffer, and then it does a put on the buffer. Finally, *print*( ) is used for debugging and prints a one-line summary of the superblock data. There's one other key superblock function we've encountered. It is *superream*( ), which creates an initial superblock for an empty file system.

```
superream(dev : ref Device, addr : int)
{
    fsize := wrensize(dev);
    if (fsize ≤ 0)
        panic("file system device size");
    p := Iobuf.get(dev, addr, Bmod | Bimm);
    p.iobuf[0 :] = emptyblock;
    p.settag(Tsuper, QPSUPER);
    sb := ref Superb;
    sb.iob = p;
    sb.fstart = 1;
    sb.fsize = fsize;
```

```
        sb.qidgen = 10;
        sb.tfree = 0;
        sb.fsok = 0;
        sb.fbuf = p.iobuf[Super1size :];
        put4(sb.fbuf, 0, 1);   #nfree = 1
        for (i := fsize − 1; i ≥ addr + 2; i−−)
            addfree(dev, i, sb);
        sb.put();
    }
```

19.4.7.2   Directory Entries

Unlike UNIX, Inferno does not have an i-node structure separate from the directory entry. Instead, all of the metadata about a file are stored in the directory entry. In this structure, we store the name and the ID numbers of the user and the group that own the file. The *mode* member is used to store a number of flags that describe the file. **DALLOC** is a flag that indicates whether a directory entry is currently in use. **DDIR** identifies this entry as describing a subdirectory. The **DAPND** bit is set for files that are append-only. Finally, **DLOCK** is used when a file is opened for exclusive access. The low-order 9 bits of *mode* are used to determine who is allowed to access the file. The *size* member gives the size of the file in bytes. Access to the blocks that make up the file is governed by the *dblock*, *iblock*, and *diblock* members. They identify the direct data blocks, a single-indirect block, and a double-indirect block, respectively. They are an example of the tree-structured file allocation technique discussed in Section 17.4.4 and serve the same function as the block pointers in a UNIX i-node. The *atime* and *mtime* members give the last access time and the last modification time, respectively. The in-memory ADT is defined as:

Dentry : adt
{
   name : **string**;
   uid : **int**;
   gid : **int**;
   muid : **int**;   # not set by plan 9's kfs
   mode : **int**;   # mode bits on disc: **DALLOC** etc
   qid : **Qid**;   # 9p1 format on disc
   size : **big**;   # only 32-bits on disc, and Plan 9 limits it to signed
   atime : **int**;
   mtime : **int**;

   iob : **ref Iobuf**;   # locked block containing directory entry, when in memory
   buf : **array of byte**;   # pointer into block to packed
      # directory entry, when in memory
   mod : **int**;   # bits of buf that need updating

   unpack : **fn**(*a* : **array of byte**) : **ref Dentry**;
   get : **fn**(*p* : **ref Iobuf**, *slot* : **int**) : **ref Dentry**;

```
geta : fn(d : ref Device, addr : int, slot : int, qpath : int,
    mode : int) : (ref Dentry, string);
getd : fn(f : ref File, mode : int) : (ref Dentry, string);
put : fn(d : self ref Dentry);
access : fn(d : self ref Dentry, f : int, uid : int);
change : fn(d : self ref Dentry, f : int);
release : fn(d : self ref Dentry);
getblk : fn(d : self ref Dentry, a : int, tag : int) : ref Iobuf;
getblk1 : fn(d : self ref Dentry, a : int, tag : int) : ref Iobuf;
rel2abs : fn(d : self ref Dentry, a : int, tag : int, putb : int) : int;
trunc : fn(d : self ref Dentry, uid : int);
update : fn(d : self ref Dentry);
print : fn(d : self ref Dentry);
};
```

while the on-disk representation is defined as

```
# this is the disk structure:
# char name[NAMELEN];
# short uid;
# short gid;    [2 * 2]
# ushort mode;
#    #define DALLOC #8000
#    #define DDIR  #4000
#    #define DAPND #2000
#    #define DLOCK #1000
#    #define DREAD #4
#    #define DWRITE #2
#    #define DEXEC #1
# [ushort muid][2 * 2]
# Qid.path; [4]
# Qid.version; [4]
# long size; [4]
# long dblock[NDBLOCK];
# long iblock;
# long diblock;
# long atime;
# long mtime;

Oname : con 0;
Ouid : con Oname + NAMELEN;
Ogid : con Ouid + 2;
Omode : con Ogid + 2;
Omuid : con Omode + 2;
Opath : con Omuid + 2;
```

```
Overs : con Opath + 4;
Osize : con Overs + 4;
Odblock : con Osize + 4;
Oiblock : con Odblock + NDBLOCK * 4;
Odiblock : con Oiblock + 4;
Oatime : con Odiblock + 4;
Omtime : con Oatime + 4;
Dentrysize : con Omtime + 4;
#
# don't change, these are the mode bits on disc
#
DALLOC : con 16r8000;
DDIR : con 16r4000;
DAPND : con 16r2000;
DLOCK : con 16r1000;
DREAD : con 4;
DWRITE : con 2;
DEXEC : con 1;
```

19.4.8   Reading a Directory Entry

The first function we look at here is the one that fetches a directory entry. The gist of this is that the *slot* parameter is treated as an index into the array. The only trick is that we're actually looking only at a window into the directory file.

```
Dentry.get(p : ref Iobuf, slot : int) : ref Dentry
{
    if (p ≡ nil)
        return nil;
    buf := p.iobuf[(slot%DIRPERBUF) * Dentrysize :];
    d := Dentry.unpack(buf);
    d.iob = p;
    d.buf = buf;
    return d;
}
```

19.4.9   Reading a File Block

The next function we want to study is the one that looks up blocks in files. This function, *getblk1* ( ), essentially takes a directory entry and a block number, fetches the block, and returns a reference to it.

```
Dentry.getblk1 (d : self ref Dentry, a : int, tag : int) : ref Iobuf
{
    addr := d.rel2abs(a, tag, 1);
    if (addr ≡ 0)
        return nil;
    return Iobuf.get(thedevice, addr, Bread);
}
```

19.4.10   Locating a File Block

Most of the work in *getblk1* ( ) is done in *rel2abs*( ), which finds where the desired block is located within the file system.

```
Dentry.rel2abs(d : self ref Dentry, a : int, tag : int, putb : int) : int
{
    if (a < 0) {
        sys→print("Dentry.rel2abs: neg\n");
        return 0;
    }
    p := d.iob;
    if (p ≡ nil ∨ d.buf ≡ nil)
        panic("nil iob");
    data := d.buf;
    qpath := int d.qid.path;
    dev := p.dev;
```

19.4.10.1   Handling Direct Block Pointers

The first case we take is one where the block number we want is small enough that it falls in the set of directly accessible blocks. In that case, we just need to get the block number out of the *dblock* array and load the block into memory. This block number (which we store in *addr*) is an absolute block number within the file system, whereas *a* is a block number within the file. This is a little like a virtual-to-physical address translation. Note that because the case we're examining here is the read case, *tag* will be 0, so we won't be allocating new blocks. If, on the other hand, we are writing to the file and the block doesn't yet exist as part of the file, then we allocate a block for it.

```
    if (a < NDBLOCK) {
        addr := get4(data, Odblock + a * 4);
        if (addr ≡ 0 ∧ tag) {
            addr = balloc(dev, tag, qpath);
            put4(data, Odblock + a * 4, addr);
            p.flags |= Bmod | Bimm;
        }
        if (putb)
```

```
        d.release( );
    return addr;
}
```

19.4.10.2 Handling Single-Indirect Blocks

If the block number is not small enough to be directly addressed but is small enough to be handled by the single-indirect block, then we handle that case here. The idea is that the indirect block contains a number of pointers to additional data blocks in the file. To be more concrete, the number of direct blocks that can be accessed (NDBLOCK) is 6, and blocks are 1024 bytes each. So the first 6 KB of the file can be accessed directly. Because each block index is 4 bytes, a disk block can hold 256 of these block indices. The indirect block then lists the block numbers that make up file positions from the 6 KB point to the 262 KB point. We let *indfetch*( ) handle looking up the desired block number in the indirect block.

```
    a −= NDBLOCK;
    if (a < INDPERBUF) {
        addr := get4 (data, Oiblock);
        if (addr ≡ 0 ∧ tag) {
            addr = balloc(dev, Tind1, qpath);
            put4 (data, Oiblock, addr);
            p.flags |= Bmod | Bimm;
        }
        if (putb)
            d.release( );
        return indfetch(dev, qpath, addr, a, Tind1, tag);
    }
```

19.4.10.3 Handling Double-Indirect Blocks

If the position we want to access is beyond the 262 KB point, but can be accessed through the double-indirect block, we handle that case here. The double-indirect block is a list of 256 addresses of single-indirect blocks, each of which is a list of 256 data blocks. So, we use *indfetch*( ) first to determine the address of the single-indirect block that will list the desired data block. Then, we use *indfetch*( ) again to look into that single-indirect block to get the desired data block.

```
    a −= INDPERBUF;
    if(a < INDPERBUF2) {
        addr := get4 (data, Odiblock);
        if (addr ≡ 0 ∧ tag) {
            addr = balloc(dev, Tind2, qpath);
            put4 (data, Odiblock, addr);
            p.flags |= Bmod | Bimm;
```

```
        }
        if (putb)
           d.release( );
        addr = indfetch(dev, qpath, addr, a/INDPERBUF, Tind2, Tind1);
        return indfetch(dev, qpath, addr, a%INDPERBUF, Tind1, tag);
     }
     if (putb)
        d.release( );
     sys→print("Dentry.buf: trip indirect\n");
     return 0;
  }
```

19.4.11   Processing Indirect Blocks

We make substantial use of *indfetch*( ) in the previous function. It's quite straightforward, especially for reads. We first fetch the indirect block from the disk. Then, we index it by *a*, which is the block number (data block if we're reading a single-indirect block or single-indirect block number if we're reading a double-indirect block). If there was no block and we're writing, then we allocate one. Finally, we release the indirect block that we loaded with a call to *putbuf*( ).

```
  indfetch(dev : ref Device, path : int, addr : int, a : int, itag : int, tag : int) : int
  {
     if (addr ≡ 0)
        return 0;
     bp := Iobuf.get(dev, addr, Bread);
     if (bp ≡ nil) {
        sys→print("ind fetch bp = nil\n");
        return 0;
     }
     if (bp.checktag(itag, path)) {
        sys→print("ind fetch tag\n");
        bp.put( );
        return 0;
     }
     addr = get4(bp.iobuf, a * 4);
     if (addr ≡ 0 ∧ tag) {
        addr = balloc(dev, tag, path);
        if (addr ≠ 0) {
           put4(bp.iobuf, a * 4, addr);
           bp.flags |= Bmod;
           if (localfs ∨ tag ≡ Tdir)
              bp.flags |= Bimm;
           bp.settag(itag, path);
```

```
      }
    }
    bp.put( );
    return addr;
}
```

19.4.12   Fetching from the Buffer Cache

We now turn our attention to the buffer management code. Like most other systems, Inferno maintains a set of buffers that hold recently accessed blocks in memory so that we don't have to access the disk for every reference to frequently accessed blocks. The only function we're going to examine in detail is **Iobuf**.*get*( ), which takes an absolute file system block number and returns a pointer to a buffer that contains the data from that disk block. If we do not already have a buffer with that data, then **Iobuf**.*get*( ) allocates one and reads the block in from the disk.

```
Iobuf.get(dev : ref Device, addr : int, flags : int) : ref Iobuf
{
```

First, we compute a hashing function to speed the lookup of the block in our buffer list.

```
hb := hiob[addr % len hiob];
p : ref Iobuf;
```

19.4.12.1   Searching the Hash Table

Because there can be more than one block that hashes to the same value, we might have to search through the list of blocks, starting with the first one that has this hash value. If we find it, we move it to the front of the list. This keeps the list sorted in increasing order of time since the last access. Finally, we return the pointer to it.

```
Search :
    for (;; ) {
        hb.lk.lock( );
        s := hb.link;
        # see if it's active
        p = s;
        do {
            if (p.addr ≡ addr ∧ p.dev ≡ dev) {
                if (p ≠ s) {
                    p.back.fore = p.fore;
                    p.fore.back = p.back;
                    p.fore = s;
                    p.back = s.back;
                    s.back = p;
```

```
            p.back.fore = p;
            hb.link = p;
        }
        hb.lk.unlock();
        p.lock();
        if (p.addr ≠ addr ∨ p.dev ≠ dev) {
            # lost race
            p.unlock();
            continue Search;
        }
        p.flags |= flags;
        p.iobuf = p.xiobuf;
        return p;
    }
} while ((p = p.fore) ≠ s);
if (flags ≡ Bprobe) {
    hb.lk.unlock();
    return nil;
}
```

19.4.12.2 Evicting an Old Block

If we make it all the way through the list and don't find a match, then we don't have the block in our buffers. So it's time to throw one out to make room for this one. We use the policy of least recently used and flush out the oldest block. The only thing we are careful about is that we need to keep any blocks that are currently locked.

```
    # steal the oldest unlocked buffer
    do {
        p = s.back;
        if (p.canlock()) {
            # TO DO: if Bmod, write it out and restart Hashed
            # for now we needn't because Iobuf.put is
            # synchronous
            if (p.flags & Bmod)
                sys→print("Bmod unexpected (%ud)\n", p.addr);
            hb.link = p;
            p.dev = dev;
            p.addr = addr;
            p.flags = flags;
            break Search;
        }
        s = p;
    } while (p ≠ hb.link);
```

```
        # no unlocked blocks available; add a new one
        p = hb.newbuf( );
        p.lock( );   # return it locked
        break;
}
```

19.4.12.3   Reading a New Block

Now we have a block that we can use for the new block. The rest of the function is dedicated to loading the block from the disk and setting all the correct administrative overhead. The call to *wrenread*( ) issues a read request to the server that is providing the file or device where our file system is stored. This is the connection to the device driver covered in Chapter 15.

```
    p.dev = dev;
    p.addr = addr;
    p.flags = flags;
    hb.lk.unlock( );
    p.iobuf = p.xiobuf;
    if (flags & Bread) {
        if (wrenread(dev.fd, addr, p.iobuf)) {
            eprint(sys→sprint("error reading block %ud: %r", addr));
            p.flags = 0;
            p.dev = devnone;
            p.addr = −1;
            p.iobuf = nil;
            p.unlock( );
            return nil;
        }
    }
    return p;
}
```

19.5   Summary

Inferno stands out as an example of an operating system that makes use of the distinction between managing name space and managing storage space. File servers that manage small name spaces provide access to a number of traditional OS services, including device drivers. Because all servers use the Styx protocol, they can be accessed on the same machine as the client or on a different machine. The Styx protocol also makes it possible for servers to be both built in to the kernel and implemented as regular user processes. The conventional persistent storage file system examined in this chapter is an example of a file server implemented as a normal user process.

19.6   Exercises

1. Can device drivers in Inferno be implemented as user application servers? Why or why not?

2. In *devwalk*( ), no call is made to (∗)*gen*( ) for the case of ., where it is called for all other cases including .. the parent directory. Why is that the case?

3. The inner **for** loop (the one iterating over the variable *i*) in *devwalk*( ) doesn't have a terminating condition. Is there a danger of an infinite loop here? Why or why not?

4. Assuming that none of the needed blocks are in memory (including the directory), how many disk accesses are required to access the byte located 1 MB into a file on Inferno? Why?

5. Given the default block size of 1024 bytes, what is the largest file that can be represented in kfs?

6. Hard links in UNIX are a result of aliases in the name space (in other words, more than one directory entry gives the same metadata). Why are such hard links not natural in Inferno?

7. In *walkname*( ) in kfs, nothing is done for the name . and likewise for .. under certain conditions. Why is there no search in these two cases?

8. Modify kfs to make it case-insensitive. A file called Foo should be accessible with the names foo, FOO, and fOO.

9. In kfs, NAMELEN is defined to be 28. Modify kfs to support large file names (similar to those in BSD) using a variable-sized directory entry.

10. Write a file server that provides a simple counter. It should serve a single file, and each time that file is read, an integer is incremented and returned.

11. Write a simple associative file system. If a file called foo is created and the string xyz written to it, then a process should be able to either read foo and get xyz or read xyz and get foo.

12. Add symbolic links to kfs.

Chapter 20

File Systems in Linux

Each of the operating systems in Chapter 18 has one, or at most a few, associated file systems. Linux, however, is representative of a more recent trend in which an operating system includes support for a wide range of file systems, including some of those described in Chapter 18. To support these various file systems, Linux uses a division of labor with two levels of abstraction. At the higher level of abstraction, we find the **Virtual File System** (VFS), which implements a number of common services and generic file system operations. For any operations that are dependent on the semantics or data structure details of a particular file system, that file system's support is invoked. In this chapter, we discuss the Linux VFS design. We follow that with a discussion of some of the details of one of the file system implementations, namely the third extended file system (EXT3).

20.1 Virtual File System

One way to conceptualize the Linux Virtual File System (VFS) is as a base class in an object-oriented style of programming. In this view, each specific file system is an instantiation of this base class. Where the generic implementation of an operation is sufficient, it is used. Where an operation depends on the details of this file system, that operation is provided by the particular file system, in effect overriding any generic version that might be there.

In terms of implementation, the VFS is organized as a collection of base classes, one for each of several areas of file system activity. These parts of the VFS are discussed in more detail in the subsections that follow. For each of these parts, the specific file system has a structure containing function pointers defining the operations it provides. Pointers to these structures are stored in the generic data structures representing mounted file systems, open files, and so on. The starting point for associating file system–specific functions with generic operations comes when a file system registers itself, passing a structure with a pointer to the function that loads the superblock when a file system is mounted. From there, each step sets up the list of functions necessary for subsequent operations.

Another perspective on the VFS organization is that of a two- or, in some cases, a three-layered design. At the top layer are the functions that comprise the system call interface. These are the functions that are called when a process issues a file-related system call. These functions handle anything that is common to all file systems, such as parsing a path name. When these functions reach a point when they need to carry out some operation specific to a particular file system, they refer to the relevant structure of function pointers. In some cases, generic functions are available for these operations. For these, a null pointer indicates that the appropriate generic function should be called. These generic support functions make up the lower layer in this design. For those operations where there is no generic function, a null pointer indicates an error of an unsupported operation. If the pointer is nonnull, then the pointer is dereferenced, and the function is called. In some cases, the file system–specific function in turn calls the generic function. The file system–specific code serves as a middle layer in these cases.

20.1.1   Superblocks

When a file system is mounted, a file system–specific function is called to load an internal representation of the file system's metadata. Named after the original UNIX on-disk metadata, this is called the superblock. A member of the internal superblock structure points to a structure of type **struct super_operations**. This structure contains a number of function pointers that are needed to carry out operations on a mounted file system. Although the name suggests that these functions are primarily related to the superblock, most are actually functions needed to fetch and manipulate other metadata structures called **i-nodes**. Some of the more interesting members of the structure include:

- *alloc_inode*( ): Allocate the memory for and initialize an in-memory i-node structure.

- *read_inode*( ): Read an i-node from the file system. In the case of most UNIX-like file systems, the i-node is read from the disk, and the relevant data are copied into the in-memory representation. For other file systems, an internal i-node structure must be synthesized from the file metadata of that file system.

- *write_inode*( ): Write a modified i-node back to the file system. Again for file systems that do not natively have i-nodes, the metadata of the internal i-node must be translated into whatever representation is used for that file system.

- *write_super*( ): Similarly handle a modified superblock.

- *sync_fs*( ): Ensure that the file system as stored on the device is up to date with respect to any cached data.

20.1.2   I-Nodes

As discussed in Chapter 18, file metadata in UNIX file systems are kept in i-nodes. When an internal i-node structure is loaded, one of its members is set to point to a structure of type **struct inode_operations**, which contains function pointers for the operations needed for operating on i-nodes. Although some of the entries do operate directly on an i-node, many actually operate on directories described by the i-node. Some of the relevant operations include:

- *create*( ): Create a new file in a directory.

- *lookup*( ): Fetch a directory entry from a directory.

- *mkdir*( ): Create a new subdirectory.

- *getattr*( ): Return the metadata from an i-node.

20.1.3   Directory Entries

Directories are implemented as lists of directory entries. For the most part, directory entries are sufficiently abstracted away from the details of a file system's implementation that the generic set of operations can be used. Consequently, though a file system implementation might override directory entry operations, we do not concern ourselves with the details of doing so. What is of interest to us is the role of directory entries in the VFS. The VFS maintains a cache of directory entries. These provide a mapping from file names to i-nodes, which can be quickly searched to avoid unnecessary disk accesses.

20.1.4   Files

In addition to the i-node operations, the internal i-node structure also points to a structure of type **struct file_operations**. When a file is opened, an internal structure representing the open file is created. This structure also points to the file operations structure. Most of the file operations correspond to familiar file-oriented system calls, including *open*( ), *read*( ), *write*( ), *ioctl*( ), and *llseek*( ). There are two lesser-known Linux system calls that we encounter in our discussion here and are found in the operations structure. They are *aio_read*( ) and *aio_write*( ), which implement asynchronous reads and writes, respectively.

20.2   The EXT3 File System

We now turn from the generic file system interface as implemented by the VFS to a specific example of a file system in Linux. The example we discuss here is the third extended (EXT3) file system. It, along with its predecessor EXT2, are probably the most widely used file systems in Linux.

The design of EXT3 is similar in many ways to the BSD Fast File System (FFS). In any disk or partition holding an EXT3 file system, the first block is reserved for a boot block. Following the boot block is a superblock, which is replicated in numerous places in the file system. The superblock and all other blocks within the file system occupy the block size, which is determined at the time the file system is initialized. Block sizes of 1024, 2048, and 4096 bytes are supported. For architectures that support page sizes larger than 4096 bytes, a block can also be 8192 bytes.

Whereas the BSD FFS divided a file system into cylinder groups, EXT3 divides it into block groups. The reason we don't attempt to organize the file system in cylinders is that with most modern drives, we have no way of knowing the actual cylinder boundaries. Thus, grouping ranges of blocks is good enough. Within each block group, we often have a copy of the superblock. After the superblock (if present), we have a one-block group descriptor table, followed by two blocks of free bitmaps. One block shows the free data blocks within the group, and the other shows the free i-nodes within the group. Following the free bitmaps, there are a number of blocks that hold i-nodes within the group. The remaining blocks in the group are data blocks. When allocating blocks to a file, we attempt to keep the blocks of a file together in the same block group along with its i-node. This overall structure is illustrated in Figure 20-1.

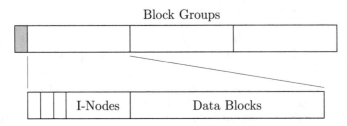

Figure 20-1: EXT3 File System Layout

EXT3 also uses a directory structure which is similar to that in BSD FFS. Each entry is a variable-sized structure primarily containing the file name and the i-number. In addition to the linear directory design, EXT3 also provides an option to speed up directory searches by adding a hash table to a directory.

The last major enhancement of EXT3 over its predecessors is the addition of journaling. As discussed in Section 17.6, this technique helps in ensuring that a file system remains consistent and in recovering after a system crash. The journal in EXT3 is stored in a regular file on the file system and can even be stored on another file system altogether. Typically, only metadata are recorded to the journal; however, file data can also be optionally recorded.

20.3   EXT3 Disk Structure

We begin looking at the details of the EXT3 file system with the data structures as they are stored on disk. All of these structures are defined in include/linux/ext3_fs.h. Rather than describe every structure member in detail, we focus on those that illustrate the principles discussed in Chapter 17 and that are used in the code discussed later in this chapter.

20.3.1   EXT3 Superblock

The first data structure we consider is the superblock. As with other UNIX-type file systems, the superblock holds metadata for the file system as a whole.

```
struct ext3_super_block {
    __le32 s_inodes_count;        /* Inodes count */
    __le32 s_blocks_count;        /* Blocks count */
    __le32 s_r_blocks_count;      /* Reserved blocks count */
    __le32 s_free_blocks_count;   /* Free blocks count */
    __le32 s_free_inodes_count;   /* Free inodes count */
    __le32 s_first_data_block;    /* First Data Block */
    __le32 s_log_block_size;      /* Block size */
    __le32 s_log_frag_size;       /* Fragment size */
    __le32 s_blocks_per_group;    /* # Blocks per group */
    __le32 s_frags_per_group;     /* # Fragments per group */
    __le32 s_inodes_per_group;    /* # Inodes per group */
    __le32 s_mtime;               /* Mount time */
    __le32 s_wtime;               /* Write time */
    __le16 s_mnt_count;           /* Mount count */
    __le16 s_max_mnt_count;       /* Maximal mount count */
    __le16 s_magic;               /* Magic signature */
    __le16 s_state;               /* File system state */
    __le16 s_errors;              /* Behavior when detecting errors */
    __le16 s_minor_rev_level;     /* minor revision level */
    __le32 s_lastcheck;           /* time of last check */
    __le32 s_checkinterval;       /* max. time between checks */
    __le32 s_creator_os;          /* OS */
    __le32 s_rev_level;           /* Revision level */
    __le16 s_def_resuid;          /* Default uid for reserved blocks */
    __le16 s_def_resgid;          /* Default gid for reserved blocks */
    __le32 s_first_ino;           /* First non-reserved inode */
    __le16 s_inode_size;          /* size of inode structure */
    __le16 s_block_group_nr;      /* block group # of this superblock */
    __le32 s_feature_compat;      /* compatible feature set */
    __le32 s_feature_incompat;    /* incompatible feature set */
    __le32 s_feature_ro_compat;   /* readonly-compatible feature set */
    __u8   s_uuid[16];            /* 128-bit uuid for volume */
    char   s_volume_name[16];     /* volume name */
    char   s_last_mounted[64];    /* directory where last mounted */
    __le32 s_algorithm_usage_bitmap; /* For compression */
    __u8   s_prealloc_blocks;     /* Nr of blocks to try to preallocate */
    __u8   s_prealloc_dir_blocks; /* Nr to preallocate for dirs */
    __u16  s_reserved_gdt_blocks; /* Per group desc for online growth */
    __u8   s_journal_uuid[16];    /* uuid of journal superblock */
    __le32 s_journal_inum;        /* inode number of journal file */
    __le32 s_journal_dev;         /* device number of journal file */
    __le32 s_last_orphan;         /* start of list of inodes to delete */
    __le32 s_hash_seed[4];        /* HTREE hash seed */
```

```
    __u8 s_def_hash_version;        /* Default hash version to use */
    __u8 s_reserved_char_pad;
    __u16 s_reserved_word_pad;
    __le32 s_default_mount_opts;
    __le32 s_first_meta_bg;         /* First metablock block group */
    __u32 s_reserved[190];          /* Padding to the end of the block */
};
```

As defined, this structure is 1024 bytes in size, which matches the smallest block size
that can be configured for an EXT3 file system. Before delving into the details of the
structure, we should point out a couple of things about the data types used. Except for
some arrays of type **char**, we don't use the standard C data types at all. In a number of
places, we use types such as __**u8** and __**u16**. These types are defined to be unsigned 8-
and 16-bit integers, respectively. Because C doesn't specify exact sizes for its data types,
such types are often defined in an architecture-specific way to ensure that data structures
like these are a known size. We also see the use of types like __**le32**. This is a 32-bit
integer like the long integer on most architectures. The **le** part of the name is a reminder
to the reader that the data stored on the disk are stored in little endian order (least
significant byte first). By defining the order, we can ensure that a file system written
on one machine architecture will be read correctly by any other. Each architecture has
macros that convert between the little endian order used on the disk and whatever byte
ordering is used on that architecture. With these ideas in hand, we can now turn to look
at several of the data members in the superblock structure.

- *s_inodes_count* and *s_blocks_count*: One of the most fundamental attributes of a file
  system is its size. These two members give the number of i-nodes and the number
  of data blocks, respectively.

- *s_r_blocks_count*: We often reserve some fraction of the file system for use by the
  superuser so that the system administrator will have room to work when cleaning
  up a problem that might have exhausted the rest of the disk space. This member
  specifies the number of such reserved blocks.

- *s_free_blocks_count* and *s_free_inodes_count*: These members tell the number of free
  data blocks and the number of free i-nodes in the file system.

- *s_first_data_block*: Within the file system data structures, the data blocks are always
  relative to the first data block in the system. On the other hand, block references
  by device drivers are always relative to the beginning of a disk or a partition. The
  s_first_data_block member tells the location of the first data block and thus gives the
  offset necessary to calculate the physical block number.

- *s_log_block_size*: Because EXT3 file systems can be initialized with various block
  sizes, we need to know when one is mounted what block size it uses. This member
  gives us the $\log_2$ of the block size.

- *s_blocks_per_group* and *s_inodes_per_group*: As discussed in the previous section, EXT3 divides the file system into a number of block groups. These members specify the number of data blocks and the number of i-nodes stored in each group, respectively.

- *s_mnt_count* and *s_max_mnt_count*: Even when the file system is cleanly unmounted every time, we still want to periodically check its consistency. These members tell us how often (in terms of the number of times it's mounted) we need to check and how close we are to the next check.

- *s_lastcheck* and *s_checkinterval*: These serve the same role for checks based on the amount of time between checks rather than the number of mounts.

- *s_magic*: It is quite common for us to put some unique value in a known place in the superblock. The idea is that if an attempt is made to mount this file system, but the "magic number" isn't what we expect, then we know that the type of this file system isn't the same as the type we're assuming.

- *s_state*: As the name implies, this member gives the state of the file system. The part of that which interests us most is whether it's been cleanly unmounted. If an attempt is made to mount the file system and it was not cleanly unmounted last time, then we want to force a consistency check.

- *s_journal_inum* and *s_journal_dev*: These uniquely identify the location of the journaling file. Because it is a regular file, its i-number and device are sufficient to locate it. This also implies that the journal can actually be on a different device from the one containing this file system, though we rarely do so.

20.3.2 EXT3 I-Node

As with other UNIX-type file systems, EXT3 uses i-nodes to represent files. This structure contains all the metadata for a particular file. As defined, it occupies 132 bytes. However, normally only 128 bytes are stored on the disk and are used. The final four bytes are used only when the file system is initialized with larger i-nodes to hold extended attributes. In other words, in the absence of extended attributes, if we have one of these structures in memory and we write it to the disk, the *osd2* member is the last thing written; neither *i_extra_isize* nor *i_pad1* are stored in the i-node on the disk.

```
struct ext3_inode {
    __le16 i_mode;      /* File mode */
    __le16 i_uid;       /* Low 16 bits of Owner Uid */
    __le32 i_size;      /* Size in bytes */
    __le32 i_atime;     /* Access time */
    __le32 i_ctime;     /* Creation time */
    __le32 i_mtime;     /* Modification time */
    __le32 i_dtime;     /* Deletion Time */
    __le16 i_gid;       /* Low 16 bits of Group Id */
```

```
__le16 i_links_count;     /* Links count */
__le32 i_blocks;       /* Blocks count */
__le32 i_flags;       /* File flags */
union {
  struct {
    __u32 l_i_reserved1;
  } linux1;
  struct {
    __u32 h_i_translator;
  } hurd1;
  struct {
    __u32 m_i_reserved1;
  } masix1;
} osd1;     /* OS dependent 1 */
__le32 i_block[EXT3_N_BLOCKS];     /* Pointers to blocks */
__le32 i_generation;     /* File version (for NFS) */
__le32 i_file_acl;     /* File ACL */
__le32 i_dir_acl;     /* Directory ACL */
__le32 i_faddr;      /* Fragment address */
union {
  struct {
    __u8 l_i_frag;     /* Fragment number */
    __u8 l_i_fsize;      /* Fragment size */
    __u16 i_pad1;
    __le16 l_i_uid_high;      /* these 2 fields */
    __le16 l_i_gid_high;      /* were reserved2[0] */
    __u32 l_i_reserved2;
  } linux2;
  struct {
    __u8 h_i_frag;     /* Fragment number */
    __u8 h_i_fsize;      /* Fragment size */
    __u16 h_i_mode_high;
    __u16 h_i_uid_high;
    __u16 h_i_gid_high;
    __u32 h_i_author;
  } hurd2;
  struct {
    __u8 m_i_frag;     /* Fragment number */
    __u8 m_i_fsize;      /* Fragment size */
    __u16 m_pad1;
    __u32 m_i_reserved2[2];
  } masix2;
} osd2;     /* OS dependent 2 */
__le16 i_extra_isize;
```

```
    __le16 i_pad1;
};
```

Notice that as with the superblock, the data in the i-node are all stored in little endian order. Most of the members of this structure represent the same metadata described generically in Chapter 17.

- *i_mode*: This member is a collection of bits that indicates the permissions on the file and the type of file. Three of the bits indicate the permissions for the owner of the file, three for the group that owns the file, and three for everyone else. Four of the bits indicate the type of the file: regular, directory, symbolic link, block special file, character special file, and so on.

- *i_uid* and *i_gid*: These specify the IDs of the user and group that own the file.

- *i_size*: The number of bytes in the file is found in this member. Note that any bytes included in a sparse file are counted here. As a result, this value doesn't actually give the amount of space used on the disk.

- *i_atime*, *i_ctime*, *i_mtime*, and *i_dtime*: These timestamps give the time of last access, the time of creation, the time of last modification, and the time of deletion, respectively. They are all measured in seconds since midnight January 1, 1970.

- *i_links_count*: As with other UNIX-type file systems, there can be multiple directory entries that point to the same i-node. This member gives the number of such entries that point to this i-node.

- *i_blocks*: This is the number of disk blocks allocated to this file. If it is a sparse file, this number might be smaller than suggested by the *i_size* member.

- *i_block*: This is an array of block pointers. It follows the same basic design as for the BSD Fast File System discussed in Section 18.5. The first 12 pointers point directly to the first 12 data blocks of the file. The next pointer identifies an indirect block containing pointers to data blocks. The fourteenth pointer points to a double-indirect block that contains pointers to indirect blocks that, in turn, contain pointers to data blocks. Finally, the fifteenth pointer points to a triple-indirect block, the pointers of which point to double-indirect blocks.

20.3.3   EXT3 Directory Entries

The design of directory entries in the EXT3 file system is similar to those of the BSD Fast File System. The primary difference is the addition of a type member.

```
struct ext3_dir_entry_2 {
    __le32 inode;      /* Inode number */
    __le16 rec_len;    /* Directory entry length */
    __u8 name_len;     /* Name length */
```

```
        __u8 file_type;
        char name[EXT3_NAME_LEN];        /* File name */
    };
```

As with the other on-disk structures, the members of the directory entry structure are all stored in little endian order. Directory entry structures do not span disk block boundaries. If an entry is added and there is not enough room to store the whole structure in the block, a new block is allocated, and the structure is stored there.

- *inode*: This is the i-number for this entry. It is used as an index into the i-node table.

- *rec_len*: This member gives the number of bytes for the whole directory entry. It is used to locate the beginning of the next entry.

- *name_len*: The number of characters in the file name is given by this member.

- *file_type*: We keep a copy of the type data from the file mode here so that the file type can be quickly determined without having to read the i-node into memory.

- *name*: Here we store the name of the file. The actual amount of space used in this field isn't EXT3_NAME_LEN. It's the length of the name rounded up to the nearest multiple of four.

20.4   EXT3 Name Lookup

To illustrate the way EXT3 implements file system support principles, we examine two representative operations. The first of these is translating a path name to an i-node as part of the *open*() system call. In the remainder of the chapter, we follow with an examination of some elements of the *write*() system call, including the translation from a logical block number within the file to the physical block number on the disk. Much of the code in these two sections is part of the VFS layer and not specific to the EXT3 file system. The series of functions we examine for name lookup is shown in Figure 20-2. The functions above the dashed line are part of the VFS layer, and those below the dashed line are specific to the EXT3 file system. All of the EXT3 functions that can be called by the VFS layer are easily identified by having names that start with *ext3_*. (The only other EXT3-specific function we cover here is *search_dirblock*().) Along the way, we point out where control transfers from the VFS layer to the EXT3-specific code.

20.4.1   Walking a Path

The *open*() system call enters the kernel with the function *sys_open*(). One of the major tasks of opening a file is locating the i-node that corresponds to the path name passed by the application program. With the i-node, the open system call support code can then check the permissions on the operation and can build the internal open file data structure. After about seven nested function calls, we arrive at the VFS function *__link_path_walk*(), defined in fs/namei.c, to follow the path name along the directory tree.

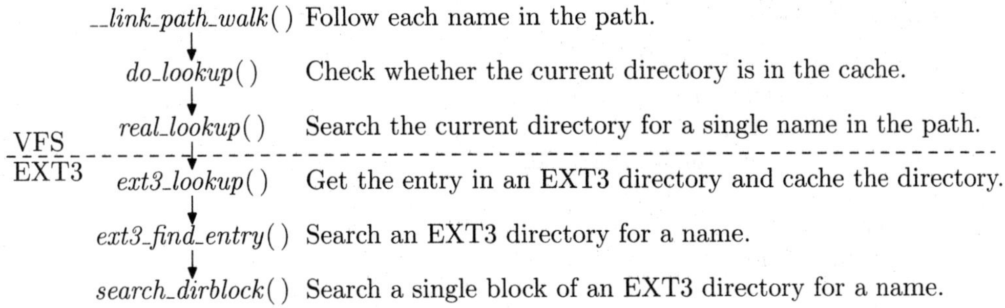

__link_path_walk( ) Follow each name in the path.

  ↓

    do_lookup( )   Check whether the current directory is in the cache.

  ↓

VFS *real_lookup*( )   Search the current directory for a single name in the path.

——

EXT3 *ext3_lookup*( )   Get the entry in an EXT3 directory and cache the directory.

  ↓

  ext3_find_entry( ) Search an EXT3 directory for a name.

  ↓

search_dirblock( ) Search a single block of an EXT3 directory for a name.

Figure 20-2: Functions Called to Walk a Path

static fastcall int *__link_path_walk*(**const char** **name*, **struct nameidata** **nd*)
{
  struct path *next*;
  struct inode **inode*;
  int *err*;
  unsigned int *lookup_flags* = *nd→flags*;

20.4.1.1 Preparing to Walk

The path name we receive might either be absolute or relative. For an absolute path name, one leading slash is sufficient, but we also want to tolerate as many as are there. Regardless, we really want to find the first nonslash character.

  while (**name* ≡ '*/*')
    name++;
  if (¬**name*)
    goto *return_reval*;

When this function is called, *nd* points to a structure that includes a pointer to the directory entry (which, in turn, points to the i-node) for the starting point of our search. If the path name is absolute, then it's the root directory. For relative path names, we start with the current working directory.

  inode = *nd→dentry→d_inode*;
  if (*nd→depth*)
    lookup_flags = LOOKUP_FOLLOW | (*nd→flags* & LOOKUP_CONTINUE);

This loop is repeated once for each element of the path.

  for (; ;) {
    unsigned long *hash*;
    struct qstr *this*;

```
unsigned int c;
nd→flags |= LOOKUP_CONTINUE;
err = exec_permission_lite(inode, nd);
if (err ≡ −EAGAIN)
    err = vfs_permission(nd, MAY_EXEC);
if (err)
    break;
this.name = name;
```

We now compute a hash on this component of the name. Of course, a path name component is delimited by a slash or the end of the string.

```
c = *(const unsigned char *) name;
hash = init_name_hash();
do {
    name++;
    hash = partial_name_hash(c, hash);
    c = *(const unsigned char *) name;
} while (c ∧ (c ≠ '/'));
this.len = name − (const char *) this.name;
this.hash = end_name_hash(hash);
if (¬c)
    goto last_component;
```

As with the beginning of the string, we might have more than one slash delimiting the components in the path. This step is not just preparing for the next iteration of the loop. We also need to determine if this is the last component in the path. If the last character is a slash, then we must be referring to a directory.

```
while (*++name ≡ '/') ;
if (¬*name)
    goto last_with_slashes;
```

20.4.1.2 Handling Interior Components

This section of the code is entered for all path components except for the last one. We want to handle the two names dot (.) and dot-dot (..) specially. The . case is simple; we just move on to the next component of the path. In the .. case, we use the parent information in the in-memory directory entry to follow this component. These steps allow us to follow these two cases more quickly than searching the directory for them.

```
if (this.name[0] ≡ '.')
    switch (this.len) {
    default:
        break;
```

```
        case 2:
          if (this.name[1] ≠ '.')
              break;
          follow_dotdot(nd);
          inode = nd→dentry→d_inode;
        case 1:
          continue;
        }
    if (nd→dentry→d_op ∧ nd→dentry→d_op→d_hash) {
        err = nd→dentry→d_op→d_hash(nd→dentry, &this);
        if (err < 0) break;
    }
```

Here is where we search the current directory for this name. This is done in *do_lookup( )*, which we examine later.

```
    err = do_lookup(nd, &this, &next);
    if (err)
        break;
    err = -ENOENT;
    inode = next.dentry→d_inode;
    if (¬inode)
        goto out_dput;
    err = -ENOTDIR;
    if (¬inode→i_op)
        goto out_dput;
```

If we have a symbolic link, we need to follow it. All we do is set the *follow_link* member of the operation structure if the file is indeed a symbolic link. Otherwise, it's null, and we take the **else** branch, which prepares *nd* for the next iteration of the loop.

```
    if (inode→i_op→follow_link) {
        err = do_follow_link(&next, nd);
        if (err)
            goto return_err;
        err = -ENOENT;
        inode = nd→dentry→d_inode;
        if (¬inode)
            break;
        err = -ENOTDIR;
        if (¬inode→i_op) break;
    }
    else
        path_to_nameidata(&next, nd);
```

```
    err = −ENOTDIR;
    if (¬inode→i_op→lookup)
        break;
```

At this point, we reach the end of the case handling all names except the last. The **continue** essentially says it's time to move on to the next name in the path.

```
    continue;
```

20.4.1.3   Handling the Final Name in the Path

This next section of code handles the lookup and link following when we reach the last name in the path. The reason this one is broken out separately is that there are some special cases where we want different behavior. For example, we might be doing this lookup to find the contents of a symbolic link rather than to follow it. However, because we are following the case of a lookup driven by an *open( )* system call, these special cases aren't an issue for us. Consequently, we skip most of the details of the remainder of this function.

```
    last_with_slashes:
        lookup_flags |= LOOKUP_FOLLOW | LOOKUP_DIRECTORY;
    last_component:
        nd→flags &= lookup_flags | ~LOOKUP_CONTINUE;
        if (lookup_flags & LOOKUP_PARENT)
            goto lookup_parent;
        if (this.name[0] ≡ '.')
            switch (this.len) {
            default:
                break;
            case 2:
                if (this.name[1] ≠ '.')
                    break;
                follow_dotdot(nd);
                inode = nd→dentry→d_inode;
            case 1:
                goto return_reval;
            }
        if (nd→dentry→d_op ∧ nd→dentry→d_op→d_hash) {
            err = nd→dentry→d_op→d_hash(nd→dentry, &this);
            if (err < 0)
                break;
        }
        err = do_lookup(nd, &this, &next);
        if (err)
            break;
```

```
        inode = next.dentry⁃d_inode;
     if ((lookup_flags & LOOKUP_FOLLOW) ∧ inode
            ∧ inode⁃i_op ∧ inode⁃i_op⁃follow_link) {
        err = do_follow_link(&next, nd);
        if (err)
           goto return_err;
        inode = nd⁃dentry⁃d_inode;
     }
     else
        path_to_nameidata(&next, nd);
     err = −ENOENT;
     if (¬inode)
        break;
     if (lookup_flags & LOOKUP_DIRECTORY) {
        err = −ENOTDIR;
        if (¬inode⁃i_op ∨ ¬inode⁃i_op⁃lookup)
           break;
     }
```

20.4.1.4 Wrapping Up

This is the place where we normally finish the path evaluation.

```
        goto return_base;
     lookup_parent:
        nd⁃last = this;
        nd⁃last_type = LAST_NORM;
        if (this.name[0] ≠ '.')
           goto return_base;
        if (this.len ≡ 1)
           nd⁃last_type = LAST_DOT;
        else if (this.len ≡ 2 ∧ this.name[1] ≡ '.')
           nd⁃last_type = LAST_DOTDOT;
        else
           goto return_base;
     return_reval:
        if (nd⁃dentry ∧ nd⁃dentry⁃d_sb
              ∧ (nd⁃dentry⁃d_sb⁃s_type⁃fs_flags & FS_REVAL_DOT)) {
           err = −ESTALE;
           if (¬nd⁃dentry⁃d_op⁃d_revalidate(nd⁃dentry, nd))
              break;
        }
```

We are now ready to return. At each step along the way, we modified *nd* to refer to each name in the path. Now that we have reached the end of the path, *nd* corresponds to the file identified by the full path name. Included in this structure, we have the directory entry, which points to the i-node. As a result, our objective is complete.

```
return_base:
    return 0;
out_dput:
    dput_path(&next, nd);
    break;
}
path_release(nd);
return_err:
    return err;
}
```

20.4.2 Generic Directory Lookup (Part 1)

This function is the first stage in looking up a directory entry as part of the VFS layer and is found in fs/namei.c. Its primary role is to distinguish between the fast case, where we already have the directory entry in our cache, and the slower one, where we actually have to search a directory for it. It might look a bit like spaghetti code, but it's organized so that the fastest case falls straight through.

```
static int do_lookup (struct nameidata *nd, struct qstr *name,
        struct path *path )
{
    struct vfsmount *mnt = nd→mnt;
```

The call to __d_lookup( ) checks the cache of directory entries for the object of our search. If we find it, we return a pointer to its directory entry. Otherwise, we return a null pointer.

```
    struct dentry *dentry = __d_lookup(nd→dentry, name);
```

These next several lines distinguish between the fast case (we have the entry in cache) and the other case (we need to look it up). If it is in the cache, we fall through, recording the **dentry** structure we found before returning.

```
    if (¬dentry)
        goto need_lookup;
    if (dentry→d_op ∧ dentry→d_op→d_revalidate)
        goto need_revalidate;
done:
    path→mnt = mnt;
    path→dentry = dentry;
```

```
    __follow_mount(path);
    return 0;
```

If we did not find the directory entry in the cache, then we reach this point in the code where we call *real_lookup( )* to carry out the actual search. If it succeeds, then we go back to the return path labeled by *done*.

```
  need_lookup:
    dentry = real_lookup(nd→dentry, name, nd);
    if (IS_ERR(dentry))
       goto fail;
    goto done;
```

Revalidation is not used in the EXT3 file system, so we ignore this code in the interest of clarity and space.

```
  need_revalidate:
    if (dentry→d_op→d_revalidate(dentry, nd))
       goto done;
    if (d_invalidate(dentry))
       goto done;
    dput(dentry);
    goto need_lookup;
  fail:
    return PTR_ERR(dentry);
}
```

When we return from this function, we either have the directory entry we want, or we failed to find it. In the latter case, the application was probably trying to open a file that does not exist.

20.4.3 Generic Directory Lookup (Part 2)

Now that we've handled the fast and (we hope) common case where the directory entry is in the cache, we turn to the case where it's not there. Of course, actually carrying out the directory search is a file system–specific operation. Consequently, this VFS function is little more than a wrapper around a call to the directory lookup function for the particular file system. We find this function defined in fs/namei.c.

```
static struct dentry *real_lookup(struct dentry *parent, struct qstr *name,
    struct nameidata *nd)
{
    struct dentry *result;
    struct inode *dir = parent→d_inode;
```

It might seem redundant for us to call *d_lookup*( ) when we just called __*d_lookup*( ). The reason for this is that the earlier call was made without any mutex locking. As a result, it's possible (though unlikely) that between the time we made that call and now, the directory entry we want has made its way into the cache.

```
mutex_lock(&dir→i_mutex);
result = d_lookup(parent, name);
```

Normally, we don't expect to have succeeded in finding the directory entry we want. Here is where we call the underlying directory lookup function for the specific file system. In our case, that is EXT3. It is at this point where control transfers from the VFS layer to the EXT3-specific code.

```
if (¬result) {
    struct dentry *dentry = d_alloc(parent, name);
    result = ERR_PTR(−ENOMEM);
    if (dentry) {
        result = dir→i_op→lookup(dir, dentry, nd);
        if (result)
            dput(dentry);
        else
            result = dentry;
    }
    mutex_unlock(&dir→i_mutex);
    return result;
}
```

Finally, here's where we return the cached entry if we found one on the second search.

```
mutex_unlock(&dir→i_mutex);
if (result→d_op ∧ result→d_op→d_revalidate) {
    if (¬result→d_op→d_revalidate(result, nd) ∧ ¬d_invalidate(result)) {
        dput(result);
        result = ERR_PTR(−ENOENT);
    }
}
return result;
}
```

20.4.4 EXT3 Directory Lookup

Here is where we make the transition from the generic VFS code to the EXT3-specific code. This first function basically does three things: It calls the actual directory search, loads the i-node, and adds the new directory entry to the cache. Its definition is found in fs/ext3/namei.c.

```
static struct dentry *ext3_lookup(struct inode *dir, struct dentry *dentry,
    struct nameidata *nd)
{
  struct inode *inode;
  struct ext3_dir_entry_2 *de;
  struct buffer_head *bh;
```

Before we do anything else, we check for an error condition, namely that the application is asking for a file name that is too long for EXT3. For EXT3, the maximum file name length is 255 characters.

```
if (dentry→d_name.len > EXT3_NAME_LEN)
    return ERR_PTR(−ENAMETOOLONG);
```

Next, we call *ext3_find_entry*( ) to carry out the actual directory search. If it fails, it returns a null pointer.

```
bh = ext3_find_entry(dentry, &de);
```

If the directory search succeeded, then we load the i-node for the entry.

```
inode = Λ;
if (bh) {
  unsigned long ino = le32_to_cpu(de→inode);
  brelse(bh);
  if (¬ext3_valid_inum(dir→i_sb, ino)) {
    ext3_error(dir→i_sb, "ext3_lookup",
      "bad inode number: %lu", ino);
    inode = Λ;
  }
  else
    inode = iget(dir→i_sb, ino);
  if (¬inode)
    return ERR_PTR(−EACCES);
}
```

Finally, we add the newly found directory entry to the cache. This call correctly handles the case where this entry is an alias for one already in the cache. Notice that we don't have to worry about some other directory search putting the entry there before us. This function is called with a mutex lock in place.

```
  return d_splice_alias(inode, dentry);
}
```

20.4.5   EXT3 Directory Search

The actual directory search itself is more involved than might be expected. Because the directory is spread out over potentially many blocks, we have to load and search each block. If the directory is large, this could be time consuming. For this reason, the EXT3 file system provides the ability to create a hash table index for a directory. In the interest of simplicity, however, we assume that the directory we are searching is not indexed. This function which handles the multiblock search is also found in fs/ext3/namei.c.

```
static struct buffer_head *ext3_find_entry(struct dentry *dentry,
    struct ext3_dir_entry_2 **res_dir)
{
  struct super_block *sb;
  struct buffer_head *bh_use[NAMEI_RA_SIZE];
  struct buffer_head *bh, *ret = Λ;
  unsigned long start, block, b;
  int ra_max = 0;
  int ra_ptr = 0;
  int num = 0;
  int nblocks, i, err;
  struct inode *dir = dentry→d_parent→d_inode;
  int namelen;
  const u8 *name;
  unsigned blocksize;
```

We start out by setting up some variables that govern the search process. We also do a little error checking, making sure that we have a valid file name.

```
  *res_dir = Λ;
  sb = dir→i_sb;
  blocksize = sb→s_blocksize;
  namelen = dentry→d_name.len;
  name = dentry→d_name.name;
  if (namelen > EXT3_NAME_LEN)
    return Λ;
```

Here is where we handle the case of a directory with an index. In the interest of demonstrating basic principles, we assume that the directory we're currently searching is not such a directory.

```
#ifdef CONFIG_EXT3_INDEX
  if (is_dx(dir)) {
    bh = ext3_dx_find_entry(dentry, res_dir, &err);
    if (bh ∨ (err ≠ ERR_BAD_DX_DIR))
      return bh;
```

```
      dxtrace (printk ("ext3_find_entry:␣dx␣failed,␣falling␣back\n"));
   }
#endif
```

Next, we set up the loop that will be executed once for each block in the directory.

```
    nblocks = dir→i_size ≫ EXT3_BLOCK_SIZE_BITS(sb);
    start = EXT3_I(dir)→i_dir_start_lookup;
    if (start ≥ nblocks)
       start = 0;
    block = start;
restart:
    do {
```

20.4.5.1   Read-Ahead

This next section of code handles read-ahead. The idea here is that rather than issuing a request for the disk blocks one at a time, we're better off getting several at once. It is very likely that they are close together on the disk and, among other things, this potentially reduces head movement. The call to *ext3_getblk*( ) handles the management of buffers of disk blocks. The call to *ll_rw_block*( ) is where we request a block from the device driver. This is the connection to the code in the case of a floppy disk drive, which we discussed in Section 16.4. (We should note, however, that it is unusual to use the EXT3 file system on a floppy. Normally, EXT3 is found on larger hard disk drives.)

```
    if (ra_ptr ≥ ra_max) {
       ra_ptr = 0;
       b = block;
       for (ra_max = 0; ra_max < NAMEI_RA_SIZE; ra_max ++) {
          if (b ≥ nblocks ∨ (num ∧ block ≡ start)) {
             bh_use[ra_max] = Λ;
             break;
          }
          num ++;
          bh = ext3_getblk(Λ, dir, b++, 0, &err);
          bh_use[ra_max] = bh;
          if (bh)
             ll_rw_block(READ, 1, &bh);
       }
    }
```

Now that we have some blocks preloaded, we get the next one to search.

```
    if ((bh = bh_use[ra_ptr ++]) ≡ Λ)
       goto next;
```

$wait\_on\_buffer(bh);$
if $(\neg buffer\_uptodate(bh))$ {
$\quad ext3\_error(sb, \verb|__FUNCTION__|,$
$\quad\quad$ `"reading directory #%lu " "offset %lu"`, $dir\rightarrow i\_ino, block);$
$\quad brelse(bh);$
$\quad$ **goto** $next;$
}

20.4.5.2 Searching a Directory Block

Now we do the actual search. If we are successful, we can stop going through the blocks and return. Likewise, if we hit an error in the search process, we quit early and return.

$i = search\_dirblock(bh, dir, dentry, block \ll \texttt{EXT3\_BLOCK\_SIZE\_BITS}(sb), res\_dir);$
if $(i \equiv 1)$ {
$\quad \texttt{EXT3\_I}(dir)\rightarrow i\_dir\_start\_lookup = block;$
$\quad ret = bh;$
$\quad$ **goto** $cleanup\_and\_exit;$
}
else {
$\quad brelse(bh);$
$\quad$ **if** $(i < 0)$
$\quad\quad$ **goto** $cleanup\_and\_exit;$
}

We haven't found it yet, so we move on to the next block. Of course, if we run out of blocks and still haven't found the name for which we're searching, we fall out of the loop.

$next:$
$\quad$ **if** $(++block \geq nblocks)$
$\quad\quad block = 0;$
} **while** $(block \neq start);$

There is a slim chance that the directory grew while we were searching. In particular, more files might have been added. If we didn't find the file we want and the directory did grow, then we try looking in the new part of the directory.

$block = nblocks;$
$nblocks = dir\rightarrow i\_size \gg \texttt{EXT3\_BLOCK\_SIZE\_BITS}(sb);$
if $(block < nblocks)$ {
$\quad start = 0;$
$\quad$ **goto** $restart;$
}

Whether we found the file or not, we are now finished with the buffers we used for the read-ahead, and we're ready to return our results.

```
cleanup_and_exit:
    for ( ; ra_ptr < ra_max; ra_ptr++)
        brelse(bh_use[ra_ptr]);
    return ret;
}
```

20.4.6   EXT3 Directory Block Search

The last function we examine as part of name lookups is *search_dirblock*( ), found in fs/ext3/namei.c. This function looks through all the directory entries in a single file system block to see if any of them matches the name that's the object of our search.

```
static inline int search_dirblock(struct buffer_head *bh, struct inode *dir,
        struct dentry *dentry, unsigned long offset,
        struct ext3_dir_entry_2 **res_dir)
{
    struct ext3_dir_entry_2 *de;
    char *dlimit;
    int de_len;
    const char *name = dentry→d_name.name;
    int namelen = dentry→d_name.len;
```

As we loop through the entries in this block, *de* always points to this iteration's entry, and *dlimit* tells us when we stop so that *ext3_find_entry*( ) can move on to the next block.

```
    de = (struct ext3_dir_entry_2 *) bh→b_data;
    dlimit = bh→b_data + dir→i_sb→s_blocksize;
    while ((char *) de < dlimit) {
```

If this entry's name matches the one for which we're searching, then we can declare success and return.

```
        if ((char *) de + namelen ≤ dlimit ∧ ext3_match(namelen, name, de)) {
            if (¬ext3_check_dir_entry("ext3_find_entry", dir, de, bh, offset))
                return −1;
            *res_dir = de;
            return 1;
        }
```

If we didn't find the one we need, then we move on to the next entry. Because the entries are not fixed size, we use the *rec_len* member of the structure to tell us where the next one is.

```
        de_len = le16_to_cpu(de→rec_len);
        if (de_len ≤ 0)
            return −1;
        offset += de_len;
        de = (struct ext3_dir_entry_2 *)((char *) de + de_len);
    }
    return 0;
}
```

After we've found the name we need, we return back to *ext3_find_entry*( ), which returns back to *ext3_lookup*( ), where the i-node is loaded and the directory entry is cached. From that point on, the path name traversal can continue, and any future references to this file are found in the cache (until its entry must be flushed to make room for new entries).

20.5   File Writing

As long as the file is open, the application can issue other file-oriented system calls on it. The most common ones are, of course, *read*( ) and *write*( ). In this section, we take a brief look at the mechanics of the implementation of the *write*( ) system call. The sequence of functions we consider is shown in Figure 20-3. At a high level, writing to a file begins with determining the point at which we're writing. After that, we turn control over to the VFS layer, where the request is checked to make sure that it doesn't violate security or other limitations on writing. After verifying that the request is permissible, we pass control to the EXT3-specific write function, which implements the write by means of the support for memory-mapped files in the memory management subsystem.

$$sys\_write(\ ) \qquad \text{Handle the } write(\ ) \text{ system call.}$$
$$\downarrow$$
$$vfs\_write(\ ) \qquad \text{Perform VFS write operations.}$$
$$\downarrow$$
$$ext3\_file\_write(\ ) \quad \text{Write to a file in an EXT3 file system.}$$

Figure 20-3: Calls to Write to an EXT3 File

20.5.1   Linux Write System Call

The entry point for the *write*( ) system call is *sys_write*( ), as defined in fs/read_write.c. It's actually little more than a wrapper around a generic write implementation for the VFS.

```
asmlinkage ssize_t sys_write(unsigned int fd, const char __user *buf,
        size_t count)
{
    struct file *file;
```

```
    ssize_t ret = −EBADF;
    int fput_needed;
```

The application gave us a file descriptor; we need a pointer to the internal open file structure. A call to *fget_light( )* is the right way to do that in this context.

```
    file = fget_light(fd, &fput_needed);
    if (file) {
```

Before writing, we need to find out where to write. That's stored in the open file structure. Likewise, after we're done with the write operation, we need to update the file position in the structure.

```
        loff_t pos = file_pos_read(file);
        ret = vfs_write(file, buf, count, &pos);
        file_pos_write(file, pos);
```

At this point, we're done using the struture for now, and we're ready to return.

```
        fput_light(file, fput_needed);
    }
    return ret;
}
```

20.5.2 Generic File Writing

Here is where we take care of the parts of the write operation that are independent of the specific file system and are, therefore, part of the VFS layer. The code for this function is found in fs/read_write.c. Much of this is checking the validity of the request.

```
    ssize_t vfs_write(struct file *file, const char __user *buf, size_t count,
        loff_t *pos)
    {
        ssize_t ret;
```

The first test is making sure that the file is actually opened for writing. Even if the user is allowed to write to the file, if it was opened read-only, then it's an error to try to write.

```
        if (¬(file→f_mode & FMODE_WRITE))
            return −EBADF;
```

If the file system involved doesn't define a way to handle writes, this is not a valid request.

```
        if (¬file→f_op ∨ (¬file→f_op→write ∧ ¬file→f_op→aio_write))
            return −EINVAL;
```

Next, we make sure that we are allowed to read the memory space from which the process told us to take the data.

> **if** $(unlikely(\neg access\_ok(\texttt{VERIFY\_READ}, buf, count)))$
>   **return** $-\texttt{EFAULT}$;

Here we make sure we're working on a valid area of the file. One part of this is making sure we're not starting or ending at a negative file offset. Another check verifies that the area we're writing isn't locked against writes.

> $ret = rw\_verify\_area(\texttt{WRITE}, file, pos, count)$;
> **if** $(ret \geq 0)$ {
> $count = ret$;

Next, we check the file permissions to make sure this user is allowed to write to the file.

> $ret = security\_file\_permission(file, \texttt{MAY\_WRITE})$;
>   **if** $(\neg ret)$ {

Now we are ready to call the file system–specific write function. If one is not defined, we fall back on a generic one. In our case, we do have one defined for the EXT3 file system, and we transfer control from the VFS layer to the EXT3-specific code.

> **if** $(file \rightarrow f\_op \rightarrow write)$
> $ret = file \rightarrow f\_op \rightarrow write(file, buf, count, pos)$;
> **else**
> $ret = do\_sync\_write(file, buf, count, pos)$;

If the write is successful, we update some bookkeeping and return. The value returned is the number of bytes successfully written.

> **if** $(ret > 0)$ {
> $fsnotify\_modify(file \rightarrow f\_dentry)$;
> $current \rightarrow wchar \mathrel{+}= ret$;
> }
> $current \rightarrow syscw \mathbin{+\!+}$;
>   }
> }
> **return** ret;
> }

20.5.3   EXT3 File Writing

The EXT3-specific write code is found in *ext3_file_write*( ) in fs/ext3/file.c. There's actually not much EXT3-specific activity here. Most of the work is done by a generic call.

> **static ssize_t** *ext3_file_write*(**struct kiocb** *∗iocb*, **const char __user** *∗buf*,
>   **size_t** *count*, **loff_t** *pos*)
> {
>   **struct file** *∗file = iocb→ki_filp*;
>   **struct inode** *∗inode = file→f_dentry→d_inode*;
>   **ssize_t** *ret*;
>   **int** *err*;

The first step is calling a generic file write routine, which is actually defined as part of the memory management subsystem. It is built on the support for memory-mapped files.

> *ret = generic_file_aio_write*(*iocb*, *buf*, *count*, *pos*);
> **if** (*ret ≤* 0)
>   **return** *ret*;

The remainder of this function handles the journaling supported by EXT3. Usually only metadata are journaled in an EXT3 file system. However, the option to journal file data as well does exist. If this file is marked for journaling, then we do so through the call to *ext3_force_commit*( ). Otherwise, we fall through to the final return and pass control back to *vfs_write*( ).

> **if** (*file→f_flags* & O_SYNC) {
>   **if** (¬*ext3_should_journal_data*(*inode*))
>   **return** *ret*;
>   **goto** *force_commit*;
> }
> **if** (¬IS_SYNC(*inode*))
>   **return** *ret*;
> *force_commit*:
>   *err = ext3_force_commit*(*inode→i_sb*);
>   **if** (*err*)
>   **return** *err*;
>   **return** *ret*;
> }

20.6   Locating File Blocks in EXT3

We now turn to one final responsibility of the EXT3 file system, namely locating the physical block containing a particular logical block of a file. The two functions we consider are called one after the other when we are locating a block of a file.

20.6.1   Identifying the Indirect Blocks

In fs/ext3/inode.c, we find this function that builds a list of indirect blocks we need to go through to get to the desired data block. Depending on the size of the file, the blocks may be listed in a one-, two-, or three-level tree, and we want the path from the root of the tree to the data block. We specify the desired logical block number with the parameter *i_block*. The result of this function is an array where each element is one offset either into the array of direct block pointers or into an indirect block.

> **static int** *ext3_block_to_path*(**struct inode** **inode*, **long** *i_block*, **int** *offsets*[4],
>   **int** **boundary*)
> {

These first few declarations give us the numbers of block pointers we find in the direct block list and in indirect blocks. As discussed earlier, the number of direct pointers is fixed as part of the design for i-nodes, so *direct_blocks* is the same, regardless of other file system parameters. On the other hand, the number of block pointers that can be stored in an indirect block depends on the number of bytes per block. The macro `EXT3_ADDR_PER_BLOCK` gives us the number of pointers in an indirect block. The computation of *double_blocks* is a little more subtle. This value gives us the number of data blocks that can be accessed through the i-node's pointer to the double-indirect block. It is the square of the number of blocks an indirect block can point to. For example, if an indirect block can hold 256 pointers, then the double-indirect block can point to 256 single-indirect blocks, each of which can point to 256 data blocks, for a total of 65,536 data blocks. Here, we calculate the square with the expression $2^{2 \log_2 n}$, where n is the number of pointers in a block.

> **int** *ptrs* = `EXT3_ADDR_PER_BLOCK`(*inode→i_sb*);
> **int** *ptrs_bits* = `EXT3_ADDR_PER_BLOCK_BITS`(*inode→i_sb*);
> **const long** *direct_blocks* = `EXT3_NDIR_BLOCKS`, *indirect_blocks* = *ptrs*,
>   *double_blocks* = (1 ≪ (*ptrs_bits* * 2));
> **int** *n* = 0;
> **int** *final* = 0;
> **if** (*i_block* < 0) {
>   *ext3_warning*(*inode→i_sb*, "ext3_block_to_path", "block␣<␣0");
> }

The first case is a block number that is small enough to be identified by the data block pointers in the i-node.

> **else if** (*i_block* < *direct_blocks*) {
>   *offsets*[*n*++] = *i_block*;
>   *final* = *direct_blocks*;
> }

The second case is the one where the block number is too large to be addressed by the direct pointers, but is small enough that it is addressed by a single-indirect block. Here, the path in the tree includes two nodes.

> **else if** $((i\_block -= direct\_blocks) < indirect\_blocks)$ {
> $offsets[n++] = $ `EXT3_IND_BLOCK`;
> $offsets[n++] = i\_block$;
> $final = ptrs$;
> }

In this case, we deal with the double-indirect block. We encounter this when the block number is too large for the single-indirect block, but can be addressed by the single-indirect blocks pointed to by the double-indirect block. Because we are going first through the double-indirect block, then to a single-indirect block, and then to the data block, we have a path of length three.

> **else if** $((i\_block -= indirect\_blocks) < double\_blocks)$ {
> $offsets[n++] = $ `EXT3_DIND_BLOCK`;
> $offsets[n++] = i\_block \gg ptrs\_bits$;
> $offsets[n++] = i\_block \,\&\, (ptrs - 1)$;
> $final = ptrs$;
> }

Finally, if the block number is large enough, we make use of the triple-indirect block. Our path of length four goes through the triple-indirect block, a double-indirect block, a single-indirect block, and the data block.

> **else if** $(((i\_block -= double\_blocks) \gg (ptrs\_bits * 2)) < ptrs)$ {
> $offsets[n++] = $ `EXT3_TIND_BLOCK`;
> $offsets[n++] = i\_block \gg (ptrs\_bits * 2)$;
> $offsets[n++] = (i\_block \gg ptrs\_bits) \,\&\, (ptrs - 1)$;
> $offsets[n++] = i\_block \,\&\, (ptrs - 1)$;
> $final = ptrs$;
> }
> **else** {
> $ext3\_warning(inode\text{-}i\_sb,$ `"ext3_block_to_path"`, `"block_>_big"`);
> }
> **if** $(boundary)$
> $*boundary = final - 1 - (i\_block \,\&\, (ptrs - 1))$;
> **return** n;
> }

20.6.2 Reading the Indirect Blocks

After building the path through the tree, we can now follow that path by reading the relevant blocks. This is handled by this function, which is also defined in fs/ext3/inode.c.

```
static Indirect *ext3_get_branch(struct inode *inode, int depth, int *offsets,
    Indirect chain[4], int *err)
{
    struct super_block *sb = inode→i_sb;
    Indirect *p = chain;
    struct buffer_head *bh;
```

This function is implemented around calls to a very simple function called *add_chain( )*. For our purposes, its operation can be described as taking the third argument as a pointer to a block number, dereferencing it, and assigning it to *p→key*. This first call takes care of the first node on the path, which will always be a block number stored in the i-node.

```
    *err = 0;
    add_chain(chain, Λ, EXT3_I(inode)→i_data + *offsets);
    if (¬p→key)
        goto no_block;
```

With the first block pointer in hand, we now run through the remaining nodes on the path. Of course, if the first node is a direct pointer to a data block, then decrementing *depth* will give us zero, and the loop will be skipped. Otherwise, we fetch the identified block from the disk with a call to *sb_bread* and index into the block to get the address of the next one.

```
    while (-- depth) {
        bh = sb_bread(sb, le32_to_cpu(p→key));
        if (¬bh)
            goto failure;
        if (¬verify_chain(chain, p))
            goto changed;
        add_chain(++p, bh, (__le32 *) bh→b_data + *++offsets);
        if (¬p→key)
            goto no_block;
    }
```

As we've seen for a number of other cases, the Linux implementation often uses this style of function cleanup and return. The successful case is the one we fall through to if we complete the loop. In other words, we were able to traverse the full path to the desired data block.

```
        return Λ;
    changed:
      brelse(bh);
      *err = −EAGAIN;
      goto no_block;
    failure:
      *err = −EIO;
    no_block:
      return p;
    }
```

20.7 Summary

Linux is an example of the modern trend toward supporting a wide variety of file systems. This support allows Linux to use disks and partitions written by other operating systems. It also allows system administrators to select the file system best suited to the application at hand. To provide this support, Linux defines a Virtual File System (VFS) infrastructure. The VFS provides much of the generic functionality for file system support. As a result, individual file systems, such as the EXT3 file system examined here, can be written more simply. The implementation details we have studied here illustrate a number of the basic principles covered in Chapter 17.

20.8 Exercises

1. What are the advantages and disadvantages of 1024-byte blocks versus 4096-byte blocks?

2. If we use a 1024-byte block size, and if each block pointer is 4 bytes, then how large can a file be using all of the pointers available in the i-node?

3. What is the maximum size of a block group for each of the allowable block sizes in EXT3?

4. What advantage would there be in storing the journal for one file system on another?

5. In _link_path_walk( ), we make provision for a file system to provide its own hashing function. What might be a reason why a file system should do so?

6. Why do we check the execute permission at the beginning of the main **for** loop in _link_path_walk( )?

7. In ext3_find_entry( ), when we find the entry we're looking for, we set the structure member i_dir_start_lookup to the block where we found it. Why do we do that? Why not start at the first block every time?

8. Modify *ext3_find_entry( )* to ignore *i_dir_start_lookup* and always start at the beginning of the directory. Measure any performance difference.

9. Create a new version of EXT3, called EXT3I, which is case-insensitive. If a file is stored with the name Foo, then it can be opened with the names foo, FOO, and fOO.

10. Write a program that determines and prints out the amount of disk space used by the journal of an EXT3 file system.

Chapter 21

Principles of Operating System Security

In Chapter 1, we discussed the major functions of an operating system. One of these is allocating resources among competing entities. By the very nature of competition, some requests for resources must be denied. In some cases, denial of a request is simply a matter of scarcity. A file cannot grow if there's no more available disk space.

However, denial of a request might also be for protecting a resource. We often want to prevent one process from inadvertently or maliciously accessing the resources used by another. Enforcing access policies is the objective of operating system security. We see examples of this throughout the OS as it manages each of the resources.

We begin our discussion of security with a look at how we know if users are who they claim to be. Next, we look at each of the types of resources and examine the basic protection techniques for each. We follow that with a brief look at some of the types of compromises often seen. We next examine the specifications of the Orange Book, followed by a brief introduction to encryption. We wrap up this chapter with an overview of security in Multics, Inferno, and Linux.

21.1   User Authentication

The starting point for any security system is establishing who is making the request. Nearly universally, processes run on behalf of users, and any request made by a process is taken as coming from its user. Before granting the request, the operating system tests it against a policy that specifies what the user may or may not do. If the user has permission to access the requested resource, the request is carried out. Otherwise, it is denied.

In addition to individual identification, many systems allow a user to be part of one or more groups. A user might not have permission to access a resource as an individual, but could have permission by virtue of membership in a group. For example, suppose we have a user named Rachel who is part of the group Students. As an individual user, she would be denied access to the file class_notes. However, we might allow any member of the group Students to read the file. Because Rachel is a member of that group, system calls to read that file would be allowed.

Because permission is dependent on the identity of the requester, it is imperative that we are confident in that identity. A successful imposter will fool us into allowing undesirable access. The process of verifying a user's identity is referred to as **authenticating** the user. Techniques for authenticating a user are dependent on the hardware available.

21.1.1   User Names and Passwords

Using only typical input devices, our options for user identification are somewhat limited. With a keyboard and mouse available, a user can type a **user name** or select one from a list. Although in some older systems users were identified by one or more numbers, most systems today use a textual name.

Of course, such a simple form of identification can easily be falsified. Anyone could claim to be any user by merely knowing the user name, and user names should be publicly known so that users can be identified by other users. The most common method of verifying a claim of identity is by expecting the user to also provide some secret information in the form of a **password**. The password is a **shared secret** held by both the system and the user wanting to authenticate on that system.

Because the security of the system depends on keeping passwords secret, we take measures to keep them from being exposed. The first such step is keeping the password from being shown as it is being typed. If a potential intruder is watching the screen over the user's shoulder, then an echoed password would reveal the secret information. Normally, we simply don't echo anything when a password is being typed. For some systems, some symbol is echoed for each character typed. This works almost as well, but of course, exposes the length of the password.

Because the system into which a user is authenticating must have a record of passwords, we must also take steps to keep them secret on the system itself. One approach is keeping them in a file that is protected from normal user access. Only a system administrator is allowed to access a file listing the passwords. This is still less than ideal because it still exposes passwords to unscrupulous administrators. Furthermore, if the system security is compromised, then all passwords are exposed. We often enhance the security of the password file by storing encrypted passwords instead of plaintext ones. At first thought, it would seem reasonable to decrypt a password and compare it to the password entered by the user. However, this again exposes a weakness. If the encrypted passwords become available and the decryption technique is known, then it is as if the passwords are stored in plaintext form. A more secure approach is to use a "one-way" encryption technique to encrypt the password entered by the user and compare that to the stored encrypted password. In one-way encryption, there is no method for taking an encrypted password and finding the original plaintext password that is any easier than a brute force test of all possible passwords.

21.1.2   Cryptographic Hashing Functions

Certain hashing functions make good one-way encryption functions. When we design hashing functions for hash tables, we generally have relatively few values we hash to. If we have 1024 buckets in the hash table, then the result of the hashing function is really only 10 bits. Furthermore, we just accept that there will likely be collisions and account for them in the code. For cryptographic purposes, we generally design hashing functions with much larger ranges of results. Hashing functions with 64, 128, or 256 bits of output are quite common. There are two key objectives for these functions. First, we want to minimize the likelihood of a collision when operating on typical data. Furthermore, we want it to be very difficult to take a block of data and find another that collides with it. Our second objective is what makes them good for one-way encryption functions. Good cryptographic hashing functions are designed so that finding the input that produces a certain output is not much easier than trying all possible inputs.

21.1.3   Callbacks

When accessing a system remotely, particularly over normal telephone lines, we often add another security measure. The system into which the user is logging in knows where the user is expected to be. Suppose the user is expected to be calling from the number 555-1234. The user initiates the connection, but before the login process is completed, both ends hang up, and the system calls the user back at 555-1234. If an imposter attempts to connect from a different number, then the login attempt would not be successful.

21.1.4   Challenge/Response Authentication

Even with passwords stored in encrypted form and callbacks, we still have another issue to address. Because the password is transmitted as plaintext, it can be intercepted. It might be misappropriated as simply as watching the keyboard as the user types it, or it might be gained by electronically monitoring the terminal or modem line. It might even be taken with an embarrassingly simplistic program that allocates a terminal line, pretends to be the login program, and carries out the dialog while the user types the password. Typically, such a program then reports a login failure and turns control back over to the real login program. The user generally thinks that a mistake was made in typing the password and tries again without suspecting anything wrong. However the password is appropriated, the miscreant can then repeat the input given in the login procedure and gain access to the user's files. This is an example of a **playback** or **replay attack**.

The key to thwarting this type of attack is ensuring that repeating the same characters does not successfully log in a second time. There are a couple of techniques we can use for that. First, if both the user and the system to which the user connects maintain a synchronized random number generator, then the user can enter the current random number as the password. Typically, the generators change periodically, say once a minute. After they have changed, then a playback attack will fail. There are two difficulties with this technique. First, there is a window during which the same login sequence will work again. However, it is generally short enough that it's not a problem in practice. The more serious problem is keeping the two generators synchronized. Inevitably, the two clocks drift apart over time. We can deal with this by allowing the system to adjust itself to the user's generator. For example, we can generate three random numbers in a row, and if the user's matches any one of them, then we can adjust our knowledge of the user's generator's time.

We can also use a **challenge/response** technique in which the system presents the user with a challenge, and the user is expected to produce the correct response. The most common form of this uses encryption. The system presents a message (a random number), and the user is expected to encrypt it and send the encrypted number back. Both the system and the user share the encryption key, but this shared secret is never transmitted, unlike a conventional password. When one machine is authenticating itself to another, this encryption process is performed by the software that carries out the establishment of the connection. However, when human beings are being authenticated, we cannot expect them to perform the encryption manually. In these cases, the users carry devices similar to calculators where they type in the challenge string, and the device then displays the response string.

In both of these techniques, there is a danger that the user's device could be stolen (or found if lost), giving access to an unauthorized person. However, with physical devices such as these, the user is much more likely to know that it has been lost and to notify the system administrator than if a password is misappropriated. When the system administrator learns of the compromise, then the user can be locked out until a suitable replacement device is issued.

21.1.5   One-Time Passwords

Another approach to preventing an eavesdropper from gaining the information to impersonate a user is to use a password only one time. Of course, requiring the user to memorize such a list would be impractical. Rather, we use techniques that allow both ends to compute a password in a well-defined way. As a result, it is most often used between computers. We refer to the machine seeking to gain access as the client and the one being accessed as the server. One of the most commonly used one-time password techniques is S/KEY. In S/KEY, both systems start with a shared secret, usually a passphrase, which we denote as P_0. Both systems then compute a series of passwords by repeatedly running the passphrase through a secure hashing function n times, so that $P_1 = H(P_0)$, $P_2 = H(P_1)$, and so on. The server retains only P_n. The client uses the passwords in the order P_{n-1}, P_{n-2}, ..., P_1. By starting with P_{n-1}, the client is effectively pretending that it has already authenticated with P_n. If the client authenticated using P_i most recently, then the next time, it will authenticate using P_{i-1}. Upon receiving P_{i-1}, the server will pass it through the hashing function to get $P_i = H(P_{i-1})$. It compares this with the stored password, which is always the most recently used one. If they match, then the client is authenticated, and the server replaces its stored password with the one just used. Notice that it's important that we go through the list from P_{n-1} to P_1. If we went through the list the other way, an eavesdropper could listen for a password and then just run it through the hashing function to get the next one.

21.1.6   Biometric Authentication

The ultimate means of authenticating a user would be some foolproof biological identification. In some sense, this would also be the ultimate one-way encryption. Were we sufficiently motivated, and the tests sufficiently fast, we could use DNA to identify a user.

For most environments, however, asking for a DNA sample each time a person wanted to log in would be rather over the top. However, there are a couple of less invasive **biometric** identifications that are used.

The first is the fingerprint. Fingerprints have a long history of use in identification in law enforcement. Although the techniques aren't perfect, they are as good as or better than passwords for ensuring valid access. Typically, the user places the finger to be recognized on a glass plate, and an image of the the fingerprint is taken. A number of features of the fingerprint are extracted from the image and compared with features stored in a database of users. If a sufficiently close match is found, the user is considered identified and allowed to access the system. In some implementations, the image is taken as the user slides the finger across a sensor that images one line of pixels at a time. After the image is taken, the comparison process is the same as for an image taken all at once. As long as the user doesn't injure the finger used for identification, the system works well. However, even a simple cut on the finger can keep the user from being authenticated.

Another unique characteristic that is used to identify users is the pattern in a person's iris or retina. The technique is similar to that for fingerprints. An image is taken of the eye and features of the image are compared with a database of registered users. Because the eye is much less likely to be injured in day-to-day activities, it makes a more reliable identifier.

21.2   Basic Resource Protection

After we establish who is making the request, the next question is whether the request is allowed on the resource. In other words, do we carry out the request, or do we refuse and return an error? How we approach this question depends on the resource involved.

21.2.1   Privileged Users

Before looking at specific resources, we need to acknowledge that in most systems, not all users are equal. Most systems have one or more users who are given special privileges. UNIX systems provide one example of this. They include a special user, referred to as the superuser, who is immune from permission checking. The superuser logs in under the name root and has complete access to all the system resources.

There are other systems that don't take this type of "all-or-nothing" approach. VMS and Windows NT each define a set of privileges that can be assigned to users. Among these privileges are permission to directly access I/O devices, to modify user properties, to access all files, and so on. The idea is that a given user can be given only those privileges that are needed to fill that user's role in the system. So a user who performs backups needs to be able to access all files but doesn't need to be able to modify user properties. Even though these systems allow for fine-grained assignment of privileges, they commonly have a single user with all of the privileges.

One final approach to controlling privileges is found in Plan 9. In the original Plan 9 file system design, there is no specially privileged user. All users are subject to the same permissions checking. However, file permissions can be bypassed at the system console, and only at the console. (Later designs make provisions to turn off permissions even when accessing the file server remotely.) Although unusual, this approach is based on an important observation. If we have physical access to a machine, then in a real sense, we have complete access to all data stored there regardless of any security measures. We can destroy the storage devices, we can boot an alternate operating system with relaxed security measures, or we can remove the storage devices and install them on another machine we can use to access the data. Consequently, giving privileged access through the console doesn't really add any possibility of compromise beyond that which is there anyway. It is remote access where we need to focus our security measures.

The nature of access privileges is very important to the overall security of a system. Experience has shown that a large number of security problems are actually caused by mistakes in administration, rather than by flaws in the software. This is one of the reasons that experienced system administrators do not use privileged access any more than necessary.

21.2.2 Access to CPU Features

Each type of resource requires unique protection techniques. We start with the central processing unit (CPU). Because assignment of the CPU to processes is controlled by the scheduler and context switching code, we don't directly protect access to the CPU. However, access to certain features of the CPU should be restricted. The most common of these features are special instructions and special registers.

A few particular special instructions are especially worthy of note. Most processors include an instruction to halt the CPU. Clearly, allowing unprivileged processes to execute this instruction would have a detrimental effect on the operation of the system. The use of input and output instructions must also be restricted. If processes are allowed to directly control I/O devices, then any other protection mechanisms for access to I/O services and for files stored on devices are rendered moot.

Among the special registers that need restricted access are those used to control the system's address translation. We cannot allow ordinary application processes to change these registers. If we did, these processes would be able to map any part of physical memory into their virtual address spaces. This would allow processes uncontrolled access to memory allocated to other processes—an unacceptable effect.

Access to these CPU features is not controlled by the identity of the user running the process. The design of the CPU hardware doesn't generally have any idea of user identity. Instead, processors generally have two or more operating modes, each with different levels of privilege. The terminology varies, but modes such as user, kernel, executive, and supervisor are common. For most systems, access to special instructions and registers is prohibited in some modes, such as user mode, but allowed in others, such as kernel mode. Normal processes typically execute in a less privileged mode. The processor switches to a more privileged mode on interrupts, including those that implement system calls. After the OS has finished servicing the interrupt, it switches back to the less privileged mode as it returns control to the process that was interrupted. In this way, the OS has access to the restricted instructions and registers, whereas ordinary processes do not.

21.2.3   Memory Access

The second major resource the OS manages is memory. Access to memory is controlled as part of the address translation mechanism. Processors without any memory management hardware generally do not provide any form of memory protection.

When a simple base-limit register pair is used, that is typically all the memory protection provided. The physical memory space described by the base register and the limit register is accessible by the CPU without restriction. Normally, each process has its own distinct memory space. The OS sets the base and limit registers for the scheduled process as part of the context switching mechanism. The overall effect is that each process can access only that block of memory allocated to it.

The more complex segmentation and paging schemes allow for more flexibility. Most designs associate with each segment or page a set of protection bits. Although the exact role of these bits varies from design to design, we generally find at least bits that determine whether that page or segment can be written. We often want some areas of memory to be read-only, particularly those that contain executable code. Conversely, we usually don't want the data areas of memory to be executable. Not all systems support such a restriction, but some do provide a protection bit that determines whether a particular segment or page is executable.

The other security issue in memory management is that of sharing regions of memory among multiple processes. In Chapter 9, we point out that sometimes it is beneficial to allow multiple processes to share areas of memory. This sharing is easily controlled through segment and page tables. For two processes that share the same area of physical memory, we set the entries for the appropriate virtual addresses to map to the same area of physical memory.

Finally, the registers that control access to segment and page tables are normally among those that are restricted. The OS changes those registers as part of a context switch, but normal processes are prohibited from modifying them.

21.2.4   Simple Protection Codes

We now turn our attention to the protection of files, and similarly, I/O devices. Even on systems that have no user identification, we often find that files can be marked read-only. Marking a file in this way reduces the chances that we might accidentally modify the contents of an important file. For the same reason, many systems prohibit, or require confirmation for, deletion of files marked read-only.

Systems that support identification of users typically have a more involved system of protection. Many of these more involved protection schemes are based on the idea of ownership. One common approach, as used in UNIX among other systems, gives each file (and sometimes device) two owners: a user and a group. This ownership assignment partitions the set of users into three subsets: the single user who owns the file, all users who are members of the group that owns the file, and everyone else. For each file, we can assign different access rights to each of those three subsets.

Systems generally provide distinct read and write privileges for each subset of users. This allows a subset to have no access, read-only access, or read and write access. In addition to these, many file systems provide other access controls. One of the more common controls is executability. If we consider an operation such as the **spawn** statement in Limbo or the *execve*( ) system call in Linux, we specify a file that contains executable code and request that it be loaded into memory and the code executed. Although we could say that if a user can read a file then it can also be executed, we sometimes want to prevent files from being executed even though they can be read. For example, a word-processing document wouldn't mean much as an executable file. As a result, most systems specify execute privilege separately from other permissions. Similarly, some file system designs provide separate privileges for file creation, deletion, and metadata changes. Those that don't often use write permission on a directory to imply permission to create files, delete files, and change metadata on files. Example 21.1 illustrates the use of these simple protection codes.

Example 21.1: Protection Codes

For this example, suppose we have five users named Mary, Rachel, Jim, Judy, and Andrew. We also have three groups named Family, Class, and Music. The Family group includes Mary and Rachel. The Class group has Mary, Jim, and Judy as members. Finally, the Music group includes Mary, Rachel, Judy, and Andrew. Consider several files and directories. For each of them, we specify the file's metadata as a tuple, where the first element is the name, the second is the user who owns the file, and the third is the group owner of the file. The fourth element of the tuple is a flag that specifies whether it is a regular file or a directory. The last element is three sets of protection codes with the owner first, the group second, and everyone else last. We designate read permission with R, write permission with W, and execute permission with E.

- (schedule, Andrew, Music, F, (RW)(R)()): The file is named schedule, it is owned by the user Andrew and the group Music, it is a regular file, and we have three sets of permissions for owner, group, and world. In this case, Jim has no access to the file at all. Everyone else, that is all the members of the Music group, can read the file, but only Andrew can modify it.

- (submit, Mary, Class, F, (RWE)(RE)(RE)): Here, everyone can read and execute this regular file, but it can be modified only by Mary. Notice that because the group and world permissions are the same, it really doesn't matter who is in the Class group for this file.

- (lessons, Jim, Class, D, (RWE)(RE)()): Here, the members of the group Class, namely Mary, Jim, and Judy, can look at this directory and open files in it. In addition, Jim can create and delete files in it. Rachel and Andrew cannot access this directory at all.

- (letter, Rachel, Family, F, (RW)(RW)(R)): Here, both Mary and Rachel can read and modify this file. Everyone else can only read it.

There are a couple of things illustrated in these examples that are typical. Although it is possible on some systems to have the group that owns the file not include the user who owns it, we almost always see that the user owning the file is a member of the group that owns it. The other typical thing is that the set of permissions for the world is a subset of the permissions for the group, which is a subset of the permissions for the owner.

This type of protection technique can be implemented by including a permissions data structure in the file's metadata. This data structure often takes the form of one or more bytes, where each bit defines one permission. The permissions are divided into three bitfields, one for each subset of users. Within each field, we have one bit for each of the permissions we can grant on the file. When a process issues a request to open a file, the file system in the OS determines the subset in which the user falls. That determines which bitfield in the protection word contains the relevant permissions. The type of request is then compared to the permission on the file, and the request is either allowed or denied based on whether that user has permission for the request.

21.2.5   Access Control Lists

Although the set of permissions we use in a simple protection scheme covers the range of actions we want to take on a file, the simple owner/group identification can be limiting. Take the case of a file containing assignment information for a course. We might want the instructor and the teaching assistants to be able to write into the file, the enrolled students to be able to read the file, and anyone not affiliated with the class to have no access at all. Here, we have three subsets of users, each with more than one member. This does not fit with a simple owner/group model. Consequently, in some cases, we might want a more fine-grained method of defining which users have which kind of access to files.

One of the more common techniques for specifying detailed permissions is the **access control list** (ACL), which is a list of identity-permission pairs. Each user or group can be given whatever permissions are appropriate to it. The idea behind this is best illustrated in a example such as Example 21.2.

Example 21.2: Access Control Lists

Suppose we have five users named Louis, Sandra, Phillip, Susan, and Stephen all involved with a course designated CS342. If Louis is the instructor, Sandra is the teaching assistant, and the remaining people are all students, we could use an ACL such as

$$\text{(Louis,RW) (Sandra,RW) (Phillip,R) (Susan,R) (Stephen,R) (*,--)}$$

to give read and write access to the instructor and assistant, read access to the students, and no other access to anyone else. We use the asterisk (*) as a wildcard, which matches any user.

Another ACL that would accomplish the same thing is

$$\text{(Louis,RW) (Sandra,RW) (CS342,R) (*,--)}$$

if all the students are in the group CS342.

This example raises the question, "What if an ACL lists both a user and one of the user's groups?" Which element of the list is used to determine permission? There are a couple of solutions we might implement. One solution simply picks the first match that fits. If we list all the users before all the groups, this approach results in the more specifically defined permission taking precedence over the more general one. The other approach is to search the whole list and take the one that gives the most privilege. Either approach requires careful administration to allow and disallow the right forms of access.

21.2.6   Capabilities

Capabilities are another approach to providing fine-grained control over access to resources. Whereas ACLs are lists of identity-permission pairs attached to a resource, a capability list is a list of resource-permission pairs attached to a user or a group. Each resource-permission pair is called a capability. When a process requests a file to be opened, the file system searches the capability lists associated with the user and all groups including the user for the file that is being opened. If the file is found, then the permissions are examined to determine whether the requested operation is allowed. We illustrate capabilities in Example 21.3.

Example 21.3: Capabilities

Consider again the users in Example 21.2. Suppose the file we are sharing is called **assignments**. The capability for this file in the list for the user Louis would be (**assignments**,RW), and the one in the list for the group CS342 would be (**assignments**,R). With this entry in the group's capability list, we do not need a similar entry in the lists of the students Phillip, Susan, and Stephen.

Capabilities are the dual of ACLs, meaning that for any set of ACLs, there is an equivalent set of capability lists and vice versa. The exercises suggest a method of proving this duality.

The individual capabilities open up an additional use of capabilities. Many systems that use capabilities allow a user to grant a capability to some other user or process to allow it to work on the original owner's behalf. Even though capabilities are associated with users, the users are not allowed to directly manipulate them to gain additional privileges. The OS maintains control over capabilities.

21.3   Types of Threats

If these techniques accounted for all possible compromises to security, there would not be much to study. We would simply implement those techniques and know that the system is secure. However, even with protection techniques in place, systems can still be compromised.

Compromises of system security can come from a number of sources. In some situations, bugs in applications or in the OS can allow users to do things we don't want them to do. Similarly, administrative errors can also allow undesired access to resources. We also find software that is written to intentionally compromise a system's security. We often call such computer "nasties" **malware**. In some cases, the compromise is aimed at simply gaining unauthorized access. In other cases, the compromise is meant to remove or damage data. Finally, the primary motivation of some compromises is to make the system less useful to legitimate users. The remainder of this section catalogs a number of these types of hostile software and other potential compromises to system security.

21.3.1   Man-in-the-Middle Attack

Suppose Mary and Rachel are communicating across a network. Unknown to either of them, however, they are both actually communicating with Erin. Erin is pretending to be Mary when communicating with Rachel and pretending to be Rachel when communicating with Mary. In this scenario, Erin is called a **man in the middle**. If Erin passes messages from Mary and Rachel unchanged, then the man in the middle is able to eavesdrop on the communication. An even greater danger is that Erin could modify the messages. For example, if Mary sent the message "Buy XYZ stock," Erin could change the message so that Rachel receives "Sell XYZ stock." Because both Mary and Rachel believe they are talking directly to each other, neither one knows that the change has taken place.

21.3.2   Trojan Horse

A **Trojan horse** is a program that impersonates another trusted program. The purpose of the Trojan horse is often to collect sensitive information entered by a user. One particularly common (though extremely unimaginative) Trojan horse is the fake login program. This fake login program displays the same prompts as the real thing, but records the user names and passwords that are entered rather than really logging the user into the system. Typically, it prompts for the user name and password and then displays the message used for an incorrect password. When this happens, it then starts the real login program. Because passwords are usually not echoed to the screen, the user believes that the first entry of the password is mistyped and proceeds to attempt to log in normally, thinking nothing has happened. In the background, however, the creator of the Trojan login has collected a valid login and password. Because this example of a Trojan horse sits between the two parties attempting to establish authenticity, it is also a type of man-in-the-middle attack.

21.3.3   Trapdoor

The next threat we consider comes from special cases in legitimate programs. The particular cases we discuss here are called **trapdoors** or **backdoors**. These threats generally arise in one of two ways. First, a programmer can intentionally put a trapdoor into a program that allows unauthorized access to the system or to some resource. Second, a trapdoor can be the unintentional by-product of a legitimate special case. During development, we often want to provide special access to a program that makes debugging easier. If the code for these debugging modes is included in released code, then someone other than the developer can use the debugging mode to gain unauthorized access. Using the login program as an example again, the programmer could add a special case to the code that allows a user to log in to an account that's not in the administrative list. With such a trapdoor in place, anyone who knows the special identification could gain access to the system despite anything done by the system's administrators.

21.3.4   Logic/Time Bomb

Logic bombs and time bombs are characterized by when they run. They generally have no effect on the system until some condition is met. In the case of time bombs, this condition is based on time. The time bomb goes off at a particular point in time. There are many stories of disgruntled employees who leave behind time bombs when they leave the company. Logic bombs, by contrast, are triggered by other conditions. They could be triggered by almost anything, certain data values, certain system loads, amounts of disk usage, and so on.

21.3.5   Virus

Often nefarious software is not installed directly on the system by the miscreant. Sometimes the offending code is moved onto the system as part of the installation of other, legitimate software. At other times, the offending software has as a primary goal spreading itself to as many systems as it can. There are two types of these we distinguish by how they are spread. The first is the **virus**. This type of malware is distinguished by the fact that it is attached to other software. In addition to executable programs, other files can serve as hosts for viruses if they can be used to initiate running the invading code. Like their biological counterparts, computer viruses can operate and spread only in the context of a host.

One of the more well-known viruses is the Michelangelo virus. On infecting an MS-DOS machine, it replaces the disk's boot block with itself, making a copy of the boot block elsewhere. Once in place, it proceeds to infect any disk connected to the system, including removable disks. These disks then transfer the virus to other machines, which it then infects. However, most of the time the virus does nothing. This insidious virus

---

Historical Note: On Trusting Trust

In his Turing Award lecture, Ken Thompson related the results of an experiment in backdoors and Trojan horses. Although he describes the details differently, the essence of the experiment was as follows. He began by modifying the login program in UNIX to allow access with a fixed "special" password, in addition to the normal password. Although that worked, there wasn't really anything new there. The next step was to modify the compiler so that it recognized when it was compiling the login program and so that it automatically inserted the backdoor at compile time. He could then remove the source code to the backdoor from the login program, and no one would see the backdoor if they were looking at the source code for the login program. However, they would see the backdoor if they looked at the source to the compiler. His next step was then to modify the compiler so that it would recognize when it was compiling itself. When it did so, it would automatically add the code that recognized itself as well as the code that recognized the login program. Finally, he could remove the backdoor source code from the compiler. However, because the executable contained the code for inserting the backdoor, both the compiler and the login program could be compiled many times, and the backdoor would always be there.

also has elements of a time bomb. It waits until the computer is booted on March 6, the birthday of the artist Michelangelo, whence came the virus's name. On that date, rather than boot into the normal OS on the machine, the virus wipes the disk, writing null bytes to it.

21.3.6   Worm

Another type of spreading malware is the **worm**. Although a worm is sometimes mistakenly called a virus, it is a different type of code. A worm differs from a virus in that a worm is a program unto itself, and, thus, it can be spread without another program. Although many of the more famous worms were primarily exercises in software that replicated and spread itself, worms can carry with them destructive code. Both worms and viruses are often spread over networks.

Many worms take advantage of software that can be told to run other code given to it. A number of the more recent exploits are worms including Code Red and I Love You. Code Red spread itself by overflowing a buffer in Microsoft's Internet Information Services server. The code it put on the system propagated itself to other systems running the same product, and it also some time later began denial-of-service attacks on particular systems. I Love You made use of a facility of Microsoft's Outlook mail user agent. Mail messages could contain scripts that were run when the mail was opened. The script carried in the I Love You message sent itself to all the contacts in the victim's address book. As a result, it spread like wildfire on May 4, 2000, infecting a significant fraction of the PCs in the world.

Perhaps the most famous worm is the Morris worm, written by Robert T. Morris, a graduate student at Cornell at the time. On November 2, 1988, this worm worked its way through a large number of workstations and minicomputers on the Internet. It infected machines running a particular release of BSD UNIX and machines running some versions of SunOS. It took advantage of a debugging feature of the sendmail mail transport agent. This feature, which was disabled in subsequent releases, allowed the developers to send code to it to execute on the remote machine to assist in debugging sendmail itself. It also made use of a buffer overflow (as did Code Red) in the server program for the finger protocol. The worm did not carry any destructive code, but only replicated itself across the network. It was originally written to keep itself from spreading too fast, thereby calling less attention to itself. However, this worm had a mistake in it that caused it to spread much more rapidly than intended and to create a high processing load on the machines it infected.

21.3.7   Covert Channel

Our next class of compromise here is the **covert channel**. Covert channels are not generally aimed at affecting the system's behavior as a data-destroying virus is. Instead, covert channels are techniques for exporting information that should be kept secret. Suppose we have a file of sensitive information, such as the file with all the passwords. If we were to simply copy this file to a directory where an unauthorized user could access it, or if we were to simply transmit it over a network, the compromise of that file could be noticed.

However, if we write a program that affects some other, observable characteristic of the system, then we have a way to transmit data. One approach changes the load on the system. If our transmitter encodes a 1 bit by increasing the system load through a long busy loop and encodes a 0 bit by decreasing the system load through a sleep, then another program watching the system load can receive the data. System load is not the only such characteristic. We can also use things like page faults, disk usage, I/O port usage, and otherwise benign network usage to encode data. Although clearly a slow and noisy channel, this type of transmission would not likely be detected through normal security monitoring techniques.

Another form of information hiding can also be used as a covert channel. **Steganography** hides information in plain sight. Places where information can be hidden include images, audio files, movie files, executable programs, and even text files. For example, suppose we have an image of the Mona Lisa stored in a lossless image format, such as PNG. If we modify the least significant bit of each pixel, we can encode data with essentially no observable effect on the image. By sending this image out through normal communication channels, we also send our hidden data. A grayscale image of 1024×768 pixels can contain a message of up to 96 KB.

21.3.8   Denial of Service

When we think about security, we are usually thinking about an attacker who wants to gain unauthorized access to a system or one who wants to destroy data. However, not all attacks are of this form. Sometimes the attacker only wants to interfere with the usability of the system. This type of attack is called a **denial-of-service** attack. It often takes the form of the attacker sending an overwhelming number of requests to the target system. Because the system cannot service all the requests it receives, many legitimate requests go unserviced.

21.4   Orange Book Classification

In 1983, the United States Department of Defense published a document prepared by the National Security Agency (NSA) called *Department of Defense Trusted Computer System Evaluations Criteria.* In lieu of this unwieldy title, this book has become known universally as the Orange Book, owing to the color of its cover. As its title suggests, this book defines a series of criteria for classifying systems according to how trustworthy they are. From 1985 through 1995, a series of books was published largely elaborating on the Orange Book. They clarified some elements of the Orange Book and gave guidance on implementation of security mechanisms. Each book in the series had a different color cover and was generally known by its color. The whole set was called the Rainbow Series. Eventually, the security criteria and recommendations of the Rainbow Series were supplanted by a new set of criteria called the **common criteria**, which were heavily influenced by the Orange Book. Though the Orange Book is certainly not the final word on computer security, or even the most recent classification criteria, it is the starting point for most discussions on how secure a system is.

The Orange Book divides systems into four divisions labeled A, B, C, and D, with Division D having the lowest level of trust and Division A having the highest. Divisions B and C are further subdivided into classes. Each division and class beginning with D and working up to A builds on the one before, adding additional requirements. The following subsections summarize the requirements for each division, beginning with D.

21.4.1 Division D

Division D is the simplest but provides the lowest level of trust. It is called **Minimal Protection**. In fact, the Orange Book's description is simply:

> This division contains only one class. It is reserved for those systems that have been evaluated but that fail to meet the requirements for a higher evaluation class.

21.4.2 Division C

Division C is called **Discretionary Protection** and formalizes a number of the features we find in most familiar systems. It is divided into two classes, C1 and C2. In Division C, systems must require users to identify themselves and to be authenticated with a password or something similar. Based on this identity, resources are protected by specifying permissions assigned to users, groups, and the world. The simple protection codes discussed in Section 21.2.4 satisfy this requirement. The system must also enforce some separation between the OS and the users. We typically expect this to take the form of restricting memory accesses with a memory management unit (MMU). However, the virtual machine techniques of Inferno also provide separation between user code and the OS. Division C systems must also include documents describing the design, use, administration, and testing of the security mechanisms. The testing team for Division C systems must include at least two members with bachelor degrees in computer science or the equivalent.

Class C1 is called **Discretionary Security Protection**, and Class C2 is called **Controlled Access Protection**. In Class C1, a group of users may log in under a group name, but in Class C2, the groups must be defined as groups of individual users, each of which logs in with a unique identifier. In addition, Class C2 adds two major elements to the requirements of Class C1. The first of these affects allocation of storage resources. When memory or disk space is allocated in a C2 system, the system must ensure that no other user's data is in that storage space. This is frequently implemented by writing zeros to the block of memory or disk before allocating it to the requesting process. The second big addition in a C2 system is auditing. The gist of the requirement is that the system must have the ability to log all logins, file and device accesses, file deletions, and so on. Needless to say, maintaining a log of every such event would consume an enormous amount of disk space and would slow the system down considerably. For that reason, the requirement specifies that the system administrator have the ability to selectively enable logging at the level of individual users.

21.4.3   Division B

The name given to Division B is **Mandatory Protection**. This division includes three classes: B1, **Labeled Security Protection**, B2, **Structured Protection**, and B3, **Security Domains**. Compared with C2 systems, the major addition in Division B is **sensitivity labels** on all data, devices, and so on. Likewise, all users also have labels. A label is a combination of classification levels and categories. The Orange Book specifies rules against which the labels of users and resources are compared to determine whether reading or writing is allowed. Unlike the discretionary controls in Division C, which can be changed by users, only certain authorized users can modify labels. Furthermore, labels must be included with all data that is exported from the system. This includes human readable output such as that produced by printers. Before any unlabeled data is stored on the system, it must be assigned a label by an authorized user.

There are a couple of common ways in which we use labels. The first is providing restricted domains for applications or users. A mail transport agent makes a good example. Because many outside systems connect to it, there are many potential avenues for security breaches. If it is compromised, we would like to limit the extent of the damage. The agent itself doesn't need access to the entire system—only those files it maintains. By putting it and those files into a domain of their own, there can't be much damage, even if someone is able to exploit a flaw in the agent. The other common use of labels is providing **multilevel security** (MLS), which is like the security classifications and clearances used in the military. It enables those who have established a high level of trust to access all the information they need, whereas those who have not established that level of trust are prevented from accessing sensitive information. Suppose we have labels Top Secret, Secret, Classified, Sensitive, and Unclassified, going from most sensitive information to the least. If we have a file with a Secret label, then a user or program with Secret or Top Secret level clearance would be able to access a file, while those with Classified, Sensitive, or Unclassified clearance would not.

Finally, all Division B systems must be designed around a documented security policy. Division B systems must be tested by a team including at least two bachelor's level computer scientists and one master's level computer scientist.

In addition to the basic Division B requirements, which define Class B1, Class B2 adds several key elements. The first of these is a requirement that interactive users be notified if labels associated with them change. The second addition is the ability to place limits on devices that prevent storing data with labels outside the allowable security levels. Class B2 also adds a requirement for a trusted communications path over which login authentication must take place. In other words, there must be some confidence that no one can eavesdrop on the login process or tamper with the login data. Covert channels are another area where Class B2 introduces a new requirement. Essentially, an extensive effort must be made to identify and characterize all such channels. The security policy model in Class B2 must be a formal model. Furthermore, there must also exist a documented top-level specification that specifies what are described as exceptions, error messages, and effects. Finally, all B2 and higher systems must use configuration (version) management in their development.

Beyond the Class B2 requirements, Class B3 requires that systems include more finely grained access privileges. In effect, a B3 system must use ACLs or the equivalent. Another interesting addition required in B3 is audit monitoring. The system must provide administrators with the ability to monitor auditable events and to be notified if those events suggest that a violation of the security policy may have occurred. Although both B1 and B2 systems are required to have a modular design, Class B3 goes further by requiring that the design of the security mechanism be complete and conceptually simple. The overall design of the system must also be well-engineered, using layering, abstraction, and data hiding. The last addition in B3 we mention is a requirement that the top-level specification be shown to be consistent with the formal security model. This requirement stops short of a formal proof, but is described as a "convincing argument."

21.4.4   Division A

Division A, called **Verified Protection**, contains only Class A1, which is called **Verified Design**. This labeling leaves open the possibility that further classes in Division A could be defined in the future. There are two areas of additional requirements that characterize Class A1. The first of these is an increased use of formal techniques over Class B3. The top-level specification must be a formal one, and a combination of informal and formal techniques must be used to demonstrate its consistency with the security model. Although there is no attempt to require that the implementation be proved correct, evidence must be provided of a correct implementation by showing the mapping from elements of the top-level specification to the source code. Furthermore, formal methods must be used as part of the covert channel analysis. The second major addition in Division A is **trusted distribution**. The path from the developers of the OS to the installation on a system must be free from tampering. Class A1 operating systems cannot be purchased in shrink-wrap boxes from the local superstore. Although not required, the image of a man in a dark suit carrying a briefcase handcuffed to his wrist gives the right idea. Division A also has the most stringent requirements for its testing team. This team must include at least one bachelor's level computer scientist and at least two master's level computer scientists.

21.5   Encryption

Up to this point, our focus has been on limiting who can use a system and on preventing those using the system from having unauthorized access to data. However, there are other issues to consider. For instance, if we are communicating over a network, how can we be sure that the message is received only by the intended recipient? In other words, how can we be sure there are no eavesdroppers? If we receive a message, how can we be sure it came from the person the sender claims to be? Another issue relates to computer hardware and is similar to our earlier observations about physical access and privileged access. Suppose a laptop computer is stolen. Regardless of how well the owner sets protection codes and passwords, the thief can merely remove the disk drive and install it on a system that pays no attention to the security of the original system. We can summarize this by saying that physical access is the ultimate privilege.

For both of these issues, we find cryptographic solutions. There is no way we can do justice to the field of cryptography here. It is a field rich in history and deep in mathematical sophistication. We can provide only a very simple introduction to some of the terms, basic techniques, and applications.

21.5.1   Symmetric Encryption

We begin with encryption as it was from the time of ancient civilizations until the 1970s. Until relatively recently, most techniques have been based on **symmetric encryption**. In these systems, we use two functions, $E(x)$ and $D(x)$, which are the **encryption function** and the **decryption function**, respectively. They have the property that $x = D(E(x))$ and often $x = E(D(x))$ as well. Both of these functions are dependent on a piece of information called the **key**. Suppose Bob wants to send a message, m, to Alice. (In keeping with tradition, we consider two parties, named Bob and Alice, in our illustrations of cryptographic techniques.) Bob computes $c = E(m)$ and transmits it to Alice. Often, we refer to m as the **plaintext** and c as the **ciphertext**. Alice can then recover the original message by computing $m = D(c)$. Because both $E(x)$ and $D(x)$ depend on the same key, this type of communication requires that Bob and Alice have a **shared secret**.

One particularly important, though rarely practical, method of encryption is the **one-time pad**. The idea is that we can change the details of the message by adding some random data to it. This random data is the key. If the random data is known to both parties, then the recipient can simply subtract it back out and recover the original message. Assuming that random data is used for only one message and assuming that it does not fall into the hands of an eavesdropper, this technique is essentially unbreakable.

The one-time pad illustrates a general issue with shared secrets. Because the pad is the same length as the message and because it must be communicated to both parties, distributing the key is just as difficult a problem as sending the secret message itself. In general, the difficulty of shared keys has plagued the users of encrypted communication throughout history. Stealing codebooks has been a major objective of espionage agents for as long as there have been codebooks.

A particular issue with the one-time pad is the length of the key. This is why the one-time pad is rarely used in practice. When it is used, the determination of the added data is often made through some agreed-upon procedure. For example, we might take the first 365 pages of a collection of the works of Shakespeare as the source of our additive data. If we transmit only one message per day, we can use the Julian date as the page number for characters that are added to the message. In this case, the book is publicly known, so the shared secret, and effectively the key, is the procedure for finding the right part of the book.

For most applications of symmetric encryption, we use more sophisticated algorithms based on smaller keys that can more easily be delivered in secret. Many of these techniques are based on substituting one symbol for another and rearranging the letters in a message. Naturally, we want the substitution to change as we go through the message. If we substituted a T for a B once, we might want to substitute a K for the next B. Of course, the exact set of substitutions and rearrangements and the exact way in which these steps change over the course of the message is determined by the key.

There are several commonly used symmetric encryption techniques that we should mention. The first is the **Data Encryption Standard** (DES) adopted in the mid-1970s. It uses a 56-bit key, which is considered weak by today's standards. It is feasible to conduct an exhaustive search of all possible keys to discover which one is used on a particular message. This search can be done in a matter of days. Although the standard was not intended to be used for all of the 30 years since its adoption, its extensive use in government and financial applications ensured its use well into a time when brute force attacks became feasible. As an attempt to strengthen DES, the triple DES technique was developed and standardized. Effectively, the message is encrypted by DES three times using three different keys. In a real sense, triple DES was a stopgap until a new, more secure, encryption standard was adopted. In 2001, the **Advanced Encryption Standard** (AES) was published. AES has the option of using 128-bit, 192-bit, or 256-bit keys. It is considered by the NSA to be strong enough to be used in secret government communication. Because of its security and standardization by the government, it is a widely used symmetric encryption technique. Another important algorithm is the **International Data Encryption Algorithm** (IDEA). It is used in the **pretty good privacy** (PGP) system and a number of other noncommercial applications. It is, however, encumbered by patents for commercial use. With a 128-bit key, it is considered a fairly secure encryption. The final technique we examine is RC4, a very simple encryption technique and one that is better suited to streaming data than the other ones we consider. (Each of them encrypts a block of data of either 64 or 128 bits.) Consequently, we find RC4 often used in network communications including such protocols as **Secure Sockets Layer** (SSL) and the **Wired Equivalent Privacy** (WEP) used on wireless LANs. Despite having a key of up to 256 bytes, RC4 is not particularly secure. As a result, we find that most applications of RC4 have other options available.

21.5.2   Public Key Cryptography

In the 1970s, a new approach to cryptography was discovered. This new approach is called **public key cryptography** and is characterized by the lack of a shared secret. In a public key system, we have two keys instead of just one. One of the keys is used for encryption, and one is used for decryption. The encryption keys are made public, whereas the decryption keys are kept secret. When encrypting a message or a file, we do so with the public encryption key of the intended recipient. The recipient's decryption key is then used to return the message or file to plaintext. The encryption functions associated with these key pairs are, however, much more computationally intensive than symmetric encryption techniques.

Because of the computational complexity of public key techniques, some of the earliest public key techniques revolved around the idea that we still want to use conventional symmetric encryption, but that we want a way to exchange a key without anyone ever seeing it. As a result, several of the early techniques are described as key exchange techniques. One simple key exchange technique was independently developed by Williamson in England and by Diffie and Hellman in the United States. Because Williamson worked for the British government as a cryptologist, his work was kept secret. On the other hand,

Diffie and Hellman were in academia and published their results. As a result, the following algorithm is generally known as the Diffie-Hellman key exchange.

Diffie-Hellman Key Exchange Algorithm: Allow two parties to both arrive at the same secret, but never transmit the secret. Each party generates part of the secret and transmits a message computed from the partial secret, but from which it is very difficult to recover the partial secret. Each party combines the received message with its partial secret to arrive at a shared secret. As a prerequisite, two numbers, g and p, where p is prime, are published publicly or transmitted in the clear.

1. Alice generates a random number a.

2. Bob generates a random number b.

3. Alice transmits $g^a \bmod p$ to Bob.

4. Bob transmits $g^b \bmod p$ to Alice.

5. Alice computes $\left(g^b\right)^a \bmod p = g^{(ba)} \bmod p$.

6. Bob computes $\left(g^a\right)^b \bmod p = g^{(ab)} \bmod p$.

Because of the commutivity of multiplication (and by extension exponentiation), Bob and Alice now share a number that is a shared secret, but one that is never transmitted openly. This number can be used as a key for a symmetric encryption algorithm.

We can ask, "What if Eve intercepts the two messages containing $g^a \bmod p$ and $g^b \bmod p$?" Could she compute the logarithm base g of the two numbers to get a and b, and then compute $g^{ab} \bmod p$? In effect, she would have to solve the discrete logarithm problem. However, this problem is very difficult, especially when our modulus, p, is large. In fact, there is no known solution to the problem where the running time is polynomial in the number of bits in p. In other words, we can't do much better than trying all the values of a (or b) starting at 1 and counting up until we find the right one. For a values of a and b with 64 or more bits, the time to test all possible values is so large that by time the correct value is found, the protected information is unlikely to still be relevant. The security of this technique depends on the difficulty of solving the discrete logarithm problem.

There is another type of public key technique where we still have the two functions $E(x)$ and $D(x)$, and they still share the property that $x = D(E(x))$. However, these two functions are not directly based on the same key. Instead, $E(x)$ is based on one key, and $D(x)$ is based on another. Obviously, there has to be some relationship between the two keys, but the security of the technique is based on the choices of them so that knowing one does not easily reveal the other.

One of the most influential such techniques was developed by Rivest, Shamir, and Adleman. It is generally known as the RSA algorithm. We begin by describing the technique for generating keys:

RSA Key Generation Algorithm: Generate an encryption/decryption key pair. The pair of numbers e and n is published as the encryption key. The number d is kept private as the decryption key.

1. Select two large random prime numbers, p and q.
2. Compute $n = pq$.
3. Compute $\phi(n) = (p-1)(q-1)$.
4. Select e such that e and $\phi(n)$ are relatively prime.
5. Solve for d such that $ed = 1 \bmod \phi(n)$.

Using these keys, we can define our encryption and decryption functions as follows:

$$E(x) = x^e \bmod n \quad \text{and} \quad D(x) = x^d \bmod n$$

Without proving it, we observe that the properties of e, d, and n imply that

$$x = E(D(x)) = D(E(x)) = x^{ed} \bmod n$$

Consider Bob transmitting an encrypted message to Alice. Equivalently, Bob could be encrypting a file intended for only Alice to read. Bob looks up Alice's public key, which we designate as (e_a, n_a). With these numbers and his plaintext m, Bob computes the ciphertext $c = E_a(m)$ and transmits it to Alice. Alice can then recover the message by computing $m = D_a(c)$. In this way, Bob has confidence that only Alice can read the message. However, there is another issue here. How does Alice know that Bob is the one who sent the message? After all, anyone can look up Alice's public key and send her a message. Alice can have confidence that only Bob could have sent the message if Bob includes a **signature** in the message. Bob computes a hash function over the message and then encrypts it with his decryption key. The message Bob sends is actually $(c, D_b(s))$, where s is the result of the hash function computed on m. At the other end, Alice decrypts the signature $s = E_b(D_b(s))$ and compares that with the hash computed on m. If they match, then she can be confident that Bob did indeed send the message. Furthermore, she knows that the message arrived intact and that no one tampered with it. It is important that Bob sends a signature that is different every time, to make sure that Eve cannot append Bob's encrypted signature to a message she sends to Alice. The hash function computed on the message accomplishes this.

There's one more aspect of this that we need to consider. How does Bob get Alice's public key in the first place, and how does he know that it really is hers? The answer is to have a mutually trusted **certifying authority** (CA). The CA is a well-known entity that provides assurance of the validity of a public key. In some cases, the CA is also the repository of public keys. By well-known, we mean that everyone who wants to communicate is aware of the CA's existence, knows how to communicate with the CA, and knows the CA's public key. When Bob queries the CA for Alice's public key, he receives a **certificate** with Alice's public key and a signature that Bob can use to verify that it came from the CA and not someone pretending to be the CA.

21.6   Protection Rings in Multics

Multics is a very interesting system from a security perspective for a number of reasons. First, in August 1985 it became the first system to be evaluated as a Class B2 system, only two years after the Orange Book was originally published. In examining the design of Multics and reading the Orange Book, it is clear that Multics had a great deal of influence on the definitions of the various classes of trust. Our primary interest in the security of Multics, however, is the way it provides protection of data through the use of protection rings as discussed in Section 2.2 and illustrated in Figure 2-1.

Security in Multics, like most systems, begins with authenticating the user at login. It uses a fairly typical user name and password approach. Each user is a member of one or more projects, much like the groups discussed throughout this chapter. Users identify which project they are working on when they log in.

We now turn to the protection mechanisms themselves. Because of the one-to-one correspondence between segments and files, the protection mechanism used by the segmentation hardware and that used by the file system are closely linked. Therefore, it is best to view protection of data both in memory and on disk in a unified way. It is easiest to understand the Multics protection mechanisms by tracing what happens when we try to call a function located in a segment we don't yet have in memory. As mentioned in Section 10.2, new segments must be made known to the process. After the file has been located, we must check to see if the user has access to it. Multics uses ACLs to govern which users and groups have access to files. The matching ACL entry specifies which of read, write, and execute permissions that user has. These three permissions are copied into the new segment descriptor.

The ACL entry also contains a triple defining several ring brackets. Ring brackets determine what access is given to code in other segments. Suppose the ring bracket for our new segment is (i, j, k), and we have a function running in ring r. We start with the case where our new segment is a data segment. For data segments, $j = k$. If $r \leq i$, then the function may read and write the new segment if the appropriate access bit is set. If $i < r \leq j$, then the function may only read from the new segment. No access is allowed if $r > k$ (or alternatively, $r > j$). Now let us consider the case where the new segment is a code segment. The first case, where $r < i$, is the unusual case where a more privileged routine is calling a less privileged one. However, this case is allowed, and the called function runs in ring i. If $i \leq r \leq j$, then we allow the call, and the called function runs in ring r. If $j < r \leq k$, we want to restrict the call. In this case, the new segment is providing a service to higher layers, but the set of functions the caller can execute is restricted. Each segment has a set of **call gates** that lists the valid entry points for calls from rings in that range. Finally, if $r > k$, then the call is not allowed. Of course, in all these cases, execute access must be allowed for that user. All of the comparisons necessary to determine access are performed in hardware.

This combination of per-user read/write/execute permission and the finer-grained ring bracketing allows Multics to address several competing requirements. First, the ring system generalizes the common kernel and user modes most processors have. This more general structure allows Multics to be more careful about which segments can access others. It also allows for data sharing in a controlled way. One user may be able to write into that segment, whereas all others may only read from it by assigning different ring brackets to the different users. The result is that Multics is often the starting point for discussing and designing highly secure systems.

21.7   Security in Inferno

As we have seen throughout this book, Inferno is not a typical operating system. It is an eclectic collection of standard techniques and novel ideas in a compact package. Security in Inferno is no different, beginning with the protection of data in memory. We have mentioned several times that Inferno can run on machines with no memory management unit, because applications run as interpreted Dis code. Not only does the Dis code obviate the need for address translation, it does the same for the need for memory protection. The semantics of the Limbo language and the details of the Dis code produced by the Limbo compiler effectively prevent a program from accessing memory not allocated to it. When using the just-in-time compiler, we rely on it to generate only native code that does the same thing. In general, then, security for memory is not an issue in Inferno.

Inferno uses a fairly conventional approach to protecting files. Whether they are conventional persistent data files or other names served by one of the servers, files all have a user and a group as owner. For the user, the group, and everyone else, there are read, write, and execute permissions specified. It follows a strategy much like that described in Section 21.2.4.

Security in Inferno gets particularly interesting, however, when we remember that all servers communicate using the Styx protocol and that servers and clients need not be on the same machine. As a result, resource sharing across networks is an inherent part of the Inferno design. This means that network security is also a major part of Inferno.

Secure communication in Inferno is built around two general mechanisms. First, most communication is secured using an algorithm such as RC4, DES, AES, or IDEA. Keys for these encryption techniques are exchanged using the Diffie-Hellman key exchange. Authentication is accomplished with digital signatures using public key techniques. To provide confidence in the signatures, Inferno builds authentication around a certifying authority. Processes do not query the CA to get other other entities' public keys. Instead, they ask the CA for certificates for their own public keys, and these certificates are exchanged in an initial authentication procedure. After authentication is complete, each party has the other's public key and can then verify signatures. The Diffie-Hellman key exchange also takes place as part of the authentication procedure. After authentication is complete and keys are exchanged, processes can use a **Secure Sockets Layer** (SSL) file server to send and receive encrypted and signed messages.

21.8   Security in Linux

For the most part, Linux security is much like the security we find in other implementations of the UNIX design. Protection of memory depends on the MMU and its protection of pages. For pages to which we don't want a process to have any access, we simply don't map those pages into the process's virtual space. For those we want to be read-only, we set the page table entry to prohibit writes. We can share pages between processes by including those pages in the page tables for both processes.

Because of the virtual file system (VFS) design of Linux, protection of files depends on the individual file systems. Their developers are free to implement any form of protection they choose. Most of them follow the usual UNIX model based on a user ID and a group ID. When users log in, they are identified with integer user IDs (UIDs) and group IDs (GIDs). Naturally, a user may be a member of several groups, but one is assigned as the initial or primary group. For purposes of querying and setting metadata, all file systems implement (or at least simulate) the user/group/world model with read, write, and execute permissions. They generally use this model for determining access permissions. If the process's UID matches the one that owns the file, then the user's access permissions are used. If the user is a member of the group whose GID owns the file, then the group's access permissions are used. Otherwise, the world's access permissions are used. Some file systems also optionally implement ACLs.

There is a special user in all UNIX-based systems. The user whose UID is 0 is called the **superuser**. The superuser's login name is generally root. When the superuser attempts to access a file, the normal access permission checking is bypassed. This allows a system administrator to access all files in order to fix problems, perform backups, and other administrative duties.

There's one more feature of the UNIX file system design that has major security implications. In addition to the nine permission bits we've already discussed, there are two more that affect the security of a file. They are the **set UID** (SUID) bit and the **set GID** (SGID) bit. If a file is executed with the *execve( )* system call, and one of these bits is set, then that process begins to run using the UID or GID, respectively, of the owner of the file. To understand how this could be useful, consider Example 21.4.

Example 21.4: Set UID Application

An instructor wants the students in the class to have access to a file, but only in a controlled way. One possible example is the grading file. In this example, the students should not be allowed to read the whole file; otherwise, they'd be able to see other students' grades. Likewise, they should not be allowed to modify any part of the file. Preventing them from writing the file is easy with the normal permissions, but read access applies to the whole file. To handle this case, the instructor makes the grade file nonreadable by the group and world and makes it readable only by the owner. Then the instructor provides a program that reads the file and displays only the appropriately selected information. The program is executable by the students and has the SUID bit set. When a student runs the program, it runs as if it were the instructor and has access to the grade file. If the student attempts to access the grade file in any other way, the lack of read permission prevents access. The exercises ask how this feature could lead to security breaches.

The SUID and SGID ideas have a fascinating history. This creative and powerful idea is the only part of the original UNIX implementation that was patented, with the patent being dedicated to the public domain soon after being issued. In many years of use, however, it became clear that it is very easy to misuse the SUID and SGID bits, creating security vulnerabilities. As a result, when designing Plan 9, the original UNIX designers dropped SUID and SGID.

If we have a system that supports the mandatory access control of the Orange Book Class B, then we could solve the instructor's problem in a different way. The access program could be given the clearance for one domain, the grade file placed in that domain, but no students given clearance for it. In recent versions of the kernel (since version 2.6), Linux has had support for such mandatory access control. This support is known as **security enhanced Linux** or SELinux. It was developed by the NSA and has been released for general use. SELinux provides general support for mandatory access controls that can be configured in a number of ways. Not only can domains, as in our example, be supported, it can be configured to provide multilevel security. SELinux does not by itself, however, put Linux at a Class B level of trust. Work is being done on some of the other requirements of Class B trust, such as auditing and security documentation.

21.9 Summary

The resource management elements of an operating system handle many issues that result from having numerous competing entities. However, when it comes to the data on the system and the data transmitted over a network, particular attention must be paid to preventing unauthorized access. In this chapter, we have examined basic file protection techniques based on users identifying themselves when logging in. We have looked at more elaborate protection techniques, such as ACLs. Knowing how much trust should be put into a system based on its features is the focus of the Orange Book. Any data that is to be secured can be encrypted with any of a number of techniques. Finally, we have examined some of the techniques used in Multics, Inferno, and Linux.

21.10 Exercises

1. Even if passwords are encrypted with a one-way cipher, why should the encrypted passwords still not be made public?

2. Because we rarely use modems and phone lines to connect to remote systems today, how would a callback technique work in today's world?

3. In a challenge/response authentication system, what is to stop the algorithm used for encryption from becoming known and used to log in to any account even without acquiring an encryption device?

4. In Example 21.1, what would the ownerships and permissions be if we wanted Judy to have complete access to a file, we wanted Jim and Mary to be able to read and execute a file, but we wanted Rachel and Andrew to only be able to execute it?

5. For each file discussed in Example 21.1, give an equivalent ACL without using groups. Do the same where groups can be listed in the ACL.

6. For each user and group discussed in Example 21.1, show the capabilities that provide the same protection as discussed.

7. In the Orange Book, why do we have a greater degree of trust in a Class A1 system than a Class B3 system?

8. Poor system administration decisions, rather than flaws in software design, are often the cause of security holes. How can mandatory access controls help with this issue? Are mandatory access controls still susceptible to administrative errors? Why or why not?

9. If a SUID program behaves as expected, there isn't much to worry about in terms of security, as long as its designed behavior is secure. How could a SUID program be a security risk if it has bugs leading to unexpected behavior?

10. This problem requires outside resources. Look up the common criteria and describe the correspondence between the various classes of trust in the Orange Book and the levels in the common criteria.

11. The protection rings in Multics can be implemented in hardware or in software. What advantage does a hardware implementation have?

12. Describe how the Multics protection rings can be implemented in software taking advantage of a paged MMU?

13. The CA in Inferno provides the certificate for a public key when the client logs in using a user name and password. Examine the Inferno documentation and determine whether the use of a shared secret (the password) is a problem. Why or why not?

14. Show how a set of ACLs can be mapped to a set of capabilities and vice versa. It will help to start by describing the full set of users, resources, and permissions in an organized way.

15. How does public key encryption with signatures prevent man-in-the-middle attacks?

Chapter 22

Principles of Distributed Systems

In Chapter 1, we discussed the idea that computer systems should rarely be viewed as a single computer running a single program for a single user. Most of this book looks at principles, examples, and techniques for breaking the one-user and one-program assumptions. Along the way, however, we have usually assumed that we were dealing primarily with a single computer. In this chapter, we break the one-computer assumption. We examine techniques for treating a collection of computing resources as a single resource. This idea has been succinctly expressed by the Sun Microsystems advertising campaign which says, "the network is the computer."

The subject of distributed systems is a rich one, with complete books written on the subject. Therefore, we necessarily take a selective approach here, discussing a number of techniques that span a number of different approaches, ranging from loose confederations of systems that share files to tightly integrated systems where multiple CPUs share the same memory and are managed by a single instance of the operating system. We also examine the difficulty in maintaining a representation of time that is consistent across all the systems. The final set of techniques we examine are election algorithms. Regardless of the way in which systems cooperate, there are times when a single system must play a coordinating role for the whole collection. Election algorithms are used to establish which system has that responsibility.

22.1 Basic Concepts

Before delving into details of distributed system organization and techniques, we should ask some basic questions about the value and implications of using multiple systems. First, what exactly goes on among systems, and what is the advantage in using multiple systems? Second, do systems in a distributed environment behave differently when running in lockstep as opposed to running with no synchronization? Third, if multiple systems have access to the same resources, how do we ensure mutual exclusion? Finally, what are the implications of distributed systems for reliability? We consider these questions in the rest of this section.

22.1.1 Resource Sharing

Distributed systems, at their heart, are systems that share resources. Throughout our study, we have focused on four resources: the CPU, memory, I/O devices, and files. All of these are candidates for sharing. We have already made some references to sharing resources in earlier chapters. For example, we have talked about multiple processes that share areas of memory. When we talk about distributed systems, we are generally talking about systems where multiple CPUs are involved.

22.1.1.1 Files

The most natural and familiar shared resource is the file system. We often need to make files available to multiple users using multiple computers connected by a network. One reason to do this is to make a user's files available from any computer that person uses. Another motivation is making common data and programs available to many users without having to maintain many copies.

Regardless of our motivation for file sharing, we often create a central repository of files in a system often called a **file server**. All the other systems on the local network, usually called **clients**, get some or all of their files from the file server.

Typically, this file sharing is accomplished over a network, where the client machine sends a message requesting a file system operation. The server carries out the operation and returns the results over the network. The first of the two most common protocols that define this communication is the Network File System (NFS), developed by Sun Microsystems and implemented in a wide variety of OSs. The other predominant file system sharing protocol is the Common Internet File System (CIFS), which was developed by Microsoft for resource sharing in Windows. It is also often known by its earlier name of Server Message Block (SMB). Like NFS, CIFS has been implemented on a variety of operating systems.

22.1.1.2 I/O Devices

There is no single approach to sharing I/O devices; different devices are handled in different ways. For the most part, storage devices are not shared directly. Instead, we share the file systems stored on them. Likewise, it is rare that we share communications ports, such as RS-232 ports, parallel ports, and USB interfaces directly. However, we often share printers connected to these interfaces. As with file sharing, client machines send requests over a network to the server machine to which the printer is connected. One of the protocols used for printer sharing is the same CIFS protocol used for file sharing. Other systems frequently use a protocol sometimes called LPD and sometimes called LPR. These two names come from the names of two programs used for printing on those systems.

22.1.1.3 Memory

We have already talked about processes sharing memory and a number of mutual exclusion techniques to protect critical sections. There is another form of sharing that also deserves our attention. In particular, if we have multiple CPUs that all have access to memory, areas of memory can be shared among the processors.

In the most common implementations of multiple CPUs sharing memory, all processors have equal access to the memory. That is, aside from delays due to contention, the time to access a given memory location is the same for all CPUs. With a large number of processors, the contention for memory becomes severe. One approach to dealing with this contention that is becoming more common is the NonUniform Memory Access (NUMA) design, in which a processor may access some of the memory faster than other areas of memory. In particular, we usually see each area of memory associated with a CPU. We think of that CPU as owning the memory associated with it. The CPU that owns an area of memory can access it quickly, just as in the single processor case. Access times are greater when accessing memory that belongs to another processor.

22.1.1.4   CPU

Sharing CPUs is a fundamentally different form of sharing than sharing the other resources. For the other resources, multiple threads of control all use a single resource. From that perspective, all time-sharing is a form of sharing the CPU.

We can, however, flip our perspective around. Instead of thinking in terms of multiple processes on a single CPU, we can think of multiple CPUs cooperating on a single task. It is this scenario of multiple threads of control executing simultaneously that makes distributed systems an interesting area of study.

The primary motivation for applying multiple CPUs to a problem is performance. If the problem is suitable for breaking down into smaller subproblems that can be solved in parallel, then we can complete the solution in less time by using more than one CPU, as illustrated in Example 22.1.

Example 22.1: Distributed Sorting

Consider any of the recursive sorting algorithms, such as the mergesort or the quicksort. On a single processor, the two recursive sorts of the two sublists must be done sequentially. However, if we have more than one processor available, we can give each of the two sublists to separate processors, which can then sort the sublists in parallel. Finally, the sorted sublists are passed back to the original processor, which combines them into the complete sorted list.

Even this simple example exhibits a couple of important features of creating an algorithm that can run in parallel. First, notice that there is one processor that has a controlling or coordinating role. It splits the problem into component subproblems and dispatches them to individual processors. This is quite common in implementing parallel algorithms. Second, notice that some parts of the task do not benefit from multiple processors. Some parts of an algorithm are inherently serial in nature, and additional processors are idle when those parts of the algorithm execute. In other words, some fraction of the execution time is sped up by using multiple processors, and the remaining time is not. The net effect of this is that the speedup is no greater, and generally less, than the number of processors. If we use four processors, the algorithm will take at least one-fourth (and almost certainly more) of the time it would take to run on a single processor. A more formal statement of this idea is known as **Amdahl's law**.

In the previous example, each CPU dispatches a problem to two other CPUs and awaits their results. For each sublist, one CPU acts as a master node controlling the others. This type of structure is not uncommon. However, we also see another general approach. Each CPU can execute the same code, performing its computations, as if it were its own master. From time to time, the CPUs do need to exchange information, but because they're all running the same code, they exchange information that serves the same role at about the same time. Weather simulation fits well into this structure. Each CPU computes the equations of fluid flow on a cube of the atmosphere and exchanges information about its temperature, atmospheric pressure, humidity, and so on to each of the six CPUs simulating adjacent cubes. Example 22.2 considers another such algorithm in more detail.

Example 22.2: Distributed Breadth-First Search

In most distributed applications, there is a set of logical connections between pairs of CPUs. The set of paths where one CPU sends data to another forms a graph. Note, however, that the edges in this graph are not necessarily physical connections. We frequently want to find a spanning tree of minimum depth embedded in this graph. Among other things, this tree gives us the ability to broadcast a message to all nodes in the most efficient way possible. We can find such a tree using the following breadth-first search algorithm:

Distributed Breadth-First Search Algorithm: All nodes start unmarked. One node is identified as the root of the spanning tree. Upon completion, each node will know its parent and its children in the tree. We have three types of messages: *search*, *child*, and *nonchild*. All messages are sent to those nodes that are directly connected in the graph. *Search* messages are used to initiate the breadth-first search on a subgraph. *Child* messages are sent back to parents by those nodes that are its children in the spanning tree. *Nonchild* messages are sent from P_i to P_j in response to a *search* message from P_j but where P_i is not a child of P_j in the spanning tree. For simplicity, we assume all communications channels are bidirectional.

1. The root node, P_r, marks itself and sends a *search* message to all nodes directly connected to it.

2. If node P_i receives a *search* message from node P_j but it is already marked, P_i responds to P_j with a *nonchild* message.

3. If node P_i receives a *search* message from node P_j and is unmarked, P_i marks itself and sends a *search* message to each node directly connected to it. It also records node P_j as its parent.

4. If node P_i receives response messages from all those directly connected to it, it sends a *child* message back to its parent.

5. The algorithm terminates when P_r receives responses from all those nodes directly connected to it.

22.1.2   Synchronous Operation

In all our examples, we've made it sound as if each process just sends messages whenever it has something to say; that would seem the most natural way to do it. However, this **asynchronous** approach is problematic. Consider the weather simulation example. If each process is allowed to run freely, the simulated time in one cube of the atmosphere might get ahead of another. The simulation would not be accurate if one CPU sends atmospheric data that exists an hour later than the receiving node expects. Another issue raised by asynchronous behavior is the question of detecting a fault. If the systems are not in some way synchronized, we don't know when we should expect an incoming message. If we don't know when one should arrive, we don't know if one fails to arrive as a result of a failure in the communications channel or a failure of a node. Although some problems are known to be solvable by asynchronous algorithms, some are known not to be.

These weaknesses in asynchronous algorithms lead us to frequently implement **synchronous** algorithms. Whereas asynchronous algorithms allow messages to be sent at any time, and consequently allow failures we don't detect, synchronous algorithms operate all nodes in lockstep, sending messages at well-defined times. Informally, we can describe synchronous algorithms as having the following properties:

- All nodes operate in a cycle of exchanging data and computing. At any point in time, all nodes are in the same iteration of this cycle.

- There is an upper bound on the time it takes to send and deliver a message. If a message does not arrive within this time, we know it will never arrive.

Of course, for the nodes to operate in lockstep, they must all have the same idea of when to begin each cycle. In other words, they must have some synchronization of their clocks, an issue we discuss in a later section.

22.1.3   Consensus

There are a substantial number of times when the CPUs in a distributed system need to come to some agreement. The distributed breadth-first search provides a good example of this. Before we can begin the algorithm, one system must be identified as the root—but how is this done? If the nodes themselves are to make this determination, they might well start out claiming, "I am the root." However, they must reach a state where one of them believes it is the root and all the others agree. Reaching this agreement is called the **consensus problem**. Consensus is one of those tasks where it is known that a synchronous solution must be applied; it cannot in general be solved by an asynchronous approach. The election algorithms we examine later in this chapter are good examples of techniques for solving the consensus problem.

22.1.4   Distributed Mutual Exclusion

Suppose we have several processes on multiple processors all sharing a resource, such as a file, an I/O device, or a block of memory. Naturally, sharing resources implies the need for mutex locks. However, we can use only certain mutual exclusion techniques.

In particular, we often use interrupt disabling to provide the lowest-level exclusion in an operating system. However, this does not solve the problem when we have multiple CPUs. Disabling interrupts on one processor does not prevent another from accessing the shared resource. Test and set instructions are included in processor designs particularly for this application. Operating on a shared lock variable, these instructions allow us to implement a low-level mutual exclusion lock. We then build higher-level lock mechanisms, such as semaphores, on top of the lower-level spin lock. This technique works very well on systems where multiple CPUs physically share one memory space and where one copy of the OS manages all the CPUs.

For systems that are less tightly integrated, and in particular where each CPU has its own memory and OS, we take a different approach. In those cases, we use the message passing operations to provide synchronization. Most of the time, a process running on one system requests a lock by sending a message indicating this. That process then blocks on the receive, waiting for the reply. The system that maintains the lock sends the reply only when the lock is given to that process. In some cases, the system that owns a particular resource (for example, a file) maintains the lock for that resource. When implemented in this way, it's not uncommon for the lock operation to be another message in the protocol for accessing the resource. Another approach to providing lock services is to create a central **lock server**. All requests for locks are made of the lock server, and it manages the locks for all resources. When implemented like this, we generally have a separate protocol for lock management.

Using a lock server is not always the best approach. It creates a single point of failure and can also become overwhelmed if it is asked to serve too many requests. There are a couple of decentralized approaches that are commonly used. First, we can use an organization similar to a token ring network. The systems can cyclically pass a token among themselves, as if around a ring. The token represents permission to enter the critical section. If a system receives the token but does not need access to the critical section, it passes the token on to the next system in the ring. If a system does need access to the critical section when it receives the token, it enters the critical section, holding the token while there. When it leaves the critical section, it passes the token on to the next system in the ring.

The other distributed approach we consider is essentially one of asking permission from all the other systems. When a system wants access to the critical section, it sends a message to the other systems asking for that access. In addition to the request, the message includes the time at which it is sent. Only when that process receives responses from every other system can it enter the critical section. Systems that receive requests and that do not need access themselves immediately respond with their permission. Systems that receive requests that are currently in the critical section wait until they leave the critical section and then send permission to the processes that were put on hold. Of course, a system that has sent a request for permission and is still waiting for the responses can also receive another request. In this case, the one that is sent earlier is given the first priority. If the newly received request was sent before ours, we send back permission. Otherwise, we behave as if we already have the lock and withhold permission until we leave the critical section.

22.1.5   Fault Tolerance

In addition to the desire for increased performance, we often implement multiple systems to gain a degree of fault tolerance. If we have 10 systems and one of them goes out of service, we still have nine on which we can do useful work. In comparison, if we have a single high-performance system and it develops a fault, then no useful work can be done while it is being repaired.

Fault tolerance through replication does, however, present us with a sort of paradox. Because we have a larger number of components, there is a greater likelihood that at least one of them has a fault, as illustrated in Example 22.3.

Example 22.3: Probability of a Fault

In this example, we consider the case where we have a large system composed of a number of smaller systems. If the probability that any given system has a fault is p, then the probability that it is working correctly is $1 - p$. Furthermore, if the overall system is composed of n smaller systems, then the probability that all n are working correctly is $(1 - p)^n$, which implies that the probability that there is at least one fault is $1 - (1 - p)^n$.

Now, suppose we have a large system made from 1024 smaller systems, and there is 0.1% probability that a given system will have a fault. In this case, the probability of at least one fault is

$$1 - (1 - p)^n = 1 - (1 - 0.001)^{1024} = 1 - (0.999)^{1024} = 1 - 0.359 = 0.641$$

In other words, there is approximately a 64% chance that at least one system is not working properly.

Because a large degree of replication implies a relatively high probability that at least one system is faulty, we generally build such systems with a number of spare systems that can be put into operation to replace faulty ones while they are being repaired or replaced.

22.1.6   Self-Stabilization

Another issue related to fault tolerance is what happens when a processor or communications fault occurs. The algorithm that's running at the time might be put into an illegal state. If this happens, do we kill the processes and restart, or do we attempt to recover in some way? Ideally, the algorithm itself includes some features that cause it to return to normal operation. The process of an algorithm moving from any state to a legal state is known as **self-stabilization** or **stabilization**.

The work on self-stabilization was pioneered by Edsger Dijkstra. In his work over the course of several synchronous steps, the nodes move to a valid global state. These initial results are very formal. Our focus here is not on these formal definitions and proofs. Rather, we consider a few general ideas in self-stabilization.

One of the most intuitive approaches to self-stabilization is often called **reset stabilization**. In this technique, one of the systems detects the illegal state. When it detects a faulty global state, it initiates a reset operation in all the nodes. This reset message is broadcast using a technique such as the breadth-first spanning tree in Example 22.2.

Because the reset message is sent to every node, reset stabilization takes time proportional to the diameter of the network. (The diameter is the largest of the minimum distances between any pair of nodes.) This running time applies, regardless of how many nodes are actually affected by the fault.

In an attempt to improve the worst-case behavior of reset protocols, some researchers have developed **time-adaptive stabilization** protocols. This approach identifies those nodes that are affected by the fault, and only those nodes are sent messages to correct the fault. As a result, time-adaptive protocols run in time proportional to the number of affected nodes.

22.2   Processor Sharing

Because it is the case of multiple CPUs that interests us most here, we now turn our attention to some of the various organizations of multiple processors. There is one class of organization we omit, however. During a period from the 1970s into the 1990s, some of the highest-performance systems were made from large numbers of processors, each with their own local memory, and all connected with a special-purpose communication network. Because of the combination of decreasing cost of commodity systems and increasing performance of standard networks, this type of design has fallen out of favor.

22.2.1   Symmetric Multiprocessing

Perhaps the most intuitive way to construct a system with multiple CPUs is to connect them all to the same memory. Frequently, the CPUs are also connected to the same I/O devices in these **shared memory** designs. When all the processors can perform the same actions, including accessing the same memory and I/O devices and handling all interrupts, we call this design **symmetric multiprocessing** (SMP). Because of the contention of multiple processors all accessing the same physical memory, we usually see only two or four processors in an SMP system.

In recent years, we have begun seeing CPU manufacturers develop processors with multiple cores. These devices contain more than one set of registers, more than one ALU, and more than one control unit. To a large extent, these multicore processors are really multiple processors in a single chip. With these multicore designs, SMP is no longer a specialized design, but is becoming more and more common.

Operating system support for SMP is actually quite straightforward, though the implementation can be tricky. Because we have multiple CPUs, we need to use a scheduler implementation that accounts for them. There are a couple of approaches that are common. In the first, we maintain a single ready list, just as in a single-processor kernel. When a time slice runs out on any of the processors, the next process to be scheduled is dispatched to run on the newly available processor. In the second approach, we keep a separate ready list for each processor. Any given process will tend to stay on one processor. This increases the chance that a newly scheduled process will have some of its memory locations already stored in the processor cache. Periodically, we look at the set of ready lists and migrate processes from one to another to keep the loads on the various processors balanced.

There is another major consideration when implementing an OS on an SMP system. When a kernel runs on a single processor, the only way one part of the kernel can run while another is running is as the result of an interrupt. However, when running on multiple processors, several processors can be executing kernel code simultaneously. This substantially increases the number of places where we need mutex locking. The simplest approach is to consider the entire kernel as a single critical section. Whenever we enter the kernel through an interrupt or a system call, we lock the kernel and then unlock it before returning. Of course, this isn't the most effective solution, as it prevents multiple processors from simultaneously executing kernel code even when they would not interfere with each other. The preferred approach is to carefully identify all the critical sections and lock the relevant data structures as they are used. The downside to this approach is that it can be difficult to properly identify all the critical sections, and bugs in locking tend to show up only sporadically.

The most obvious performance benefit from SMP is the ability to run more than one process from the ready list at a time. On a time-sharing system where there are generally a significant number of ready processes at any time, the multiple processors can be kept busy. However, even a single application can take advantage of multiple processors. If it is written as a set of cooperating threads or processes, then those threads can run in parallel, increasing the overall speed of the application.

22.2.2 Clusters

The next organization we consider is composed of a number of distinct computers connected with a standard network, where each computer runs its own copy of the operating system. Such **clusters** can consist of any number of machines from two to tens of thousands. Clusters comprise over 70% of the most recent top 500 supercomputer list (June 2007). A typical cluster consists of some number of commodity computers running Linux and connected by gigabit Ethernet. They use NFS to share data, but often have local disks for booting and for storing system programs and libraries. Normally, the machines in a cluster are all located in the same physical location and are all administered in the same way by the same organization.

Applications that are written to take advantage of clusters normally have a distinct structure. Generally, an initial process runs on one machine. One of the first things it does is to create a number of associated processes, one on each of some or all of the other machines in the cluster. Programs that benefit from parallelization have a substantial amount of repetition in the form of loops, often with one major loop in which all the computation is done. In the most common cases, each iteration of a loop performs some computation on a number of data items. For example, in a weather simulation, each interval of time is one iteration through a large outer loop. Inside that loop, the program simulates the behavior of each of many blocks of the atmosphere. This repetition is the key to applying these sorts of problems to clusters. For a cluster implementation, in the major loop, the program sends each data item, such as a simulated block of the atmosphere, to one of the processes created on the various machines. This spreading the data across many machines is often called **scattering**. After each process has finished its computations on that item, it sends its results back to the process executing the major loop. That process collects the results from the various machines in the cluster and uses those data to prepare the next iteration of the major loop. The collecting of results is often referred to as **gathering**.

22.2.3   Grids

Grids are distinguished from clusters by their geography and administration. Whereas clusters are contained in a single facility and are administered together, grids are more physically separated and span multiple administrative domains. Often, machines in a grid are widely separated geographically and are connected through the Internet.

These characteristics imply certain usage differences when compared with clusters. In particular, the interconnection among machines in a grid is generally significantly slower than in a cluster—up to 1000 times slower. Allowing access from other administrative domains creates a significant number of security considerations. Both of these factors imply that the process of passing work off to another machine in the grid is much more time-consuming than it is in a cluster. As a result, we need to break problems into coarser components when scattering them across a grid. In some cases, we scatter tasks that are full programs themselves. For example, when compiling an operating system kernel, we might spread compiles of several source code files across various machines in a grid. By compiling a number of files in parallel, we can compile the whole kernel faster than on a single machine.

Both the SETI@home and the Folding@home projects are examples of grid computing. In each of these projects, the problem is divided into relatively small subproblems, and participants across the world download parts of the problem to their local systems over the Internet. These distributed machines then carry out relatively lengthy computations on the data and then send the results back to the central, coordinating system. In SETI@home, these computations examine radio telescope data, looking for signals that could have been generated by an extraterresterial intelligence. In Folding@home, the distributed systems compute the folding of complex proteins.

22.3   Distributed Clocks

Each machine in a distributed system keeps its own idea of the current time. At boot time, the kernel sets its understanding of the current time. As the system runs, clock interrupts are handled, and for each, a value is added to the current time. However, all the clocks on all the machines won't run at exactly the same rate. Over time they will drift relative to each other.

For many applications, however, it is important for all the systems to have the same notion of current time. For example, when compiling a large system, we usually avoid compiling source files that have not changed since the corresponding object file was created. However, if the time of the last edit of the source file and the time of the creation of the object file are written by two different machines, then the two times might not have the correct relationship. If the clocks are far enough apart, one time could be seen on another machine as being in the future!

22.3.1   Logical Clocks

In some cases, our primary concern is knowing which of two events happened first. As long as we can ensure that the relative timing of events is preserved, the system will work properly. For this type of application, we can maintain a **logical clock**, which doesn't necessarily bear any relationship to real time. Lamport presented a technique for maintaining logical clocks based on a couple of key observations. First, when two processes do not communicate with each other, it doesn't matter how fast their clocks are, relative to each other. Therefore, in the absence of messages, the logical clocks can be allowed to free run. Second, a message must arrive after it was sent. To make things work correctly, there are a couple of other things that we much ensure. A logical clock can never run backwards, and no two events happen at exactly the same time. With these ideas in place, the technique is quite simple. Each message is sent with the sender's logical clock value at the time of transmission. We denote the sending time included in the message as t_s and the time on the receiver's logical clock when the message arrives as t_r. When a machine receives a message where $t_s > t_r$, the receiver advances its logical clock to the value $t_s + 1$. In this way, the relative order of events is preserved.

22.3.2   Physical Clocks

Sometimes, the relative order of events is not enough; we need clocks that closely represent real time. This turns out not to be a simple task. One of the most common approaches is for a system to periodically inquire of a time server what the current time is. However, by the time the client machine gets the message containing the current time, the current time has actually changed by the amount of time it took the message to be sent and processed. So, the client should actually add some time to what it receives in the response message. As an approximation to the time it needs to add, the client can measure the time that elapsed between sending the query and receiving the response. If we assume that half of that time was taken to send the query and half to send the response, the client can then add half of the round-trip time before setting its own clock.

Network transmission time is not the only issue we face. As with logical clocks, it's not a good idea to allow a physical clock to run backwards. Then, what if the client's clock has run fast and it receives a message from the server that says time is earlier than the client's clock says? Typically, the client reduces the amount of time that's added for each clock interrupt. If this amount is reduced enough, the client's clock will slow down, allowing real time to catch up to it. Similarly, we often do the same thing when moving time forward to prevent sudden jumps in time.

Finally, if a system consistently runs fast or slow, we would like to fix that. This can be accomplished by fine-tuning the time increment for each clock interrupt. The most accurate way to do this is to implement a phase-locked loop, the details of which are beyond the scope of this book.

All of these ideas are included in some implementations of the network time protocol (NTP). Using this protocol, one system can synchronize and maintain its clock to within milliseconds of another system's clock. NTP operates in an infrastructure where systems are divided into **strata**, which identify how far a system is from an authoritative time source. Stratum 0 includes devices that are the sources of authoritative time, such as atomic clocks and GPS receivers. Stratum 1 systems are called **primary time servers** and get their time from the Stratum 0 devices. For the most part, Stratum 1 systems are operated by government agencies or large research organizations. Stratum 2 systems use NTP to synchronize to Stratum 1 devices, and so on. Systems of Stratum 2 or higher are referred to as **secondary time servers**. Often an organization, such as a corporation or a university, will operate a Stratum 2 server for systems within its domain. It is also common for routers in the organization's network to serve as Stratum 3 servers. Most systems in the organization, then, synchronize to their local router, making them Stratum 4 systems.

Although we have not been explicit in stating it, one observation about physical clock synchronization needs to be mentioned. Just because we are using physical clocks doesn't mean we can relax the requirement to preserve relative ordering of events. The relative ordering must be maintained. However, if we can keep the physical clocks synchronized to within a time difference that's smaller than the time to transmit a message, the physical clocks will preserve the relative ordering of events.

22.4   Election Algorithms

Several times in this chapter, we have referred to situations where we need to identify a unique machine or processor among all those we are using. We often call this unique machine a **leader** or **coordinator**. A lock server is a good example of this. However, our observations about the probability that all the systems will be functioning properly raises some issues here. If we have one machine that is serving the unique role and it fails, then what do we do? With grids, the situation is even worse. In addition to system failures, a system might be down for administrative reasons or a local power failure. Communication links between networks can fail, rendering possibly many systems unreachable. In this section, we consider two **election algorithms**. We use these algorithms to select the initial leader or to select a new one if the old one becomes unavailable.

22.4.1   Bully Algorithm

The first election algorithm we consider is called the **bully algorithm**. When using this algorithm, each processor is assigned a priority, and the one of highest priority among those that are available is selected as the leader. If there is no difference among the processors, the priority can be any other unique number, such as a network address. The name comes from the fact that whenever a processor of higher priority receives a request to be elected from a lower-priority processor, it sends out its own request for election.

The basic idea behind the algorithm is straightforward. Some processor, P_i, sends a message to the leader but doesn't receive a response before it times out. At this point, P_i determines that a new leader needs to be chosen, and it starts the process by sending a message to all higher-priority processors asking to be elected. Any higher-priority processors that receive that message start elections of their own and send a message back to P_i to stop. At some point, there will be one that either has no higher-priority processors or that gets no response. That is the new leader, which broadcasts a message to everyone announcing that fact. We can state the bully algorithm, as illustrated in Example 22.4, more formally as follows:

Bully Algorithm: We start with a set of processors P_i, where $1 \leq i \leq n$. Each processor has a unique priority. We denote the priority of processor P_i by $p(i)$. The processors comprising an unknown subset determine which processor in the subset has the highest priority. That processor is selected as the leader. The following list should be thought of as rules, rather than as a sequential list. We label these statements with letters, rather than numbers, to highlight this.

    A. If processor P_i fails to receive a response from the leader within the allowed time, it begins an election by sending the message *elect* P_i to all processors P_j, for all $p(j) > p(i)$. In other words, it sends the message to all processors of greater priority.

    B. If processor P_i receives the message *elect* P_j, where $p(j) < p(i)$, then it sends a *stop* message to P_j. If it is not already conducting an election, it also starts another election by sending *elect* P_i to all processors of higher priority. If no processors of higher priority exist, P_i broadcasts the message *elected* P_i to all processors to indicate that P_i is the new leader.

    C. If processor P_i times out after sending an election message without receiving either a *stop* or an *elected* message, it is the highest-priority processor still available. It broadcasts the message *elected* P_i to all processors indicating that it is the new leader.

    D. If processor P_i was down and comes back up, it initiates an election, sending *elect* P_i to all processors of higher priority.

Example 22.4: Bully Algorithm Election

To illustrate the bully algorithm, let us take an example with five processors, whose priorities are 0–4. For simplicity, let $p(i) = i$. Initially, all five processors are up, and P_4 is the leader. Now, consider what happens if P_4 goes down and P_1 recognizes this before any others do. P_1 then begins an election, sending the message *elect* P_1 to P_2, P_3, and P_4. Both P_2 and P_3 send *stop* messages back to P_1 and start elections of their own, with P_2 sending to P_3 and P_4 and with P_3 sending to P_4. P_2 receives a *stop* message from P_3. Because P_4 is down, P_3 never receives a response, which indicates that it is the new leader. In the final step, P_3 broadcasts the message *elected* P_3 to all the processors. The flow of messages is shown in Figure 22-1.

There are a couple of facets of Figure 22-1 that are worth pointing out. Notice that P_0 does not take part in the election, except to be notified of the result when P_3 broadcasts the *elected* message. Also notice that P_3 is the only processor that never gets a response to the election message it sends. This is because it is the highest-priority processor still available. It is this lack of a response that tells P_3 that it is the new leader.

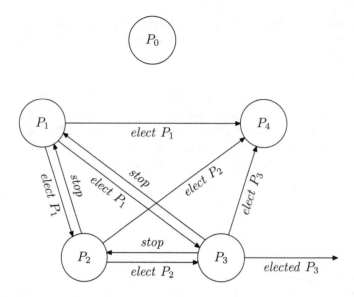

Figure 22-1: Example of Messages in the Bully Algorithm

It's pretty clear how the bully algorithm works when only one processor detects the loss of a leader. However, we need to also consider what happens if more than one processor detects the loss of a leader before a new one is elected. To see that this case works as well, consider any two processors that both detect a loss of leader. We denote these two processors by P_i and P_j, where $p(i) < p(j)$. There are two cases: P_j detects it first, and P_i detects it first. If P_j detects the loss first, then it will have already initiated an election when P_i detects the loss. Consequently, P_i's election messages will not affect the election already going on, and it will receive a *stop* message from at least the processor that started the election first, namely P_j. In the second case, P_i starts an election before P_j detects the loss. In this case, P_j must not have gotten the *elect* message from P_i, or else it would already know there was no leader. As a result, P_j begins an election. However, regardless of whether P_i's election message or P_j's election message arrives at a higher-priority processor, it will send a *stop* message to both and will start an election of its own. Putting all this together, we will always have the highest-priority processor receiving an *elect* message and timing out, establishing it as the leader.

22.4.2   Ring Algorithm

The next election algorithm we look at is called the **ring algorithm**. Like the bully algorithm, the ring algorithm assumes that each processor has a unique priority. It also assumes that the processors can be treated as being logically in a ring. To a certain extent, the algorithm assumes that the physical network is more fully connected.

The ring algorithm follows a simple strategy. We go around the ring making a list of all processors that are available and skipping over those that are not. When we get back to our starting place, we then pass that list around the ring again. The second time around, each processor records the new leader, which is the processor on the list with the highest priority. More formally, we can state the algorithm, which is illustrated in Example 22.5, as follows:

Ring Algorithm: We start with a set of processors P_i, where $1 \leq i \leq n$. Each processor has a unique priority. We denote the priority of processor P_i by $p(i)$. The processors comprising an unknown subset determine which processor in the subset has the highest priority. That processor is selected as the leader. The following list should be thought of as rules, rather than as a sequential list. We label these statements with letters, rather than numbers, to highlight this.

A. If processor P_i fails to receive a response from the leader within the allowed time, it begins an election by sending an *elect* message with a list containing only P_i to the next available processor in the ring.

B. If processor P_i receives an *elect* message and it does not include P_i in the list, the processor adds P_i to the list and sends the new message to the next available processor in the ring.

C. If processor P_i receives an *elect* message that includes P_i in the list, it constructs an *elected* message with the same list and passes it to the next available processor in the ring. P_i also records the processor of maximum priority in the list as the new leader.

D. If processor P_i receives an *elected* message that it did not send, it records the processor of maximum priority in the list as the new leader and passes the message on to the next available processor in the ring.

E. If processor P_i receives the same *elected* message it sent earlier, then the election is complete and no more action is taken.

Example 22.5: Ring Algorithm Election

Let us now consider how the ring algorithm handles the scenario used in Example 22.4. For simplicity, assume that the order of the processors in the ring follows the order of their priorities. When P_4 goes down, P_1 detects it and begins the election process by sending an *elect* message around the ring. Each processor passes it on to the next, except for P_3. Because P_4 is down, P_3 bypasses it and sends the message to P_0. When it gets back to P_1, the highest-priority processor in the list is P_3. As the *elected* message circulates around the ring, each processor recognizes P_3 as the new leader. These messages are shown in Figure 22-2 where the inner arrows are the first messages and the outer arrows are the second set of messages.

As with the bully algorithm, we want to ask what happens if more than one processor detects the loss of leader before a new one is elected. Again, let the two processors be P_i and P_j, where $p(i) < p(j)$. Here both P_i and P_j initiate an election message going around the ring. Assuming no new processors become unavailable or available during the election,

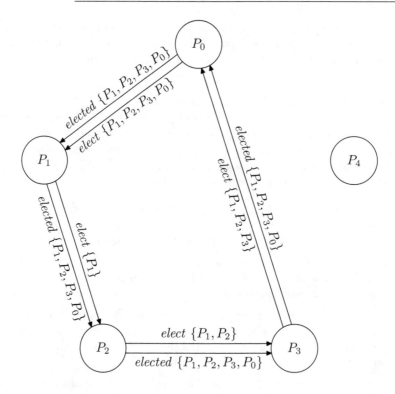

Figure 22-2: Example of Messages in the Ring Algorithm

both messages will generate the same list before they return to their respective processors. Two *elected* messages will then circulate through the ring with the same leader identified. Whichever message a given processor receives last is redundant, but does not interfere with the correct functioning of the algorithm.

22.5 Summary

As the operating system has evolved, one key trend is moving toward more forms of concurrency. Throughout this book, we have discussed techniques for supporting multiple concurrent users and multiple concurrent processes. In this chapter, we consider concurrency in the form of multiple cooperating processors, often in the form of multiple independent, but cooperating, computers. We have discussed how various resources can be shared and the implications on mutual exclusion as a result of sharing by multiple processors. We have looked at the advantages of distributed systems in terms of administration, performance, and fault tolerance. A survey of some ways of organizing multiple processors comprised the next major topic. Finally, we took a look at a couple of algorithms for selecting a unique leader from a set of otherwise identical systems.

22.6   Exercises

1. If we build a relatively small cluster with 32 machines, and each machine has a 99.99% uptime, then what is the probability that at least one machine will be down?

2. Consider a cluster with 512 machines, where each machine has a 0.1% probability of a fault. How many spare machines are necessary to ensure that there are at least 512 available machines 90% of the time?

3. Given the basic strategy presented here, give an algorithm for a mergesort that takes advantage of a cluster.

4. In this chapter, we state that memory contention constrains many SMP implementations to a small number of processors. What exactly would be the problem with a large number of processors sharing memory? What are some techniques that could help make it practical to have a shared memory machine with a relatively large number of processors?

5. In comparing clusters with grids, we find that the difference in communication speed affects how much it's practical to break a problem down into subproblems. How can we tell if we have broken the problem into a set of subproblems that's too fine-grained? In other words, how can we tell if breaking a problem down any further would be counterproductive?

6. If the majority of the machines in a cluster use NFS for their file systems, and the NFS server is a single machine, does this create a significantly greater probability of a fault? Why or why not? What can we do to reduce the probability of the cluster being down as a result of the file server?

7. As we've described it, in a system with no faults, every run of the bully algorithm selects the same machine. Suppose we have leaders with several different roles. How can we keep from putting all of the leaders on the same machine?

8. Give an expression for the amount of time that the ring algorithm takes to run for n processors, where each message takes T seconds to send. Assume the processing time at each processor is negligible.

9. Write a program that implements the bully algorithm in a simulated network.

10. Write a program that implements the ring algorithm in a simulated network.

Appendix A

Compiling Hosted Inferno

In this appendix, we discuss compiling Inferno to run hosted by another OS. Most of our discussion is focused on configuring Inferno for the host environment, setting up the compilation tools, and setting the host environment.

A.1 Setting Up the Configuration

Before attempting to build an Inferno kernel, the file /mkconfig needs to be edited. This file defines what operating system is being used to build the new Inferno and defines the target. As it comes in the installation, this file reads:

```
#
# Set the following 4 variables.  The host system is the
# system where the software will be built; the target
# system is where it will run.  They are almost always
# the same.

# On Nt systems, the ROOT path MUST be of the form 'drive:/path'
ROOT=/usr/inferno

#
# Specify the flavour of Tk (std for standard builds)
#
TKSTYLE=std

#
# Except for building kernels, SYSTARG must always
# be the same as SYSHOST
#
# build system OS type (Hp, Inferno, Irix, Linux, Nt,
```

```
# Plan9, Solaris)
SYSHOST=Plan9
# target system OS type (Hp, Inferno, Irix, Linux, Nt,
# Plan9, Solaris)
SYSTARG=$SYSHOST


#
# specify the architecture of the target system
#  - Plan 9 imports it from the
# environment; for other systems it is usually just hard-coded
#
# target system object type (s800, mips, 386, arm, sparc)
#OBJTYPE=386
OBJTYPE=$objtype


#
# no changes required beyond this point
#
OBJDIR=$SYSTARG/$OBJTYPE


# variables appropriate for host system
<$ROOT/mkfiles/mkhost-$SYSHOST
# variables used to build target object type
<$ROOT/mkfiles/mkfile-$SYSTARG-$OBJTYPE
```

If we are building a hosted Inferno system on Plan 9, then the mkconfig file is correct as it comes. Otherwise, there are three lines that need to be changed. First, the line defining ROOT should be changed to identify the root directory of the Inferno install. Next, the SYSHOST line should be changed to indicate what type of system is being used to do the compile. This will also be the system hosting the newly compiled Inferno. Finally, OBJTYPE should be defined so that the correct compilers and libraries are used.

For example, an individual installing Inferno into a home directory on Linux might change these lines to:

```
ROOT=/home/stuart/inferno
SYSHOST=Linux
OBJTYPE=386
```

and an NT user who installed into the default directory would set these lines to:

```
ROOT=c:/Users/Inferno
SYSHOST=Nt
OBJTYPE=386
```

(Note the use of the forward slashes for directory separators in contrast to the Windows convention of backslashes.) Be careful when setting these values because they can be case-sensitive.

A.2 Compiler and Development Tools

If you are building Inferno in Plan 9, then all the necessary tools are already in place. If you are building Inferno in a UNIX or UNIX-like environment, then it is very likely that you have the correct tools in place. In most cases, the mkfiles expect that the cc command will be the correct compiler. In open source UNIX-like systems, this command will invoke the gcc compiler. For Solaris, the mkfiles explicitly expect gcc. The mkfile for HP-UX expects the compiler to be named c89. For NT (and otherwise named NT-based Microsoft Windows systems), the Microsoft Visual C compiler is necessary. You do not need the integrated development environment (IDE), just the compiler and linker themselves.

Assuming the correct compiler is in place, there is one additional piece that you need to make sure you have installed in UNIX environments. Because hosted Inferno in UNIX is an X application, you need to ensure that the development header files and libraries for the X windowing system are installed. Otherwise, you will get errors indicating that the compiler is unable to find files like X11.h.

A.3 The PATH Environment Variable

For Plan 9 users, there is no PATH environment variable, so this section may be skipped. For users of UNIX and UNIX-like systems (for example, Linux or FreeBSD), the PATH environment variable is likely to include everything needed to use the local compiler. The only thing that needs to be added is the directory containing mk and other tools specific to Inferno. In your .bashrc (or other shell initialization file), include a line like:

```
export PATH=/home/stuart/inferno/Linux/386/bin:${PATH}
```

where the directory you're adding to the path is constructed from your Inferno root directory and the host OS name.

For users of NT-based host systems, there are a couple of ways to set up the path. If you have administrator access to the system, then you can set the environment variable PATH and you'll have what you need in any command window you create. The details for this vary a bit depending on which NT incarnation you're using (NT, 2000, XP, and so on). The easiest common first step is to click the right mouse button on the My Computer desktop icon and select Properties from the menu. You are looking for a tab labeled Environment or a button labeled Environment Variables. If there is no tab by that name, you will probably find a button or a tab labeled Advanced. When you get to the window that shows you the environment variables, select the one called PATH and click Edit. (You are likely to find such a variable only in the system variables part of the window. It is also possible to set a user-specific PATH variable. If you do not have administrator access, you will not be able to change the system variables.) At this point, you can add the directories you need. The other approach is to create a batch (.bat) file that you would run in each command window where you intend to do a compile. This batch file would have to be run manually each time you open a window, so it is less convenient than setting PATH through the GUI. In such a batch file, you would include a line such as:

```
PATH=c:\Users\Inferno\Nt\386\bin;%PATH%
```

In addition to the directory containing the Inferno-specific tools, you'll need to add the directories necessary for using the Microsoft Visual C compiler. Exactly which directories are needed depends on which version of the compiler you have installed. The easiest way to determine which directories you need is to start by finding the file cl.exe on the system. Put that directory into the path. Then iteratively attempt to compile the system. If the compiler throws an error with a dialog box indicating that there is a .dll file it can't find, locate that file and add its directory to the path. After a couple of iterations of this, you should have identified all the directories you need, and the system should compile fully.

A.4   Other Environment Variables

When using some versions of the Microsoft Visual C compiler, it is necessary to also set the environment variable `Include`. It should be set to the name of the directory containing the file windows.h in the install. The default location for this file is:

C:\Program Files\MicrosoftVisual Studio\VC98\Include

for the Visual C '98 version. (Substitute the appropriate name, for example \Vc7, for this part of the path name.) Similarly, the variable `Lib` also needs to be set for some installations. The default value for this directory is:

C:\Program Files\Microsoft\Visual Studio\VC98\Lib

Note that in some cases (particularly the .NET versions of the compiler), there is an additional directory called PlatformSDK in the path. For example,

C:\Program Files\Microsoft\Visual Studio .NET 2003\Vc7\PlatformSDK\Include

and

C:\Program Files\Microsoft\Visual Studio .NET 2003\Vc7\PlatformSDK\Lib

A.5   Compiling the System

After everything is set up, to compile the system, simply go to the emu directory in the Inferno root and issue the mk command. Do not attempt to compile using an IDE for your local compiler. The effort to get it set up so that it knows how to compile Inferno is far more trouble than it's worth. Using the mkfiles, mk understands exactly how the system needs to be compiled and you'd have to replicate its behavior in the IDE to make it work. There is no problem if you want to use the editor that's part of the IDE to edit code, but always go to a normal command prompt and issue the mk command to compile the system.

NT users might find one additional change to be helpful. Out of the box, the mkfiles for Inferno on NT build both the NT hosted Inferno executable and a Microsoft Internet

Explorer plug-in. Unless you have specific reason to want the plug-in, you can safely remove it from the build list and save yourself a little time (and perhaps confusion) each time you compile. In emu\Nt\mkfile, there is a line that reads:

```
CONFLIST=emu ie
```

You can safely remove the part that reads ie.

A.6   Running the New Version

In each environment, the build process leaves the newly created executable in the emu subdirectory named by the host system (for example, emu/Linux). On a Plan 9 system, the newly created executable is called 8.emu on a 386-type platform (with the 8 being replaced by the appropriate character on other architectures). In POSIX (UNIX-like) environments, the new executable is called o.emu. For an NT-based system, the executable file is called iemu.exe. These programs can be run as they are created and will take the same command-line arguments as the original. (However, you'll find that the -r option to set the Inferno root will now default to the place you have Inferno installed.) If you want this version to be installed over the top of the original version of emu, then issue the command:

```
mk install
```

and future invocations of emu will start your newly compiled one.

A.7   Summary

To summarize, these steps should be done once before building a hosted image:

1. Edit the mkconfig file, with particular focus on the variables ROOT, SYSHOST, and OBJTYPE.

2. Make sure the necessary compiler is installed on the host system and properly configured, including any necessary environment variables.

3. Set the PATH environment variable.

4. On Windows NT, change the CONF entry in emu/Nt/mkfile to remove ie.

Each time you create a new kernel, do the following:

1. From the host command prompt, issue the mk command in the emu directory.

Appendix B

Compiling Native Inferno

Although most of our attention has been on Inferno as it runs hosted by another OS, it can also be built to run natively on the PC, among other platforms. This appendix contains instructions for creating a floppy that will boot into Inferno running natively.

Assuming you are working in a windowing environment, it will be easiest to have two windows open, one with a host OS command prompt and one running Inferno (without its window manager). Most of the steps described in this appendix are carried out in the host OS window. We point out those steps that should be carried out in the Inferno window.

The instructions presented here build only a minimal kernel image. It has virtually no support for graphics, and it lacks the administrative tools to set up networking. Furthermore, it lacks kfs, the native file system. Although support for all of these is possible (assuming the relevant hardware is supported), we opt for an approach in keeping with the KISS principle. (KISS stands for "Keep It Simple, Stupid.") However, there is nothing to prevent anyone from going further than these instructions and configuring a system that can be the basis for a more full-fledged installation.

B.1 Setting Up the Configuration

Much of the configuration necessary for building hosted Inferno is also necessary for native Inferno. In particular, the /mkconfig file needs to be set up, as described in Section A.1. Likewise, the PATH environment variable also needs to be set, as we discussed in Section A.3. Rather than repeat those descriptions here, if you have not already set those up to build hosted Inferno, refer to those sections now.

B.2 Building the Tool Chain

Unlike hosted Inferno, native Inferno can be built using only tools supplied with the Inferno distribution. If you have installed the distribution on a version of Windows NT,

Irix, or Solaris, then you already have the necessary compilers and other tools installed. The changes made to the `PATH` variable make the necessary compilers and other tools available.

For other host systems, including Linux, FreeBSD, Mac OS X, and Plan 9, the necessary tools must be built. These systems must already have the normal compiler installed. With everything configured and the local compiler installed, issue the `mk install` command in the Inferno root. This command will build all the libraries, the compiler suite, a new executable for hosted Inferno, and all the Inferno applications. Not all of this must be compiled to build a native kernel. However, running `mk` in the Inferno root directory is the easiest way to get the programs that are necessary.

B.3 Building the Bootstrapping Code

The directory os/boot/pc contains the code necessary to build the bootstrapping code for a PC. Several versions of this code are contained there. However, to build a bootable floppy, only two files need to be built. To build those two, issue in that directory the command `mk pbs.install 9load.install`. The results of this command are the files Inferno/386/pbs and Inferno/386/9load.

B.4 Setting Up the Kernel Configuration

The directory os/pc contains the PC-specific code for a native kernel. It also contains a number of files that can be used to configure the kernel. We will work with one of the simpler configuration files called pc. There are some changes we need to make to pc for our purposes. Make the following changes to pc:

- In the `init` section, change `wminit` to `shell`. This will run a shell after Inferno is booted.

- In the `code` section, change the line that reads `int consoleprint=0;` to `int consoleprint=1;`. This change causes the kernel output to be printed to the console.

- In the `root` section, add `/dis/lib/arg.dis` and `/dis/lib/filepat.dis`. These two libraries are needed in addition to those already listed in pc to support the shell and the applications included in the Inferno image file.

These are just a minimal set of changes to get a bootable floppy that boots to a shell with a few commands available. If you want to add support for networking, graphics, or disks, other parts of the file will need to be modified.

B.5 Creating the Loader Configuration

The boot loader, 9load, can take a configuration file that controls which kernel image to load, as well as other things. For our purposes, we need to specify only the kernel image file. Create a file called plan9.ini containing the single line:

```
bootfile=fd0!ipc.gz
```

This file can be created with any text editor either in the host OS window or in the Inferno window.

B.6   Building the Kernel Image

With all of these configurations in place, building the kernel image is simple. Just issue the mk command in the os/pc directory. The result is a file called ipc.

To make the kernel image fit on a floppy, we need to compress it. Here is where we switch to the window running Inferno. From the Inferno prompt and in the os/pc directory, issue the command gzip ipc. This will compress the kernel image, creating a file called ipc.gz.

B.7   Making the Floppy Image

Again from the Inferno window and in the os/pc directory, we will now create a file containing an image of the floppy disk. The command to do this is:

```
disk/format -b /Inferno/386/pbs -df disk /Inferno/386/9load plan9.ini ipc.gz
```

There is a common mistake worth pointing out here. If you leave out the parameter disk, the file that will be formatted as a disk image is the 9load file generated in Section B.3. If you do this, re-create 9load as described in that section.

B.8   Running the New Kernel

The disk image file can be used in several ways. First, it can be run with any of a number of PC emulators. For example, the freely available qemu system can run the native Inferno disk with the command:

```
qemu -fda disk
```

If you are using a version of Windows NT as the host OS, Microsoft also has a package called Virtual PC available for free download.

Alternatively, we can create an actual floppy and boot a computer with it. The file disk can be copied to a floppy using the dd command in various UNIX-like systems. On Windows NT, there are several freely available applications that can write the disk image to a floppy. Among these are rawrite for Windows, imgtool, NTRawrite, rawrite32, rawritent, rawwritewin, DiskWritie, DImage, as well as Windows versions of dd.

Note that there are limitations on how the floppy image can be used. You cannot use it to build a bootable USB memory device. If you do try to boot Inferno from such a device, pbs will be loaded by the BIOS, and pbs will load 9load, because it also uses the BIOS. However, 9load does not use the BIOS to load the kernel image, and 9load does not include support for USB storage devices. Likewise, 9load also generally fails on USB-connected floppy drives.

Finally, the floppy image we've created here can also be used to create a bootable CD-ROM. In this case, however, the plan9.ini file should include the line:

```
bootfile=sdD0!cdboot!ipc.gz
```

instead of the one described earlier. This particular line assumes that the CD drive is connected as the master drive on the secondary IDE controller. The sdD0 will have to be changed for other arrangements. The Inferno man page for 9load contains more details.

B.9 Summary

To summarize, these steps should be done once before building a native image:

1. Edit the mkconfig file, with particular focus on the variables ROOT, SYSHOST, and OBJTYPE.

2. Set the PATH environment variable.

3. If running on a UNIX-like host OS, run mk install from a host command prompt in the Inferno root directory to build the tool chain.

4. From a host command prompt, issue the command mk pbs.install 9load.install in the os/boot/pc directory.

5. Edit the os/pc/pc file to set up the desired Inferno kernel configuration. The necessary changes include at least the init, code, and root sections.

6. Create the file plan9.ini in the directory os/pc with a bootfile line.

Each time you create a new kernel, do the following:

1. From the host command prompt, issue the mk command in the os/pc directory.

2. From the Inferno command prompt, issue the command gzip ipc in the os/pc directory.

3. From the Inferno command prompt, issue the command:

    disk/format -b /Inferno/386/pbs -df disk /Inferno/386/9load plan9.ini
    ipc.gz

Suggested Readings

Aho, A.V., Denning, P.J., and Ullman, J.D., "Principles of Optimal Page Replacement," *Journal of the ACM*, Vol 18, No 1, pp 89–93, 1971

Barham, P., Dragovic, B., Fraser, K., Hand, S., Harris, T., Ho, A., Neugebauer, R., Pratt, I., and Warfield, A., "Xen and the Art of Virtualization," *Proceedings of the Nineteenth ACM Symposium on Operating Systems Principles*, pp 164–177, 2003

Belady, L.A., Nelson, R.A., and Shedler, G.S., "An Anomaly in Space-Time Characteristics of Certain Programs Running in a Paging Machine," *Communications of the ACM*, Vol 12, No 6, pp 349–353, 1969

Bensoussan, A., Clingen, C.T., and Daley, R.C., "The Multics Virtual Memory: Concepts and Design," *Communications of the ACM*, Vol 15, No 5, pp 308–318, 1972, *http://www.multicians.org*

Bic, L.F. and Shaw, A.C., *Operating Systems Principles*, Upper Saddle River, NJ, Pearson Education, 2003

Bowman, I.T., Hold, R.C., and Brewster, N.V., "Linux as a Case Study: Its Extracted Software Architecture," Proceedings of the 1999 International Conference on Software Engineering, pp 555–563, 1999

Comer, D., *Operating System Design: The XINU Approach*, Englewood Cliffs, NJ, Prentice-Hall, 1984

Corbató, F.J., Clingen, C.T., and Saltzer, J.H., "Multics—The First Seven Years," *Proc SJCC*, pp 571–583, 1972, *http://www.multicians.org*

Corbotó, F.J. and Vyssotsky, V.A., "Introduction and Overview of the Multics System," 1965 Fall Joint Computer Conference, *http://www.multicians.org*

Cox, R., Grosse, E., Pike, R., Presotto, D., and Quinlan, S., "Security in Plan 9," USENIX Security Symposium, 2002, *http://plan9.bell-labs.com*

Daley, R.C. and Neumann, P.G., "A General-Purpose File System for Secondary Storage," 1965 Fall Joint Computer Conference, *http://www.multicians.org*

Deitel, H.M., Deitel, P.J., and Choffnes, D.R., *Operating Systems*, Upper Saddle River, NJ, Pearson Education, 2004

Digital Equipment Corporation, *VAX Software Handbook*, Digital Equipment Corporation, 1980

Dijkstra, E.W., "Self-Stabilizing Systems in Spite of Distributed Control," *Communications of the ACM*, Vol 17, No 11, pp 643–644, 1974

DoD Computer Security Center, *Department of Defense Trusted Computer System Evaluation Criteria*, CSC-STD-001-83, Fort George G. Meade, MD, Department of Defense, 1983

Doward, S., Pike, R., Presotto, D.L., Ritchie, D.M., Trickey, H., and Winterbottom, P., "The Inferno Operating System," *Bell Labs Technical Journal*, Vol 2, No 1, pp 5-18, 1997, *http://www.vitanuova.com*

Duda, K.J. and Cheriton, D.R., "Borrowed-Virtual-Time (BVT) Scheduling: Supporting Latency-Sensitive Threads in a General-Purpose Scheduler," *Proceedings of the Seventeenth ACM Symposium on Operating Systems Principles*, pp 261–276, 1999

Flatebo, M., Datta, A.K., and Ghosh, S., "Self-Stabilization in Distributed Systems," *Readings in Distributed Computing Systems*, pp 100–114, IEEE Computer Society Press, 1994

Friedman, M.B., "Windows NT Page Replacement Policies," Computer Measurement Group Conference, 1999, *http://www.demantech.com*

Galli, D.L., *Distributed Operating Systems: Concepts & Practice*, Upper Saddle River, NJ, Prentice Hall, 2000

Glaser, E.L., Couleur, J.F., and Oliver, G.A., "System Design of a Computer for Time-Sharing Applications," 1965 Fall Joint Computer Conference, *http://www.multicians.org*

Glass, G. and Cao, P., "Adaptive Page Replacement Based on Memory Reference Behavior," *Proceedings of the 1997 ACM SIGMETRICS International Conference on Measurement and Modeling of Computer Systems*, pp 115–126, 1997

Goldenberg, R.E. and Kenah, L.J., *VAX/VMS Internals and Data Structures*, Boston, MA, Digital Press, 1991

Goldenberg, R.E., Dumas, D.E., and Saravanan, S., *OpenVMS Alpha Internals: Scheduling and Process Control*, Boston, MA, Digital Press, 1997

Goldenberg, R.E., *OpenVMS Alpha Internals and Data Structures*, Boston, MA, Digital Press, 2003

Gorman, M., *Understanding the Linux Virtual Memory Manager*, Upper Saddle River, NJ, Pearson Education, 2004

Graham, R.M., "Protection in an Information Processing Utility," *Communications of the ACM*, Vol 11, No 5, pp 365–369, 1968

Green, P., "Multics Virtual Memory—Tutorial and Reflections," *ftp://ftp.stratus.com/-pub/vos/multics/pg/mvm.html*

Hall, E.C., *Journey to the Moon: The History of the Apollo Guidance Computer*, Reston, VA, American Institute of Aeronautics and Astronautics, 1996

Hill, J., Szewczyk, R., Woo, A., Hollar, S., Culler, D., and Pister, K., "System Architecture Directions for Networked Sensors," *ACM SIGPLAN Notices*, pp 93–104, 2000, *http://www.tinos.net*

Honeywell, *The Multics Virtual Memory*, Honeywell, 1972

Kernighan, B.W., "A Descent into Limbo," *http://www.vitanuova.com*

Kronenberg, N., Benson, T.R., Cardoze, W.M., Jagannathan, R., and Thomas, B.J., "Porting OpenVMS from VAX to Alpha AXP," *Communications of the ACM*, Vol 36, No 2, pp 45–53, 1993

Landwehr, C.E., Bull, A.R., McDermott, J.P., and Choi, W.S., "A Taxonomy of Computer Program Security Flaws, with Examples," *ACM Computing Surveys*, Vol 26, No 3, pp 211–254, 1994

Lavington, S.H., "The Manchester Mark I and Atlas: A Historical Perspective," *Communications of the ACM*, Vol 21, No 1, pp 4–12, 1978

Leffler, S.J., McKusick, M.K., Karels, M.J., and Quaterman, J.S., *The Design and Implementation of the 4.3BSD UNIX Operating System*, Reading, MA, Addison-Wesley, 1989

Lions, J., *Lions' Commentary on UNIX 6th Edition*, Florence, KY, Peer-to-Peer Communications, 1996

Love, R., *Linux Kernel Development*, Indianapolis, IN, Novell Press, 2005

Mattson, R.L., Gecsei, J., Slutz, D.R., and Traiger, I.L., "Evaluation Techniques for Storage Hierarchies," *IBM Systems Journal*, Vol 9, No 2, pp 78–117, 1970

McCoy, K., *VMS File System Internals*, Boston, MA, Digital Press, 1990

Nutt, G., *Operating Systems*, Boston, MA, Pearson Education, 2004

Organick, E.I., *The Multics System: An Examination of Its Structure*, Boston, MA, MIT Press, 1972

Ossanna, J.F., Mikus, L.E., and Dunten, S.D., "Communications and Input/Output Switching in a Multiplex Computing System," 1965 Fall Joint Computer Conference, *http://www.multicians.org*

Patterson, D.A., Gibson, G., and Katz, R.H., "A Case for Redundant Arrays of Inexpensive Disks (RAID)," *ACM SIGMOD Record*, Vol 17, No 3, pp 109–116, 1988, *http://techreports.lib.berkeley.edu*

Pike, R., Presotto, D., Thompson, K., Trickey, H., and Winterbottom, P., "The Use of Name Spaces in Plan 9," *Proceedings of the 5th ACM SIGOPS Workshop*, 1992, *http://plan9.bell-labs.com*

Pike, R., Presotto, D., Doward, S., Flandrena, B., Thompson, K., Trickey, H., and Winterbottom, P., "Plan 9 from Bell Labs," *Computing Systems*, Vol 8, No 3, pp 221–254, 1995, *http://plan9.bell-labs.com*

Pike, R. and Ritchie, D.M., "The Styx Architecture for Distributed Systems," *Bell Labs Technical Journal*, Vol 4, No 2, pp 146–152, 1999, *http://www.vitanuova.com*

Quinlan, S. and Doward, S., "Venti: a new approach to archival storage," First USENIX Conference on File and Storage Technologies, 2002, *http://plan9.bell-labs.com*

Ritchie, D.M. and Thompson, K., "The UNIX Time-Sharing System," *Communications of the ACM*, Vol 17, No 7, pp 365–375, 1974, *http://plan9.bell-labs.com/who/dmr/*

Ritchie, D.M., "The Evolution of the UNIX Time-Sharing System," *BSTJ*, Vol 68, No 8, pp 1577–1594, 1984 and *Proceedings of a Symposium on Language Design and Programming Methodology*, pp 25–36, 1979, *http://plan9.bell-labs.com/who/dmr/*

Ritchie, D.M., "The Limbo Programming Language," *http://www.vitanuova.com*

Saltzer, J.H., "CTSS Technical Notes," MAC-TR-16, Boston, MA, Massachusetts Institute of Technology, *http://www.multicians.org*

Saltzer, J.H., "A Simple Linear Model of Demand Paging Performance," *Communication of the ACM*, Vol 17, No 4, pp 181–186, 1974

Saltzer, J.H., "Protection and the Control of Information Sharing in Multics," *Communications of the ACM*, Vol 17, No 7, pp 388–402, 1974

Salus, P.H., *A Quarter Century of UNIX*, Reading, MA, Addison-Wesley, 1994

Schroeder, M.D. and Saltzer, J.H., "A Hardware Architecture for Implementing Protection Rings," *Communications of the ACM*, Vol 15, No 3, pp 157–170, 1972

Silberschatz, A., Galvin, P., and Gagne, G., *Applied Operating Systems Concepts*, New York, NY, John Wiley & Sons, 2000

Solomon, D.A. and Russinovich, M.E., *Inside Microsoft Windows 2000*, Redmond, WA, Microsoft Press, 2000

Stallings,W., *Operating Systems*, Upper Saddle River, NJ, Prentice-Hall, 2005

Tanenbaum, A.S., *Distributed Operating Systems*, Englewood Cliffs, NJ, Prentice-Hall, 1995

Tanenbaum, A.S., *Modern Operating Systems*, Upper Saddle River, NJ, Prentice-Hall, 2001

Tanenbaum, A.S. and Woodhull, A.S., *Operating Systems: Design and Implementation*, Upper Saddle River, NJ, Prentice-Hall, 2006

Thompson, K., "Reflections on Trusting Trust," *ACM Turing Award Lectures: The First Twenty Years 1966–1985*, pp 171–177, New York, NY, ACM Press, 1987

Torvalds, L. and Diamond, D., *Just for Fun*, New York, NY, Harper Business, 2001

Turner, R. and Levy, H., "Segmented FIFO Page Replacement," *Proceedings of the 1981 ACM SIGMETRICS Conference on Measurement and Modeling of Computer Systems*, pp 48–51, 1981

Vita Nuova Limited, "Dis Virtual Machine Specification," 2000, *http://www.vitanuova.com*

Vyssotsky, V.A., Corbotó, F.J., and Graham, R.M., "Structure of the Multics Supervisor," 1965 Fall Joint Computer Conference, *http://www.multicians.org*

Winterbottom, P. and Pike, R., "The Design of the Inferno Virtual Machine," *Proceedings of IEEE Compcon 97*, 1997, *http://www.vitanuova.com*

Wood, P.H. and Kochan, S.G., *UNIX System Security*, Hasbrouck Heights, NJ, Hayden Book Company, 1985

Index

4.3BSD, 21, 29, 129, 241, 243–246, 339,
    431, 432, 481, 482, 487, 523
802.11, 342
802.15, 342

AƂBA, 259
absolute path name, 412, 427, 489
abstract data type, 82, 451, 456, 466–469
access control list, 433, 519, 520, 527, 532,
    534
access time, 311, 324
accessed bit, 200, 216, 218–221, 244, 246,
    288, 302
account number, 408
account specifier, 408–410
acme, 438, 439, 442
activation record, 205
address bus, 63
address translation, 198–201, 205, 206,
    214, 225, 229, 233, 238, 239, 242,
    250, 251, 253, 255, 286, 337, 516,
    517, 533
Adleman, Leonard, 530
Advanced Configuration and Power
    Interface (ACPI), 72
advanced power management (APM), 63
AES, 529
aging, 220, 249
alias, 406, 420, 426, 427, 497
Alpha, 27, 29, 30, 132, 239, 245
alternate data stream, 435
Amdahl's Law, 539
analog computer, 317
analog-to-digital converter, 317
Apollo 11, 97
Apollo Guidance Computer (AGC), 97
Apple, 418
ASCII, 350, 354, 355, 430
asynchronous I/O, 320, 481

asynchronous operation, 541
AT&T, 55
ATA, 312, 366
atomic execution, 101, 103
automata theory, 407

B+ tree, 434, 435
B-tree, 402
backdoor, 521, 522
background process, 22, 26, 123, 125, 126,
    235–238
backing store, 196, 214, 215, 253
backup, 197, 420, 515, 534
bad block relocation, 326, 429
banker's algorithm, 115
bar-code reader, 312, 330, 340
barrel processor, 309
base priority, 92, 133, 135
base register, 198–200, 242, 517
basis vector, 407
batch operating system, 10, 87
batch processing, 123, 137
baud, 313
Belady, Lazlo, 217, 228
Belady's anomaly, 227–229
Belady's min, 217, 221
Bell Labs, 23, 26, 29, 35
Bellard, Fabrice, 15
Berkeley Software Distribution (BSD), 29
binary search tree, 207, 254, 257, 260, 261,
    266, 271
binary semaphore, 105, 374
biometric identification, 515
BIOS, 62, 63
Bliss, 28
block caching, 423
block device, 314, 318, 333, 334, 337, 338,
    371, 372
block group, 481, 485

block special file, 431, 487

blocking I/O, 319, 335, 340, 341

Bluetooth, 342

BogoMIPS, 71

boot block, 62, 433, 481, 522

boot loader, 16, 61, 62, 76, 208

bootstrapping, 15, 28, 42, 59, 61, 62, 337, 356, 387, 405, 420, 429, 431, 433, 434, 545

BSDI, 29

buffering, 313, 315, 320, 322–324, 328–330, 334, 338, 339, 367, 372, 374–376, 378, 380, 381, 391, 420, 445, 453–455, 465, 468, 475, 476, 481, 494–497, 499, 501, 502

bully algorithm, 548–551

Burroughs, 3

bus driver, 341, 342

busy waiting, 104

cache, 196, 201, 215, 225, 326, 544

call gate, 24, 532

callback, 513

canonical mode, 331

capability, 520

Cartesian coordinates, 407

CCI Power 6, 29

CD-ROM, 318, 320

CDC 6000, 309

certificate, 531

certifying authority, 531, 533

challenge/response, 514

channel, 149, 308, 348, 441, 443, 455

character device, 318, 333, 338–340, 374

character special file, 431, 487

child process, 127, 165–167, 172–179, 226, 238, 241, 289, 430, 455, 456

CIFS, 538

ciphertext, 528

circular array, 323

circular buffer, 422

class driver, 341

clock, 95, 99, 103, 129, 318, 333, 546–548

clock interrupt, 187, 193, 318, 333, 334, 546, 547

clock tick, 182, 184, 185

cluster, 11, 545, 546

Code Red, 523

code segment, 198, 204, 205, 214, 216, 238–242, 244, 283, 284, 290, 293

Coffman, 111

cold start, 15

Comer, Douglas, 12

command interpreter, 22, 28, 121, 126, 131, 168, 236

common criteria, 524

communications device, 309, 312–314, 317, 318, 330, 342, 538

Compaq, 27

compiler, 213, 225, 350, 385, 410, 522

computing utility, 22, 32

concensus, 541

Connection Machine-2 (CM-2), 327

console, 49, 75, 123, 242, 356, 358, 516

console computer, 16

context switch, 161, 517

context switching, 4, 11, 57, 83, 86, 94, 98–100, 102, 122, 128, 134, 137, 141, 160, 161, 172, 179, 191, 192, 250, 516, 517

contiguous file, 415, 419, 429

Control Data Corporation, 309

controller, 347

cooked mode, 331

copy on write (COW), 166, 226, 284, 300–302, 304

Corbató, F.J., 22

covert channel, 523, 524, 526

CP/M, 30, 213

critical section, 101, 102, 105, 109, 538, 542, 545

cryptographic hashing function, 513, 514

CSR, 314, 315

CTSS, 21, 28, 94, 121, 124, 233, 333, 334, 338, 425, 426

current directory, 412, 426, 427, 431, 489, 491

Cutler, David, 27, 30
cylinder group, 432, 481

data segment, 198, 204, 205, 214, 216, 238, 240, 242, 283, 284, 290, 293–297
datagram, 319
DataVault, 327
dead start, 15
deadline, 135
deadlock, 81, 109, 111
debugger, 123, 144, 168
deferred procedure call, 342
demand paging, 215, 244, 284, 427
denial of service, 524
dependency graph, 111, 113, 114
DES, 529
device, 307, 308, 340, 342, 345, 347, 381, 383
device controller, 308, 309, 314–317, 320, 321, 323–325, 327, 334, 335, 338–342, 348, 349, 352, 354, 358, 360–369, 373, 375, 378, 383, 384, 386, 388, 389, 391–394
device driver, 40, 58, 60, 308–311, 313, 314, 317, 320–327, 330, 331, 334, 337–343, 345–347, 352, 356, 357, 359, 364, 366, 368, 371–375, 385, 387, 395, 396, 404, 406, 431, 437, 440, 477, 499
device file, 411, 431
device specifier, 411, 429, 433, 434
differential analyzer, 317
Diffie, Whitfield, 529
Diffie-Hellman key exchange, 530, 533
Digital Equipment Corporation (DEC), 15, 24, 238, 241, 245, 246, 432
digital-to-analog converter, 317
Dijkstra, Edsger, 543
dining philosophers problem, 108
directory, 411, 419, 420, 426–431, 434, 435, 443, 445–449, 462, 465, 481, 482, 487, 490, 498–501
directory entry, 419–421, 427–433, 443, 444, 446, 448, 451, 454, 461–464,

469, 471, 481, 488, 489, 494–497, 502
directory tree, 409–412, 420, 429, 430, 433, 437, 439, 442, 443, 447, 448, 458, 488
dirty bit, 200, 219, 221, 249, 302
Dis, 3, 36, 38, 39, 43, 47, 50, 52, 141, 150, 151, 157, 160, 162, 163, 254, 437, 533
disk controller, 310
disk drive
    arm, 310, 311, 324–326
    cylinder, 310, 311, 314, 324–326, 362, 363, 389, 391, 432, 481
    head, 310, 314, 323, 324, 362, 363, 389, 499
    platter, 309, 323, 324
    sector, 310, 311, 314, 323, 324, 360–363, 367, 372, 389, 391, 413
    spindle, 310
    track, 310, 323, 324, 362, 363, 426
distributed computing, 39
distributed operating system, 11
DMA, 282, 314, 363, 365, 367, 368, 385, 391–394, 421
double-indirect block, 430, 432, 469, 473, 474, 487, 506, 507
DragonflyBSD, 29, 241
drive specifier, 407, 408, 410
dynamic linking, 59
dynamic priority, 91, 93, 135, 136, 167, 171

eavesdropping, 514, 527, 530
echo, 330, 357
election algorithm, 548
elevator, 325
elevator algorithm, 324–326, 334, 371, 387, 413
EMACS, 23
embedded system, 1, 42, 97, 229, 250, 253, 317
encryption, 7, 40, 41, 60, 342, 512–514, 527–531, 533
ENIAC, 9

environment variable, 130, 151, 155, 167, 441

error handling, 159, 311, 314, 319, 348, 361, 366, 381–383, 385, 386, 393, 394, 456, 462, 497, 498

error-correcting code (ECC), 327

ESDI, 312

Ethernet, 7, 312, 545

eve, 44

exception, 100, 150

exclusive open, 400, 401, 464, 469

executable file, 60, 244, 284, 337, 410, 411, 418, 451, 518, 522, 524

exit status, 127, 154, 155, 167, 168, 172

explicit allocation, 202

EXT3, 481, 482, 484, 485, 487, 488, 495–499, 502, 504, 505

extension, 410, 411, 433

extent, 434, 435

Fast File System (FFS), 432, 481, 482, 487

fault tolerance, 328, 543

Ferranti Atlas, 216

file access
    byte stream, 402
    indexed, 402
    records, 402, 403
    text, 402

file access time, 403, 426, 430, 469, 487

file allocation, 422

file allocation list, 415, 416, 418

file allocation table (FAT), 416, 434

file allocation tree, 416, 418, 430, 451, 469, 506–508

file descriptor, 49, 75, 411, 430, 441, 455, 458

file fork, 418

file locking, 105, 400, 403, 406

file owner, 403, 408, 418, 419, 430, 433, 435, 469, 487, 517–519, 533, 534

file position, 401

file protection, 403, 419, 428, 430, 431, 433, 435, 469, 487, 488, 502, 511, 512, 515, 517–519, 532–534

file server, 38–40, 43, 49, 52, 345, 411, 423, 437–444, 446, 448, 450, 452, 453, 455, 456, 458, 477, 516, 533, 538

file sharing, 400, 406

file size, 419

file system, 6, 24, 28, 36, 40, 56, 58, 60, 74, 196, 309, 318, 334, 337–339, 341, 371, 399–423, 425–510, 532, 538

file system consistency, 420, 421, 423, 450, 455, 482, 485

file system synchronization, 423, 455

File Transfer Protocol (FTP), 442

file type, 403, 410, 426, 428, 487, 488

file version, 411, 433

Files-11, 28

filter driver, 342

fingerprint, 515

FireWire, 308, 341

floppy disk, 310, 385, 389, 413

floppy drive, 499

flow control, 313, 328

foreground process, 126, 127, 135, 235, 236

fork, 418

fragmentation, 209, 263, 272, 429
    external, 208, 210–212, 254
    internal, 208, 212

frame, 319

frame table, 202

framing error, 314

free bitmap, 206, 413, 414, 432, 434, 482

free list, 207, 208, 210, 235, 240, 243–247, 249, 254, 257, 260, 264, 266, 272, 414, 415, 431, 451, 467

free space, 413

FreeBSD, 29, 33, 38, 241, 557

front panel, 15

garbage collection, 159, 161, 203, 255, 259, 273–279

GCC, 174, 189

GE-645, 23, 234, 335

General Electric, 23

global page replacement, 217

Gourd, Roger, 27

graphical user interface (GUI), 36, 42, 126, 135, 403
grid, 11, 546, 548
group, 419
group ID, 45, 47, 408
GRUB, 62
grub, 208
guard page, 404
guest OS, 137

halting theorem, 114
hard link, 420, 431
Hardware Abstraction Layer (HAL), 31, 248, 341
hardware flow control, 313
hash table, 150, 151, 153, 156, 207, 402, 475, 482, 498, 512
Hellman, Martin, 529
Hewlett-Packard, 27
HFS+, 418
hierarchical naming, 409–412, 420, 427, 429, 433, 439
Honeywell, 23
Honeywell 6180, 23, 234, 335
HP-UX, 38, 557
Hurd, The, 14
Hustvedt, Dick, 27
hybrid computer, 317
Hypertext Transfer Protocol (HTTP), 7
hyperthreading, 190

I Love You, 523
i-node, 430–432, 451, 469, 480–482, 484, 485, 487–489, 494, 496, 497, 502, 506, 508
i-number, 430, 431, 482, 485, 488
I/O devices, 5, 28, 32, 48, 58, 113, 204, 236, 239
I/O port, 315, 316, 348, 352, 358, 383
I/O processor, 308, 309
IBM, 14, 63, 217
IBM 7094, 21, 334
IDE, 309, 312, 341, 357–360, 362, 366, 439
IDEA, 529

idle process, 184, 188, 190
idle task, 159
IEEE, 86
IEEE 1394, 308
ignition control computer, 94
implicit allocation, 203
in-band flow control, 313, 329
Incompatible Time-sharing System (ITS), 23
index block, 416
indirect block, 430, 432, 469, 473, 474, 487, 506, 507
Inferno, 21, 35, 36
initial program load (IPL), 15
instruction count, 157
instruction counter, see program counter
Intel x86, 15, 32, 56, 64, 65, 67, 137, 170, 173, 190, 248, 250, 281, 283, 286, 290, 292, 295, 298, 299, 391
interleaving, 323, 324
Internet, 6, 56, 546
Internet Protocol (IP), 7
interprocess communication, 58, 124
interrupt, 18, 63, 95, 97–100, 102, 103, 129, 137, 167, 170, 172, 187, 192, 198, 200, 205, 226, 240, 304, 313–316, 321–323, 334, 335, 340, 342, 346, 347, 349, 350, 352–354, 366–369, 373, 383, 386, 390–394, 516, 542, 544, 545
interrupt controller, 341
interrupt descriptor table, 65
interrupt handler, 67, 99, 102, 308, 313, 320, 323–325, 334, 337, 339, 340, 342, 346, 347, 353, 366, 373, 391–393
interrupt vector, 99, 204, 236, 239, 241, 380
inverted page table, 202
iPAQ, 38
IPsec, 60
iris, 515
IRIX, 38
ISA, 312, 341
iSCSI, 312

Itanium, 27, 30

Java, 418
Java Virtual Machine, 3, 36
Javastation 1, 38
job, 87
job control, 168
journaling file system, 421, 422, 434, 482, 485, 505
just-in-time compiling, 3, 35, 38, 42, 44, 141, 162, 533

kernel process, 141, 142, 145, 157, 160, 163
kernel thread, 86, 131, 165, 288
Kernighan, Brian, 26
key, 514, 528–531, 533
keyboard, 46, 63, 142, 236, 317, 330, 350, 352–354, 357, 358
keycode, 350, 354, 355
Kilburn, 216
Kildall, Gary, 30
KISS, 561
Knuth, Donald, xxvi

Lamport, Leslie, 547
large block addressing (LBA), 312, 362
latency, 311
    rotational, 311
    seek time, 311
layered OS, 12, 31, 136
LBA48, 364
least recently used, 423
Lego Mindstorms, 38
library, 9, 17, 24, 28, 41, 60, 86, 131, 135, 166, 179, 225, 254, 341, 356, 402, 427, 432, 545
LILO, 62
Limbo, 36, 38, 39, 41, 47, 52, 142, 149, 151, 253, 255, 273, 418, 441, 450–456, 458, 459, 463, 468, 533
limit register, 198–200, 242, 517
link, 420, 426, 427, 430, 431
linker, 59, 250, 385, 428
Linux, 21, 33, 38, 40, 43, 45, 47, 556

Linux Conceptual Architecture, 57
Linux Kernel Modules (LKM), 59
Lions, John, 26, 55
Lipman, Peter, 27
load balancing, 184, 190
local page replacement, 217
lock, 542
lock server, 542
locked memory, 296, 298
log-structured file system, 422
logic bomb, 522
logical clock, 547
logical volume name, 407
lower half, 321, 322, 334, 337, 340, 346, 373
LPD, 538
Lucent, 36

Mac OS, 14, 38, 418
MACH, 14
Macintosh, 14, 418
Maclisp, 23
Macsyma, 23
mailbox, 341
major device number, 431
malware, 521
man-in-the-middle attack, 521
mark and sweep, 203, 255, 273
Mars, 405
Master Boot Record, 62
Master Control Program, 3
math coprocessor, 65
McCarthy, John, 21
memory access time, 226
memory allocation, 206
    best fit, 210, 211
    best-fit, 254, 261, 262
    buddy system, 211, 212, 251, 285
    first fit, 209, 210, 229, 240
    next fit, 210
    worst fit, 211
memory hierarchy, 195, 197, 202
memory layout, 170, 197, 203–205, 235, 236, 241, 245, 247, 248, 250, 255, 281, 282

memory management, 4, 28, 61, 64, 124, 137

memory management unit (MMU), 24, 62, 63, 65, 198, 208, 214, 215, 226, 229, 234–236, 238, 242–244, 250, 282, 302, 375, 525, 533

memory-mapped file, 203, 225, 235, 247, 248, 283, 284, 292, 301, 403, 404, 427, 430, 502, 505

memory protection, 198, 200, 226, 233, 235, 247, 253, 291, 517, 533

memory sharing, 203, 214, 238–240, 248, 253, 284, 343, 400, 404, 517, 533, 538, 539, 541, 544

Mentec, Inc., 24

message passing, 107, 322, 405, 542

metadata, 6, 40, 400, 402, 403, 405, 406, 408, 410–413, 418–422, 426–435, 438, 446, 451, 469, 480, 482, 485, 487, 505, 518, 519, 534

Michelangelo virus, 522

microkernel, 12, 23, 39, 57, 91, 405

Microsoft, 30, 538

Microsoft Windows, 557

MINIX, 14, 56

minor device number, 431

Minsky, Marvin, 21

MINX, 57

MIPS R4000, 30

mirroring, 328

MIT, 22, 23

modem, 313, 339, 513

modified bit, see dirty bit

module, 59, 60, 153–155, 162, 255, 256, 273, 451

Mona Lisa, 524

monitor, 2, 106

monolithic OS, 12, 23, 27, 31, 39, 57, 59, 405

Morris worm, 523

Morris, Robert T., 523

mote, 31, 342

mount, 48

mount table, 406

mounting, 405, 406, 412, 420, 423, 442, 480, 485

mouse, 63

MS-DOS, 30, 213, 522

Multics, 21, 22, 26, 28, 32, 124, 234, 235, 334, 338, 404, 425–430, 531, 532

multilevel feedback queue, 92, 123, 125, 130, 132, 135, 171, 181–183, 191

multilevel queue, 91

multilevel security, 526, 535

multiprogramming, 11

multitasking, 11

mutex lock, 102, 124, 145, 148, 182, 185, 257, 262, 263, 296, 301, 304, 322, 347, 360, 365, 374, 375, 377, 386, 400, 456, 496, 497, 541, 545

mutual exclusion, 68, 81, 102, 105, 106, 108, 109, 111, 115, 203, 321, 538, 541

name space, 6, 37, 40, 43, 48, 49, 151, 155, 235, 345, 399, 405–412, 420, 425, 427, 429–431, 433, 434, 437, 439, 441, 442

NASA, 405

NetBSD, 29, 33, 241

network, 7, 523, 533, 538, 545, 548

network interface, 308, 314, 317, 319

network protocol, 7

Neumann, Peter, 26

Newton's third law, 324

NFS, 538, 545

nice, 181, 182, 186

nonblocking I/O, 320, 335, 340, 341

normal mode, 331

NSA, 524, 529, 535

NTFS, 418, 434

NTP, 547

null device, 331, 341

NUMA, 73, 539

ODS-1,2,5, 432, 433

one-time pad, 528

one-time password, 514

one-way encryption, 512, 514
onion-skin algorithm, 233
open file table, 405, 488
OpenBSD, 29, 241
oracle, 114
Orange Book, 524–527, 532, 534
OS/2, 31
ostrich algorithm, 112
out-of-band flow control, 313
overlay, 213

packet, 319
page, 199
page directory, 201
page fault, 200, 216, 217, 219–221,
        224–228, 235, 244, 249, 283, 292,
        293, 298–300, 302–304, 404, 524
page frame, 199, 206, 208, 215, 218, 221,
        225, 227, 228, 235, 246, 249, 286,
        298, 301, 302
page frame number, 200–202
page number, 199–202, 234, 242, 245, 295
page reference string, 217, 221, 228
page replacement, 216, 224, 227, 228, 287
    Belady's min, 217
    clock algorithm, 218, 219, 221, 235,
        244, 287
    FIFO, 217–219, 221, 228, 229, 246, 248
    least recently used, 220, 221, 227, 229,
        246, 287
    not frequently used, 216, 220, 221,
        229, 249
    not recently used, 219, 221, 229, 287
    page fault frequency, 224, 247
    second chance, 218, 229, 246, 287, 288
    two-handed clock, 219, 244, 246
page table, 65, 66, 135, 200–202, 235, 242,
        245, 248, 250, 251, 284, 286,
        299–302, 304, 416, 428, 517, 533
    four-level, 286, 299
    three-level, 202, 245, 299
    two-level, 201, 286, 299
page table entry, 200–202, 218, 246, 286,
        300, 301, 303, 304

paging, 65, 199, 205, 206, 208, 213–216,
        224, 225, 227, 230, 234, 235, 241,
        243, 246, 247, 253, 286, 292, 296,
        298, 300, 301, 309, 375, 403, 423,
        517, 533
parent directory, 412, 420, 427, 431, 433,
        443, 448, 461, 462, 490
parent process, 127, 130, 153, 154,
        165–168, 172–179, 226, 238, 241,
        284, 289, 430, 437
parity, 313, 328
parity error, 314
partition, 408, 413, 431, 432, 452
partitioning, 208, 250
Pascal, 451, 456
password, 330, 512–515, 521–523, 532
password file, 512
Paterson, Tim, 30
PCI, 341
PDP-1, 21
PDP-11, 15, 24, 26, 27, 30, 129, 235, 238,
        239, 337, 421, 429
PDP-7, 26, 333
peripheral processor, 309
persistent storage, 197
Peterson's algorithm, 104
PGP, 529
physical address, 66, 197, 238, 286
physical address space, 200, 205, 239, 241,
        243, 247, 255, 300, 516, 517
physical memory, 196, 198, 206, 213, 214,
        225–227, 229, 236, 239, 241, 244,
        246, 248, 250, 251, 254, 281, 285,
        292, 296, 298, 300, 517, 544
physical memory address, 204
Pike, Rob, 36
pipe, 430
PL/I, 23
plaintext, 512, 528, 529, 531
Plan 9, 33, 36, 40, 448, 450, 515, 534, 556,
        557
playback attack, 513
polling, 314, 349, 350, 352, 375
port driver, 341

POSIX, 31, 40, 41, 48, 49, 56, 86, 106, 107, 131, 166, 341, 434

PowerPC, 30, 38

powersave, 137

preemption, 85, 90, 95, 102, 111, 127, 150, 157, 184, 186–188, 192, 318

prefetching, 244

prepaging, 216, 224

present bit, 200, 215, 220, 244, 300

primary storage, 196, 214

priority, 85, 95, 105, 123, 125, 126, 132, 160, 167, 171, 172, 181–183, 185, 186, 191, 337

priority boost, 92, 172, 182, 186

priority inheritance, 93

priority inversion, 92

privilege, 515–517, 527

process, 4, 81

process creation, 4, 5, 17, 27, 36, 43, 47, 50–52, 62, 73, 82, 83, 86, 94, 100–101, 123, 124, 126–128, 130, 131, 133, 134, 141, 142, 150–155, 159, 162, 165–167, 170, 173–181, 206, 226, 238, 241, 250, 255, 281, 285, 288, 290, 430, 455, 518, 545

process group, 150, 152, 154, 156, 165, 455

process ID, 73, 85, 127, 135, 145, 150, 152, 153, 172–174, 176, 337, 441

process management, 82

process state, 84, 91, 99, 121, 124, 126, 128, 130, 132, 134, 142, 150, 156, 158, 168–170, 173, 175, 186, 299

process synchronization, 58

process table, 48, 85, 100, 127, 128, 130, 134, 143, 145, 149, 151, 153, 168, 170, 404, 405

process table entry, 85, 100, 126, 147–153, 155, 156, 161, 163, 168, 170, 172, 176, 178, 188, 289, 293

process termination, 4, 6, 17, 36, 83, 84, 89, 100–101, 113, 123, 124, 126, 127, 131, 145, 155–157, 166, 168, 170, 172, 173, 236, 250, 259, 283, 285, 293, 298, 427

processor mode, 27, 28, 30, 239, 245, 247, 248, 250, 284, 516, 532

producer-consumer problem, 110

program counter, 99, 151, 162, 163, 178, 179, 261

protected mode, 64

protection rings, 23, 235, 532

pseudo-device, 331, 341

public key cryptography, 529–531, 533

punched cards, 10, 16, 22, 318, 333, 334

QDOS, 30

QEMU, 15

quantum, 90, 92, 94, 99, 123, 125, 133, 135, 136, 150, 157, 159, 160, 162, 163, 172

race condition, 102, 110

radix priority search tree, 291

RAID, 326–328

RAM disk, 71, 74

ramdisk, 331

random access, 401

raw mode, 330

read-ahead, 499, 501

read-only memory (ROM), 16

read-time, 429

ready list, 87, 95, 154–158, 160, 172, 175, 181, 182

real address, 197

real-time, 132, 135, 167, 168, 171, 181, 182, 185

real-time scheduling, 95

receiver overrun error, 314

red-black tree, 290, 291, 298

reference, 273

reference count, 100, 153, 154, 157, 255, 273, 290

register, 99, 100, 149, 160, 161, 172, 195, 197, 314–316, 320, 337, 347–349, 352, 360, 362, 364, 383, 384, 389, 390, 393, 516, 517, 544

register set, 162, 163, 173, 176, 178, 179, 190, 353

relative path name, 412, 427, 489

relocation, 198

rendezvous principle, 107

replay attack, *see* playback attack

request queue, 320–322, 324–326, 334, 337,
        339, 340, 342, 347, 360, 371, 372,
        385, 387, 388, 394, 396

reset stabilization, 543, 544

resource fork, 418

resource manager, 2

resource sharing, 2, 538

retina, 515

return value, 166

rewind, 401

Rice's Theorem, 114

ring algorithm, 550, 551

Ritchie, Dennis, 26

Rivest, Ron, 530

root directory, 420, 427, 433, 439, 442, 443,
        446, 448, 453, 454, 489

RS-232, 308, 312, 313, 330, 337, 538

RSA, 530

RSX-11, 432

RT-11, 21, 24, 126, 235–238, 335, 337, 338,
        428, 429, 433

S/KEY, 514

SATA, 312

scatter/gather, 545

scheduler, 32, 124, 137, 333, 377, 516, 544
    class, 133
    slotted, 96
    workclass, 125

scheduling, 4, 57, 73, 81, 83, 86, 100, 123,
        137, 142, 157, 160, 170, 181, 237
    borrowed virtual time, 137
    EDF, 95, 125, 137
    event-driven, 95
    FCFS, 87
    FIFO, 92, 181, 185
    priority, 90, 95, 127, 128, 130
    real time, 94
    round-robin, 90–92, 94, 97, 160, 181,
        185

SJF, 87, 90, 325
    two-level, 94

SCSI, 60, 308, 312, 321, 341, 359, 360

Seattle Computer Products, 30

secondary storage, 196, 214, 229, 235, 309

security, 6, 13

seek, 391, 393, 401, 413, 430–432

segment descriptor, 180, 235, 239, 428, 532

segment fault, 235, 428

segment number, 427

segment table, 65, 178, 250, 427, 517

segmentation, 64, 65, 199, 204, 205, 224,
        225, 234, 235, 238, 283, 404,
        427–429, 517, 532

self-stabilization, 543

SELinux, 61, 535

semaphore, 105, 106, 110, 542

sensitivity label, 526

sensor, 31, 95, 342

sequential access, 401

service provider, 3

SGID bit, 534

Shakespeare, 528

Shamir, Adi, 530

shared memory, 58

shared secret, 512, 528–530

shell, *see* command interpreter

shortest seek time first (SSTF), 325

shutdown, 45

signal, 46, 127, 167, 168, 172, 177, 298,
        376, 382

signature, 531, 533

sixth edition UNIX, 21

SMB, 538

soft interrupt, 373

software flow control, 313

software interrupt, 18, 29, 46, 76

Solaris, 38

spanning tree, 540, 543

sparse file, 418, 487

special file, 411, 431

spin lock, 104, 542

Spirit, 405

SSL, 529, 533

stack, 47, 99, 100, 134, 135, 170–172, 176, 179, 199, 205, 236, 238, 240, 241, 245, 247, 250, 255, 265, 278, 283, 284, 290, 293, 298

stack algorithm, 228

stack pointer, 99, 170, 173, 250

stack segment, 198, 205, 214, 238, 240, 242, 290

Stallman, Richard, 23

start bit, 313

starvation, 87, 92, 123, 136, 186, 372

static linking, 59

static priority, 182

steganography, 524

stop bit, 313, 314

storage area network (SAN), 312

storage device, 309, 314, 317, 318, 345, 359, 401, 404, 406, 413, 421, 423, 427, 441, 443, 445, 538

stream device, 318, 322

striping, 327, 328

Styx, 38, 40, 345, 346, 348, 437–442, 445, 450, 451, 456, 458, 464, 533

SUID bit, 534

Sun Microsystems, 41, 537, 538

SunOS, 241, 523

superblock, 431, 432, 451, 453, 454, 467, 468, 479–482, 484, 485, 487

superuser, 484, 515, 534

supervisor, 2, 22

swapping, 94, 128, 131, 132, 134, 196, 213–215, 233, 238, 240, 243, 244, 246, 247, 253, 309

swapping space, 196, 233, 241, 244, 301, 431

symbolic link, 420, 427, 431, 487, 491, 492

symmetric encryption, 528–530

symmetric multiprocessing (SMP), 11, 188, 544, 545

synchronous I/O, 320

synchronous operation, 541

system call, 17, 24, 27, 29, 30, 38, 52, 76, 122, 124, 126, 127, 129, 131, 133, 138, 166, 168, 170, 172–175, 178, 179, 205, 234–236, 238, 240–242, 247, 248, 250, 255, 284, 292, 293, 300, 320, 334, 337–341, 346, 347, 374, 385, 400, 401, 404, 405, 425, 426, 428, 430, 431, 434, 437, 440, 455, 480, 481, 488, 502, 511, 516

Tanenbaum, Andrew, 56, 112

tar, 442

tasklet, 373

TCL/Tk, 40

TCP/IP, 7, 61, 312

Teager, Herb, 21

terminal, 46, 76, 122, 127, 312, 330, 331, 333, 334, 337, 339, 341, 513

test-and-set, 103

text segment, *see* code segment

thermostat, 317

Thinking Machines, Inc., 327

Thompson, Ken, 26, 36, 450

thrashing, 94, 227

thread, 50, 86, 131, 133, 142, 157, 165, 190, 303

time bomb, 522, 523

time slice, 90, 92, 94, 95, 98, 104, 125, 141, 162, 163, 168, 170–172, 177, 181, 182, 185, 186, 225, 320, 544

time-sharing, 10, 11, 29, 43, 52, 62, 72, 76, 81, 86, 90, 97, 99, 123, 127, 137, 159, 167, 171, 181, 182, 185, 227, 279, 320, 335, 408, 539, 545

timer, 318

TinyOS, 21, 31, 136, 250, 342, 425

Torvalds, Linus, 56

translation lookaside buffer (TLB), 201, 202, 246

Transmission Control Protocol (TCP), 7

transmitter underrun error, 314

trap, 18, 27, 30

trap vector, 236

trapdoor, 521

Trojan horse, 521, 522

Tron, 3

Turing machine, 81, 98
turnaround time, 88
TX-0, 21

UC Berkeley, 29, 31
UCSD Pascal, 3, 36
Unicode, 434
University of Cambridge, 32
UNIX, 15, 17, 26, 35, 55, 57, 128, 129, 131,
    181, 226, 238, 239, 241, 243, 255,
    284, 338–340, 421, 429–431, 433,
    448, 451, 467, 469, 480, 482, 485,
    487, 515, 517, 522, 523, 533, 534,
    557
UNIX Systems Laboratories (USL), 29
upper half, 321, 322, 325, 334, 337, 340,
    346, 372, 385
USB, 308, 312, 321, 341, 538
user authentication, 512, 514, 517, 532
user ID, 45, 47, 408, 469, 487, 534
user input, 330, 331, 337, 339, 357, 358
user interface, 8, 399
user name, 512

valid bit, *see* present bit
VAX, 27, 29, 129, 239, 241, 242, 244–246
VFS, 479, 481, 488, 494–496, 502–504, 533
virtual address, 66, 197–201, 205, 213, 234,
    238, 242, 286, 290, 299, 300, 517
virtual address space, 129, 131, 198, 199,
    201, 205, 206, 213, 224, 226, 235,
    238, 239, 242, 245, 247, 248, 255,
    282, 284, 290, 295, 300, 404, 429,
    516, 533
virtual device, 331
virtual machine, 3, 24, 32, 38, 39, 43, 44,
    48, 141, 149, 151, 153, 159–161,
    163, 253, 254
virtual machine OS, 3, 14
virtual memory, 5, 213
virus, 522, 523
Vita Nuova, 36, 450
VM, 14, 32

VMS, 21, 27, 131, 245–248, 287, 340, 341,
    432, 433, 515
VMware, 15
volatile storage, 197
vsyscall, 284

water mark, 328, 329
watermark, 224
WEP, 529
Whirlwind, 21
Williamson, Malcolm J., 529
Win32, 31, 434
Windows NT, 21, 30, 38, 40, 94, 133,
    247–249, 287, 341, 342, 418, 434,
    515
work queue, 373, 385, 386, 390
working set, 224, 225, 246–249, 287
worm, 523

Xen, 15, 21, 32, 137, 208, 250, 251, 342,
    343, 425
Xenoserver, 32
XINU, 12
XON/XOFF, 313

zombie, 128, 168